God as Poet of the World

God as Poet of the World

Exploring Process Theologies

Roland Faber

Translated by Douglas W. Stott

Westminster John Knox Press
LOUISVILLE • LONDON

Translated by Douglas W. Stott from the German *Gott als Poet der Welt: Anliegen und Perspektiven der Prozesstheologie,* second edition, published in 2004 by Wissenschaftliche Buchgesellschaft, Darmstadt.

© 2004 by Wissenschaftliche Buchgesellschaft, Darmstadt
English translation © 2008 Westminster John Knox Press

Book design by Sharon Adams
Cover design by Night & Day Design

Published by Westminster John Knox Press
Louisville, Kentucky

This book is printed on acid-free paper that meets the American National Standards Institute Z39.48 standard. ∞

PRINTED IN THE UNITED STATES OF AMERICA

08 09 10 11 12 13 14 15 16 17 — 10 9 8 7 6 5 4 3 2 1

Library of Congress Cataloging-in-Publication Data is on file at the Library of Congress, Washington, D.C.

ISBN 978-0-664-23076-0

"[God] is the ideal companion who transmutes what has been lost into a living fact within [God's] own nature. [God] is the mirror which discloses to every creature its own greatness."

Alfred North Whitehead

Contents

Abbreviations

AJThPh	*American Journal of Theology and Philosophy*
BZAW	Beihefte zur Zeitschrift für alttestamentliche Wissenschaft
Conc	*Concilium*
CPS	Library of the Center for Process Studies, Claremont School of Theology
EKL	*Evangelisches Kirchenlexikon.* Edited by Erwin Fahlbusch et al. 4 vols. 3rd ed. Göttingen, 1985-96.
ESPT	Journal of the European Society for Process Thought
EvK	Evangelische Kommentare
EvTh	*Zeitschrift für Evangelische Theologie*
FZPhTh	*Freiburger Zeitschrift für Philosophie und Theologie*
IPhQ	*Irish Philosophy Quarterly*
JAAR	*Journal of the American Academy of Religion*
JR	*Journal of Religion*
KD	*Kerygma und Dogma*
LThK	*Lexikon für Theologie und Kirche*
MTZ	*Münchener theologische Zeitschrift*
NZSTh	*Neue Zeitschrift für Systematische Theologie und Religionsphilosophie*
PhR	*Philosophische Rundschau*
PS	*Process Studies*
SzTh	*Salzburger Zeitschrift für Theologie*
TP	*Theologie und Philosophie*
TRE	*Theologische Realenzyklopädie.* Edited by G. Krause and G. Müller. Berlin, 1977—.
ZPhF	*Zeitschrift für Philosophische Forschung*
ZTK	*Zeitschrift für Theologie und Kirche*

Abbreviations of the Works of A. N. Whitehead

AI	*Adventures of Ideas.* New York: Free Press, 1967.
CN	*Concept of Nature.* 1964. Cambridge: Cambridge University Press, 1993.
Conv.	"A. H. Johnson, Some Conversations with Whitehead concerning God and Creativity." In *Explorations in Whitehead's Philosophy*, ed. Lewis S. Ford and George L. Kline, 3–13. New York: Fordham, 1983.
ESP	*Essays in Science and Philosophy.* New York: Greenwood Press, 1968.
FR	*Function of Reason.* Boston: Beacon Press, 1958.
HL	"Harvard Lectures 1925-1926 (Charles Hartshorne's Handwritten Notes on A. N. Whitehead's Harvard Lectures 1925–26)," edited by Roland Faber. *PS* 30/2 (2001): 301–73.
IM	*An Introduction to Mathematics.* London: Oxford University Press, 1958.

Imm.	"Immortality." In ESP 77–96.
Let.	"Letters to Guy Emerson," 5 May 1944. The Houghton Library, Harvard University, Cambridge, MA.
MC	"Mathematical Concepts of the Material World." 1905. Reprint in *Alfred North Whitehead: An Anthology*, ed. F. S. C. Northrop and Mason W. Gross, 11–82. New York: Macmillan, 1953.
MG	"Mathematics and the Good." In ESP 97–113.
MT	*Modes of Thought*. New York: Free Press, 1966.
PM	*Principia Mathematica. With Bertrand Russell*. Vols. 1–3. Cambridge: Cambridge University Press, 1910–13.
PMd	*Principia Mathematica: Vorwort und Einleitungen*. Mit einem vorwort von Kurt Gödel. Frankfurt: Suhrkamp, 2008.
PNK	*An Enquiry Concerning the Principles of Natural Knowledge*. Reprint 1925. New York: Dover Publications, 1982.
PR	*Process and Reality: An Essay in Cosmology*. Corrected edition, ed. David Ray Griffin and D. W. Sherburne. New York: Free Press, 1978.
PRd	*Prozess und Realität: Entwurf einer Kosmologie*. Überschung und Nechwort von J. Hall. Frankfort: Suhrkamp, 2001.
RM	*Religion in the Making*. New York: Meridian Books, 1960.
RMn	*Religion in the Making*. New York: Meridian Books, 1996.
S	*Symbolism: Its Meaning and Effect*. New York: Fordham University Press, 1985.
SMW	*Science and the Modern World*. New York: Free Press, 1967.

Voices

I asked each of the following fourteen theologians to articulate his or her personal understanding of process theology in a succinct statement for inclusion in this book. In effect, these voices offer fourteen answers to the question, "What is process theology?"

James Bradley, Canada. "As developed by Peirce and Whitehead, process theology is essentially an elaboration of various Trinitarian themes. Its close convergence with the modern logic of relations arises out of its generalization of the strictly relational definition of the three persons to all things. It abandons any notion of the necessary existence and self-completeness of the divine and makes the incarnational theme of immanence fundamental. Thus theology becomes divine cosmology: the serial procession of the godhead is realized only within the infinite evolution of creation. That is the coming of the Spirit, in which all things freely participate and where evil, which is not just lack but destruction, is met only by the immutability of the agapeic gift of the community of all things."

John Cobb, California. "Process theology affirms that the deepest reality of the world is a vastly complex network of interrelated events. Even God is affected by what happens, just as God participates in the constitution of every creaturely event. Theology cannot be segregated as one academic discipline among others:

interdisciplinary

it brings the Christian perspective to bear on important questions everywhere. Process theology has dealt extensively with the relations of Christianity to other religious traditions and to the natural sciences. Today ecology and economics seem particularly urgent topics. Process theology seeks an inclusive vision of a processive and historical world in which Jesus Christ is the center."

James W. Felt, S.J., California. "From the viewpoint of an outsider occasionally looking in, process theology seems chiefly characterized by both its special interests and its special methodology. It is specially interested in describing God's literal interaction with the components of the world and its history, to the point of introducing time into God's own life. This is in reaction to what was perceived as a substantialist, nonrelational, static outlook of traditional theology in which God seemed unrelated to the world. As to its methodology, process theology, as usually understood, is grounded on the conceptual scheme of Alfred North Whitehead, perhaps as adapted by Charles Hartshorne or other thinkers indebted to Whitehead's basic conceptuality. Whiteheadian metaphysics seems to me to have become for many process theologians a kind of privileged Procrustean bed into which the cardinal beliefs of Christian Revelation must fit if they are to be regarded as intelligible. The question is open whether this approach can lead to a credible Christian theology."

Lewis S. Ford, United States. "Process theology is based on the thought of Alfred North Whitehead and his intellectual associates, most notably Charles Hartshorne. Process Theology is a temporalistic understanding of God requiring both divine initiative and creaturely response."

David Griffin, California. "Process theology, based on the 'process philosophy' of Alfred North Whitehead, is a constructively postmodern type of theology— advocated thus far primarily but not exclusively by Christian thinkers—that provides unique solutions to various problems of modern philosophy and theology. These solutions are rooted in the Whiteheadian worldview, which is naturalistic, in the sense of rejecting the possibility of supernatural interruptions of the world's normal causal processes, while rejecting the modern version of naturalism, with its atheism, materialism, and sensationist doctrine of perception. Whitehead's naturalism instead affirms panentheism, panexperientialism, and the primacy of nonsensory perception. According to panentheism, the world exists in God, and God influences all creatures in terms of ideal, normative possibilities (so that the world is 're-enchanted'), but this influence is a regular part of the world's normal causal processes, never an interruption thereof. Besides overcoming the apparent conflict between theistic religion and scientific naturalism, this doctrine avoids the problem of evil (which was created by the nonbiblical doctrine of *creatio ex nihilo*, which process theology rejects). Panexperientialism, which says that all genuine individuals are experiential processes with spontaneity (while recognizing that there are aggregates, such as sticks and stones, which are as such devoid of experience and spontaneity), avoids ontological (Cartesian) dualism and hence its successor, reductionist materialism. . . . Process theology thus achieves a 'reenchantment without supernaturalism' that grounds a communitarian cosmopolitan ethic."

Science

Thomas E. Hosinski, United States. "Process theology uses Alfred North White-head's profound philosophical analysis of reality to rethink and reinterpret Christian religious experience and doctrine. It seeks to express Christian faith in a way compatible with the established theories of contemporary empirical science. Equally important, it tries to construct an understanding of God better suited to the implications of Christian religious experience than the traditional view, while purifying the Christian doctrine of God of ideas offensive to the religious sensibilities of many, Christian and non-Christian alike. At its heart is a vision of God as empowering, persuading, and saving love (and a correlative rejection of the idea of God as coercive determiner of history)."

Kurian Kachappilly, India. "In this wider sense, I view 'process thought' as a 'method of inquiry into a background frame of understanding.' And process has rightly become for me 'a way of doing philosophy and theology.' . . . [B]asic concepts are that the whole of everything is not made up of things, but of 'events,' and that all events, however small they are, affect other events. . . . If God is viewed in 'process-relational' terms, the cross of Christ can be interpreted as proof for God's love for the world: 'God so loved the world that he gave his only Son, so that everyone who believes in him may not perish but may have eternal life' (John 3:16). Whitehead's vision of God as 'great companion—the fellow sufferer who understands,' resonates this biblical reality. . . . An important implication of God's relatedness to the world is that the world has the opportunity to 'contribute to the color and richness' of divine life. The idea of God's ongoing enrichment is not merely a logical deduction, but it matches with the religious idea as well."

Catherine Keller, New York. "Process theology, in microcosm, means the rearticulation of faith through flows of relationship. Rather than assuming that it speaks as and to human beings bonded in separate communities of stable identity, it develops a theology of becoming, in which identity unfolds as a complex negotiation within our social and ecological situations. Process theology on one level is a faithful adjustment of Christian doctrine to contemporary possibilities. . . . It challenges the Western worldview—which most Christian practice today presumes and in some ways intensifies—in which the mind appears as a separate entity 'knowing' and 'controlling' a world of material, mechanical things. Behind that modern worldview lies the nonbiblical, classical Christian myth of an all-controlling immutable paternal God presiding over a sin-and-death ridden creation, the 'theatre' for salvageable and separate souls which 'He' will eventually save from transience and mortality. Process thought offers a systematic alternative that at once preserves aspects of the classical sensibility but shifts its terms beyond modernity: thus God is redescribed . . . as not changeless but rather faithful, not controlling by might but inviting by wisdom, as 'creating' and 'saving' not by coercive but by persuasive power. This God is not a Lord of power and might, but Spirit of love and wisdom. At another level, however, process thought does not content itself with theological deconstruction and reconstruction. It is driven by a certain prophetic visionary sensibility to transfigure the practice of theology by lowering its defenses against competing perspectives. For instance, in its attunement to the nonreductionist science that began to emerge a century ago . . . Whiteheadian thought has imported into faith an excitement and sense of discovery that seemed to be available only to the natural sciences, and that seemed dead in the traditional languages of the church. Similarly, it has embraced genuine dialogue with other religions—not just among the sibling rivals of the family of Abraham but with Buddhist, Hindu, Taoist and Aboriginal traditions. It finds in its own sense of the intimate presence of the divine in all things (its pan-en-theism, which is not pantheism but also not classical theism) affinities with other paths, especially in their mystical insights. Yet it upholds a strong—biblical—sense of relationship with the divine, which does not thus dissolve into a divinized universe. In this radical relationality, God-in-all and all-in-God, process theology has also embraced rather than repelled the challenge of feminist theology. For women seek not just a modern 'equality' within the church but a transformation of the symbolic imagery of the West, in which the divine may be addressed analogically in the images of both genders, while always transcending all personal, indeed all creaturely language. Yet for feminist theology, as for the ecological and social justice movements with which process theology mingles in the English-speaking contexts, the transdisciplinary movement of theology serves a God who sends us back to care for our little portion of the creation. The 'divine lure' or 'cosmic Eros' of process theology inspires work with the interstices of church and society, spirituality and politics, humanity and its ecology, *Wissenschaft* and art. Thus it does not fit comfortably with the modernism of Protestant and Catholic dogmatic options. Yet it negotiates its transcontextual and transforming discourse at the boundaries of the traditional discourses, not in a utopian, new age nowhere."

Helmut Maassen, Germany. "Process theology is the attempt to make Christian reference to the creator God credible. In this respect, Christian theology must necessarily draw from philosophical and scientific findings in developing its own propositions of faith. Here the Whiteheadian understanding of metaphysics can provide a theoretical construct in which traditional Judeo-Christian tenets of faith can be linked to philosophical-scientific findings within a multi-perspectival view of reality. This construct in its own turn guarantees a fundamental openness toward correctives and changes, dispenses with the notion of a single or solely privileged perspective, and solicits verification from experience itself. Whitehead's cosmology, understood as a metaphysics of experience, is thus also open to specific experiences such as that of the Judeo-Christian tradition."

Gregory James Moses, Australia. "Process theology believes in a God who is unmetaphorically a God of mercy and compassion, affecting all and affected by all, a God who is relational through and through, and constituting a relational base to a thoroughly relational Universe. It strives to be faithful to and continually provoked by the special focussing of the Divine Lure to be found in the Jesus Event and the early Jesus Movement. It strives in Whiteheadian fashion to be adequate to the totality of experiences, whether to be found in everyday life, or in the natural, social, human sciences and arts, as well as in what the Spirit has to say to all the churches and the work of the Spirit in other religious traditions. Finally, of its very nature it tends to be socially and environmentally sensitive, with God in whom it believes constituting as it were the final environment for all our activities, luring us into new deeds appropriate to the third millennium."

Tokiyuki Nobuhara, Tokyo. "In this vast universe each small unit of life is breathing along with the rest of the innumerable units of life. Individual units of life are interconnected, and are concrete appearances of the entire universe (which is at every moment growing and advancing while containing them in itself). If we call the all-embracing universe Reality, each and every unit of life, as its concrete appearance, is an ever-new Process. And God really works at once in connection with the entire universe and in connection with each new process of life. God is inclusive of the entirety (the ever-new entirety) of the universe, and is the source of the appearance of each and every unit of life. As such, God is the one who is 'with' all units of life in the universe. . . . The task of philosophy is to consider and explore all the interconnections of the universe or the world, of each and every unit of life (in our human case, the human self), and of God in a thoroughgoing and holistic manner. When I speak of 'all the interconnections,' I naturally deal with their metaphysical background (such as what Kitaro Nishida calls the 'place of absolute Nothingness') and with their actual embodiment (such as Whitehead's concept of an 'Adventure in the Universe as One')."

John Quiring, California. "Process third-way thinking mediates dualistic positions in education, religion, philosophy, ideology, and culture; balancing polar opposites in some cases: absolute/relational, being/becoming, unity/diversity, infinite/finite. Process theologies transform the doctrinal dimension of religions in terms of 'the full circle of cognition.' For example, the doctrine of divine omnipotence is modified in light of evolution, freedom, and evil. God is beyond, behind, and within the passing flux of the world. God is eternal-temporal consciousness, knowing and including the world in God's *actuality* but not God's *essence*. The *primordial* nature of God presents options to the world. The *consequent* nature of God experiences and knows the world. Rebellion against fullness of well-being for creation is original sin against God. Separation of love, power, and justice is the demonic, but God envisions novel consequent goods to overcome evil, acting through the persuasive power of ideals and the lure of beauty and value, rather than the coercive power of force."

Gene Reeves, Japan. "Process philosophy is a liberating vision of reality as dynamic, creative, interdependent, and value intensive. That reality is dynamic means that all actuality is always becoming, changing from moment to moment, opening possibilities not present previously. That reality is creative means that the present is always more than the past, that to a limited degree freedom and novelty is to be found in all actual things. That reality is interdependent means that as actors within a vast network of relationships, all things are inheritors of a rich past and contributors to an evolving future. That reality is value intensive means that all actual things not only have past causes, but aims or purposes as well, values for themselves as well as for others. That it is a vision means that process philosophy is an aesthetic and imaginative offering as well as an intellectual one, truly a philosophy. It is liberating because it frees us from conventional and faulty conceptions and frees us to devote ourselves to creating a more beautiful world. Process theology is simply that style of theology which uses this philosophy to interpret the Christian tradition to the end of making it vital in the present. As such, it involves critical reflection on the ideas and practices of the Christian tradition, seeking always to be faithful to the tradition, as rigorous as possible in pursuit of truth, and enamored of relevance to the actual conditions of living beings."

Barry Whitney, Canada. "While still widely misunderstood and misinterpreted by most traditional theologians, process theology has provided a unique and viable alternative to traditional theology, an alternative consistent with biblical texts and that calls for a major reassessment of the traditional theology—its doctrine of God, in particular, and the attributes assigned to God as 'dipolar' rather than 'monopolar.' The vision of God in process theology as 'persuasive' rather than unilaterally coercive (the latter emphasized by most traditional theology, especially in the extremist forms of Calvinism and Thomism) represents God's power and knowledge consistently with a true 'metaphysics of freedom,' the first such theistic view wherein all life has some genuine degree of creativity (freedom at the conscious level). This view dissolves the problem of evil as traditionally formulated and advocates a God who exerts a powerful persuasive love by which the universe was created and by which it is sustained."

Introduction
What Is Process Theology?

The origin and nature of a thing do not coincide with that thing's beginning. This fundamental insight into the historical nature of all phenomena as articulated by the French philosopher Henri Bergson applies without qualification to process theology as well (Deleuze 1997). Process theology coalesced into a phenomenon in its own right only over a period of time during which the unexpected alliance of various traditions gradually generated the contours of that which was genuinely new in process theology. And that new element in its own turn invariably emerges in the guise of ever new attempts to understand the nature and form of that theology. So, what *is* process theology? The search for an answer to this question must continually keep three considerations in mind, namely, *history*, *content*, and *perspective*.

Where does one find the *historical* origins of process theology? A search for the sources into which the path already traversed by process theology leads back and eventually disappears, the sources on which process theology itself could reflect only after attaining a consciousness of itself as a separate entity, the sources from which process theology itself derives, as it were—that search reveals four "precursors": pragmatism and evolutionism, the philosophy of life and the philosophy of becoming, liberal theology, and the philosophy of the organism.

Within a narrower philosophical context, process theology was shaped in part by the *pragmatism* and *evolutionism* of William James and John Dewey, Samuel Alexander and George Santayana, and by the *philosophy of life* of Henri Bergson (Lucas 1989). The former introduced it to the teleological nature of the epistemological process, to the notion that all knowledge is characterized by both interest and goal and constructs its truth from the relation to its "function" within a whole. The latter bequeathed to it the primacy of life over reason and thereby an understanding of the impossibility of relegating the world—a world perpetually in the process of becoming—to a place within a system as something definitively known. In committing itself to this *pragmatism of truth*, process theology opposes any timeless theory of truth; instead it supports novelty or newness as a paradigm for the acquisition of knowledge, and thereby also the notion that truth is accordingly fulfilled only in an (eschatological) process whereby the world itself becomes whole. In committing itself to the *priority of life*, process theology sooner follows Nietzsche than Hegel in recognizing the irreducibility of the process of becoming over against any attempt at systematization and in thus taking as the basis for its theological reflection a view of the world as essentially suprarational and incapable of being assessed as a totality (Wiehl 1986).

Within a more distant intellectual-historical context, process theology is rooted in two traditions that began with Pharaoh Akhenaten and the pre Socratic philosopher Heraclitus. The first tradition viewed the universe as being constituted as a unity within a living, loving, wise, and creative God (Hartshorne/Reese 1976), while the second understood the world as an eternal creative process of becoming (*panta rhei*), guided by self-creative, living reason (Wolf-Gazo 1988). It is from the tradition of monotheism that process theology derives the notion of *panentheism*, according to which the world as a whole is one in God or becomes whole within the unity of God. And from the tradition of *pancreationism* ("everything flows") process theology derives its understanding of the world as a world that is constantly in the process of becoming and that within this creative emergence cannot be reconstructed or articulated in any fixed fashion. Process theology accordingly develops its understanding of God in opposition to the kind of "theism" that tends to be alienated from the world, and does so by distinguishing God and "creativity," the principle of the living, unfinished whole of the world.

Within a more recent theological context, process theology emerged against the backdrop of nineteenth-century *liberal theology* with its opposition to supernaturalism and hence to any understanding of God as being "beyond the world"; this opposition involved a concomitant commitment to the "naturalism" of an understanding of God as immanent in the world and to a Christianity of cultural and ethical responsibility (Buckley 1997). Process theology's unique interpretation of liberal theology provides the basis not only for its "naturalistic" commitment to a God who is both *engaged in and affected by the world*, a God who in fact does not withdraw into transcendence or remain otherwise unaffected by the world (Peters 1966), but also for its ethical understanding of Christianity as a theology of action, freedom, responsibility, and activity in the broader sense.

It was, however, the work of the English mathematician and American philosopher Alfred N. Whitehead (1861–1947) that provided the decisive stimulus prompting the actual emergence of process theology (Lowe 1985, 1990). His work not only provided the catalyst for the emergence of process theology, but also became the abiding reference point accompanying later development. It was in the examination and assessment of his work that process theology acquired its initial self-understanding, and in the perpetual reexamination of that same work that it derived the critical resources for subsequent developments. Within an increasingly broad conceptual framework, Whitehead set about establishing a universal theory of the world as a whole which he called "speculative philosophy" and "cosmology" (Lowe 1991). On the one hand, this "theory of the world" was to develop a schema or system of categories within which all possible experiences might be coherently interpreted or explicated; on the other, it was to replace all previous cosmologies, be they philosophical, like that of Plato, or scientific, like that of Newton (Rust 1987). At the same time, however, this new metaphysics was to reunite the various disciplines that had in the meantime been sundered from one another, for example, both strands of knowledge—experience (empirical knowledge) and thinking (rationality)—on the one hand, and the material world (the natural sciences) and the mind, spirit, or intellect (the humanities), on the other (Balz 1964).

With regard to its historical antecedents, an initial answer can now be given to the question "What is process theology?": *Process theology is the soteriological articulation of a universal "cosmology" ("general theory of the world as a whole") as developed especially by Alfred N. Whitehead, that is, as an examination and elucidation of the world with regard to its meaning as a whole and with an eye on the possibility of universal reconciliation. The systematic efforts of process theology to this end examine varied philosophical and theological traditions of the West, together with more recent results of the natural sciences (quantum physics, the theory of relativity, the theory of evolution) and with Eastern thought (especially Buddhism). In a programmatic sense it thus develops new, interdisciplinary, nondualistic categories based especially on the nature of all reality as a process of becoming and as characterized by events.*

Given the complexity of this historical background, it comes as no surprise that even those quite familiar with the history, development, and modes of operation of process theology tend to avoid succinct answers of this sort. Three reasons behind this disinclination might be adduced, reasons that, by the way, also reveal the driving force behind the internal development of process theology: its complexity, multicontextuality, and interdisciplinarity.

Complexity. The oversimplification generally characteristic of descriptive definitions and succinct formulae invariably falls short of the mark. Process theology, however, has gone so far as to take as one of its primary tenets the assertion that although simplification is indeed one of the basic functions of reason (a function without which ultimately nothing can be known), it is nonetheless incumbent on theological reflection to resist the mind's inclination to simplify within the cognitive act. The purpose of such resistance is to perceive and assess reality itself in a more commensurate, appropriate fashion. Knowledge of reality in the understanding of process theology always involves the attempt to perceive and acknowledge anew the irreducible complexity of reality both as a whole and in its particulars, to open up that reality critically over against attempts at simplification, and to render that reality bearable or accessible even amid its irreducible multiplicity—multiplicity that is, after all, often perceived as threatening and dangerous—and to do so without fostering the impression that knowledge thus acquired is on the verge of disintegrating into chaos.

Multicontextuality. Process theology arose (and has since tended to abide) in the field of tension between philosophy and theology, dynamically positioned between its *philosophical roots* especially in the "process philosophy" of the British mathematician and American philosopher Alfred North Whitehead (as whose theological articulation process theology historically emerged in the first place) and the *inherent necessities of a theology* that understands itself grounded in a revelatory event. Biblical connotations, truths of faith, a communitarian orientation, and the overall soteriological intent of theological work must be balanced with philosophical reflection on the reality of this world.

Interdisciplinarity. Process theology's universal claim to develop itself within a "theory of the world as a whole" and to explicate this theory theologically militates against simple answers to the question regarding its precise nature. On the one hand, the particular discipline providing the primary backdrop for process theology in any given interdisciplinary dialogue (physics, biology, psychology, etc.) will invariably shape the concrete form of this theology. On the other hand, it is precisely because of the fundamental interdisciplinarity of process theology itself that its findings and tenets are from the outset so fragile, since the latter necessarily remain in flux according to the *empirical findings* of the various sciences and disciplines.

Given this complex positioning of process theology, an "abbreviated definition" can be formulated drawing on at least these elements of *content*: *Process theology is the tentative draft of a theology of the universal nexus of events that is the world itself, in the processive oscillation between creative freedom and ecological evolution. Within its soteriological association of God and world process, the categories of the relational (all event happenings are related to everything else), the synthetic (all event happenings are an amalgamating of everything else), and the creative (all event happenings are something spontaneously new over against everything else) constitute an organic nexus or coherent context such that the universe as a whole comes into purview as a network of developmental contexts rendering human beings possible as knowing, free, acting subjects. Within this process, God's creative and redemptive love encompasses all that happens in the world such that it liberates this world with regard to its potentiality (mentality) and saves it with regard to its worldliness (physical nature).*

Why has such a theology of the creative, the ecological, and the organic not entered into the mainstream of theological reflection? After all, it is precisely the creative element that has so much to contribute to the search, on the one hand, for ways to shape the world in a fashion that might enhance the dignity of human beings, and, on the other, for ways to articulate and enhance the ecological interconnectedness of all constituent parts of this world. The factors preventing process theology from entering that mainstream can be explicated with the previously mentioned aspects of complexity, multicontextuality, and interdisciplinarity.

Complexity. Insofar as the intention of process theology is precisely to avoid oversimplification in order to do justice to the actual complexity of the world as a theological locus of talk about God, its fundamental principle is to *perceive precisely those fissures* otherwise covered by a conceptuality that does indeed oversimplify that complexity and in so doing abstracts away from the concrete whole of the process of God and the world. As a matter of fact, process theology has indeed developed a language that, precisely through its tendency to differentiate where simplification might otherwise seem more helpful, has made access to process theology itself more cumbersome. Considerable practice is required to familiarize oneself with the terminological terra incognita it discloses and to apply the subtle categories it constructs and then shapes into instruments of thought. The path leading away from simplified terminological and conceptual construction demands a fundamental change of perspective regarding the task of theological cognition: differentiation instead of simplification; the sundering of conceptual boundaries instead of the construction of protective enclosures; and a striving for openness instead of the expectation of secure foundations. Process theology requires unusual theological virtues, especially curiosity and an acknowledgment of the primacy of questioning over the potential attainment of answers, of searching over finding, of joy in movement and activity over acquiescence to stasis. It is the conviction of process theology that the question of redemption and consummation, a question that is part and parcel of theological thought and work as such, can be meaningfully raised and indeed is even possible in the first place only by entering into rather than avoiding the adventure of an irreducibly complex world (Moltmann 1995).

Multicontextuality. Precisely because process theology has always been positioned within the field of tension between philosophy and theology, its philosophical roots have often caused its methodology to be misunderstood, thwarting any further spread of its agenda. *On the one hand,* its focus on the paradigm of life over against system and doctrine, its global ethical and secular orientation, its search for a pragmatic means of soteriological change in the world, and its universal, cosmological interest has led it to embrace the primacy of what might be called vibrant, living chaos over against lifeless order. *On the other hand,* especially Whitehead's philosophy—a philosophy that, after all, understands itself as "speculative philosophy"—has prompted the theological work of process theology to acquire a pronounced systematic or system-immanent character. Whereas in the first case it was the systematically inaccessible element of chaos under the paradigm of living flux that seemed suspect to a theology that understood itself as a system of coherently ordered, incontrovertible truths of faith, in the second it was precisely the fundamental systematic-metaphysical assumptions of Whiteheadian philosophy that were perceived as being incompatible with theology. And in all fairness, these theological concerns do indeed reflect profound anxieties. *Either* one feared a dissolution of cherished truths into a relative and wholly incalculable process of truth, *or* one found oneself confronted by a system quite capable of sucking virtually everything into its vortex, a system moreover to be rejected as an illegitimate metaphysical preoccupation of and philosophical intrusion on theology itself. In response, process theology in its various representatives has apparently been unable to explain how the solution to this dilemma might be precisely to understand "system" consistently as *hypothetical*, that is, as a system whose *formal* relativity is reflected in the *relationality* (and thus in the coherent, albeit vibrant interconnection) of its grounds, its facts, and its mediated content (Faber 2000e).

Interdisciplinarity. The awareness that process theology can do justice to the larger world process only if the envisioned universality is acquired through intensive contact with the concrete world has prompted not only the integration of scientific findings into its work, but also an openness toward numerous aesthetic, ethical, and religious traditions in the same context. The differentiated language process theology then developed on the basis of this dialectic between universality and concretion, however, unfortunately made process theology itself more difficult to understand, since in any case the operational language of theological discourse must first learn how to engage regional concepts from a specific area (be it nature, society, or religion) in universal discourse. This appropriation in its own turn takes place within a complex process through which language is *critiqued* and then *expanded* into a universal context in which the context as such, and ultimately, the meaning of language, are altered. Hence the language of process theology must continually be rendered transparent with regard to the *aura of its regional origins*, the *method of its expansion*, and the *new meaning* it acquires in the universal context. Considerable linguistic barriers are invariably generated by the manifold, constantly overlapping language interplay whose universality can be rendered linguistically viable only through semantic alteration. Again, representatives of process theology have apparently not yet been successful in making transparent to anyone but specialists this dialectic of concretion and abstraction, of immersion in the languages of regional disciplines or traditions and expansion of such languages into universal linguistic patterns.

These not inconsiderable obstacles to understanding the phenomenon of process theology do prompt one to wonder whether, indeed, anyone has attempted to understand process theology *systematically*. Are there any "introductions" to process theology? It is remarkable that throughout what is already a hundred-year history there have been so few reflections on the question "What is process theology?" In the broader sense, and from a few anthologies (Cousins 1971; Brown, James, and Reeves 1971) and articles in reference works (Reitz 1970; Brown 1977; Dalferth 1989; Loomer 1971, 1987; Welker 1992; Faber 1999b), one can adduce only four introductions that genuinely understand themselves as such.

Robert Mellert's book *What Is Process Theology?* (1975) focuses on the remarkable and fruitful resonance that the process thought of Alfred N. Whitehead has generated precisely among theologians since the 1960s: "Today every respectable graduate school of theology has its process theologian, or at least someone able to teach the subject adequately" (Mellert 1975, 7). Mellert's point of departure is an explication of the fundamental vocabulary, the nexus of interrelated terms and concepts in which the *event-centered thinking* of process theology unfolds. From this vantage point, Mellert then explicates the specific distinctions obtaining within such a theology with regard to various theological themes such as religion, God, creation, human beings, Christ, church, sacraments, morality, and immortality. In conclusion he considers how process theology makes it possible to conceive of God and world as "inter-related" (Mellert 1975, 131), as *mutually beneficial and enriching.*

The introduction of John Cobb and David Griffin, *Process Theology: An Introductory Exposition* (1976), which in translation also influenced the reception of process theology in German-speaking theology, places process theology into a *critical context*. Beginning with the typical understanding of God's nature in prcoess theology as "creative-responsive love" (Cobb and Griffin 1976, 41), the authors explicate an ecological theology of nature (of the world) on whose basis human existence is then defined, Christ in his pervasive interconnection with the world is presented within the parameters of a Logos-Christology (as God's wisdom), and completion is explicated as "eschatological peace" for the perishing world. It is the *critical concept of God*, however, from which for these authors process theology acquires determinatively critical potential. On this view, God's pervasive interwovenness with the world stands over against traditional notions of God, for example, God as a "cosmic moralist" whose primary interest is in the implementation of moral rules; as an immutable, passionless Absolute that ultimately remains "external" to the world; as a "controlling power" that is nonetheless not up to the task of addressing the problem of theodicy; or as a "masculine" fantasy against which feminist and ecological categories are brought to bear.

Marjorie Suchocki's *God—Christ—Church: A Practical Guide to Process Theology* (1989) takes the dominant paradigm of "interrelation" in process theology in developing doctrines of God, Christology, ecclesiology, and eschatology. Theology in this context is to be understood as "relational theology" (Suchocki 1995, 1) that speaks of God and the world in *relational categories* corresponding to an understanding of the world as a *creative community*, as a "community" in "communication." This communal world is, however, nonetheless characterized by sin, death, suffering, transgression, and in the broader sense by *breaches of communication*. The paradigm of process theology confronts this situation and responds with the notion of a *relational God* conceived as creatively and redemptively present in everything that happens. Taking these theological connections as her point of departure, Suchocki develops a relational doctrine of God that no longer conceives God's presence, wisdom, and power as a "unilaterally" determinative omnipresence, omniscience, and omnipotence, but rather as both giving *and* receiving. She then explicates this relationality with respect to the life, death, and resurrection of Jesus, to a relational ecclesiology characterized by global solidarity, and to an eschatological consummation of the world and its history.

Finally, Robert Mesle's *Process Theology: A Basic Introduction* (1993) develops process theology critically from the perspective of the new paradigm of the relationship between *power* and *freedom* as a critique of the power structures and power focus within theology itself and accordingly as a theology of liberation. Beginning with the new understanding of God's love as a relational power that, rather than coercing and overwhelming, instead liberates, accompanies, and endures creaturely existence in the very act of redeeming, Mesle develops a theology geared to address heated contemporary questions: God's power in the face of suffering in the world; God's action in a temporal world of becoming and perishing; and a theological analysis in opposition to repression and on behalf of liberation with respect to the gender problem, ethics, ecology, and the plurality of religions. Mesle's conception, by tending toward a pronounced "theological naturalism," positions itself within the context of the question whether and to what extent the paradigm of process theology inclines toward "pantheism."

Where, then, does the present "exploration" position itself with regard to the phenomenon of process theology and its complex difficulties? It is intended as an introductory outline and as a perspectival draft. It develops an *outline* of process theology that introduces its *basic conceptual positions*. It also prepares a *draft* of process theology that articulates the differing conceptual paths chosen by various process theologies and then juxtaposes its own theological path over against previous solutions. To this end, it engages three strategies: (a) Acknowledging process theology's inclination to engage in *language critique* and to employ *creative categories*, this exploration sets about disclosing the conceptual world of process theology by engaging in the not inconsiderable task of empathetically examining its linguistic rules and categories along with the attendant philosophical and historical background and systematic context. (b) By examining *problem-oriented positions, questions, discussions, and developments* within process theology, it critically considers the process theological agenda of producing a "relational theology." (c) In a *constructive reflection* on the theological problems raised by process theology, it suggests possible solutions and examines the question whether and to what extent theology might need to reexamine the work of process theology.

The *perspectival center* of this exploration is its intention to explicate process theology as *theopoetics*. Process theology, rather than being excessively subdivided into a plethora of different aspects, is to be presented against the backdrop of a coherent *formal horizon*. The context providing such structure is found in a quotation from the theological section of Whitehead's *Process and Reality* (1929) in which Whitehead *characterizes* God and God's processive relationship with the world. This characterization both examines the critical potential for speaking about God within the parameters of process theology and discloses the perspective that provides the structure for this work: God as the *poet of the world*.

3 fold creation

The universe includes a threefold creative act comprised of (i) the one infinite conceptual realization, (ii) the multiple solidarity of free physical realizations in the temporal world, (iii) the ultimate unity of the multiplicity of actual fact with the primordial conceptual fact. If we conceive the first term and the last term in their unity over against the intermediate multiple freedom of physical realizations in the temporal world, we conceive of the patience of God, tenderly saving the turmoil of the intermediate world by the completion of his own nature. The sheer force of things lies in the intermediate physical process: this is the energy of physical production. God's role is not the combat of productive force with productive force, of destructive force with destructive force; it lies in the patient operation of the overpowering rationality of his conceptual harmonization. He does not create the world, he saves it; or, more accurately, he is the poet of the world, with tender patience leading it by his vision of truth, beauty, and goodness. (PR, 346)

This *theopoetic "definition"* offers the following perspectives for the theopoetic program of process theology: (a) Everything that happens in the world is in fact an enfolded creative act in which the universe is constituted through the proximate juxtaposition of infinite possibilities and multifarious complex physical realizations. The creative *process* is the *form* of the unity of the universe. (b) God, rather than acting within this process as part of the physical universe itself, that is, as a productive or destructive force, instead constitutes the universe as process by offering possibilities and by assessing realizations in the light of these possibilities. God constitutes the world process as *one* through the saving process of joining future and past. This is the soteriological unity of the universe in contradistinction to the cosmological unity of the world process. (c) It is as the creative power of the possible, the new, and the future (Logos) *and* as the power of the saving re-collection of the realized world process (Pneuma) that truth, goodness, and beauty are actualized as God's vision with respect to God's own essence. God shapes the creative world process into a harmony in which the process itself is incorporated as the harvest. (d) As the ultimate unity of the harmony of the world, God is nonetheless its creator; but God is a saving creator, the poet of the world who shapes that world into its saving form, the poet as "saving creator" of the world harmony in the transition through both the freedom and the abyss of the world, a world that through precisely this process becomes that which it never was.

If from this theopoetic perspective we now once more ask, "What is process theology?" the following "abbreviated theopoetic definition" can be offered: *Process theology is theopoetics, that is, a theology of perichoresis (of the mutual coinherence of all things) in which the universe represents God's creative adventure and God the event of creative transformation of the world. It is within the net of interwovenness—the process itself—that God appears as the "poet of the world," as its surprising creator (the ground of its novelty), its compassionate companion (the ground of its interwoven nature), and its saving radiance (the ground of its harmony).*

I. Figures

The Emergence and Differentiation of Process Theology

Process theology is an extraordinarily complex phenomenon whose identity developed in different currents and directions; indeed, it cannot really be understood apart from these diverse expositions and versions. A survey of its overall development, however, does reveal a fundamental dynamic that has determinatively shaped its emergence and development historically, namely, the interaction between two mutually opposed tendencies. On the one hand, there is a pronounced *empiricist* inclination that gives priority to life over concept and is committed to a world characterized by infinite flux. It is this inclination that prompted the designation "process thought." On the other hand, one encounters a pronounced *rationalistic* inclination deriving from the element of systematic severity, the commitment to the notion that the world can be known systematically (Griffin 1990b; Brown/Davaney 1990). Hence, depending on accentuation and temperament, any given version of process theology may lend priority to the empiricist or rationalistic inclination and thereby also posit certain alternative accentuations, articulated personalistically or naturalistically, understood as revelatory or as natural theology, inclined to embrace an aesthetics of flux or flow or, by contrast, to posit certain structural orders within the flux of the world.

Any *portrayal* of the complex development of process theology necessarily involves a *decision* regarding its form—depending on which of its dynamic characteristics one chooses to accent. The present study will address the following elements: the *emergence* of process theology in Chicago as a reaction involving a certain theological movement, namely, the sociohistorical school (§1), and Whitehead's organic philosophy (§2); the development of the two *fundamental schools* of process theology, namely, the empiricist (§3) and rationalistic (§4); the emergence of a specifically *Christian* process theology from naturalism (§5), existentialism (§6), and revisionism (§7); and finally the differentiated development into constructive and deconstructive variants of *postmodern* process theology (§8).

§1. CHICAGO THEOLOGY (S. MATHEWS)

That process theology was constituted as *theology* in the first place is to be credited to the theological community in Chicago at the beginning of the twentieth century. The University of Chicago Divinity School laid the groundwork for the project of process theology. The original nucleus was a twofold theological accent among the faculty of this school, namely, a strong *social* interest and the consciously reflected *cosmological* dimension of theological work.

A sociopolitical movement known as the *Social Gospel movement* established itself among the faculty in Chicago at the beginning of the twentieth century. This theological movement viewed itself as a political theology determined to confront the challenges of the industrial revolution and the consequences of the unbridled capitalistic mechanisms of the period, and to do so by interpreting the gospel and its radical political, social, and ethical implications as a thorn in the side of exploitation and impoverishment. The gospel was understood *essentially* as a "social gospel," and it was theology's task to bring this particular dimension of the gospel to bear (Cobb and Griffin 1976). One defining characteristic of this *Chicago school of theology* was that the social message of the gospel be *applied* within the contemporary context—on behalf of justice, liberation, and redemption. To this end, theology itself was "functionalized" and was to *serve* this particular goal. "We have," Walter Rauschenbusch wrote in 1917, "a social gospel. We need a systematic theology large enough to match it and vital enough to back it" (*A Theology of the Social Gospel,* 1917, 1). Systematic theology exhibits three characteristics here: (a) it serves a pragmatic soteriological purpose, namely, to actualize the redemptive dynamic of the social gospel; (b) it is in this "function" that its truth is fulfilled, and it is in precisely this task that it must prove itself; (c) the phenomenon that theology serves is broad and vibrant and antecedent to any systematization. Hence systematic theology's self-definition includes the implementation of the breadth and vitality that is essentially antecedent to it and first grounds it.

The reflexive dimension that Shirley Jackson Case and Shailer Mathews brought to the *Social Gospel movement* is also part of the emergent history of process theology. The "sociohistorical school" understood that which is Christian as being characterized by *events*, that is, as a fundamentally *historical* and *social* coherent context that necessarily precedes its own systematic reconstruction. Christianity is a phenomenon of life, a moving organism whose content and teachings emerge from within and yet also develop along with Christianity itself. Christian doctrine or teaching is always the result of the active, ongoing life of this vibrant historical organism that is "Christianity." Hence theology is always socially bound and always follows, that is, is always posterior to, the historical community as whose theory it is articulated. Offices, sacraments, and religious teachings, being processively structured and accessible only to posterior systematization, necessarily possess only fragile stability, which in its own turn is historically determined and thus changes along with the social organism as whose articulation it appears at any given moment (Cobb 1982).

The *pragmatism of the sociohistorical method* consists in placing Christian teaching in the service of the church's struggle to liberate the oppressed. In order to remain adequate to the demands of that struggle, Christian teaching itself will necessarily change, depending on those demands. The central theological category is thus not the truth of Christian teachings, but rather the adequacy with which that truth fulfills its pragmatic function. In his book *The Evolution of Early Christianity* (1914), Case turned against his teacher Ernst Troeltsch, who was intent on clinging to an a priori of that which is "essentially Christian" over against historical development. Case instead now posited that which is "essentially Christian" directly in the history of the society of Christianity to the extent it contextually lives the social gospel in every age and in every community (Case 1914).

This sociohistorical focus emerged in an even more fruitful fashion of process theology in the writings of Shailer Mathews, who was appointed professor of New Testament history two years after the department was established and after 1908 was professor of theology. Mathews understood Christianity as a social movement, founded by Jesus, whose "essential nature" consists in practicing self-surrendering love in discipleship to Jesus. Its teachings are secondary products of its life and will always require alteration depending on the circumstances of the social community out of which they emerge and which they in turn serve. Mathews—not unlike Küng in the latter's paradigm theory (1994)—understands doctrinal development in connection with various "social minds" in which Christianity as a society historically shapes and alters itself throughout its history (Mathews 1915; 1923).

Although Mathews initially thought that Christianity as such remained stable as the "general type" of that which is Christian and that only its various theological forms underwent change, he later recognized that there is in fact no "essence" of that which is Christian except in the *historical continuity of the society* of Christianity itself. Although the "identity" of Christianity in its perpetually changing life is now grounded in the confession to Jesus as the initiator of redemption (Mathews 1940, 71), that identity must nonetheless be interpreted *ever anew* in light of that confession, which itself is continually new, depending on the age. Continuity is established only through the community that consti-tutes itself in an identifiable fashion as Christianity through reflection on its own origin. Even if the designation "process theology" is rarely applied to the socio-historical theological initiative, it is not surprising that it is often "remembered as *process theology* . . . whose primary representative was Shailer Mathews (1863–1941)" (Clayton 1985, 465).

It was, finally, Shailer Mathews and Gerald Berney who incorporated an ele-ment of *cosmological* reflection into sociohistorical theology. Mathews realized that within the parameters of such sociohistorical commitment, the concept of God too was subject to the same sort of relativization, that is, needed a new, transhis-torical grounding. He developed the requisite cosmological foundation in his book *The Growth of the Idea of God* (1931), maintaining that even though the meaning of the word "God" emerges only within the history of its use in religious life, it is nonetheless *not* merely a projection, since a genuine, real ground is thereby projected into religious experience. Mathews finds this "ground" in the *real process of the universe* to the extent this process constructs "personality-evolving and per-sonally responsive elements of our cosmic environment" (Mathews 1931, 226). We speak of "God" insofar as we relate these personality-evolving powers of the world process to social givens in which they acquire theological relevance. For his part, Gerald Birney was able to develop the cosmological aspects of this initiative by placing Christianity into the new context that simultaneously directly affects everything else, namely, that of evolution. He guided Chicago theology onto the same track taken by Henri Bergson, Alfred N. Whitehead, Lloyd Morgan, and Samuel Alexander (Cobb 1982). Here the primacy of life over concept, a cos-mological focus, an evolutive paradigm, and pragmatism all became the heirs of emergent process theology.

To a certain extent, this historical situation represented the general model ulti-mately leading from Chicago to the crystallization of that which, as process the-ology, ultimately proved to be so fruitful for theology. The most significant event, the event that more than any other amalgamated the elements deriving from the previously discussed origins into a new unity and at the same time catalytically generated all further developments, was doubtless Chicago theology's encounter with the thinking of Alfred N. Whitehead. In 1926 Whitehead delivered four lectures in King's Chapel in Boston—his Lowell Lectures—in which he expressly addressed the topics of religion, theology, God, and cosmology and which he sub-sequently published as *Religion in the Making* in 1926 (Lowe 1990). These lec-tures were Whitehead's most concentrated presentation to date of the theological implications of his cosmological concept. The key symbolic foundational event in the history of process theology was when Whitehead's *Religion in the Making* began to attract attention among the faculty at the Chicago Divinity School, and Shailer Mathews, who was dean at the time, invited Henry Wieman, a guest pro-fessor in Chicago, to deliver a lecture that same year in which he would not only explicate Whitehead's ideas but also discuss their theological implications before the faculty (Williams 1970). In 1927 Mathews then appointed Wieman to the faculty itself as professor of theology. Finally, in 1928 Charles Hartshorne, Whitehead's assistant at Harvard, became professor of philosophy in Chicago. This particular coincidence of events and appointments can be viewed both as the terminus a quo and as the basis for the subsequent developmental differentiation of process theology (Cobb 1982).

§2. ECOLOGICAL DOCTRINE OF GOD (A. N. WHITEHEAD)

Alfred N. Whitehead's philosophical work must be viewed as the determinative catalyst for the emergence of process theology from the mid-1920s. Even though Whitehead himself was no theologian and had no intention of initiating a new theology, the nature and structure of his thinking generated particular interest precisely among theologians. The result was that, paradoxically, the resonance his philosophy generated in theology was more enduring than in either philosophy or scientific theory—areas to which he had dedicated himself practically his entire life. It was particularly the independent abiding of his "cosmology" within the field of theology that generated a peculiar dynamic within the reception of his work in the larger sense. The more pronounced Whitehead's influence on theology became, the more suspect did he himself become to philosophy proper. The more daring aspects of his thinking were forgotten in the discussion of key areas of his work, while those same aspects developed into independent constructions in theology that were, however, no less alien to Whitehead's original intentions. Two dates are of symbolic significance in this respect. When in 1925 Whitehead introduced the concept of God into his philosophical discussion in his first series of Lowell Lectures, which he published as *Science and the Modern World* (1925), Rudolf Carnap, who had previously been following Whitehead's work, ceased to do so (Carnap 1961). On the other hand, the interpretation by Whitehead's assistant, the philosopher of religion Hartshorne, provided the determinative impetus initiating the theological development of Whitehead's work; what Hartshorne did, however, was to establish process theology as a philosophy of religion. Curiously, both Carnap and Hartshorne taught philosophy in the same department in Chicago (Hahn 1991).

This dilemma has accompanied process theology ever since. Precisely the connection between scientific theory, philosophy, and the notion of God in Whitehead's work was bound to be attractive to a theology that viewed dialogue with modern science and philosophy as essential to its own identity; that same connection, however, was similarly bound to seem to secular philosophy like an encroachment—quite in the sense of the medieval notion of philosophy as the "handmaid of theology" (*ancilla theologiae*). On the other hand, however, precisely a "theology" that constituted itself both as philosophical theology *and* as philosophy of religion was setting out on its own independent path, and thus was bound to be suspect to a Christian theology that feared an encroachment of philosophy into its proprietary sphere of revelatory theology. Hence from the very outset, Whitehead's interpretation of process theology was positioned on the boundaries and at the front between these two disciplines.

What in Whitehead's work generated this theological interest? It was Whitehead's "cosmology," his theory of the world as a whole, in which all empirical reality, be it scientific or subjective, was to be rationally and coherently interpreted and understood. Within ever broader circles—beginning with physical mathematics and extending on to scientific theory and the philosophy of nature, all the way to metaphysics—Whitehead's works addressed the question of how one might redress the seemingly irreversible breach between knowledge and wisdom, natural science and philosophy, objectivity and subjectivity, cognition of nature and religious, ethical, and aesthetic experience. Whitehead viewed this bifurcation of nature into two spheres, that of nature and that of the mind, as the fundamental problem of a development that found its final articulation in Descartes's division of reality into a world of extension (*res extensa*) and a world of the intellect (*res cogitans*) and its unfortunate petrifaction in Kant's distinction between a transcendental a priori antecedent to all experience, on the one hand, and an empirical a posteriori that in and of itself is inaccessible (*ignotum x*), on the other. The effects were disastrous. Scientific knowledge became uncoupled from intellectual phenomena in such a fashion that henceforth allowed nothing beyond mutual reconstruction. Either intellect, subjectivity, and personality had to be reduced to material processes—ultimately to the local movements of elementary particles—or knowledge of nature had to recede into an insurmountably remote distance as a projection of human conceptual patterns (the inaccessibility of the "thing in itself"). Whitehead's thought resisted both alternatives and instead sought to reattain the *unity of experience* (Lotter 1991).

Whitehead's project was to reestablish the unity between the sundered spheres of experience and reality. This project, however, is the source of both its theological attractiveness and the hostility directed toward it. (a) *All* experience— including religious experience and theological thought—is to be accounted for in its *inner integrity*. (b) *Every* experience—one's personal veneration of God no less than scientific knowledge—is to be coherently comprehensible within the *same* context of the *one* unified world. (c) *No* experience may be understood beyond the *mutual transition* from matter to mind, subjectivity to objectivity, knowledge to reality. (d) *Nothing* isolated from experience can be real; in the larger sense, nothing isolated "in and of itself" is to be viewed as real. The genuinely volatile aspect of Whitehead's initiative is precisely that *all reality must be viewed as real* insofar as the overall agenda of "cosmology" is indeed to reconstruct all spheres of reality, all levels of experiences, and all modes of cognition within the parameters of *differentiated unity* beyond (or antecedent to) any disjunction. More yet: all knowledge of reality and indeed reality itself must be viewed as constituting *a continuous nexus or coherent context*. And more provocatively still: subjectivity and objectivity, mind and matter, cognition and being must be viewed as being *essentially* the same (Lucas 1989).

This prospect, however, is both a blessing and a curse for a theology intent on resisting exclusion by the sciences. Although divine revelation and religious experience do indeed acquire immediate relevance within the wholeness of the one, unified world, at the same time they are also transformed into relative phenomena within that world; God now appears in a world-immanent fashion as an element of that world's totality. For philosophy too, this prospect is both blessing and curse. If it does indeed overcome the fissure between cognition and reality, it is accused not only of passing beyond subjectivity and objectivity, but also of dissolving the one in the other. Because such cosmology runs the risk of collapsing into monism, Whitehead developed the notion of *ecological unity* in revising the bifurcation of reality in a fashion resisting such undifferentiated monism. The "unitexturality of reality" implies an *irreducibly pluralistic differentiation* of all reality that is in fact actualized in a *dynamic rhythm of transition*; that is, this view recognizes ecological unity as both differentiation and transition (Hampe 1991).

Whitehead's unique solution to the problem of the bifurcation of reality is to understand reality not as a given, but as a "moving whole" that *constitutes* itself within a perpetual creative transition from multiplicity to unity. This new unity of the many, however, rather than occupying all reality as a monistic unity, is instead *relativized* into *one unity among many* within a single, plural universe (which it thereby expands) of possible further unities. Although the one universe does indeed attain unity beyond all splitting into mutually alien and ultimately inaccessible spheres of reality, it does so only within a *creative process* of a mutual transition of matter and mind, object and subject, reality and cognition. Whitehead calls his reconstruction of the creative process the "category of the ultimate" in his cosmology; its function is to describe the otherwise irreducible, coherent interconnection between unity, multiplicity, and creativity.

> Creativity is the principle of novelty. An actual occasion [event] is a novel entity diverse from any entity in the "many" which it unifies. . . . The ultimate metaphysical principle is the advance from disjunction to conjunction, creating a novel entity other than the entities given in disjunction. The novel entity is at once the togetherness of the "many" which it finds, and also it is one among the disjunctive "many" which it leaves; it is a novel entity, disjunctively among the many entities which it synthesizes. (PR, 21)

Three characteristics of the "category of the ultimate" shape the universe as a movement of transition (Faber 2000e). (a) *Relationality*. There are no isolated realities, only transitions from multiplicity to unities. Every unity within the universe is composed of its relation with other unities, which in their own turn constitute the multiplicity from which the novel unity emerges. Hence it is not enough to say merely that every unity in the universe, which is always merely one among many, always stands in a (although not undifferentiated) relationship with all others; it is indeed *only* in relationship to those others which are not itself that it is *constituted* in its "inner essence" as a unity. (b) *Concrescence*. The universe exhibits unity only as the "*becoming* concrete" of unity from relationships, as the "growing together" (concrescence) of plural reality into a new unity that integrates all its relationships. Hence every process through which a unity is created is an *experiential process,* and every *emergence* ("becoming") of reality is a process integrating physical reality within the horizon of mental unity. (c) *Creativity.* Unity is always integration (synthesis) that *happens.* It is not merely that *this particular* unity emerges from within the universe; instead, the *universe* itself as a "moving whole" *becomes* within *this* unity. On the one hand, a unity emerges as creative novelty out of multiplicity; on the other, this unity is relativized into one unity among many in a universe that precisely thereby is creatively renewed. The universe *moves* within unities that in their own turn are *happenings* that become and perish. Hence Whitehead's universe is an ecological process of integration and relativization, a process of processes.

How does God fit into this ecological universe of moving relationships? In his work *Religion in the Making,* which integrates the question of God into cosmology and contributed considerably to the emergence of process theology in Chicago, Whitehead understands the movement of the universe as determined by three characteristics, which in their own turn constitute as it were the *conditio sine qua non* of such a universe, namely, creativity, the sphere of forms, and God (RMn, 90). In thus presenting the primal elements of the universe (recalling Plato's *Timaeus*), Whitehead is in fact stipulating within the movement of the universe that without which the universe cannot move in the first place, that which without actually creating this process does immanently determine its *character.* (a) *Creativity* refers to the *activity* of becoming and perishing. It describes the *pure happening* of the moving quality of the universe as the emergence of perpetually new happening. (b) The *sphere of forms* refers to the pure *potentiality* of the possible, which can be actualized in every new process. It describes *pure* longing for the unrealized and toward that which is new as actualized in every happening, and it points to the forms and structures in a universe that is apparently organized in a complex fashion. (c) But what does *God* refer to? God *integrates* creativity and forms. Only when activity and form become *concrete,* that is, are actualized in concrete happenings, does a concrete universe come into being. Here God is the "principle of concretion," the principle of limitation of pure activity and pure potentiality (§27). That which is concrete is always a finite happening, and God refers to the concretion of that which is concrete and thus to the historical form, the moving order, and the concrete development of the universe as a moving whole (SMW, 178f.).

What does God's ecological function within the framework of Whitehead's cosmology mean for the development of process theology's own understanding of God? It was at latest in the mature cosmological draft in *Process and Reality* (1929) that Whitehead recognized that a God who guarantees the concreteness of the ecological process of the universe must *itself* be concrete (Jung 1965). Hence God must not only have an "ecological function" within this process (as formative principle and determining character of the universe), but also *itself* be positioned within that process ecologically *as* "ecological happening." This notion led to the development of Whitehead's later "ecological doctrine of God," which understands God as a *concrete event* within the process of processes but simultaneously as a particular type, namely, as the concrete happening *in which* everything (and without which nothing) becomes concrete, that is, in which everything is relationally constituted and creatively relativized. God now emerges as the happening that *encompasses* the universe in its ecological relationality and creative motion, as *the empowering and saving event per se* and in which the universe, as the process of processes, creatively constitutes itself, ecologically enters into its network of relationships, and acquires enduring character even amid its perishing.

In Whitehead's ecological doctrine of God, God is the "poet of the world" who encompasses all that is processual, that is, is the creatively formative and saving process in the grand sense. Whitehead articulates God's pervasive ecological interwovenness by distinguishing between God's "primordial nature" and "consequent nature." Every happening in the world is constituted ecologically into a new totality (mental reality) from relationships with other happenings (physical reality) and with new possibilities of its own realization (Fetz 1981). In this process of becoming concrete, God is that particular dipolar—"mental" and "physical"—event from which, on the one hand, every event acquires, as its beginning, the possibility of new becoming (the ideas as God's mental reality), *and* into which, on the other hand, every event happening that has become concrete is then taken up (the concrete world as God's physical reality). The ecological process of processes—the cosmos—is, in its ultimate, perfected form, reflected in the countermovement of God's process: While the world acquires creative form and deliverance in God, God, who happens as event *Godself,* gives Godself the world as possibility and takes it up as reality (§29). With this "theopoetic concept of God," Whitehead's ecological doctrine of God became the initiator, driving force, and catalyst for the subsequent development of process theology.

§3. EMPIRICAL THEOLOGY
(H. WIEMAN, H. MELAND, D. D. WILLIAMS)

Henry Wieman's encounter with Whitehead and his subsequent interpretation of Whitehead's work within the context of the sociohistorical school in Chicago resulted in the development of the particular form of process theology known as "empirical theology," one of the three schools of process theology in the twentieth century. After examining Whitehead's work on the philosophy of nature, *Concept of Nature* (1920), and after delivering his guest lecture at the Chicago Divinity School in 1927, Wieman published the essay "Professor Whitehead's Concept of God" (Wieman 1927b) and his interpretation of Whitehead in *The Wrestle of Religion with Truth* (1927). Here Wieman not only followed the empiricist inclination of Whitehead's cosmology, but also directly picked up its early empiricist concept of God as the principle of concretion; he did *not*, however, follow the further development of Whitehead's ecological concept of God, through which Whitehead was at just that time trying to comprehend God as an event rather than as an abstract principle. It was only Wieman's own students Bernard Meland, Bernard Loomer, and Daniel Day Williams who found this "loss of transcendence" in Wieman's thought unsatisfactory and tried, each in his own way, to think through the problem anew (Brown 1977). Unlike his students, however, Wieman himself later turned away from Whitehead, finding his philosophical home instead particularly in the pragmatism of John Dewey (Reeves and Brown 1971). Nonetheless, through the radical experiential focus in his theology, Wieman not only became one of the founders of process theology, but also shaped American theology in the larger sense, so much so that his influence could occasionally be compared to that which Karl Barth had on European theology (Meland 1963).

One of the foundations of empirical theology is Whitehead's revolutionary *understanding of experience*. Whitehead maintained that the basis for every experience was a concrete connection between the experiencing subject and that which is experienced, a connection which he understood as an *event* of concretion whereby multiplicity becomes a new, creative unity; here experience is viewed as an ecological connection—within the event of experience itself—between the experiencing subject and that which is experienced. Notwithstanding the complexity of the experiential process in the mode of sense perception and reflected cognition, in its most elementary form we perceive something as being truly real if it truly *affects* or acts on us in some way, something with which we stand in some relation even *before* we experience the perception of reality as *our own* activity (S, 43f.; PR, 176). From this relational reference to reality as a whole, empirical theology deduces the *relativity* of reality and of its knowledge within the process of reality itself. As Bernard Loomer points out, this means first of all that since everything results from the experience *of* something, nothing independent of everything else can be comprehended at all (Loomer 1968). Moreover, as Bernard Meland (1976) demonstrates, this relativity generates a fundamental distrust of the rationalistic assumption that experience might be comprehensible in a completely rational fashion (Inbody 1995).

By embracing empiricism in this way, process theology to a certain extent is an heir to the empiricist philosophy of David Hume, from which even Whitehead himself had already critically drawn. Empirical theology, however, radicalizes this empiricism after the fashion of the "radical empiricism" of William James, who maintained that it is not general or universal knowledge that is accessible in knowledge (i.e., ideas), but rather only the singularity of *concrete* experiences, experiences that precisely in their singularity cannot be reconstructed by any schema or system (Dean 1990). Empirical theology operates with "a methodology which accepts the general empirical axiom that all ideas are reflections of concrete experience" (Loomer 1968, 160). Here empirical theology closes the circle with the sociohistorical school and Whitehead. The sociohistorical method maintained that no rational foundation for the course of history can be found that can be incorporated into a universal, timeless, a priori system *apart from* or *beyond* the social organisms in which it is reflected (§1). Whitehead for his part maintained that every general process of understanding is possible *only* on the basis of *concrete events* of experience and is categorically impossible apart from experience (§2). Empirical theology accordingly understands its task to be that of disclosing *empiristically* the theological dimension of the fundamental happening of experience with regard to its relativity and suprarationality (Meland 1976).

But how is God present within this "immediate experience (of the creative advance)"? For Wieman, God discloses Godself in human experience as *that particular process that leads to the ever-greater good*, the "good" being defined here as the ever richer fullness and ever greater intensity of experience that can be attained in the processes of the world (Wieman 1946). The task is to distinguish within the woven complexity of the world as the process of processes that particular process which as the good is to be accorded *ultimate trust*. Paradoxically, we trust God *not* because God, as the good, guarantees our own experiential process, that is, preserves the good we have already attained, but rather precisely because, quite in contrast to all other processes, God in fact *breaks up* everything that has already been attained, doing so for the sake of moving toward ever greater good. The *event* "God" refers to the happening of *creative transformation* within the process of experience. Trusting anything else would be idolatry (Cobb 1982). God alone is the "creative good," that is, the power of good through which "created good" can emerge within the world process in general and the human experiential process specifically. A theological reconstruction of the experiential process illuminates precisely the dimension of reality itself that cannot be controlled; here God is understood as inhering within the event of our experience of reality as its surprising, creative, and unanticipated saving dimension (Haught 1986). In the empiricist analysis of experience, "God" is the event of that which is unconditionally bequeathed, that which is creatively novel, and that which is unforeseeably saving.

Empirical theology was accused of having developed a concept of God that was so intertwined with the experiential process of the world that, inevitably, the impression arose that God was in fact dispersed within the world in a distinctly *immanentist* fashion. This charge, however, is justified only with some qualification (§5). God's transcendence remains even in Wieman's "theological naturalism," albeit with a twofold turn in the tradition of negative theology. (a) Wieman was a naturalist "for God's sake" (Cobb 1993, 135). Not unlike in the case of Karl Barth, the question of God's *presence* was more important to him than that of God's existence. Unlike Barth, however, he sought a point of departure not in biblical revelation or, for that matter, in any other tradition, but rather in the analysis of experience, where God appears not as a person or—as for Whitehead—as concrete event, but as the principle of creative transformation. Nonetheless, Wieman did understand God as a "personality-evolving" power. The reason is not naturalistic, that is, not a low estimation of personality or subjectivity, but rather *theological*. Wieman maintains that God represents something "more" than can be expressed by the notion of the human "person." Ultimately this position is an expression of the biblical injunction against images, that is, a version of negative theology. Understanding God according to the image of the human personal being would constitute idolatry and would mistake the "creative good" with a "created good." (b) Wieman defines God as the principle that sets into motion the dynamic of good within all happening. God always appears as the power of change toward the ever new, toward that which has as yet not been attained. Within "creative transformation," God becomes visible not only as the creator over against all creatures, but as that particular sovereign principle that places things into the very *situation* of creative transformation. This situation is not caused by any world process; it cannot be produced as such. It is pure grace. It is the negative-theological situation of exodus, of setting out without knowing the future into which God is directing us; and it is the situation of saving grace that breaks through all evil, that is, through all clinging to the good that has already been attained.

§4. NEOCLASSICAL THEISM (C. HARTSHORNE)

The beginning of process theology is often associated with the name of the American philosopher of religion Charles Hartshorne. His work can indeed be read as an interpretation of the interior theological side of Whitehead cosmology, so much so that people gradually began to perceive Hartshorne's thought in service to Whitehead virtually as, in a reverse fashion, the orthodox glasses required for every theological interpretation of Whitehead. In the assessment of later generations of process theologians, as well as in the public perception of process theology, the result was that, "in many respects, process theology has been as much Hartshornean as Whiteheadian" (Cobb and Griffin 1976, 167). This assessment is not entirely unjustified, insofar as it was indeed Hartshorne's theological intuition that made it possible for Whitehead's concept of God to enter into broader philosophical and theological discourse in the first place and thereby into the context of tradition of both philosophy and theology. Amid these considerations, however, many failed to recognize that Hartshorne did not actually found process theology as such; instead, he prompted the emergence of what was perhaps its most prominent and influential school in the twentieth century. Two defining characteristics of that school might be adduced. (a) With regard to its *methodology*, as an ideal type it represents the pole opposite empirical theology and in this capacity appears as *rationalistic theology* (Brown and Davaney 1990). (b) With regard to its *positioning* within philosophy and theology, from whose traditions it does indeed wish to draw, it appears as *neoclassical theism* (Hartshorne 1962).

Hartshorne, too, taught in Chicago from 1928 on, developing his rationalistic and neoclassical initiative parallel to Wieman's empirical theology. Hartshorne's authenticity in the interpretation of Whitehead derives from his time after 1925 as an assistant to Whitehead himself, who had received an appointment in 1924 as professor of philosophy at Harvard, where he actually developed the mature version of his cosmology. Although Hartshorne was certainly capable of bringing contemporary philosophical experience to bear as a result of his time in Germany as a student of Martin Heidegger, Edmund Husserl, and Nicolai Hartmann, he understood himself as coming from the tradition of American pragmatism, especially that of Charles Sanders Peirce, an edition of whose writings on the philosophy of religion Hartshorne himself edited; one of Hartshorne's areas of interest was the philosophical question of God (Hartshorne and Reese 1976). In any event, his activity in Chicago and his reputation for being an authentic exegete of Whitehead explain, on the one hand, how almost all second-generation process theologians passed through Hartshorne's school, and, on the other, how many of the points of contention raised by theological criticism with regard to the teachings of process theology are in fact grounded in Hartshorne's own theological positions and accentuations (Tracy 1990).

What, then, are the particular accents of Hartshorne's thinking that process theology inherited? Three particularly significant elements can be adduced: rationalistic theology, neoclassical theism, and panentheism.

(1) *Rationalistic theology.* Unlike empirical theology, Hartshorne began with the rational rather than the empirical side of Whitehead's cosmology. Even though the event-oriented nature of all experience prompted Whitehead, as it were, to protect its singularity by viewing it as systematically irreducible within the moving whole of the universe, he nonetheless maintained that the organization of the universe was both discernible and thus also capable of reconstruction. Whitehead's metaphysical project—given the "unitexturality of reality"—of making all experience accessible to interpretation within a *single* schema of categories, virtually begs for a logical, coherent, and necessary system in terms of which the moving whole of the universe is comprehensible as a unity (Rust 1987). Hartshorne seized on precisely this agenda in enhancing the rationality of the system such that it became the ultimate criterion. Although Hartshorne was indeed aware of the abstract nature of such a metaphysical system over against the concrete becoming of the world process itself, he interpreted that abstractness as an expression of the eternity of ideas, and furthermore interpreted the primordial nature of God in Whitehead's thought as a coherent system of ideas to which *logical necessity* is to be ascribed. The consequence of this rationalistic initiative was Hartshorne's pronounced and persistent interest in the *necessity of God.* When the analysis of the experiential process focuses on the "most general aspects of experience," what they in fact reveal is the a priori of all experience as the *necessary structure* of the world, a structure that ultimately *is* God. This position prompted the rationalistic demand that God *necessarily be demonstrable.* Hartshorne made repeated attempts to prove Anselm of Canterbury's "ontological argument" (Hartshorne 1962, 1965). In his own variant of the ontological proof of God—which derives God's being from his idea of "that which a greater cannot be thought"—God is *either* necessary *or* impossible. God is either discernible rationally in the mode of the *impossibility of not being,* or God is *merely* possible and thus contingent. But a God who "may not be" must not only not be, God also does not exist, since necessity (that is, that God necessarily be) is part of the concept of God in any case (Dalferth 1986).

(2) *Neoclassical theism.* Hartshorne's rationalism exerted its greatest and most enduring influence on process theology's understanding of God. Unlike Whitehead, Hartshorne does not understand God as *a single* event that creatively releases the entire world from within God's own primordial nature according to the possibility of its "becoming" and then takes it back up again, in a saving fashion, into God's own consequent nature according to the reality of its "having become." Hartshorne instead understands God as a *sequence (or succession) of events.* He interprets God not as a concrete event moving *counter* to the world process, but, *after the manner* of the world process itself, as a nexus of "events of God." Hence the "mental pole" of the event "God" is transformed into the *abstract character* of God in which all ideas fit together in a logically necessary system, while God's "physical pole" is transformed into *a succession of concrete events* in which, in effect, God first becomes God. That is to say, it is in this succession of events—from one event to the next—that God *becomes* within the world according to God's unchangeable, ideal character. God is integrated into the temporal world process by Godself becoming temporal in and with the world. Hence Hartshorne in fact represents a certain form of *temporal theism* (Hartshorne and Reese 1967). That notwithstanding, Hartshorne did believe that he not only preserved the authentic intention of Whitehead's ecological doctrine of God, but also made it possible to "position" it theologically within his own version. The abstract primordial nature of God, in which God is to be understood as necessary, unchanging, and eternal, corresponds to the unchangeable God of classical theism as understood, for example, by Thomas Aquinas. The enhancement of this doctrine through the understanding of his temporal theism, however, does, one might point out, overcome the weakness of the classical conception, in which God was *only* unchangeable, unmoved, and passionless in God's remoteness from the world. By contrast, the *neo*classical God is living, vibrant, interwoven into the world itself, sensitive to time, and passionately involved in the world in God's very becoming (Hartshorne 1962). More yet, these two positions can now be fused into a harmonious whole insofar as the unchangeable, remote God, rather than standing *over against* the vibrant, living, world-oriented God, instead now appears coherently integrated *within* that God (Griffin 1993). The unchangeable relates to the vital or living the same way the abstract relates to the concrete, or the way the character of a person relates to that person's history; it is, after all, an abstraction *from* the concrete, living element of vitality, and is the structure *of* that which is alive (§22). Virtually all second-generation process theologians (beyond the empiricist school) adopted this aspect of Hartshorne's thought, namely, God as the *consequence of concrete events*, which do not simply subdivide into different gods, since they are necessarily actualizing the *same character* of God (Hartshorne 1948; 1984).

(3) *Panentheism.* Unlike Whitehead, Hartshorne no longer understands God as a novel event that perpetually sunders the unity of the world (a position in which empirical theology actually stands closer to Whitehead); instead he understands God as that through which the unity of the world happens. God's primordial nature now supplies not a sphere of ever new possibilities, but the

necessary character itself of the world's structural unity. And God's consequent nature now no longer refers to God's renewal through God's saving integration of the perishing world, but rather a succession of divine events that repeat the same character. In Hartshorne's "panentheism," the *world is one in God* on the basis of its integration into the one, unified character within the concrete experiencing of God (Hartshorne 1937; 1953). To articulate more clearly his understanding of God as the unity *of* the world, Hartshorne directly and quite consciously contradicts Whitehead by drawing from one of Plato's metaphors describing the relationship between God and the world as that between the soul and the body. For Hartshorne, God is the *life principle of the world*, its *world soul*, and the world itself God's *physical body*. Within this extraordinarily intimate connection, God appears profoundly interconnected and interwoven with the world and as being wholly world immanent (Hartshorne 1991). Even though in Hartshorne's version God does not entirely become identical with the world, one may legitimately suspect that beyond God's "function" of giving unity to God's body—the world—God is nothing other than abstraction. On the other hand, however, Hartshorne's body-soul metaphor no longer conceives God as a principle (empirical theology) or event (Whitehead), but as a *person*, that is, as a life history constituted through God's integration of the world (body) within God's character (soul) (§22). This notion provided the basis for a wider reception of process theology quite apart from specialized discussions.

§5. THEOLOGICAL NATURALISM (B. LOOMER)

Alongside and together with the two more prominent schools of process theology—the empiricist and rationalistic—a "third school" is often named as well, namely, *Christian* process theology (Welker 1992). To the extent it deals with specifically Christian theological questions, it may well be designated as a "school," though what is at issue is a common *interest* whose articulation transcends the notion of school in generating many different initiatives (§§5–8). What specifically Christian process theologians have in common is that they all tend to develop Christologies. Alongside the various Christian process theologies that arose especially as a result of Hartshorne's own theological reception, the version that emerged from Wieman's empirical theology is often overlooked, perhaps because its articulation has naturalistic implications that are generally not understood as being motivated by Christian concerns and thus often not immediately recognized as part of Christian theology. Such is particularly the case with the "theological naturalism" of Bernard Loomer, a student of H. Wieman and C. Hartshorne, who from 1945 taught theology in Chicago and later at Berkeley (Cobb and Griffin 1976). The expression "process theology" itself may even go back to him (Ford 1974; Loomer 1978).

From Wieman Loomer adopted the "naturalistic" inclination to understand God as an event happening *in* the world or as a principle of the world's creatively transformational event happening. Hartshorne's panentheism taught him to understand God as a form of the unity of the world. And both drew Loomer's attention to Whitehead, who taught him to understand the unity of the world as a creative happening, as a moving whole, and as creativity. Loomer's own explicitly theological naturalism, however, is not interested in sublating God into the concept of "nature" (*physis*), into that which emerges or grows forth from within itself. Nor was he interested in allowing the distinct "subject" of theology to disappear, as later interpreters of empirical theology believe (Mesle 1993). Instead, Loomer was interested in *radicalizing* the object of theology and in conceiving God *beyond* all simple differences. Hence "[t]he world is God because it is the source and preserver of meaning" within "the creative advance of the world in its adventure." For Loomer, God symbolizes "the ultimate mystery inherent within existence itself" (Loomer 1987, 42). Hence, although unlike Whitehead Loomer does not understand God as a universal process of departure moving counter to the world, he does share Whitehead's view that God refers to the adventure of the world, to its creative departure into novelty. Unlike Hartshorne, however, he does not conceive God as the "subject of the world" (world soul), though he too acknowledges that God is comprehensible only within the horizon of the wholeness of the world. Unlike Wieman, he does not understand God as an event *in* the world, but rather as the creative event *of* the world itself. This concept of God acquires theological relevance once its religious meaning is recognized, since here God refers to a *wholeness* of the world *insofar as* that totality is understood as referring to a *loving conferral*, as it were, *of wholeness* as the ultimate mystery of the world. His determinative insight is that God is not to be interpreted beyond the world and thus beyond all experience, but as the expression of the *redeemed wholeness of all experience.*

Loomer consistently defended himself against the charge of having taken God away from theology with this "naturalism," of having developed a "headless theology" (Loomer 1948). He is indeed militating against the traditional Christian understanding of God's transcendence according to which God affects or influences the world, as it were, "from the outside" (Loomer 1949). In that sense, his "naturalism" is resisting what he sees to be the regnant element in the traditional theological understanding of God, namely, the "supernaturalism" of a *deus ex machina*. His naturalistic slant in talking about God is not, however, directed against God's creative sovereignty over against the (physical) world (Loomer 1971) or against God's self-revelation in Jesus Christ (Loomer 1948). Loomer's naturalism is, however, based on the realization that this faith can succeed only by illuminating the *experiential structures* in the world, which on the most fundamental level reveal that everything *is* (and thus can be experienced) only because it stands *in relation* to something else. Hence God, rather than being remote or beyond the world, is instead eminently world-related, eminently relational, and indeed is the source of all relationality. Even though God cannot simply be conceived as an "event" in the world, God cannot be directly distinguished from the world even though God is not identical with it. Hence Loomer understands God neither as an abstract "relation" nor as a "person," that is, as a distinct structure of events and relations (different from others), but rather as *the* universal *network of interrelated individuals* (Loomer 1987, 258).

God's relationship *with* the world is God's relation *as* world insofar as within the weave of relationships the world itself is creatively transcended toward redemption. God as the redeemed relational wealth of the world is love (*agape*). Loomer's concept of God is profoundly shaped by an understanding of God's loving surrender to the world, God's suffering with it, and God's sacrifice for it. God's love alone is capable of integrating the world—with all its contradictions, tragedy, disharmony, defeats, and failures—into a (redeemed) whole. Loomer speaks here of God's *size* and *stature* (Dean and Axel 1987). Here Loomer's understanding of transcendence becomes accessible. God is capable of withstanding the world with all its contradictions and discordance. The "size" of a person is the degree to which that person is able to endure dissonance without collapsing (Dean 1990). God's "size" is infinite; God's *agape* is "completely selfless love" (Loomer 1987b, 251); that is, it is the power or capacity to integrate all dissonances and all evil. *Thus* does God distinguish Godself from and transcend the world without positioning Godself "over against" it. God's "size" interprets God's "goodness" as that particular *fullness* capable of bearing everything without losing itself, and of integrating everything without collapsing (§45) (Faber 2000e).

Loomer's God, rather than being the unity of the world as manifested in unambiguous order (as is the case in the classical understanding of the *Logos*), instead creates living unity *as* adventure. Because Loomer's God is in this sense a living God, God also remains *ambiguous*. God is never "unambiguous," since only "order" is unambiguous; and order is "dead." Loomer's God remains perpetually ambivalent and the source of the world as adventure. Quite contrary to any predestined and merely unfolding "preestablished harmony" of the world in God (Leibniz), Loomer's understanding conceives the harmony of the world as the *integration of the tragic*—following the lead of Whitehead's later thought. Hence he also understands the world as being profoundly permeated, informed, as it were, by the cross of Christ. God's *size* consists not in relieving the world of its ambivalence (by elevating it into eternal order), but rather, to the contrary, in spurring it on to ever new adventure, an adventure to which Godself, however, is coextensive by way of God's capacity for encountering its tragedy and disharmony in God's love (§45) (Faber 2000a).

§6. EXISTENTIAL THEOLOGY (S. OGDEN, J. COBB)

The development of process theology into a respected theological enterprise must doubtless be examined together with two theologians, namely, Schubert Ogden and John Cobb, whose thinking derives not only from Chicago theology, but also from the influence of "existential theology" (Cobb 1982, 40) in the reception of Heidegger and Bultmann. This theology, by the way, is by no means a recent phenomenon, going back rather to Hartshorne's own time as a student of Heidegger (Hartshorne 1990). Whereas Cobb wrote various articles concerning the relationship between Heidegger and Whitehead (Cobb 1964), and Ogden developed his own theology in conscious critical dialogue with Bultmann (Ogden 1970), both were concerned with genuinely merging process thought and existential categories within theological discourse. To that extent they can be viewed as the catalysts and examples of process theologians' interest in existentialist philosophy and theology during the 1960s.

These two theologians' affinity for a philosophically *open* field of inquiry not tied to any *one* philosophy (notwithstanding the considerable affinity for certain philosophical positions) made it possible to develop a form of process theology which found its identity in a revelatory theology, that is, beyond those particular reflections of a philosophy of religion in so far as it is not shaped in any essential or determinative way by the concrete Christian context. This philosophical relativity in its own turn enabled process theology to understand itself in a conscious fashion as theology within the context of the church (Ogden 1996). Especially Ogden's existential analysis of faith and Cobb's existential analysis of Christian modes of existence indicated the path along which one might establish this theological orientation toward the church. Both thinkers view philosophy as an adequate *mode of understanding* for dealing with the challenges of Christian existence, and both genuinely integrate not only the initiatives of Heidegger, Bultmann, and Whitehead into their theologies, but also—and each in his own way—the empiricism of the Chicago school and the rationalism of Hartshorne. Moreover they pay special attention to questions of the meaning and sense, the rationality and credibility of the Christian faith in the contemporary world and initiate connections with political theology, liberation theology, and feminism (Cobb 1982; Suchocki 1994).

Schubert Ogden follows Bultmann in seeking to provide a "radical demythologization and existential interpretation" of faith (Ogden 1980). In the process, he tries to do justice in a unique way both to the *empiricist* side by reflecting on the existential experience of faith and to the *rationalist* demand for an "*objective*" grounding of existential experiences such that, in some way, God is "real" for every person (Ogden 1991, 22). The grounding for this assertion is provided by (Whitehead's) metaphysics. In his main work, *The Reality of God* (1964), Ogden takes this step away from the "non-objectifying" and thus "existential" act of faith to the objectivity of the truth of faith by engaging in a reflection specific to process theology. Faith in God (which cannot otherwise be objectified) becomes unavoidable, as it were, only when based on a *universal* experiential *structure*, of which we can indeed become aware through our own *existential* experience. It is by employing Whiteheadian categories that he now completes his analysis of experience, which—contra the supernaturalism of earlier "theism"—discloses faith in God from within the "integral secularity" of the very structures of our experience. In Whitehead's categories, "God" emerges as the expression of the existential experience of the *elementary value* of our life, albeit an experience that cannot be further reconstructed. Our self-experience is grounded in an otherwise ineradicable, primal trust in the value of our existence, the latter of whose "objective" ground is "God." Hence "the reality of God" is already affirmed where our existence emerges, believing, free of anxiety, and in a state of trust. In a fashion counter to a mythological interpretation of this reality of God, however, Ogden preserves an element of existential certainty for which the "objective existence" of God no longer represents a meaningful category (Buri 1970). This position corresponds not only to the biblical God of universal love at the foundation of our existence, but also to Hartshorne's relational understanding of God, according to which God is both eminently relative and eminently absolute. It is only God's *dipolarity* in this sense that first secures the eminently relative, existential relationality of God's love, which is by no means lost in the sense of not being objectively offset, grounding instead— by virtue of its own absoluteness—the absolute value of existence as such.

John Cobb has been widely recognized as the founder of Christian process theology (Hanselmann and Swarat 1996). After studying under Hartshorne in Chicago, he received an appointment at the renowned Claremont School of Theology near Los Angeles, establishing the Center for Process Studies in 1973, which did indeed provide a stable center for American process studies beyond theological discussion proper, ensuring it a broader forum (Welker 1993). His book *A Christian Natural Theology* (1965), a classic of process theology, provided a theological assessment of Whitehead's understanding of God. Without any further argumentative support, Cobb chose there to follow Hartshorne instead of Whitehead in understanding God not as an event, but as a "person," that is, as an event nexus with a distinctive life story, which in the case of God is the world itself (Cobb 1974). Cobb is concerned with the *biblical* God, which he tries to approach by way of Hartshorne's "neoclassical theism." On his view, the "neoclassical" expansion of the unchangeable God by way of God's integrative world relationality— Hartshorne's living "person"—frees the biblical God from those particular aspects that make it more difficult to understand God as self-surrendering, responsive *love* that is genuinely affected by the world itself; such aspects include unchangeability, the inclination to implement eternal principles of order, and moral superiority in dealing with the suffering world. By contrast, the loving God, rather than already knowing everything, instead waits for our own knowledge and understanding. And instead of striving for absolute control, the loving God provides the possibility itself for the adventure of the world. To articulate this liberating, relational view of a God who is itself Godself interwoven with the world, Cobb adopts Whitehead's useful distinction between God and creativity, a distinction that defines the biblical God of love as a concrete event, as a living happening, rather than as a metaphysical principle, *also* incorporating into this view the idea of the creative freedom exercised by creatures themselves, a freedom *not* capable of being controlled or guided by omnipotence. Cobb understands these two aspects in a theologically cogent fashion as the relationship between "ultimate reality" (creativity) and the "ultimate actuality" of that reality (God) (Cobb 1982a). Although God does actualize this creative freedom archetypically, God does not do so by dominating creaturely creativity, but rather by lovingly accompanying and encompassing it. Creativity is that particular power of self-creation grounding the intrinsic value and independent status of every creature, value and status moreover that God has no interest in breaking by coercive force, since God Godself is the ultimate actualization of precisely this reality. From this perspective, a fundamental theological criticism of repressive power came to dominate Cobb's thinking, which in subsequent decades was also applied in areas transcending theological discourse proper, including in dialogue with ecology, economics, politics, the feminist analysis of power, and the realities of the church.

Unlike Ogden's rationalistic reconstruction of God from universal experiential structures in faith, Cobb's existential theology actually tends toward an *empirical theology of historicity* even though Cobb shares with Ogden the same vision of a dipolar God and a creative world. In his book *The Structure of Christian Existence* (1967), Cobb does commit to existential theology insofar as he understands faith not primarily as an acceptance of certain truths, but as a mode of existence; at the same time, however, he resists an unhistorical analysis of human existence that simply identifies that which is truly Christian with that which is truly human. Contrary to the assumption that Christian existence accordingly represents the *true* version of genuinely human existence (while simultaneously devaluing all other modes of existence as unactual in this sense), Cobb understands Christian existence as *one* possible *structure* of genuine human existence alongside and with others. In an analysis (recalling Shailer Mathews) of the historical relativity of human "essence," an essence that can never be accessed in any pure fashion, insofar as it is actualized only in a changing, creative succession of historical forms, Cobb understands the identity of specifically Christian existence in terms of relativity that is historical in a twofold fashion and thus inaccessible to rational reconstruction. (a) That existence is *what* it is through *how*—through which historical forms—it has become what it is. Just as Buddhist existence emerged from Hindu existence, so also Christian existence emerged from Israelite and Hellenistic existence. (b) Every mode of existence can in its own turn be actualized in various modes—in the prophetic mode, for example, within the biblical context. Hence the identity of Christianity is always historically determined, and is so in a way commensurate with the axiomatic dipolarity between relativity and absoluteness of process theology and always in connection with the Christ event. In fact, the Christ event itself represents the constitutive element in that identity, albeit always exclusively in creative "re-cycling" within different historical contexts.

§7. SPECULATIVE THEOLOGY
(L. S. FORD, J. BRACKEN, M. SUCHOCKI)

In John Cobb's work, there came to the forefront within process theology a methodological reflection that sought to unite the mutual inner *dynamic* of its two prominent currents, the empiricist and the rationalistic. Because Whitehead called it "speculative" (PR, 4f., 7–9, 203–5), some referred to this "third method-ological direction" of process theology as *speculative theology*. Speculative process theology is inclined to develop a general, anticipatory schema of ideas in which everything can be adequately interpreted (Brown and Davaney 1990, 79), a schema it ultimately borrows from Whitehead's framework of categories. The *self-referential* result of this specifically *dynamic* juxtaposition of rational system and empirical experiential adventure, however, is not only that new empirical ele-ments are constantly being integrated into the system, but also that *the system itself is changed.* The consequence is the permanent *revision* of Whitehead's eco-logical doctrine of God—in a fashion taking it beyond the fundamental decisions of empirical theology and neoclassical theism. This revisionism of "speculative" process theology generated several interesting versions of process theology, such as those of Lewis Ford, Joseph Bracken, and Marjorie Suchocki. Bracken follows Hartshorne's inclination to understand God as a "person" (event nexus) but does interpret that position anew. Ford and Suchocki return to Whitehead's inclina-tion to understand God as an "event" while nonetheless fundamentally rethink-ing the position of the God-event with respect to the event-world.

Marjorie Suchocki, a systematic theologian in Claremont, California, under-stands her own revisionism as serving the soteriological function of all theology. In interpreting process theology as a "relational theology"—an expression going back to Bernard Loomer (1978, 518; 1984, 321f.)—she engages a differentiation of Whiteheadian categories in interpreting God more strictly as the *reality of the future* that is world oriented, creative, and redemptive. Commensurate with the dipolar perspective, this interpretation means, first, that God's primordial nature creatively discloses to every creature, as its future, possibilities of becoming (or attaining to) its identity; second, it means that God's consequent nature then redemptively takes up and transforms into Godself precisely that which has become in its historicity. That is, God now emerges as the *power of the creative and redemptive future*—a notion also expressed by Pannenberg and Moltmann (§39). By embracing the world thus, God becomes the power of liberation from the power of sin (Suchocki 1995). Yet because in Hartshorne's thinking God *becomes,* as part of the world, like a world event and oriented toward God's own future, and because the "person" of God is wholly involved in the temporal process of the world, God cannot be conceived within these categories as the power of the future. Hence Suchocki follows Whitehead's assertion that God can-not be a succession of events that unifies itself only in a fashion oriented *toward* the future; instead, God must be an event that unites everything else in a fashion coming toward the world *from* the future. Here she draws on the insight that although God, like every world event, is indeed *dipolar*—grounded *mentally* from within a sphere of possibilities and *physically* from within the history of its origins—one must assume a "reversal of poles" within God. Unlike other world events, God's primordial nature encompasses *all* possibilities as the vision of harmony, not just a restricted developmental space. Hence instead of developing or constituting God-self in a fashion oriented *toward* the future as God's own identity, God instead already *is* every possible future of every possible world. And unlike other world events, God does not ground or constitute Godself out of a history "antecedent" to God; God's consequent nature instead takes up the *entire* history of the world into itself without restriction commensurate with God's primordial vision. In this reversal of poles, God is always already perfect and creative—commensurate with the absolute aspect of God's primordial nature. For *precisely* this reason, however, God can be understood as utterly and wholly *sensitive to the world* and *capable* of redeeming the world—commensurate with the relative aspect of God's consequent nature. Suchocki's God is the loving God and the God capable of selfless love. God "grows" from within the world—"accrues" on the world, as it were—insofar as God, in a saving fashion, takes it up into Godself. God does not, however, (first) "become" (God) with the world in this sense, since God is already the completed future of all becoming and thus the future of the world as well.

Lewis Ford goes one step further and interprets God as *the event of the future* as such (Ford 1981). Like Marjorie Suchocki, Ford severely criticizes Hartshorne's interpretation of God as an event succession but radicalizes Suchocki's own position by partially suspending process theology's distinction between God and creativity and then interpreting it anew (Ford 1986). He interprets creativity, the power of creative self-constitution of every event, as fundamentally *temporal,* that is, as a movement within time through the three temporal modes of future, present, and past. In the present, every event is conceived as happening and as being self-creative; here creativity grounds the plurality of all happenings in the universe. In the past, this process of event happening has been concluded and has acquired objective status; here creativity grounds causality, that is, the formative pressure of the past as the history of newly arising events. This distinction between past and present modes of events corresponds to Whitehead's distinction between immanent creativity (self-constitution) and transcendent creativity (causality) (PR, 129; AI, 230; S; Stokes 1960). Unlike Whitehead, however, Ford adds a new mode of creativity in order to complete the symmetry, a mode he identifies with God, namely, the *creativity of the future* (Ford 1986). Here creativity grounds the font of time as the unity of God and future creativity *and* the creativity of God as the unity of the world process itself. This identity encompasses God as creator of the world and the font of all creativity, a creativity which, as it were, self-creatively pluralizes itself in the present of all creatures in order to objectify itself in the past in self-transcendence. Whitehead's primordial nature, God's ideal, mental aspect, is united with creative activity to become the power of differentiation, a power that by always being future is also (from the perspective of the past) always nonobjectifiable, and at the same time (from the perspective of the present) presubjective and which as such both grounds the world and releases the world from within itself. Hence in the future, and unlike in the conception of John Cobb, elementary reality (creativity) and elementary actuality (God) are one and are for *precisely that reason* the ground of the world (Ford 2000).

Joseph Bracken, a Jesuit and systematic theologian in Cincinnati, initially did not follow this understanding of God as an event of and from the future, maintaining instead Hartshorne's temporal concept of God while simultaneously revising it to accord with a *Trinitarian* understanding of God. He radicalizes Hartshorne by understanding God not only as a "person," but as a "community of persons," that is, not just as a *single* event succession, but as a *community of event successions* (to wit, those of the Father, Son, and Spirit) (Bracken 1985). This choice does, however, force him to provide an answer to one fundamental structural problem in Whitehead's own conception of event, namely, that concerning the *unity* of event *nexuses*. If, that is, all events represent the "growing together" of multiplicity into an organic unity, while this unity itself, when it perishes, is really only one among many, then must not the unity of organisms in the macrocosmos necessarily be *secondary* over against the inner unity of the events as "atoms" of the community? Bracken solves this problem by understanding events in an organism not as representing atoms merely "at their unique location," but rather as representing ecological unities constituting an interwoven network. Every event in an organism is as it were present *everywhere* in that organism. That is, every event is at once both itself and all others. Bracken calls the common sphere of all events in a community the *energy field* of that organism (Bracken 1989). Paradoxically this consideration brings Bracken close to Ford's identification of God and creativity; since this energy field, constituting a community of events, is pure activity, it ultimately corresponds quite closely to the notion of creativity. Hence Bracken interprets the unity of God as an energy field of the community of the three divine "persons" (event successions) as creativity that is the *one* essence or nature of God (Bracken 1991). Bracken's revisionism thus ends in the mystical theology of a thinker like Meister Eckhart with his differentiation between "God" as actuality distinct from everything (the Trinity as the community of communities) and the "Godhead" as activity that is, by contrast, identical with everything (the essence of God as undifferentiated unity) (Bracken 1995).

§8. POSTMODERN PROCESS THEOLOGY (D. GRIFFIN, C. KELLER)

A person's self-perception and the assessment of that person by others rarely coincide. David Griffin understood himself as a "speculative theologian" even though, wholly positioned as he is within Hartshorne's conceptual framework, he is more easily called a rationalistic theologian (Griffin 1990b). Moreover, in referring to John Cobb as "postmodern," Griffin is in fact referring more to his own program. Griffin understands postmodernism as the attempt to establish a new, *integrated worldview* over against the disjunction of modernity by the Cartesian dualism of mind and matter, phenomena of the mind and the reality of the natural sciences, subjectivity and objectivity (Griffin 1977). For the enterprise of establishing a new, holistic worldview, he advocates a *constructive* postmodernism and views process theology (in the tradition of Hartshorne) as capable of implementing precisely this postmodern project (Griffin et al. 1993). Wholly counter to this position, postmodern philosophy within American (neo-)pragmatism (J. Dewey, R. Rorty) and French deconstructionism (M. Foucault, J. Derrida, G. Deleuze) constituted itself as a position of radical relativity, irreducible plurality, and infinite *différance*. A number of process theologians, especially Catherine Keller, accepted this *condition postmoderne* for the theological project and reconsidered Whitehead's ecological, relational, and processual paradigm from this perspective (Keller/Daniell 2002). They advocate a *deconstructive*, pluralistic postmodernism over against integralism, the latter being no longer accessible and not desirable in any case.

David Griffin, a theologian and philosopher in Claremont, California, understands his own constructive postmodernism as a reaction to a modernism irretrievably lost in insuperable dichotomies. Methodologically Griffin follows Whitehead's understanding of how (scientific) objectivism and (philosophical) subjectivism can be overcome by the vision of the *one* world in which everything is coherently interrelated such that, despite all plurality from the perspective of individual detail, no dualism emerges; instead, everything in the world is included within a *single texture* (Lotter 1990). Because philosophically Griffin does indeed intend to establish a new worldview capable of integrating all the more important epistemological methodologies, he is convinced that the future will see the advent of a worldview of holism in which there will no longer be any dualism. Griffin understands this holism as an alternative expression for his "postmodern constructive thought," which in its own turn is an alternative description of process theology as such (Griffin 1989). Indeed, process theology itself now emerges as an integrative program that will no longer fit into any scholarly discipline, not even that of academic theology (Cobb 1996, 198). This expansive cross- and interdisciplinary character of process theology prompts Griffin not only to engage in intensive dialogue with scientific disciplines such as physics, biology, and psychology, it also almost forces him to adapt other epistemological forms and modes such as parapsychology (noncausal contact) and transpersonal psychology (other levels of consciousness) (Griffin 2000). In implementing this holistic program, Griffin theologically accepts Hartshorne's fundamental understanding of God as a "person," as an event succession integrated into the world itself, which is distinguished from that world insofar as it is always antecedent to the world with God's vision of world (God's primordial nature) and at once always posterior to it within the concrete events of God in which God constitutes Godself "physically" within and from the world which God then takes up into Godself (God's consequent nature). Here God is understood antisupernaturally within a *rigorously temporal theism* as the creatively ideal power of the universe, a power that moreover moves within a universe characterized by Einstein's theory of relativity (Fitzgerald 1972; Hartshorne 1977). Many process theologians today follow this concept (partially or completely), particularly where process theology is identified with the influence and tradition of Hartshorne (Griffin 1986).

Catherine Keller, a systematic theologian in New Jersey, is one of the most respected representatives of a form of postmodern thought—a *deconstructive* program—diametrically opposed to constructive postmodernism. In this version, process theology is a critical discipline engaged in analyzing human reality and its unexamined foundations with the goal of *liberation from repressive forms* of these foundations (Keller 1997). She understands Whitehead not as a "fundamentalist" of otherwise inaccessible and self-evident grounds (as does Griffin in constructing a holistic worldview), but in an "anti-fundamentalist" fashion as a creative adventure of deconstruction of unexamined claims, or—as Whitehead himself puts it— as a critic of abstractions that are held to be concrete (Keller and Daniell 2002). Keller associates Whitehead's analysis of coercive power with French deconstruction of the foundations of Western thought, especially as articulated by Foucault, Derrida, and Deleuze. Such includes a critique of the myth of historical unity (postmodernism), a critique of structures guided by political interests in preserving constellations of dominion (postcolonialism), a (feminist) critique of constructive conceptual forms in theology (poststructuralism), and a new theology of gender difference (queer theory). The metaphysical character of Whitehead's metaphysics is suspended, and from the perspective of his thought the axiom of reconstructed plurality and of irreducible difference is then fruitfully engaged anew on behalf of "cosmology" over against all monopolizing "unity." Keller has engaged this critical, anti-repressive, pluralizing agenda in a theologically enlightening fashion, especially with regard to apocalyptic thinking and the theme of creation. Apocalyptic expectation, which has repeatedly managed to dominate theology in one form or another, is deconstructed as the seduction of absolute discontinuity, which believes itself capable of taking leave of this world. Apocalyptic ultimately issues in a Platonic dualism that strives for the "beyond" at the cost of an ecological ethics of engagement on behalf of *this* world, at the cost of a focus on the notion of network, from the perspective of which every absolute emergence is invariably seen to be merely the remnant of supernaturalism, as the actions of a deus ex machina for whom the world serves merely as the material for another world or even merely as a source of pleasure (Keller 1986). Keller circumscribes the same theological wound with regard to creation theology. The notion of creation from nothing (*creatio ex nihilo*) sunders the fundamental relationality of the world and merely establishes unilateral, repressive power structures. The basis for this entire conception is a feminist distinction: the masculine desire to do away with the feminine, with the world as an interwoven unity, the masculine condemnation of the "primal sea"—with which many creation myths begin (cf. also Gen. 1:2)—as either "nothing" (nihilation) or as "evil" (condemnation) (Keller 2000). Whitehead's concept of God emerges in new attire in Keller's revivified focus on biblical and mythological sources, namely, as depth (in the image of the sea, *tehom*), as creative power (in the image of the spirit, *ruach*), and as a plurisingularity (in the image of the highest God, *elohim*) (Keller 2003). Although a number of younger theologians have embarked on this path as well, the discussion of potential theological consequences is still in its infancy (Keller and Daniell 2002).

Given the challenges theology faces in this century, I would suggest understanding process theology as an enterprise that builds on the goals of constructive and deconstructive methods in process theology and at the same time maintains ties with the three earlier methodological versions of empiricist, rationalistic, and speculative process theology—albeit in an altered form, namely, as *reconstructive theology* refocused on Whitehead's ecological theology, and, in its *critical reconstruction*, as the basis for a (permanent) *reformation* of process theology (Faber 2000). The articulation of such a reconstructive theology will address three considerations.

(1) Unlike an "orthodox" canonization of Whitehead's philosophy for use in process theology, here even the inherent inconsistencies of that philosophy are to be acknowledged. Indeed, to the extent these inconsistencies emerge from the inner logic of that philosophy rather than being imposed from without, they serve to thwart the construction of any (closed) system. Whitehead himself never believed he had created a "system" in any case; nor does his thinking suggest he did so, since *any* theory exhibits event character and as such must be subject to creative transformation if it is to abide. Long before French poststructuralist deconstruction, Whitehead sought a *nonessentialist departure* from dependence on fixed, self-evident "substances" and "subjects" (Keller 2002, 6).

(2) A reconstructed Whitehead facilitates a critical reformation of initiatives of process theology beyond their inherent systematic restrictions. Renewed focus on Whitehead's thought might illuminate anew an element of theological breadth that is more open than the successively emergent "Whitehead orthodoxy" in process theology might have been willing to acknowledge. Renewed focus on the *theological* roots of process theology in empirical theology might moreover illuminate anew system-critical perspectives at the foundation of process theology that allow priority to be given to *vibrant, living development* over the rigidity of system.

(3) The theological reasoning of process theology thus faces a twofold task of mediation. First is the reconciliation of nature and spirit, science and wisdom, reason and history. Second, this reconciliation, however, cannot be carried out within the framework of premodern holism, but only in a transition through a postconstructivist relativization of reason itself, which is to be the instrument of reconciliation (Welsch 1995). Put differently, reason in process theology is always positioned within the field of tension between empiricist and rationalistic tendencies, constructive and deconstructive methodologies, that is, within a field of *irresoluble* antagonism in which *all parties* must nonetheless be accorded their rights. The best way for any future process theology to deal with these *contrasts* will be to engage them all *simultaneously*, albeit not with misguided irenic goals, but precisely in an acknowledgment of *their mutual negation* as the driving force for creative theological reason.

Unlike the situation in constructive theology, the *deconstructive* element is accorded particular significance here. Similarly unlike in the American variant of deconstructionism (R. Rorty, M. Taylor), which Griffin justifiably criticizes as "eliminative postmodernism" intent on fleeing into pure constructionism (Griffin 1994), French deconstructionism strives not to eliminate "reality," but to discern its "trace" in language, in the text, and in *différance*. This "other of the text," however, emerges only in the deconstruction of all essentialism, substantialism, and epistemological fundamentalism, and only by abandoning faith in the "fulfilled present" of uninterpreted "reality" within our own cognition. Nonetheless, as Keller points out, such deconstructionism does strive for the "other" (Keller 2002). Reality is by no means exhausted by the concepts in which we mediate it; put theologically, "God" is not a pure construct of our language. Process theology as "theopoetics" deconstructs all substantialism—including that of "God"— but does not understand itself as poetic (in the sense of fanciful) construction of subjective experiences, but as the *poetics of the "trace" of God* as the other of the language of God. It is in this sense that I understand postmodern (reconstructive) process theology neither as a constructive nor as primarily deconstructive (Derrida) or poststructuralist (Deleuze) enterprise, but more as a *postconstructive theology* that seeks the *other* in the language of God of process theology itself (§30), but is able to find that other only *in* that language, namely, in the process itself of deconstruction and reconstruction.

II. Foundations

The Philosophical Background

A. N. Whitehead's "organic philosophy" or "philosophy of organism" provided the determinative theoretical stimulus behind the emergence of process theology (PR 18f. et passim). Process theology is characterized by a fundamental commitment to a new paradigm of an ecological, relational, and processual worldview, just as this ecological, relational, and processual theology will correlate this new worldview into an organic whole. In critically turning away from obsolete paradigms of the world with an eye on establishing a new "cosmology," process theology is fundamentally committed to overcoming materialism and idealism (§9); to coming to a new understanding of subjectivity (§10); to coming to know that which is singular (§11); to reconstructing real things from events (§12); to combining connection (relationship) and change ecologically (§13); to constructing space-time as an expression of communication and freedom in the universe (§14); to acknowledging a new paradigm of "living vibrancy" and creative disorder in the cosmos (§15); and to acknowledging creativity as the principle of all continuity (§16). This agenda prompts process theology to call into question many of the most important fundamental philosophical insights in Western cosmology, both ancient and modern, something not only contributing to the sometimes strangeness of process theology, but also turning it into a fascinating conceptual model.

§9. MATTER AND MIND
(RECONSTRUCTED PHILOSOPHY OF SCIENCE)

Even before Whitehead arrived at the metaphysical dimension in his thought, his examination of questions of mathematics, logic, and physics finally led to his writings on the philosophy of science around 1919. Even at that time, Whitehead's intentions were already shaped by his vision of integrating matter and mind (CN chaps. 1–2). The disjunction of mutually independent spheres of being, namely, that of nature with its material structures, structures accessible to the natural sciences, on the one hand, and that of the mind or intellect as characterized by subjectivity, on the other, turned out to be an error in our own process of perception (and the epistemological ideal based on that process) (Klose 2002). This disjunction or separation, one might point out, is extremely old and has essentially always permeated Western philosophy in the distinction between the world of becoming and that of ideas, in the body-soul problem, and in the self-distinction between the natural sciences, on the one hand, and the humanities, on the other (FR, 61). This separation was fixed both ontologically and in philosophy of science in Descartes's bifurcation of two substances, the *res extensa* and the *res cogitans*; ever since, this distinction has prompted powerful attempts to reduce all that is mental to the material. The naturalistic program has traditionally included methodological claims to derive consciousness, human freedom, and the phenomena of subjective perception from causally determined natural processes. For example, colors are viewed as the subjective illusion of various wavelengths, consciousness as an evolutive epiphenomenon of brain processes, and freedom of decision as the anticipatory reflection of the predetermined natural course of events. Materialism appears to be the natural implication of the construction of a philosophy of science (§44) (Sayer 1999).

In his book *Concept of Nature* (1920), Whitehead traces this philosophy of science back to its beginnings in ancient philosophy and finds in it an ideology of the "bifurcation of nature" (CN, 26ff.). (a) Materialistic reductionism illegitimately takes control of the scientific method, since that method was originally introduced to explain natural phenomena, not, however, to be abused in establishing the causal derivation of mental or intellectual phenomena (Rohmer 2000). (b) Because, for Whitehead, the concept of nature includes the experience of nature, any abstraction of the processes of perception, experience, and cognition from nature will inevitably lead to an abstract nature, which must not, however, be further applied in an explanatory fashion to the experiential processes themselves from which the abstraction was made in the first place (Klose 2002). (c) The separation into spheres of nature and mind is based on the philosophical decision to recognize as real only that for which a clear (mathematical) concept can be constructed, while anything known in this way exists independently and thus as a causal reality. By contrast, Whitehead reconstructs nature from the *experience* of nature such that every act of *perceiving* nature constructs the *ground of knowledge* of nature "in itself." A "perceptive event" then constitutes not only a mental phenomenon that in some fashion stands over against nature, but an occurrence *within* nature itself. In its own turn, nature is now released from its mindless condition and is viewed instead as a process in which cognition represents a natural process (Löw 1990).

What, however, is the source of the illusion of this separation of mind and nature? Within our own *thought*, we are accustomed to constructing a clear concept of whatever it is we "know," something that can happen only by "separating" or "isolating" that which is to be known, that is, by observing it "in and of itself" without considering its relationships to anything else. In the *perception* itself, however, which represents the basis of our thought, we initially find ourselves situated within the one, single sphere of nature as our frame of reference. In *perceiving* we evaluate the foreground and background, emphasize certain "factors" within the framework or weave of nature, focus on those factors and allow everything else to merge into a diffuse relational background. In *thinking*, however, we lose the sense of interconnectedness between all the various "factors" in the one "fact" of nature and *believe* that the otherwise relationally complex "factor" thus thrown into relief is actually an independent being, an independent, substantial "entity." This process of *substantiation*, in reversing the relationships attendant on the original perception, causes us to view the reference framework now merely as the attribute of independent things and to view these now as the *substrate* of all relationships. The result is a world consisting of material particles with posterior (accidental) relationships (CN, 12–16). The world now appears as an accumulation of independent things that merely bump up against one another like billiard balls, though only in an external fashion within the "container" of time and space (external causality). The relational arrangement of nature within perception (which established the entire epistemological process) now becomes a subjective question mark within dead nature, void of meaning insofar as it can now be derived wholly from the causal chain of (what is now abstract) external nature. The fundamental error of this bifurcation is precisely that it views that which appears within thought (causal particles void of relation) as concrete nature.

If, however, the experiential process itself represents a natural process, and if, in a reverse fashion, nature itself, rather than being mindless, is itself a cognitive process, what emerges is a new paradigm of nature as an *organic network of relationships*. Whitehead examines this network and transforms it into a "metaphysics of experience" in which nature and mind, causality and freedom mutually determine, permeate, and produce each other (Beelitz 1991). Two insights prompt this view: (a) Because nothing is without relationships to other things, any conception of an independent substance and a material substrate is obsolete. Hence also nothing can really be said to abide, that is, to subsist intact through change; there can be only moments of emergence and perishing. Nature itself consists not in "things" in the traditional sense; instead it continually *becomes* within events and event nexuses (Hampe 1990). (b) Nothing is without perception and experience. There is nothing beyond experience (PR, 167). Whitehead initially distinguishes between "perceptive events" within the nexus of natural events before realizing that a perceptive structure must inhere within *all* events if they are to be fully relational (Rapp 1990). Every event constitutes itself from the "perception" of other events that enter into it as relationships, from which then the new event becomes that what it is. Nature, rather than consisting of passive particles, instead consists of organisms that constitute themselves within an active perception of their surroundings (Emmet 1966).

Here Whitehead positions himself within a series of thinkers who reconstruct matter and mind as an original unity. The "Copenhagen interpretation" of quantum reality as described by Niels Bohr finds in quantum events, to the extent they are not measured, a characterless *ignotum x*, which thus also cannot be denied mental characteristics (Casti 1989). Bertrand Russell's "neutral monism" understands every atom of reality as being at once both material *and* mental depending on the epistemological angle of vision (Popper and Eccles 1997). Recently Donald Davidson's "theory of supervenience" has articulated something similar on the basis of a philosophy of science that maintains that mind emerges along the entire range of causal happenings without intervening in them, which is also why it need not be disputed (Brüntrup 1996) (§44). In contrast to these thinkers, Whitehead views *fully relational happenings* as the locus of the distinction and relationship between the material and the mental. (a) Every event is *dipolar*, that is, includes both a material and a mental side (PR, 45), distinguished as two poles of a single whole through their *relationship* with other events. Events forming a new event constitute its *physical* pole; those possibilities representing the developmental sphere of a new event constitute its *mental* pole (PR, 108). (b) Fully relational nature occurs as a *moving nexus of relationships* of happenings that both become and perish and that constitute time and space; the physical pole perceives the past, the mental pole future possibilities. Present events are independent of one another and thus external in the fashion of being expanded into space (AI, 191–200). The universal event nexus thus prompts the emergence of two fundamental characteristics: the *passage of events* and the *extensiveness of events* (CN, 34). (c) All natural events constitute a *nexus of causality and freedom* insofar as they derive causally from their own past and yet still maintain a free element of self-determination within the sphere of their own possibilities (PR, 27f.; Categoreal Obligation IX). Nature itself is a *creative* process with its own history, albeit one that cannot be reconstructed through laws, and in its own turn gives birth to an otherwise indeterminate surplus of novelty (PR, 28, 46, 128, 146).

The significance of this new paradigm of nature as an organism cannot be overestimated. Time and space, history and the actual processes, causality and freedom, subjectivity and objectivity, quality and quantity, value and measure all emerge from the *same* coherent context of the event structure of reality (Altizer 1975). This view implies an *evolutive* concept of mind and matter in which both appear not as unreconciled opposites, but within a *gradual differentiation within the organizational form of organisms*, extending from the stability of elementary physical particles to the "living vibrancy" of biological organisms on to intellectual freedom and reflexivity within the context of human brain functions (§§19, 44) (Fetz 1981). With respect to the "organicity of the mind" (the essential corporeality of all allegedly immaterial mental activity) and the "creativity of matter" (the activity and indeterminate causal character of the allegedly passive material substrate), all of Whitehead's subsequent philosophical commitments acquire meaning that direct themselves against the previously mentioned "bifurcation of nature" thereby articulating the *fundamental ecological thrust* of his "philosophy of the organic" (Hampe 1990).

§10. SUBSTANCE AND SUBJECT (REFORMED HISTORY OF PHILOSOPHY)

In his critical discussion of philosophical tradition, Whitehead found his assertion confirmed that the organic paradigm, although indeed influential, was nonetheless always threatened by the "bifurcation of nature." His analysis revealed that the cause was the emergence of a manner of thinking focused on substance and a commensurate reinterpretation of the fully relational happenings of nature as relationless encounters between otherwise isolated entities (Wolf-Gazo 1980). One further result was that the concept of substance attached to this understanding of that which is relationless but enduring overwhelmed the understanding of subjectivity in transforming subjects into relationless phantoms surrounded by lifeless matter, and into irrelevant epiphenomena superfluously produced and captured within self-enclosed, predictable circles of causality (Lotter 1996). Plato, Aristotle, the English empiricists, Leibniz, Kant—all contributed to the victory of "inorganic" thinking, even though Whitehead does discern and accordingly emphasize the places where vital elements of the organic paradigm are at work among all of them, to wit, precisely at those junctures where they made false "substantialist" decisions (Kann 2001).

In Whitehead's view, within the history of tradition of such philosophical decisions the dualism between idealists and materialists is already discernible in the antagonism between the Platonic doctrine of ideas and the atomism of Democritus (PR, 96; AI, 121–22). Plato's ideas are eternal with respect to the concrete arising and perishing of the world insofar as they can be isolated as the *forms* of that which becomes concrete and as such acquire the function of perfect prototypes for what is the (then) imperfect world of becoming. They not only remain the same even amid temporal changes in the world itself; they also determine the *essence* of that which becomes in that world and which moreover finds its act of being in precisely those ideas as forms (Rorty 1983). Because the idea, as the essence of the concrete, remains the same amid the chaos of the arising and perishing that takes place in this world, the real relationships or connections of the concrete can represent nothing more than marginal additions. By contrast, Democritus's atoms are mutually independent particles within empty space whose external (as it were, statistical) movement generates relations that do not, however, affect the material essence of those particles. They, too, remain the same, moving independently and unaffected by any of their constellations. It was on the basis of these decisions that in both philosophical and scientific theory stable concepts of idealism and materialism of substance have prevailed until today that are based on the same presupposition, namely, that substances themselves remain untouched or unaffected by their relations (Kann 2001). Whitehead's organic paradigm radically transforms both conceptions, maintaining that Platonic forms in fact do not represent substances that ground the act of being, but rather potentialities for the actualization of events, for whose creative act they provide room for play, which in its own turn does, however, emerge from within a *real* nexus of relationships. Democritus's atoms, then, do not represent static stuff, fluctuating in unrelated particles, but are instead the expression of quantum-physical interconnectedness of flowing energy, in which each quantum of energy represents a relationally determined event within the entire field at its locus within that nexus (PR, 309).

Whitehead believes that the most significant mistake effective in the history of philosophy with respect to inorganic substantiality emerged from Descartes's reception of Aristotle's concept of substance and its subsequent application to the understanding of subjectivity (Kann 2001). Although Aristotle did—as Whitehead himself was aware (PR, 209)—develop an organic concept of substance in his *Metaphysics*, it was precisely the concept developed in his writing on the *Categories* that exerted the most lasting und unfortunate influence, namely, the determination of the essence of a thing as that which abides amid all change, that is, that which remains the *same* amid all change (Fetz 1981). Descartes picks up this definition of substance and makes its decisively inorganic implications even more specific in defining *substance* as that which needs nothing more for its being than itself. Equipped with this relationless, independent being as that which is ultimately real, Descartes now defines two substances: the extensive (*res extensa*) and thinking (*res cogitans*). Substantialism ends up not only in the familiar dualism of matter and mind, but also in an essential definition of subjectivity as relationless self-thought. The *res cogitans* is referring to subjects with respect to their power of self-being, even though ultimately this "power" turns out to be that of the impotence of isolation, of the loneliness of the subject that ultimately knows *only itself*. This concept of the subject, overgrown as it is by an excessive focus on substance, leads to a subjectivism which has lost all relationality and all objective reality, ultimately ending in an egoism of free-floating individuals. While it is true that Descartes himself tried to avoid this immanent implication of his position by positing that God (as the ultimate independent substance) provided the necessary relationality of subjects to the world beyond themselves (*realitas objectiva*), his position nonetheless opened the door to the inexorable development of modern individualism, subjectivism, and relativism (Lotter 1990).

Although Whitehead adopts Descartes's subjectivist ideal (objective knowledge is always that of subjects of the act of knowing) and understands subjectivity as the ultimate (metaphysically unavoidable) "situation" of all cognition, he frees the concept of the subject from any distortion by an inorganic concept of substance. If for Whitehead the concept of substance itself already represents an *abstraction* articulating not that which actually happens within nature, but that which within those happenings is *possible* (the constancy of a given form), then all the more should the concept of the subject itself be understood anew on the basis of its *concrete activity*, that is, without the assumption of some antecedent, constant substrate. But what *is* the concrete activity of a subject? It is the activity of *becoming* a subject (Lotter 1990). Even though this concrete activity or subjectivity of the subject does contain abstractions—as the past (physical reality) in relation to which it becomes what it is; as possibilities (mental reality) that it realizes; as anticipation of its self-transcending (objective reality) in which it is cast beyond itself into the becoming of other subjects—these abstractions are always elements of *subsequent* constancy and continuity *brought forth* or *transformed* precisely by the activity of its becoming. Because the abiding or stability of substance represents an abstraction in the processive emergence of subjects, subjects themselves can "become" only as *relational texture*; that is, rather than being isolated, they instead are fully relational unity, *and* they possess *event structure*, that is, they become and then perish. Subjects are nonsubstantialist, discontinuous activities of subject becoming (Busch 1993). There is no element of constancy behind them that abides and determines that which they are. They are not in any substantialist fashion substrates of their own becoming (so that they cannot become anything other than what they already are); it is rather in a nonsubstantialist fashion that subjects first become that what (once they *have* become) they are (Faber 2000e).

Three considerations shape Whitehead's concept of the subject: (a) Subjects come to their existence insofar as they become *out of others*. They represent a self-becoming out of a past, on the one hand, and into a future, on the other, a future into which they bring *themselves* forth. Furthermore, subjects always constitute themselves out of the experience of reality which is *not* they themselves. A subject always emerges *out of other subjects*, subjects that objectivize themselves in that subject, represent its physical reality, and exert an influence within it as its history. At the same time, subjects always perceive this past from a certain *perspective*, a sphere of possibilities, which indicates what the history that a subject "re-collects" might become, once *this particular* subject has become concrete (Lachmann 1990). (b) Subjects are meaningful *for themselves* insofar as they *become*. Their concrete becoming constitutes their being. Indeed, their becoming *is* to a certain extent their "being" *as* subjects. Subjects arise from a *creative activity* in which, precisely in their arising, they combine their past (physical pole) and their sphere of possibility (mental pole) into a *unity of immediacy*. In this capacity, they represent not only transitions of a past—a past that recollects itself within them—into a future of potential self-exceeding in which they acquire meaning for the becoming of other subjects, but also *self-meaningful processes* of self-acquisition (Sayer 1999). (c) Subjects become meaningful *for others* by *perishing*; they possess no constancy with regard to their own immediacy, since otherwise they could not be experienced by others. Because of the relationality of subjects, they must transcend or move beyond themselves toward other subjects, that is, in their completion they become *objective* by losing their own immediacy, and *as* objects they simultaneously become moments of experience of other subjects, which constitute themselves as subjects only through precisely these experiences (PR, 88).

In Whitehead's organic paradigm, the "subject" no longer has the sense of "underlying" in the essentialist sense, but rather of "lying ahead (in the future)" in a nonessentialist sense; that is, no underlying substrate inheres in the subject ("sub-ject"), but rather is it ahead of its self-acquisition. The subject is actually "superject" (PR, 28f.). Subjectivity/superjectivity exhibits an open dipolar structure, namely, an inner polarity of being brought forth *causally* from the other and of bringing itself forth *finally* (*causa sui*), on the one hand, and an external polarity of self-constitution and self-transcendence, on the other. In its open dipolarity, a subject "becomes" in three phases. First, it preposits itself ideally in its becoming (as the simple possibility of its arising); second, it aims at itself in its becoming by collecting its past (actualizes its immediacy) in order, finally and third, to transcend itself in its self-acquisition (to become an object, to lose its immediacy) and in so doing to be "present" in other subjects (to act causally without being "self-present") (Lotter 1990).

The *rhythm of the subject/superject* in the *reformed subjectivist principle* (PR, 79f.) is Whitehead's corrective of the subjectivism not only of Descartes, but also of Hume and Kant (Faber 2000e). (a) Contra Descartes, who did after all thoroughly think through the "subjectivist principle" himself, Whitehead's own principle means that subjects, rather than being isolated substances, instead represent *relations in becoming*, the gathering of relations into a subjective unity and the self-transcending of subjects as relations within other subjects. (b) Contra Hume, who was aware of the finitude of the subject as a chain of impressions, Whitehead's principle means that subjects themselves can be *present in* other subjects, namely, as "subjects of the experiences (of others)" in which they bring themselves forth out of other superjects, and as "superjects of their (own) experiences," in which capacity they acquire meaning in others (Welten 1984). (c) Contra Kant, who with his transcendental principle removed subjectivity from empirical experience and degraded objects into projections of subjects, Whitehead's principle emphasizes that subjects can also become *objects of experience* (contra the "transcendental subject," which is always merely the presupposition of experience) and can *become subjects out of objects* (contra Kant's *ignotum x* of the transcendental categories of the knowledge of subjects) (Busch 1993).

Whitehead's reformed subjectivist principle removes from the concept of subject not only the substantialism that has exerted such considerable influence throughout the history of philosophy, but also its skeptical and relativistic consequences, and in so doing paves the way for a *new realism through relationalism* (Faber 2000e). In Whitehead's *organic* paradigm of subjectivity, one finds a critique of the inorganic paradigm of substantiality as such; the organic now

becomes the paradigm for *all* reality (Kann 2001). In Whitehead's nonessentialism (antifundamentalism), a kind of "pansubjectivism" acquires universal character and renders reality as such, that is, *its universal structure*, a texture of events
(Wiehl 1990).

§11. THE SINGULAR AND THE UNIVERSAL
(COPERNICAN EPISTEMOLOGY)

Although Whitehead's "pansubjectivism" does involve considerable consequences for epistemology, it must be correctly interpreted so that it not be misunderstood as "pan-psychism" (Hampe 1990), that is, as the simple assumption
of the universal animation of nature. This pansubjectivism refers not to "omni-
animation," but to the epistemological insistence on the *unitexturality of reality*,
without which according to Whitehead no knowledge of reality is possible, insofar as isolated substances cannot be known and insofar as substantialist subjects
can only know themselves (Faber 2000e). Here "cognition" itself becomes an
integral part of the structure of reality as such (Wiehl 1990). But what does this
mean? (a) If indeed subjectivity determines reality as such, moreover reality is
stripped of its alleged substance character, that is, the assumption that everything
consists of self-enclosed, incommensurable substances. Insofar as subjects are in
fact *fully relational events* rather than substances, reality in its own turn is to be
understood as a *relational arrangement of events*. (b) *All* events exhibit the structure of subject/superject. They arise from the perception of other subjects that
objectify themselves within them. They become what they are and then perish as
moments of becoming for other subjects. Reality as an organic texture of events
is manifested as the *primal rhythm* of becoming (as subject) and perishing (as
superject); of causal determination and then final self-determination; of self-aim-
ing in becoming and then, by contrast, becoming a cause in perishing; of becoming a subject and then an object. (c) Reality arises as an organic texture of events
that individualizes itself out of relations and then generalizes itself to relations;
that is, as "subject," every event is *singular* and meaningful for itself; as "superject," it then acquires *general* meaning for others. (d) Structurally every event is
a "cognitive process." Since reality consists in *singular* events and *their* general
meaning or significance within other events, knowledge is knowledge of the *singular* in *its* general significance (Störig 1997) (§47).

The fundamental assumption of the "unitexturality of reality" as fully relational reality in which every existing thing is in fact a cognitive process and in
which knowing as such is a constituent part of being—this assumption deconstructs not only substantialism in the broader sense, but also the epistemology
attaching to it. Here Whitehead's critique of substantialism is linked to his critique of the substantialist epistemologies of Aristotle, Descartes, Hume, and
Kant insofar as, commensurate with their understanding of substance, they
maintain that one can know *only* the universal, never the singular. In what

amounts virtually to a *Copernican revolution in epistemology*, Whitehead consistently understands knowledge as *knowledge of the singular* (Wiehl 1990). In Whitehead's *reformed-subjectivist epistemology*, the universal represents only a (necessary) *abstraction* in (and on the basis of) the event activity constituting the singular, which the universal cannot grasp or cover. On the other hand, the singular can become an object of the cognitive process only if, rather than being utterly inaccessible, it is somehow "knowable" (PR, 49, 211, 230). This is precisely what the event structure seeks to accomplish. The complex dialectic of singularity and universality *corresponds* to the complex process of the becoming and perishing of events, insofar as universality always represents *abstraction within the process of singular events*, whereas singularity itself implies *a process of the constitution of an event* out of other events and their abstractions (Hampe 1990).

The fundamental argument in Whitehead's Copernican turn in epistemology is found in his critique of Aristotelian substantialism. For Aristotle, individual substances are *unknowable*; the goal of knowing is the *universal*. By contrast, Whitehead demands knowledge of the *singular* and in so doing demonstrates the status of singular events *as* cognitive processes (which accordingly are not only knowable, but also indicate the cognitive process as such). Whitehead argues that if, as is the case in Aristotle, the world is conceived within a dualism of substance and nonsubstance (*accidens*, predicate, character, attribute), then something can only either be substance itself or occur as something nonsubstantial *in* a substance. Everything substantial is independent, everything nonsubstantial dependent. If it is also true that substances too are always subjects rather than predicates, then subjects too are always substances. In that case, however, as far as subjects are concerned, something is *always* either subject or nonsubject (object, predicate, activity). The result is that substances and subjects are *unknowable* because, *first*, substances can never enter into other substances—they are independent (only dependent nonsubstances occur "in" or "on" substances)—and, *second*, subjects (as substances) can know only *one* substance, namely, *themselves*. The isolation of substances and subjects makes them *ineffable* (unknowable *in principle*); their nonsubstantial *characteristics* become the object of cognition, since they are knowable precisely because they are universally accessible. So their universality indirectly attests, as it were, the knowledge of substances *by way of* the *universal characteristic structures* surrounding them (PR, 157f.). The result is that subjects as substances are *isolated mysteries*, and knowledge of the universal, that is, of the communicable characteristics of subjects, *never* grasps the *essential* (hence, according to Thomas Aquinas, we cannot know the essence of so much as a gnat) (Wolf-Gazo 1988).

The grave consequences of the substantialist epistemological concept come to the fore in Descartes's thinking. The "knowing substance" is one of two mutually independent substances that are not really connected with each other. Knowledge can never be *real*; it must always be *ideal*, that is, knowledge of ideas as the universal, as universals, as thoughts. "I think, therefore I am" (*cogito ergo sum*). This sentence more than anything else demonstrates not only that the innermost essence of knowledge is now no longer merely knowledge of the universal within thinking, but that the innermost essence of substantial *subjects* is nothing other than *thinking*, that is, a knowing of the universal. The substantialist subject disappears in its cognitive ideal, namely, the universal. This, however, is merely commensurate with the untenability of the substantialist concept of subject, which necessarily ends in monistic collapse. That is, the definition of substance as that which is (completely) independent introduces a concept of God into the discussion. But if God is indeed the ultimate independence and thus the substantial subject *as such*, then it will invariably suck into itself the two "substances," *res extensa* and *res cogitans*. Descartes ends in Spinoza, whose *single* substance, the primordial nature (*natura naturans*), produces an infinite number of dependent attributes, including extension and thinking. Ultimately there can be only *one* subject that fulfills the substantialist condition; and precisely by fulfilling that condition, the world in its own turn is reduced to its *attributes*. Ultimately God knows only Godself by way of the universality of the world. And since God must thus be unknowable, only God's universal ideas are discernible; indeed, they are the essence equally of our cognition and subjectivity. And again we end in a solipsism of the subject and of its unknowability beyond its ideas (Kann 2001).

Although David Hume brings fresh energy to the largely immobile substantialist epistemology, according to Whitehead he nonetheless fails by having not sufficiently resisted its temptations. As one of the first in the Western tradition, Hume initially challenges the very notion itself of the substantiality of the subject. There *are* no substances, he asserts, but only *series of impressions* whose knowing-together (from habit and because of repetition) awakens the impression of substance. And this assertion is indeed revolutionary. That which is seemingly constant and which as such grounds a substance as independent, self-sufficient reality, now turns out to be merely *appearance*, namely, as the *repetition* of the same character pattern in ongoing or repeated impressions. It is not subjects that function as substances, but rather substances themselves that are the patterns within the *cognition of subjects*. This insight reconstructs the substantialist theory of subjectivity from a subjectivistic epistemology and deconstructs it as a delusion in the cognition of subjects. Whitehead's criticism at this point is that instead of going on to develop a nonsubstantialist theory of subjectivity, Hume now also dissolves the subject itself in his epistemology. It too is merely a result of impressions, a chimera in the knowledge of cognitive events that constitute themselves as "a subject," insofar as in the *repetition of impressions* (PR, 136) they awaken the impression of an all-encompassing "I" (Welten 1984). If, however, subjectivity is derived from the repetition of events, then it must appear as that which in them is *capable* of being repeated, namely, as the *universal*, which abides or remains constant as *idea*. Paradoxically, then, although Hume did indeed find his way through to a nonsubstantialist concept of event, by "digitalizing" cognitive events—which remain self-sufficient and unknowable particles—he nonetheless reduced his concept of subject to the illusion of a quasi-substance. Once again, the ground is the unknowability of the individual, since the individual impression itself already represents a sense impression, a character pattern, something universal; in the meantime, however, the subject is merely an illusion within the cognitive process as the repetition of the universal (Lucas 1989).

Kant, finally, by paving the way for nonsubstantialist subjectivity, remains in Whitehead's opinion all the more mired (albeit undetected) in subtly solidifying a substantialist epistemology. Kant's own "Copernican revolution" in epistemology abandoned a notion of objectivism which yet acknowledged *uninterpreted* perceptions of reality (the "thing in itself"); the knowing subject itself became the "producer" of objective reality, and cognition became an operation in which the subject itself brought forth the world commensurate with its *own* inner cognitive structures (Busch 1993). But this again dissolves the singular into the universal. The key point in Kant's concept of the subject is as a matter of fact not at all the *empirical* subject concretely perceiving the world, but the *transcendental* subject that (with its own conceptual forms) itself constitutes the *condition of the possibility of knowledge* of the world. That subject *constructs* rather than *experiences*, and as the presupposition of cognition cannot itself enter into experience (Wiehl 1990). But if the subject, rather than perceive the world, instead *constructs* it according to its own transcendental structure, then knowledge of the world comes about commensurate with the *thinking* of the subject, that is—similar to Descartes's ideas—commensurate with *universal conceptual forms* in which the singular cannot be represented, remaining instead the unknown, the *ignotum x*. Ultimately the subject and object of cognition remain experientially remote and separated from each other, mediated only through the universality of conceptual forms. And the Cartesian dualism of substances remains intact.

In Whitehead's view, only Locke and Leibniz managed to break through the unknowability of the particular. Locke did so by assuming "ideas of individual things" alongside universal ideas in the cognitive act, Leibniz by interpreting the concrete elements of the world as individuals within the framework of his doctrine of monads (Kann 2001). Yet even in these two thinkers, one finds the subliminal prevalence of substantialist epistemology. Locke was unable to maintain the notion of "ideas of concrete things," and Hume subsequently—and paradoxically—reduced in a substantialist fashion this inconsistency in Locke's epistemology by deconstructing the "ideas" as universals, ultimately as projections of the percipient event rather than as the perception of the objects of cognition themselves in their singularity. Leibniz for his part did maintain the understanding of his monads as individuals of knowledge of the world, as what amounted to holographic world centers in which the world itself, as a whole, was reflected in each individual monad. But he was forced to remove from the relational context of these monads any notion of mutual perception (causality); from the substantialist perspective, they can be reflected in one another only by way of the world (the universal) and by way of God, who brings all of them into a "preestablished harmony." As such, Leibniz's monads remain "windowless" and isolated, just as do Locke's cognitive events (Rohmer 2000).

Contra this substantialist epistemology's solipsism (a substantial subject knows only itself) and skepticism (nothing essential is cognitively accessible in the characteristics of substantial subjects; hence nothing is really known at all), Whitehead now articulates his own, nonessentialist event theory, in which a *relational* concept of subject permits subjects to become (arise) out of objects and then to perish in becoming objects (superjects) for other subjects. His Copernican revolution assesses the following insights from philosophical tradition. (a) Contra Aristotle, the individual or particular (in its concrete appearance and history) cannot be understood merely as a marginal appearance of a universal (form or essence); instead, that particular *is the essential itself*, and is so, precisely when *not* mediated merely by universal (knowable) characteristics but instead by standing *in* relation or itself being *a relation*. (b) Contra Descartes, the solipsism of the independent and self-sufficient substance—which ultimately, as Spinoza demonstrates, can be only *one* substance—must be replaced by the singularity of many events mediated not by ideas or as ideas (of God), but by *real relations*, in which the duality of extension (materiality) and ideality (conceptuality) is, if not suspended, at least relativized as *inner features* within their *constitution*. (c) Contra Locke, subjects know not just "ideas of concrete objects," but *real objects*, and do so *immediately, directly*. (d) Contra Hume, events of cognition are not merely series of isolated particles mediated through universal ideas, but the *real "inbeing" of particles within one another* (PR, 137). (e) Contra Leibniz, events are not to be understood as mutual mirrors that are "windowless" toward one another, having instead a *causal relationship* through which they concretely *produce* one another. (f) Contra Kant, finally, subjects do not construct objects of cognition from universal cognitive structures; instead, *subjects of cognition themselves arise out of their objects of cognition* (PR, 88).

Whitehead calls his new epistemology—following and replacing Kant's three critiques—the "critique of pure feeling" (PR, 157f.). In this *epistemology of feeling*, subjects are present *within* others and are knowable in their *singularity* (Wessell 1990) (§36). The epistemological "Copernican revolution" here is the impossibility that the universal (in whatever form, as ideas or conceptual forms, sense impressions or world concepts) can lead to knowledge of the concrete. Whereas philosophical tradition generally held that universals were capable of defining the concrete and of thereby leading to knowledge (of the "substantial essence" of the concrete), Whitehead now shows in a reverse fashion how the singular can *in principle not be reconstructed* by the universal at all; instead, it must be concretely *felt* in its singularity (its "inner essence") (PR, 55). In this context, "feel" refers to real perception of concrete events precisely in their singularity, shaped by their historical positioning and causally brought forth by felt events. And indeed, Whitehead formulates a new cognitive concept of "experiential events" as *processes of the (subjective) feeling of events, which are themselves (objectified) feelings*.

Whitehead's nonessentialist understanding of epistemology combines Kant's critique of uninterpreted reality (reality not guided by the subject and theory) with a critique—taking its orientation from Leibniz—of the notion that reality can be reconstructed from abstractions. With respect to Leibniz, Whitehead speaks about a return to "pre-Kantian modes of thought" (PR, XI), albeit not for the sake of embracing revivified "objectivism" (substantialism), but in order to avoid the subjectivistic consequences of Kant's own Copernican turn (Wiehl 1971). The "unitexturality of reality" as required by the "reformed subjectivist principle" comprehends reality as a *relational process*, in which subjectivity and objectivity mutually construct, deconstruct, and reconstruct each other. There is no uninterpreted foundation of knowledge, as in Descartes, nor any subjectivistic disjunction within reality rendering knowledge indistinguishable from imagination, as in Kant. Cognition is thus the deconstruction of the repressive *disjunction* of reality and knowledge. Reality *itself* is a cognitive process, as in Leibniz (Klose 2002). Contra Leibniz, however, in Whitehead's nonessentialism subjects first *become* within the cognitive process itself, and are (objectively) *real* only after having thus become. In Whitehead's postmodern epistemology, the universal must be deconstructed within a "critique of abstractions" (of clear, self-evident, and self-present ideas) as a "critique of pure feeling." The ("felt") concrete, however, is not reduced to a new kind of "uninterpreted reality"; instead, it itself, out of its very constitution, *interprets* (objective) reality, that is, arises in its own turn out of a process of integration of past interpretations (Lachmann 1990). The process of *feeling* the singular, the latter of which cannot be reconstructed from the universal, demonstrates that cognition is an interpretive operation (which, as irreducible and unavoidable, can thus never come to completion) that has *become* concrete and thus has no abstract (systematic, uninterpreted) origin, but rather one that is historical or (as Whitehead puts it) "causal," that is, not rationally self-evident, moreover an origin that thus must be interpreted ever anew in *each new instance* of feeling (Emmet 1984) (§41).

§12. EVENT AND OBJECT (DUAL METAPHYSICS)

Whitehead's event theory links general experiential *metaphysics* with the *epistemology* of feeling. Its mediation of the singular and universal interprets the "unitexturality of reality" as an ecological paradigm that not only allows for a *real* knowledge of reality, but also interprets reality itself *as* a cognitive process. Whitehead's epistemic metaphysics, thereby, introduces into all reality an element of inwardness, subjectivity, and causal indeterminateness (as the negative foil of freedom) and accords to all being an inviolable intrinsic value, indeed, even an element of noncausal spontaneity (AI, 195). In a reverse fashion, this "pansubjectivism" also expands (natural) causality from a merely *mechanistic* concept to a *historical* one; the determinative influence exerted by origin is understood not as absolute, but as historical, as tradition, as heritage, as the decision between a repetition of the past or an alteration of the given data (PR, 26–28, Categories of Obligation III, IV, IX). The question is thus how physical reality can be understood in its *givenness* if *all* that happens in the world is of a creative character. Put differently, how can there be any *constancy* in nature if everything in the cosmos possesses event character (Busch 1993)? What is the status of "objectivity"? Put differently yet again, how do the things of our world arise from events?

Even in his early writings on the philosophy of nature, Whitehead was already distinguishing between event and object—the fundamental distinction of his dual metaphysics. In his *Concept of Nature*, Whitehead understands "events" as singular occurrences, with definite spatio-temporal extension, that replace or follow one another or that arbitrarily subdivide a happening with spatial-temporal extension; they represent, as it were, *spatio-temporal slices* through the world. "Objects," by contrast, refer to that which substance metaphysics associates with what *remains the same* amid the change or through the succession of events (CN, 170). Within the epistemic weighting of this dual construction, events attain a natural character, that is, a character of organic growth. Rather than representing arbitrary slices of space-time, they instead constitute the *inner unity* of a cognitive event (Clarke 1984). Within the sequence of cognitive events, objects then represent that which is knowable over against the ultimately inaccessible singularity of events; that which in the event has already passed away (and thus no longer currently exists) remains knowable within *another* cognitive event. At this early stage, "objectivity" refers to that which abides amid a succession of fleeting events, as it were ideas, forms, or patterns, which by being repeated over a period of time within event chains thereby generate cognition and, on the other hand, constancy within nature (CN, 143ff., 166–70; Welker 1984; Ford 1984a).

Even at this early stage, at the time of Whitehead's writings on the philosophy of nature, the changes over against the substantialist view are obvious. It is now the activity of events, rather than the essential form, that guarantees actual reality. Forms are objects, that is, possibilities of actualization within events. Events, rather than being constant, are instead *abrupt*. Within them, objects constitute a *character* that can be "inherited" down along event chains. Events become and perish. Patterns remain if they are repeated in events. This is Whitehead's early nonessentialist reconstruction of allegedly self-identical substances out of event successions with objective character.

In his philosophy of science as presented in the book *Science and the Modern World* (1925), Whitehead understands an event as an *inner unity*, that is, no longer as an arbitrary spatio-temporal slice that actualizes a character, but as an *organic "atom"* of nature, as *unity of assimilating becoming (prehensive unity)* (Ford 1984), but simultaneously also as one *atomic unity* among many others (SMW, 64–66). Here Whitehead's own philosophical reflections merge with developments within physics in the theory of relativity and early quantum physics in asserting that the smallest building blocks of the universe are in fact events that—externally—constitute otherwise *indivisible* "atoms," that is, entities that *cannot* be further subdivided into yet smaller entities of equal concreteness, *and*—internally—constitute *developmental processes* that attain their inner unity by way of their *relation* with other events (Jung 1980). Events now constitute "*epochal*" *unities of time* incapable of further physical subdivision; that is, they can enter being only *at once* (epochal theory of time: SMW, 125–27; Ford 1984; 1988; Wallack 1980) (§14). The *atomicity* and *organicity* of events are indissolubly associated (SMW, 133–37). The one cannot be had without the other. If events were *only* "atoms," that is, lacking all inner relation of origin *out of* other events, they would be merely "particles" lacking any relationship with their surroundings and thus lacking organicity (Sander 1991). Yet if they had *only* organic relationships, that is, were completely lacking in abruptness and discontinuity with the world from which they become, then we would be living in a holographic universe lacking all external relationships and thus also independence and atomicity (Rust 1987). It is here that Whitehead is able to effect a turn from Descartes's substantialism, which ultimately ends in Spinoza, that is, in the one independent substance (*natura naturans*), over to the pluralism of someone like Leibniz, which included the notion of many monads (Faber 2000e). Moreover, Whitehead's concrete pluralism goes beyond even Leibniz's holism by understanding monads as *organic developmental processes* that, despite not existing without some form of inner relationships, nonetheless do represent independent processes (Ford 1984). The meaning and status of "objects" is transformed accordingly. Objects now constitute the *sphere of possibility* of the actualization of events, the latter of which react to the history of their own origin. Objects no longer appear *primarily* as the character of permanence deriving from repetition; instead they now allow events as such to *decide* whether they will repeat the past or make room for new possibilities (Fetz 1981). "Objects" now mutate into "eternal objects," that is, into abstract possibilities, which viewed in and for themselves neither become nor are, but rather, unmoved by the real world, represent the ideas, patterns, forms, and structures that events perceive as their *free developmental sphere*. They provide *at the same time* for the possibility of constancy (when they are repeated) and change (when new objects are actualized counter to the event history) (Hampe 1990).

In Whitehead's philosophy of science, events and objects now take on the meaning of *development* and *structure*. A "development" is in and for itself neither constant nor changeable, but rather the actualization of timeless structures in situations of organic determinacy, a *becoming* in which "structures" may imply constancy or change (Wiehl 1991). Unlike in the substantialist view, here the "essence" of a thing is *decided*. That is, forms do not determine what would otherwise be indeterminate (matter); instead, they represent certain possibilities available for a decision concerning that which *could* become real. That which is real is a *decision* among possibilities (Rorty 1983). The nonessentialist consequence of the duality of event and object now becomes clearer than was earlier the case. Whitehead not only deconstructs self-identical substances as *repeated structures of event successions*; he also reconstructs subjects—so misunderstood from the essentialist perspective—as the inner development of events into that which, once they have become, they will then be, namely, *these* particular subjects with the structure that *they* have *decided*.

In the cosmology of *Process and Reality* (1929), this organic concept leads to a significant consequence, namely, to a distinction *within* the concepts of "event" and "object." Because events represent internal decisions of unity between possibilities, Whitehead now distinguishes between the *event as the becoming* of the organic unity of an "atom," on the one hand, and *event as a change* within the relational unity of many "atoms," on the other (Lachmann 1990). Whitehead accords *indivisible* unity only to microcosmic unities of becoming, which form from relations with other unities of becoming; they can perish, but never change (PR, 35). He calls this event "actual entity" (PR, 22: Category of Existence I). By contrast, Whitehead reconstructs macrocosmic events as a nexus of change involving many microscopic unities of becoming (actual entities). Events in the genuine sense—the microcosmic unities of becoming —arise and perish and in so doing macrocosmically constitute either constant things or changeable events. This differentiation in its own turn emerges from the manner in which *becoming* events are related to objects. Because events (actual entities) are themselves constructed both from their own *history* and also from their *sphere of possibilities* insofar as both represent a *new unity* of their history and their decision regarding their sphere of possibilities, the macrocosmic constancy of things and the change in events depends on the *relation* between history and the sphere of possibility (Hampe 1990). *Both* represent "objects" for the decision of the actual entities. The history of the origin of an event is its "real potentiality," while its free developmental sphere is its "pure possibilities" (PR, 22f.: Categories of Explanation VI, VII; Kline 1990). An actual entity is constituted from the *feeling* (concrete perception) of both "objects," and in doing so is *singular* in both a *dipolar* and *organic* sense; it feels its history (real past actual entities as *its* past) and its possibilities (pure future of capacity for being as *its* possible future), that is, its singular physical origin within the horizon of its mental possibilities. The decision for which an event is responsible in view of its feeling, has teleological character, that is, that decision is guided and directed by the ideal of *harmony* of its potentialities (Fetz 1981).

Whitehead's cosmology differentiates between events and objects with respect to their size (macrocosm/microcosm) and time (past/future). *Organic becoming* represents the smallest indivisible unity of actuality within the cosmos. It is what grounds all macrocosmic relational nexuses—with regard to both their constancy and their change. The "becoming" of events is *not* "change," but rather its *basis*. It constitutes the *inner unity of time*, which, as long as it becomes, emerges from the objectivity of the past (temporal origin) and future (atemporal possibilities) and, once it has become, perishes in order to be efficaciously active as an object within new events. Here Whitehead deconstructs the substantialist disjunction between form and matter, subject and object, possibility and reality. Whitehead's dual metaphysics ultimately curtails any dualism between development and structure through the notion of its movement, the *oscillation between one and the other*. Events become objects and from objects become events (Faber 2000e). But Whitehead's organic paradigm also deconstructs essentialism and substantialism as an illusion of "givenness" and reconstructs them out of the *resolved constancy* of actual entities in macrocosmic things, moreover complements or completes their constancy by way of the *resolved change* within macrocosmic events, which from the substantialist perspective would otherwise be merely "nonessential."

And yet events and objects are never genuinely lost each within the other, an insight attested by one final development in Whitehead's article "Immortality" (1941), where he distinguishes between the aura of events (actual entities), on the one hand, and that of objects (structures), on the other, by juxtaposing them as *abstractions* from the *one concrete* universe. Only the intersection of the two spheres genuinely "exists" concretely; *in abstracto* these two "worlds"—the event world and the object world—are characterized by irreplaceability (Imm., 79–90). The event world is essentially the "world of activity"; it is creative, actual, finite, and temporal. The object world by contrast is essentially the "world of values"; it is systematic, potential, infinite, and eternal (Faber 2002b). Whitehead's final position was to view events as *creative happenings* and objects as *value settings for decisions*.

Whitehead thus concludes his examination of events and objects with the following nonsubstantialist nuance. "Events" cannot be utilized; they are historical unities incapable of being reconstructed by reason and with no goal apart from an unbridled striving for the *intensity of their creative act* (Lachmann 1994). Instead of following the essentialist paradigm of the "essential knowledge" of uninterpreted reality, they strive as it were without any fixed aim for intensity. "Objects," by contrast, situate the creative act in an (aesthetic and ethical) *sphere of decision* such that intensity can be actualized *only* through the *harmony of value settings*. Rather than representing "essential entities" (the uninterpreted grounds of the knowledge of reality), they instead *interpret* decisions as harmonizations of valuations (SMW, 205; RM, 95; Sayer 1999). In this sense, *intensity and harmony* constitute the ultimate connotations of events and objects. The givenness of nature, the constancy of things, the objectivity of the world—all these things are based not on constant essential entities, but on *creative acts of decision* and the valuations attaching to those decisions. Objectivity constitutes itself as *harmony* by way of the *intensity* of creative acts actualized through values—harmony of the past (realized values), of the future (possible value settings), of things (character of constancy), and of macroevents (intensity of new valuations).

§13. PROCESS AND RELATION
(THE ONTOLOGY OF FLOW)

In its challenge of substantialism, essentialism, subjectivism, and their eminent consequences in the form of relativism, skepticism, nihilism, dualism, illusionism, epistemological fundamentalism, and solipsism, Whitehead's own thought was itself always based on the priority of *relationality* over isolation (Faber 2000e)

(§§16, 24). Whitehead articulates this principle as follows: That which has no relations, cannot be known, since it is (in principle) not know*able*; that which has no "coherent context" *is* not, or is irrelevant. And in a reverse fashion, that which does stand within relations, is and is knowable—and both simultaneously. Metaphysics and epistemology merge into a unity within an *ontology of relations*. "Togetherness" in this sense is that "fundamental" (n.b., not epistemologically "fundamentalist") category that for Whitehead cannot be expressed by anything else (e.g., by higher universals or more concrete elements). "Togetherness" speaks cosmologically about the whole of the world as a concrete category, and ontologically about relationality as the irreplaceable category (incapable of being deconstructed by more concrete elements), and epistemologically about the "reformed subjectivism" of subject/object oscillation (PR, 21f.) In *Process and Reality* Whitehead finds the comprehensive expression for this universal relationalism in the concept of "necessity in universality," which implies that only what "communicates" *is*, and that what does *not* "communicate" is unknowable and thus unknown (PR, 4). For Whitehead there is an "essence of the universe which forbids all relationships beyond itself, as a violation of its rationality" (PR, 4). Rationality and relationality converge in universality; *only* the relational is rational.

And yet Whitehead did recognize early on that relationality per se was not sufficient to overcome substantialism and subjectivism *if at the same time* one could not prevent the universe from lapsing into crystalline rigidity of the sort that threatened the universal relationalism of Leibniz and the absolute idealism of F. Bradley (Jung 1980). For Leibniz, all movement within the universe is phenomenal only, since the holistic structure of the monads, which universally reflect one another, has already anticipated every movement in a "pre-established (by God) harmony," in which the monads do little more than fulfill their own ideality without, however, ever being able genuinely to *become* in their identity (Deleuze 1996). In this sense, relationalism can indeed rigidly abide in a subtle substantialism (of the "givenness" of monads that already always "are" *what* they are) and subjectivism (of the *idealist construction* of the world from the subjective reflection of the monads) (PR, 19). Substantialism and subjectivism can be radically overcome only by acknowledging the *movement* of the relational nexus. Hence in "note II" to the second edition of his early epistemology in *The Principles of Natural Knowledge* (1924), Whitehead remarks that in emphasizing relationality he had not yet sufficiently recognized "the true doctrine, [namely] that 'process' is the fundamental idea" (PNK, 202). He would thenceforth—from the *Concept of Nature* on—treat the "passage of nature" or the "creative advance to novelty" as fundamental (CN, 54).

It was only in the cosmology of *Process and Reality* that Whitehead finally found a satisfactory solution to the relationship between relationality and processuality. Universal relationality now refers to the universe as *natura naturans* (Spinoza), as *physis*, that is, as the movement of self-production, of the self-generation of the whole (PR, 93). What is at work here is what Whitehead calls the *universal singular* in his later work *Adventure of Ideas* (1933), "the singular of *The* [sic] universe, of Nature, of *physis,* which can be translated as process" (AI, 150). The universe as a relational whole is (and is *only* in the form of) "the process" (in the singular). The moving whole is the "essence" of the universe; "substance" is deconstructed here as a relational nexus within the movement of transition and self-renewal. Here Whitehead finds himself related more closely to Indian and Chinese thought, insofar as his own "absolute" (contra Western monistic or dualistic traditions) is paradoxically both highly *relational* and highly "moving," that is, is neither "absolute" (beyond relations) nor "perfect" (beyond movement in the sense of already being concluded). Precisely because Whitehead's "absolute," namely, the process, is *nothing in and for* itself beyond relationality and processuality, it is also nonsubstantialist. It does not "exist" in what might be called the substantial singular, but rather only in the *(universal) process of (concrete) processes.* *The* process is "actual in virtue of its accidents. It is only then capable of characterization through its accidental embodiments" (PR, 7). The universal singular of the process is concrete *only* in the plural of events. Moving wholeness as a connex of relationality and processuality practically demands a *concept of event* that engages temporality and thus also the finitude and transience of relationships against any inclination to view extant relations as static in a substantialist sense, to wit, "process" as the emergence and perishing of relational processes. Contra the self-identical substantiality of an unmoved relational whole, Whitehead engages his own *organic* concept of the world as a self-producing *organism in process,* that is, as a "community of actual things" currently in the state of "incompletion in process of production" (PR, 214). Whitehead's understanding of "process" in this sense is capable of withstanding *any* version of substantialism.

Three principles shape this "process of processes" in Whitehead's event theory (Sander 1991).

(1) The *principle of universal relativity* maintains that every potentially or actually existing entity, that is, objects and events, must be capable of functioning as elements in the becoming of events (PR, 22: Category of Explanation IV; Nobo 1978). Put differently (and with greater focus on nonsubstantialist conceptualizing), nothing can be *in and for itself* that has not already become *from something else* and is not capable of becoming efficacious *for something else.* Everything is relative in the sense that it must be capable of functioning within the oscillation between event and object. It is relative *for other things* and thus *relational.* "Universal relativity" as relationality includes the notion that relations are both finite and transient and as such are in motion, as well as the notion that events perish in becoming objects for new events and that new events come into being from objects that in their own turn had once been events. The ideas and forms that Whitehead calls "eternal objects" or "pure possibilities" are "real" only insofar as they participate in this process *as* possibilities. Whitehead does not recognize any metahistorical sphere of eternal ideas that as "real reality" ground the actual world of becoming; he acknowledges only a plurality of possibilities *for* realization (Fetz 1981).

(2) The *principle of process* is the bastion against essentialism, because it focuses

on the processual character of event over against the notion of antecedent or anterior determination of essence (PR, 23: Category of Explanation IX). The key assertion is that the *becoming* of an event (its self-constitution and self-production) determines its *being* (strictly speaking, its having become). Only the event that has become genuinely also *is*, though it has already perished (PR, 166; Moser 1975; Kline 1983). Precisely by perishing, it is relinquished—divested of self—in order to become objectively *efficacious* (in its resolved or decided quality). But no pure "givenness" really attaches to that which is objective; there is only that which, in its "givenness," has indeed become (Wiehl 1990). There are no "grounds" that might function as foundations, because that which does "ground" something is itself something that in its own turn has been grounded. Hence this principle is directed *internally*—with respect to the self-production of events—against the assumption that becoming, *before* actually having become, in some way represents the preformed fulfillment of its own essence (the principle of substantiality) (Hardt 1995; Faber 2002b), and *externally* against an understanding of origins that tries to attain an irreducible foundation (Descartes's *fundamentum inconcussum*). The case is rather that "essence" (substance) *becomes*, and givens (origins) *have* become (Keller 2002a).

(3) The *ontological principle* values the significance of the concrete-singular, which cannot be (even remotely) known through any systematic analysis of abstractions. The assertion is that *reasons* can only be events (Moser 1975; Ford 1993), a position that thus understands rationality itself as *historical*. For if reasons can only be events, then there are no systematic reasons that in their own "givenness" have not similarly become (or come into being) from concrete situations of concrete event nexuses. There are rational reasons, to be sure, but no origins (reasons) lacking context and becoming (Krämer 1994). If, however, within the rational analysis of reasons this recourse to universals (reasons independent of context) is inadequate, on the one hand, and recourse to concrete events necessary, on the other, then the overall movement of reality can never be completely analyzed. Life becomes the principle of rationality (Wiehl 1986).

"Togetherness" as the basis of the ecological community of the universe is articulated in Whitehead's ontology of flow as an *organic nexus* of process and relation (Lachmann 1990). This nexus is never actualized abstractly, but only *concretely* as the *processual relation* of the swing from object into the subject and vice versa. Whitehead refers to this universal base relation as "prehension" (PR, 22: Category of Existence II; Hartshorne 1984; Hampe 1990; Ford 1984). Prehension refers to the concreteness of the relation from the outside (objects) toward the inside (the becoming of events), to self-production in perceiving the other, to the presence of the past in the emerging (becoming) present, and to the presence of that which has been decided within yet new decisions. The singular "process" exists only in the *processuality of concrete relations*. In its own plurality, however, the "process of processes" cannot be reduced to particular monads existing in and for themselves; instead it is differentiated into *relational actual entities*. For this reason too, Whitehead's relativity of events does not cultivate any form of relativistic pluralism, constituting instead a *relationalism* of the "moving whole" whose unity, rather than forcing things under its own static dominion, instead remains perpetually in flux, that is, is actualized only within self-difference (Rohmer 2000) (§24).

Here the status and significance of Whitehead's conception of "process" emerge. This conception is nothing less than Whitehead's deconstruction of all substantialism, essentialism, fundamentalism, and subjectivism of self-identity and self-presence on the most universal level. Whitehead's understanding of "process" discloses a link with the deconstructionism of Derrida and the post-structuralism of Gilles Deleuze. On the one hand, Whitehead engages the antecedence of *différance* in opposing "self-identity" as the basic metaphysical illusion of Western essentialism; on the other, he opposes essentialism with the notion of "process" (Keller 2002a, 6). At issue is always the attempt to overcome the presuppositions of Western thought insofar as they—according to White-head—are based on the "fallacy of misplaced concreteness" (PR, 7, 18, 93f.; Ford 1984): a loss of the ecological situatedness of all "identity" and "presence" within the relations of self-constitution, within the process of self-production, and in the organism of complex self-embedding in favor of abstractions, independent substances, and a solipsism inclined to oppress virtually every sphere. Hence ultimately Whitehead's "process" is a revolt against the unbroken power of abstractions, which in an illusory but nonetheless extremely forceful and influential fashion have been viewed as that which is concrete in culture, society, and religion (Faber 2002a).

§14. SPACE AND TIME
(PHILOSOPHY OF NATURE: EXTENSION AND FREEDOM)

Whitehead's relationalism has exerted significant influence in the surprising reconception of space-time/time-space through inner and outer worlds, physical space-time, and subjective experiential time-space (Fagg 1995). The inalienable connection between cosmological space-time and subjective time-space represents a premier example of how one has to overcome the bifurcation of nature in *res extensa* and *res cogitans*, the traditional Cartesian dualism. It is precisely within this context that matter and mind, the objectivity of the natural sciences and the normative subjectivity of philosophy emerge as constitutive connex within the framework of Whitehead's "reformed subjectivist principle" and its concretion within "moving relationships," namely, prehension. Accordingly, the theme of space-time plays a determinative role in Whitehead's thought, so much so that ultimately physical space-time and subjective freedom become virtually codeterminative (AI, 195f.).

Whitehead's early work with the problem of space-time in *Mathematical Concepts of the Material World* (1905) led him to an important initial insight, namely, that space and matter do *not* represent independent entities (MC, 32). Even before Einstein (who at the time was working on his special theory of relativity), Whitehead ventured the assertion that if within the cosmos entities and relations are linked through fields, then space can be comprehended as the *relation between* particles of matter (Lowe 1991). Contra Newton's understanding of "absolute space," Whitehead understands space here not as a "container" for the spatial movement of material particles, but as the *result* of their coherent connections (Rust 1987). Whitehead, however, understands particles not as dimensionless points (as Einstein's theory of relativity requires), but as relations, as *dimensional structures*, and as the results of relationships (thus already exhibiting a connotation with quantum physics and even extending to contemporary string theory) (Stolz 1995).

In *Concept of Nature* Whitehead then (having in the meantime become acquainted with Einstein's special theory of relativity) demonstrates that the universe represents a single relational nexus (a fact consisting of relational factors) in which nothing can be wholly isolated from anything else except in imagination (in the thinking of factors as independent entities)—which in its own turn has already succumbed to the error of bifurcation and substantialism (CN, chaps. 1–2) (§10). Whitehead understands space and time as *abstractions* from the concrete relational nexus of events exhibiting two fundamental characteristics, namely, "extension" and "passage" (CN, 34). Just as it is only in the passage of events that physical objects emerge (as characters that endure within the perishing of individual events), so also does physical time now *arise* as an abstraction from this concrete, passage of events, as the macrocosmic objectivity of this perishing. Physical time emerges only at the level of event nexuses to the extent they stand in the relation of passage and thus constitute an event history. By contrast, space appears as an abstraction from that particular relation of events situated in a simultaneous nexus and as such render their (mutual) extension visible. The connection between space and time is relative, as in Einstein's model; rest and motion emerge from the relativity of the event nexuses constituting enduring characters (objects) and moving toward one another with a certain, finite causal velocity (which for Whitehead is not necessarily identical with Einstein's speed of light) (CN, 169).

In *Science and the Modern World* Whitehead then articulates two extremely important insights more precisely. Because events are now understood in their *inner* constitution as actual entities that "arise," that is, produce themselves *from others*, matter localized in space, *on the one hand*, is reconstructed as the *causal* relationship *between* events and event nexuses, whereas the basis of physical time, *on the other*, is interpreted from within the *inner* becoming of events as *epochal* time (SMW, 122–27; PR, 68f.).

(1) Concerning *causal space*. Because in Whitehead's event theory "objects in space" do not represent anything concrete, constant, or substantial, but rather objects, that is, patterns, forms, or structures *of* events that maintain themselves over generations of event nexuses (and within all events attaching to this nexus as their character), the physical space of objects represents an abstraction from the

causal connection between the events themselves constituting the event nexus underlying the objects in space (Hampe 1990). A material object is thus never merely where it appears *in* space, but rather is an abstraction, the constant object *within* the flowing causal nexus. Whitehead refers to the opposing reduction, one typical of contemporary physics, as "simple location" (SMW, 80ff.)—an application of "misplaced concreteness" that mistakes the abstract for the concrete—and finds his view confirmed by the nonlocal character of quantum events in contemporary physics (Busch 1993; Kaku 1994; Casti 1989; Penrose 1991). Within a causal event chain, objects are never *merely* where they are found within abstract physical space, but rather within the *entire* chain and in all other events perceiving that chain. Whitehead reconstructs the notion of "empty space" (space containing no physical objects) on the same basis as being not "empty," but as an event nexus that does not actualize any permanent patterns (SMW, 67f., PR, 177)—here, too, ahead of his time insofar as quantum physics today understands "empty space" as an occurrence of virtual particles (Doud 1993).

(2) Concerning *epochal time*. To the extent time too represents an abstraction from the causal event nexuses, namely, their *causal result*, every causal event nexus represents its own temporal system with its own causal velocity (CN, chap. 5). Since this velocity *must* always be finite—causality does, after all, ground *time*— Whitehead's physical time is always relative, commensurate with the special theory of relativity (Stolz 1995; Ranke 1997; Hampe 1990; Tanaka 1987). Why, however, is infinite causal velocity an impossibility? The reason is that events possess their own "time" of *inner becoming* (their self-production) and become physical reality *as a whole* only after they have become. This "inner time" of becoming cannot be expressed in physical time, since events *ground* physical time only through their perishing and becoming objects themselves. As long as they are still becoming, they are "not yet" and hence also not yet *in* physical time (PR, 284f.; Klose 2002). Nonetheless they "become"—as *inner unity*, which Whitehead calls "epoch" because its wholeness refers in fact to an event's concreteness, which cannot be further reduced (to the concrete) (SMW, 122–27; Ford 1984). This "atomic" character of time is able to overcome the bifurcation of nature. *On the one hand*, the internal emergence of an event as subject is a pretemporal actual entity, that is, mental experiential time or qualitative event time (*kairos*); *on the other hand*, what arises from this is discontinuity in the sense of quantum physics, a field (of extended) time quantums (Planck time) and thus physical time as a quantitative measure of perishing (SMW, 129–38; Klose 2002).

Whitehead refines these distinctions in *Process and Reality* through the concept of *prehension* as the basic relation within the physical-subjective universe, and the concept of the *dipolarity* of all events. Since "prehension" is referring to that particular relation in which a *new* event is produced as a subjective entity from objective physical givenness, its physical space-time also enters—along with the objects—into the new events, that is, they always arise *relative* to the extant space-time and then later become elements of precisely this space-time when through their own perishing they themselves have become objective (Leclerc

1978). Hence physical space-time appears as the *continuum of the past* from which events emerge and into which they then enter such that they confirm, alter, expand, or enrich this continuum—the "extensive continuum" (PR, 97f.) (§16). Hence every event arises out of a cosmic (physical) system of coordinates; then, after having become, it becomes a quantum of this very system of coordinates, the latter of which it now codetermines through its own objectivity. Within the *inner* self-constitution of events, this space-time is *produced* perpetually anew and subjectively (PR, 283ff.; Hampe 1990). Commensurate with the nonphysical character of this inner constitution within the nonspatiotemporal differentiation and integration of possibilities toward the harmony of decision-based determinateness, that is, of an "epoch," the mental process that establishes unity can never be grasped physically, though it does remain the *presupposition* for the emergence of physical space-time. Physical reality designates the event nexus of the cosmos as events that have become the past; by contrast, subjectivity refers to the inner arising of new events in their immediate present. Hence every event is *dynamically dipolar*. With its *physical* pole, it persists within space-time and produces itself as the feeling of the spatiotemporal past as its physical history. With its *mental* pole, it arises as that particular mental entity that in subjective intensity is not situated within space-time, instead extending above or beyond the latter as its possible future in order later, in concluding the integration and within the resolving (deciding) of all possibilities, itself to become a quantum of the physical, spatiotemporal past (Wiehl 1991; Faber 1999c).

In *Adventures of Ideas*, Whitehead combines physical extensionality and subjective freedom into a complete, mutual determination of the subjective and objective poles of all processes—through the notion of *noncausal relations* (AI, 248; Faber 2000e). Every event becomes dipolar from the perspective of both its past, the objective universe of past events (real potentialities) and its future, its unrealized possibilities (pure possibilities). This is the causal process. Yet since every event *currently* in the process of becoming does *not* represent a physical reality, neither can it be felt by other events (Ford 1988; Griffin 1992). With respect to other events *simultaneously* in the process of becoming, it lies in their *future*, which cannot be perceived. Since the causal velocity must be finite, present events—events mutually situated within one another's inaccessible future—cannot causally influence one another and are thus causally independent of one another (Fitzgerald 1972; Fowler 1975; Hartshorne 1977). The dipolar consequence is that *externally* within the universe one finds not only causal relations, but also *causal independence*. Hence the universe itself is not merely a holistic arrangement of inner relationships or the movement of causal mediations, but rather essentially a space of freedom, chance, indeterminateness, and independence (Rust 1987). *Internally*, on the other hand, events occur *spontaneously*, free from causal determinateness. More precisely, however, this *inner* freedom from causality in its own turn *generates* an *extensional* universe. The free space of mutually independent events in *juxtaposition* is what first grounds physical space, just as in a reverse fashion this "elbow-room within the Universe" (AI, 195) disposes the inner spontaneity of events as noncausal free space (Faber 2000e). Space and freedom, time and causality codeterminately merge into a complex, nondualistic whole as the basis of what is indeed now an *organic* cosmology (AI, 190; Hampe 1990).

§15. CHAOS AND COSMOS (ORGANIC COSMOLOGY)

Whitehead's organic cosmology emerges from a critique of the one-sided nature of two paradigmatic cosmologies, namely, the *Platonic* and the *Newtonian*. Whereas Platonic cosmology stakes everything on *inner* relations, namely, on the power and reality of ideas and forms, Newtonian cosmology reduces everything to *external* relations that are exhausted in the movement of change of place (Rust 1987; Kann 2001). A profound dualism inheres within both cosmologies. Whereas the conception of antiquity understands the cosmos as a living organism (in the movement of a world soul), which can only inadequately explain the extensionality of the cosmos, the modern conception falters in being unable to integrate the mental element, indeed, even going so far as to reduce the mental in its entirety to the physical, that is, to constellations of local movement (Wiehl 1991). For Whitehead, the weakness of the two cosmological paradigms is that they render impossible any mutual, interpenetrating *translation* or *transition* of subjectivity and physicality, a reflection of the very Cartesian dualism that is to be overcome. Whitehead's organic cosmology renders this translation possible by assuming that *the* most fundamental relation in the universe mediates within itself *between* subjectivity and objectivity. *Prehension* is that particular concrete relation in which a subject constitutes itself from (physical) objects. The nature of its constitution implies a priori both external and internal relationality (Busch 1993). Local movement (*kinesis*) and becoming (*energeia*), "primary qualities" (such as mass or velocity) and "secondary qualities" (such as color and tones) are all essentially related within prehension without the possibility of being reduced to one another (Hampe 1990). As such, Whitehead's organic universe appears neither as an exemplification of eternal ideas nor as the empty whirring of dead particles (SMW, 54), but as a *colorful community of creatures full of life and relationality* (PR, 50). Whereas Platonic cosmology understands the cosmos as a *teleological* (final-causal) process, and Newtonian physics understands it as a *causal* (efficacious-deterministic) execution (of natural laws), Whitehead's organic cosmology fuses both elements into a *prehensive* (final-efficacious) process (Rust 1987).

This organic, prehensive, and causal-final initiative yields an *evolutive cosmology* (Lucas 1989). Unlike evolutionism, however, it begins not with biological evolution, that is, with living organisms, but with physical evolution. Hence Whitehead—similar in some ways to Pierre Teilhard de Chardin and in direct line from Plato's theory of chaos—posits an evolution of the cosmos *itself*, that is, not only of organisms as such, but rather of (inorganic) material and especially of natural laws (PR, 92–98; AI, 103–18; Kann 2002). In so doing, he distances himself from both vitalism and mechanism. Contra vitalism, he insists on a *nondualistic* explanation that understands *all* forms (including life) as developing from the same antecedents. Contra mechanism, he insists on a *nonreductionist* explanation that understands the appearance of both life and mind as evolving as genuine "emergences" from complex, causal-final laws (§44). In *Science and the Modern World* he refers to this position as "organic mechanism" (SMW, 80, 107).

Three fundamental assumptions apply to the evolution of the cosmos. (a) The "unitexturality of reality" precludes dualistic and monistic concepts (e.g., a realm of ideas, a deus ex machina, though also physical reduction), demanding instead a *dipolarity* of events constituting the cosmos, that is, in which the cosmos evolves. This dipolarity is itself *moving*, that is, is a *rhythm of the oscillation* between becoming (a subject) and change (of location) (Wiehl 1991). Physical objects are always a result of this oscillation of dipolar events, insofar as they constitute an enduring object character. The evolution of this character accordingly stringently includes the development of matter and of natural laws. (b) Because being and knowing are inextricably linked within events, the *process of abstraction*, that is, the process of the formation and perception of (real or pure) objects takes place as a process of *nature* itself (rather than solely of human cognition) (S, 26; Welker 1984). There inheres within all reality an irreducible element of "mentality." Rationality itself, rather than appearing only in connection with biological or even human evolution, already represents an element of the evolution of matter and of its natural laws; in more complex structures, however, it does indeed come to expression as life or mind. (c) Since every event as such represents an *activity of decision* among objects (as potences of actualization), an element of freedom inheres in *all* cosmic development that is incapable of being described deterministically. Subjectivity shapes the evolution of the cosmos from the very outset (Ford 1983a).

On the basis of these principles, Whitehead now interprets evolution as a causal-final development of *complex organisms within their environment* (PR, 110–29; Rohmer 2000; Fetz 1981). No organism lacks a "wherein," that is, an environment, without which an organism would not be that which it in fact is (§16). In Whitehead's understanding of such cosmically thoroughgoing evolution, this coherent ecological nexus applies not just to biological organisms, but to inorganic organisms as well. For Whitehead, biology is concerned with macroorganisms, physics with microorganisms (SMW, 103). Insofar as ultimately *every* organism (whether physical, biological, or psychological) is based on events and event nexuses, however, three organic relations of "in-being" apply to *every* event relationship or connection:

(a) Every event nexus simultaneously constitutes an organism that becomes an environment for others, that is, a milieu, *and* is itself situated within an environment (encompassing the organism). The cosmos itself consists in a complex, internally interconnected "organism of organisms." In this sense, the entire world becomes an environment to itself insofar as every *new* generation of organisms relates directly within its own actualization (its own actual becoming) to its objective, spatiotemporal past as its environment (Hampe 1990). (b) All actual entities are inherently microorganisms that constitute themselves out of the macroorganism (into which they are embedded) as their "actual world" (PR, 46). The microevent integrates the history and the character of the organism from which it produces itself as out of a "body." Every event of a (micro)organism constitutes the entire (macro)organism at a singular location, for which the organism simultaneously represents the environment (Busch 1993). (c) Because all physical organisms (whether inorganic or organic) are based on event nexuses, every constant nexus within the cosmos represents a character for which a specific event nexus serves as the "environment." Every cell, every thing, every elementary particle, every simple or more complex organizational structure within the cosmos is not something "given" (not an ultimate) in and for itself, but a complex of (pure and real) objects generating constancy and whose "environment" is the event nexus that through the repetition of precisely *this* character decides concerning constancy or change (Rohmer 2000; Bracken 1991).

Ultimately the evolution of complex organisms in the cosmos depends on the development of different, variously multifaceted, and dissimilarly complex event nexuses. The *most fundamental* form of event connection—and *per definitionem* no event is "alone" (Hampe 1990)—is what Whitehead calls (in a technical sense) a "nexus," that is, a connection in which no specific structure is "corporealized" (Wiehl 1990). In general, that is, abstracted from its concrete situatedness, the *nexus* possesses within itself the *potentiality* for all possible simple or complex organization, since in and for itself it is only *chaos* (PR, 72). The "chaotic," however, begins only to reveal itself against the backdrop of the potentiality of orders; but taken in and for itself, it implies something *fundamental* for the development of the "cosmos": The *basic nexus* is the *locus of the actualization* of potentiality as such (PR, 61ff.); abstracted from actualization, however, it articulates simply the existence of an ontological freedom of singular events that do not *have* to repeat anything (Busch 1993). The *basic nexus* either repeats no structure at all (an object), or must not repeat it. Its fundamental, unique feature is to be the locus of the singular, the nonrepeatable, the unpredictable. Hence Whitehead understands the *basic nexus* both as the *fundamental relationship* of events, as the most primitive (still empty) context on whose basis *all* organisms develop their organization (Griffin 1976), and as a highly complex, nonobjectifiable (i.e., not object-related) form of *vitality* within the cosmos, the latter of which transcends the organizational structures of organisms. Hence in the *basic nexus* one finds the convergence of, on the one hand, the empty "wherein" of the development of increasingly complex organisms, *and*, on the other, life, mind, and freedom on the basis of these more complex organic levels. Because the *basic nexus* stands as the *locus of novelty* at both the *foundation* and the *peak* of every organization of the "cosmos," it acquires fundamental significance in Whitehead's cosmology (§§24, 35) (Keller 2002b).

The "cosmos"—as every possible form of organism in a specific stabilization of order and novelty—arises between the *basic nexus* as "chaos," that is, as the environment of every organization, and the *basic nexus* as the living sundering of every order. The entirety of evolution is in fact a development of *structures of repetition* of objects, that is, of forms, structures, and patterns that are borne by event nexuses. Whitehead refers to any nexus that actualizes organization as a "society" of events (PR, 92ff.). Every *society of events* actualizes an order that surpasses that of the given individual event of the organism, insofar as every event actualizes the common pattern of the organism and repeats it over subsequent generations of events (Nobo 1986; Bracken 1991; Hampe 1990). In this regard, the evolution of events and organisms as the emergence of increasingly higher structures unfolds, as it were, "unitexturally"; that is, the more complex the *inner* structure of an event, the more complex the *society* that can be organized. Whitehead distinguishes essentially four evolutive stages of events and societies (Hosinski 1993):

(1) Events of *empty space.* These events actualize only the *most general* structures within the cosmos, those representing the "environment" of all further organisms. Such include the basis societies within the cosmos of extension and force fields such as the "extensive society," the "geometric society," and the "electromagnetic society." Events at this stage of evolution do not exhibit novelty, at least none that exerts any influence, but only characters that they repeat (extension, geometry, and basic forces) (PR, 177; PR, 70, 92).

(2) Events as moments in the *life histories of nonliving organisms.* Events at this stage of evolution actualize structures of the most general societies as "environment" and more specialized structures as their characters. They allow the construction of "enduring objects," that is, things with constant character (PR, 34). If this character develops in a temporally constant fashion (electrons), Whitehead speaks of a "non-living personal order"; things with coordinated spatial structure (tables) he calls "corpuscular societies." Here the overwhelming majority of the events repeats the character of the society, though there may also be some events that actualize a certain measure of novelty. Although such events spontaneously alter the repetitive element, statistically they are generally rendered less effective through the massive repetition of the characters. That notwithstanding, this sporadic spontaneity does pave the way for an evolution of structures, for the origination of new forms and types of societies (PR, 177; PR, 90f., 96).

(3) Events as moments in the *life history of living organisms.* On the basis of general, specifically nonliving structures as the "environment," "living events" can now arise that develop "living organisms" (PR, 177; PR, 102). They are characterized by *structural novelty*, which not only arises spontaneously in each individual instance, but is also *expediently* (final-teleologically) integrated into the living organisms (AI, 207). The surplus of possibilities from the past (real potentiality) and the surplus of future (pure possibility) make it possible for events not only to repeat their past (conceptual repetition), but to revise it as well (conceptual reversion) (PR, 247ff.). If this novelty is *systemically* reintegrated into the organism, a living structure arises that not only reacts to its "environment" with a stoic inclination to permanency and excludes change as far as possible, but also

adapts to its environment (PR, 101; Busch 1993). Living organisms rely on their capacity to develop permanent structures capable of making themselves as independent as possible from their environments by becoming adaptable to *many* environments. The more vibrant (alive) living organisms are, the more will they be inclined not only to adapt, but to *create* their own living space. The ecology of life cannot be interpreted merely as a conservative process of adaptation to an environment (Darwinist error). It is instead also a *creative process of "re-forming"* the environment to meet the needs of living organisms (FR, 7; Kann 2002).

(4) Events as moments in the *life history of enduring objects with conscious cognition*. The "environment" of living organisms, finally, makes possible "living persons" with consciousness (PR, 177; PR, 107). At this point, novelty in events becomes so predominant that it leads to consciousness, that is, for Whitehead to the perception of the *negation of reality within the space of many possibilities* and thus to a *reflected decision (or a decision capable of reflection)* among possibilities. In complex living structures such as the brain, an event nexus evolves in which novelty is no longer structured by any specific character; instead, here every order is sundered. The living organism becomes the environment of an "entirely living nexus," a *nonsocial event succession* of conscious events that, though constituting a "genetic nexus (a connex of inheritance)," Whitehead calls a "living person" (PR, 107; Hampe 1990; Busch 1993; Hosinski 1993).

What is the goal of evolution? A survey of the "ascending" complexity of organic organization within the universe suggests that the universe in fact has no goal, no end state toward which it might be moving (Jung 1958; Hauskeller 1994). For the ground of all order is the *basic nexus,* "chaos," whose preeminent characteristic it is to be the indeterminate "place" of potential *novelty*. A pass through the orders of the "cosmos" discovers at the "zenith" of complexity not a goal, but the "vitality" of the nexus itself as novelty that, although indeed borne by those orders, simultaneously and repeatedly breaks through them. Hence the "goal" of evolution is not order, not some final condition or state, but the "chaos" of life and vitality, that is, the process itself (in the universal singular) (§13) (Keller 2002b). The *motor* of this evolutive movement is *novelty and life*. It contributes to the *intensity* of every individual event, though within the event nexus as such it develops through *harmony* (Griffin 1976). In fact, these two elements mutually interpret each other. Intensity is possible only through complex, supporting orders of organization; in contrast, harmony needs crumbling or otherwise fragile orders that prevent intensity from becoming static. *Intensive* harmony within the event nexus does not imply "harmonization," that is, the exclusion of contradiction, but rather precisely a broken order that preserves life against systemization (AI, 256f.). On the other hand, *harmonious* intensity within the becoming of events prevents the "chaos" of collapse. Event-centered syntheses ultimately attain an "identity" that in their perishing is capable of becoming an object for *other* syntheses—and as such also a "cosmic" impulse for the advance of the universal process (AI, 238; Rohmer 2000).

If the universe as a whole thus has no *final* condition of order, but only movement itself guided by intensity and harmony, then it also has no *initial* condition of order. The universe can thus be "defined" as a nexus that through its chaotic basic constitution generates certain types of order through which it passes and which it ultimately allows to sink back into the chaos of the novel—which is simultaneously the birth of a *new* order (PR, 91). Such orders, supported by all societies of events in a universe, are its *immanent laws of nature*—and any given universe extends as far as do these laws, though such a universe must not necessarily be either the first or the last or even the only universe. The *basic "chaotic" nexus* allows for many (successive or even simultaneous) "universes" as well as, given the change in the fundamental types of order within the chaos, also "cosmoses" with a wholly different character than our own (PR, 91ff., 96ff., 112, 116, 197ff.; Busch 1993). Whitehead acknowledges that even the most fundamental types of order within our universe are themselves *contingent*. That is, a given universe must not necessarily exhibit the character of extension (PR, 91, 289, 326); there is no metaphysically compelling reason why time in a universe must necessarily proceed such that the advent of the new is *necessarily* accompanied by the perishing of that which is otherwise "past" (PR, 340) (§39). A universe that does, however, harmoniously develop such fundamental characteristics from chaos before sinking back down into it Whitehead calls a "cosmic epoch" (PR, 91ff.). With this understanding of chaos and cosmos, Whitehead pioneered contemporary cosmologies that entertain the notion of a pulsating universe as well as, in more recent versions of the inflation theory, also "multiverses."

Whitehead occupies a unique position with regard to a *critique of evolution*. In applying the notion of evolution to the development of the cosmos as a whole, he does so, not by generalizing it with regard to biology, but by taking his point of departure from Plato's "evolution of matter," assuming that at every stage of evolution the universe exhibits a *thoroughgoing developmental structure* (Kann 2002) (§35). This evolutionary universality notwithstanding, Whitehead was *not* an evolutionist, since he criticized the basic categories of evolution as *substantialist consequences* of "mechanistic materialism" in the ideological tendencies of nineteenth-century physics with the attendant bifurcation of nature (SMW, 95ff.) (§9). He similarly distances himself from Darwin in a programmatic fashion by understanding evolution not as a process of selection, but as a process of *intensity* and thus as a phenomenon whose teleological character derives from the fundamental notion of self-worth inherent in all that is real (Rohmer 2000). At the same time, however, he also distances himself from evolutionary optimism of the sort inhering within teleological conceptions—such as that of Teilhard de Chardin or vitalism—by not acknowledging any *macrocosmic* teleology. The order of the world is aesthetic precisely because it develops *without any goal* (albeit never without meaning) (Hauskeller 1994; Sayer 1999; Wessell 1990). With his basic evolutive categories of intensity and harmony, Whitehead *desubstantializes* evolution, since evolution now unfolds, not for the sake of *self-preservation* as in the Darwinian model, but for the sake of *self-intensity*, which in its own turn aims at self-transcendence (§§21–23). This ideologically critical cosmology positions

Whitehead at the beginning of postmodern cosmologies, such as that of Gilles Deleuze, who adduces Whitehead's "chaosmos" in support of his own position (Deleuze 1996; Keller 2002b).

§16. CREATIVITY AND CONTINUUM
(THE MOVING WHOLE OF EXISTENCE)

Within organic cosmology, chaos and order are related as *evolution of structures on the basis of novelty*. All four stages of organization within the cosmos develop within a "wherein," the *broadest background* of all organisms, the *pure potentiality of every possible order* (AI, 134; Kann 2002; Busch 1993) (§§15, 35). This "wherein" is always *present* as the perpetual *activity toward novelty*, also rendering possible ever new structures, through their perishing as well (§24). The nexus at the foundation of all that exists is at once both *creative* and *receptive*, ensuring the *creative process* of the whole as well as the process (in the universal singular) as the *unity of a coherent nexus* that in fact *is* "the world." In the first sense, Whitehead refers to the activity of the world process as "creativity" (§2), in the second as the "extensive continuum" (PR, 31f., 97ff.; AI, 295) (§14). These constitute the ultimate but perpetually efficacious *ground* of the cosmos as *process*, as "moving whole." Whitehead explicates these two aspects separately but as part of a single coherent context (Bracken 1995; Garland 1983).

Creativity refers to the *ground* of events and to the *ultimate principle* of cosmology (Faber 2000e), answering the most fundamental question of "why," namely, why there is something rather than nothing (Heidegger; Leibniz). Creativity is Whitehead's version of Heidegger's *ontological difference* (which the latter was contemporaneously developing). But Whitehead understands it as the difference not between Being and beings (*Sein* and *Seiendes*), but as that between activity (creativity) and actuality (event) (Ford 1985). It is not the ground of the *being* of that which is, but of the *becoming* of events. Creativity refers to the *actus essendi*, which focuses, to be sure, not on the *persistence* of that which is (substantialist danger); instead as the *activity of the act of becoming* it focuses on the *arising and perishing* of events. Here events receive their ground of the arising of the new *as well as* the ground of the efficacious influence of the old. Creativity refers at once to a principle both of *spontaneity* and *causality*. On the one hand, creativity is *pure activity*; no trace of passivity inheres within it (unlike the *materia prima*, the pure potentiality of Aristotle); as such, it always implies *self*-creativity, the power of events to bring *themselves* forth (Bradley 1994; Garland 1983). On the other hand, creativity refers to the activity of *being shaped* by the event that has already become; itself lacking character, it receives such through that which has already become and then allows it to be efficacious within the arising of new events. Whitehead refers to this dual aspect of creativity as *immanent* creativity (spontaneous *self*-creativity) and *transitory* creativity (causal production of other events) (Garland 1983). Creativity as ground is nothing "in and for itself," that is, beyond the actualization of events; it is real only *in* them (and apart from them is a pure abstraction). It refers to the power of the pure self-(giving)-surrender of the "ground" to the "events." Viewed directly, however, it is nothing (Faber 2000e).

The locus classicus of Whitehead's creativity is the "category of the ultimate" as the basis of *all* other metaphysical categories in *Process and Reality*. There it refers to the "principle of novelty" (PR, 21), which is responsible for the disjunctively many becoming a new unity (one) and at the same time for this one (*unum*) perishing as one among many (*aliquid*) (Fetz 1981) (§2). Through the entire series of dualities, this *oscillation* is Whitehead's *fundamental metaphysical principle* applying to *all* nexic connections (of all universes). Whitehead uses the term "concrescence" (PR, 224f.) to refer to the *inner* process of the *becoming* of events, a process through which a new subject produces itself as a new inner unity through constituting itself from objects, past events, in fact from many different things that it "is not," gathering itself, as it were, into a new synthesis and in that sense "growing together"—concrescing—into a new concrete reality. By contrast, he uses the term "transition" (in the sense of a "passage into something else") to refer to the *external* process through which such a synthesis *perishes* after having fully become a unity or an objective past, that is, something that precisely through its perishing efficaciously acts as an object on other things (PR, 210–29). Only these two processes together secure the *movement* of the whole, thereby avoiding ossification (concrescence only) and dissolution (transition only). These two processes together constitute the basis of a relational (holistic) but individually differentiated (atomistic) universe. Here the notion of dual creativity becomes the ecological principle of an *organic* and *communicative* universe.

This duality of creativity enables Whitehead to view *pure activity* and *pure receptivity* as two sides of the *same* fundamental ontological and cosmological principle. Whereas they are normally juxtaposed as form (activity) and matter (potentiality) or as goal and causal effect (teleology and causality), Whitehead views them as a unity. Pure activity actuates all forms without itself being a form (PR, 20). It is formless activity, "protean" (RMn, 92), wholly *undetermined* and thus *receptively determined* by the actualities (events) it activates (PR, 31f.). Nor is it any sort of matter, since it lacks all trace of passivity (Fetz 1981). It renders causality possible insofar as qua active it is self-constitution (*causa sui*) and in its receptivity relates *efficaciously* that which is perishing to that which is new (*causa efficiens*). As the "universal of universals" (PR, 21; Rohmer 2000), creativity is also in a certain sense simultaneously both goal (*causa finalis*) and the latter's sublation, since that which it represents as goal is in fact not a universal (not a coming to rest in a final, universal condition), but rather the *process of renewal as such*.

Creativity as activity grounds *discontinuity*; creativity as receptivity grounds *continuity*. The applicable principle here is that receptivity enables activity to be active by "taking up" all actualities that perish (albeit *not* in the fashion of a "container") and sending them on past the causal continuum so that new, discontinuous unities can emerge in the universe (AI, 177; Garland 1983). Although

Whitehead does not view continuity as secondary by any means, he does view it as being comprehensible only within the oscillation with the discontinuity of new events. Nothing is simply "given"; instead, everything has "become." This principle enables Whitehead to avoid the substantialist consequences of continuous existences. Since all continuity has "become," it grounds the discontinuity of becoming. Hence there is no "continuity of becoming," but only a "becoming of continuity" (PR, 35). That which the receptive creativity "takes up" to a continuum Whitehead calls the "extensive continuum," since it stretches out the event horizon of all that has become over all becoming, creates objectivity and facticity, efficacious causal force and presence within that which is coming (Bracken 1995; Nobo 1986). From within this "extensive continuum" as the past, creativity actualizes new events, which in perishing enrich the continuum and structure it anew as a whole (§32).

Activity and receptivity shape the fundamental aspects of the *unity of the universe*. Creativity as activity refers to the ontological unity of the process (in the universal singular), to *discontinuous self-renewal*; creativity as receptivity guarantees the cosmological unity of the world as a *continuum of communication*. These two aspects together establish the unity of the universe as a "moving whole" of existing.

(1) Creativity as the *active* unity of the self-renewal of the universe guarantees that its unity does not become rigid and that it is real only as *process*. Unity always implies synthesis. Every universe is in a certain sense the entire universe at the locus of this emerging event (*quodammodo omnia*). If these syntheses were *not* transient, the result would be a hierarchy of being within the universe itself whose highest level would be the unity of *the* universe—but this view generates an ontotheology that posits the unity of the world in the highest being or in a substantial ground (PR, 21; Ford 1988; PR, 333 n. 3). Whitehead, however, acknowledges unity (contra monism and pluralism) only as an *event-centered* synthesis (concrescence) that in perishing becomes one unity among many. This unity of the universe grounds *self-actuation* and *novelty*, unity as the *movement* of novelty, unity *as* process (PR, 7; Faber 2000e).

(2) Creativity as the *receptive* continuity of communication guarantees that the universe remains the *same* (or remains *itself*) within the process (Rohmer 2000). Continuity, however, is no longer conceived substantialistically as an underlying continuum, that is, as an essence that remains the same, but rather nonsubstantialistically as the "wherein" of the entire world process. Here Whitehead returns to the obscure, "third type" of being in Plato's cosmology, as addressed in *Timaeus*, namely, to that which "takes up, receives, accepts" (*hypodochē*) or to the place (*khora*) of all becoming (Kann 2001). All efficacious events and objective ideas come together in this "wherein" as the "place" of the process without which nothing would be concrete. This "place" in its own turn is something neither material nor ideal, being instead the *expression of the relationality of everything* within the one universe; that is, it is nothing "in and for itself," but merely the "medium of intercommunication" (AI, 134) or, more pre-

cisely still, the *real communication* of all things at the foundation of the world. This unity is all-relational, a "thoroughgoing relativity which infects the universe" (AI, 154), lacking any form of its own, the *fluidum*, as it were, of the process itself. In its emptiness, this element of creativity that "accepts" or "takes up" *receptively* unites "all that happens," albeit in a fashion such that it produces everything *actively* as a "modification of its environment" (AI, 154). As such it bears a resemblance not only to the emptiness (*kenon*) of Lucretius, but to the Buddhist notion of "emptiness" (*sunyata*) and Kitaro Nishida's "place" (Faber 2002d; Nishida 1999).

With this understanding of the unity and totality of the world, Whitehead developed a metaphysical concept making it possible to read his ecological cosmology within the context of deconstructionist and reconstructionist postmodern theory. In a fashion similar to deconstructionist postmodernity (and several decades earlier), Whitehead responded to the substantialist challenge by deconstructing the notion of self-enclosed entities and static totalities at the foundation of metaphysical models, except that he opposed substance not with *difference*, but with *process*—notwithstanding the fact that the relationship between these two responses is doubtless significant in its own turn (Keller 2002a). Both understand the subjectivistic variant of substantialism as the generating of basic concepts of unity and self-presence; in the notion of "fulfilled presence (in the present)," basic concepts become grounding realities that fill with presence that which is grounded, encompassing it and providing its content (§41). Derrida understands this particular essentialism of "fulfilled essentiality" as paradigmatic of metaphysical thinking as such—a grounding of the world through principles such as "being," "consciousness," "idea," "God," "the good," or "substance." All grounding comes to rest in this one ground, because everything is fulfilled in its presence. In fact, however, this entire notion of (substantialist and subjectivistic) "self-presence" and "self-identity" is an illusion of repressive unity that seeks to undermine all difference. Totality reveals an oppressive countenance precisely because it is inclined to fix things statically rather than reveal motion (Welsch 1995). By contrast, Whitehead's notion of creativity, in both its aspects—activity and receptivity—consistently understanding unity and totality as progress and movement, is a *critique* of substantialist self-presence. (a) As pure activity, an event "becomes" as long as it "is" not yet, that is, has not yet become "self-present"; but once it has become "whole" (present to itself), it perishes. It is never "self-presence," only "self-becoming," and never "self-identity," but only the "perishing" of its fulfilled self in the moment of fulfillment (PR, 82; AI, 237; Johnson 1937). Whitehead understands this "fulfillment"—he actually uses the term "satisfaction"—as the quintessence of both self-acquisition and self-loss at once (PR, 25f.; Category of Explanation XXV; Lotter 1990). Here Whitehead's *creativity* corresponds to Derrida's (epistemologically) nonfundamentalist and (ontologically) nonsubstantialist *différance*—to the connection between (spatial) "difference" and postponement of (temporal) presence (Keller 2002a). Hence one does not encounter in Whitehead's thought any "ultimate principle" of creativity as the self-evident foundation of metaphysics; instead, the "principle of novelty" is *per definitionem* the incessant renewal of principiality. Creativity articulates unity solely as *difference* or, even more severely, as the incessant production of difference. (b) The totality of creativity as pure receptivity in its own turn possesses no self-presence that might seek to grasp and define or determine itself. In its formlessness and movement, it is "empty" and as such that which is wholly opened, that which allows everything *within itself*, the "foster-mother . . . of . . . becoming" (AI, 187). Precisely in being nothing in and for itself, it provides everything as communication with everything else as moving whole. Here as well, Whitehead's notion of creativity as *hypodochē* corresponds to Derrida's adaptation of Plato's *khora*: totality as "nothing" that lacks both self and presence and that, subordinating nothing to itself (*hypostasis, substantia*) (whereby it would substantialize itself), instead *differentiates* everything (Derrida 2000). It is thus with the notion of creativity as the moving whole of existence that Whitehead effectively overcomes both substantialism and subjectivism, against which he had engaged his organic philosophy in the first place.

III. Contacts

A Place for God

How does *God* enter Whitehead's organic thinking? Where is God's "place" within the process, and what is God's importance for the process? Since Whitehead (unlike Hartshorne) nowhere provides a proof of God's existence designed to demonstrate the necessity of God (indeed, he wholly rejects such proofs in any case), one must ask instead how God can be differentiated *as* God from all event happenings of the world within an ecologically constituted, wholly relational world (Wieman 1927; Suchocki 1995). The answer emerges from the *theopoetic* "definition" of God as the "poet of the world." Whitehead's more precise formulation is that God "does not create the world, [God] saves it: or, more accurately, [God] is the poet of the world, with tender patience leading it by [God's] vision of truth, beauty, and goodness" (PR, 346). This statement possesses epistemological-theoretical status; it is interested not in creation, but in *salvation*. In organic philosophy, God's role is not to *ground* or *establish* the world (ontotheologically), but to *reconcile* it (soteriologically) (Faber 2000e). God appears as the source of genuine future (§17) and of spheres of possibility (§18), as the Logos of organic order (§19), as the ground of subjectivity (§20), as the intensive meaning of existence (§21), as the guarantor of personal identity (§22), as the eschatological meaning of the history of both life and the world (§23), and as the contrafactual

81

"unity" of the process (§24). The key insight here is not that references to God are introduced into the organic event process as such, but *how* they are introduced. God is viewed neither as that which grounds and therefore as metaphysically necessary, nor as arbitrary and therefore as metaphysically dispensable, but *theopoetically* as *reconciled nondifference* (§28). God is disclosed *within* the process as temporally transcending anteriority (foreshadow), and in *difference* to the world process as that which *opens* this process as one of *difference* by entering *into* that very process (§30). The following discussion will show *how* God leads the world "by God's vision of truth, beauty, and goodness."

[handwritten margin note: God-within + distinct from The Process]

§17. FUTURE
(THE ESSENTIALLY NOVEL)

That which is new (novelty) acquires exponential significance in Whitehead's organic paradigm (Green 1968). It refers in a basic sense to the movement of the universe as an "open whole." Even more, it is through creativity as the "principle of the new" that the creative renewal of the universe becomes the most fundamental proposition one can make concerning its "essence" (§16). Without the "novel" there can be no events, no becoming and perishing, only rigidity, and instead of process only the *stasis* of a relational structure (PR, 46) (§13). As such, the notion of "novelty" acquires key argumentative significance in the project of overcoming dualism, substantialism, subjectivism, and epistemological fundamentalism, since the oscillation between subject and object, becoming and change, concrescence and transition is mediated solely through novelty. Whitehead's understanding of novelty implies that the world cannot provide novelty for itself; instead, novelty represents to a certain extent a "Divine locus" in the world where God is absolute future (Suchocki 1995) (§39).

Is the reference here to something *essentially* new? In many responses to the question concerning the "new" within the cosmos, it is viewed simply as a variation of the old. Ernst Bloch's "matter" appears as the "primordial mother" (*mater*) of becoming and as such of renewal, as the inexhaustible primordial ground of potentiality from which perpetually new forms are actualized (Bloch 1978). Gilles Deleuze interprets the "new" with Bergson as "virtuality," as the "enfolding" of the universe in a sphere of potentiality from which new events are then continually actualized (Hardt 1995; Faber 2002b). It is no accident that the theory of immanence regarding novelty that these authors present consciously avoids theistic connotations in explaining the origin of the new. There are internally cogent reasons for doing so; if the new does not radically transcend the world, there is no need to speak about God in the first place. Bloch replaces "God" with "matter," with "primordial potentiality," Deleuze with the virtual enfolding of the world. By contrast, Whitehead resists this temptation and persists in his understanding of the new as the *radically* new. Its radical nature appears precisely where its appearance is accompanied by the unexpected, the surprising (or even frightening) element of something otherwise inaccessible that can *in no way* be derived from the old. As Deleuze points out, "virtuality" (and thus also Bloch's primordial potentiality) corresponds to Whitehead's "real potentiality," to the future openness and self-transcendence of the past with regard to the arising of new events; it is referring to the creative-transitory agency of the "extensive continuum" (PR, 62, 66f., 76; Deleuze 1996). Whitehead does, however, distinguish this from "pure (mere) possibility" (§18). The essentially new for Whitehead is that which is *wholly unrealized*, not merely that which "could be" (the form of possibility of an anticipatory prognosis), but rather that which is wholly uninvented (SMW, 87: "the light that never was on sea or land") (Sayer 1999). That which is "uninvented" (or radically "invented") is, on the one hand, *possible* insofar as new events feel and then actualize that which is radically new in connection with their origin (real possibilities); it is, on the other hand, *impossible* because it simply does not in any way reside within the horizon of the possible *before* actually entering, *wholly unexpectedly*, into that horizon.

Once having committed to radical novelty in this sense as the basis of ecological cosmology, Whitehead faces the task, on the one hand, of having to conceive the unforeseeability of new possibilities, and, on the other, of preserving the *coherent* context and connection with the continuum of the world. Otherwise, that which is (only) purely possible will simply enter the world as deus ex machina, as an element of arbitrary, *incoherent* disconnection. Whitehead's premise, namely, "necessity in universality" (§13), is that nothing lacking a relational connection with the moving whole of the world can be known, and that "the unknow*able* is [in principle] unknown" (PR, 4; my italics). What, then, is the connection between the discontinuity of the new, on the one hand, and the continuum of the possible, on the other? Whitehead solves this problem with the notion of the *temporalization of the possible* (Hampe 1990). The purely possible is the future out of which events realize themselves, in which realization they then perish and as the past become the real potentiality for new events (Ford 1986). It is in the event-present that the uninventable future is seized *as* a possibility of self-actualization. For its self-actuation, an event needs what might be called the *unexpected sphere of possibility enablement*. This sphere remains *essentially* future and as such also inaccessible, even though it does render possible the future of *the* world, of *the* act of event becoming, of *the* continuum. In a way, the radically inaccessible becomes the transcendental presupposition for the continuity of becoming (PR, 35).

But how does Whitehead avoid the breach with the continuum, that is, how does he conceive the relation between the essentially inaccessible nature of the future and the new with the relational structure of the world if, after all, it is by definition beyond relationality? Whitehead solves this problem by positioning the radically new within the "absolute future" of *God.* The inaccessible does not merely hover, as it were, "positionlessly" beyond the universal relational structure; it *must* itself have some place of its own *within* that structure, that is, a place within an *event* (since events alone are real and concrete) (Farmer 1997). God is that particular event whose defining characteristic is precisely that God is the locus of the uninvented new. God appears as the locus of the future insofar as the future has its place *within God*. And even more, Whitehead "defines" God as the quintessence of uninventable novelty and absolute future, attributing both novelty and future to the *essence* of the event "God," insofar as it designates the primordial nature of God (PR, 32, 46; Ford 1981).

Everything concrete is event. An event constitutes itself as a decision among various possibilities, between *real* possibilities (the potential of the past that exceeds facticity) and *pure* possibilities (unrealized possibilities). An event is thus a temporal process that gathers itself from the past and future into a given present. In a manner of speaking, its future must be viewed as its beginning, since it becomes possible "in the future" before it realizes itself in the present. It is from the future that an event comes to itself as the tension between the past, which it can assess and repeat, and the unrealized novelty out of which it is, as it were, bequeathed to itself. If, however, it is from the future that the entire world process renews itself and *commences* in its becoming, then the novelty of the future "grounds" every event in its existence (Faber 2002f; Hauskeller 1994). But this grounding "from the front" rather than "from behind," from the future rather than from the origin, must in its own turn also have a "place" within the process, since otherwise it remains a mere abstraction (§35). Where, however, is the location of infinite unrealized possibilities? Where is future itself grounded? It must—again, this is Whitehead's consistent premise—be grounded in an *event*; such is required by Whitehead's "ontological principle," according to which events alone can be "grounds" or "reasons" in this sense. The particular event in question here must be the locus of the infinite potential of unrealized possibilities (Jung 1965). There they must be grounded *as* possibilities, both as *infinite* and as *unrealized* (Fetz 1981; Suchocki 1995). This particular event is God. Whitehead refers to the "place" of event-centered possibility in God as *God's primordial nature*. In God's primordial nature, God feels all infinite possibilities *as such*; this primordial nature is God's "mental pole" (PR, 87, 343, 345; Fetz 1981). In this conception, unrealized possibilities have a place in event happening where *as* pure possibilities they stand in an *organic connection* with the process while simultaneously representing the *unconditional presupposition* of every world (PR, 47; Rohmer 2000). As primordial nature, God appears to the world as what might be called "enabling unconditionality" that simultaneously grounds the process as the absolute future, which, as seen above, constitutes its "beginning" (§39).

Process theology has indeed reflected further on this notion of God as the "absolute future" of the world. Marjorie Suchocki especially views such references to God from the perspective of the future as the unconditional presupposition for the process of time and the world (Suchocki 1995). At crucial junctures this is also true for the theologies of Jürgen Moltmann and Wolfhart Pannenberg, where God appears as the absolute future of the world who approaches or moves toward the world "from the future" and as such is understood as the "source of time." Karl Rahner gives this motif a soteriological interpretation, maintaining that only where God is the absolute future—that is, only where God cannot be derived in any fashion from the world—can the power to reconcile the world be attributed to God. Only where there is something *essentially* new can the circle of sin as determined by the past, the wheel of suffering of the world, and the solidarity in evil be unconditionally sundered (Faber 2000h). Hence the primary place of God within the world process is an *eschatological* one, involving the "advent" of God's ultimate *power of redemption* from God's *unconditional* future (Moltmann 1995). God is always *present* to the world precisely *as* its reconciled future, a future it cannot give itself (§39). Although God as absolute future is pure grace, which (commensurate with medieval theology) presupposes the world *to itself* (*gratia praesupponit naturam*), the variant in process theology of this theological principle of grace understands grace in a *temporal-theological* fashion as a progressive operation of reconciled nondifference. God presupposes (in the sense of prepositing) *Godself* as the future of the world—and as such is always unconditionally antecedent to (ahead of) the world—while yet, through being seized (the unexpected possibility becomes present), becoming the possibility of the event (emergence) of the *world* (Faber 2000h) (§35). Viewed thus, grace incessantly becomes nature, since future becomes past *without* grace ceasing to be unconditional grace (§37). God's unconditionality not only posits itself *antecedent* to the world as ground, but also, as source, *ahead of the world* into the future in order to enter into the world's own becoming and perishing. The unconditional nature of the *future* becomes the source of the *continuum* of the world.

§18. POTENTIALITY
(THE PRESENCE OF THE TIMELESS)

The *temporalization of the possible* (§17) corresponds to the *potentialization of time.* The past, present, and future are grounded in the differing status of possibility. Time itself is an expression of the process of realization of potentialities. The *past* is that which has been realized and as such is that which is factual. Since the past is gathered into *new* unity in the constitution of new events, the relationality among past, actively efficacious facts also acquires significance. That relationality must not necessarily be harmoniously arranged; it can instead, amid considerable tensions between facts, also contain a *potential* for further future developments that will decide concerning the status of precisely these contradictions within the past. Whitehead speaks about the energy of the past, a kind of causal pressure or even struggle that creates space or latitude for future decisions (AI, 198; Frankenberry 1983; Faber 2000e). By contrast, the *future* is that which, though unrealized, is provided, indeed intended for realization. It brings the unrealized into play as that which though uninvented is yet possible, or introduces the possible as that which might be realized again, as that which is "re-realizable." Although not everything future is per se something new, it does always

open up a tension between fact, on the one hand, and the decision for realization, on the other—either for a realization of the factual in a repetition of that
which has already been realized, or of a different and thus (with regard to that
factual) *new* possibility (as a revision of the past) (PR, 26: Categoreal Obligations
IV, V). The sphere of free play between that which has already been realized and
a repetition/revision is the *present* of decision among various possibilities. It is in
that space that the factual is gathered as that which is received (felt), that is, as
"real potentiality" *for* the becoming of an event, and the possible as that which is
as yet *un*realized, that is, as "pure potentiality" *for* the decision that will in fact
realize an event. That is to say, it is within a becoming event itself that both past
and future come together as the potential for realization; as such it is the presence *of* both past and future.

What, however, is the actual status of this "potential" within events? As surprising at it may initially seem, Whitehead paradoxically defines it as the *presence
of the timeless* within the process (PR, 23: Category of Existence VII). *In and of
itself,* the possible is not temporal, but rather is that which is time*less* within *all*
time. That notwithstanding, it is the *ground* of the *temporality* and status of time
within the history of events and event nexuses. That which is timelessly possible
in and of itself appears within the process of the self-actuation of events as the
future with regard to its nonrealized status, as the present with regard to the deci
sion for realization as such, and as the past with regard to its factual realization
(Hampe 1990). Possibilities in and of themselves have the status of "pure objects"
for the realization of events; that is, in no way can subjectivity be attributed to
them, and their objectivity is *pure abstraction* from the process itself (Fetz 1981).
Hence Whitehead calls them "eternal objects," since their timeless nature appears
within events in the differentiation of time, whereas it is in them that events in
their own turn encounter *eternity* (Ford 1973).

The meaning of these "eternal objects" corresponds to that of the *ideas* in Platonic cosmology. As Whitehead explains, temporal things exist, as they do in
Plato's cosmology, through participation (*methexis*) in the eternal things—albeit
with several key differences in Whitehead's thought. (a) For Whitehead, these
eternal objects do not represent some ultimate reality; they are neither active nor
concrete, but rather *abstractions* within the process and *possibilities* for that
process. They are real solely in events and event nexuses. With respect to their
relation with events, in *Concept of Nature* Whitehead refers to them as the
"ingression" of the timeless into certain situations (CN, 144ff.). They refer to
that which transcends the singularity of every event, since they can actually be
realized in *many* events if a *situation* emerges allowing for their realization. They
represent the *universal* positioned beyond every temporal structure insofar as it
is realiz*able* at *any time* (PR, 22f., 40, 44; Sayer 1999) (§12). (b) Although the
eternal objects are indeed timeless, they do make it possible to understand events
as a *process of decision*. They are atemporal or timeless because they are as yet
undecided (Rorty 1983). By establishing *contrafactual tension* within events, however, with their timeless presence the eternal objects grant to events the possibil-

ity of being processes of decision among various alternatives toward the factual. Hence rather than being active in the Platonic sense or representing the "essence" of events, they instead *make it possible* for events to become that what their "essence" is (PR, 53, 59f.; Faber 2000e; Fetz 1981). (c) Within the timeless presence of the "eternal objects," an event in its becoming *posits* both past and future as *present*. Their timelessness thus mediates the *in-being* both of past reality and of the unrealized future within the event process (Hampe 1990). From the timeless presence of the "eternal objects," the becoming of events as the process of *presentation* or *manifestation* beyond physical time extends itself to a *unity of presence/present* (§20). Through "participation" in them, events become "actual entities" that enjoy presence as long as they are in the process of becoming but also always only as process of perishing. (d) The past (facticity) arises out of perishing because events, as unities of presence/present, themselves perish to the status of real objects. Participation of the past in "eternal objects" *mediates* their objectivity within objective quanta of past unities of presence/present and simultaneously their presence within new becoming (PR, 283ff.; Kasprzik 1988).

What, however, is the ground of the timeless? Once again, the "ontological principle" applies (§13). The timeless ground of the actual world must be grounded in an *event*. This event must itself be *the* timeless ground of the actual world, that is, the infinite potential of all possibilities must not only be present within it in its timelessness, that event must also be that *eternal unity of presence/present* that is never within time and yet is the unconditional ground of the arising of all time and all *presence within time* (Rohmer 2000). This event is God (§16). Whitehead understands the primordial nature of God as that eternal unity of presence/present in which God is eternal and *as* eternal renders possible time, identity (within time), actuality as decision and the objectivity of that which is past. By virtue of the infinity of the "mental pole" in God, with which God orders all potentialities into a unity of presence/present, the timelessness of objects within God is simultaneously God's eternity, who in turn can never perish because, unlike temporal events, God can never exhaust God's own sphere of possibilities (Ford 1973). In God's eternity, God is thus *imperishable* because God can never be "objectified." Paradoxically God's eternity discloses *unconditional subjectivity*; since it cannot be objectified, it is *independent* of the world process, but for just that reason also the *unconditional condition* of that world process (Faber 2000e). As eternal, God is conditioned by no world, no facticity, no history (PR, 47). Yet God's unconditional presence is *essentially turned toward the world*, that is, is the unconditional presupposition for world. Without ever losing God's eternity (and precisely *because* God never loses it), God *presents* or *manifests* Godself, through God's eternity, within the world as time, as *its* activity of becoming, as *its* identity within the unity of presence/present, and as *its* objectivity of that which is past (Clarke 1988) (§25).

What is the theological relevance of God's eternity, understood in this sense? (a) It does not stand counter to the process of time. It is not the other of time that must ultimately be discarded or "shaken off" for the sake of eternity. Instead, it is God's eternity itself that *makes the process of time possible.* (b) The *presence* of

[margin note: primordial nature]

God's eternity in *every* event positions that event in a sphere of decision in the face of what that event completes itself and moves toward its own identity. Indeed, within the interior of every event, God is more intimate to the event than is the event to itself. (c) The presence of God's eternity within the event process makes events *possible* as pretemporal (but always time-related) unities of presence/present. Within God's presence, events becomes present *to themselves*. (d) Within God's presence, that which is past remains *efficaciously active*, that is, God becomes the witness of the facticity of real history, making it possible both to have solidarity with the victims of history, whose cumulative activities remain present, as well as to maintain the unavoidability of "standing before God" (*coram Deo*). (e) God's eternity can be known (discerned) within the presence of the possible in the becoming of events. The experience of God in any case always precedes or is antecedent to our experience of the world, albeit never directly, because the presence of God's eternity is *turned toward the world*, that is, is encountered in the guise of the primordial, unique possibilities of each event within *its* unique situation. In the presence of the timeless, a certain spirituality of time, capable of feeling God's presence, acquires contours (§48).

The common objection leveled against process theology, that God is invariably lost in being merged with the world process (Küng 1980; Scheffczyk 1984), finds a theologically adequate solution in the reminder that God's eternity opens up world *unconditionally* and precisely in this unconditionality is *never* exhausted or absorbed by the world process (Clarke 1984). This particular criticism affects only Hartshorne's rational theology, for which God's primordial nature does indeed represent an abstraction that is real *only* within a concrete temporal process of God events (§4). This view, however, is based on the assumption that God's primordial nature can objectify itself, that is, that God is in fact a succession of transient events, and God's primordial nature thus not a creative subject, but merely the quintessence of abstractions (Hartshorne 1948; Faber 2000e). For Whitehead, however, because God's primordial nature is infinite, God's timelessness has *subjective* character, that is, cannot be objectified. Hence God's primordial nature is the *creative* locus of "eternal objects" (Ford 2000). The primordial nature is not merely a "pool" of possibilities, but the *subject of their creative constitution* (§41). In its subjective timelessness, God's eternity (similar to Boethius's classical concept of infinity) refers to the subjective self-possession of God's *unconditional vitality in the infinite unity of presence/present.*

§19. ORDER
(THE ADVENTURE OF IDEAS)

How does order arise in the world? How is it that the world appears not as chaos, but as cosmos? What is the relationship between chaos and cosmos, order and novelty? Whitehead's organic paradigm understands order only on the basis of *creative* processes developing and shaping a certain *structure (pattern)* that lends *constancy* to them amid their becoming and perishing. At the basis of such constancy, however, the creative act leads structures into *decision* (Hampe 1990). The ground of orders is thus the basic "chaotic nexus" that *can* but must *not necessarily* develop structures (§15). Commensurate with the "ontological principle," orders that as structural elements within the becoming of events are potentialities of becoming can "define" that becoming, that is, exhibit both delimiting and ordering character; they cannot, however, *determine* the essence of becoming (PR, 25f.: Categories of Explanation XX, XV; Rorty 1983). As abstractions in the process, they become real and actively efficacious only in the concretion of events; but they do not replace those events. Although events are grounds of the "entry" or "ingression" of potentials in their becoming, they are not (temporal) "representations" of ideas that, within their ordered status, might in some fashion constitute the *real* reality of the world (§12). The not inconsiderable consequence is that if indeed such orders are *always* relative with regard to the process of the world, never "sublating" that process into some final, ultimate order, then the world can *never* attain its goal in a certain order (§15). The purpose of orders is the *adventure* of the world in its multifarious creative event happening, *not* a situation in which that adventure is shut down, as it were, in some final, ultimate order (AI, 273ff.) (§39).

Potentials predispose the world as adventure by allowing for *coherent structural connections and differences* within the process (Kasprzik 1988). Because "in and of themselves" potentials represent *defined* coherent contexts of difference, their "entry" into the event nexuses makes it possible to differentiate orders within the world process. Potentials *as* orders can be distinguished with regard to at least four different functions they fulfill within the process. *Within* events they articulate "qualities," *between* events they refer to "characters," *between* event *nexuses* they form "patterns," and *within the whole* they define "(natural) laws."

(1) In Whitehead's organic thinking, *qualities*, rather than being attributed to substances as attributes, are instead possibilities within the becoming of events (§12). Essentially they are eternal objects felt by events either physically (as potential of the past of that which has already become) or mentally (as alternatives of becoming in certain situations) (§18). They always provide preliminary potentials of becoming by suggesting the repetition within new events of that which was acquired in the past *or* by allowing for the entry of *new* qualities (AI, 192f.; Welker 1988). In this sense, they stand for both constancy *and* change depending on whether an event, in its becoming, rerealizes that which is available to it or which it takes over from its own past *or* alters it toward the realization of alternatives (PR, 40, 46, 164, 187, 238; Rohmer 2000). The basis for constancy and change resides in what makes the concrete concrete in the first place, namely, its *decision* among various possibilities. Depending on the level of events and the organisms to which they belong, this decision will be made more or less freely, more or less consciously (§15). However, because qualities do not occur *inherent in* something, emerging instead only as objects within the relation of subjects to one another, one cannot really say that an event "has" qualities

(Faber 2000e). They instead represent the *objectification of a process of decision* that already has a past and that extends to coming events. That is, qualities enter into events only insofar as the latter are already positioned within a nexus.

(2) Within event nexuses, qualities develop *characters* that define a given organism, that is, shape it inwardly into this particular organism and at the same time also differentiate it from all others (PR, 40, 238ff.; Fetz 1981). Every nexus that "has" qualities has already fixed its potentials into specific characters that in their own turn determine that nexus as that which it abidingly is (amid the flux of time and space). Through its character, a nexus becomes a *society of events* sharing that character (Bracken 1991). As long as all the events in the society maintain that character, the society remains "identical" and "identifiable" as *this particular* society (PR, 34, 89; AI, 203). Such a society can be an elementary particle that remains what it is through time, or a "fixed object" in our macroworld, such as a table or a computer, or even a human society that develops certain, characteristic social and political features. At this level Whitehead introduces, from a processive philosophical perspective, the earlier concept of substance as a practical abstraction of organic processes. Wherever simple or more complex qualities becomes fixed as the characteristics of a given macroorganism, that macroorganism appears to us as a "substance" that sustains certain qualities over time (PR, 79) Constancy in this sense, however, is not something *given*, but something that has *become*, that is, the repetition of qualities of the defining character of organisms through "generations" of events that become and then perish. Hence that which is "substantial" in this sense, the "essence" of a "thing" (organism) actually refers to a *collective objectivization of a process of decision* within an event nexus, and "substantial change" then refers to the gradual or also sudden appearance of new characters on the basis of complex changes that in their own turn are grounded in new decisions, in spontaneous or deliberate innovations that the organism itself—as a whole— adopts (Hosinski 1993). Characters are thus subject to the evolution of organisms, evolution that in its own turn is based on the creativity of those organisms' events.

(3) Within the organic paradigm, the world discloses itself as an organism *of organisms*, the latter of which are related in various structural, coherent nexuses. These *structures* or *patterns*, however, are subject not only to the arbitrary decision of events, but also possess a *well-defined inner correlation*. And this point is significant, since only if possibilities form patterns in becoming, only if they organize clearly defined differences, can structures emerge in the cosmos in the first place that extend beyond mere accidents (Kasprzik 1988). Whitehead, a mathematician himself, was well aware of the remarkable mystery that the world can itself be represented mathematically, that is, that there obviously exists some order in nature that follows laws of the sort we imagine in our own intellect (MG; IM; PM; Henry 1983; Mays 1961). This realization that mathematics "functions" when applied to nature was one of the fundamental convictions that made the natural sciences possible to begin with. Whitehead reconstructs this insight with the inner structural connex of the eternal objects, which always

"enter" the world in an ordered, structured fashion and between which the decisions of events in their becoming *cannot* be arbitrary, that is, independent of their logical structure (Henry 1993; Harris 1992). The inner structure of the "realm of eternal ideas" guarantees harmonious, reasonable, and meaningful order. Every eternal object thus has a twofold nature: (a) An eternal object (e.g., blueness) has an "individual nature" differentiating it from all other objects, and it has a "relational nature" through which it is related to all other objects within a *systematic* nexus or context (SMW, 157ff.). (b) The systematic connex of all eternal objects is itself a "hierarchical structure" of structures oriented in two directions. In one direction, the object abstracts from the *concrete*, that is, analyzes the concrete event into increasingly simple objects; here the simplest eternal objects are the most abstract (the blueness of the table). In the other direction, the object abstracts from the *abstract* itself, that is, from the simple object, thereby formulating increasingly complex patterns of objects that approach ever closer to the concrete event nexus being analyzed (without, however, ever attaining it in its *concreteness*) (Beelitz 1991). Eternal objects thus stand in a *structural relation* to one another, that is, within a systematic connex (independent of the processual world). In *Science and the Modern World*, Whitehead calls this connex of coherent context the "abstract hierarchy" of eternal objects (SMW, 168f.). This hierarchy guarantees *inner coherence* in the realization of patterns as possibilities within the process of becoming and thereby also the *discernible* or *knowable nature* of the actual world.

(4) The world as a whole realizes its potentials as *natural laws.* Because patterns themselves are internally ordered, these laws correspond to an inner logic. They are neither arbitrary nor indiscernible in the sense of being nontransparent. Instead they *explicate* the actual ordered relations regnant within the world (Busch 1993). Given the coherence of patterns in their abstractness, natural laws cannot be merely an arbitrary volitional imposition; instead they themselves express the *immanent reasonableness of potentials* that the world either genuinely realizes or could realize. But because natural laws become efficacious only in concrete event nexuses and in being borne or supported by the patterns of decision of organisms themselves, Whitehead maintains that natural laws are *immanent* in nature, that is, are neither ordained nor prescribed "from the outside" (e.g., by a God) nor unchangeable (AI, 103ff.). Instead they represent the order of the background nexus adopted by *all* societies within the cosmos and remain actively efficacious as long as all societies adopt them. Laws constitute the broadest pattern of the comprehensive nexus of *this* particular cosmos (Rust 1987). Hence they are *not at all necessary*; that is, *other* laws might well apply in a *different* "cosmic epoch." Hence in the broadest sense they are characterized by *historicity* (AI, 112f.; Lucas 1989). Here Whitehead positions himself within the context of contemporary physical cosmology in the search for the contingency not only of natural laws in the narrower sense, but of universes as such (§15).

What, however, is the relationship between God and the world order? Because qualities, characters, patterns, and laws are *potentials,* that is, possibilities within the becoming of events and organisms, they are grounded in the *one* event that unites all potentials as such within itself and actuates them for the world, namely, in the primordial nature of God (§18). As before, Whitehead is not attempting to provide a "cosmological argument for the existence of God," that is, is not attempting to derive God as "organizer" from the order of the world itself. Instead he is wrestling with the *inner logic of the experiential structure.* In its metaphysical analysis, Whitehead considers it impossible to *derive* the ordered character of the world from the evolution of the world (Jung 1965). The order of nature is a "deep conviction" that is already *(pre-)given in* experience itself even though it is efficacious only within that experience (Busch 1993; Kann 2002). Although an *immanent* explanation of the ordered nature of the world, that is, one that does not take recourse in an "essence residing beyond the world," can indeed explain the arising, becoming, and perishing of orders, it cannot explain how within the current process such orders "enter" *in the first place* (RMn, 89ff.; AI, 103ff., 119ff.; PR, 244; Rohmer 2000). As was the case with the future of the radically novel (§17) and the "ingression" of possibilities into the process (§18), order also requires an *event-locus* in which it inheres *as such*—and this locus is God's primordial nature as the mental feeling of all possible orders of world (Suchocki 1995).

Understanding God thus as the *event locus of all possible orders of world* has considerable theological consequences, not only for the divine ordering of the world, but also with respect to the manner in which order is grounded in God.

(1) Because God is the locus of all *possible* orders of world, God does not prescribe any *specific* order to the world. In this sense, God's Logos (in the Augustinian sense) may well be understood as the "divine order of ideas" of world, as God's vision of world whose "aim," however, promises a *release or opening up for adventure* rather than the execution (or implementation) of a certain order (§38). Hence Whitehead does not at all entertain the notion of the *one* (a "single") world order that renders *this particular* world the only possible, only meaningful, and "best of all possible worlds" (Leibniz) (Maassen 1988). To the contrary, *many* different worlds (cosmic epochs) may represent meaningful orders within the divine Logos. The determinative consideration is that the synthesis of events can never be sublated in abstract orders and that orders themselves (be they not repressive) instead express the divine wealth that bequeaths itself without any *one* "purpose" or "aim." The aim of divine ordering in this sense is not at all some "pre-established harmony" of the sort that for Leibniz preordains—a priori—the *one,* divinely "best" order of the world, but rather the *intensity and harmony of the adventure of world* (AI, 295f.; Deleuze 1996).

(2) Because all orders simultaneously "exist" as *possible* orders in God, God's primordial nature can indeed be conceived as the eternal, but not as the *unalterable* order of ideas, being understood instead as the *living valuation* of orders for the world (Ford 1978a; 1984a; Faber 2000e). This insight underwent a lengthy development in Whitehead's thought. As long as he was convinced—as

was indeed still the case in *Science and the Modern World*—that God was a principle of the world rather than an event, he was inclined to interpret the order of eternal objects as being *systematic* itself, whereby also its internal reason, its "logicity" was grounded (RMn, 73; SMW, 164f.). And even as late as *Process and Reality*, he found in the divine order of eternal objects in God's primordial nature a guarantee that there is such a thing as "metaphysical stability" in the larger sense—principles that make experience itself possible, and patterns that make novelty valuable (PR, 40; Ford 1973b). Parallel with Whitehead's critique of his own mathematical magnum opus, *Principia Mathematica* (1910–13), however, in which together with Bertrand Russell he tried to ground all mathematical order on a logical system of axioms, Whitehead was also developing his metaphysical assessment of the systematic order of ideas (PMd, V–XXXIV; Faber 2000e; Rust 1987). The Austrian mathematician Kurt Gödel took Whitehead's *Principia Mathematica* as the occasion to prove mathematically that there *can* be *no* self-enclosed mathematical logic (Gödel's incompleteness theorem), a proof that had one particularly significant consequence, namely, that there is not just *one* mathematics (Penrose 1991; MC, 17; Mays 1961). With respect to metaphysics, Whitehead recognized that every order can be based only on a *current* synthesis of events (concrescence) and that the *one* order of all eternal objects can thus *never* be systematically reconstructed (Maassen 1988). Whitehead then logically maintains that there can be no eternal object of all eternal objects (that is, no ultimate, systematic idea of all ideas); what is the case instead is that the "universal of *all* universals" (my italics) is *creativity* (PR, 46; PR, 21: Category of the Ultimate). Although Whitehead does refer to God's primordial nature as being *perfect* or *complete* (as containing the infinite fullness of all orders), that perfection refers not to systematic order, but to *creative* order (Maassen 1988; Ford 2000). The divine Logos is basically *creative*. Rather than seeking to execute or implement a definitive vision, God instead is the *creative locus of the valuation of all ideas* with respect to the concrete process of the world (Imm., 89f.; Faber 2000c; Rohmer 2000).

A *theopoetic* interpretation discloses the relation between God and the order of the world. As poet of the world, God guides the world with God's *living* vision, a vision that rather than imposing (orders) instead frees up (patterns for decision). One of the most interesting consequences is that it is within *reconciled nondifference* that God bequeaths Godself in God's Logos, in God's vision of world, *both* as order *and* as novelty (Fetz 1981) (§15). Because orders represent not only potentials for the becoming of event nexuses but also the novel element of as yet unrealized potentials, the divine Logos consistently bequeaths its vision as the possibility for ordering or, by contrast, for sundering orders. The ultimate ground is that within God's primordial nature, order and novelty are *the same* or, more specifically, are undistinguished yet *reconciled* within the Logos. The "goal" of the world turns out to be the inexhaustible harmony between orders and novelty within the Logos and the infinite adventure of the divine ideas in the world process (§38).

§20. SUBJECTIVITY
(THE INITIAL AIM)

Whitehead's nonsubstantialist position accords special significance to the character of subjectivity in becoming (§10). Subjectivity *is* the becoming and perishing of subjects of experience, which become out of objects (facts of history, real
and pure potentials) and perish to the status of objects of experience of other subjects. The subject is *subject/superject* as the concrescence ("growing together" into
itself) and transition (becoming an object for other subjects), or self-creativity
and causality (PR, 45ff., 84ff.; Lotter 1990; Klose 2002). Whitehead understands
the causal agency of past objects within the self-constitution of a subject as a relation of "prehension," referring both to the concrescence of a subject from the
experiences of past subjects and to the continued "agency" of past subjects in the
becoming of new subjects (Busch 1993; Hampe 1990) (§§12–13).

Prehensions always exhibit a *subjective* tone, referring as they do to a *subjectively attuned perception* of the past and transporting, as it were, the tone of past
objects in the latter's *subjective constitution of their objectivity* (Hosinski 1993).
Whitehead refers to this *subjective mode* of perception (concrescence) and trans-
ference (transition) of objectivity as the "subjective form" of prehension (PR,
85–89; Nobo 1986). It is *form* because it refers to the transfer of objectivity from
past to new subjects of experience as well as to a character in which a new subjects constitutes itself from past objects of experience (PR, 155; AI, 183f.; Busch
1993; PR, 25: Category of Explanation XXIV). Nevertheless, however, this
"form" is not simply an "eternal object," that is, not an objective (nonsubjective)
form or idea, but an expression of *subjectivity*, that is, the feeling of a private manner in which a past object constituted itself and constitutes a present subject. Precisely in this subjectivity of form the *emotional tone of perception* manifests itself,
which cannot be conceptually analyzed, representing instead the result of the *singularity* of a subject in its becoming (PR, 162; Fetz 1981). Whitehead provides
the following example in *Adventures of Ideas*. A past event (I at that time) that
experienced anger transports not only the "content" of that anger into a new
event (I now), but also the *manner* in which the event constituted itself *as* angry.
Within the becoming of the past event, a new tone was constituted that is *transferred* in its emotional form (AI, 183f.).

It is the subjective form of prehensions that represents the genuinely connec-
tive or linking element within prehensions. On the one hand, it is the subjective
feeling of a past event that *objectifies* itself in subsequent events as the *subjectivity of the past event*. On the other hand, it represents the subjective manner in
which a subject in its present becoming perceives its own past *in private subjectivity* (Faber 1999a). From this Whitehead also concludes that new events are
inclined to repeat their origin, which they objectify within their own becoming.
Constancy within the world derives from their subjectivity, the feeling of the reality of *others* in *their* feeling and the feeling of other reality as one's *own* feeling.

Whitehead refers to this as the "conformation of feeling" (AI, 183; AI, 238: "emotional conformity"; Emmet 1966; Faber 2000).

What at the level of individual prehensions Whitehead calls the "subjective form," he calls "subjective aim" at a level of (microscopic) events or actual entities, that is, at the level of the integration of multiple prehensive processes into a unity of subject/superject (PR, 19, 25, 224; 27: Categoreal Obligation VIII). The subjective aim is that particular *wholeness* of an event's becoming to which an event, as it were, gathers itself, the *unity* of having become as a subject/superject (Lotter 1990). It is an *aim* in its objective content (a complex eternal object) *and at once also* possesses this content only within a subjective character, in the subjective *singularity* of an event, in the identity of *this particular* subject. Over against prehensions, a certain completeness inheres within events; events constitute themselves out of processes of prehension but are themselves a (complex) prehensive operation through which subjects arise from objects and, in a reverse fashion, perish to the status of objects (PR, 151, 156; Farmer 1997). This completeness means that events constitute *ultimate unities* of becoming—as completion (concrescently) and object (transitionally)—because in them the integrative process of subjective forms comes to *completion,* insofar as the event attains *internal wholeness* while simultaneously—at the same moment—coming to a *standstill.* In other words, becoming whole in this sense simultaneously means *perishing* to the status of *one* object among others (§16). Whitehead refers to this condition of completion—in which all prehensions are integrated and all possibilities decided—as the "satisfaction" of events. Such "satisfaction" is at once both completion and end, namely, the completion of subjective becoming (subject) and the perishing into a completed object (superject) (PR, 84–89; Lotter 1990; Faber 2000e; Klose 2002). The subjective aim is thus that particular subjective form in which an event finds its wholeness, which *in its subjective tone objectifies the event's singularity* and at once also *transports* that singularity for the becoming of new subjects (Hampe 1990).

Commensurate with Whitehead's nonsubstantialist "process principle," the unique feature in his theory of subjectivity is that the "becoming" of an event determines its "being" as *having become* (§12). A subject is not antecedent to its experiences (as is a substance to its qualities, attributes, and movements); instead it is only in *becoming* out of its own experiences that a subject first "comes to itself" (Busch 1993). Its identity constitutes not a presupposition, but the *result of its becoming.* Hence the totality toward which an event in its becoming *strives* as toward its identity must in a certain fashion *precede its becoming.* To ensure that an event does indeed become itself, as it were, the subjective aim in which a subject will ultimately have "gathered itself" in completion must in a certain fashion already constitute the *beginning* of its becoming (Lotter 1990; Suchocki 1995). Whitehead refers to this as the "initial aim" of an event, the self-presupposition of an event for its becoming (PR, 244). Of course, an event presupposes itself only according to *its possibility* of *having the capacity to become* at *this particular* location within the process (Rohmer 2000). Events arise out of a *possible profile of their arising*; the "initial aim" designates this *potential of specific becoming*. A *final* structure inheres in this totality or wholeness of events; that is, every event arises from its specific possibility for having a certain capacity to become, a possibility it eventually reaches (either altered or unaltered) within its concrete becoming. From the *initial* aim of being able to become, in the larger sense, the *subjective* aim then arises within the process of becoming, namely the becoming-whole and the bequest of final subjectivity of this event in the becoming of *other* events (Suchocki 1995).

The initial aim of an event refers to the *beginning*, the *creation* of an event, not merely with respect to its objective content (of eternal objects that a given event *could*, in its becoming, form or fuse into a subjective totality), but also with respect to its *subjectivity*, its *singularity*, its irreplaceable *self-creativity* (PR, 69; Faber 2000h). The initial aim of an event designates the place at which potentiality becomes subjectivity. Just as the "ingression" of potentiality into events is an act of God's primordial nature, so also the initial ignition of events—which are God's act of grounding, of the creation of new events. Here God constitutes nothing less that the "immediacy of the concrescent subject" by "its living aim at is own self-constitution" (PR, 244). God is the beginning of the autonomy of self-creativity (concrescence) of every event and thus also the presupposition of its subjectivity. The initial aim of a subject is not merely a bundle of more or less structured eternal objects (not a loose gathering of possibilities of becoming), but God's own *valuation* of possibilities precisely at *this* particular place (of time and space) within the process, that is, with respect to the facts, history, and developments at hand and with respect to *relevant* possibilities of becoming in view of the historicity of all arising (Suchocki 1995; Rohmer 2000). Hence this initial aim already outlines in an anticipatory fashion the possible unity of any given event, the unity that it "will be" after it "has become." Nonetheless it is within God's valuation of the potentials that an event is bequeathed to itself such that within its *subjective feeling* of both God and world it can indeed become itself (Sayer 1999).

Process theology draws on God's creative activity in this sense to provide a complex interpretation of creation itself. (a) God's gift of this initial aim makes it possible to retrieve the classical term from creation theology concerning "continuing creation" (*creatio continua*), which maintains that in a sense of process theology as well, God is—stubborn rumors to the contrary (Moltmann 1995; Küng 1980)—the creator of *every* event happening in the world (PR, 225, 342; Faber 2000h) (§§28, 30). God is not only inherent within every event, but is also the *beginning of its inwardness*. (b) Through this creative initiative, within the interior of every event God is more intimate to the event than is the event to itself. In this act, the creature is constituted and bequeathed *to itself* precisely *as* creature. It is not the self-power of self-creativity *against* God, but rather God-given autonomy (Pannenberg 1986; Ford 1981, 1986). The (nonsubstantialist) "subject" of process theology is a *relational subject* through and through, so much so that it constitutes itself *as* itself only out of the relation that God opens for it (§13). (c) Every event, as subject, has a genuine origin that, though inconceivable without historicity, cannot be derived from the world. Divine grounding endows to it its self-worth, which cannot be relativized by history, in the form of its *immediacy*, that is, its singularity and irreplaceable significance before God (Sayer 1999). Since every subject takes its beginning in God, it accordingly also stands *unavoidably* before God and *for precisely that reason* with its own dignity and value.

The specifically *theopoetic* aspect of this theology of subjectivity manifests itself when the creative activity of God is confronted with the assertion that God as the poet of the world *saves* rather than *creates* (§35). Whitehead is opposing not the notion of God's creative agency as such, but its nontheopoetic interpretation (§§28, 29). Although with respect to the initial aim God does indeed act in a *genuinely* creative fashion, God does so in the sense neither of some transcendent imposition nor of physical production. In a subtle fashion, God acts as creator as the *future of subjectivity* rather than as its *origin*. Here God's creating activity emerges as something profoundly *immanent* to the creature itself and at once also as an *ideal* operation. The power of divine agency nonetheless becomes visible in creating that initial aim, that is, in creating subjectivity and the provisions for the becoming of events (world as world) in the larger sense. Whitehead's conception of God acting ideally rather than physically (in the poetological "definition"), instead of weakening God's being creator, *transforms* it into tender agency through possibilities, ideas, gifts, and offers. Such creative agency always discloses relation, freedom, difference. And yet nothing would come about if God were not also—by virtue of the power of God's primordial nature and the power of God's ideas—creatively efficacious. God creates differently, namely, *from the front*, from the perspective of the aim, from the future through God's ad-vent and *out of* the future of the event (Faber 2000h) (§35). It is in this sense that the beginning and end of an event meet in reconciled nondifference as the immanence and transcendence of divine creating.

Such theopoetic reference to God's creative agency makes it possible to entertain an interesting concept of God's "presence" that must by no means fall victim to Derrida's criticism of self-presence (Suchocki 1995; Faber 2000h) (§48). God is "present" for every event *as* its beginning and aim. The implication is that God grounds every event as its future, God's presence in the event being simultaneously the event's future. God is in any case from the very outset in the "presence" of the event—before that event began to become—as that which makes its becoming possible (Ford 1986a). As immediate and direct as God's "presence" within every event may seem, however, it is far from constituting what we understand by the notion of fulfilled self-presence. Such "presence" speaks instead about the *trace* of God (Levinas) within the event, in the sense that God is there before the event "becomes" (Davis 1996). This "presence" of God as prefuture and trace, however, never allows the assumption of a self-evident divine principle of the world or the appropriation of the *other* within one's own subjectivity. Instead the subject discloses itself as one that is always snatched from itself, as it were, before it becomes itself (Faber 2000e). With this notion of God's "presence" as the immanent creator of subjectivity (§35) Whitehead paradoxically also articulates the true *transcendence* of God, God's unappropriable exteriority (§40).

§21. INTENSITY
(SELF-FULFILLMENT AND RELATIVIZATION)

In the nonsubstantialist understanding, the essence or nature of an event reveals itself only in (never prior to) the becoming of the event itself. Whitehead distinguishes three generative phases within this becoming, that is, phases that cannot be set off chronologically "one after the other." (a) The *constitution* of an event as *possibility of its becoming* in the context of a certain history of the cosmos, at this particular place and at this particular time. This is the phase of the initial aim, of the constitution of a subjective aim that the event must yet attain or reach (PR, 244). (b) The *process of decision* as a process of subjectivity through which the initial aim is transformed into the subjective aim. As the tension between history and possible future, this phase unfolds within the dipolarity of physical (past) and mental (future) acts of feeling (PR, 88). (c) The phase during which the process *comes to rest* (*satisfaction*), when the process of decision ceases as a tension between past and future, reality and possibility, and is finally resolved. At this phase, the subject attains both its perfection or completion *and* its end. Through its "satisfaction" (*satis facere*, satiation, saturation), the immanent creativity of its self-becoming turns into transcendent creativity, whereby the completed event now acquires meaning for *other* becoming. Concrescence completes itself to the point of saturation and becomes transition, the delivery of completion for others (PR, 88; Sayer 1999). Subjectivity is relativized into objectivity; "subjective immediacy" turns into "objective immortality." The subject perishes and becomes superject (PR, 29, 82–85; Lotter 1990).

The *aim* or *goal* of the process is from the very outset, that is, from the perspective of the *initial* aim, the completion of the subjectivity of the event, the attainment of its *subjective* aim. What, however, makes that aim a specifically *subjective* aim? It is the "self-enjoyment" of its becoming (PR, 145, 289; Cobb and Griffin 1976). It is true that through the process of decision various possibilities are assessed, accepted or rejected, realized or excluded, such that a complex, eternal object emerges, namely, the event as the actualized idea of itself (PR, 43, 45, 50, 58, 232f., 225; Nobo 1986). Nevertheless, it is the subjective *mode* in which that process of decision unfolds that determines the *self-significance of the attained goal*, namely, whether it corresponds to its initial ideal (which can then be enjoyed), falls short of it, thereby becoming a "cripple" of its own possibilities with regard to its "completion," or even completely fails. In any case, in its saturation (satisfaction) the event always attains a *certain self-fulfillment* whose "enjoyment" realizes a measure of *intensity* (PR, 27; Sander 1990). The intensity of the self-fulfillment of an event derives both from the particular history it finds at hand (and its real potentials) and from the possibilities for altering that history, though ultimately also from the event's capacity, within its process of decision, to *reach* or *attain subjectively* its initial aim as its own, unique *highest possible ideal*. The goal of subjectivity is the intensity that a subject experiences in its becoming (in its immediacy) and with respect to its meaning (its immortality) (Lachmann 1994).

How a subject *deals* with the tension between reality and possibility, history and ideal, past and future determines the measure of intensity of an event. Put differently, the subject's process of decision itself is a process of emergent intensity. *As a process of decision among various possibilities of becoming, it is always a process of reduction* (of possibilities), indeed ultimately of self-relativization (with respect to the initial sphere of possibilities) (Faber 2000e; Hauskeller 1994). The relation of a becoming subject with the world and the possibilities is determined by the *integration of acts of feeling* (Lango 1972), of the prehensions of the world and the sphere of possibilities, an integration that in its own turn can be positive or negative, either positively taking up the potentials the subject finds before it or negatively rejecting them (Fetz 1981; Farmer 1997) (§13). *Positive prehensions* perceive the (real and eternal) objects of self-constitution in an *integrative* fashion. By contrast, *negative prehensions* explicitly exclude an object from integration (Leclerc 1978). In this sense, a becoming subject not only makes certain decisions among the various possibilities it finds before it, it also either integrates *or* negates them and in so doing alters its own "objective basis"—its world, its room for free play, its initial aim. The subject, through *interpreting* its world, brings itself forth as *subjective interpretation* (Lachmann 1994). *Negation* is of considerable importance in Whitehead's theory of experience, allowing events to make genuine decisions, interpreting "spontaneity" in both nature and history, and allowing for the appearance of that which is new or novel. As such, negation represents an evolutive power in the world process (Busch 1993). Nonetheless Whitehead's "prehensive negation" does not result in reality constructionism of the sort he criticized in contemporary subjectivism. Instead it leads to a deconstruction of the notion of a "purely" accessible foundation (Descartes's *fundamentum inconcussum*), since although the negation of the past does exclude the potentials of this particular past from the event's operation of self-construction, it does not exclude the *subjective form of their nonintegration*; that is, exclusion, rather than destroying these facts as such, instead feels them *as* facts, albeit in the *mode* of rejection (PR, 226, 231f., 237; Suchocki 1995; Fetz 1981). Within each interpretation, reality remains given as the point of integration, not, however, as "fulfilled presence," but—with Derrida—solely in integration itself as the trace of differentiation (§13).

This process of integration of prehensions unfolds its evolutive power on *structural levels of intensity*. Within the organic cosmos, the complexity of the interior structure of events corresponds to the organizational complexity of societies of events (§15). The more novelty and freedom an event is able to realize within its interior structure, the more living vibrancy can the organization of the event nexuses set free; an intensification of the subjectivity of the process of integration extends from empty space all the way to living persons (Hosinski 1993). Highly structured intensity is found, on the one hand, in *conscious events* and, on the other, in *living personal organisms*. The determinative feature with respect to intensity is the subject's and society's *power of integration*. The more an event is able to integrate its spontaneity with the multifarious data it finds before it, the more intensively will the subject live. The more freedom, novelty, and conscious awareness can be "organized," the higher the degree of structural intensity. Whitehead speaks about the "canalization" (PR, 107f.) of freedom and novelty and about the "coordination of the mental spontaneities" within the organism (AI, 207). The greater the *capacity for integrating differences, alternatives, and contradictions* within events and societies, the higher the intensity of those events and event nexuses (PR, 340). Whitehead understands the measure of intensity as deriving from the power to develop "contrasts" (PR, 83; Wiehl 1984). *Contrasts* are *integrated differences* between reality and possibility, between past and future, between physical and mental acts of feeling, between contradictions in origin, mutually exclusive alternatives of realization, and ultimately between *all* subjective forms of integration of acts of feeling and the *one* subjective aim integrating them (Lango 1972).

There is, however, no ascending evolutive schema here (as in Teilhard de Chardin). No element of necessity inheres within the *structure of intensity*, and every *development of contrast* constitutes a risk (is subject to decision). Ultimately the power of negative prehensions provides for the possibility that this process of integration can also fail. When such is the case, the *process of intensification* (evolution) is abruptly transformed into a *process of disintegration* (de-evolution), resulting in a *loss of intensity* (Welker 1988; Jung 1958). In *Adventures of Ideas* Whitehead adduces different forms in which the development of contrasts fails. (a) In a general sense, the contrastive process is an *aesthetic* process of differentiation and integration of differences, even if such include "discord." Whitehead speaks of an "inhibition" of contrastive development when such discord is tolerated only by excluding some of the discordant parts for the sake of attaining the "aesthetic unity" of an event's subjective aim (AI, 252, 356f., 260ff.). Every inhibition involves a loss of intensity for the sake of maintaining a reductive harmony in the event. (b) Whitehead speaks about an "anaesthesia" of the event (AI, 259) if such inhibition of contrast development comes about through excluding parts of a discordant history of the new event (because of mutual incompatibility), resulting in a complete suppression of the discords or contradictions of the history. In these cases, the loss of intensity is enormous, since here facts are excluded from the subjective form of their "perception" as if they did not exist. This exclusion results in a loss of the conscious awareness of discordances for the sake of unity, which in its own turn results in a *horrible* repression, shock, suppression, and loss of event depth. (c) If on the other hand contradiction, mutual incompatibility, or an extreme case of discordance enters into the subjective form, the event then *feels* this discordance *as such* ("discordant feeling"). If it is unable to calm the contradiction within feeling or "re-solve" it into a sustainable contrast, the result is "aesthetic destruction" (AI, 256), which comes to expression in conscious suffering because of the contradiction. Here intensity is reduced to pain caused by disharmony (Hauskeller 1994).

Intensity expresses the *aesthetic goal* of every event, its sense, and its purposeless, that is, functionless and not utilizable, meaning (Sayer 1999). Such *aesthetics of becoming* is concerned with the development of contrasts, with beauty, and with harmony (Sander 1991). The greater an event's capacity for transforming into *harmonious differences* or *aesthetic contrasts* the contradictions or discordances within the history of its origin or between that history and its possibilities, the more intensively will it experience its self-fulfillment (Maassen 1988). The subjective aim of an event is indeed the result of its own creativity, the creativity rendering it capable (or incapable, as the case may be) of transforming the subjective forms of its prehensions into differentiated harmony (Lango 1972). Hence it cannot be understood as a "preformation" of events such as the "preformation" of things through the Platonic ideas. Instead it is an *offer* concerning whose selections the event must yet decide (Rorty 1983). It is in this process of transformation of the initial aim into the subjective aim that the event's *singular* response to the world it finds before it is manifested. In reaching the initial aim, this can mean the subjective harmony of all contradictions of becoming; in the ideal case, it can mean the highest aesthetic intensity. In the worst case, however, it can also mean a complete loss of intensity, amid which events lose themselves in a stupefaction (anesthetization) of their very selves. Finally, one determinative element in the development of intensity is the contrast between concrescence and transition, between the becoming and perishing of an event. The more an event is in a position to adopt its finitude and view itself within the context of a world beyond itself, the more intensive will its self-fulfillment be (PR, 56, 215; PR, 27: Categoreal Obligation VIII; Faber 2000e). In biblical terms, an event can experience itself in the highest intensity of self-fulfillment when it is able to accept its relativization for a world for which it thereby acquires meaning as potential and then, in its *satisfaction*, dies "full of days."

God is both involved in and affected by this process of intensity in a complex fashion:

(a) If intensity is the meaning of an event, then (as Kant would put it, albeit in a cosmologically more extended sense here) the "worth" of every event resides in its *aesthetic purposelessness*. In the initial aim, God grants to every event this ultimate functionlessness in which every event is bequeathed to itself; that is, here every event both is bequeathed to itself *and* is the goal of itself—never the "cause of itself" (*causa sui*) in any antidivine sense (§20). God's *primordial nature* is the origin of the intensity process of every event. Because the purposeless self-givenness of an event is unaccompanied by any subjectivistic or solipsistic implications, the aesthetic self-worth of an event (the intensity of its subjectivity) is disclosed only in a *final contrast* between self-constitution from a past and relativization toward a communal future beyond itself. Hence God is also involved in this self-relativization—this time through God's receptive aspect, God's *consequent nature,* in which God gathers the harvest of that event into Godself (§30). By virtue of this sublation of the event amid its perishing, the event can now accept its relativity within its becoming and die "full of days." (b) God is not only involved in the process with both God's primordial and consequent natures as the basis of the intensity process, but is *infinite intensity* "in and of Godself." In *Process and Reality* Whitehead refers to God's primordial nature as the *absolute standard of intensity,* since "it arises out of no actual world," representing instead a priori the *infinite aesthetic harmony of all possibilities of all worlds* (PR, 47). And the consequent nature, that is, God's physical prehension of the real world in its state of having become, is able to translate every real situation, even that of utmost discordance, into a meaningful contrast; it can do this because in God's infinite primordial nature, God knows of no negative prehensions (Maassen 1988). While intensity within world events can lead to negative prehensions and to a reduction of intensity, God is able to perceive everything *positively* in infinite intensity (§45).

God once again appears in soteriological nondifference. On the one hand, God's infinite intensity guarantees that every event is "purposelessly" meaningful. God pursues *no* purpose with the world process except to bequeath God's own purposeless intensity and to perceive every event undistorted in its intensity. On the other hand, *all* events (and thus the world *in and of itself*) exist for their own sake, for God gives Godself selflessly/purposelessly. In the "appropriation" (selfless gift) of the initial aim, divine possibilities arise for the *initiation of the intensification process.* Insofar as a superject is then taken up in God, the event itself becomes part of God's *saving reception* of world, albeit without becoming God. Contra the occasional assumption that God's intensity "needs" the world and for that reason also renders it purposive (Küng 1980), closer examination reveals that precisely the opposite is the case. God's primordial nature, rather than needing a world, is instead itself a pure gift for the self-fulfillment of events. God's consequent nature, on the other hand, does not acquire extra intensity through its reception of world events—for God is already *infinitely intensive* by virtue of God's own primordial nature; instead, God's consequent nature purposelessly heals all contradictions and discordances in the world. This is what enables God to perceive the world *undistorted* in its freedom from purpose and save it in a surprising, unanticipated integration in divine harmony (groundlessly and without "functional" intention) (Maassen 1988). God's infinite intensity pours itself out, without any dark reserve, like the good (*bonum diffusivum sui*) of negative theology (Faber 2001c).

§22. PERSON
(ORIGINALITY AND IDENTITY)

Whitehead's conception also attributes aesthetic intensity and purposeless meaningfulness in a particular form to "persons" (Busch 1993), something occasionally overlooked insofar as Whitehead *reconstructs* persons *ecologically.* From the perspective of such ecological reconstruction, persons, which Whitehead under-stands as the highest level of structural intensity, represent a *living nexus* within a complex society, an event nexus that "internally" (with respect to the individual events of the nexus) contains *conscious events* and "externally" (with respect to the social network or arrangement of events) represents a *temporally ordered, living nexus* (§15). (a) Conscious events develop such an intensive subjectivity that the integration of past (reality) and future (possibility) takes on the subjective form of *alert awareness* and *decision*. By contrast, consciousness first emerges only—here Whitehead's theory of consciousness coincides with contemporary brain research (§44)—where reality is perceived with respect to its capacity for *not* being (i.e., its contingency in the alternative sphere) or the *possibility* of its capacity to *be* (its degree of realization) (Hosinski 1993). Consciousness requires the *highest structural intensity of integration* of given data (past, facticity, historicity) and freedom (future, novelty, spontaneity) within the situation of decision. (b) In societies of events with this highest structural intensity constituting a "purely living nexus" within a protecting organism (the corpuscular society of the body and brain), there can be living persons only because their conscious events not only *happen* spontaneously, but are also thus *transmitted* (Busch 1993).

Several considerations merit attention in Whitehead's reconstruction of personal being. First, persons are positioned within a cosmological, evolutive, ecological context in which their "structural position" discloses them as an *advanced form of intensity*. In a general sense, by "person" Whitehead understands a *cosmological* organization of a given event nexus, an organization moreover that—independent of the human being—represents a certain form of *temporal order*. A society of events with *personal unity* consistently arises when events follow one another in immediate series, that is, are objectified each within the next (successive) ones and as such develop a *continuous* subjective form (PR, 34f.). Every such temporal event nexus needs an organic structure, a corpuscular society into which it is embedded and which supports it. The more complex the organism, the more intensive the personal society this organism is able to shelter. Living persons arise in living organisms that "canalize" a high degree of spontaneity. Personal societies become "guiding organs" of complex organisms, thereby shaping them into a higher unity. In this sense, animals can be viewed as "living persons" (in contradistinction to plants, which do not bear any such temporal, guiding organization) (Fetz 1981). The transitions, however, are fluid (PR, 102). Human beings organize their organism with the help of a "personal society," which harbors so much novelty and spontaneity that the society bursts the character of a "society" and develops a *purely living nexus*, that is, a nexus not bound by any (societal) "character." Whitehead thus calls this nexus a "non-social nexus" (PR, 106f.). Such a nexus, however, is by no means "asocial," but rather simply no longer defined by a "character." It experiences its intensity to the highest degree in consciousness, creativity, and freedom "along the borders of chaos" (PR, 105f., 111; Keller 2002b).

Whitehead is well aware that "personal unity is an inescapable fact," and hence that it is incumbent on every philosophy to "provide some doctrine of personal identity" (AI, 186). His own, ecological reconstruction, far from being interested in dissolving or otherwise reducing personal being, instead is reacting to a *fundamental philosophical dilemma*, namely, how personal *unity* is to be conceived if persons in their own turn stand for *living vitality*? For "unity" as such is always restrictive, describing the development of objectivity, of a character, a "defining element." By contrast, "living vitality" consistently strives to remove all such "definition" (restriction, enclosure) and to embrace spontaneity and novelty and burst through any restrictive characterization that might "capture" or "enclose" it (§24).

This dilemma has traditionally been resolved in favor of restrictive unity. The paradigmatic locus of such resolution is the Platonic-Aristotelian doctrine of the soul as *form*. As long as ideas are understood as the principle of actuality of an organism that "inform" matter, unity can be only be defined *formally*. Commitment to this understanding constitutes one of the unfortunate mishaps of classical substantialism, namely, the understanding of the soul as form that sustains itself or endures (substance), as the principle of activity (*anima forma corporis*), and as something with independent being (Cartesian subject). Whitehead, however, follows the critique of "self-identical Soul-Substance" (AI, 186) of David Hume and William James. In Whitehead's critique, such forms appear not as subjects, but as *objects* actualized as possibilities within events (ontological principle). Whitehead reconstructs "substantial forms" as *macrocosmic repetition of patterns* in series of events, as the development of a formal structure of temporal societies (Nobo 1986) (§19). By contrast, *all* societal characterization is overcome in an *entirely* living nexus; in its *nonsocial spontaneity*, such a nexus cannot in any way be defined as "form." The traditional response is in fact an example of how concreteness (living vitality) can be mistaken for abstraction (form), the originality and spontaneity of the soul having been shut down, as it were, in repeated characters (enduring form-patterns) (PR, 104; Faber 2002d). In this sense, Whitehead understands personal self-identity as an intensification process of nonsocial events in a complex organism that shapes itself into a *historical* unity, a *unity of genuinely lived life* of the entire "personal society" (as body and soul). If both identity and originality are to receive due and equal consideration, one must be able to understand human personal being as a highly *creative integration of intensity*.

(1) Personal being refers to the complex whole of a living organism that an *entirely living nexus* consciously experiences, guides in freedom, and through its spontaneity places into a creative history of interaction with the world and other persons. This "soul" of the person is embedded in the organism and is rendered possible only on the basis of that organism's complexity. By contrast, the "body" is that particular complex society of corporeal/mental events of all degrees and kinds providing support for the "soul," which in return lends to that body intensity and spontaneity. In this sense, the "body" and "soul" constitute in persons an indivisible unity of organization of originality and depth of intensity (Hosin-

ski 1993). In that unity, spontaneity is "canalized" such that it can attain personal depth.

(2) As the *nonsocial vitality of an entirely living nexus*, human personal being is *immediately* connected or linked with the ground of the cosmos, the *basic (chaotic) nexus* at the foundation of all orders, societies, and spontaneity within the cosmos (§19). Although that foundation or ground is commonly conceived as "chaos," it is nonetheless the ground of complexity, evolution, and creativity (§24). Personal being makes the world transparent with respect to its own creative ground; in it, that ground reemerges as it were (traversing all forms and types of order) in *pure vivacity*. It is no accident that in *Adventures of Ideas* Whitehead suggests locating the *unity* of personal being, its self-identity—for which every philosophy, as previously indicated, must adduce grounds—in the unity of the world in the larger sense, in the nonformal, all-encompassing, *"chaotic" nexus*, the broadest horizon of the "All," the boundary of nothingness, the (Platonic) "Wherein" (AI, 134; Wessell 1990) (§32). Despite the criticism that Whitehead is unable to adduce any specifically *antecedent* unity of personal being (in contrast to its cumulative unity within its history) (Rohmer 2000), it is indeed articulated in this "Wherein" (*khora*)—except that it is not of a *formal* nature (AI, 187; Faber 2002d).

(3) Personal being does not possess any substantialist anteriority; it is instead a *cumulative process of the history* of the entire personal society (Farmer 1997). Persons "attain" *themselves* in their history, the becoming of their organism, their lived life (S, 27). The entirely living nexus does *not* establish any structural "form," nor any integral anterior character (PR, 104); it does, however, establish a *mutual immanence* of its events (AI, 207f.; Faber 2000e) (§§34, 44). Such conscious events do not by any means live their intensity within "chaotic" isolation, instead "canalizing" such into a *single* history that *transmits*, as subjective form within the nexus, the intensities of past events while also including to the greatest extent possible their subjective aim. In this way, the personal nexus acquires a singularity of "style," a "historical character" (Rohmer 2000). A person *shapes* or *develops itself* into its identity, emerging from the cumulated intensity of its life as long as there is no faltering of spontaneity and as long as it acquires depth within its "style."

(4) When the *spontaneous ground of the world* breaks through in persons, it is experienced as the communicative *common* creative ground between persons. This spontaneity may appear to them as the element of *inexhaustibility* when they are attracted each to the other. Persons never exist alone, but rather always in connection as community (§35). Not only are they positioned ecologically on a complex evolutive basis of mutually intertwined organisms—organisms that render their "being" possible in the first place and turn them into a highly social phenomenon. They are positioned within the openness of personal encounter that acquires space within the nexus itself and becomes visible in the mutual attraction of spontaneity. In a sense transcending Whitehead's own understanding, personal being can be understood as a *community of inexhaustible spontaneity*—and

in the *"chaotic" nexus* as *communication* expressing the "foundation" of the world (AI, 150). Personal being is disclosed at the "place of emptiness"—Plato's "place" (*khora*) or "receptacle" (*hypodochē*) where communication and creativity become intertwined (Faber 2002d) (§16).

Whitehead's elaborated understanding of person can easily be read against the background of Derrida's critical deconstructive project of overcoming the substantialism of "self-presence." Within the phenomenon of "person," "self-presence" proves to be an illusion with respect to the becoming of individual events, insofar as it is misconstrued in the sense of "self-possession," and also an illusion with respect to the "wholeness" of persons that refers *not* to a sustaining "personal identity," but to a self-differentiation of the nonsocial living nexus of the person. Within every new event of the nexus, the person "has" or "possesses" itself only as *intensity, not* as duration, only in *difference, not* as "self-identity." One can almost maintain that Whitehead's "person" (the entirely living personal nexus) is realized as concrete *différance*, differentiating itself through self-grasping and perpetually displacing its identity into an *eschatological* hope, into the cumulative identity that emerges as the entire nexus itself becomes (moves toward being) whole. Here the theological dimension becomes particularly virulent, insofar as this move toward wholeness (becoming whole) is conceivable *only* as something that happens redemptively, as a *person in God* (PR, 350).

What does this personal being have to do with God? No less than in other philosophical conceptions that provide a plea *on behalf* of personal being, in Whitehead's ecological reconstruction too, personal being ultimately is disclosed *theologically* (and is untenable without this horizon). Within the becoming of persons, God is in a certain sense involved with everything which in a sense of process theology involves God's orientation toward the world itself. God is disclosed in persons as the future of their originality and ultimate identity, as the presence of the sphere of possibility and developmental potential, as the granting of the structure whereby originality acquires depth and this depth acquires identity, as the final origin or source of subjectivity in each of its events, and as the gift of its intensity. In this sense, divine involvement in the world *culminates* in personal being. This understanding underscores the central significance of personal being in any discussion of process theology, albeit more as desideratum (to the extent one must grant that such has rarely been clearly recognized) (Faber 2000e). Whitehead articulates four specific divine reference points for human personal being.

(1) *Opening*. More than in many substantialist and subjectivistic conceptions, in Whitehead's understanding of "person," God is *immediately* engaged in *each* of God's events through God's *primordial nature*. The person's originality as well as its "personal style" are mediated and supported by God's gift of the initial aim. God stands as it were at the very beginning of the *différance* of personal becoming; similarly and in a reverse fashion, person as *différance* is never without God. In Whitehead's ecological reconstruction, personal being emerges as a reinterpretation of Richard of St. Victor's understanding of (Trinitarian) personal being as "ex-(s)istence"—as *relational* and *communicative* existence (Faber 1995a).

(2) *Reception*. Every "personal event" is taken up by God's *consequent nature*. In its superjectivity, God receives that which the event has produced from its initial aim in order to preserve it undistorted in its completion and to transform it into the wholeness of the becoming person. In *Process and Reality* Whitehead can thus refer to persons becoming in a *twofold fashion*: (a) their *earthly becoming*, in which every *new* personal event objectifies all preceding ones with its subjective form, thereby also transmitting them in their originality, such that over the course of its life the person develops a singular character and grows into its unique identity; (b) their *theological becoming* in God's consequent nature, in which every event is not merely partially objectified, but instead transformed in its comprehensive relevance into the redeemed wholeness of its divine identity. This is the "person in God" (PR, 350).

(3) *Loving attention*. Once a personal event is completed, it perishes and is "objectified" in new events. This direct cumulation of the personal nexus corresponds to a divine turn in loving attention through which God appears not only as the *future* that makes originality possible, but also as a *salutary attention* in which the person's objectified past becomes anew a *loving gift* from the future. Whitehead is thinking here of an *interaction* between the earthly person and the person in God. God not only transforms every personal event into a divine reality; God also lets this transformed reality flow back into the earthly process. At every moment of its becoming, a person receives itself not only in originality (future) and continuity (past), but also as the *future of its redeemed past* (§30). Here Whitehead's theological grounding of personal being passes beyond deconstructionist *différance*, transforming it into the *vision* of redeemed wholeness *within* the process of differentiation (Keller 2002a). Whitehead's basis for personal being is *being loved unconditionally*.

(4) *Immortality*. The intensive interwovenness of personal being with the evolutive process that lends corporeality to an entirely living nexus may view personal societies as being so intimately bound to their corporeal conditions that persons then come to an end when these conditions themselves perish (Fetz 1981). The notion of an intensive interconnection through love, however, enables Whitehead to speak of the immortality of persons in God. His point of departure in *Adventures of Ideas* is that there is good reason to speak of an existence of the soul beyond its (earthly) body. The nontemporal aspect of God's own "everlasting nature" (God's receptive consequent nature) could "establish with the soul a peculiarly intense relationship of mutual immanence" such that the entirely living nexus of the person could partake of immortality as everlasting, sublated reception in God's life (AI, 208). Through *communicative immanence* between God and world, personal being is elevated above worldly corporeality and attains an eschatologically redeemed state in divine encorporeality.

One interesting question is the extent to which God is to be regarded as a "person." Whitehead himself initially vacillates with regard to this question. In *Science and the Modern World*, he views God as a principle that makes personal being possible but is itself not to be regarded as a person (SMW, 178). In *Religion in the Making*, he still begins by maintaining that God (in view of Buddhism) may not *necessarily* be understood as a person even though Whitehead himself simultaneously attributes *personal actions* to God (RMn, 62f., 154f.). What is in any case clear is that God can always be said to have a character that *develops* personality, and that thus God is *never less* than a personal reality (he never identifies God with an apersonal world law) (Jung 1965; Faber 2000e). An examination of process theologies shows that they in their own turn can take quite different positions on this subject. Empirical theology conceives God as a transpersonal power providing the ground for persons in the world (Wieman) (§3) (Cobb 1993). Rational theology interprets God as a cumulative person consisting of divine events ("God events"; consequent nature) or as a personal individual (personal society) (§4) (Auxier 1998). Speculative theology understands God as a Trinitarian community of personal societies (Bracken 1985) (§7). But even if with Whitehead we understand God as *event*, this divine event can never be *less* than a person. If the defining feature of personal being is its originality, then God's primordial nature is virtually the unmeasured and unmeasurable standard of this originality (infinitely anterior to every entirely living nexus as regards "chaotic harmony") (§32). If personal being implies cumulative identity, then God's consequent nature is the quintessence of the reception of life within cumulative unity. If personal being is based on communication, then God's *active, caring concern* toward every event reality within the latter's nexuses in the world constitutes virtually *the* expression of divine personal being. If God is nonetheless still understood as "event," then it is not as something that happens on a subpersonal level, but rather *amid love on a suprapersonal level*, overcoming the particularity, temporality, and chaotic endangerment of all personal being by standing in a relation of redemptive nondifference to persons (§§34, 40).

§23. VALUE
(SELF-TRANSCENDENCE)

Whitehead associates personal being not only with intensity, originality, and identity, but at least just as closely with death. In a way, death is the mode of existence of the person. Put differently, "person" refers not only to the aesthetic reality of self-identity, but also to the ethical reality of self-transcendence. This juxtaposition may seem somewhat surprising at first: death as an "ethical" reality? Is death not the anticipatory model of the finite wholeness of personal life (Martin Heidegger) or the absurd pulling down of existence on its path toward freedom (Jean-Paul Sartre)? Is it not *the* crisis of our existence as such (Karl Jaspers) in which we become aware of ourselves—as finite but also in our precious singularity (Küng 1996)? Whitehead's understanding of person positions the person's existence directly in the *existentiality of each of its events*; they are not only finite, but are also conscious of being such, being aware of their *hereafter* as well as their *disappearance*, through which they *become objective*. The person dies at every moment in order thereby to become person in the highest intensity. Put differently, a person lives its originality "along the borders of chaos," that is, aware of its "existence in death," an *existence in self-transcendence* (§22). Here the person is aware of being cast beyond itself at every moment of its existence. *In death* it then becomes an *ethical existence* (Lachmann 1990). Its *existential intensity* is simultaneously grounded not in enjoying its purposeless freedom, but in being conscious precisely of a final *aesthetic-ethical contrast* (§21).

Whitehead uses the term "value" to refer to this *transpersonal* moment in personal being, a moment that at once also lends a depth of existence to personal being. By "value," however, he is referring not to "exchange value," but is retrieving the earlier (Platonic and, subsequently, Christian) *doctrine of the good*, but now from the perspective of nonsubstantialist premises (Sayer 1999). "Value" in this sense refers to the *importance, meaning, worth* (MT, 1–19, 109, 117; FR, 30; SMW, 178; AI, 235) of an event *with regard to its process of decision*. It is "the good" with respect to the *process* (Lachmann 1990). Because this process has three phases (§10), the meaning of "value" is realized differently with regard to each of the three phases of becoming:

(a) With regard to the initial constitution of an event out of its initial aim, "value" means that the potentials from God's primordial nature do not represent merely a conglomerate of eternal objects, but God's *primordial valuation* of this particular sphere of possibility commensurate with the past (real possibility) and best future of the incipient event (Ford 1981; Suchocki 1995). Here "value" refers to the *proposition* of a process of becoming as the standard (of possible meaning) of its becoming (it cannot be subjectively relativized, possessing instead ontological quality) (Sayer 1999). (b) In the process itself of becoming, in which the event prehends all potentials (both physical and mental), an event decides on a *certain valuation* of these potentials, either including them (positive prehension), excluding them (negative prehension), enhancing their value (enhancing the importance for itself), or devaluing them (diminishing their importance) (Hosinski 1993). Here value refers to the functionless, independent, free valuation of the event's own process, to its becoming as a development of values for enriching intensity and self-enjoyment. Here value refers to "the good" as *self-value* (self-worth), as that which exists for its own sake, the *worth* or *dignity* of every event occurrence (Sayer 1999). (c) With respect to the "satisfaction" of the process of becoming in which the subject of becoming transitions into the status of a *superject of its "having become,"* value refers to this process of having become as the generation of a value (a subjective aim). In it, every event attains objective immortality for the continuing process (Lachmann 1990). Here value refers to the importance of an event as the *fruit of its own becoming* in its *effective value beyond itself* (Hauskeller 1994). Here value refers to the objective obligation of the cosmos to perceive the self-value of this completed process of becoming and to allow it to remain efficacious (S 39).

Of course, commensurate with the "unitexturality of reality," this three-phase value process—*primordial valuation* (the good as proposition for the process of becoming), *self-enjoyment/satisfaction* (the good as self-value), and *importance/meaning* (the good as value for the becoming of others)—applies not only to persons, but in general to *all* events, a view thereby also opposing the substantialist and subjectivistic "fallacy of misplaced concreteness," for which all (material) existence is passive, meaningless, and empty ("vacuous actuality") (PR, 29; SMW, 49; PR, 18). Whitehead's theory of value unmasks this "valueless" materialism as an abstraction and instead consistently understands concrete actuality as *meaningful*—in its becoming (as an event happening incapable of objectification) as well as its having become (facticity) (Lachmann 1990). The determinative (antisubstantialist and antimaterialistic) *aesthetic axiom* of Whiteheadian philosophy is that all facticity is immanently valuable (echoing the Platonic assertion concerning the *ens et bonum convertuntur*) (Sayer 1999). This capacity for value reaches its highest intensity in the personal nexus, for it is in persons that the *aesthetic* process of value appears as an *ethical* process of meaning. The *center* of this ethical existence is its *immanent value structure* as *self-transcendence*. In all three phases, "value" is consistently that which within the process of decision itself surpasses subjectivity:

(a) In the *first* phase, the goal of the process appears as the teleological proposition for the incipient process. Here God's valuation constitutes the process as "transcendent" *anteriority* in the double sense, namely, in the *temporal* sense of the aim yet to be attained, and in the *grounding* sense as the inauguration (opening up) of the process itself. This transcendence grounds subjectivity, but always with respect to an aim in which it will ultimately pass beyond itself. (b) In the *second* phase, although value does refer to the development of self-value, such self-value acquires its highest intensity precisely insofar as it is aware of the transcendence of its self (the aesthetic-ethical contrast). (c) It is in the *third* phase that this self-transcendence becomes overt insofar as the event now, at its end, completes itself and in so doing acquires immortality and value *for other* becoming. From the very outset, the event was focused on attaining its subjective aim, an aim in which it passes beyond itself. From the very outset, the process of becoming is in fact an ethical process of self-surpassing, insofar as it happens with the existential awareness of responsibility for efficacious agency in other processes, in processes beyond its own subjectivity. Self-transcendence is its "goal." In death it acquires meaning beyond itself. In a reverse fashion, awareness of this situation similarly constitutes part of the subjective process itself, of subjective intensity, and of the immanent aesthetic meaning of an event (PR, 27f.: Categoreal Obligations VIII, IX; Faber 2000e).

These considerations have considerable consequences for the "value" of a person. The "assessment" of the value of an event within the ongoing process proceeds not with an eye on supply and demand, nor on the current market for sympathy and antipathy, nor on the current stock of being popular or unpopular, but on an event's *immanent process of intensity*, its *self-value*, its functionless, nonfunctionalizeable "self-functioning" (PR, 25: Categories of Explanation XXVf.). Value is not a history of reception (even though the value of a past event can be revalued in such), but a moment of immanent self-value arising as self-transcending value in the process of becoming. Here fact and value enter into an immediate coherent unity that remains both indissoluble and incapable of relativization within the ongoing process (Altizer 1975). This value is grounded in the *immediacy* of subjective self-becoming; it is *there* that an event acquires *transcendent* meaning. And in a reverse fashion, it is only in the awareness of self-transcendence *as a moment* within the process of becoming that self-becoming also acquires self-value. The *anticipation* of ethical relevance "beyond death" makes aesthetic intensity possible (PR, 27: Categoreal Obligation VIII: Category of Subjective Intensity). Aesthetics and ethics, self-value and self-transcendence mutually determine one another (Hauskeller 1994). Even though values *arise* only as *subjective acts of decision* (Whitehead acknowledges no material values as does, e.g., Max Scheler in the latter's "value ethics"; for Whitehead, "value" always means *valuation*), they always *refer* to the *objective relevance* of these acts beyond themselves (Maassen 1988; Sayer 1999). Self-transcendence refers to an *event's ethical claim* that it be perceived beyond itself, as well as to the *world's claim* to acquire meaning beyond the event in its becoming. The value of a person depends not on the evaluation of others, but on the self-value and the self-transcendence implied therein as the person's mode of existence.

The concept of value discloses personal being with respect to the *existential meaning* of self-transcendence, that is, of "ethical death" as a *form of existence* of the person. If every event of a person already constitutes an existential exodus such that it does *not* live the "self-enjoyment" of its individual events "for itself," but rather within self-transcendence for the *entirety* of the person (which is yet outstanding), then for the person as a whole its *transpersonal transcendence* is actually its meaning. Whitehead refers to this *trans*personal meaning of *the* person as "peace" (§39). Peace consists in the acquisition of value structures (the coordination of value). The first effect of the awareness that persons acquire transpersonal meaning when they complete themselves *as* persons becomes palpable for Whitehead in being liberated from a preoccupation with itself. Peace always involves the surpassing of personality, but in a fashion such that its *existence* is thereby fulfilled (AI, 284ff.). In "ethical death" as a form of existence of the person, a person comes to the conscious realization that ultimately its cumulation is directed *not* toward itself as relative value, but toward release beyond itself as "an appeal beyond boundaries" (SMW 285). In a key passage in *Adventures of Ideas*, Whitehead refers to this *transpersonal generation of meaning* as the attainment of "self-control at its widest—at the width where the 'self' has been lost, and [self-] interest has been transferred to coördinations [of value] wider than personality" (AI, 285). Self-transcendence as the transpersonal meaning of personal being does not refer to the eclipse of personal being, disclosing instead the *form of existence* of persons directed toward extinguishing the "self" (Suchocki 1995). This transpersonal expansion of personal being reminiscent of the Buddhist doctrine of "not-self" (*anatta*) intends not to overcome personality, but to disclose its *essence*. Value discloses the *process of personal being* as a process of the becoming of *self-value* (Inada 1971; Faber 2002d).

The crowning achievement of this transpersonal theory of value is a *deconstruction* of substantialism and subjectivism, precisely with respect to human personal being. Value refers first of all to the "inner reality" of a happening (SMW, 93), to its intensification process and self-value. This self-value, however, is not fulfilled aesthetically in a final act of self-enjoyment of the personal event or person as a whole, but in a final *meaningful* death through self-transcendence. The "reversal" of the subject into superject means that the event ends in a full state of completion. In "satisfaction" as the "essence" of that completion, an event *could* enjoy itself; instead, however, it *perishes*. Becoming fully complete (whole) simultaneously means "having become" (Kline 1983). No personal event attains fulfillment within itself, within its own self-presence, but rather solely through its transcending self-loss. "Completion" is the perishing of immediacy; "it never really is" (PR, 85). Since this constitutes the intensive existence of human persons, personal being does indeed appear in Whitehead's thought as concrete *différance*. At the moment of self-grasping, the person differentiates itself (*différe*) and defers (*déferre*) its meaning within the process of differentiation. The person never really participates in self-possession, self-fulfillment, or self-presence in any substantialist or subjectivistic sense, but it consistently realizes the intensity of self-transcendence (Faber 2000e).

Différance is deeply ingrained *existentially* in personal being and as such characterizes it as a profoundly *theological existence*. Within essential self-transcendence, the eschatological meaning of person becomes concentrated *beyond* itself, namely, in its *meaning* in God's consequent nature (§22). The "person in God" fulfills this self-transcendence by first acquiring identity within God, except that this identity resides *beyond* its self, namely, in God's own *reception* of the person. There the person becomes *wholly* its "self" and *wholly* "self"-less; it is in this "self-lessness" in God, however, that it attains its "peace" (Suchocki 1988). Here one encounters reflections of notions such as the mystical death the soul dies in order to be able to see God (Dionysius the Areopagite), dying in order to live, and an essentially *communicative* understanding of person beyond all substantialist theories of the self that focus on how the self allegedly endures, remains the same, and partakes of self-presence. Persons attain "presence" *beyond* themselves in God and only *there* fulfill *themselves* (mystical death) (Faber 2000e). God bequeaths the final *theopoetic meaning of the world* as value as a *self-meaningful self-transcendence* (SMW, 93). On Whitehead's view, the *genuine task of theology* is precisely to search for *this particular* meaning, to understand "how [the] life [of persons] includes a mode of satisfaction deeper than joy or sorrow" (AI, 172).

The question of value includes the question of identity. By opening up the theological dimension of the concept of value, Whitehead finds that *ultimate* identity is of a theopoetic nature, that is, must be understood from a perspective moving from aesthetic identity (self-value) to ethical identity (self-transcendence) to religious identity (value in God) (Sayer 1999). This religious value discloses God's reconciled nondifference with the world. We become *wholly* "ourselves" through being expanded in God *beyond* our own "selves"—and in being expanded into our meaning within the whole in God. Put *theopoetically*, God's primordial vision (God's primordial nature) is that particular self-transcendent value structure of God in which God wholly *bequeaths Godself* to the world (acquires *meaning* for it) in order to redeem everything in its *self-transcendent self-value* through divine appreciation (the *meaning* of the world in God's consequent nature) (Inada 1975) (§39).

§24. UNITY
(WHOLENESS AND INFINITE OPENNESS)

It is not just the entirely living nexus of the person that first makes the question of "unity" within the cosmos become so pressing. This question is instead one of the fundamental questions of philosophy as such and even today occupies a central position in poststructuralist discussion, albeit as one that has received a negative response (Keller 2002a). Whitehead himself stands within this long tradition in taking "unity" as one of the fundamental tenets of his own philosophical construction of categories. In his "Category of the Ultimate" (PR, 21f.) (Whitehead's basic nonfundamentalist category), unity represents one of the key words used to articulate his ecological conception in the form of the "togetherness" of things, a notion not otherwise capable of being grounded. Such togetherness, however, rather than being static or substantial, is instead a *process* unfolding within a *twofold creative swing* from multiplicity into unity and from unity into multiplicity (§§2, 16). The structural locus of "unity" in Whitehead's thought defines it not as something "given," but as something *happening* or *occurring* in the rhythm of events becoming and perishing. Moreover Whitehead departs radically from tradition in maintaining that this ultimate rhythm prevents one both from understanding the universe as unfolding from some state of basic unity (*physis* in the ontotheological use) and from understanding it as moving toward some static end condition of comprehensive unity (substantialist ontotheology) (Faber 2000e). That is, unity is neither the ground of unfolding nor the highest being (the unity of the universe); instead it consistently represents a *finite moment* within the overall creative process. While it is true that the *entire* universe is gathered within every unity, every event at *this* particular place (PR, 36), nonetheless, within the act of perishing, this world perspective itself is simultaneously merely *one* moment within the multiplicity of the world—a world whose genuine unity it has itself thereby expanded. Unity is always both *processual* and *relational*, the becoming and perishing of unity—unity as "becoming one internally" (*unum*) and "becoming one among others" (*aliquid*) (PR, 21; Fetz 1986).

This understanding of unity clearly demonstrates how Whitehead's "flat ontology" prevents the notion of a layered universe in which everything is gathered toward ever greater unities until everything eventually flows together in the unity of God (Wilber 1996). In fact, Whitehead explicitly refuses to acknowledge any

Plurality

"inclusive unity " that might muzzle the universe, as it were, by bracing and layering it (Ford 1988). On the other hand, this position also reveals the internal difficulties that have since critically beset Whitehead's initiative. For if indeed all unity is *finite*, then plurality must be accorded the *same* ontological status as unity itself—a clearly *radical* conception of plurality (Welker 1985). There is no unity that can encompass a plurality without at the same time itself perishing as a moment of a new plurality surpassing this very unity. To that extent, Whitehead is a radical pluralist, understanding every unity as *smaller* (in transition) than the multiplicity it encompasses (within concrescence) (Faber 2003). Here Whitehead is operating as a deconstructionist and precursor of French *philosophy of difference* (Foucault, Deleuze) (Welsch 1995; Keller 2002a), realizing Derrida's *différance*—even before its formulation—as *process*. Unity is understood in an antisubstantialist fashion, losing the status of self-presence and acquiring instead the status of *différance/process*. Unlike deconstructionism and poststructuralism, however, Whitehead is interested not in differentiation itself, but in the *connex* of that which is differentiated—the way the one is able to be *in* the other (PR, 50; Keller 2000) (§8), and thus in the "mutual immanence" within the process of differentiation (§34). His "plural chaos" is a *nexus*, that is, "togetherness" (§35). To that extent Whitehead, rather than being a relativistic pluralist whose thought issues in indifference and indecision, is instead a *relationalist* for whom everything is *connected* or *linked as* difference (Faber 2000e).

But how is such "unity" to be conceived as "connex"? In what way is a nexus "one"? In what way a society of events? A macrocosmic "event"? A thing? Something living? The human person? If unity is in any case always smaller than the multiplicity it unites, and if every unity perishes in order to become part of a multiplicity encompassing it, then how can *any* more complex structure in the cosmos be "one"? Initially it is easier to indicate how cosmic structures and organisms are *not* one. Commensurate with the *ontological principle*, events alone can be the grounds of unity, not real or pure objects (qualities, characters, patterns, or laws) (§15). Unlike tradition, for which ideas or forms guaranteed not only actuality but also unity, for Whitehead such can be discerned only within the concrete *becoming* of events (Rorty 1983) (§13). Because this becoming constitutes itself *prehensively* from *relations* with other events (concrescence), however, and then perishes *in relation* to other events (transition), unity itself (within an event nexus) can only be *event-centered*, never *structural*. Although structures do indeed fulfill an important function within the process of unity, that process itself can never even remotely be understood on that basis (PR, 43, 48) (§11). The radical nature of the ontological principle suggests understanding unity as something that we are not initially inclined to comprehend as unity in any case, namely, as the *process itself* (PR, 7; Rohmer 2000).

And Whitehead does indeed understand *process* as the *innermost essence* of events and thus of *concrete unity* in the world ("the very essence of real actuality") (AI, 274). How, however, can "process" constitute the unity of complex organisms? Although Whitehead is thinking of extremely variable modes of unity in this context, they all remain oriented toward "process" as unity (Jung 1980). Critics subsequently frequently questioned whether Whitehead could conceive unity in an adequate fashion along these lines, finding instead that his solution (unity as process) was unsatisfactory (Pannenberg 1986; Rohmer 2000; Fetz 1981). Critics found that Whitehead seemed to give the unity of events ontological precedence over that of event nexuses. Misconstrued "atomism" in this sense then prompted the unity of event nexuses to appear secondary and thus as being ontologically derivative (Nobo 1986; Bracken 1989). Not understanding Whitehead's solution, critics objected that he is in fact unable to conceive the *ontological* unity of larger organisms, not to speak of living beings or, certainly, persons (Scheffczyk 1984; Schulte 1989; Sander 1990). What critics overlooked is that one must differentiate strictly between what one sought—but did not find—as "unity" in Whitehead, and that which Whitehead himself ultimately understood by unity. What critics sought was *structural* unity—unity as *form*. Although Whitehead is indeed familiar with such, he deconstructs it as an abstraction of concrete processes (ontological principle). And that is the problem, namely, that critics reject Whitehead's deconstructionist notion of unity while simultaneously searching for *substantialist (formal)* unity. From the substantialist perspective, however, "process" must necessarily appear as the negation of unity.

How, then, does Whitehead resolve the problem of *unity as process* with respect to complex structures within the cosmos? His solution is to understand "unity" with respect to all cosmic unities both *structurally* (formally) and *processually*. Here his thinking consistently tries to avoid the notion of a "static morphological universe" (PR, 222), seeking instead a perspective from which "existence" and "process" "presuppose each other" (MT, 96) such that *ultimately* they are grounded in processual, nonformal unity.

(1) The unity of *actualities* (microscopic events) is structurally determined by *subjective forms* in which real and pure objects are prehended. Hence, although they constitute the *structural* unity of a *form*, they also demonstrate, to the extent they are *subjective* (i.e., nonobjectifiable), that they cannot simply be reduced to or understood solely as structure, being instead the *creative arising* of unity (process principle). The unity of actualities cannot be objectified and in their nontemporal mentality (intellectuality, subjectivity) cannot be comprehended other than *processually* (Klose 2002).

(2) Unlike microscopic events or actual entities whose mental pole generates unity beyond chronological time (Lango 1972), *event nexuses* are positioned within chronological time (Ford 1988). But how is their unity to be conceived, given their *diachronic differentiation* within time? Whitehead adduces three modes of unity, namely, macroscopic events, societies, and super-actualities: (a) *Macroscopic events* emerge from the differentiation of actualities that produce a temporal nexus (coherent context) without repeating a common character (PR, 73). Their unity is that of something that happens macrocosmically without structural constancy. Although certain structures may persist or endure within individual moments of the sequence of actualities, as a whole this unity cannot

be objectified structurally. Unlike microcosmic events (actual entities), they develop not a teleological (mental) nexus, but a *causal* one, in which they generate themselves (§§15, 20) (PR, 80). Ultimately their unity is processual (causal) rather than formal. (b) By contrast, *societies* possess a strong structural connex that can occasionally even take on the form of a quasi-substantial unity, especially in the case of fixed objects whose character is predominant and moreover is repeated in all members of the society (PR, 89) (Nobo 1986; Fetz 1981). Have we found the sought-after structural unity here? Whitehead immediately relativizes this notion commensurate with the ontological principle, maintaining that only as long as the events continue the repetition of structure does the unified character of societies remain intact. Formal constancy (still) remains subject to causal conditions, and here too unity ultimately remains processual. (c) Whitehead discloses a special form of balance between formal and causal unity by assuming that certain societies exhibit a *teleological* structure *like* microcosmic events. Event nexuses then "become" *like* individual actual entities, in which case their unity is not only causal (as with macrocosmic events) or predominantly formal (as with societies), but final (PR, 286). *Superactualities* link their microcosmic actualities like prehensions into a "super-concrescence" capable of attaining a subjective goal superordinate to the event nexus—that is, a mental, atemporal, final unity (Lachmann 1990). Even though formal elements of teleological structure do inhere within the unity of a superactuality, such is always included within the *processual* unity of "becoming" of the "super-concrescence," which cannot be objectified formally.

(3) It is especially with regard to the notion of *personal unity* that criticism of Whitehead's processual understanding of unity is unmasked as a variation of substantialism. Whitehead defines personal unity in a wholly nonsubstantialist, indeed antisubstantialist fashion, maintaining that as the unity of an entirely living nexus, it cannot *in any way* be *formally* defined (§22); instead it is of a consistently and wholly nonformal nature, constituting indeed the expression par excellence of nonformal, processual unity. For it is in the personal nexus that the *basic chaotic nexus* becomes visible that is to be understood as *the* basis of the unity of the cosmos in Whitehead's organic cosmology, namely, as *that* event nexus in which *all others* come to their existence (§15). As such, it functions in an *unqualified* fashion as the unity for that which is to be called "cosmos" in the larger sense. If, however, *the* unity of the cosmos is to be understood as being *wholly* processual rather than formal, then how can unity *within* this nexus not also always *ultimately* be processual (even if in its details it may well exhibit structural evolution)? The transparency between the "structurally" *highest* unity in the universe (personal being) and the *broadest* unity of the universe (the chaotic nexus) shows that Whitehead *rigorously* understands unity in a nonsubstantialist fashion as being consistently processual. Organic cosmology understands unity ultimately as being borne by the *uniqueness* of the chaotic nexus (§16); that is, *creativity* and *receptivity* (*khora*) stand for this unity, which in principle is nonformal, all-receptive, and creative (AI, 187).

With Henri Bergson before him and Gilles Deleuze after him, Whitehead understands unity as wholeness and wholeness as "openness" (Deleuze 1997b) (§16). Something is "whole" if and as long as it *is becoming*. Wholeness is the *openness* and *living vitality* of a process, a process that cannot be reduced to the "totality" of the structural moments that "are becoming" within it (Deleuze 1997b). The paradigm for wholeness is mentality, spirit (intellect), subjectivity, life, that which according to the ontological principle cannot be reduced to or understood in terms of structures, universals, or objectivity (PR, 40, 80). Unlike the (alleged) irrationalism of Bergson's philosophy of life, however, which needs no structural abstraction to account for the becoming of the whole, and Deleuze's immanentism, for which (similar to Bloch's "matter") structures represent concretizations of virtual potentials of the past, Whitehead maintains both the *rationality* and the *transcendence* of the process (Rohmer 2000): The process attests *structures* that remain points of crystallization of unity (§18), as well as the *radical novelty* that cannot be grounded from the world itself (Wiehl 1986) (§17). Whitehead understands both as being embedded in God's primordial nature, which structures all eternal objects as possibilities for world and generates them as novelty over against the world itself. The primordial nature, however, demonstrates that wholeness means life, since in it all forms are subject to divine *valuation* and emerge from an act of divine creativity (§23)—it is *this* act that is unity as living wholeness and infinite openness, as divine-living process (Ford 1981).

Substantialist criticism maintains that macrocosmic unity dissolves in the alleged "atomism" of events and that *formal* unity is thus required to attain *real* unity. The allegation is that Whitehead instead temporalizes macrocosmic unity and atomizes it through extension and perishability (Sander 1990). In that case, the oneness of a person would indeed come about only *indirectly* through objectivized past events no longer positioned in living unity within the whole of the person and which thus preclude the concrete person from being "given" in any antecedent or anterior fashion (before its becoming as an event) (Rohmer 2000) (§22). The response to this objection is that extensional and temporal difference (§14) identify a person in an almost paradigmatic fashion as concrete *différance*, whose unity cannot be defined by way of self-presence. *Processual* unity, however, is not only difference (the collapse of unity), but also *connex*—nonsubstantialist but *relational* unity, *nexic* unity (§13). A nexus always realizes the "mutual immanence" of its events (AI, 191ff., 201ff.) (§34). Even though this immanence *must* be *indirect* as long as one is inclined to allow for "external relations" and thereby also space-time (commensurate with our cosmos), nonetheless against the background of the *basic chaotic nexus,* unity is to be interpreted as a creative process. As the unity of activity and receptivity, the *basic chaotic nexus* (and all structural unities within it) constitutes a *field* in which every event appears as a moment of the *same* field (Bracken 1989). Everything that happens within that field affects all events that concretize ("atomize") the field. In a reverse fashion, every event is always a result of the entire field (Busch 1993). Here unity acquires an *event-oriented* ground that is nonetheless *truthful* without falling into the trap of "self-presence."

Ultimately Whitehead will provide a Trinitarian theological grounding for this relational understanding of unity as a "field of mutual immanence" (§34).

What role does God play with respect to the processual wholeness of the universe? The understanding of unity as open wholeness and of the latter as the infinite openness of the cosmos (chaotic nexus) (§16) explains why Whitehead ultimately associates unity with the concept of "adventure," which suggests the notion that it is only through *creative self-transcendence* that the world can attain "self-identity," that is, within the infinitely open wholeness of the process itself (AI, 274ff.). In the grand concluding vision of *Adventure of Ideas*, Whitehead interprets this wholeness of the process as the creative and receptive unity of self-transcendence (creativity/receptacle/self-transcendence) in which God appears threefold, namely, as "Eros," as the "Adventure of the Universe as One" (AI, 295), and as "Harmony of Harmonies" (AI, 296). (a) "Eros" places the world into the openness of creativity by freeing up everything as a potential of creative becoming, such that the creature is offered to itself as that which becomes. Eros entices, lures the creature into the openness of becoming, into the new, the novelty of its genuine existence. As Eros, God's primordial nature is the beginning of every creature, is its future, and is the reflection of its *best* possible existence. As Eros, God sends Godself as "the good" to all that becomes and entices it toward Godself. (b) When God receives the world, God knows about it "from the inside" and accepts the world as that which it has become and in all its truthfulness. God does not, however, assemble or organize the unity of the universe into a fixed order that "has become," as it were, once and for all; instead God arranges it as an adventure, placing it squarely into openness, accompanying it as open wholeness, and *keeping its wholeness open* (§30). (c) As the "Harmony of Harmonies," God guarantees that all the adventurous movements of the universe will ultimately be organized into a harmonious whole. This harmony, however, does *not* represent any preordained idea, or any particular order or system to which the world must eventually correspond if it is to be saved; it is instead the power of God to bring everything that might happen into a "harmonious wholeness" in which the world in fact cannot perish. God appears as the reconciling radiance of the beauty of the world (§39).

The suspicion that Whitehead's concept of God serves merely to comprehend the unity of the world in a subtle fashion (Welker 1984; Dalferth 1986) fails to recognize Whitehead's concept of the "unity of the world" as a living whole and as infinite openness. Whitehead uses the term "creativity," *not* God, to refer to this processual, nonformal unity. By contrast, "God" refers to that particular power that preserves precisely *this* unity by *keeping it open* (Faber 2000e). God acts efficaciously as the power of the future (Eros, adventure, harmony) that perpetually prevents the emergence of frozen formal unity (Moltmann 1995). *Theopoetically* God acts not as a creator who grounds unity (ontotheological unity) or formally justifies unities, but as the redeemer who shows the way to openness and liberates from all oppressive unities. Within both God's primordial and God's consequent natures, God embraces the world process and in so doing expresses God's love for the adventure of the world. In this love, God fulfills God-self as the patient advocate of the beautiful—through the contrast of Eros, harmony, and adventure. Within such theopoetics, unity emerges as *living unity* (unity of living self-becoming and self-valuation), which cannot be reconstructed morphologically, while God emerges as the *intensely living unity* whose agency means poetics, the escape from morphological occlusion and rigidity into the unity of life, life that comes to fulfillment only within the infinite openness of life itself, that is, within its eroticism, harmonics, and adventurousness—for which God stands within the world process (§35).

IV. Horizons

The Relationship between God and the World

The center of theopoetics is *God's world poetics*, God's *patient vision* of world; its goal is *salvation*. The focal point of reflection in process theology is the relationship between God and world (Cobb 1971a). This center, rather than involving one topic among others, instead represents the *inclusive brace* for all theological inquiry, the "matrix" or generative pattern for theological themes, problems, and solutions as such. The center of the present chapter is this world poetics of God, namely: God as a "dipolar" event that assembles or collects together the world *panentheistically* and as such allows God's relationship with the world to appear as open monotheism (§25); the *theistic triad*, through which God's immanence and transcendence are reconceived as the *mutual immanence* of God and the world(§26); God as concrete event in which everything is concretized and without which nothing is concrete in the world (§27); God's *self-creativity*, which is God's very essence, and God's overflowing creative power (§28); God's *alterity* in God's relationship with the world, which comes to expression in the reversal of movement of God and world (§29); the *radical reciprocity* of God's relationship with the world, and God's relationship with the world in Whitehead's "six antitheses" (§30); the *processual juxtaposition* of God and world in the concrete creative process, structurally discernible in four phases (§31); and finally the continuity of the world toward (and in) God as a *common field of a divine matrix* (§32). These juxtapositions and relationships will disclose *the extent to which* from the perspective of process theology God is to be called the "poet of the world" (and in which sense God is not to be so designated). Process theology has developed a "theological cosmology" as a new brace for theological assertions and inquiry, namely, the *theological relevance of world*.

§25. DIPOLARITY
(PANENTHEISM AND OPEN MONOTHEISM)

The principle of organic relationalism of "necessity in universality" (§13) stipulates that everything not standing in some relation is unknowable. Process theology thus understands God as "God in relation." This relationality of "God in relation" unfolds through three principles. (a) The "unitexturality of reality," according to which everything is to be taken as real and concrete in the same fashion (flat ontology), allows God to move into purview as *event*. (b) The three principles of event structure disclose God as a *dipolar event*. Commensurate with the principle of relationality, one must be able to refer to God as "existent" and as being capable of entering into the becoming of world events. Commensurate with the ontological principle, God (lest God be conceived as a mere idea) can act efficaciously only if God is genuinely *concrete*. Commensurate with the principle of process, God "becomes" what God "is," that is, God is a *concrescence* that comes about within the difference of the mental and physical poles. (c) Commensurate with the singularity of everything that happens, however, God as a concrete, dipolar event is *singular subjectivity* and as such dipolar in a unique way. God stands in an irreplaceable relationality to the world, a relationality within which the world itself first attains its identity. Although the dipolarity of God and that of all events in the world are indeed characterized by irreplaceable singularity, they are nonetheless positioned within an *organic nexus*.

   "Dipolarity" means that every event carries out *mental* and *physical* acts of *prehensions* through which it constitutes or indeed concretizes itself as a *synthesis* emerging from the perception of physical reality and a sphere of possibility (§§ 9f., 12). This synthetic activity (creativity) of every event has a twofold origin: first, the past of that which has already happened, a past that it transforms within synthesis into the history of its origin, *and*, second, the future of its own possibility as *capacity for becoming*, its capacity for being a new event. Every event begins (to become itself) from the world and God, from the past of the world that has already become and from God's bequeathed future (in the initial aim) (Fetz 1981; Hosinski 1993; Rohmer 2000). As far as God's dipolarity is concerned, this means (Reeves 1984) that (a) *every* event is positioned within the tension between mentality and physicality, intellectuality and materiality—*including* God (PR, 108). That is to say, God too (in relation to the world) is *not* merely abstract "spirit" in contrast to the materiality of the world, but is instead—precisely within this dipolarity—both mental and physical, spiritual and "material" (Cobb 1974). In this sense, dipolarity articulates the corporeality of every event and thus also implies that God Godself is *corporeal* (Hartshorne 1991c). (b) Within dipolarity every event completes the synthesis of its becoming—*including* God (PR, 239, 244)—incorporating not only possibilities but also the reality of the actualized world itself. God too is "concretized" from a sphere of possibility, on the one hand, and the reality of the world, on the other, that is, from the infinite sphere of possibility of all possible worlds *and* from a perception of all previously actualized worlds with regard to that which they have actually become and to their truth (PR, 338). God's mental pole is God's *primordial nature*; God's physical pole is God's *consequent nature* (PR, 32), and in this regard "dipolarity" refers to God's *organic nexus* with the world (Suchocki 1995; Hosinski 1993). (c) By virtue of its dipolarity, every event is positioned within a nontemporal unity of the mind (the mental pole) and a temporal relationality involving its corporeality (physical pole) (PR, 45). Beyond time, God too is characterized by a temporally independent, atemporal and pretemporal eternity of the primordial nature; God is *also*, however, characterized in God's consequent nature by a temporally sensitive, temporally relative, and temporally perceptive integration of the temporal world (PR, 31). Here dipolarity refers to the organic nexus of time and timelessness and articulates God's *organic realization of eternity and temporality* (Clarke 1984; Ford 1973b; Cobb 1974).

As unusual as it may at first appear, this understanding of God's dipolarity picks up and lends a contemporary interpretation to the biblical horizon of a corporeal God who is both world perceptive and temporally sensitive (Faber 2002f). In effect, these three dimensions of dipolarity allow for understanding the organic juxtaposition of God and world *without* losing or submerging God in the world (Welker 1988). From the dipolar perspective, this "God in relation" appears as the creative and saving origin of the world. The creativity of every event in the world is constituted not from some nothingness of its "not yet being," but from the inaccessibly anterior future that is God's primordial nature, out of the divine-compassionate gift of the initial aim, of a sphere of both possibility and freedom for decision, out of the bequeathal of self in inaccessible anteriority, and out of the personal proposition of and to the self (§21). Nor is any event ever lost into the nothingness of "no longer being"; instead, it falls into God's perception of all that has become, namely, into God's consequent nature, the compassionate saving of the life fragment of every event, the "putting aright" of all that happened, its integration into divine harmony, where it abides eternally in God (§39). It is in this way that God and world "become" *for each other*.

In *this* sense one can cautiously agree with Hartshorne's description of the world as the "body" of God and God as the "soul" of the world (Hartshorne 1991). In delimiting this position over against the threat of pantheism, Hartshorne refers to this organic nexus of God and world as *panentheism* (Franklin 1984) (§4), the assertion that everything is *one* in God.

Negatively, then, that is, in critical delimitation over against pantheism, this "panentheism" is characterized by the following: (a) The *world does not become God*, for everything is one in God such that God unites it in its *difference* from God and from everything else, that is, in its plurality and differentiation (Bracken

1997). Everything is one within God's primordial nature insofar as it is *released* from God (according to its possibility) for its *own* realization. Here unity implies providing space for the uniqueness of the plurality of creatures. Within God's consequent nature, by contrast, God unites everything through saving reception and by transforming it into its own truth and into a reconciliation completing everything in its uniqueness. Although everything is united *relationally* within God's consequent nature (in both difference and connex), it is *never* transformed into God (Reese 1991). (b) *God never becomes world*, since everything is received so that it may become itself within difference. There is no concrete event as such in God's primordial nature, only the *possibility* of every event as a divine possibility. In God's consequent nature, God *perceives* events that have already happened; rather than becoming God, they instead become themselves in being prehended by God (Christian 1967).

Positively, this "panentheism" is characterized by the following. (a) Panentheism interprets the *biblical God*, who is anticipated eschatologically as the God who will be "all in all" (1 Cor. 15:28) (Faber 2000e). Jürgen Moltmann has referred to himself as a "panentheist" in this sense, albeit not because he understands everything as being "divinized" in God's unity, but because *without* God's unifying activity nothing could become itself in the first place (Moltmann 1993). The ultimate *divine predicate* is then *world relationality*, being "all in all." (b) Panentheism interprets God's event-nature as concrescence, understanding God's "becoming" as prehensive activity that not only is *world related* but instead *world sensitive* (Faber 2001c). Through "uniting" the world, God *experiences* world, *knows* about it (its truth), and *reconciles* it.

In his article "Peirce, Whitehead, and the Sixteen Views about God" (1991), Hartshorne highlights the meaning of this dipolar panentheism by situating it within a matrix of *all possible variations* of the relationship between God and world. Within this context, his interpretation of the dipolarity of God and world understands the mental pole as *necessity* and *absoluteness* (timelessness, reason, structure, unity) and the physical pole as an expression of *contingency* and *incompleteness* (temporality, fortuitousness, historicity, multiplicity) (Hartshorne 1946). He now classifies all possible understandings of the God-world relationship such that their relationship with dipolarity is depicted within the matrix as either affirmation, negation, or partial affirmation/negation (Figure 1).

Figure 1: Sixteen Views of God

Columns: God's relationship with the world

		I (N)	II (C)	III (NC)	IV (X)
Lines: relationship between the world and God	1 (n)	N.n (1)	C.n (2)	NC.n (3)	X.n (4)
	2 (c)	N.c (5)	C.c (6)	NC.c (7)	X.c (8)
	3 (cn)	N.cn (9)	C.cn (10)	NC.cn (11)	X.cn (12)
	4 (X)	N.X (13)	C.X (14)	NC.X (15)	X.X (16)

God.world **N/n**: necessity (absoluteness); **C/c**: contingency (relativity); **X**: not applicable

All forms of "theism" and "atheism" are disclosed from their position with respect to dipolarity. The *columns* formulate four basic positions with regard to God's necessity (completeness) or contingency (incompleteness). *Column I* attributes *only* infinity/completeness to God. For these positions, God is necessary/absolute *in every regard* and is contingent in no regard—hence (uppercase) N. This column refers to all positions that attribute *nondual transcendence* to God or accept *theological transcendentalism*. *Column II* includes all positions that understand God as being contingent/relative *in every regard* and as necessary/complete in no regard—hence (uppercase) C. This column refers to God's *nondual immanence*, commensurate with *theological immanentism*. *Column III* describes those positions for which from varying perspectives God can be both necessary/absolute *as well as* contingent/relative—hence (uppercase) NC. These positions refer to God's *dual transcendence and immanence* or to various forms of *panentheism*. Finally, *column IV* articulates those positions for which God either *does not exist* or in any case does not mean anything with respect to the contrast between N and C—hence X. These positions are those of atheism. The *lines* formulate the same four basic positions with respect to the world's necessity or contingency. *Line 1* refers to those positions for which the world is necessary/complete (intransient, abiding) in every regard—hence (lowercase) n. *Line 2* views the world as being contingent/relative in every regard—hence (lowercase) c. In *line 3* the world appears from varying perspectives as simultaneously necessary/absolute and contingent/relative—hence (lowercase) cn. Finally, *line 4* denies the existence of the world or considers it irrelevant with regard to the contrast between n and c—hence X.

The various positions taken in philosophy and theology throughout history can be effortlessly classified among these sixteen views. Classical/Platonic theism has the form N.c. or N.cn, Aristotelianism N.cn, classical/Spinozistic pantheism N.n, Hindu monism or acosmism N.X, atheism X.c, X.n, or X.cn, skepticism X.X or X.c.

Panentheism appears different, depending on the assessment of the world. (a) With respect to the creation of the world, it can assume the form NC.n if it accepts relationality in God but renders the world necessary, or the form NC.c if it does maintain contingent creation. (b) With respect to the meaning of the world for God, it assumes either the form NC.c if the world is viewed as emerging completely and solely from God, or the form NC.cn if it assumes that the world means something for God that God receives relationally from the world. (c) Because panentheism in *process theology* assumes *dipolarity* applies to both God and world, it thus exhibits the form NC.cn; it can speak about God's eternity *and* about God's sensitivity to time, though also about the world possessing a certain meaning that it receives from God *and* that God must allow the world to present to God in its own turn. At the same time, however—and this is quite clear to Hartshorne—divine necessity/contingency is *not* to be equated with worldly contingency/necessity; each means something different for God and world, representing a *unique (and different)* predication for each.

The dipolarity of God and world providing the basis for panentheism of process theology is best viewed as *open monotheism.* The *one* God is at once also a highly *relational* God (§26). This relationality comes to expression in the fact that God and world mutually *enrich* each other, gathering themselves each from the other in "becoming" (Moltmann 1995), the world insofar as every event takes both its beginning and departure *mentally in God* (the gift of the initial aim), God by *physically* "becoming" *from God's perception of the world* (not from the world itself!) (Faber 2000e; Christian 1967). This is why Whitehead understands God not only as *unity* (primordial nature), but in a certain sense also as *plurality* (consequent nature), to the extent that the unity of the world is transformed into God's heavenly reign (Welker 1988), without, however, disappearing within God (RMn, 154; PR, 351). This dipolar monotheism is *open* because, on the one hand, the *one* God (primordial nature) creates *differences* within Godself from which the world is then begotten in all its multiplicity and variety, and because, on the other, the *uniting, synthesizing* God (consequent nature) assembles within Godself *the reconciling connex of all differences* (God as "consequent multiplicity") (PR, 349). This monotheism is *inclusive* insofar as it does not stand against (or in exclusion from) multiplicity in God—the Platonist risk of reducing God to the "One" (*hen*). Finally, this monotheism is also *dynamic* to the extent it assumes not some static unity/multiplicity, but a dipolar movement of *difference out of unity* and *connex in unification* (§24). From the perspective of theopoetics, the dipolar God is the "poet of the world" insofar as God *differentiates* everything *in reconciliation*, thereby also interpreting anew the biblical monotheism of God as "all in all." This open, inclusive, and dynamic monotheism thereby becomes the horizon for the *essential relationality* and *mutual immanence* of God and world of the sort that has emerged from the Christian doctrine of the Trinity (Faber 1995a).

§26. ESSENTIAL RELATIONALITY
(GOD'S IMMANENCE AND TRANSCENDENCE)

In equal delimitation over against both pantheism and supernaturalism, the panentheism of process theology interprets God's immanence and transcendence amid the new conditions of organic cosmology as the *essential relationality* and *mutual immanence* of God and world in an emphatic ecological engagement of processuality, relationality, and temporality (§2). In this view, God's immanence does not issue in pantheistic identity between God and world, or God's transcendence in arbitrary externality (separation from world) (Faber 2000h). The motif of a complex juxtaposition of immanence and transcendence can be disclosed *theopoetically* in the notion that God as poet of the world is related to the world process as "*reconciled nondifference*"; that is, God's dipolar process does not unfold *like* the world process; God's *reconciliation* unfolds such that within God everything that is yet in processual tension within the world process (relationally and temporally) is *non-differently integrated* (PR, 348: "reconciliation"; AI, 295; Faber 2000e). Whitehead's dipolar panentheism (NC.cn) seeks an interwoven relationship between God's immanence and transcendence through which God and world process mutually enrich each other in processual oscillation, without God disappearing into the world or becoming knowable other than as "God in relation" (Suchocki 1988).

Nonetheless, Whitehead's doctrine of God and process theology in general have been accused of *immanentism* or even pantheism. Leo Scheffczyk maintains that Whitehead (and with him process theology) follows an immanentism that fails to preserve the essential otherness of God (1984, 103), while Oswald Bayer moves him into proximity with Spinozism (Bayer 1999)—at first glance not entirely without some justification, given the development of Whitehead's doctrine of God along with certain further developments with process theology itself.

(1) After introducing the concept of God as such (Jung 1965), Whitehead himself seems to have interpreted it immanentistically. In *Science and the Modern World*, God appears as an *attribute of creativity* (SMW, 173ff.), as that particular, basic cosmological force that since Whitehead's *Concept of Nature* is considered responsible for the "passage of nature" (CN, 54) (Emmet 1986) (§16). Here, however, Whitehead interprets it as "substantial activity" (SMW, 107, 123, 165), in which all attributes—hence also God—and all events as modes inhere immanently. This notion in particular had a pantheistic ring, and creativity in its own turn a Spinozistic tone, insofar as everything is taken as a mode of the *same* activity, while God is understood as *one* of its *immanent attributes*, responsible for the concreteness of events ("principle of concretions") (SMW, 178) (§27). In *Process and Reality*, in a turn away from a Spinozistic and toward a Leibnizian understanding (Kann 2002), Whitehead completely desubstantializes "substantial activity," interpreting it instead as an activity *immanent* to events themselves (PR, 9; Faber 2000e). God now appears not as a principle or attribute, but as a concrete *event* (Jung 1965). Within the general parameters of Whitehead's flat ontology, however, this assertion seems to mean that within the overall nexus of all events God has been immanentistically abbreviated into one *moment of the world*. In *Adventures of Ideas*, Whitehead apparently further retracts God's transcendence in favor of creativity, in no longer understanding God as "transcendent creator" at all, but as "immanent creator," the latter being then identified with "immanent creativity" (AI, 236) (§§28, 35). Is Whitehead then an immanentist after all, unable to preserve God's transcendence, an immanentist whose concept of God ultimately (and necessarily) ends in pantheism?

(2) Later developments in process theology itself also initially encourage this conclusion. Wieman's empirical theology emphatically renounces—"for God's sake" (Cobb 1993)—any transcendent concept of God, understanding God instead as the principle of creative transformation in the world (§3). Hartshorne's rational theology treats God not only as an event *like* other events, but also as a society of events *like* other societies (Hartshorne 1948). Here God appears as the "world soul" and the world as "God's body," albeit in the strict sense of God as a

"defined character," more than an "entirely living nexus," *of the world* (§§15, 22). The poetic intensification of Loomer's naturalistic position can even speak about the "identity" of the universe and God (Loomer 1987) (§5). Is that not proof enough of process theology's inclination toward pantheism? Thus does Griffin's constructivist theology advocate completely overcoming all theological super-naturalism, which in essence means overcoming all notions of God's "other-worldliness" (Griffin 2000) (§8).

Is process theology's "panentheism" not thereby unmasked, if not as strict "pan-theism," then at least as a form of "panencosmism," for which everything in the world (including God) is *in* the world, and nothing (including God) is *outside* that world (Mesle 1993)? On the other hand, one should bear in mind how subtly the organic paradigms of Whitehead and later process theology tried to avoid the simple alternatives of monism *and* dualism—even at the risk (and consciously and abidingly accepting that risk) that their nondualist alternative might itself be mis-understood (§9). The motif of avoiding substantialism resulted in a paradox of the *complexity of mutually opposing (and in and of themselves false) propositions* of non-dualist and nonmonist language: God's transcendence, but no supernaturalism; God's immanence, but no pantheism. But how? A little-noticed passage in *Religion in the Making* provides the key reference point. By way of a "theistic triad" (Faber 2000e, 482), that is, a juxtaposition of three understandings of God's immanence and transcendence, Whitehead triangulates the imponderable alternatives before finally presenting his paradoxical solution, namely, to understand God as *relation-ally* transcendent and as *differently* immanent (RM, 66f.) (Figure 2).

Figure 2: Beyond Immanentism and Externality

Transcendentalism
("Semitic concept")
Extreme doctrine of transcendence

"direct opposition"		*"fluid transition"*
Immanentism		**Monism**
("East Asian concept")	*"Reversal"*	*("pantheistic concept")*
Extreme doctrine of immanence		Extreme doctrine of monism

Relationalism
(Christian concept)
Integration of the three extreme concepts through the doctrine of the Trinity

It is worth noting first that Whitehead does not choose a "third path" between immanentism and transcendentalism, instead illuminating the juxtaposition of God's immanence and transcendence in three positions and their constructive rejection. The rejected positions are as follows: (a) The *East Asian* concept cor-responds to *immanentism*, identifying God (pantheistically) with the immanent world order. Whitehead (contrary to the prejudices of his critics) explicitly rejects

[handwritten margin note: Process Panentheism ?]

this "extreme doctrine of immanence." (b) The *Semitic concept* archetypically represents a *transcendentalism* that understands God as being absolutely external to the world and yet simultaneously also an individual (or personal) being. Whitehead rejects this position (one often theologically advocated) as the "extreme doctrine of transcendence." (c) In an unconventional move, Whitehead then adds a *pantheistic concept* that differs from immanent pantheism (the first position) by speaking not about the dissolution of God in the world, but about the world itself being a phase of the divine life. Whitehead also rejects this monistic pantheism, what he calls the "extreme doctrine of monism," a doctrine corresponding to certain conceptions of "panentheism" for which the world is conceived as being "one in God" such that it now becomes part of God's life (§25: Figure 1). One should be mindful not to confuse this particular monism with Whitehead's own "panentheism."

Whitehead's rejection of these positions highlights his own understanding of God's immanence and transcendence. (a) Contra the *immanentist* concept, Whitehead is *not* advocating that God be understood as a world-immanent natural law, or as a world-immanent Logos, or as the world soul. Whitehead was well acquainted with the vagaries of early Christian Logos-Christology that doomed such Christology to failure (Pannenberg 1976) (§38). He similarly "distances himself" here from those process theologies that would appropriate him pantheistically (Mesle 1993). What Whitehead is seeking instead is to articulate God's *nonimmanentist immanence*. (b) Whitehead also opposes the *transcendentalist* conception of God as a being external to the world, since such externality merely means that though God is not conceived *as* a world-immanent being, God is nonetheless (in a hermeneutically uncritical move) placed beyond the world *like* a world-internal entity. Here Whitehead is by default also opposing theologies that conceive God as a volitional person beyond the world who acts on the world from outside—a very real danger attaching to Christian theology (Faber 1995b). What Whitehead seeks instead is to understand God's *transcendence* as *nonexternal*. (c) Finally, Whitehead also opposes a *monistic* conception for which the world is merely a phase within God's life. This mythological sublation of the world in God, through which the world risks becoming merely a partial moment within God's history, can also be viewed as one of the dangers attaching to the Christian (internal divine) theodrama (Hans Urs von Balthasar) (Faber 1995a). Whitehead seeks instead a *nondualist understanding of immanence and transcendence*. [queer]

Whitehead now arranges the positions of this "theistic triad" into a context demonstrating how his own position overcomes them. (a) The immanentist and monistic conceptions are *inversely* related. Whereas immanentism develops propositions about God as propositions about the world, every monistic proposition about the world implies a proposition about God. The inverse immanentism of *both* concepts consistently permits only propositions involving the similarity, equality, or identity of God and world; it does not permit propositions involving dissimilarity, otherness, or alterity. (b) The transcendentalist and the immanentist concepts are *mutually exclusive*. Whereas immanentism

acknowledges no reality beyond the world, such is the presupposition for transcendentalism, which in its own turn cannot acknowledge any immanent world
law not ultimately dependent on the arbitrary will of the God beyond the world.
Both conceptions depend on the (absolutely posited) alternative of nature and
will within their conceptions of God. Whereas immanentism rejects volition on
the part of God and as a result is generally also prepared to deny personality to
God, the transcendentalist variant juxtaposes God in an absolute fashion over
against the world by positing God's volitional personality against natural necessity and thus also juxtaposing God in a dualistic fashion as spirit against nature.
Both positions exemplify the weaknesses of the *substantialist dualism* of matter
and mind, nature and will, law and person, body and soul (§§9–10). (c) Surprisingly, the transcendentalist and the monistic concepts are related in *continuous transition*. Whereas in transcendentalism the world represents a volitional
act of God that God "substantializes," that is, God posits *outside Godself* as a self-
surpassing act, the monistic conception understands the act of world generation
as abiding *immanently* within God as part of the divine life. Transcendentalism
accordingly is not just antithetical to pantheism, but also continuous with it,
demonstrating once again the considerable extent to which transcendentalism,
which understands itself as a bastion against pantheism, in truth represents
merely the dualistic variant of monism that hermeneutically has not sufficiently
considered that it is conceiving God *arbitrarily*, that is, without any essential
coherent, contextual connection with the world.

Whitehead's own solution to the consequences of these three positions can
be described as follows. (a) God is to be conceived neither monistically by way
of simple similarity to the world, nor fixed dualistically by way of simple alternatives (such as that between immanence and transcendence). God does *not*
stand in an *arbitrary (external) relationship* with the world. (b) What is needed
is a *relational conception* for which God stands in *nondualistic alterity* to the
world and is thereby tied to it in an *essential (nonarbitrary)* fashion. Whitehead
finds these criteria fulfilled in the Christian God of *loving concern* (RM, 69f.),
the "God in relation." (c) The relational juxtaposition of God's immanence and
transcendence is nonsimple, that is, irreducibly complex. The principle in which
Whitehead articulates this maintains that we "may discover an immanent God,
but not a God wholly transcendent" (RM, 69), meaning that although God may
be transcendent, God is know*able* only through God's *relation* with the world;
hence even in God's transcendence God must already have made Godself immanent, if God is to be known *as* the transcendent God. Whitehead is not saying
that God cannot be *wholly* transcendent, only that our relational knowledge of
God precludes speaking about God's transcendence without *also* speaking about
this relationality. The paradox is thus not whether God is "not wholly" transcendent, that is, is *partially* immanent and *partially* transcendent (Philipson
1982), but rather how God is to be conceived as *neither* external-transcendent
(as an otherworldly piece of the world) *nor* as an "as if" of our own immanent
projection (Luhmann 1989). God's relationality surpasses or passes beyond the

simple distinction between *relative* immanence and *relative* transcendence as presupposed by the three concepts of the "theistic triad." Put differently, *God neither can be grasped nor is God conceived in an adequate theological fashion by the simple alternatives "transcendence" and "immanence"* (Faber 2000e, 2001c). Pantheistic misunderstanding and Spinozistic suspicions arise only where this principle is not heeded. By contrast, what one can now say is that God is *wholly* transcendent and *wholly* immanent in God's relationality, but is such in nonexternal *and* nonimmanentist *nondifference* (§40).

God's relationality can now be understood as a conception *beyond immanentism and externality.* (a) Relationality obtains in a nondualistic fashion beyond the antitheses of immanence and transcendence. (b) Relationality does not realize mere similarity between God and world such that God remains a part of the world or is yet conceived "like" world (albeit outside it). (c) Relationality, rather than realizing a fortuitous or accidental relationship between God and world, instead articulates the *essential* relationship between God and world. Precisely this notion is what Whitehead envisioned in his attempts to conceive the proper juxtaposition of God and world and what he finally also solved in *Adventures of Ideas* with his relational concept of the "mutual immanence" of God and world (AI, 119ff., 191ff., 201ff.) (Faber 2000e).

Taking as his point of departure the early Christian doctrines of the Trinity, Christology, and pneumatology, Whitehead draws attention to the genuine initiative undertaken by the Alexandrian school to confess the mutual immanence of the divine persons in one another, that of God in Christ, and that of God in the world within God's Pneuma (§34), an initiative Whitehead considers to be *the* most significant philosophical development since Plato (AI, 167). The theological doctrine of the *direct, immediate immanence* of the persons in God and of God in the world expresses the fundamental metaphysical position of *nonsubstantialist relationality* as such (AI, 168f.), namely, that something can be *present within something else* (PR, 50: "being present within another entity") (Böhme 1980) (§34). From this, one derives (a) the *essential* relationality of all reality, that particular "necessity in universality" whose premise is that nothing can be without relationships, (b) the "unitexturality of reality," according to which everything is to be taken as concrete in the "same" sense, and (c) the relational event structure, in which nothing can exist alone, since everything arises from the prehensive unifying synthesis of others (§13). What then follows from the theological category of the mutual immanence of God and world is that God (a) cannot exist "beyond" the world and can be *transcendent* to the world only *relationally*, (b) as a concrete event must be simultaneously both immanent and transcendent, and (c) in God's self-unfolding must be "God in relation" (Faber 2000e).

In *Adventures of Ideas*, this position leads to the thesis that God and world are related *essentially*, that relation residing "beyond the accidents of will" and commensurate (not unlike in the position of Paul Tillich) with the "necessities of the nature of God and the nature of the World" (AI, 168) (§28). This assertion is to be interpreted *nondualistically*, albeit while maintaining God's alterity, from the perspective of the *essential relationality* of *all* events. God as "dipolar event" is profoundly *immanent* to the world insofar as God, in a fashion *antecedent* or *anterior* to the world, is perpetually *present* as the "primordial conceptual fact" of the primordial nature, *and* insofar as the world itself is profoundly immanent to God, since God as "ultimate unity" of all that has happened "tenderly [saves] the turmoil of the intermediate world by the completion of [God's] own nature" (PR, 346), that is, by gathering it into reconciliation within God's consequent nature. At the same time, God perpetually remains overwhelmingly *transcendent* to the world process insofar as the primordial nature is God's infinite vision of world that does *not*, however, presuppose any world, while God's consequent nature refers to God's infinite reconciliation of the fragmentariness of what has become, which without this reconciliation would be mere past and would ultimately sink into nothingness (Cobb 1971b) (§30). The theopoetic category of *reconciled non-difference* articulates this situation; beyond the simple distinction between immanence and transcendence, God opens up the *différance* (between God and world) and retrieves its connex in reconciliation.

Within this theopoetic conception, immanence and transcendence represent not static categories, but *categories of the relational movement* of God and world that can be translated neither into spatial metaphors of God's "presence" in the world nor into substantialist propositions about Being (Faber 2000b) (§8). Instead they constitute *processual* propositions regarding mutual concretization of God and world and as such (like all propositions concerning events) are to be taken *temporally* as having a critical, nonsubstantialist intent. God's transcendence is God's "anteriority" of absolute future and God's "posteriority" of saving recollection; God's immanence is God's *coming* into the world as its future and God's *inward recollection* of that which no longer is (Faber 2002b). Quite in the sense of the critical (postmodern) categories of *difference* and *connex*, God in God's immanence is never comprehensible as "fulfilled presence"; instead, the world must *die* into God in order to live (§40). The immediacy attending this notion of mutual immanence is disclosed not as God's "presence," but as the "(free) space" and "time (of decision)" associated with the self-becoming or concretization opened up and embraced by God's nondualistic immanence/transcendence. In this sense Whitehead understands God as the *principle of concretion*.

§27. THE PRINCIPLE OF CONCRETION
(GOD'S CONCRETENESS
AND THE CONCRETION OF THE WORLD)

In Whitehead's organic cosmology, that which is "concrete" (what he calls "concrete fact") results from the *process* of "concretion" (RM, 90). According to the principle of process, nothing is what it is without having *become* what it is. With respect to "givenness" (the *what* of being), everything is something that has become (the *how* of being) and is something concrete insofar as it *became* concrete (Fetz 1981). Whitehead understands this activity of *becoming* concrete, the process of *self*-concretization, furthermore, as "concrescence," as the "growing together" or collection of relations (prehensions) into the unity of a new event (PR, 41f., 211; AI, 236) (Wiehl 1971) (§§12–13). The concrete world is an incessant, ongoing process of concretion, of the synthesis from the objectively concrete within a subjective process. The "de-*cisional*" nature of concrescence shows it to be a process of "de-*cision*" among the various relations of actual reality into something objectively real that includes both the past (causal efficacy) and the purely possible of the future (the nonreal) (PR, 21; Rorty 1983). Concretion is a process involving *decision* in its "root sense of 'cutting off'" among both real and pure potentials (PR, 43; Kline 1983). Through concretion, a subject experiences self-value and worth, because it becomes itself through the process of decision. In a reverse fashion, the process of decision itself is self-becoming *as* self-*valuation* (§23) (Sayer 1999).

"Self-valuation" is the mystery, deriving as it does not from the *possibilities* (eternal objects) among which an event decides "itself," for it is only in the subjective process that such are in fact valuated. Nor does it derive from the subject's *act* of becoming, its self-creativity, since the latter is pure activity (prior to any form) rather than determined (protean) (§16). Nor does it derive from the *past* of events, since self-creativity (the elementary freedom of every event) does not permit deterministic causality of the concrete (Ford 1990). Whence, then, does the power of valuation derive that allows a subject to become and that constitutes its identity? How is it that—amid the *unspecific nature* of creativity, the *undecided nature* of possibilities, and the *undetermined nature* of the concrete—a *specific* event, a *specific* value process, a *specific* subjective identity emerges?

Whitehead's response to these questions is the "principle of concretion" (AI, 178; Faber 1997). His introduction is based on the following consideration. In the midst of infinite activity (creativity), potentiality (future), and facticity (past), some principle of individuation (*principium individuationis*) is needed. For Whitehead, however, one can attribute that principle neither to matter (Platonically, as the individuation of ideas and forms) nor to spirit (Thomistically, as the form of the soul) (Fetz 1981), nor to the activity of form (like in Aristotle) (Rorty 1983). One can attribute it only to the individual as *value process* (Rohmer 2000). In Whitehead's conception of event, the *principle of individuation* of self-valuation is the *initial aim* (Sayer 1999) (§20), determining the *beginning* of every event and representing the *singular ideal* presented for the event to actualize. It is the *establishment of the foundation* of its *identity*, the *presupposition* of the process of becoming, fulfilling itself in that particular saturation through which the event completes itself in its *subjective aim* and then perishes as superject in passing into its *factual identity*. The initial aim is the key to Whitehead's nonsubstantialist explanation of how an event is *anterior to itself* within the concrete process of decision and valuation that, from the very outset, includes its goal (*telos*), future, completion, as well as its end, identity, and ideal. Within this anteriority or what might be called "initiality," this initial aim grounds a concrete event—prior to that event's own valuation process—as *God's valuation*. That is, even before an event commences as a subjective value process, God has already assessed (valuated) the past, discerned the best possible potentialities for a new event, and bequeathed the event *to itself* in the initial aim (Ford 1981; Suchocki 1995). A new event begins to "become" itself only because within the infinite space of creativity, potentiality, and facticity, God *initializes* a value process through a valuation of creativity, potentiality, and facticity *for* a new self-value (§15).

In the chapter "God" in *Science and the Modern World*, Whitehead introduces and conceives God as the *principle of concretion* (SMW, 177f.), though this meaning of God will be subjected to considerable change. Its formulation still derives from Whitehead's understanding that since God is not concrete, God is thus a *principle* rather than an event (§26). Here he still understands God in a thoroughly Spinozistic fashion as one of the attributes of "substantial activity" ("it is Spinoza's one infinite substance") alongside potentiality ("realm of eternal objects") and facticity ("individuation into a multiplicity of modes") (SMW, 177). Since the other two attributes are both *infinite*, that is, underdetermined with respect of the concrete process, some "principle of limitation" is needed so that amid this underdetermined nature *something* can become concrete. Because events are "the emergence of values which require such limitation" (SMW, 178), concretion thus means limitation, and limitation the emergence of values. Concretion always represents a *value process* and God the *principle of valuation* as such (Maassen 1988). In *Religion in the Making*, Whitehead desubstantializes "substantial activity" (Spinoza's "one infinite substance") in favor of an understanding—oriented toward Leibniz—of multiplicity of many concrete events (Deleuze 1996) in which creativity (which cannot be substantialized) functions as the *principle of self-creation* and God as *concrete event* (§2). Nonetheless God does appear in this context as one of the three "formative elements" (RM, 88) of event constitution whose irreplaceable divine act is God's valuation, decision, and limitation amid infinite freedom (creativity as pure activity) and pure potentiality (the realm of eternal objects as pure possibilities), an act through which God permits the two infinities to interact, thereby rendering concretion possible (RM, 115). Even though, from *Religion in the Making* on, this divine limitation can take place only as *event*, Whitehead continues to refer to God as the "principle" of concretion (Jung 1965). In *Process and Reality*, he then explicitly assigns this act of concretion and limitation to God's primordial nature, understanding it now as the determination of the eternal objects inhering within the primordial nature with respect to the potential subjective aim of every event (PR, 244). Whitehead now understands God's primordial nature as the valuation process of possibilities with respect to a new event (Ford 1981), and he understands God's immanent valuation of the infinite possibilities in God's nature as God's *caring concern* for the world, as prevision (*provisio*) and foreknowledge (*pronoia*) of the prevailing *best* world within the concrete situation of an emergent event (Peters 1966). Whitehead now also interprets the principle of concretion as the "principle of determination" and "principle of order" (PR, 345; RM, 142–45).

Within Whitehead's organic cosmology, the principle of concretion in fact represents the *universal principle of meaning*, supporting as it does the concreteness of the world with respect not only to the initiation of *intensity* (private subjectivity), but also to its *harmony* (public order) (§15). As *principle of valuation*, it provides the foundation for the *subjective value process* as well as for the *objective value capacity* of the world (its meaning) (Sayer 1999), rendering possible both individuality and sociality (Lotter 1990). By serving the meaning of the world with regard to both intensity and harmony, it is above all the *principle of aesthetic valuation* (and only subsequently a logical and ethical principle). In its own turn, subjective intensity with its united contrasts represents a *subjective principle of harmony*. On the other hand, the world order generates its objective harmony from the relationality of intensities, whence also subjective harmony becomes the *objective principle of intensity*. Within Whitehead's theopoetics the principle of concretion ultimately grounds the world as an aesthetic world (Sayer 2000; Wessell 1990), that is, as a world of aesthetic freedom (purposeless bequeathal of self) and of beautiful order (as purposeless "cosmos") (Rohmer 2000), of the creation (*poiesis*) of identity (Sander 1991), and of a vision of the good, true, and beautiful, with which God guides the world so that it indeed becomes its own meaning.

But how is God *engaged* with God's *own* concretion as a generative principle of meaning in the concretion of world? One too easily overlooks the fact that God as the principle of concretion—the principle with which *every* concrescence commences—can be efficacious only such that the "concretizing" element in concretion must in fact be the *value process of Godself*. And this insight is of considerable significance insofar as *God's concrescence* in precisely this sense—as the process of infinite intensity and valuation with respect to infinite creativity, potentiality, and facticity—represents the *beginning of all subjectivity* (self-valuation, self-decision, self-identity) (Faber 2000e). Since what is involved here is a valuation process, God's concreteness *as a whole* must provide the ground for the concretization of world, *not* merely God's primordial nature, which bequeaths the subjective aim of every world event. Since the unfolding of every valuation process involves *all ontological temporal modes*—namely, the present of self-creativity, the past of facticity, and the future of potentiality—God must necessarily also be engaged *with the entirety of God's dipolar concrescence* (PR, 277) involving God's self-creativity, God's primordial nature (mental pole), *and* God's consequent nature (physical pole) if God is to allow a concrete event to commence *as itself* (§30). That is, just as the initial aim initiates (and must initiate) the *entire* event with both its physical and mental poles if it is to attain its subjective aim, so also does God become the origin of that event with the entire weight of God's complete dipolarity. Hence the valuation process that concretizes the world is in fact a process directed *both* internally and externally. The significant consequence is that God creates a new event externally (*ad extra*) *only* by becoming *completely* engaged internally (*ad intra*) (§32). Not only does God limit all possibilities by initiating a specific initial aim, this particular valuation of the primordial nature in its own turn also presupposes the perception and valuation of the actual world by God's conse-quent nature. Only thus does God know about the concrete world, valuate it, and bequeath it a new vision of its future (Lansing 1973).

What is the relationship between the concreteness of God and that of the world? Put differently, how does the concrete God appear *within* the world of concretion, whose *principle* God simultaneously is? The response to this question attributes a noteworthy function to the principle of concretion. If, that is, God provides the possibility of concretion in the world through God's *own concretion*—doing so by virtue of the *otherwise irreducible un- and underdetermined nature* of creativity, potentiality, and facticity—then the condition for all concreteness in the world is that it *cannot be reconstructed through abstract grounds* (§11). Put differently, just as commensurate with the ontological principle only concrete events can function as grounds (Whitehead speaks of "reasons") for the way the concrete world is, precluding any adequate reconstruction of that which happens in the world concretely through recourse to universals, so also can there be no rendering of the ultimate grounds for the actual course of the world as abstract logical or ethical orders or transcendental patterns. The *rational* ground for this final *irrationality* of the world is precisely its *concreteness*, which can unfold only self-creatively as *concrescence*, that is, as an ultimately irreducible act of freedom. This ultimately irrational concreteness is based on *God's* concreteness—on the *self-creative act of divine concrescence* (Faber 1997). Limitation—namely, God's act of freedom and valuation—grounds the world as ultimate "irrationality," since, as Whitehead underscores in *Science in the Modern World*, "no reason can be given for just that limitation which stands in [God's] nature to impose"; Godself is "the ultimate limitation, and [God's] existence is the ultimate irrationality" (SMW, 178). Although God's nature is *not* rational ("no reason can be given for God's nature"), nonetheless precisely as the subjective valuation of creativity, potentiality, and facticity, it is the "ground of rationality." Theologically this means that the world cannot be accounted for rationally, grounding instead in an aesthetic process of intensification and harmony (Hauskeller 1994; Lachmann 1990) initiated by God's own concreteness. The meaning of the world is not ensured by the evidence or discernment of eternal orders, but rather solely by God's *concrete engagement* for intensity and harmony.

Is God's *caring concern* not then the *predetermination* of any concrete or even arbitrary (qua rationally indeterminate) world order? Although Whitehead does indeed refer to his principle of concretion as a principle of *determination*, two cogent reasons militate explicitly against misunderstanding the principle of concretion *deterministically*.

(1) Divine limitation qua determination is an *aesthetic* happening of divine valuation with regard to intensity and harmony. Such *divine harmonics*, however, implies neither an essentialist rationalism grounding the order of creation in God's *being* in the fashion of Thomas Aquinas (§36), nor volitional irrationalism grounding the order of creation in the ultimately obscure arbitrariness of the

divine *will* in the fashion of William of Occam (§34). For the divine harmonics is fundamentally *relational* (AI, 168f.) (§34), deriving, on the one hand, from the incommensurable plethora of intensity and harmony within the divine primordial nature and, directing itself, on the other hand, in an overflowing exuberance of divine goodness (*bonum diffusivum sui*) toward the highest possible meaning of the world within God's consequent nature (Maassen 1988; Faber 2000e). The theological consequence is that God is *not* encountered in the world as the result of some analysis of the grounds of the world. Whitehead's God is neither an Aristotelian ground that with necessity must be rationally discovered, nor an arbitrary God standing like a tyrant over against and determining the world. God is instead (somewhat similar to the Thomistic God) encountered as *freedom* (Greshake 1983). The world is fundamentally neither simply rational nor simply irrational, being instead a meaningful happening out of God's relational affection, meaning that the concrete God is *never* to be encountered in an ontological world order accessible to the probing of reason or in the transcendental conditions of being, but—as the *concrete God*—*only* in concrete revelation and as concrete history. From this perspective—and contra occasional attempts to reduce the agenda of process theology to metaphysics—the principle of concretion grounds the genuine meaning of religion as the source of knowledge of God that cannot be achieved or supplanted by philosophy (§35).

(2) God's limitation comes about through the bequeathal of the initial aim, which inaugurates every process of intensity and harmony, doing so not only *privately* by constituting an event's subjectivity, but also *publicly* by constituting an objective world order (Sayer 1999). Since, however, the objective world order is grounded in the *aesthetic value process of subjects*, it can be conceived only as resulting from a process of freedom. Although in the initial aim God does indeed bequeath to each event the *possibility* of becoming itself, God does *not* relieve the event of the actual decisions involved in that becoming (PR, 47, 69, 167, 224). What the initial aim opens up instead is the *difference* between ideality and creativity, placing the event into its *own* becoming, its *own* process of decision. Although the subject does aim for itself as subjective goal within the event's becoming, it is also the subject itself that determines the extent to which it either accepts, rejects, or alters God's offer. Only the event itself can relieve the tension between ideality (its *possible* goal) and creativity (its *self-creativity*) in reaching its subjective aim (Hauskeller 1994). Once an event "has become," it perishes as something concrete, having now become its own value—both for itself (satisfaction) and for the world process (superject). The world order is thus an open process of aesthetic harmonics, that is, a valuation process not subject to any determination from divine being or volition, emerging instead from the process of decision of events within the world that God renders possible ideally but does *not* determine in reality. The theologically not insignificant consequence is that the *same* principle (of concretion, limitation, determination) stands for both order *and* freedom, for both structure *and* novelty (§§17–18). For Whitehead, divine "determination" in this sense is always

a *possibility* or offer, rather than a verdict or necessity, and as such requires freedom. Divine "limitation" is thus always *relational*, taking its orientation from
the history of an event and bequeathing to that event its own ideal of highest
intensity and harmony within the specific situation into which it is born.
Divine "concretion" always commences with a *vision* of intensity and harmony
in order to provide for the possibility of the *new* with regard to intensity and
harmony *contrary* to all static order (Suchocki 1988). In the initial aim, an
event "feels" the world with God's eyes—within the sphere of all possible
worlds—before deciding, within its own process of emergence, the extent to
which it will repeat the order of its world or, as it were, set out for new shores.
In this context, God functions as "supreme Eros" (AI, 198), who implants
"desire" and "appetition" (*appetitus*) (PR, 348) for the world to break forth
toward ever greater intensity and harmony. It is in this way that God summons
the world forth from the determinateness of prevailing orders (Sander 1991).
But Eros, rather than coerce the world, instead positions it within its own
adventure (AI, 295) (§§35, 39).

Although the principle of concretion is indeed a principle of God's "presence"
in the world (in which God with tender patience leads it "by his vision of truth,
beauty, and goodness" [PR, 346]), it is so in a *critical* sense, namely, as a principle of exodus, of theodicy, and of *différance*.

(1) God's presence does not establish any order through which God might be
ontologically determined, logically known, or ethically called to account from
evidence within the world (Faber 2000e; Connelly 1962) (PR, 93; MT, 113);
nor, therefore, does God establish any order in which the world itself might be
ontologically fixed, logically defined, or ethically assessed (Jung 1958). What
God establishes instead is *creative* order and freedom directed against ossification
and rigidity. That order grounds not the status quo, but an exodus from prevailing relationships. Its inherent revolutionary element includes the ethical, social,
and political charge to change the world for the sake of universal justice (Mesle
1993). It demands—to speak with Vatican II—the transformation of the world
into God's creation (*Gaudium et spes,* 39). The aesthetics of the vision of divine
harmony requires an ethics of self-transcendence (§23); anything else is mere
"anaesthesia" (§21).

(2) God's presence is not some oppressive determination of what happens in
the world. God is not a glorious "tyrant" who shapes or measures the world
according to abstract standards, structures, or orders (Pittenger 1971; Hartshorne
1967). If such were the case, then God would indeed be responsible for the evil
in the world (Griffin 1991). With respect to theodicy, the aesthetic harmonics of
the principle of concretion means critically that God's presence, rather than
restricting, instead places creatures into the *freedom* with which they themselves
then determine what they "will be" once they "have become." The world order,
along with the evil and wickedness attaching to it and the disharmony it generates, rather than being something (pre)determined out of the divine nature, arises
instead from a *self-creative process*; its social nature determines itself from the *man-*

the initial aim is always unfolding

ner in which events subjectively actualize themselves and objectively affect others (both individually and structurally) (§45).

(3) In the concretion of the world, God's presence exhibits the character of *transcendent* immanence. It knows about the past world in the consequent nature and approaches as the future in the initial aim. Never, however, does God become so present within an event that the event might lose its *own* presence of becoming, deciding, and valuing. The embrace of God's "presence" instead releases an event into the "space" of its *self-creativity*. In this way, the principle of concretion functions as the *critical difference between creator and creature*, God and world, actual past and possible future, tradition and renewal. God's "presence" can never be called "fulfilled presence" within God's creature; instead one can refer (with Levinas) to *diachronic* transcendence, to a temporally tensed transcendence that never becomes present, instead always remaining the future that was, however, already present wherever a new event becomes (§48). It is *God's trace* within the emergent event (Faber 2000e; Faber 2002b). The Whiteheadian principle of concretion is thus a *critical principle of différance*. It follows *différance* because it never becomes presence (Welsch 1995), but it also contradicts it, since instead of only deferring (*différer*) meaning into the ever new future, it instead also gathers into meaning that which is perishing.

A structural peculiarity in Whitehead's theology makes this *critical potential* of the principle of concretion possible, namely, his *differentiation between God and creativity* (Stokes 1960; Cobb 1975; Sander 1991; Faber 2000e) (§28). The agency of the divine Eros is always *ideal*, that is, God never takes from any event the self-creativity through which it becomes the "cause of itself" (*causa sui*) and an unalterable activity of freedom. God never becomes fulfilled presence, since within the present every event is *self*-creative. This distinction between God and creativity is so fundamental that Whitehead articulates and grounds it in *Science and the Modern World* simultaneously with his initial systematic introduction of God—and virtually in the same passage. Whitehead maintains that if there were *no* distinction between God and creativity, then God would *have* to be understood as the total determination of the world (SMW, 179), in which case the principle of concretion would be nothing more than a Spinozistic variant that grounds the world from the necessity of the *natura naturans*. Whitehead's concept of God, to the contrary, is already formed *from the outset* by the awareness of the theodicy so that the notion that God solely and alone is responsible for the evil in the world would become unavoidable (§45). Therefore, Whitehead's introduction of the principle of concretion demands a *critical distinction* between a *metaphysical ground and cosmological moving principle* of the world—which Whitehead calls "creativity"—and an *aesthetic valuation process* that meaningfully creates and reconciles the world—which Whitehead calls "God" (Cobb 1971; 1982; Faber 2001c). In Whitehead's theopoetics, every event has an ontological self-status within the universal and (universally) immanent self-creativity of the world. By contrast, God acts efficaciously "*wholly* in all" rather than effecting "*all* in all" (§25).

§28. SUPERJECT OF CREATIVITY
(GOD'S SELF-CREATIVITY AND CREATIVE POWER)

As one of the fundamental givens of Whiteheadian thought, this distinction between God and creativity is thus also one of the most important problems in process theology (Neville 1995; Cobb 1975; Ford 1983a). Whitehead articulated this distinction with respect to the question of God at the very outset of his discourse in *Science and the Modern World* and then rigorously maintained its presence up to his final writings of note, namely, the two articles "Mathematics and the Good" and "Immortality" (1941). It thus represents one of the fundamental and original constituent elements of Whiteheadian philosophy and theology, notwithstanding the significant change it underwent (Faber 2000e).

Prior to *Science and the Modern World*, creativity still appears in the guise of what Whitehead calls the "passage of nature/events"; God does not yet play any role in Whitehead's participation in the discourse of philosophy of science (§§9–11). Nonetheless, in this preliminary form as "passage in *Concept of Nature*," creativity does not simply refer to the flowing character of nature in and of itself (Heraclitus), supporting instead the fundamental temporalization of all that happens, in this case as the coming of the new and the perishing of that which has already happened (CN, 34, 54, 178). In *Science and the Modern World*, creativity then appears in the Spinozistic guise of the one "substantial activity" or "general activity" (SMW, 107). Unlike Spinoza's *natura naturans*, however, this activity, rather than referring to a necessary streaming of divine substance, is already being understood in an unambiguously nondivine fashion as *pure activity*, neither generating forms of the world nor exuding them as the essence of the world (§16). Here Whitehead is still attempting—and only here does he genuinely pick up on Spinoza—not only to conceive this ultimately groundless, spontaneous activity of existing as the "form" of the unity of the universe, but also to express it *rationally* as such unity. Whitehead is accordingly able to interpret the concrete events—from whose relations the world obtains—as modes of the *one* activity; at the same time, however, since the reference is to *pure* activity, he must additionally provide for forms and some principle of limitation enabling those forms and activity to interact, whereby concrete events are concretized as modes (SMW, 177) (§27)—they are attributes of activity. The fundamental distinction between creativity and God that Whitehead introduces and simultaneously systematically grounds here, however, has an even deeper ground. Even though Whitehead had been dealing with theology for decades, he was intent on not formally introducing God into his thinking before solving *the* (in his own eyes) fundamental theological problem of how to define God as creator, given the presence of evil in the world (Price 1958). And he did indeed end up taking the problem of theodicy and its possible resolution as his point of departure for introducing the concept of God in his thought, doing so moreover by distinguishing between God and creativity. Whereas creativity refers to a "neutral activity" grounding all becoming—be it good or evil—God represents the good, the process that establishes value (SMW, 179).

The term "creativity" itself appears for the first time on December 19, 1925, in Whitehead's *Harvard Lectures*, which he delivered in 1925/26 (Faber 2001d; HL, 301–73). Between *Science and the Modern World* and *Religion in the Making*, the term occurs in some of Hartshorne's lecture notes as a genuine *transitional concept* from general activity (conceived as a universal concept of unity) to the insubstantial (substanceless) self-creativity of Whitehead's later period. Whitehead is still referring indirectly to it with Spinoza's notion of (quasi-active) substance to the extent that "everything that is" is thereby an attribute of creativity (HL, 341). What Whitehead intends to provide here, however, is clearly something new, namely, a temporal reconstruction of events in their *creative* becoming and their *causal* agency. Everything that perishes "is" *causally* efficacious as the ground of the characterization of that which is coming, to the extent it becomes an attribute of creativity and transmits to the new events everything characterizing it (Garland 1983). Here it appears yet intact in both its active and receptive aspects as simultaneously *immanent* and *transcendent* activity (§16). Creativity in this sense has a "character" (HL, 330); it is something that has been determined by everything that has previously become, by creatures; and as it were, as the *witness to the activity of the past* and as the power of facticity, it passes this determinateness on to new events (HL, 342). In a general fashion, abstracted from its specific characterization by creatures that have already become, Whitehead understands creativity as the expression of *universal* or *general relationality* (HL, 330), albeit *not* as static structure, but as an expression of the unity of the world as a *moving whole* (§24). It is no longer quasi-actual substance, but the "locus" of the characters that shape and define it—as is the case later with the "receptacle" (AI, 295)—characters that, however, it immediately "reactivates" without passivity (PR, 277). Whitehead articulates this causal-creative transition with the assertion that creativity *for* creatures becomes creativity *with* creatures (HL, 343). This creativity, the power of world movement that generates unity, is never even remotely identified with God (God plays no role in the *Harvard Lectures,* in any case), referring instead to the *togetherness of world events* within their *moving relationality*, which, in a simultaneously causal and creative fashion, provides the foundation for connectedness *and* freedom.

In *Religion in the Making*, creativity enters the public arena in the new guise in which it will henceforth shape Whitehead's thought in a fundamental fashion, namely, as the *substanceless, indeterminate, undefined act of existence* of concrete events within their self-emergence, moreover as something that is consistently given only *in actu*, being determined already *in concreto* by forms of the process. It refers to sheer, pure activity at the foundation of the universe; it is untamed (protean) and expresses the *infinite freedom* at the foundation of all that happens in the world (RMn, 90ff.). The plural world of multiple events—not creativity— now provides the parameter of unity from which Whitehead takes his orientation. Accordingly, three fundamental characteristics of this world can now be discerned: creativity, forms, and God (§2). To the same degree that creativity was "desubstantialized," God acquired concreteness (Faber 2000e). God, instead of referring to an abstract principle of concretion, now indicates that particular *concrete* event *in* which form and activity interact in creating world. God is now no longer an attribute of a substantial activity; instead, substanceless activity in its own turn is a moment in the ongoing becoming nature of God (Jung 1965) (§25). This relationship finally sealed in *Process and Reality*, where forms are integrated into God's primordial nature (Welker 1984) and creativity is completely desubstantialized. Creativity is now real only *within* its instances, the events, namely, as their (each event's unique) *self*-activity (PR, 7; Faber 2000e). In providing the ground for the swing from subject to superject, it is now viewed as having two primordial aspects—the *active* aspect of *immanent creativity* (self-creativity), whereby events are comprehended in their ontological freedom as being self-caused (*causa sui*), and the *receptive* aspect of *transcendent creativity*, through which the causally interwoven nature of the ontological connectedness of the world is expressed (Garland 1983). God is now the *primordially determinative* element of formless creativity, while creativity itself now appears as God's original *self-creativity* (PR, 222).

An increasing polarization between creativity and God becomes discernible in Whitehead's later philosophy (1933–41). These two primal aspects were already being distinguished terminologically more sharply as early as *Adventures of Ideas*, where creativity refers to pure activity, the receptacle to pure receptivity (AI, 295) (§16), and God being juxtaposed to *both* cosmological aspects as a soteriological process integrating and reconciling them in God's two natures. The *spontaneous activity* on the part of the world corresponds to God as the *supreme Eros*, as the valuating, alluring pendant of ideal freedom, novelty, and the capacity for meaning. On the other hand, the pure *receptive oneness* of the universe in the *receptacle* corresponds to *God as the unity* of the adventure of the universe ("Adventures in the Universe as One"), through which everything is brought into meaningful harmony (AI, 295). Finally, in Whitehead's last work of note, "Immortality" (1941), this polarity enters a final stage in the differentiating of two worlds. The "World of creativity" or the "World of fact" is the actual world of the spontaneous happening and perishing of finite events whose "energy" is the formless *creativity* that nonetheless generates and preserves all event happening. By contrast, the "World of value" contains all the world's potentiality, structurality, and determination of content in its abstract quality *as valuation*; its foundation is *God*, the occurrence of value as such that provides meaning (Imm., 82). It is worth noting that Whitehead, rather than separating the two "worlds" within some ultimate duality, instead comprehends them as an *abstraction of the one universe* (Imm., 80); *this* universe is the concrete, moving, and valuing whole, the *concretum* of universal relationality (Faber 2002b). Whitehead has consistently and strictly maintained the distinction with which he originally started; *activity* and *valuation* ground the distinction between *creativity* and *God* (Imm., 90). These two, however, never stand juxtaposed in separation in Whitehead's work; instead they constantly intersect. Ultimately, in their final form in "Immortality," and despite various imbalances, they stand in a relation of *mutual immanence*, inseparable insofar as in separation they would be merely pure abstractions. God as a *concrete* event is always a moment of the world of activity; God's self-creativity, however, is an *act* of valuation that turns creativity into a moment of the world of value (§40).

Given the functions that creativity has acquired over the course of this development, one is immediately confronted with the volatile theological issue of whether key divine predicates are not being attributed here to a neutral ontological principle, while God—albeit for the sake of God's religious and ethical justification (theodicy)—is thereby impoverished (Schulte 1989; Koch 1983). What, that is, remains for God if creativity becomes responsible for the ontological *act of existence* (*actus essendi*), guaranteeing freedom and novelty within the universe, regulating both becoming and perishing, securing spontaneity and causality, and if in a certain sense it even makes teleology and the value process (as act and novelty) possible in the first place? If creativity now refers to *all* that is "creative," can God still be "creator" (and if so, in what abiding or enduring sense)? Indeed, does such a self-creative universe even *need* a creator (Scheffczyk 1984)? The answer may come as somewhat of a surprise. Even though—for the aforementioned reasons associated with theodicy and encroaching pandeterminism—Whitehead was not really interested in maintaining the figure of God as "creator," and even though he does indeed adopt the creative function of "immanent creativity" (over against a "transcendent creator") (AI, 236), his theopoetic concentration of the concept of God in the elements of *redemption*, *valuation*, and *meaning/sense*, rather than *relieving* God of God's creative power, instead paradoxically virtually *rescues* that power amid the conditions of postmodernity—as God's unmistakable *poiesis* (§26). Even if one must concede that Whitehead's differentiation and complex juxtaposition of creativity and God have led to various and sundry discussions and positions of process theology that were subsequently charged with having disempowered or curtailed God—or even eliminated God from the Judeo-Christian tradition as such—this criticism in its own turn (Pannenberg 1986; Moltmann 1993) along with several versions of process theology itself (Griffin 1987; Ford 1983b), is itself based on presuppositions that Whitehead's *own* distinctions essentially already rendered obsolete (§35). To wit, some criticized (or adopted) Whitehead from the perspective of an *ontotheology* that neither can be called "biblical" nor (in the contemporary postmodern context) is philosophically tenable in any case. Here, indeed, God had to be conceived as the "supreme being" or "ultimate ground," as ultimate unity, and this unity in its own turn as the creative principle of the whole (Welker 1988). That is, this criticism stumbled directly into the trap of transcendentalism, which Whitehead himself had explicitly criticized for having indeed removed God from the world (as its ground or supreme guide), while nonetheless conceiving God as a "piece of the world," that is, *commensurate* with the world (§26). Given these ontotheological premises, creation necessarily had to appear as *causation*. And it still appears thus, even in the most subtle form of differentiation between cause (*causa*) and ground (*principium*), because the guiding notion is not God's singular creating (*bara*), but the *sovereign grounding* of the world that one could discern in the actions of potentates or in the agency of physical forces (AI, 169; Haught 1995). Whitehead's theopoetic initiative explicitly criticizes this analogous basis of the understanding of ontotheological creation for removing an element of the "energy of physical production" from the physical process and transferring it to divine creative activity, which as a result then inevitably appears as a "combat of productive force with productive force, of destructive force with destructive force" (PR, 346). Whitehead does not, however, as he has been accused, counter this notion with immanentism, which he clearly rejects, but with his *relational concept* of God, for which God's nature means "relationality" and "creativity" (§26).

A consideration of the relational framework within which God and creativity must be conceived makes the *relationality of God's creative agency* (with respect to creativity) more comprehensible. First, one has to consider that *unitexturality of reality* precludes assuming anything concrete that is not real in the same way everything else is real. Hence God refers to a concrete event. The other consideration is that the notion of *universal relationality* ("necessity in universality") precludes propositions about anything lacking relations (such propositions being considered meaningless). Creativity refers precisely to this second premise, namely, *universal relationality as actual relationality within actualities.* These two premises together lend sense and meaning to the *differentiation between God and creativity.* I refer to this distinction as "*theopoetic difference.*" Universal relationality is not an event, but rather its ontological ground; that is creativity. Because there can be no "beyond" with respect to universal relationality, however, creativity is a ground immanent to the concrete "moving relations" (events in concrescence) (Bradley 1994). But because, at latest by *Religion in the Making,* it became clear to Whitehead that the limitation or restriction of that which is possible in the larger sense must be viewed as an act of synthesis, as a valuative sketch of the world (Jung 1965, 606), God must be a *concrete* event and may *not* be identified with the ontological ground of the world. Though this *theopoetic difference* between ontological ground and concrete God may seem rather unusual at first glance, similar evidence can indeed be adduced from philosophical and theological tradition. One might mention Heidegger's differentiation between "Being"—which he does not want interpreted as "God"—and "God" (the creator), or Thomas Aquinas's differentiation between the "Being of beings," the "Being common to all beings" (*esse commune*), and God as "self-subsisting being" (*esse ipse subsistens*). As within Whitehead's theopoetic difference, "Being" is immanent to beings, but *without* its own nature or essence, instead wholly flowing and nonconcrete. God, however, is *concrete* being, self-being, subject and essence "for Godself" (Faber 2001c).

This theopoetic difference between creativity and God contains two unprecedented, nonsubstantialist, and nonsubjectivistic consequences for the understanding of God's creative power, namely, that God is the *original creature of creativity* and is the *original fact of creativity.* (a) The concept of "creation" has been altered, referring now not to causation, but to the relational creating of self-value, that is, of self-creativity within the process of a concrescence. Hence, as a concrete event God is, like every other event, *relationally self-grounded*, that is, within the dignity of God's own, purposeless, meaningful existence (Franklin 2000). In this sense, God too is a "primordial creature" (PR, 31). God is not, however, the "creature" of a "creator"—again, such notions represent a nonrelational regression back to the notion of causation—but rather a "creature" of *the* "creative," of the principle of the *self*-creative, of creativity (PR, 47, 69, 85, 289). This means—to articulate the implications once more in all clarity—that God is a creature of *God's own* self-creativity; put differently, God is *creator of Godself* and *creation of Godself*. (b) Because creativity refers to the concept of universal relationality *in actu*, self-creation always simultaneously means creating an *other*. Immanent creativity requires transcendent creativity (PR, 43, 85, 87, 102, 237, 280; Rohmer 2000). As an event, God is not only self-creative, but also—as Whitehead again articulates in a unique fashion amid altered conditions—the "primordial created fact," which in its "objectivity" becomes creatively efficacious *for others* (PR, 31). God constitutes Godself from God's own self-creativity such that God thereby *primordially* "characterizes" the otherwise wholly undetermined activity. God is thus the "eternal primordial character" of creativity and the "aboriginal condition which qualifies its action" through which God first renders it *transcendentally* efficacious (PR, 225).

Just as Heidegger's ontological distinction becomes *concrete* in a nondifference of "Being" (*Sein*) and "being-in-the-world" (or "being-there," *Dasein*) (Stegmair 1988), so also does Whitehead conceive the theopoetic difference as *concrete nondifference* of God and creativity, God thereby being the "primordial superject *of creativity*" (§29). This nondifference then issues in a new relational understanding of creation. On the one hand, God is not only the subject of *God's own* creativity, but also the superject of God's creativity *for others*—and thereby creator in the *primordial* sense of "making" all that which is produced "in creativity" in order to "make" or create itself (PR, 32). On the other hand, because God as superject must not perish to become "objectively," transcendentally efficacious beyond Godself, God is perpetually *simultaneously* both subject and superject of creativity (Suchocki 1988). God's creating thus always simultaneously acts both *internally* and *externally* (§§32, 35). God never creates something without simultaneously being self-creative, and God is never self-creative without simultaneously—similar to Tillich's understanding (Moltmann 1995)—creating something outside (external to) Godself. This conception grounds God's creative power *relationally*, understanding it neither as natural causation (of a *natura naturans*) nor as arbitrary positing (voluntarism) (§26). This relationality represents neither necessity nor arbitrariness within God's creative act, instead elevating both *freedom* and *relation* (and both simultaneously) to the status of foundation. Creativity, after all, does not refer here in any way to necessity, but to *creative freedom*. To the extent creativity does articulate *universal relationality*, the *latter* is at least "necessary." Hence as *superject of creativity*,

God creates both freely and relationally at the same time. As the *primordial* superject of creativity, God is the "aboriginal instance of this creativity" (PR, 225), creating externally in a primordial fashion such that *all* creatures thereby attain their own self-creativity. Hence creativity finds its initial *departure* in God's own concrescence and then is efficacious (acquires agency) in God's superjectivity as *creation* of a relational world.

§29. CONVERSION OF PROCESSES (GOD'S ALTERITY AND ORIENTATION TOWARD THE WORLD)

Within the framework of process theology's ecological paradigm, the volatile question was bound to arise concerning how God's relationship with the world might be conceived such that God did not simply disappear from the universal ecology as such; for the principle of universal relationality *precludes* God being conceived transcendentally without simultaneously implying immanence (§26). In its own turn, however, Whitehead's flat ontology regarding the event-nature of *everything* concrete *must* interpret God as a concrete *event*, since otherwise God would be an abstraction and as such neither subjective nor efficacious. Hence Whitehead conceived God as a *dipolar* event that is simultaneously concrete and relational (§25), such that God appears as the crowning conclusion to Whitehead's cosmology (Ford 1983). Whitehead combines these two principles into a *radical axiom* in *Process and Reality*, maintaining that "God is not to be treated as an exception to all metaphysical principles, invoked to save their collapse. God is their chief exemplification" (PR, 343). But does this not mean that God exists only within the framework of the metaphysical principles, thereby becoming a creation of our own metaphysics?

Because many versions of process theology began by resolving not to pay God any "metaphysical compliments" (SMW, 176) (Griffin 2000), there was a desire to make the concept of God coherent *within* Whitehead's metaphysical system. The result was that God was *coerced* into the conceptual schema of process theology and *subordinated* to metaphysical principles, the latter of which became increasingly oppressive as they tended to "define" God (Gilkey 1973). On the other hand, precisely the *divergent plurality* of such attempts demonstrates that there *is no* metaphysically coherent understanding of the concept of God in process theology. Over against such projects, Whitehead himself quite consciously maintained that there *can* be *no* definitive metaphysical system that would not perpetually risk becoming obsolete (PR, 7; Price 1954). Indeed, in a retrospective on his life's work in a 1944 letter to Guy Emerson, he confessed that he himself never had any intention of providing such a "system." (Let., 1f.).

One can easily show that the concept of God in Whitehead's organic philosophy is an *open* concept resistant to any and all classification, exhibiting instead almost system-destructive tendencies (Faber 2000e). In Whitehead's cosmology,

God is (measured against the categories of that cosmology) not a principle at all, nor a category, nor an event (in the usual sense). (a) Even though Whitehead did occasionally refer to God as the "principle of concretion," he eventually abandoned this principled character of God in favor of a concrete synthesis of decision (God as concretion), even confessing later—by way of self-correction—that God, rather than being a principle as such, instead "provides" (Latin, *providere*) a principle of concretion (Conv., 5; PR, 244). (b) God does not appear among the categories of Whitehead's "Categoreal Scheme" at the beginning of *Process and Reality*. Notwithstanding that God is called the primordial superject of creativity, God does *not* appear in the "Category of the Ultimate" that formulates the creative swing of the one and many (PR, 21f.). Nor is God attested among the "Categories of Existence," of which Whitehead acknowledges eight (events ["actual entities"], prehensions, nexuses, subjective forms, eternal objects, theories, multiplicities, contrasts) (PR, 22). One does not encounter God until the section on "derivative notions" (PR, 31ff), which complement the system of categories (Christian 1964). The ground is God's concreteness (§27). (c) Surprisingly, God is also not understood as an event in the defined sense of the categories. Neither is God finite (mortal) like all other actual events (Conv. 9), nor does God constitute Godself from God's own past (PR, 345). God is instead infinitely living and (in God's primordial nature) lacks all presupposition of a world (PR, 345). God's concreteness is *different* from that of all events. Whitehead calls God a nontemporal event, in Whitehead's parlance a "nontemporal act," "nontemporal entity," "nontemporal actuality" (PR, 31f.; RM, 88), which he further describes as a nonderivative event, in his parlance a "non-derivative actuality" (PR, 32), and as "everlasting" (PR, 345ff.). He *differentiates* God terminologically from every other actual event as that particular actuality (he uses the expression "actual entity") that is *not* to be identified with any other actual event ("actual occasion") (PR, 88). In a certain sense, God *breaks through* all the principles of organic cosmology, and all the categories in that cosmology change when the reference is to God. In conversations with A. H. Johnson, Whitehead admitted that in key points his concept of God was systematically inconsistent (Conv., 9).

Considerable problems arise if God's concretion is conceived *in accordance with* the organic event categories. (a) If God is an event *like* every other actual event, then God would "arise" from God's physical prehensions (taking up the world into God's consequent nature). In that case, however, God not only would be dependent on the world, but would in fact only be *constituted* as God in the first place on the basis of world. Thus did Richard Rorty interpret Whitehead's God, as a being that precedes us on the path to a better world, thereby reducing God to a "higher being" (Rorty 1994). (b) If, as Whitehead himself concedes, God in God's primordial nature can be called an actuality ("actual entity") only in a *deficient* sense (PR, 345), then that primordial nature is reduced from a subjective synthesis of possibilities to a complex eternal object realized *only* through "concrete divine events" (of the consequent nature). This is the path taken by Hartshorne in understanding God as a temporally organized society of "God events" (Hartshorne 1991c), thereby also reducing God to a "world soul." (c) If both these considerations are accurate, then whence does God have God's subjective aim? Not only would God now be the victim of an eternal world from which God constitutes Godself; God in God's own turn would need a "God" to open up God's becoming for Godself. Whence, however, would such a deus ex machina come from for *God's own* concrescence (Suchocki 1988)? Here, of course, the idea of God as such is taken *ad absurdum*, which is why David Sherburne declared Whitehead's God finished and advocated instead interpreting Whitehead "without God" (Sherburne 1971). (d) If, however (contra Hartshorne), God's concretion does not end, how then can God perceive the world and be perceived by it? Every event can perceive only as long as it is engaged subjectively in becoming; it can itself be perceived only after having passed away, that is, only when it becomes a real object in the becoming of other subjects. If, however, God's primordial nature were abstract rather than subjective, then God could not perceive world without perishing Godself. If on the other hand God "becomes" in a timelessly incessant fashion, God cannot be perceived, since in that case God would never be objectivized (Suchocki 1988; Ford 1988).

To remain true to Whitehead's intuition, one must clearly understand that God can never be taken as *an examplar of a rule*; God instead creates for Godself the rules of God's self-execution (Faber 2000e) (§47). Ultimately one of the most fundamental principles of organic cosmology precludes God from ever being *capable* of occupying a place within a system that understands God as an examplar, namely, the *ontological principle*. Its assertion that only events can be grounds (reasons) precludes the possibility of a concrete event being the examplar of a rule, remaining instead—precisely qua its concreteness—inaccessible to abstraction (Faber 2000e; Faber 2000g). Hence, as only John Lango among classical interpreters has recognized, Whitehead's axiom—the axiom denying metaphysical compliments to God—can also be interpreted commensurate with his ontological principle to mean that God is *not* a metaphysical principle invoked to explain what other principles cannot (Lango 1972, 32). Hence neither is God an element of a metaphysical system. Within God's own concreteness, God is antecedent to all principles through which God might be comprehended. This assertion does not, however, open the door to arbitrary irrationalism, deriving instead from the "system" itself insofar as it follows a deconstructionist rather than rationalistic strategy during whose implementation it maintains itself "in process" without becoming fixed or rigid (Keller and Daniell 2002a). The concept of God thus stands for *living openness*—its rationality perpetually *in flux*—to *singularity* amid the coherence of any system's principles. Here one catches a glimpse into a coherent self-transcendence with respect to all considerations of God that prevents the concept of God itself from falling back into the clutches of the notion of "self-presence" as entertained by antiquated metaphysics (Faber 2000b). Instead, God's concreteness forcefully tends toward *différance*.

Given this nonfundamentalist but postconstructionist insistence that God be articulated *beyond* metaphysical rules intent on "comprehending" God, and yet

to do so such that God is not positioned "absolutely"—that is, without any relation to them—beyond them, one solution is to understand God as "event" in
God's *otherness*. In the final pages of *Process and Reality*, Whitehead's introduction of the notion of a *reversal* of the concept of "process" with respect to God
intimates God's *alterity* in this sense without abandoning the notion of God's
relationality (Faber 1997). This "reversal of process" effects an *inner reversal* of the
dipolarity of the event "God" over against every actual event through a "reversal
of the poles." Whereas with respect to every event there are "two concrescent
poles of realization—'enjoyment' and 'appetition,' that is, the 'physical' and the
'conceptual' [poles]," "for God," *unlike for all other events*, "the conceptual [pole]
is prior to the physical, [while] for the World the physical poles are prior to the
conceptual poles" (PR, 348). This simple *priority* of the mental pole in God, however, changes absolutely everything theologically. God's infinite primordial nature
precedes every world and derives from no world. It is the primordial concrescence
of divine subjectivity (God's life for Godself) (§40). In it, God is the transcendent creator of the world. The perception of the world is then not God's becoming God, but the redemptive gathering within God's consequent nature, to which
Whitehead refers with a *purposeless-soteriological* implication (given the immanence of the world in God) as the "kingdom of heaven" (God's life *for* the world)
(PR, 351).

Lewis Ford (1968; 1973b) and Marjorie Suchocki (1975) have picked up on
this core statement concerning the "reversion of poles" and considered its consequences. Their findings can be summarized as the *four characteristics* of a reverse
process of God.

(1) *Everlasting concrescence.* God's reverse process is complete, unlimited, and
free (Suchocki 1995). God's subjective aim, rather than being determined by a
prevailing world, instead derives—quite independently of the course of things—
"from the completeness of [God's] primordial nature" (PR, 345). The subjective
aim, like the primordial nature itself, is a free act of divine self-creation ("free creative act") (PR, 344). Therefore, as an initial consequence, God's inexhaustible
process must be unlimited—"everlasting concrescence" (Ford 1968, 66; 1988,
116; Suchocki 1988, 148). God's primordial nature is not characterized by any
lack of actuality (that is, it is not an "abstraction" as in Hartshorne's understanding) (§§4, 22), being instead the unlimited fullness of the divine life. God's transcendence in this sense appears as free (independent of the world) and yet
relational, that is, as the overflowing fullness of infinite concrescence that makes
the world itself possible. God is world-relational without being coerced to engage
in creation. Here God appears in the guise of the "self-diffusing good" (*bonum
diffusivum sui*) of mystical theology (§40).

(2) *Inclusive actuality.* God's reverse process makes it possible for God to perceive the world in a *real* fashion beyond perspectival limitations, that is, to perceive
the world *really* (as it is) and to redeem it *ideally* (as it could be). Because God does
not have to bring about God's own concrescence by deciding among possibilities,
that is, does not become concrete by *reducing* possibilities and harmonizing the

world through *exclusion* (God having no negative prehensions in any case), God is able to perceive everything from the perspective of *its* emergence, though also to complement it in view of the whole by means of an ideal of itself. In God there is no concrescence through reduction and negation, but rather—as Lewis Ford puts it—only through "conceptual supplementation" (Ford 1973b, 348f.) (§39). Because God does not have to exclude anything within God's physical perception of the world in order to realize harmony, God is able to receive everything that has been perceived *as itself* and to liberate it in a "redemptive glance" for the "kingdom of God" (Maassen 1988). Within the context of the reverse process, not only does God not presuppose any world, God can in God's own turn (and for precisely that reason) be understood as the infinite power of redemption (Suchocki 1988).

(3) *Primordial satisfaction.* The process of God "begins" without presupposing any subjective aim that might, as in the case of other events, come to completion (and its end) only in its satisfaction. As Marjorie Suchocki has demonstrated, God's reverse process is instead to be understood as "primordial satisfaction" (Suchocki 1988, 142). Whereas all other world processes move toward their satisfaction as toward their identity (§20), the divine process takes as its point of departure *from its primordial satisfaction* in "beginning" to develop its own concrescence (PR, 32, 88). That is, God thus does not "need" any world for God's concrescence (as if God were a "process toward fullness"); God is instead "process *in* fullness," self-creativity in the highest sense, namely, as the movement of purposeless love, the self-exuding of fullness (*Summa theologica* 1 q. 44). Because God's concrescence is not directed toward the "unity" of satisfaction, happening instead prior to it, from the perspective of that unity of satisfaction God's concrescence is thus *movement toward diversity*, creative self-overflowing toward the multiplicity of the world (Faber 2002b; 2001a; 1997).

(4) *Primordial superject.* This primordial "unity of satisfaction" designates God as the "primordial superject of creativity" (PR, 32). Whereas world processes become objective only when they perish, after which they are efficacious within others, God's reverse process is "at the beginning" not only subjectively self-creative, but also *superjectively efficacious* (Suchocki 1975; 1995), meaning that God is the creator of the world in the *most primordial* sense (§26). Freedom and relationality are again united. God is free in God's concretion as self-creativity; as superject *of* creativity, however, God is already also, *in one and the same*, conceived as creator of the world, not only as *causa sui*, but as *causa mundi* (§25).

Whitehead even takes this notion a step further, albeit only in the form of hints, now understanding the divine process in "conversion" to the world process. "In every respect," Whitehead writes, "God and the World move conversely to each other in respect to their process" (PR, 349). I understand this "conversion" as Whitehead's most significant proposition concerning God's alterity *and* orientation toward the world—that is, both in one and both simultaneous. On the one hand, this conversion of processes of God and world is in its essence more than merely a reversion of poles, encompassing instead the *entire movement* of the process. It is not just the *elements* of the dipolar process that are reversed, producing such surprising displacement within the concept of God itself; instead the *entirety* of the process itself becomes *something different*. The conversion is the *complete inversion* of the process (Faber 1997). The "other" of the process already represents an other *with respect to* the "process" (as applicable to the world); whereas the world process takes place within the *arc of tension* attending a dual swing of subjectivity and objectivity, concretion and transition, immediacy and past, God for God's own part *is* this duality in the *reconciled nondifference* of God's moments, stages, contradictions, and antagonisms (Faber 2000e). It is the reconciled nature of the divine process in its otherness that first allows God's specifically *reconciling* activity in the world. This *conversion as alterity* is virtually the presupposition of the *conversion as world orientation* with regard to the divine process (Faber 2002b; 2001c; 2001a). God's process, in its reconciled relationality, *opens up* the world process *toward God*. And that is the mystery of conversion, namely, that the world process is creatively grounded from the reconciled nondifference of the divine alterity such that in it, the process simultaneously finds reconciliation. This is the point of Whitehead's theopoetic assertion that God *saves* rather than creates (§§20, 28); reconciliation is the beginning and end of God's conversion to the world (Faber 2000e) (§40).

In process thinking, this reconciled nondifference that simultaneously opens and reconciles all differences refers to the *radically other*. It now no longer suffices to differentiate the concept of God within Whitehead's "categoreal" matrix, since instead God now extirpates Godself from that very matrix. The divine process is not an "exemplar" of a cosmological rule, but rather the event of the new, of the inaccessibly inscrutable, indeed an interruption of categoreal continuity (Faber 2000e). In this conversion of processes, God appears as *différance*, as an *other process*, as the *process of the other*, or even as the *other with respect to the process*. Paradoxically, acknowledgment of the other beyond categoreal exemplarism, rather than leading to a collapse of the principles, instead discloses them almost dialectically in their inner *reconciled state* (Faber 2000c). Here a key point is attained for theopoetics, since now it is the *negative theology* of God's alterity—albeit a God who in God's orientation toward the world, rather than disappearing into speechlessness (and irrelevance), instead through God's own transcendence possesses *poetic* character in creating the world in a reconciled light. This concept of God, with its reconciled and reconciling nondifference at the center of the poetics, does not, however, lead to a new ontotheological resubstantialization of God; such is precluded by the *exteriority* of the divine process, which never manifests itself as fulfilled presence of the "selfsame," but rather only as the *other* with respect to the process. Nondifference, as theopoetic substitution for the divine process, refers to God's true alterity under the regime of *différance* (§40) *in which* God is manifested as *converse process*, as the countermovement of differentiation (Faber 2001c). Because this process can be called both reconciled and reconciling, it does not relieve us of speaking about God (Faber 2002b).

§30. FOUR PHASES OF THE CREATIVE PROCESS
(THE ECOLOGY OF LOVE)

The notion of God's converse/world-oriented process interprets God's reconciled nondifference within the world process as a *reconciling process* (Faber 2000b) (§29). Whitehead ends the concluding theological section of *Process and Reality* with reference to that particular *soteriological interwovenness* in which this conversion of world process and divine process is realized as the *ecology of love* (PR, 350f.; Pittenger 1981)—a concept rarely discussed in process theology (Hosinski 1993) even though in it the *concrete juxtaposition* of God and world comes to expression as nowhere else (§§25–28). In four phases, deriving from the inner structure of the processes, that is, from the *dipolarity of events* and their *swing between subject and superject*, the processes of God and the world lovingly engage or mesh with each other (§§17–18, 20–21). Cosmologically they arise from the phases of concrescence/transition, namely, initial aim, physical prehensions, satisfaction, and agency for others (PR, 87f.; Moser 1975). To be sure, the specifically soteriological form of this process structure is revealed only when one focuses on God's own agency within it; moreover it is only when God's *otherness* is perceived—in which these creative phases are realized *within* the divine process—that its reconciling character as the ecology of love can fully enter our purview (Faber 2000e).

First phase—"conceptual origination." Whitehead accepts the *empirical* principle of all cognition (contra Plato and the illuminists, and with Aristotle), namely, that all cognition begins with the perception of (physical) reality rather with innate (inborn) ideas (Fetz 1981) (§§3, 11). Whitehead nonetheless sides with Plato to a certain extent in accepting that no perception of reality can happen without *comprehension* ("com-prehending," "grasping") as physical reality (§18), though Whitehead does differ insofar as he presupposes not ideas, but rather the initial aim of an event, that is, its *possibility* of becoming. Hence every world process is grounded, even before its actual beginning, in the ideal presupposition of *being able* to become—here and now, in the context of its concrete past—as harmonious unity of self-being (§20). In this sense, every process *begins* with God, from God's gift of the initial aim, in which one finds not only its anterior teleological form (the best of all possibilities) of its self-realization, but also the constitution of the event's mental pole. In a certain sense, *every* actual event begins with a reversion of poles—albeit not as *causa sui* (*like* God), but as being bequeathed to itself from God (PR, 224) (§29).

Second phase—"physical origination." The event now *becomes in actual fact* by self-creatively realizing itself from its physical prehensions and synthesizing the physically given into a self-interpretation in its mental pole (Fetz 1981). Whereas the first phase indicates the origination of every event *from God*, the second refers to the origination of every event *from the world*.

Third phase—"satisfaction." The event reaches its subjective aim and becomes a "perfected actuality." The *completion* or *perfection* of the event process is significant in that it indicates that the event is entering a qualitatively different movement. Whereas the event was earlier a concrescence toward the completion of itself, now—*in* completion—it transforms into its perishing and thus enters into the process of transition (§23). This transformation itself is of a peculiar nature, being neither simply the enjoyment of the "self-presence" it "has become," nor simply the disappearance of an event. Instead it is the *moment* at which the event "is" *simultaneously* both subject *and* superject (Suchocki 1988). Yet whereas God—in the conversion of processes—must be called the primordial *superject qua subject*, this "simultaneity" and "oneness" of subject and superject flashes into view within the actual event only as a timeless (albeit time-generative) vision of reconciliation. Whitehead thus views this phase as *negative*, as a phase in which the event "has not yet lost itself." Yet it is also a paradox, insofar as "time has stood still—if only it could" (PR, 154). It is not that time stands still (as the self-enjoyment of completion); it is that time *would have* stood still if such were possible to begin with. This "presence" is not substantialist *self*-presence, but nonsubstantialist presence as *past* ("has stood still"), completion as end, satisfaction as *différance* (Faber 2000e). "Perfection" is always a creative production of difference (AI, 257); an event is "perfect" (*perfectio*) only "in the perfect (tense)" (*perfectum*).

Fourth phase—"swing back." The completed event that objectifies itself as past is now *efficaciously causal* as superject in the becoming of other, new processes; it becomes part of the "actual world" of new events. It "passes back into the temporal world" and "swings back" as datum for new events. Now it is a *fact* and a *concrete value* and is fruitful in its self-transcendence (§23). If there were no third phase, one could express causal efficacy in a purely immanent fashion—without recourse to God. Because, however, satisfaction always represents an end as well, a death, a loss, the event is efficacious not only through mechanical causality, but also through its *interruption*. Because the "swing back" includes at its center a *translation (in the sense of displacement) of self*, God acts efficaciously within this fourth phase as the *flowing back* into the world of that which has been harvested into God (§21). And this is God's love, namely, the reception or taking up of that which is lost into God's consequent nature *and* the gift of new events from the *divine knowing and valuing of the concrete world* (PR, 346). A past event is causally efficacious not only with respect to the *second* phase, but also—given God's *caring concern* for the best realization of the new—with respect to the *first* phase of the new event.

For the world, God acts efficaciously in these four phases as the *creative motor* of the process, as the concrete, world-oriented love. Put differently, through God's involvement in the creative phases of the process, this process appears as a creative process rather than as a disparately chaotic one. In the *first phase*, God bequeaths each event to itself, since God knows about the world that has become concrete (third phase). The primordial nature presupposes the consequent nature, through which alone God knows about the world not only in the possibilities of its capacity for being, but also in its concreteness (its "having become" concrete) (Lansing 1978). In the *second phase*, God lets the event become itself, through its own decision, through its own synthesis of the world. God's love liberates or sets free; it is not totalitarian. It respects concrete history in that what it has become. That is, the world is not a result of God's decree. The world has become that what it is through self-creativity; it is value resulting from self-valuation (§§23, 41). In the *third phase* God takes up into Godself that which has become—now as that which perishes. An event not only perishes into a past, but is also saved into God's memory (Reeves 1984). To the same extent that God continually saves the world, God also knows about it and *valuates* within God's consequent nature that which has become (PR, 346). In this third phase, the event is translated out of itself (wrenched out of its self-becoming) and saved *as itself* within God's eternity. God is efficacious in this regard as the kingdom of heaven (PR, 351). Through this action of saving into God, however—and this is noteworthy—the world process, rather than being interrupted by God, is instead *opened up* or *inaugurated*, for in the *fourth phase* God approaches the world in a renewed fashion in order to accompany the creative process as love. In this phase, God manifests Godself as the kingdom of God *"with us today"* (RM, 72) (§39).

One might point out that *within God's own concretion*, these four phases emerge differently, insofar as they realize themselves *inversely* commensurate with the "inner conversion." Because they take place *simultaneously* in a *reconciled* fashion within the divine process, that is, without the arc of tension attaching to world processes, the four phases of God's "inner" creative process correspond to the *four characteristics* of God's reverse process (§29) (Faber 2000e). In the *first phase*, God sets into motion the primordiality of God's primordial nature, that is, the groundless-creative valuation of all possible worlds out of God's inscrutable and boundless fullness. Here God is *everlasting concrescence*, and because this concrescence is infinite, God's "unity" flows into the multiplicity of the world ("multiplicity of actualities"). This first phase is thus the phase of divine creativity beyond itself—the creation of the world in the divine Logos (§28). In the *second phase*, God is manifested as *inclusive actuality*, that is, as the "locus" of the perception of the world in God's consequent nature, the reception of all events as God's physical prehensions, their valuation, their judgment, and their reconciliation in God. Here God "grows" from the world without ever having been "needy." Now God is the "place" in which everything is not only perceived, but also transformed in light of the whole. Reconciliation appears as process "in" completion (§39). The *third phase* discloses God as *primordial satisfaction*, that is, as an everlasting process of the fullness of divine life at the highest intensity. At this phase, God lavishly dispenses Godself as the highest self-enjoyment and as the kingdom of heaven. In connection with the displacement of events in the third phase, the satisfaction, Whitehead speaks about an "Apotheosis of the World" (PR, 348). What this implies is not a "divinization" of the world (through which the world becomes God) (Welker 1984), but in the biblical sense participation in the divine nature (2 Pet. 1:4) through eschatological transformation or metamorphosis into a spiritual body (*soma pneumatikon*) (1 Cor. 15:44f.) (§38). The *fourth phase* discloses God as the *primordial superject of creativity* and thus as the primordial cre-

ative power. God's power is not only ideal (first phase), but also *effective,* since superjectivity always implies objective agency and causality (Conv., 9; Frankenbury 1983). God as *causa mundi,* however, is love, affection for the concrete world, *caring concern* (*providence*) (Hosinski 1993). God's "providence" is not "untouched" foresight of that which has not yet become, that is, foresight void of consideration of that which the world has become, but the result of God's sympathetic love for that which is past and that what has been displaced from itself—within God's "swing back" to the transient and perishable, which in this light appears as that which is coming. Paradoxically, the kingdom of heaven appears not as the end of the world, but as the *eschatological beginning* of the world process (Faber 2000h).

World process and divine process appear intensively interwoven within the four phases of the creative process (contra supernaturalistic transcendentalism). The conversion of processes, however, prevents this mutual processual immanence of God and world from ever being transformed into a pantheistic dissolution of God (immanentist danger) or into a mythological sublation of world into the life of God (monistic danger) (§26). Instead, this processual network of God and world comes about as mutual interpenetration of *freedom* and *relationality* (§28). That is, God appears as intensively engaged in *each* of the four phases of the world process without ever being reduced to or disappearing within the world process or being "functionally" exhausted within that process (Faber 2000e). Instead, God is efficacious within all four phases *as* God (not as "part" of the world process) in loving affection for the world process by being present in each of its individual events as *concrete* love—opening that event up creatively (ideally and efficaciously), sym-pathetically accompanying it, reconciling it "in God," and revealing it "in the world" as reconciling (§22).

This entire ecology of love is rendered possible by the conversion of the processes of God and world (§29). The "simultaneity" of freedom and relationality in this conversion guards the *theopoetic process* against *immanentist misinterpretation* (and from those versions of process theology) that would deny free creativity to God's immanence within the process, as well as against *substantialist misinterpretations* that fear God's sovereign presence within the process as a reintroduction of a "transcendent signified" (Derrida 1978, 278ff.) in its ontotheological "self-presence." One can counter both misinterpretations by analyzing and illuminating this conversion of processes. On the one hand—deriving terminologically as it does from the ancient doctrine of the Trinity (Faber 1995a)—it is an *immanent* conversion, that is, an inner otherness of the divine process, and on the other hand an *ecumenical* conversion in the sense of representing a different turn or orientation of the divine process toward the world process.

(1) Because of the *immanent conversion* or *inversion* of God's concrescence, it comes about not in four phases, but rather as self-differentiation of that which in the world constitutes—in temporal extension—the open whole of the cosmos (Faber 2002b) (§40). The divine process flows over into the world as a *reconciling* process amid the *inner reconciliation* of all its moments and in primordial

groundlessness (Faber 2000e). Because of this reconciled nondifference of all creative phases "in God," God is never merely a moment or element of the world process, being instead the perpetual ground of its creative character and its soteriological cogency. God's process is the origin of the temporal process of the cosmos, that is, is itself both sensitive to and affected by time, while yet *not* being temporal itself, but rather eternal and everlasting, world-perceptive and world-receptive, perpetually growing without ever becoming world (PR, 349; Faber 1995b) (§29). In this sense, the "poet of the world" is the *free creator* of the world.

(2) Because of the *economic conversion* of the processes of God and world, that is, on the basis of the *nature* of the economy (*oikonomia*) of God's world-orientation and the world's God-orientation, this reconciled nondifference of the process has a *differentiating* effect in the world, constituting the world process as *différance* (Faber 2002b). God manifests Godself in the creative phases of events not as "fulfilled presence," but in the temporal arc of tension of the world process as a *temporal countermovement*, that is, as the *eschatological approach* toward every process in each of its phases (Faber 2000h). The unique feature of God's poetics is that God affects the world both by creating and reconciling it *from the eschatological future* (§§35, 39). With respect to the individual creative phases, in the *first phase* God is present *as the future* of the potential event that will yet arise; once that event actually "becomes," God has already always *been there*. Here God's "presence" appears as creative "trace" (§20). In the *second phase*, in which every event is "present" for itself, God is *absent*, providing space, freedom, and the horizon of the event's self-becoming (§28). In the *third phase*, the event is displaced out of its own present, is "perfect" (simultaneously both complete and past), and has been transfigured over into God. Here God affects the world as *memory*; that which is past is now present within God as "having been" and God present for it as its *reconciling future*. In the *fourth phase* finally, God approaches the world as *eschatological future (ad-vent) of the kingdom of heaven*, approaching each of its events and becoming present for them as *caring concern*. Theopoetically the creator of the world is the *eschatological creator*, and God's presence is always presence within *différance*, as trace, as the saving memory of that which is past, and as the creative "ad-vent" of that which comes (§39).

This economy of love in the four creative phases discloses a *creative conversion* of the processes of God and world in the sense that God and world mutually enrich each other *without* God's alterity obtaining at the cost of God's relationality and vice versa (Faber 2000e) (§29). *Within the prevailing otherness* of both God and world, they constitute a *single* creative process, an *interprocess of creativity* (§32). God's reconciled nondifference allows this creativity to operate harmoniously (albeit in a complex and living, vibrant manner in the sense of the "chaotic nexus") rather than chaotically (with a loss of intensity). That nondifference, by differentiating itself into the world, thereby constitutes the world process as an unfathomable process of *différance*, arranging it in reconciling *connexio* rather than abandoning it into arbitrary chaotic differentiation. Here theopoetics of process theology can draw on the deconstructionist criticism of the ontotheological substantializing of God without having to share its constructivist implications (Keller 2002) (§8). Within this economy of love, God does not construe the world, nor the world itself or God. The world is not merely an illusion of God or of our own yearning; nor is God a fantasy of our longing for sense and meaning (§41). The *postconstructionist* consequence is that God differentiates the world freely but always relationally, that is, on the basis of the knowledge and desire for its emancipated status. God cannot (constructivistically) "foresee" the world; instead God must initially seek to perceive it for the sake of God's caring concern (§25). Similarly, the world cannot (analytically) construe God for itself; it can only let God reveal Godself *empirically* within the alterity of God's process (§36). The creative process is a *synthetic* process of concrescence, of *growing* together. Within their relationship of mutual creativity, God and world are in any case always oriented toward each other *concrescently*, in mutual sensitivity rather than projection, in sym-pathy rather than phantasmagoria, in mutual receptivity rather than repression. In this way, the theopoetic process implies creative conversion in the sense of the *reciprocity of God and world for each other*.

§31. SIX ANTITHESES
(THE RECIPROCITY OF GOD AND WORLD)

Within the creative process, God does not merely manifest Godself as "present" in *every* concrete process, in *every* event of the world (as whatever, whenever, and however such may take place) (§29); God is also active in a distinctly creative, caring, and reconciling fashion in *each* creative *phase*—phases immanent to it—of its arising (§30). This insight is an overwhelming testimony to process theology's interpretation of God's everlasting presence in God's creation (*creatio continua*), God's gracious, liberating, sym-pathetic but simultaneously redemptive and eschatological agency. Whereas the four creative phases theologically express God as the alpha and omega (Rev. 1:8) of the world process (Reeves 1984), doing so moreover concretely with respect to *every individual* process (PR, 350f.), what are known as Whitehead's *antitheses* consider this with respect to the world process *as a whole* (PR, 347f.). These antitheses articulate the intensively interwoven character of the processes of God and world as *a single, grand, creative, free, and relational happening* (Faber 2000e). These antitheses—as such unique in Whitehead's work—constitute to a certain extent the "final summary" (PR, 347f.) of process theology's understanding of the relationship between God and world and as such a synopsis of the creative process as a whole.

> The final summary can only be expressed in terms of a group of antitheses, whose apparent self-contradictions depend on neglect of the diverse categories of existence. In each antithesis there is a shift of meaning which converts the opposition into a contrast.
> It is as true to say that God is permanent and the World fluent, as that the World is permanent and God is fluent.

> It is as true to say that God is one and the World many, as that the World is one and God many.
>
> It is as true to say that, in comparison with the World, God is actual eminently, as that, in comparison with God, the World is actual eminently.
>
> It is as true to say that the World is immanent in God, as that God is immanent in the World.
>
> It is as true to say that God transcends the World, as that the World transcends God.
>
> It is as true to say that God creates the World, as that the World Creates God.
>
> God and the World are the contrasted opposites in terms of which Creativity achieves its supreme task of transforming disjoined multiplicity, with its diversities in opposition, into concrescent unity, with its diversities in contrast. (PR, 347f.)

In these antitheses, Whitehead articulates the fundamental *creative relationality* between God and world in *radical mutuality*. This relationality encompasses the determinative features of mutual relatedness—permanence and flux, transcendence and immanence, unity and multiplicity, actuality and creativity (Faber 2000e)—that Whitehead himself variously attributes *mutually* to both God and the world. What this means is that all these concepts can be applied both to God with respect to God's relation with the world *as well as* to the world with respect to its relation with God. The *relational meaning* that God and world have *for each other* comes to expression in these antitheses as a *single* process of mutual sensitivity, openness, and life, as a process in which the mutual reciprocity of God and world generates a *field of mutual, open wholeness*, what might be called the *interfield of mutual relatedness* (§32).

It is no accident that these antitheses, given their formulaic presentation above, subsequently exerted great influence. They have either been taken as a confession of process theology, that is, as an "abbreviated formula" of process theology (Sander 1991), or have been adduced over against process theology itself as final proof of its strange or even (with respect to traditional theology) irreconcilable view of things (Küng 1980). The antitheses do reveal a key point for verifying any given understanding of process theology (Faber 2000e). Either they are read within the horizon of a linear analogy between God and world (God as event or society *like* an actual event or an actual society) (Hartshorne 1991) (§5), or are understood in light of a *complex* interpretation of the juxtaposition of God and world (PR, 100) of the sort illustrated by the conversion of processes (§29). The text itself, however, provides ample evidence that one cannot simply choose arbitrarily between these interpretations, consisting as it does of *three separate parts*: (a) a *hermeneutical introduction*, (b) the *six antitheses*, and (c) an *ecological reminiscence* explicating the process-ontological basis of the antitheses. Only a *synopsis of these three parts*—rather than their contextual isolation (Küng 1980)—makes a balanced understanding of the antitheses possible. Such interpretation must also take into account the differentiating qualifications of the theopoetic relationship between God and world, all of which are contextually positioned:

the dipolarity of the processes of God and world (§25), the mutual immanence of God and world (§§26, 34), the creative swing between God and world in the creative process (§§28, 30), and the conversion of processes (§29).

(1) The *hermeneutical introduction* formulates a *hermeneutics of transformation*. As Whitehead emphasizes, the coherent nexus of God and world involves a *contradictory* relationship. Placing God and world *together* in a coherent nexus obviously results in *oppositional juxtaposition*, a contradiction that can be resolved only by being understood as *process*. This hermeneutical process emerges not through *changing* the juxtaposition of the interpenetration of the processes of God and world, but by *comprehending* that opposition precisely *as* a coherent nexus (§21). What is sought is thus a criterion that transforms this contradiction into a *contrast*, into *mutual relatedness*. A contrast is that particular category of the process of concrescence that articulates how an event transforms itself from its data (the often contradictory facts of its past) into a "subjective unity" commensurate with its subjective aim, a unity that, rather than extinguishing the contradictions, instead transforms them into *complex harmony* (PR, 109ff., 228; AI, 252f.; Wiehl 1984) (§27). For Whitehead, these antitheses to a certain extent constitute such "concrescence," that is, they become an *event* precisely and only when *transformed* interpretively into a harmonious contrast (Krämer 1994). "Processual unity" and "subjective harmony" of the interpretive process itself emerge abruptly, happening like an event, within the interpreter, that is, it cannot be coerced, being *rational* only with respect to an *acknowledgment* of the moments of the "subjective aim" of the cognitive process presupposed by these antitheses, namely, intensity and harmony (Griffin 1976; Hauskeller 1994), freedom and relationality (Cobb 1983; Loomer 1976; Ford 1976), rationality and creativity (Wiehl 1986; Rohmer 2000).

The process of *transformation* in the interpretation of the antitheses comes about through an abrupt *shift of meaning* that in its own turn happens when that which these antitheses formulate—but which can also be overlooked (Küng 1980)—is understood *as* contrast rather than as opposition. To this end, it is important to *remain mindful* of the "categories of existence" (Sander 1991). To wit, if the interplay of event, prehension, nexus, subjective form, eternal object, theory, multiplicity, and contrast (PR, 22: Categories of Existence) is overlooked both within the process of concrescence itself and in its interpretation—or if such are not grasped in their coherent organic context (PR, 255), then these antitheses will necessarily fail within the "event framework" (FR, 2f.; Krämer 1994) (§21). Put differently, if the "categories of existence" are not applied *concretely* to the relationship God/world, namely, with respect to dipolarity, mutual immanence, concretion, superjectivity, and conversion of processes, then the antitheses themselves will *not* establish any "aesthetic harmony of contrasts" (Sayer 1999). To be successful, they require hermeneutical transformation.

Just what happens when Whitehead's hermeneutical instructions regarding the antitheses are not followed can be seen in Hans Küng's interpretation, which can stand representatively for all those interpretations that understand antitheses as antinomy. Küng constructs not a relational field of mutual openness, but an antinomy of leveling; that is, the opposition within the antitheses appears only from the perspective of its radical mutual opposition, *not* from that of the shift of meaning through which such leveling is sublated into a *contrast of mutual otherness*. Küng maintains that Whitehead "oversimplifies in his thought the relationship between God and the world, reducing it to complete reciprocity. Is the problem really solved by regarding God and the world as eternally related to one another, as ultimately interchangeable factors, so that in the end it is just as true that God is before the world as that the world is before God? The problem lies precisely in this 'just as true.'" (Küng 1987, 180). On the other hand, however, a problem does inhere in the "as true" because it *is* a problem, because it *does* formulate an "apparent self-contradiction" that Whitehead as a matter of fact does *not* deny, a contradiction that, however, represents *not* the end, but rather—and to the contrary—the point of departure of the transformative interpretive process. An interpretation ends up in the antinomy of leveling only if it perceives the "as true" only in its radical mutuality and not *also* with its shift in meaning (Faber 2000e). This antinomy expresses a static opposition within the antitheses, not the goal of the transformative process it sets into motion.

Within the ontological, epistemological, or linguistic processual structure of Whitehead's organic cosmology, *opposites* consistently represent moments *in a process*; being otherwise nothing but static abstractions to which no meaning is attributed (PR, 341; Faber 1995b). They acquire such meaning only through incorporation or inclusion (*ingression*) within a *concrete process* (PR, 40ff.; Hampe 1990). Antinomies (as dualities of mutual incompatibility) are interpreted in Whitehead's ecological interlinking *as process*, and it is only *in process* that they are realized as contrast (PR, 83, 100, 106). Not unlike Derrida's deconstruction of dualities of "self-presence" in metaphysical "first principles," Whitehead dissolves these dualities into differences that are always involved in the process of differentiation; unlike Derrida, however, with regard to process, Whitehead is concerned not with *difference*, but with *connex* (§24). The differentiations of dualities are always involved in an ecological swing one into the other (Klose 2002; Wiehl 1986) (§§12–13). (a) With respect to *ontological opposition*, Whitehead always views an *event* as *subject and superject*, albeit never simultaneously and in the same respect, but rather in the process of differentiation and swing (of concrescence in transition). On the one hand, the "event as the *subject* of experience is not 'in' the real world, but rather the world is 'in the subject'" to the extent it is constituted through "its subjective aim and the subjective forms of world comprehension emerging from it"; on the other hand, the "event *as superject* is 'in' its environment to the extent it belongs to a causal chain of events" (Lotter 1996, 7). (b) With respect to *epistemological opposition*, Whitehead juxtaposes the in-being of events within the world and of the world within events such that no leveling is implied, but rather that *the same is expressed from always different perspectives* (Nobo 1978). Whitehead thus speaks about these *different relations of opposites* as "antithetical relations" (MT, 163). In his definition, antitheses express those relations in a way that say the same thing *differently*, whereby the qualification "differently" *must* derive from the *mutual relation* (appearing rational within it), whereas the relation itself always represents a dynamic process. (c) With respect to the *linguistic structure* of the antitheses, a qualification of "as true" thus applies to the *entire* proposition, *even though* the "theses" themselves, that is, the different parts of the proposition constituting the opposition, move counter to one another, which is why *the same thing* in the "theses" in fact possesses a *different* meaning, one in mutual orientation and emerging from the *relation*. I use the term *immersion* to refer to this shift of meaning (one frequently encountered in Whitehead) in antithetical relations with respect to a common content emerging from the "subjects" in relation (Faber 2000e, 473). The antitheses have an *immersive structure* insofar as the various "theses in opposition" appear *immanent within* the various other "theses" with which they constitute antitheses, albeit *without* there being any "outside"—even in the form of a "unifying guiding idea" (Lotter 1996, 27)—from the perspective of which the antitheses might be viewed "objectively." It is solely within *mutual immanence* that the antitheses are disclosed as contrasts. Their meaning is disclosed solely through the *immanent shift* emerging from within the *relation of opposites*.

(2) These *six antitheses* articulate the interwoven nature of the processes of God and world with respect to the *fundamental features* of *relationality of the creative process* as a whole. (a) Their content revolves around *four thematic contrasts*, namely, permanence and flux, multiplicity and unity, immanence and transcendence, and actuality and creativity. (b) With respect to these contrasts, God and world are then opposed (posited in opposition) in order to disclose thematically their mutual relation so that God and world form *four kinds of opposition*: (1) the opposition of *mutual otherness*, God on the one side, the world on the other ("<->"); (2) the opposition of *mutual comparison*, God and world in comparison with each other ("/"); (3) the opposition of *mutual relatedness*, God and world in their various relatedness to each other ("—"); and (4) the opposition of *mutual generation*, God and world in "production" of each other ("> <"). (c) Together these different oppositions are disclosed in *six mutual relations* between God and world: (1) God's permanence/flux and the world's flux/permanence, (2) God's unity/multiplicity and the world's multiplicity/unity (both representing the first type of opposition), (3) God's eminent actuality in comparison with the world and the world's eminent actuality in comparison with God (second type of opposition), (4) the world's immanence in God and God's immanence in the world, (5) God's transcendence over against the world and the world's transcendence over against God (both representing the third type of opposition), and (6) God's creative causality over against the world and the world's creative causality over against God (fourth type of opposition). Viewed thus, the six antitheses, through the harmony of their various moments, can disclose the theopoetic process as a whole (Figure 3).

Figure 3: The Contrast Structure of the Six Antitheses

Six Antitheses	Six Relations	Four Contrasts	Four Opposites
1. Permanence/Flux	1. Permanence/Flux	1. Permanence/Flux	1. God<->World
2. Unity/Multiplicity	2. Unity/Multiplicity	2. Unity/Multiplicity	2. God / World
3. Actuality	3. Eminence/Actuality	3. Immanence/Transcendence	3. God—World
4. Immanence	4. Immanence/Immanence	4. Actuality/Creativity	4. God >< World
5. Transcendence	5. Transcendence/Transcendence		
6. Creativity	6. Creativity (Causality)		

The *contingency of the four thematic contrasts* underlying these oppositions and relations is not simply arbitrary. Although they cannot be reduced one to the other, insofar as each can also be stated individually, their confluence results from the *inner rationality* of the ecological process paradigm. Flux/permanence, unity/multiplicity, immanence/transcendence, and actuality/creativity reflect the principles of the creative process itself. (a) The contrast flux/permanence expresses Whitehead's *fundamental*, nonsystematic principle (i.e., the principle not represented in the system of categories), namely, the *countermovement* of God and world in the conversion of their processes (PR, 351; Faber 2000e). (b) The contrast unity/multiplicity expresses the "category of the ultimate," that is, *the* systematic principle, the principle grounding the system of categories itself and articulating the processuality of reality as a movement from multiplicity to unity and from unity to multiplicity (PR, 21f.). (c) The contrast immanence/tran-scendence expresses the fundamental principles characterizing the process as *dif-férance*, namely, inside/outside, subject/superject, private/public, and concrescence/transition (Hampe 1990; Lotter 1990; Kline 1983). (d) The con-trast actuality/creativity takes into account the process-ontological difference between "event" as a concrete process and "creativity" as an ultimate principle of the process (Ford 1986; Garland 1983).

The *eight characteristics of the four contrasts* are not "concepts," representing instead as it were an articulation of the "transcendentals" of the creative process (*notae*); because of their universality, they (like the classical transcendentals unity, truth, goodness, and beauty) cannot be conceptually grasped and defined in delimitation over against a hierarchy of concepts (Fetz 1986). In their "potency," they instead *encompass* both God *and* world—not through delimiting definition, but as *processual and relational modes* in which the mutual movement of the processes of God and world comes about. They thus mean nothing "in and of themselves," but rather *only* in their immersion within the processes of God and world. Hence the concrete relation between God and world as *process* emerges *only* through a shift of meaning, which is why these antitheses express nothing "common" with respect to the characteristics of the creative process that might be substantialized as a "third something" over against the processes of God and world. Instead they only formulate *universal features of the mutual otherness of the processes in conversion* (Faber 2002b); that is, in *inner* conversion they acquire exteriority (mutual otherness) and in *external* conversion universal truth (they become "as true"). Hence in them God and world are not juxtaposed *simply*, but rather *mutually*. It is not that *both* God *and* the world are for each other *both* this one *and* that one. Instead, with respect to the same proposition the world has a relation with God that in the *reversal of processes* continues to obtain as well, namely, in God's relation to the world (§29). *With the aid* of the universal features, God and world are always brought into a *reversal of movement* and thus become visible in their alterity precisely through their universality.

The *first antithesis* attributes *permanence and flux* to the processes of God and world such that both can be said to apply to both processes *in relationship to each other*. Permanence refers within the world process to an abstraction from the event process constituting constancy within the flux of the nexus. In its own turn, flux refers to the event process itself, its vitality and nonpermanence, its chaotic nature and concreteness (PR, 167, 209, 328ff., 341ff.) (§12). By attributing flux and permanence to both God and the world process, Whitehead avoids the ontotheological separation of "an entirely static God, with eminent reality" (PR, 346) from the merely perishing world. Because of the conversion of processes, however, Whitehead understands permanence and flux within the divine process in *reversion*. Whereas flux is primary within the world, its permanence derives ultimately from God, so that "in God's nature, permanence is primordial and flux is derivative from the World" (PR, 348). A shift of meaning accompanies this reversion. In the world, permanence always appears only in *abstraction* from the process, the latter of which always happens amid "perpetual perishing," such that permanence is able to develop merely qualities, characters, structures, or laws (§19). Yet in relation to God, the permanence in the world appears also as *both* a gift of creative Eros to the process itself—a gift of ideas, objects, and goals through God's primordial nature (§§18, 20)—*and* an expression of hope in God's eschatological activity, namely, that that which perishes may remain—in full integrity—in God's reconciling recollection (§39). In God's process, by contrast, divine permanence emerges from the everlasting concrescence and primordial superjectivity of God (§28); the everlasting event "God" neither perishes nor is efficacious through abstraction (objectification) of itself (with a loss of subjective immediacy) (Conv., 9). God's concrescence is *primordially permanent* both in the "ideal" sense (of the inexhaustibility of nature) and in the sense of the "everlastingness" of the inexhaustibility of the consequent nature (Clarke 1984; Hosinski 1993). God's *concrescent flux* then does *not* mean that God needs the world, without which God would not be God. What it means instead is that, since God's primordial nature is the measure of all intensity, God *reconciles* the world through the fluent reception of actual events in God's consequent nature (Maassen 1988; Christian 1967). It is in God's dipolar intertwining of primordial nature/consequent nature and permanence/flux that "the reconciliation of permanence and flux" happens (PR, 348).

The *second antithesis* understands God and world as *unity and multiplicity* for each other. One of the classical propositions of theism, after the manner of Plato, Plotinus, early Christianity, and ontotheology, is to interpret God as the unity for the world that releases from itself the multiplicity of the world. Whitehead does *not* take this path, since he understands the unity of the world as a characteristic feature of the process, a characteristic he locates in creativity. Nor does Whitehead—as in the first antithesis—speak about a relational opposition in which God might stand *for* the unity of the world; instead he speaks about an *opposition of mutual otherness.* Unity and multiplicity are attributed to *both processes*—God and world—in each instance differently. Whereas the multiplicity of the world expresses the universal nexus of the myriad events, God must appear as *one* event, as *one* concrescence (Cobb 1989). But as *event,* God's unity is conceived neither as the cause of multiplicity (creation-theological unity) nor as the goal of multiplicity (eschatological unity); rather theopoetically it indicates the reconciled unity of an everlasting concrescence *over against* the multiplicity of processes in the world. This interpretation is supported by the reversal of the second "thesis," which may initially seem absurd. Whereas the unity of the world is that of the *process* in which everything is connected processually in a relational universe, God *must* appear *as multiplicity.* In God's dipolar nature God embraces the creative multiplicity of all possible worlds (primordial nature) and the redeeming multiplicity of all events, societies, and nexuses that have already happened (consequent nature)—that is, the process itself (§39). Here God is *multiplicity* (PR, 350), a reconciling "society" of (saved) events (Conv., 9). That is God as the "kingdom of heaven" (PR, 350). Thus the shift in meaning: Whereas there is unity in the world commensurate with the category of the ultimate only as process of *différance,* in God there is always *différance* as (reconciled) *connex.*

The *third antithesis* speaks about God and world with respect to their *eminent actuality* for each other. Although Whitehead naturally understands God as actuality and the world process as a process of actualities, in what does the *eminence* of actuality consist? After Whitehead—commensurate with the first antithesis—rejects the ontotheological assumption of God's "eminent reality" over against the world (God as "supreme being") (SMW, 179; PR, 343; AI, 169; Cobb and Griffin 1976; Griffin 1989b), an event can be viewed as "eminently actual" *only* in the sense of its singularity and irreplaceableness within the process (Suchocki 1988). Here Whitehead does not speak about an opposition of mutual otherness (as in the first two antitheses), but about an opposition of *mutual comparison.* There is no "pair" of process characteristics that might constitute a contrast and then be differently attributed to God and world; there is only a *single* characteristic feature that is now differentiated *internally* itself, namely, as "actuality" over against "eminent actuality." *By comparison,* the "juxtaposed character" of eminence generates not nonactuality (an object), but a *different mode* of actuality. A singular event is "eminently actual" when viewed from the perspective of its *self-*creativity, which characterizes its singularity (Faber 1999a). By contrast, an event is "actual" when its concrescence comes into purview as a "growing *together,*" that is, as an act of reception of *other* events and objects (§11). Insofar as God can receive the world only as it has "created" or "made" itself through its own self-creativity, the world is "eminently actual" over against God. Insofar as God opens up or inaugurates the entire process as such for every event through the gift of the initial aim, God is "eminently actual" over against the world, and the world now appears in all its processes as the reception of its own creativity. Here the shift in meaning also becomes visible. The world is always first constituted in its eminence (self-creativity) through an *external act* in which it receives itself for its becoming. By contrast, in God's primordial subjectivity, the creation of the world is initially an *inner* act and thus *identical* with an act of God's self-creativity (§28). Given God's everlasting concrescence, God's reception of the world thus does *not* imply any constitution of Godself, but rather (precisely because such is not the case), in the *freedom* of God's consequent nature, a reconciling act through which the world itself is saved (Felt 1972) (§25).

The *fourth* and *fifth antitheses* each juxtapose God and the world's *immanence and transcendence* in their relation to each other. It is worth noting here that Whitehead articulates this opposition of immanence and transcendence neither in mutual otherness nor in mutual comparison, but as an opposition of *mutual relation*. That is, *neither* do immanence and transcendence constitute a "pair" of characteristic features attributed differently to God and world, *nor* does Whitehead compare God and world with respect to some inner difference involving immanence and transcendence, a difference through which God and world might be distinguished through comparison. Instead, these two antitheses view God and world in *mutual relation* with regard to the *same* immanence or transcendence. *Just as* God must be called immanent in the world, *so also* is the world immanent in God; and *just as* God transcends the world, *so also* does the world transcend God. These two antitheses thus say *nothing* about the relationship between immanence and transcendence (of God and the world)—a topic Whitehead addresses in his "theistic triad" in *Religion in the Making* (§26)—but *only* about the relationship between God and world with regard to their *mutual transcendence* and their *mutual immanence*. This mutuality with regard to common immanence and transcendence derives from the interwoven dipolar character of the creative process (§25) in all its phases (§30). God bequeaths to the world its ideality (here God is immanent in the world) and receives its materiality (here the world is immanent in God). The world bequeaths to God its actuality (here the world transcends God) and receives from God its potentiality (here God transcends the world) (Suchocki 1995). Within this *common creative process*, God and world are so interwoven that they continually are one in the other and yet simultaneously exceed or pass beyond each other (PR, 93f.) Within this process, immanence and transcendence are *basically the same* (PR, 88). By taking up the world into Godself (in God's consequent nature), God transcends the world with regard to that which it has become (and as which it has perished), to the extent that the world becomes immanent in God *through the same act*. Insofar as God (through God's primordial nature) bequeaths to the world the potentiality of its own becoming (the initial aim), the world in its concrete becoming transcends God to the extent that God becomes immanent in it *through the same act* that releases the world into self-creativity. But is there any shift of meaning in this opposition of mutual relation? Yes, there is; for while the world always transcends God only *in its singularity* (the privacy of its subjectivity) and (as subjectively perishing) is immanent in God, God is always *erotically immanent* and *transcendent in reconciliation* in the world *with regard to the whole* of the process (AI, 295f.)—and thereby always with respect to the universal process (§§28–29), its public meaning (§§26–27), and its eschatological peace (§39).

The *sixth antithesis* speaks about God and world *mutually creating* each other (Cobb 1974). It occupies a special position among the antitheses insofar as its implication must necessarily seem shocking to many interpreters: namely, that the world creates God! What this antithesis seems to be saying is that although God does indeed create the world, the world does the same thing with respect to God. Must the "world" not appear as a kind of "contra-God" here, and God at most as its demiurge (as in Plato's *Timaeus*) (Moltmann 1995)? Does one not run the risk here that the world has "its own origin," one *not* deriving from God and thus independent of God (Haught 1986)? Does one not ultimately end in a radical dualism that at the very least contradicts the Christian concept of creation, according to which God is the *sole* creator (Welker 1988), who creates the world through God's singular word of creation (*bara*) "out of nothing" (*creatio ex nihilo*) (Küng 1980; Scheffczyk 1984)? Many process theologians have indeed adopted the thesis that God does *not* create the world "out of nothing" (Ford 1983b; Cobb and Griffin 1976), and many are inclined to maintain that God must be understood more as the Platonic demiurge than as creator (Maassen 1991b). Quite apart, however, from however else one may respond to this notion (§35), *this particular* "creation-theological thesis" is neither compelling (§28) nor even implied by the sixth antithesis in any case. One must initially concede that this antithesis represents a *radical* opposition, to wit, that of *mutual production*, an opposition extending considerably further than all the others, precisely in expressing the *creation* of relationality, capacity for comparison, and otherness. Even more than in the case of the opposition of mutual relation (in the fourth and fifth antitheses), here the *same* creativity is asserted as applying to both God and the world with respect to their mutual relationship, and the relationship itself is understood as one of causal mutual production. Yet this sixth antithesis—like all the others—can be properly understood only against the background of the conversion of processes (§29). God's *self*-creativity is *simultaneously* the primordial act of creation of world, since God's primordial superjectivity is what first *constitutes* the world in its self-creativity (§29). The result is a significant shift with respect to the meaning of the "theses." Whereas God creates the world primordially, that is, unconditionally (without preconditions, yet relationally), the world creates God only insofar as it is taken up in reconciliation into God's everlasting concrescence (Suchocki 1988). God's creation of the world is a *liberating act of God,* whereas the world's creation of God is in its own turn *also* an *act of God* through which God *saves* the world.

All six antitheses address an *ultimate opposition*—that between God and world in their process toward each other. Whitehead understands this duality of "final opposites" as the *key* formulation of the "cosmological problem" that emerges when one penetrates through to its insoluble ultimates: "joy and sorrow, good and evil, disjunction and conjunction—that is to say, the many in one—flux and permanence, greatness and triviality, freedom and necessity" (PR, 341) (Faber 1997). At *this* juncture, God and world "embody the interpretation of the cosmological problem in terms of fundamental metaphysical doctrine as to the quality of creative origination, namely, conceptual appetition and physical realization" (PR, 341) (Beelitz 1991). The ultimate opposition between God and world is positioned within the context of the interpretation of the creative process as a dipolar oscillation, and precisely here becomes visible the *ultimate shift of meaning* that is at work in *all* these antitheses. Commensurate with the "conversion of processes," that which with respect to the world process is a *process of oscillation* (§§17–24), is transformed in relation to God into a *process of nondifference* (§§29–30). That which in the world requires a process of *différance* of flux and permanence happens in God as *reconciled movement* (Faber 2000e). That which in the world is variously a *receptive*, alternating movement of unity and multiplicity is reconciled in God as the *productive* movement of world creation (Faber 2002b). That which in the world diverges as differentiation in the ontological difference of event and creativity implies nondifferentiation (and primordial unity) in God (Faber 2001d). That which in the world appears as the primal rhythm of the oscillation of concrescence and transition, the creative movement of becoming and perishing, happens in God as God's reconciled movement—something about which theopoetics, at the boundary or utmost limits of language, can speak about only through paradoxes such as "primordial superjectivity" or "everlasting concrescence" (§29). All the unconventional "theses" contained in these six antitheses—that the world is unity and God multiplicity, that the world is permanent and God fluent, that the world is eminently actual in comparison with God, that the world is immanent in God and yet simultaneously transcends God, that the world creates God—can be read theopoetically as the expression of God's *reconciled movement of nondifference* (§26) in which all the differences of the world are sublated (for God) while yet being permitted (for the world) (§40).

(3) Following the six antitheses, the *ecological reminiscence* explicates the ultimate opposition between God and world as an *interprocess of creativity* (§§30, 32). In fact, however, the radical nature of the opposition of mutual production addressed by the sixth antithesis is already focusing on the theme of the *same* creativity in the mutual relation of God and world. It may thus be viewed as a logical progression when the creative process is now, as a whole, subjected to a cosmological interpretation in which God and world appear as a mutual movement *of* creativity (Van der Veken 1986; Garland 1983; Ford 1986). In a linguistic shift away from the two "subjects" of opposition—God and world—toward creativity itself as a "quasi subject" (in the universal singular) (§13), the cosmological happening as a whole can now be viewed, in its innermost essence, as a *creative process* whose core is *concrescence*, the *transformation of*

opposites into contrasts (PR, 24: Categories of Explanation XII–XVII). Several items in the ecological reminiscence are noteworthy in this regard: the looping of interpretive and ontological process; the central, almost "quasi-subjective" position of creativity itself "over against" the opposites of the process (God and world); and concrescence with its transformative character as the creative process's "super-feature."

Insofar as the *hermeneutical introduction* and the *ecological reminiscence* correspond, they attest the inner harmony of the interpretive process and the cosmological propositions of the antitheses. As is the case elsewhere in Whitehead (PR, 3f.; Kasprzik 1988), content and interpretation, reality and harmony mutually disclose each other. Whereas the interpretive process requires a transformation of opposites within the antitheses into a contrast, the *content* of these antitheses is nothing other than precisely that transformation of opposites into contrasts within the cosmological process. Through the looping between interpretation and content, the shift in the meaning of the "theses"—which alone discloses the *sense* of the antitheses as *contrast*—itself appears as a cosmic process subject to the same axioms it is interpreting as content. Here, at this important juncture, Whitehead is consistent in taking seriously the "unitexturality of reality," in which cognition and being imply the *same* kind of process, namely, creative concrescence (Wiehl 1990). Whereas the *hermeneutical introduction* summons to a creative concrescence of the antitheses, the *ecological reminiscence* interprets the cosmological ground for this very concrescence as the essence of the creative process itself.

Whitehead refers to the *essence of the creative process* in the oscillation, interpenetration, and mutual embrace of the processes of God and world as *creativity* (§16), the driving force, the motor, the meaning of the overall movement (Garland 1983; Ford 1983c; Neville 1983). Hence God and world appear as the embodiment of its essence, as fulfillment of its "supreme task," namely, to allow this creative swing itself to happen, to execute the primal rhythm of the process (concrescence and transition), and perpetually to render possible the dynamic of the open whole. This special status of creativity has prompted speculation. Some thinkers maintain it recalls the *monistic* (Spinozistic) interpretation of *Science and the Modern World* as "substantial activity" (SMW, 177ff.; Van der Veken 1986); others view the passage merely with a *linguistic description* of the process, a description Whitehead completed as a pluralistic (Leibnizian) interpretation of creativity once and for all in *Process and Reality* (Christian 1967). Insofar as creativity appears as a "quasi subject" that allegedly executes an *ontological act*—the fulfillment of the supreme task of the process—a monistic interpretation seems cogent (Bracken 1995; Wilcox 1986). But since Whitehead declares that creativity is *not* to be understood substantialistically and thus can be called nonabstract only in its instances (events), a pluralistic interpretation seems more appropriate (Bradley 1994) (§24). The theological implications of a monistic or pluralistic interpretation of creativity are similarly not inconsiderable. In the *monistic* interpretation, God appears as an attribute of creativity, the latter of which would then represent the actual subject of the process. In the *pluralistic* interpretation, creativity is defined merely as an expression of the self-creation of every process, thereby leaving room for God's primordial creativity (God's primordial superjectivity) (Pailin 1984; Bracken 1995).

Whitehead himself explicitly opposed both a monistic universe of the One (of either the Spinozistic or Bradleyan sort) and a pluralistic universe of multiple monads (Leibnizian universe) (PR, 9). In the particular form through which Whitehead overcomes *all* dualism (the Cartesian universe)—dualism to which in any case the monistic and pluralistic alternatives invariably remain obliged—pluralism and monism merge into a new configuration, namely, an *oscillation* of external and internal relations, externality and interiority, publicity and privacy, subject and object, concrescence and transition *into each other*. Creativity refers to this *creative oscillation* (Faber 2000e), which is why creativity may be interpreted neither monistic-substantialistically nor static-pluralistically, neither as "substance" (*natura naturans*) nor as a pure principle of description, but rather as the *ecological principle* of the process, as the swing of the final opposites into each other (joy and sorrow, good and evil, disjunction and conjunction, flux and permanence, greatness and triviality, freedom and necessity), as the swing of the ultimate characteristics of the process into each other (the thematic contrasts of permanence and flux, multiplicity and unity, immanence and transcendence, and actuality and creativity), and—finally—as the swing of the ultimate opposites into each other (God and world). Creativity accordingly constitutes neither a "super God" (Spinozistically) nor a (Leibnizian) plural principle of the many. Instead it designates the immanent process of self-creativity of every event—and as such designates both a *plural happening* (Bradley) and *an ontological act* (Bracken) transcending every happening. In this sense, creativity refers to the simultaneously *dynamic*-monistic (unifying and immanent) and *dynamic*-pluralistic (differentiating and transcendent) *interprocess between God and world*.

The ecological reminiscence then summarizes the six antitheses with respect to that which holds them together internally, namely, the essence of the creative process as *process of intercreativity*. No substantialist interpretation of creativity is reintroduced—it remains instead the principle of self-creativity, a principle becoming concrete *only* in its instances (PR, 9; Bradley 1994); nor is the "essence" of the process defined essentialistically, since creativity refers to the *pure activity of the creative swing itself* in its radical openness and determination through its "opposites," God and world (Faber 2000e). The *structure* of this intercreativity between God and world is the *swing of transformation*, in which the opposites themselves are transformed into a contrast. The *goal* of intercreativity is to fulfill what creativity means, namely, as the *principle of novelty* to lead the way into the *dynamic of intensity and harmony* (§16). "Neither God, nor the World, reaches static completion. Both are in the grip of the ultimate metaphysical ground, the creative advance into novelty. Either of them, God and the World, is the instrument of novelty for the other" (PR, 349).

The "quasi-substantialist" language concerning the "supreme task" and the "grip of the ultimate metaphysical ground" merely clarify the *ultimate nature* of the proposition concerning the meaning and structure of the creative swing—to be an ultimacy for which no further ground can be adduced than its own immanent meaningfulness. This is the reason why *concrescence* as the transformation of opposites into contrasts is designated as the "super-characteristic" of the creative swing; *there is no further ground* outside the process itself in which this swing and the creative transformation into contrasts take place (PR, 21). The ultimate push for novelty, defined as *contrast*, is the striving for intensity and harmony. The ultimate feature of the creative process is neither *chaos* (novelty without order and harmony) nor static *dualism* (order without intensity), but *transformation*. Insofar, however, as within the transformative process itself God does not act "just as" does the world process, instead affecting the world in a *primordially reconciled* fashion, God as the *superject of the creative swing* is the ultimate ground of intensity and harmony (§28). The ultimacy of the transformation of opposites into contrasts thus finds its final ground in *God's* superjectivity (of reconciled nondifference). Whitehead, emphasizing the *theopoetic* implication and context, describes this ultimacy as follows: "All the 'opposites' are elements in the nature of things, and are incorrigibly there. The concept of 'God' is the way in which we understand this incredible fact—that what cannot be, yet is" (PR, 350). In the conversion of processes, God—as the principle of concretion and as superject of creativity—in Whitehead's antitheses is the final creative, gracious-surprising, freely self-giving ground of structure and meaning of the creative process—so that what cannot be, yet may be.

§32. DIVINE MATRIX (THE CONTINUUM BETWEEN GOD AND WORLD)

[handwritten annotation: The creative mission of God + World]

God and world stand in reciprocity, that is, in an interprocess of creativity. The *same* creative relation obtains *between* God and world as an expression of precisely the *same common intercreativity* whereby their inner processes also "become" what they are (§31). This "between" with regard to God and world in their common "inter-creativity" is, as it were, the common "creative field" in which God and world "encounter" each other and *communicate*. And more yet, the *creative field* to a certain extent constitutes the *presupposition* of their creative self-realization *as* God and world. In this sense, *intercreativity* appears as the *creative matrix* describing the mutual "in-being" of God and world, their mutual immanence, such that this immanence is *essential* to both God and world beyond the distinction between "nature" and "volition" (§28). Since God's freedom is not sublated by God's relationality in the conversion, God as the superject of creativity also remains the *primordial superject of intercreativity*. Mutual immanence is grounded *in* God, in divine nondifference, and is to be understood as the *divine matrix of communication of all existence*. Yet this divine matrix is not simply "God," but rather the "wherein" of common communication. Hence the divine matrix can be considered only in the *theopoetic difference/nondifference* of God and creativity (§29). Among process theologians Joseph Bracken has undertaken the task of working out such a concept of a divine matrix (Bracken 1995).

The meaning of intercreativity as a "matrix" of all existence derives from the two fundamental aspects of creativity itself (§16)—the active aspect of *pure activity* and the receptive aspect of *pure receptivity*. As activity, creativity refers to the process of self-renewal, discontinuity and novelty, chaos and finality, a harmony that acquires meaning only through intensity. As receptivity, creativity refers, in contrast, to the process of communication, continuity and recollection, relationality amid all novelty, an intensity that acquires depth only in communicative harmony. Whitehead himself speaks about immanent and transcendent creativity. Whereas *immanent* creativity refers to the self-activity through which every event founds itself as its own ground (*causa sui*), *transcendent* creativity grounds the essential coherent nexus of every event with all others—either as the *causality* through which every new event's origination becomes immanent within it (extensive continuum), or as the *superjectivity* through which every event unfolds its agency in others (objective immortality) (Garland 1983). Both aspects disclose creativity as the ground of both spontaneity *and* communication within the universe (AI, 295).

What, in my perspective, is decisive for the understanding of intercreativity is the *coherent context* of spontaneity and communication against the backdrop of a critical reconstruction of their origin in the history of philosophy and its theological implications.

(1) Aristotelian philosophy (and with it various influential theologies) developed a distinction between a principle of activity and a principle of potentiality. Aristotle identifies the former with the form of substance (the active form of essence, *morphē*, soul) and the latter with matter (the substrate of form, *hylē*, body) (Böhme 1980; Rorty 1983). The consequences of this distinction, as is well known, ultimately led to substantialist and subjectivistic ontology, cosmology, and epistemology (Lucas 1990) (§§9–10). With respect to the grounds of the world Aristotle acknowledges a principle of potentiality as a boundary concept, his *materia prima*, the all-formable formless, but he must juxtapose a supreme principle of activity alongside it, the "unmoved mover" (*primus movens*) (Fetz 1981). An ontotheology inheres within this Aristotelian hylemorphism as a result of the ultimate implications of its substantialism, namely, God as supreme being, and "first matter" as the unformed nothingness from which God creates (Rorty 1995) (§§28, 35).

(2) Notwithstanding that this distinction between activity and potentiality can be viewed as a genuine accomplishment of Aristotelian philosophy (Fetz 1981), Plato was already familiar with such a distinction—as something far more fundamental and complex, but also hidden and mysterious. The notion of the "wherein" (*khora*) or "receptivity" (*hypodochē*) in the cosmology of his *Timaeus* refers to the "third type" of being (Derrida 2000), being neither form (idea) nor material happening (concrete actual event) as for Aristotle. It is instead formless and nonmaterial, the all-receptive mother of being (*mater*) (AI, 187; Kann

2001) (§§15–16). Yet as receptive ground of the world it too is juxtaposed with a hierarchy of ideas as whose highest embodiment the super-idea of the good reigns. Here one encounters the first intimations of the ontotheological distinction between a supreme formative principle and a principle of passivity (Maassen 1991b).

(3) The classic doctrine of "creation from nothing" (*creatio ex nihilo*) draws nourishment from this substantialist and ontotheological dualism (§35). Whereas the "wherein" (or "first matter") is declared to be a "nothing," God remains the supreme formative principle "from above" (May 1994; Keller 2003). Process theology criticizes the theological implications of this *ontotheological connex* of the principles activity/form and potentiality/passivity and reformulates it in a nonsubstantialist fashion under postmodern conditions through the notion of *theopoetic difference* (§28). Whitehead transforms the *ontotheological* connex into a *theopoetic* one by *identifying* in a nonsubstantialist fashion the two principles—which in ontotheological substantialism are *antagonistically* juxtaposed—within the *same* principle, namely, that of creativity, while yet allowing that creativity to be grounded in a nondifferent fashion in God. In an important disentanglement, this identification eliminates, on the one hand, the classical connex between activity and form, since for Whitehead forms (eternal objects) are not active, and, on the other, the equally unfortunate connex between matter and passivity, since for Whitehead events are active and causally efficacious (Fetz 1981). This in its own turn frees up space again for that "third," mysterious type, the "wherein," as the relation of events to one another, as the universal memory of the universe in which nothing is lost. Insofar, however, as it is now the *same* creativity that both recollects and prompts agency, the all-receptive "wherein" now no longer exhibits passivity, being now understood instead as the principle of pure activity. And the *theological consequences* here are significant, since if the two principle now no longer diverge, referring instead to the ground of the same happening within nondifference, then they must similarly no longer be *distributed* to God and world. Instead, Whitehead's fundamental insight is that as the *same* principle of spontaneous communicative activity they are vibrating *both* in the world *and* in God (Ford 1977b). Within theopoetic difference, creativity is disclosed as the *same ground of activity of both God and the world* (Bracken 1995), that is, as the *intercreativity between God and world* (§§30–31).

Under the conditions of universal relationality and the unitexturality of all reality as posited by process theology (§28), creativity must then be understood as the "essential relatedness of all things" (MG, 106), not as an "arrangement" (as formal "order"), but as the all-receptive and itself formless "wherein" (receptacle) of the concrete process (with its unforeseeable spontaneity). Here creativity refers not only to a principle of activity, but also to a "locus" or place (*khora*) of *communication* of all event happenings (AI, 134; Faber 2000e). It is the self-grounding and all-affective processual unity of the universe as an open whole, the unity of the world as the *basic nexus* (§24). And Whitehead does indeed define the basic nexus of all cosmic epochs (of this universe and all universes) as a *chaotic nexus* (§15) grounded not in some "order," but solely in the "general metaphysical obligation of mutual immanence"; Whitehead maintains that "in Platonic language, this is the function of belonging to a common Receptacle" (AI, 201). *Mutual immanence* refers to the chaotic nexus as the *broadest* coherent context of all event happenings, as the "medium of intercommunication" (AI, 134). *Within* the chaotic nexus itself, many cosmic epochs are possible, epochs shaped through "formal orders" in God's Logos for the creation of intensity and harmony and that develop organically as "unity" (cosmos). Theologically this means that because intercreativity implies communication, *including* that *in* God and *between* God and world, it constitutes a *divine matrix* or the *common medium of creative communication between God and world* (Figure 4).

Figure 4: The Divine Matrix of Universal Communication

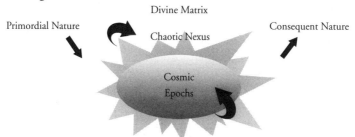

The divine matrix has not only *theological* consequences with respect to theopoetic difference, but also—beyond that—*cosmological* consequences with respect to ontological difference and interesting *religiophilosophical* and *deconstructionist* implications.

(1) The *theological consequence* involves theopoetic difference. The divine matrix basically allows the common "wherein" of communication between God and world to appear as a *common continuum* without either God disappearing within the world or the world within God. Nor do God and world merely obey the same principle of activity. Within theopoetic difference, it is possible to view God as the *source* of difference without wholly identifying God with God's inner principle of activity (Ford 1981; 1986). Instead, God as superject of intercreativity initially creates the divine matrix in a creative act *inwardly* that God may then freely, in a creative act, have overflow into the world *outwardly* (§§27–28). (a) The principle of activity is a principle of communication. Intercreativity thus might suggest understanding Godself as *inner-divine communication*. Bracken accordingly developed the divine matrix within the context of *inner-trinitarian communication* as the principle of God's communicative activity, of *God's Trinitarian nature* (Bracken 1978; 1981; 1985) (§34). Within God's own nature, God is the spontaneous communication of the three divine persons, whose matrix thus refers to the medium of communication—common to all three divine persons—as the principle of divine activity. Creativity is then God's nature as communication (Bracken 1997). (b) Through an act of *free* (but relational) creation directed outwardly, God creates a "wherein" of common communication

grounded by the *same* principle of activity (Bracken 1995) (§26). This common matrix, however, instead of being *identical* with inner-divine communication, opens up for the world a "locus" for its *own* spontaneity. In this sense, divine grace bequeaths self-creativity. (c) This divine matrix as intercreativity is not only God's principle of (self-)creativity and divine communication, but *also* the principle of communication between God and world and, *as such,* the principle of activity between all events within the world nexus. Divine grace bequeaths the world to itself as "nature," that is, as communication. Because, however, the divine matrix is *not* simply God, instead being mediated within the world through the *chaotic nexus,* creatures have the possibility of *refusing* communication, that is, they have the freedom to sin (§37). (d) In a fashion similar to Jürgen Moltmann's pneumatology, the divine matrix speaks about the Holy Spirit as the medium of the mutual immanence of God with and in the world (Moltmann 1993). And similar to the understanding of the Spirit of God in Pannenberg's Trinitarian theology, it represents God's nonrepresentational (insubstantial) nature (Pannenberg 1976) (§38). Within the communicative nondifference of the Spirit to the world, God appears as the *first self-giving foreshadowing* of its eschatological redemption (§39). (e) Just as in mystical theology, God appears in the world not only *as God* in personal encounter, but as the principle of activity *of the world itself;* God encounters the world as *its* "innermost," as *its* own mystical ground (Bracken 1995) (§40).

(2) The *cosmological consequence* of the divine matrix involves the world as "locus" of *communication.* Since the chaotic nexus is defined from the perspective of mutual immanence, Whitehead's cosmos cannot exhibit absolute chaos (§15), which would constitute solipsism (PR, 81, 92), the consequence of substantialism and its implications, namely, skepticism and relativism (Lotter 1990; Faber 2000e). To the contrary, the real world is (from a postconstructivist perspective) a *continuum of communication* of solidarity between all creatures and the perception or sensation of a world grounded in the causal nexus (PR, 71f.; Nobo 1987) (§41). In it, "chaos" is the *expression* of communication that takes place in living vibrancy, novelty, intensity, and freedom (§24). The chaotic nexus is thus a "communicative 'wherein,'" a "field" of creative communication in which all orders, structures, intensities, and harmonies freely develop (commensurate with causal and self-creative rules) (AI, 201; Loomer 1978b). *Every* individual nexus within the chaotic nexus creates its own field of communicative unity inwardly and a field of organic delimitation externally (Busch 1993). This organic constitution of the universe makes it possible to understand the evolutive phases of events and societies (§15) as well as the functions of orders (§19) as moments of *organic fields* (Bracken 2001). Within this organic and processual arrangement of mutually exclusive, overlapping, or inclusive fields, it is social and nonsocial event nexuses (societies or entirely living nexuses) that define an *evolutive* cosmos of degrees and stages of order, freedom, intensity, harmony, and complexity (Rust 1987).

Within a grand arc extending from quantum-physical fields to the "divine field," Bracken integrates the overall evolutive cosmos as a plethora of discontinuous organism forms, levels, and movements against the background of the continuity of communication; here events are the *centers* of field-energy, a field-effect of the overall field at a specific place (a quantum-physical organism of universal relationality). Societies represent an energy field as the "wherein" for each of the events emerging within their milieu, and themselves constitute a *center* for an environment of surrounding fields (Bracken 1989). Every organism *is* an "environment," an energy-field of its own existence, an "onto*genetic* field" of the *arising* of the events and event nexuses it structures (Nobo 1998); every organism is also, however, *in* an "environment" (or in many further fields) of surrounding organisms, in which an organism becomes precisely that which it is (Busch 1993). *All* fields, however, are grounded and positioned within the *divine* field (Bracken 1995). The divine matrix represents the broadest "environment" of all fields and their manifestations (events, nexuses, societies, and structures). In this sense the divine field constitutes a continuum of communication between God and world in which all that is past (extensive continuum and consequent nature) as well as all that is yet future (potentiality and primordial nature), everything structural (objects) as well as everything actual (prehensions, events, nexuses), everything receptive (the "wherein"), as well as everything creative (activity), merges into a processual whole of the universe as the adventure of God-world (Bracken 2001) (Figure 4).

(3) The *religiophilosophical implication* involves dialogue between religions. Within theopoetic difference, when such appears as the divine matrix, God is encountered both as *actuality*, that is, as event, as "entity," as concrete unity, as person and subject of communication, *and* as *activity*, as the ground of every actuality, as the pure activity of every event, as the ground of communication (§40). Because actuality and activity coincide *in God*, indeed, because God must be called the very source of the difference between actuality and activity (Faber 2002b), God is always simultaneously both person and nature, both concrete personal event of communication (or "in" communication) *and* ground of activity as communication (Faber 2001c). In the world itself, however, actuality and activity diverge in theopoetic difference; God is encountered "in" communication as personal event "over against" the world *and* as ground of the activity *of* the world as communication, that is, as divine matrix (Bracken 1995) (§§29–30).

Bracken engages this distinction for the sake of entering into dialogue not only with religions that have a personal concept of God, but also with those that instead acknowledge a "nonpersonal" ground such as *Tao, brahman,* or *nirvana.* The Buddhist notion of "ultimate reality"—emptiness, nothingness, *sunyata*— exhibits striking affinity with the divine matrix (Bracken 1995). An animated discussion continues with the Buddhist Kyoto school (Kitaro Nishida, Seiji Nishitani, Massao Abe) concerning the concept of "absolute nothingness" (Cobb 1982a; von Brück and Lai 1997). In understanding the concept of ultimate emptiness, Nishida adduces the notion of Plato's "place" as the communicative "wherein" of mutual emptying (Nishida 1999; Faber 2002d). Abe compares the Buddhist *sunyata*, absolute nothingness, with the Christian concept of *kenosis,* the self-emptying of God (Abe 1990), in which God is encountered not as a personal counterpart, but as ultimate reality (Abe 1985). This nonsubstantialist reality of self-emptying communication corresponds to the divine matrix (Cobb 1990; Faber 2002e), insofar as within the divine matrix God is encountered *not as* God, but as *incognito*, world oriented, kenotic, allowing for the possibility of an anonymous language of God. God appears within the divine matrix *empty of Godself* and as such *as pure communication* (Inada 1975), corresponding thus to the Mahayana Buddhist concept of "interdependent arising" (*pratitya samutpada*), or even to the concept of ultimate reality as "interdependent interpenetration without resistance" of Hua Yen Buddhism (Odin 1988). The limitless communicability of the divine matrix is indeed reflected in the identity of *nirvana* and the cycle of rebirth (*samsara*) within absolute emptiness (*sunyata*). Since communication "at the foundation of the world" is both pretemporal and prespatial in the divine matrix (space-time accordingly representing a certain, contingent type of order of the matrix), the divine matrix thus refers to the universal and unhindered relationality of all events and event nexuses (Inada 1975).

In Christian contexts as well, concepts of God's *secularity* arise that find a response in the conception of the divine matrix, for example Dietrich Bonhoeffer's religionless, secular God (1997), the nontheistic God of the God-is-dead theology of Thomas J. J. Altizer (1966), and the closely related idea of a divine "matrix of all being" that draws from the ecological Gaia-hypothesis of Rosemary Radford Ruether (1993; Moltmann 1995). In contradistinction to these conceptions, within the concept of the divine matrix as understood by process theology, God—notwithstanding God's being as ground—remains *personal* actuality (Faber 2000e). In a reverse fashion, however, and contra all ontotheological theism, God—notwithstanding God's being as person—in God's creative and simultaneously kenotic form remains the common communicative matrix of all existence. This notion includes God not only as God, but as the "between" and "wherein" that opens up communication for the community of all creatures; God as God *and* nothingness, as person *and* "self-less" communication, as counterpart *and* innermost element (§48)—from the perspective of theopoetic difference, God appears yet *sub contrario* as the ground of the world, the "ultimate reality" of the world as divine, the "divine element" of the world as its limitless communicability, and this communicability itself as (divinely generated) continuum of God and world. This continuum, however, does not allow an undeconstructed "natural theology" (as *theologia gloriae*) that ignores the question of theodicy (§45), being based instead on a *kenotic* moment of God's "receptive bestowal of space" (§35).

Even in the context of "nontheistic" process theologies (or those critical of theism), this conception of a divine matrix acquires comprehensive, mediative, and corrective significance (Ford 1977a; Mesle 1993; Hardwick 1996). Such can follow a relational but naturalistic concept of God that understands God as the interrelational universe as a whole, as in Bernard Loomer (§5), or as creative event of transformation beyond all personality (yet simultaneously grounding such personality), as in Henry Wieman (Reitz 1977) (§3), and can do so without succumbing to purely naturalistic implications (Cobb 1993). For on the one hand, God—notwithstanding God's kenotic form as matrix (activity)—remains personal reality (actuality); on the other, within theopoetic difference one avoids any final (supernaturalistic) dualism of the sort empirical and naturalistic process theology are denying, since *in God* activity and actuality are *non*different (§40), while yet representing God's creative difference *in the world* (Faber 2002b; 2001c; 2001a).

(4) Finally, the *deconstructive implication* of this conception of the divine matrix involves its critical significance within the framework of a postmodern criticism of the ontotheological idea of God. Following Heidegger's criticism of ontotheology and together with Derrida's deconstruction of Heidegger, process theology opposes *supernaturalism, substantialism,* and *logocentrism* in theology (Faber 2002b) (§13). The theopoetic (non)difference between God and creativity grounds this criticism with its understanding of the genuine conception of a divine matrix. What all three (supernaturalism, substantialism, and logocentrism) have in common is that they take recourse in an "ultimate essence" that—as supreme being or as ground of the world—is simply "given" in self-presence as being both relationless and wholly self-grounding and as such either allowing everything else (as derivative) to participate in itself or repressing and excluding such (§35).

Derrida directs his own criticism at the notion of a self-evident principle of "fulfilled presence"—be it the human being, God, consciousness, spirit, or being. Indeed, even Heidegger's ontological difference yet reminds Derrida of a "transcendent signified" beyond the context of all "signifieds." Only *différance* is allegedly "older" than ontological difference, since in and of itself it signifies nothing (no self-present being), but is merely the infinite interplay of differences (Welsch 1995). The ontotheological God of self-presence, rigidly fixed, and juxtaposed as the "highest reality" over against everything else, is removed from the interplay of differences. Here Derrida finds not more than the repressive element of logocentrism, which champions only a *single* Logos pure and independent from the relational interplay of differences. Logocentric thinking formulates itself in conceptual pairs of which one, as the primal concept, fulfills the pure whole of the pair in self-fulfillment and represses the other of itself; such binaries include, for example, being/nothingness, God/world, soul/body, unity/multiplicity—within which one member always appears as that which ought not be (Plato's *mē ōn*) (Welsch 1995). The theological consequence of such logocentrism is substantialism and supernaturalism. Self-present being grounds itself solely from within itself and the presence of all its moments, being otherwise related to nothing else; *the Other* escapes it (Faber 2000e; Faber 2002b). This in its own turn leads to a relationless concept of God, to pure self-presence, on the one hand, and a diminishment or reduction of the world—its multiplicity, its relational differences—to the meaningless play of its finite elements, on the other.

In averting ontotheology, Whitehead also avoids paying any "metaphysical compliments" to God (SMW, 179). His *six antitheses* show that rather than resolving the "ultimate opposites" logocentrically, he conversely maintains them as contrasts (§31). Bracken has demonstrated how Whitehead's *creativity* functions the same as Derrida's *différance*. Both relate to Plato's *khora* as an expression of the interplay of differences, interplay that cannot be summarized as an "entity" of any sort (a unity of being) and thereby self-presently extracted, as it were, from the process of differentiation. Rather than represent a "reality" (of any sort) or "subject" (concept, substantive), the *khora* instead is the *name* of the process of differentiation as such, of relationality toward the *Other*, of temporalization (temporal difference) and spatialization (heterogeneous nonidentity) itself. Neither is identified with "God" (Bracken 2002).

The acknowledgment of an intercreative divine matrix does not logocentrically "remove" God from the interplay of differences as a self-present, relationless, supernaturalistic "supreme being," for God *as matrix* does not represent a "being" or even an actuality (event, society, thing, something that "is," person, counterpart, something concrete) at all. Instead God *as matrix* refers to *pure activity*—as the underlying *principle of activity* of God and world, as the encompassing *principle of communication* in God, between God and world, and in the world (Bracken 1995). In this sense, God appears *distributively* "present" within the interplay of differences not as transcendent Logos, but as immanent communication (Faber 2002b). From the perspective of the divine matrix, God must now no longer be conceived ontotheologically as the "soul of the world" (as such still resonates in Hartshorne) (§§4, 26), as the logocentric unity of the (subsequently repressed) multiplicity of the world, which in and of itself would be nothing, but as the nonsupernaturalistic, nonsubstantialist, and nonlogocentric "between-field" of God and world. As the pure "wherein" of interdependent reference in this sense, God is thus the open space of *différance*, of essential relatedness toward *the Other*, the non-self-present.

In a theopoetics whose full articulation is yet outstanding, this divine matrix occupies a distinctly *forward-looking and promising position*. It represents the hitherto most succinct name for the vision of God as poet of the world in process theology. All the attributes of the God/world relationship—dipolarity, mutual immanence, the principle of concretion, superject of creativity, the creative phases, the contrasts of the six antitheses—are concentrated within it anew, acquiring thereby cosmic-theological power. As communicative ground, it facilitates understanding God as communication *in and of itself*. As the field of mutual immanence, it appears as the field of communication *between* God and world. As the "wherein," she is the *mother* of all being, becoming, and life. Here one can see how God creates simultaneously both relationally and freely: (a) "inwardly"—recalling Moltmann's reference to the cabalistic zimzum (God's self-limitation) (Moltmann 1993)—through God's "creating space" for nondivine creatures in common (and in participation in innerdivine) communication; (b) "outwardly" through God's distribution of creativity, freedom, and self-formation within the creative chaotic nexus, which Godself risks and shares (Faber 2000e; 2001a). That is, within this shared, common field, God participates in the world, senses it, takes it up (into his consequent nature), simultaneously guiding it poetically with the power of God's ideality (primordial nature). Within this common field, *all* creatures are coparticipants in common communication—including God—as "creations" of intercreativity (§§16, 31). God's *superjectivity* of intercreativity now reveals a kenotic God who surrenders Godself to the world, "objectifies" Godself for it, "hands" Godself to it—in the kenotic form of the chaotic nexus. Here one also finds the *fundamental structure* of a relational, communicative world revealed. *Basically* nothing is separated; everything is instead mutually immanent in ontological solidarity. *Basically* everything derives from something else and is oriented toward something else, everything positioned in *différance*, within the arc of becoming and perishing, subjectivity and superjectivity. *Basically* everything that happens is "self-less," implying self-loss amid self-acquisition, and the acquisition of self-identity in self-transcendence. *Basically* no order can logocentrically adequately render this process of differences. At the core of God's kenotic self-gift, however, everything is already sublated within the connex of the divine matrix, *différance* transforming itself into the *differential connex* of that which is differentiated, into a nexus of mutual immanence. Finally, Whitehead's *principle of concretion* acquires radical meaning in referring to God not as *event* (as such, God as concretion rather than principle), but as *matrix*, as the principle of creative communication, as the principle of universal concrescence, and as the principle of universal meaning—notwithstanding God's actuality as juxtaposed "counterpart" to the world (§27). It is from this perspective that the divine matrix—like theopoetic difference as such—acquires a soteriological meaning; universal harmony and abiding adventure intertwine into *soteriological différance* within the nexus of God and world (§39). Within the nondifference of God's concretion, and God as principle of concretion, God is the *poet of the matrix* who saves all differences *as* relations (in recollection, renewal, transformation).

V. Accesses

Visions of God

Within the history of reception of process theology itself, the view has become entrenched that since process theology is concerned primarily with cosmology, it fails to pay adequate attention to various theologically relevant questions and issues (Sayer 1999; Scheffczyk 1984). Is process theology actually metaphysics or theology? Does it restrict itself to Whitehead's ecological cosmology and its theological implications, or does it understand itself from the perspective of a specifically Christian self-understanding (Gilkey 1973; Ford 1973c; 1974)? Historically process theology's double origins have contributed to this "dipolarity" of its identity. On the one hand, it did indeed arise as philosophical theology in the wake of Whitehead's thought (Hartshorne) (Koch 1983). On the other hand, however, *genuine* theological concerns also drove its development (Shailer Mathews) (Welker 1992) (§§1–4). And indeed, the development of a specifically "Christian process theology" (Hanselmann and Swarat 1996) in the work of John Cobb confirms this fundamental dipolar structure. For he understands Christian theology as such first of all not as a Christian "theory of God," but (quite in the Thomistic sense) as a consideration of all relevant content from the perspective of Christian interest in the world. In that case, theology is actually a consideration of the "whole"—as Pannenberg puts it (Pannenberg 1996)—that is, an understanding of the whole "under the aspect of its relation to God" (*sub ratione Dei*), and is always theology of Christians *and* of human culture, always philosophy and a revelatory theology (Cobb 1996).

Process theology has indeed developed as Christian theology (Cousins 1971). Whitehead himself studied theology intensively for almost a decade, had a voluminous theological library, and was in conversation with Cardinal John Newman (Lowe 1985; Price 1954). His own cosmology refers essentially to a Christian understanding of God and grounds key intuitions by referencing them back to Jesus and his proclamation of a God of love (RM, 71ff.) as well as to early Christian theology of the Alexandrian and Antiochian schools (AI, 130, 167ff.). From its very origins in the *Social Gospel movement* (§1), process theology has understood itself as an untimely and critical but contemporary reformulation of the *biblical* divine impulse (Pittenger 1968; Cobb and Griffin 1976; Ford 1978). The center both of Whitehead's own doctrine of God and of process theology itself is occupied above all by a *soteriological impulse* and a *God of love* (Pittenger 1968; 1969; Faber 1999b). It is from the perspective of this "teleology" that it has addressed various specifically theological questions and issues and even produced varied dogmatic outlines (Ford 1970) (§7).

Within its own peculiar *access*, process theology tries to move toward a *genuine vision of* God for which process theology's specific doctrine of God is groundbreaking insofar as it acknowledges "three natures" in God (§33)—a position affecting all other issues, including the development of a doctrine of the Trinity (§34), a genuine theology of creation that considers the problem of power and love (§35), an independent theology of religion and doctrine of revelation based on God's concreteness (§36), specific doctrines of grace, sin, and redemption shaped by the interrelationality of the divine matrix (§37), a unique Christology that takes biblical wisdom (*Sophia*) as its point of departure in confronting the problem of Christ's divine-human person and Christ's pneumatological presence (§38), a genuine historical eschatology that addresses not only God's complex "ad-vent," but also the consummation of the world in an "eschatological peace" and the abiding adventure of the world (§39), and finally an implicit negative theology deriving from God's nondifference—addressing essentially the question of God's "existence" (§40).

§33. THREEFOLD CHARACTER (GOD'S RELATIONAL NATURE)

Process theology consistently speaks about God's dipolarity (§25), understanding the "dipolar God" terminologically as God in *two natures*—the primordial nature and the consequent nature (PR, 344). This notion of dipolarity is in fact so central (Wood 1986) that occasionally it is even formulated as an alternative to the doctrine of the Trinity (Ford 1975) (§34). Closer inspection, however, prompts us to question not only the apparent arrangement of the doctrine of dipolarity as such, but also its function as an alternative to the doctrine of the Trinity, since Whitehead himself acknowledges a "third nature" in God, namely, God's *superjectivity* or *superjective nature* (PR, 88). Discourse in process theology has paid little attention to this notion of God's "superjective nature," attributing little fundamental significance to it, perhaps because Whitehead himself really mentions it only once in *Process and Reality* (Ford 1973a). Yet from the perspective of the "third nature" the sense of the "two natures" is altered, insofar as God's dipolarity, rather than standing off unto itself, is now positioned within an *interpretive horizon* (§31).

Whitehead introduces the cohesive hermeneutical connection between God's dipolarity and the "third nature" within the context of his analysis of the *complex process structure* of events (§21). Events develop *two poles*, a physical and a mental pole (§§9, 25); they proceed in *three phases*, an initial physical phase of perception, a subsequent phase of mental cogitation, and a third phase of saturation (satisfaction), of consummation and termination of the process (§§16, 28), and ultimately the overall process of an event always happens within the *dual swing* of "two processes," the microcosmic process *within* events and the macrocosmic process *between* events, subjectivity and superjectivity, immanent and transcendent creativity (§§21, 23, 30). Whitehead summarizes this multilayered, overlapping process structure as a theory of the "threefold character" of an event: "the character 'given' for it by the past . . . the subjective character aimed at in its process of concrescence . . . [and] the superjective character . . . qualifying the transcendent creativity" (PR, 87). These *three characters* now also apply to the "primordial event" (Whitehead speaks of "primordial actual entity"), which is God (albeit acknowledging the *specific difference of God's processuality* over against every world process).

> In the case of the primordial actual entity, which is God, there is no past. Thus the ideal realization of conceptual feeling takes the precedence. God differs from other actual entities in the fact that Hume's principle, of the derivative character of conceptual feelings, does not hold for him. There is still, however, the same threefold character: (i) The "primordial nature" of God is the concrescence of a unity of conceptual feelings, including among their data all eternal objects. The concrescence is directed by the subjective aim, that the subjective forms of the feelings shall be such as to constitute the eternal objects into relevant lures of feeling severally appropriate for all realizable basic conditions. (ii) The "consequent nature" of God is the physical prehension by God of the actualities of the evolving universe. His primordial nature directs such perspectives of objectification that each novel actuality in the temporal world contributes such elements as it can to a realization in God free from inhibitions of intensity by reason of discordance. (iii) The "superjective nature" of God is the character of the pragmatic value of his specific satisfaction qualifying the transcendent creativity in the various temporal instances. (PR, 87f.)

Here God is an *event* to which initially the *same* process structure applies as to every other actual event, namely, that particular *threefold character* encompassing its internal and external, subjective and objective, physical and mental complexity. If God were understood only analogously to events (which is not Whitehead's intention), God would then constitute (in Hartshorne's sense) an event succession collected from the world (the event's given past) in its physical feeling (prehension), out of which it "grows together" through an integrative inner mental process and then, finally, becomes objective (for itself and the world) in the satisfaction of its concrescence in order to constitute a temporal, living, personal community of events in everlasting or perpetual swing (§25); this is the sense of God as "world soul" (Griffin 1992) (§4). Whitehead, however, whose perspective is that of the "conversion of processes," understands the divine process in *internal and external inversion* with respect to all nondivine processes (Suchocki 1988; Faber 2000e) (§30), which is why God's threefold character takes on a quite different appearance. Hume's principle that all knowledge comes from experience and that all being has a primarily physical constitution (Fetz 1981) does *not* apply to God, who in fact has *no* past and is *not* constituted from a world (PR, 344f.) (§28). What applies instead is a reversion of poles, according to which God's concrescence has a primarily ideal character that "commences" with the infinite valuation of potentials (of all possible worlds), that is, commences from "within itself" *without origin* (Ford 2000; Franklin 2000). Within God's *primordial nature,* God has no prevailing or given past, no "antecedent," and (for that reason) is *nontemporally eternal,* without end, without perishing, without limitation (PR, 7, 13, 31, 40, 46, 345) (Ford 1973b; Clarke 1984). Whitehead conceives the event "God" strictly *not* as a temporally ordered society of events (Conv., 9; Ford 1986c), but—commensurate with the conversion of processes—as *primordial and everlasting concrescence* (Suchocki 1975) (§29). As a little-recognized consequence, God's *consequent nature* also does not refer to *God's* concrescence out of the prehension of world (something the primordial nature already accomplishes in God), but to the freedom of the "universal concrescence" of world (§32), to its *redeemed transformation* into God guided, through God's caring concern, by intensity and harmony. God's consequent nature is God's orientation toward the world, in which God perceives and salvifically receives the world in order then to bequeath it to *itself* in caring concern. The *superjective nature,* however, refers to the *objectivization* of God's concrescence for the world and as such to the *consummation* (completion, satisfaction) of the salvific transformation of the world, insofar as such then *qualifies* the world (§30). In it, God *acts efficaciously* (as agent, creating and redeeming) by characterizing transcendent creativity and thereby determinatively shaping the divine matrix (§32). In this regard, Whitehead speaks—in an unequivocally bold fashion and at the very boundaries of his own categories—about God's *real efficacious power or agency* within the world, all the while also implying, however, that God's inner process takes place in the *reconciled nondifference* of subjectivity and superjectivity (§28), so that this "third nature," then, attests not only to God's superjectivity as being *primordial,* but thereby also being the *origin of God's dipolar subjectivity,* that is, to God's "primordiality" as such (for Godself and the world).

The consequence of God's threefold character, a character fully disclosed only in the conversion of processes, is that God's dipolarity speaks not about a God that "becomes god" after the fashion of actual events, but about a *divine process characterized by abundance*. The *sense* of this threefold character (and thus of God's integrated dipolarity) is *not* primarily metaphysical (Farmer 1997), but *theological* (Takeda and Cobb 1974). Because of this abundance of God's ineffable primordiality with its absence of origin, it is not that God must somehow "functionalize" the world (for God's process of becoming); that abundance instead is an expression of God's *gracious orientation toward the world* and of *overflowing, saving love* (Faber 2000e). Whitehead's doctrine of God can ultimately be understood as a critical attempt to provide justice anew for the *biblical God of love* contra inappropriate metaphysical intrusion. Contra ontotheological conceptions of God as a metaphysical principle, as transcendental moralist, or as arbitrary ruler of the world, Whitehead explicitly commits to the "Galilean origin of Christianity" (PR, 343) with its *God of love* (§35). In fact, God's threefold character can be explicated as *threefold love*—as an "economic process" of threefold world love and as "immanent threefold love" within the divine process.

Within the world process, the threefold world orientation of God's process of love has soteriological meaning. God's *primordial* nature is not simply the "locus" of all possible worlds, but rather their concrescence, that is, their free *valuation* (RM, 78; PR, 246f.; Ford 1983; Franklin 2000). God as *valuation process* establishes a *process of universal communication saturated by meaning*—relational, intensive, and harmonious. Thus does the primordial nature *act efficaciously* in the world as its unconditional, *serendipitous novelty* that constantly seeks intensity, and as its *lively order* that constantly strives for harmony, as its *tender, caring concern*, with which God simultaneously "lures" the world toward its own self-creativity ("lure for feeling," PR, 189) and "seduces" it toward God ("appetition," PR, 348). The primordial nature appears in the figure of *Eros*, as the gift and promise of infinite vivacity, as *abundance of the not-yet*, and as *salvific future* (AI, 198). The *consequent nature* is God's redeeming perception, effecting the process of transformative redemption of the world (Suchocki 1988). In it, God's central soteriological and eschatological acts boldly merge into a synthesis in which God appears as infinitely understanding patience, as the judge who valuates the world process, as unconditional reconciler, as sym-pathetic fellow sufferer with the world, and as the promise of immortality (Hosinski 1993). In it, the world process is *unfolded* and *released* for maximal intensity and then *enfolded* in reconciled unity. In the world, God appears through the consequent nature as a *communio universalis* (Faber 1992) in the guise of the "Adventure in the Universe as One" (AI, 295). Although the world's adventure is not thereby taken from it, its "unity" as communication, however, is salvifically assured. God's *superjective nature*, finally, refers to God's gracious and salvific activity in the world—but does so in a quite specific sense. In it God bequeaths to the world God's undivided affection for every event, doing such not only by opening up its future and positing it in community, but also by allowing it to *feel* the real world, that is, its past—

which it "re-collects" in its becoming—*as being reconciled in God* (Peters 1966). In the superjective nature, God appears as *concrete caring concern*. By holding up to the world its own reconciled past as a mirror of its becoming (RMn, 155), God provides *hope* for completion and consummation. Such becomes a primal motif not only of action for the world, but also of knowledge of self-transcendence *into* God (Faber 2000e and h).

In the *divine process* as well, the "three natures" similarly possess soteriological significance with respect to the *reception of the world* within God's threefold process of love. In God, God's *primordial nature* is the "locus" of divine concrescence and thus the infinite, unconditional, and primordially reconciled measure of all communication (concrescence). As such, it refers to God's *primordial wisdom* for the world (PR, 347). In God, God's *consequent nature* denotes the "locus" of the world within divine concrescence. The "apotheosis of the world," or its saving reception into God's "nature," represents a complex process of reconciliation including unconditional perception, judgment, and unfolding (releasing) transformation into divine communication (PR, 346). Hence in it, everything is without inhibition (discordance). By virtue of this comprehensively unfolding and enfolding reconciliation, God encounters the world in it as the *kingdom of heaven*, thereby bequeathing to its (physical) *resurrection* (Suchocki 1995). In a certain sense, however, the *superjective nature* is the also "locus" of unity—or even of origination of both the primordial nature and the consequent nature; for in the conversion of processes, God's everlasting concrescence "begins" *from* the primordial superjectivity which is God's "third nature" (Faber 1997). In God, it is God's own *reconciled* process and for that reason also God's primordial *power* of reconciliation.

These "three natures," however, should not be misconstrued as God's "threefold essence" (nor, certainly, as three essences or three gods). Whitehead is quite careful to designate this distinction of God's "characters/natures" not as a "real distinction"—such that God would actually be three gods—but as "distinction of reason" (PR, 344). Marjorie Suchocki speaks about a "functional" distinction within the *one* nature of God (Suchocki 1975). The "three natures" name the *one* "threefold character" of the event "God." On the one hand, this view maintains that the "three folds" are folds of the *same* nature of God; on the other, however, this "folded" quality, rather than multiply the "nature" of God instead *differentiates* it regarding its concrete *character*. That is, the "three natures" refer not to tritheism, but to God's *relational* nature, through which God simultaneously acquires both unity and difference (§26). Hence this distinction between the "three characters" in the one nature of God already implies a *disposition* for *Trinitarian language*; rather than assembling an arbitrary triad (Johnson 1963), it articulates a *coherent internal correlation* (PR, 344; Sayer 1999) (§34). With respect to the complex process structure (dipolarity, three phases, and subject/superject duality), the "three natures" can be explicated as a *coherent order of their swing into one another*.

(1) The "three natures" constitute a *structural* unity/difference insofar as they constitute an *inverse contrast*. From the dipolarity and subject/superject duality

of the process itself follows that what in the divine matrix comes to light as the ultimate opposition of all other oppositions, namely, that between God and world, is reflected (or even takes its point of departure) *in God* as the opposition between God's primordial nature and consequent nature (§34). Through an *inner-divine antithesis* analogous to the previously discussed "six antitheses," Whitehead boldly attributes the following oppositional features to God's dipolar nature. He maintains that God's primordial nature is "infinite," "devoid of all negative prehensions," "free," "complete," "primordial," "eternal," "actually deficient," and "unconscious." By contrast, God's consequent nature is allegedly "determined," "incomplete," "consequent," "everlasting," "fully actual," and "conscious" (PR, 345) (§25). As an antithesis, however, the inner-divine opposition must establish itself as a *creative process*, that is, transform itself into a *complex contrast of mutual otherness* (§31). Since, however, the dipolar opposition of physical and mental poles applies to *every* event, such transformation of poles into a contrast constitutes nothing other than the process of becoming itself, which precisely in its contrast attains the goal of satisfaction. By virtue of the *inversion* of processes, however, in God this dipolar contrast is grounded in God's primordial superjectivity—that is, precisely in the "third nature." It is the *origin* of the contrast within God and, as such, the *source* of the opposition between primordial nature and consequent nature (§28). The consequence is an *understanding* of the divine process *with Trinitarian inclinations*.

(a) The "third nature" sublates the "inner-divine antithesis" of oppositional features into an *innerdivine contrast* of primordial satisfaction. The seeming incompleteness of the two natures—the deficient actuality and unconsciousness of the primordial nature, the determined quality and incompleteness of the consequent nature—has a different meaning in God, functioning now in the abundance of the "third nature" to express the *essential relationality* of these other natures. God's primordial nature, independent of the world, is thus initially also "unconscious" *of that world* (not subconscious in the fashion of animals); it is not "completely actual" (Whitehead uses the expression "actually deficient") (PR, 345), since actuality applies to the *entire* threefold divine process (PR, 344f.; Hosinski 1993). In its own turn, God's consequent nature is "incomplete," because, without ever having been in need, it "grows" or "increases" in actual events (PR, 12, 346); it is determined (by the world) because it lets itself be determined (Felt 1974), not because it in any way "needs" the world for its own becoming (Franklin 2000).

(b) In God's "third nature," dipolarity and subject/superject duality is sublated into a Trinitarian form. The "third nature" now appears as the *origin of the divine process* and as such is the *ground of the difference* between primordial nature and consequent nature as well as of its *efficacious power* internally (for God) and externally (for creation). Whitehead already attributes "objective immortality" and thus objective efficacious power to *both* natures (PR, 32); God's superjective efficacious power *within the world* is at once also the origin of the first two natures *inwardly* and *implements itself*—both inwardly and outwardly—in *both* modes. Whereas the world process happens within the difference of opposites and within the arc of tension of the process itself, God's inverse process manifests itself in the "third nature" as the *reconciled nondifference* of opposition, relation, and efficacious power both inwardly and outwardly (§29–31).

(2) The "three natures" constitute *processual* unity/difference insofar as they are engaged in a *swing into one another,* a swing in connection with which each aspect of the threefold character has an irreplaceable function. That is, they in fact constitute a coherent correlation of *mutual immanence,* rather than being merely fortuitously juxtaposed (Lansing 1973). Whitehead understands this correlation as the *center of the Christian doctrine of the Trinity.* In it, the "three natures" exhibit an essentially *Trinitarian inclination.*

(a) The "three natures" are arranged in a coherent unity because they *transgress into one another* within the three phases of the process itself. The ecological swing of the "three natures" into each other is revealed especially in the four phases of the creative process (§30), in which the world process and divine process conversely interpenetrate each other. Within the ecological interpenetration in the world process, physicality, mentality, and satisfaction "follow" one another. In the superjectivity of the satisfied event, it then again becomes the causal point of departure for the first phase of new events. In God's *converse* process, however, the source of the process is *satisfaction,* that is, God's superjective nature, from which originates God's everlasting concrescence as borne by God's primordial nature. This in its own turn develops as *inclusive actuality* (Ford 1988), as the reception of the world's multiplicity into the consequent nature (PR, 345f.) (§29). The everlasting satisfaction of this physical reception of the world in God, however, is nothing other than God's *primordial superjectivity,* so that the "third nature"—which is actually the *first* nature—arcs back into the primordiality of the primordial nature.

(b) The "three natures" constitute a coherent unity because they *mutually presuppose* one another. On the one hand, the primordiality of the primordial nature is indeed unconditional insofar as it expresses God's *lack* of presupposition (insofar as God does not constitute Godself from any world). In order to fulfill what its essence is, however, namely, in wisdom to bequeath the potentialities—it nonetheless *presupposes,* within the concrete process, that God knows in which (past) context new potentialities are to become important either in breaking forth, renewing, or ordering. In this sense, the primordial nature presupposes the consequent nature. In a reverse fashion, the consequent nature, if it is to fulfill its own essence—namely, to save the world into God in judgment and transformation—*needs* the primordial nature as the standard for judgment and for the visionary goal of transformation (PR, 346) (Lansing 1973). The situation is more difficult with respect to the "third nature." According to process theology oriented toward Hartshorne, which thinks in terms of event analogy, there can be only a saturation of God if God perishes in God's individual events and ceases, being reconstituted in ever new events. Here the first two natures of every "God event" would be completed in the "third nature" such that the latter would presuppose the two polar natures. In a reverse fashion, however, the polar natures would presuppose God's superjectivity only if God were a "nexus of events," that is, only if each prevailing God event that has perished would also, superjectively, affect the coming dipolar God event (Lansing 1973). Following a conversion of processes, however, everything merges coherently into a unity of mutual presupposition (Suchocki 1975). In this case, the polar natures necessarily presuppose God's superjective nature insofar as they emerge from it. The superjective nature in its own turn presupposes the polar natures insofar as it takes place only within their difference, as superject *of* the difference between primordial nature and consequent nature.

Even though within the context of theopoetics God's "three natures" have primarily soteriological and Trinitarian-theological rather than metaphysical significance, their role within a *critique of metaphysics* should not be overlooked (McCool 1988). The doctrine of the "three natures" *radically* affects the philosophical implications of the understanding of God.

(1) The classic paradigm of tradition viewed God as "pure act" (*actus purus*), to which no possibilities might be attributed that were not already actualized. Otherwise one would have to assume that God has unrealized possibilities that God must yet realize, an assumption implying incompleteness, changeability, and dependency on God's part. Potentiality was thus viewed as a "deficiency of being," which cannot be attributed to God (Faber 1995b). The *primordial nature*, however, provides a place within God for such potential, a place where it may be precisely what it is *as such*, namely, novelty, future, order, structure, vision. The primordial nature unites all possible worlds as the living concrescence of divine harmony and all relationality as valuable and meaningful (Ford 1977d). In the process paradigm, God is understood not as a "fulfilled act" incapable of being enriched or augmented by anything "outside itself"—already "being" everything it could "become"—but as an "act" that "provides space," an act that *withdraws* in bequeathing possibility (§§28, 35). God's act is at once both chaotic and relational. Within the primordial nature, the primordial act of being is not understood as an autocratic act of self-sufficient abundance. Here—as later in Tillich as well—the "*actus purus*" is understood as an act of *creative communication* (Moltmann 1995; Ford 1984b).

(2) According to the classical doctrine of God that views God's perfection as lacking all potentiality, God could subsequently not receive anything that had not already had God wholly as its own point of departure (Faber 1995b). The notion of God's satiation allowed only for a world of God's incomplete *expression*, never a *perception* of a world that might realize its *own* creativity. God was both "unreceptive of world" and "incapable of suffering." The "unmoved mover" was an *apathic* God (Fiddes 1988). By contrast, the process paradigm understands God as a communicative God who can be enriched by the world. God's act of "providing space" creates a world to which God also "listens." God is now a *sym-pathetic* God capable of suffering and indeed of accompanying the world and of allowing the world to bequeath self-creativity to God (Suchocki 1995). The *consequent nature* manifests a God who is profoundly moved, a God who

receives rather than rules, who unconditionally loves rather than implements standards. "Love neither rules, nor is it unmoved" (PR, 343). God's *primal act* is now understood not in an archetypal sense as a "moving beyond" outwardly, but rather as a "growing together" *inwardly*, not as a transcending act *ad extra*, but as a *receptive* act *ad intra* (Ford 1977d). God's creative act is thus essentially communicative and relational (§28).

(3) In a reverse of the doctrine of the "unmoved mover," a doctrine of the "only-moved God" developed (Hartshorne and Rees 1976). The concept of God from tradition—in the sense of the Kantian differentiation between analysis and synthesis—was *analytical*, viewing the world (as "predicate") as being already contained in the concept of God (as "subject"). Hence it could not really mean anything new; it could only mean that which God let it be. Even Leibniz still understood all movement of the world as ultimately representing the unfolding or development of concepts, that is, as "pre-established harmony" lacking causality and adventure (Kann 2001). Although Hegel was indeed able to conceive movement and concept simultaneously through his dialectic of negation, he ultimately dissolved movement also into the "pure concept" (Wiehl 1986; Lucas and Braeckmann 1990). By contrast, the *synthetic* concept of God transformed God into a *result* of the world movement in the sense that God arises from the world. In contrast to tradition, God now appeared as a "God becoming (God)," as a temporal God (Alexander 1920), as a becoming being out of the course of the All (Rorty 1994), as a being coalescing from the world (Hartshorne 1991). Whitehead's notion of the *superjective nature* (in inversion and conversion) took a path different from both these views. In contradistinction to "analysis" and "synthesis," I refer to this path as *reverse synthesis* deriving from God's *inverse concrescence* (§29). Over against a synthetic concept of God, which results from a concrescence of God, God's *inverse superjectivity* is not a synthesis growing out of God's experience of world. On the other hand, God's inverse concrescence is also not a form of analysis, no mere development or unfolding of implications, but genuine inclusion, a process of growth from the world. Hence God is neither an autocratic dictator of a world whose conditions and appearance would a priori be implications of God, nor an epiphenomenon of the becoming world. Instead, God manifests Godself as world-sensitive affection that provides space and is capable of receiving without thereby becoming in need. Relationally, God is understood as God in abundance who is *capable* of redeeming and whose redemption dictates *nothing*.

The theopoetic doctrine of God's "threefold character" does not imply *any* ontotheology of autocratic presence of some supreme being or self-present grounding of the world (Welsch 1995). On the contrary, in all three characters, God is positioned as both *future* and *past* for the world within a "tensed present," as both *trace* and *brace* (Faber 2000e; Faber 2002b) (§25). In the primordial nature, God was already present at the locus of the future emergence of *every* event, even before it began its process of becoming; and when it does enter that process of becoming, God is then but the trace of its origination. The consequent nature transforms the future of past events as *past* into God's presence. The superjective nature recalls the past of events as a saved past, and bequeaths it in each new event's presence as the possibility, hope, and radiance of its future. From the perspective of the deconstruction of a God of fulfilled self-presence, this God of the "three natures" appears as a *relational* God of *différance*, and as such as an *eschatological* God, as the promise of "threefold future." It is precisely on this basis that process theology now develops its relational doctrine of *creative communication* and *communicative creativity*.

§34. MUTUAL IMMANENCE (TRINITARIAN COMMUNICATION)

The doctrine of the Trinity was never an easy topic for process theologians (Ford 1975). Even though this theme has counted more among the variables than the constants of process theology (Faber 2000e), Christian process theologians have consistently addressed it, even when its interpretation took non-Trinitarian directions (Bracken 1978; 1981). The result has been that within the process paradigm as such, what at first glance seems like a bewildering variety of initiatives toward a Trinitarian theology emerges (Bracken and Suchocki 1997). Implicit and explicit Trinitarian conceptions emerged against the backdrop both of an "entitative" understanding of God (God as *one* event) and a "nexic" understanding (God as a society of events). In their attempts to conceive a Trinitarian theology, models of process theology generally also do not seek simple triadic conceptions for the sake of following externally (at least) the Christian model. Instead they try to articulate a genuinely Trinitarian concept of God. Typologically, (at least) the following five Trinitarian models of process theology can be distinguished.

Model I: the Trinity as *creative dipolarity*. Unlike their teacher Hartshorne, Cobb and Griffin tried to provide an appropriate place for the doctrine of the Trinity in the discourse of process theology, albeit with a not inconsiderable critical edge (Cobb and Griffin 1976; Bracken and Suchocki 1997). Their model is based on process theology's fundamental assumption of God's creative dipolarity (§33). Every event concresces in dipolar self-creativity. The same holds true for God, and in this case also in the original sense; God as concrescence in the primordial nature and consequent nature is the primal implementation of creativity in God. Within an intensive interpenetration of economic (world-oriented) and immanent (God-related) Trinity, the primordial nature refers to God's immanence in the world, to the divine Logos, the Son. By contrast, the consequent nature refers to the world's immanence in God, to God's Spirit. God's self-creativity functions in the place of the Father as the primal divine ground and act of the dipolar nature. In this sense, the "three persons" are positioned *within God* (immanent Trinity) in a relationship of mutual determination. Within the two natures, the creativity that is otherwise without origin acquires its initial embodiment (without which it—creativity—would remain merely a pure abstraction from the process rather than something concrete); and the two natures then characterize that creativity in a primordial fashion such that it—and with it the two natures—is also capable of agency in the world. *In the world* (economic Trinity), the "three persons" act as the creative origin of all creativity, as creative and responsive love (Cobb and Griffin 1976). Through the Logos, the Son, the primordial (inner-divine) character (of creativity), that is, the primordial nature, overflows into the inexhaustible variety of creatures and affects the world as *creative love*. Within the perception and reception of the world in God, in the Spirit of God, God's *responsive love* acts as accompanying, cosuffering, but also *life-giving power* (Cobb 1997; Lee 1997). Here Griffin's conception is directed critically against the notion of a supernaturalistic God who merely produces (and is responsible for) everything, since the dipolar God acts with *receptive creativity* (Griffin 1997). Furthermore, Cobb's understanding of God's creative dipolarity deconstructs the repressive power of classical conceptions of the Trinity (Cobb 1997). Contra the notion of an almighty Father or omnipotent creator who determines everything, the above understanding of creativity by default prompts the powerful, monarchical principle virtually to disappear from the Trinity altogether (Ford 1975). One of the objections to this model has been that it does not really articulate a "genuine" Trinity, that it is actually a "binitarian" model (Tracy 1990), leaving the Father for all practical purposes out of the picture (Schulte 1986; Koch 1983) or at least not conceiving him as an "actuality" ("entity") like the Son and Spirit (Cobb and Griffin 1976). In consequence, critics have turned Cobb and Griffin's initiative around and taken it instead as proof that their peculiar heterodox doctrines are incapable of developing any genuine Trinitarian understanding of person (Scheffczyk 1984). On the other hand, in the light of *différance* such creativity (commensurate with Derrida's view) proves to be "older," because it relieves the ontotheological model of the Father as "principle without principle" (*principium sine principio*) of its political innocence (Faber 1997). The world-sensitive character of "binitarian," creative-responsive love merely reflects God's biblical modes of immanence in the word (*dabar/logos*) and spirit (*ruach/pneuma*). This model's pronounced salvific-economical cast enables it to develop an eminently critical potential insofar as its ultimate principle is not dominion (pantocracy) at all, but noncoercive tenderness (creativity) (Lee 1997) (§35).

Model II: the Trinity as *complex dipolarity*. Ford (1997) and Suchocki (1995) undertook to articulate further distinctions to counter the structural weaknesses of the dipolar Trinitarian construction without abandoning its critical edge. To facilitate a more coherent understanding of the immanent Trinity, they interpreted the act of the event "God" in a more pronounced fashion as a threefold act, though without abandoning dipolarity as the basis. Although with respect to the *immanent Trinity* both—like Cobb and Griffin—identify God's Spirit with the consequent nature, they do differentiate the Father and Son *within* God's primordial nature. Ford identifies two of its functions as Father and Son. The "primordial envisagement" as primal act of God's concrescence, in which the primordial nature orders (and in a certain sense creates) all potentialities, corresponds to the origin of the Trinity (the Father). By contrast, the "entirety of the primordial nature" corresponds to the Logos, the creative order in God and the world (Ford 1975). Suchocki by contrast assigns the "amorphous realm of possibilities," which is void of both order and form, to the Father, and the "primordial vision" generated from it with its "primordial character" to the Logos/Son (Suchocki 1995). Both Cobb and Suchocki view the Father as the groundless beginning—Ford more specifically as an expression of the primordial will, Suchocki as an expression of amorphous, formless (or preformal) nature (as *principium operationis*)—and the Son as the principle of order, as Logos (Bracken 1978; 1981). With respect to the *economic Trinity*, Ford and Suchocki differentiate the Son and Spirit within the intertwining of primordial and consequent nature. Ford addresses especially the question of the *contingent nature* of the Trinity in the juxtaposition of Father and Son. Counter to a "necessary relationship" of the sort inhering within inner-Trinitarian speculation, the economic Trinity first appears only in connection with the actual economy, that is, in the history of Israel and Christianity. The Father refers to the God of Israel, the Son to the Christ event. The economic Trinity represents the relationship between Judaism and Christianity, elevating both to the status of coprinciples in God. That is, without Christ there is no Trinity, but without the God of Israel there is similarly no Trinity. The Spirit appears in the world as the *inverse* consequent nature and represents an aspect of the primordial nature. Within a unique intertwining of Son and Spirit within the economy of salvation—an intertwining also biblically attested—God acts efficaciously within the Spirit in events (§30) insofar as the Son bequeaths to them their initial aim (§38) (1997). It is precisely this function of God's Spirit within the economy of salvation that interests Suchocki (1995). She draws on Cobb's theory of conceiving the Spirit as the operation of the consequent nature that both perceives and vivifies the world (1997) but makes it clear that only if God's consequent nature is also *active* in the world (not simply taking the world up into God) can it be addressed as the Spirit of God. Since Cobb, however, attributes this activity to the primordial nature, the Logos, the distinction between God's agency in Christ (Son) and in us all (Spirit) must remain *undifferentiated* within the world. Hence Suchocki understands God's Spirit as the creative transformation that takes place in every event when it forms itself according to the initial aim bequeathed to it by the Logos (Suchocki 1995; 1997). Ford and Suchocki thus succeed in portraying the specific "functions" of the three persons in a fashion differentiating them in both an inner-Trinitarian and a salvific-economical perspective (Faber 2000e). By understanding the Trinity wholly from the perspective of God's actuality (concrescence), they enable creativity (activity) to be associated with God's nature, God's act-principle (*principium operationis*).

Model III: Trinity as *creative binarity* (of God and world). Whereas the dipolar Trinitarian concepts focus on inner-Trinitarian distinctions, the binary concept tries to think wholly from the perspective of the *economy of salvation*, taking advantage of the fact that the ultimate oppositions within the cosmology (*oikonomia*) and the "inner-divine antithesis" of the dual nature in God (*theologia*) are mutually translatable (§33). Lawrence Wilmot and (in concurrence with him) Joseph Bracken thus interpret the triad "world," "God," and "creativity" as formulated in the "ecological reminiscence" (§31) as the genuine locus of a processive theological doctrine of the Trinity (Wilmot 1979; Bracken 1981). Wilmot believes that in his later work, Whitehead, who in *Adventures in Ideas* addressed the topic of Trinitarian theology in antiquity—implicitly mediated by the Neoplatonic/Plotinian triad of the One (*hen*), spirit (*pneuma*), and world soul (*psychē*)— tended toward an explicitly Trinitarian economy (Wilmot 1979). According to Bracken, in the context of the economy of salvation, *God* (the Father, the origin, the unity of the "three [inner-divine] natures") and *world* (the "society of the divine Son" with all finite *events of all moments* [Bracken 1981, 89f.], that is, the world within the creative Logos) communicate *in mutual creativity* such that within this unifying relation of Father and Son in their "oppositional contrast" the world is sublated by their salvific mediation (Bracken 1981, 91). Here the Trinity, without disappearing into the world process, becomes the salvific economic structure for the overall process and (in a fashion reminiscent of the theology of the church fathers) becomes *soteriologically* mediated communication between God and world that yet leaves space for an inner-Trinitarian grounding (of the world in God) (Moltmann 1993).

Model IV: Trinity as *ultimate category*. In a rather cryptic remark, Günter Holl points out how in Whitehead's "category of the ultimate" the "Christian doctrine of the Trinity takes on a secularized form" (PRd, 644). If this idea possessed *structural significance*, it would anchor the doctrine of the Trinity at the very *center* of Whiteheadian thought and take it (reminiscent of Hegel) as the very *principle* of his thinking. In that case, the innermost motor of the creative process, namely, the creative swing of unity and multiplicity, would constitute both structurally and processually the *vestigium trinitatis* of process theology. This does indeed obtain an eminent, coherent correlation between the *category of the ultimate* (§§2, 16, 24) and the *ecological reminiscence* (§31). Suchocki remarks that Whitehead firstly views the "ecological Trinity" of the ecological reminiscence, namely, "God," "world," and "creativity" immediately as correlated in the form of "creator," "creature," and "creativity"; that is, they have no meaning independent of one another (PR, 225) and that secondly their creative swing is nothing other than a "restatement of the Category of the Ultimate (one, many, and creativity)" (Suchocki 1988, 168 n. 9). In this sense, there is indeed a correspondence between Father/God/unity/creator, Son/world/multiplicity/creature, and Spirit/creativity/swing. This particular initiative toward a doctrine of the Trinity of process theology would ground the salvific-economic meaning of "creative binarity," that is, of the "ecological Trinity," even as far as within the creative principle itself; similarly, and in a reverse fashion, it would recognize the creative principle of Whitehead's ecological cosmology as a *Trinitarian nucleus* of the overall creative process (in the world, between God and world, and in God). On this view, creative principle and ecology would mediate each other within the same basic Trinitarian form and the Trinity itself would be universally efficacious, constituting the innermost essence of all concrete processes (Faber 1997).

Model V: Trinity as *society*. Hartshorne interprets God as a society of God-events, that is, as a "person," as a "personally organized society" that gathers all of God's physical prehensions of the world (consequent nature) into the concrete *personal character* of God's mental prehensions (primordial nature) (§§22, 25). The world process appears as God's body and the divine character as the world soul. Unlike the severe criticism Ford levels against Hartshorne's societal model of God, which allegedly transforms God into a temporal being (Ford 1986c), Bracken constructively develops Hartshorne's initiative into a "social model" of the Trinity (Bracken 1985; 1997), articulating three transformative moments. (a) Bracken maintains that process theology's traditional reference to God's dipolar nature or, as outlined above, to the "third nature," *insufficiently* grounds Trinitarian theology, insofar as in the light of tradition, God's "natures" in fact run counter to the features attributed to the divine persons, sooner referring—commensurate with the expression "nature"—to aspects of the one essence of God than to three "persons" (Bracken 1981). And the various models do indeed intersect and overlap in attributing the "natures" to the divine persons. The Father as creativity can be an aspect of the primordial nature. The Son expresses functions of the primordial or consequent nature. The Spirit can be associated with both natures, depending on whether the function is immanent or economic, or even with creativity. (b) Since no *three* persons can be expressed in a *single* event, Bracken—contra Whitehead—adopts Hartshorne's understanding of the "divine person" as a *successively organized society* of God-events, though he does postulate—commensurate with Christian revelation—*three* such "persons." God is then a society consisting of three personally organized societies—Father, Son, and Spirit (Bracken 1985). Here the philosophical conception would not really have (speculatively) *reconstructed* God's actual revelation as Trinity according to reason (as do the other speculative constructions), it being instead merely *employed* or *applied*; the social dimensions of the relationships of the divine persons, their characteristic features, and their "subjective" difference would be maintained (Bracken 1978). (c) Bracken, however, must rethink the unity of the divine being if he is to counter the criticism of his "social model," leveled not only by followers of Hartshorne, who allege that his model tends arbitrarily to duplicate or multiply the person of God, thereby expanding Hartshorne's concept into tritheism (Cobb), but also by followers of Whitehead, who allege that his model merely multiplies the temporal dissolution of God into the world process (Suchocki). He counters by conceiving creativity as the *intersubjective* nature of the three personal societies (Bracken 1997) and the latter as divine matrix (Bracken 1995) (§32), enabling him to associate the *entire processual coherent correlation* of act and form, immanence and transcendence, and creative and soteriological dimensions as expressed in the "three natures" *and* in creativity entirely with the divine *nature*. By contrast, the three *persons*—freed from these "functions" and *characteristically* differentiated from one another—now *embody* this one nature of God (Bracken 1981). Finally, Bracken is now able to formulate a unity of creator and creature as continuity within the *same* nature, albeit in gracious difference, neither dissolving

God and world one into the other nor understanding the world as a necessary emanation of God (Bracken 2001). Bracken's model is a model of *Trinitarian perichoresis* that is at once both complex and communicative, integrating both immanent and economic Trinity, and is moreover a model that broadly communicates with tradition (Moltmann 1994; Faber 1995).

If amid these multiple initiatives one now looks for explicit Trinitarian connotations in Whitehead's own work, one quite specific context proves particularly fruitful. *Religion in the Making* uses Trinitarian language to protect God's *essential relationality* against one-sided intrusions by notions of God's immanence and transcendence (RM, 66ff.) (§26). In *Adventures of Ideas*, Whitehead adduces the Trinitarian doctrine of antiquity (particularly of the Alexandrian school) in grounding this essential relationality universally as *mutual immanence* (AI, 168f.). "Essential relationality" and "mutual immanence" mutually translate each other and merge into a *Trinitarian perichoresis* (§26). More than process theologians have perhaps realized, Trinitarian thinking touches the very roots of ecological cosmology, while in a reverse fashion—revealed as its innermost source of movement—it prompts a genuine Christian reconstruction of its various issues and concerns.

"Mutual immanence" expresses the essential coherent nexus of everything within the process, the ecological interpenetration and universal relationality of the process itself. It is absolutely central to Whitehead's entire cosmology, insofar as it enables Whitehead critically to unhinge both substantialism and subjectivism as well as all nonprocessual essentialism (Faber 2000e). The question framing Whitehead's philosophical project is *how something may be conceived as being "in" something else* (Hampe 1990). His response is his event theory, according to which everything mutually inheres within everything else insofar as it constitutes itself from the other, growing "together" (concrescing) self-creatively from the other in a dipolar fashion (physically and mentally), and, after it has "become," it then perishes and enters superjectively into the becoming of others (§26). In Christian Trinitarian theology, Whitehead discovers this same mutual immanence as an expression of the essence of Godself (Wilmot 1979). Three different propositions describe the economic and immanent Trinity as mutual immanence in this sense. (a) Contra the "orthodox Platonism" of Arianism, which accepted only a "derivative image" of God in the world (thereby also excluding God from the world), Christian theologians accepted the assertion of "a multiplicity in the nature of God," "each component being unqualifiedly Divine." This view articulates the doctrine of "mutual immanence in the divine nature." (b) With respect to the development of a "doctrine of the person of Christ," Christian theologians "rejected the doctrine of an association of the human individual with a divine individual, involving responsive imitations [of God] in the human person," opting instead for the notion of "direct immanence of God in the one person of Christ." (c) Finally, the doctrine of "some sort of direct immanence of God in the World generally" is the doctrine of the "third person of the Trinity" (AI, 168–69).

Without theologically judging the doctrine of the Trinity one way or the other, Whitehead does lament that it was never developed into a "general metaphysics" (AI, 169). And indeed, if the relationality of mutual and direct immanence had become the basis not only of a doctrine of God, but also—quite in the sense of universal relationality and the unitexturality of reality—the basis of cosmology, Trinitarian theology could have been influential in a more universal sense (something that was, however, rarely the case). Notwithstanding the fact that substantialism deeply influenced both the doctrine of God and cosmology, there always lurked—at the very center of the Christian doctrine of God—a potent resource for its revision, because in its foundation, the Christian doctrine of God—with its economic and immanent doctrine of the Trinity, its *threefold direct immanence* of the divine persons each within the other, in the person of Christ (christological immanence), and in the world (pneumatological immanence), as well as with the notion of the world's own threefold immanence in God—is already *essentially relational.*

Accepting the fundamental status of this mutual translation of theology and cosmology through mutual immanence, one clearly sees that a Trinitarian interpretation of the doctrine of God of process theology is indispensable. In my opinion—and despite Bracken's reserve (1981)—the search for a perspective from which the "mutual immanence" in process theology can be translated into *Trinitarian theology* must necessarily focus on the *threefold character* of God's nature (Faber 2000e; Rae 1984) (§33). One can demonstrate that the threefold character (1) provides a *structural explication* of mutual immanence, (2) addresses questions and issues of *Trinitarian theology* as such, (3) accommodates *Trinitarian distinctions* within the discourse of process theology, and (4) unites the advantages of the *five Trinitarian models* without adopting their weaknesses.

(1) The "threefold character" refers to the *internal structure of every event* and, *conversely*, to the internal structure of the process of God, namely, the *divine nature as threefold* (§33). In this function, however, it is nothing other than precisely that which mutual immanence intends, namely, that the "in-being" of one event in another comes about through *prehensions*, that is, feelings of the other *as* other as a moment of the concretion unique to that event (§25). Mutual in-being is thus always *relational* happening of concrescence out of prehensions (ontological principle) and its transitory presence within new prehensions (principle of universal relativity). The "essence" of an event—understood nonessentially in this sense—consists in these *prehensive relations* from which it *grows together* (process principle). The *structures* in which these prehensive relations gather *processually* consist in those particular moments associated with the threefold character, namely, dipolarity, tripartite phases, and subject/superject duality (§33). The threefold character explicates an event as that *inner* relational happening through which everything is *mutually* immanent; that is, it determines not only the "inner essence" of events, but also the prehensive and nexic structure of *all* event nexuses (PR, Category of Explanation XVIII). In this sense, the "threefold character" becomes the *indispensable* locus for a *genuine* doctrine

of the Trinity in process theology, a doctrine moreover that can be shaped by Whitehead's Trinitarian connotation of mutual immanence.

(2) The threefold character of the divine nature is also commensurate with the requirements of a *differentiated* Trinitarian theology. Although it may appear that by "character/nature" in God Whitehead is referring to essence/nature, "character" actually refers to a coherent nexus or correlation of events that is *personally generative* in the sense of developing a personal style (§22) through which a person first genuinely attains its identity and unmistakable value (PR, 35) (§23). In the language of Christian theology, the "three characters" are *not* to be interpreted as God's "three natures," but as "three persons" of the one nature of God (Faber 1997), a *personal interpretation* in favor of which the following considerations militate. (a) The meaning of the mutually irreplaceable uniqueness of each "character" has Trinitarian inclinations insofar as the "three natures" are positioned within mutual immanence, within *noninterchangeable* relations, each fulfilling an irreplaceable "function" within the process (Faber 1997). (b) *Personal freedom* is to be attributed to each of the "three characters." The primordial nature, rather than referring to a structure of ideas, instead addresses the freedom of God's concrescence. The consequent nature, rather than representing a "hard drive" that registers everything (Moltmann 1993), instead is the free transformation of the world in God's vision (Felt 1974). The superjective nature, finally, articulates the freedom of the origination of all processes ("primordial superject of creativity") in God and the world (§28). (c) Unique immanence within the world process and distinctive transcendence from the world process applies to all "three natures." The superjective nature, as the origin of all process, expresses divine transcendence as such; it is immanent in the world as caring concern. The primordial nature, as the living "order" of divine concrescence and as the unconditional measure of intensity, is transcendent per se; it is immanent in the world as the beginning of every process within the initial aim and as the ground of novelty and order in the world. The consequent nature, as the reception of the world in God, is transcendent per se; it is immanent as communicative matrix (§32). It is in this sense that the "three natures" correspond to the "functions" of the divine persons as origin (Father), Logos (Son), and Pneuma (Spirit).

(3) Within the discussion of the concept of God among process theologians, these three characters are fully capable—criticism notwithstanding—of articulating *Trinitarian distinctions*. (a) The central Trinitarian-theological determination of "person" is *difference*. In God, "person" is that (and only that) which cannot be said in common of God, that is, that which in God stands in *relational opposition* (DH, 1330). Whitehead refers to the process of integrating relations within events as a self-diversity of "roles," which in satisfaction are then transformed into contrasts. Within the conversion of processes, with respect to God this means that the one event "God" develops its *inverse concrescence* within a *self-diversification of "persons"* through oppositionally contrasting the three characters (Faber 1997). (b) The communication shared by the divine persons attests them as *relations* rather than as "three subjects." From the perspective of process theol-

ogy, the corresponding notion is that the "three natures" are relations that are understood not substantialistically as three "subjects" each with its own "consciousness," but nonsubstantialistically as three primordial differences and relations of the same concrete event "God" that *mutually emerge one from the other* (Faber 1995a). (c) The relation of origin between the Trinitarian persons, being *noninterchangeable*, unequivocally separates them one from the other. The three characters fulfill this criterion if the focus is on the inner *complexity* of the process *structure* they express, rather than on their "triplicity" as such. The superjective nature stands over against the "subjective nature"; that is, the dipolarity of primordial nature (Son) and consequent nature (Spirit) derives from the superjective nature—though the reverse is not the case. The distinction between primordial nature and consequent nature reveals their "order of mutual otherness," the primordial nature (primordiality) "logically" preceding the consequent nature (consequence). *Reciprocal* relations, however, also obtain. From the perspective of the economy of salvation, an "inversion" (to use a term suggested by Hans Urs von Balthasar) between Son and Spirit takes place, that is, the primordial nature presupposes the consequent nature. The superjective nature is concrete caring concern only *through* the primordial nature (Logos). In its own turn, the consequent nature presupposes both "primordial natures," namely, the "primordial superject" (Father) and the "primordial nature" (Son) (Faber 2000e).

(4) The threefold character of God's nature is able to address and coherently integrate all *five Trinitarian models*. (a) *Genuine tripartite relations*. Contra the weaknesses of models I–IV, which begin with pronounced dipolarity or binarity, this model engages genuine tripartition grounded by the inversion of the divine process, that is, by the primordiality of the "third nature" (§§28, 33). In contrast to model I, here the primordial nature (Son) and consequent nature (Spirit) are no longer without origin, flowing instead out of the superjective nature, eliminating the need for differentiations "within" the dipolar natures (model II) and the utilization of creativity in determining the uniqueness of the Father. (b) *Both personal and natural origin*. The weakness inhering in all the models, which posit creativity instead of a "third relation of origin" (models I–IV), can be addressed insofar as within the conversion of processes the superjective nature appears as the primordial superject *of* creativity and thus is discernible the origin *both* of the personal differences in God *and* of shared creativity as activity and common nature of the persons (§28). This view provides both for a *principium sine principio* (personal origination) and for an origin for the *principium operationis* (natural origination). Quite in the sense of Alexandrian theology, the Father is now understood as the origin both of the "deity" (God's essence/nature) and of the divine persons, though also as the personal origin of the creativity of the world (models III–IV) (DH, 112–15; Faber 1995a and b). (c) *Personal difference and subjective/superjective unity*. Over against the social interpretation of the three persons as "personal societies" (model V), personal difference is now conceived as inhering within *one* event. This view avoids the connotation of "person" and "subject"/"consciousness," while still maintaining the coherent correlation of

character, person, and relation. The conversion of processes addresses all the problems of God's temporality attaching to the social model (§29). Yet the communicative field of the divine matrix (model V) is preserved, since God, by virtue of God's threefold character, is genuine multiplicity, also allowing the world to exist both creatively and in reconciliation within the common matrix (§32).

Perhaps the most interesting consequence of the Trinitarian perspective with regard to the "*threefold character*" *of the inverse process* "God" is that it transforms the oppositions of the five models into a coherent contrast. Whereas models I, II, and V are developed within the *opposition of event and nexus*, from the *inverse* perspective both are expressed simultaneously. Whereas models III and IV focus on the *opposition of creative principle and larger ecological structure*, God's *inverse* process is able to ground the mutual mediation between principle, God event, and ecological macrostructure. Whereas models I, III, and V presuppose the difference between God and creativity as being ungrounded, *inversion* is able to ground that difference. God's threefold process thus yields the *Trinitarian structure of the process* at all levels (Figure 5).

Figure 5: The Trinitarian Structure of the Process

Microstructure	*Mutual Mediation*	*Macrostructure*
"Category of the Ultimate"	"Threefold Character"	"Ecological Reminiscence"
"Prehension"	"Event"	"Nexus"
Process	*Inversion of the Process*	*Conversion of the Processes*
(Opposition/Contrast)	(Opposition/Contrast)	(Opposition/Contrast)
Multiplicity → Unity	Consequent Nature ← Primordial Nature	World ↔ God
↑	↑	↑
Creativity	Superject of Creativity	Intercreativity
(Creative Ground)	(Groundless Source)	(Immanent Matrix)
	"Mutual Immanence"	

Trinitarian Principle		*Immanent/Economic Trinity*		*Trinitarian Ecology*
Ecological Microstructure	←	Ecological Structure	←	Ecological Macrostructure
Trinitarian Microstructure	→	Trinitarian Structure	→	Trinitarian Macrostructure

These levels are identified as follows. (a) The level of the creative principle as expressed by the category of the ultimate, corresponding to the smallest concrete component of the process, namely, the *prehension*. It is the *microstructure of concrescence*, through which self-creativity becomes concrete. (b) The level of the *event* with its threefold character; it is *complete concreteness*, causal and final wholeness, the (relational) "atom" of the process within which self-creativity and transcendent creativity, becoming and perishing, subjectivity and objectivity are mediated. (c) The level of the *nexus*, which in its totality refers to the cosmos with all event nexuses and societies on the basis of the chaotic nexus. This is the locus at which the organic and ecological dimension of the process of the mutual immanence of events and their multifarious coherent nexuses takes place. It corresponds to the "ecological reminiscence" (§31), the cooperative activity of God and world within the mutual immanence within creativity.

These three levels are arranged into a *coherent nexus* mediated by the event "God." The Trinitarian structure of the inverse process of God represents the concrete implementation of the *Trinitarian principle of all processes* and simultaneously the *ground of the Trinitarian ecology of the cosmos*. In it, the creative microstructure and the ecological macrostructure are *actively mediated*. (a) The opposition between creative principle and overall ecological structure becomes transparent as a contrast within God's Trinitarian concrescence, which grounds both. (b) The opposition between event and nexus is broken because all concretion displays the *same* Trinitarian structure through God's Trinitarian concrescence, and because, at the same time, the interprocess between God and world becomes the *expression* of Trinitarian life. That is, God must be neither principle nor nexus in order to ground both the creative principle as such and the chaotic nexus (and all organisms in it) as a specifically *Trinitarian* nexus, though God does unite the creative principle and nexic variety as a Trinitarian event. (c) The opposition between creativity and dipolar event, divine matrix and God, as juxtaposed at the microlevel and macrolevel, is grounded in God's Trinitarian concrescence out of the *creative difference* opened up by the original superject of creativity. This difference (the opposition between actuality and activity, or between matrix and nexus, person and nature) arises in light of the Trinitarian process as a *contrast*, since God's superjectivity is the primal enactment of *différance* (§28).

The integrative power of the Trinitarian event structure moves more clearly into focus when one considers not only how it provides a place for the Trinity at the very *center* of process theology's doctrine of God, but also how a Trinitarian concept of God, precisely as such, provides a critical counter to ontotheological substantialism. The *consistent and thoroughgoing relationalism* evident within the Trinitarian event structure affects all issues associated with a revelatory theology (§§35–40). Unlike many theologies of the Trinity, the theopoetic Trinity—which even underpins theopoetic difference—affects the *entire* process (equally in its *nexic form* and its *creative principle*). It is in this sense as well that the Trinitarian event structure also *grounds* that particular universal relationality and unitexturality of reality, providing the point of departure for their knowledge, since the mutual immanence they express is grounded in the *threefold character of the process* itself.

§35. POET OF THE WORLD
(COERCIVE POWER, CREATIVE WEAKNESS, AND THE POWER OF LOVE)

No other topic has provoked as much discussion as has process theology's understanding of *creation* (Küng 1980; Scheffczyk 1984; Koch 1983). Insofar as process theology itself unfolds within the context of cosmology, that is, within the context of the *relation* between God and world (part IV of this book), God's creative love must necessarily constitute the quintessence and touchstone of its theoretical reflections. It is especially in connection with the *four phases of the creative process* (§30) and the *six antitheses* (§31) that process theology has developed the pronounced thesis that God does *not* create the world "out of nothing" (Ford 1983b), and that the critics of process theology have found support for their suspicion that process theology *denies* God as creator (Moltmann 1993). Cobb and Griffin accordingly openly admit that "process theology rejects the notion of *creatio ex nihilo*, if that means creation out of absolute nothingness" (Cobb and Griffin 1979, 65). Pannenberg counters that the resulting idea of radical "self-creative capacity" demonstrates the irreconcilability of Whitehead's metaphysics with the biblical idea of creation and hence also the biblical idea of God (Pannenberg 1986, 194). It is clear that both assumptions—the assertion of process theology and the theological objection to it—are referring to the *theopoetic difference* of God and creativity, which thus quite justifiably stands at the center of theopoetics (§28). The interpretation of that difference will determine how God is to be understood as creator and in what sense thesis and antithesis are in fact accurate. Ultimately, however, *both* assumptions (assertion and objection) can be refuted *to the extent* one interprets this theopoetic difference against the background of the *conversion of processes* (§29) and *God's superjectivity* (§28) (Faber 2000h). To that end, let us examine the *central passage concerning theopoetics*—the passage providing the original point of departure for this book—to the extent it describes what happens *theopoetically* in the *threefold creative act*.

> The universe includes a threefold creative act composed of (i) the one infinite conceptual realization, (ii) the multiple solidarity of free physical realizations in the temporal world, (iii) the ultimate unity of the multiplicity of actual fact with the primordial conceptual fact. If we conceive the first term and the last term in their unity over against the intermediate multiple freedom of physical realizations in the temporal world, we conceive of the patience of God, tenderly saving the turmoil of the intermediate world by the completion of his own nature. The sheer force of things lies in the intermediate physical process: this is the energy of physical production. God's rôle is not the combat of productive force with productive force, of destructive force with destructive force; it lies in the patient operation of the overpowering rationality of his conceptual harmonization. He does not create the world, he saves it; or, more accurately, he is the poet of the world, with tender patience leading it by his vision of truth, beauty, and goodness. (PR, 346)

God is the poet of the world. The first thing this means is that God certainly is the creator of the world (PR, 47, 225, 346ff.). God's *poiesis*, however, is a *relational* act of tender patience and saving love, not a *unilateral* act of physical production or destructive force (Mesle 1993). Within the threefold creative act, God's *poiesis* appears as the unity of creative beginning and reconciling end, as the tender embrace of the self-creativity of the world with its productivity, destruction, and its turmoil (§30). In its threefold structure, the creative process opens up to the world an "intermediacy" between God as vision and completeness, an *intercreativity* extending between God's creative and reconciling love, a divine matrix in which God—world sensitive—is Godself engaged in the tender, caring concern of a "great companion—the fellow-sufferer who understands" (PR, 351) (§34: Figure 5). This specifically *relational* understanding of creator, creativity, creation, and creature leads not only to the source of the negation of creation from nothing (*creatio ex nihilo*), but also—following the same line of thought—to a perspective from which one can refute the objection that this view robs God of God's creative capacity. The basis as well as the goal of process theology's thesis is not to attack God as creator, but to deconstruct the *ontotheological context of interpretation* of God's creative power (Franklin 2000). Whitehead concurs with many process theologians that classical creation theology is formulated within a *context of coercive (or impositional) power*, whereas the theopoetic difference of God and creativity inhering as countermetaphor in the threefold creative act is an attempt to reestablish the *original biblical context* for understanding God's creative power from the perspective of God's *relational love* and *alterity* (Ford 1983b) (§28).

If one follows the *traces of coercive power* in the doctrine of creation, viewed from the perspective of Cobb and Griffin's assumption that the classical doctrine of *creatio ex nihilo* "is part and parcel of the doctrine of God as absolute controller" (Cobb and Griffin 1979, 65), one encounters first of all Whitehead's own *complex theory of coercive power* in connection with cosmology, religion, and creation theology. Even in his initial systematic introduction of God into his work—in *Science and the Modern World*—Whitehead rejected attributing any coercive characteristics to God. Theodicy prevents Whitehead from interpreting God as the "all-producer"" (§27) or from paying God "metaphysical compliments" (§29). In this sense, the notion of theopoetic difference inheres in Whitehead's work from the very outset (§28). In *Religion in the Making*, Whitehead then traces the emergence of coercive power in religion through the latter's association with political-nationalistic currents (Roman Empire, state religion, national religion) and the concomitant morbid exaggeration of national self-consciousness (RMn, 43), the accompanying dogmatic intolerance of its doctrines, and especially the emergence of the simple concept of an arbitrary, transcendent God beyond this world (§26: Figure 2). Ontotheological (nonrelational) substantialism in politics, religion, and theology transformed the "gospel of love" into a "gospel of fear," and God into a "terrifying" concept serving solely to enhance the power of "his" representatives (RMn, 75). In *Process and Reality*, Whitehead *unmasks the structure of coercive power* in analyzing the notion of "his" ontotheological transcendence that resulted in specifically *unilateral* creative power being attributed to God. "When the Western world accepted Christianity, Caesar conquered," and the theology of the legitimization of sovereign coercive power formulated by "his lawyers" came to dominate the scene. The "deeper idolatry" inhering in that theology conceived God "in the image of the Egyptian, Persian, and Roman imperial rulers" (PR, 342), and "the Church gave unto God the attributes which belonged exclusively to Caesar" (PR, 342). The result was that

God could appear in the threefold figure of the "imperial ruler," the "personifica-
tion of moral energy," and as an "ultimate philosophical principle" (PR, 342–43).
For Whitehead, the tragedy of Christianity is that against this background of coercive power the philosophical understanding of God as "unmoved mover" and the
political understanding of God as "imperial ruler" merged in the incriminating
idea of an "aboriginal, eminently real, transcendent creator" (PR, 342). Whitehead amplifies this analysis in *Adventures of Ideas* by asserting that Christian theology adopted the *analogy of ruler* in which God "stood in the same relation to the
whole World as early Egyptian or Mesopotamian kings stood to their subject pop-
ulations" (AI, 169). The resulting ontotheological concept of God as "the one
absolute, omnipotent, omniscient source of all being, for his own existence requiring no relations to anything beyond himself," constituted in effect an apotheosis
of coercive power, or a "sublimation from its barbaric origin" (AI, 169).

Process theology subscribes to this deconstruction of ontotheology as an
expression of *structural coercive power*. One finds hardly any version of process
theology that does not direct itself in some fashion against such organized
grounding of arbitrary power and against the coercive power of repression of the
sort archetypically inhering in the concept of God as "transcendent creator," and
there is not any process theology that has not itself formulated a *theology of nonviolence* through the *countermetaphor of theopoetic difference* (Mesle 1993; Griffin 1976). Whitehead himself adduces especially *three resources*—even speaking
about "threefold revelation"—in carrying through a *theopoetic deconstruction* of
the ontotheological, nonrelational regime of coercive power. These resources
include a *philosophical* one, the Platonic conception of God as ideal force; a *religious* one, the person and message of Jesus; and a *theological* one, the early Christian doctrine of the Trinity (AI, 166f.). All three moments disclose the relational
categories that should characterize a creation theology critical of coercive power.

(1) Whitehead was fascinated by the intellectual power with which Plato freed
himself from the coercive impositional power inherent within the barbaric conceptions of God by conceiving God's creative power not as a *physically efficacious
power of coercion*—with its attendant implications for a concept of creation based
on an analogy of coercive power—but as the *ideal power of persuasion* (AI, 166).
God's creative power refers to the "power of [Godself] as ideal" of the world
(RMn, 156), the power that does *not* compete with physical power (nor is even
analogously conceivable as such), being instead the "patient operation of the overpowering rationality of [God's] conceptual harmonization" (PR, 346). Whitehead found, however, that Plato did not go far enough, insofar as instead of a
"supreme agency of compulsion," he posited merely a "supreme reality, omnipo-
tently disposing a wholly derivative world" (AI, 166).

(2) Whitehead saw in the figure of Jesus nothing less than the religious "exemplification" of the Platonic "discovery" of a noncoercive God and a concrete criticism of all claims of coercive power beyond surrendering love. The center of
Jesus' fate was his challenge of the illegitimacy of coercive power and his reaction to this power, namely, the *suffering under coercive power*, on the one hand,

and the *power of love*, on the other. His message was one of "peace, love, and sympathy" (AI, 167). If the essence of Christianity consists in nothing other than that the life of Christ itself is the revelation of the "nature of God and God's agency in the world" (AI, 167), then that life does not belong in the context of the three ontotheological traditions of the "ruling Caesar, or the ruthless moralist, or the unmoved mover," being based instead on the "tender elements in the world, which slowly and in quietness operate by love" (PR, 343). In Jesus, God's *nature* is manifested as *love*, and God's actions are determined by precisely that love (§30).

(3) The subsequent theological interpretation of the revelation of God's nature in Jesus in the Trinitarian theology especially of the Alexandrian and Antiochian schools represents for Whitehead the key source of the doctrine of *mutual immanence* (§34). It represents the decisive breakthrough—after Plato's discovery of God's noncoercive agency—in its assertion that God *in and of Godself* is that particular *noncoercive communication* that *for just that reason* God also reveals Godself in the world itself as its ultimate "wherein," as the Trinitarian communicative space of the mutual immanence of God and world. If one now expands Trinitarian immanence, over against its ontotheological restriction to the immanent Trinity, into a general metaphysics, the Platonic vision loses its final transcendent reserve concerning God's immanence, and God's own agency is revealed in its innermost essence as "persuasive agency" (AI, 169).

Whitehead's understanding of God's creative power is shaped by the notion of the noncoercive power of persuasive love, by the renunciation of such power on the part of tender love, and by the thwarting of impositional power by communicative immanence. Here God's essence (communication) and nature (concrescence) are revealed as the expression of a *necessity*. That is, God does not in some way "decide" to renounce coercive power or not to rule. God is instead *in principle* nonruling, nonviolent, and noncoercive (Ford 1986; Cobb and Griffin 1976). Contrary to the *analogy of dominion*, which attributes to the God-king a creative power accessible to "his" (arbitrary) will (AI, 130), here God and world—"beyond the accidents of will" (AI, 168)—are related relationally and nonunilaterally commensurate with their *nature*, and God's creative power is *communicative* rather than autarchic, *weak* rather than powerful, *creative* rather than restrictive. (§26). Process theology's struggle against the notion of an omnipotent God—a struggle that has shaped it from the beginning (Hartshorne 1984)—derives from its rejection of the substantialism of an ontotheologically based understanding of God's dominion of the sort culminating in references to the "transcendent creator" or in *creatio ex nihilo*; process theology itself counters with a creation theology based on the *theopoetic difference* of God and creativity (Faber 2000h) (§28). It is in *Adventures of Ideas* that Whitehead formulates his most radical understanding of his *theopoetic alternative* of a relational creation theology within theopoetic difference as the *essential relationality* of God's creative "weakness" (§26); here, without denying God's transcendence, he refers to God as the "immanent God/creator" (AI, 131, 168) conceived in *nondifference* to "immanent creativity" (AI, 236).

> There are two current doctrines as to this process. . . . One is that of the
> external Creator, eliciting this final togetherness out of nothing. The other
> doctrine is that it is a metaphysical principle belonging to the nature of
> things, that there is nothing in the Universe other than instances of this pas-
> sage and components of these instances. . . . Let this latter doctrine be
> adopted. Then the word Creativity expresses the notion that each event is a
> process issuing in novelty. Also if guarded in the phrases Immanent Cre-
> ativity, or Self-Creativity, it avoids the implication of a transcendent Cre-
> ator, so that the whole doctrine acquires an air of paradox, or of pantheism.
> Still it does convey the origination of novelty. (AI, 236)

This central passage mentions both the reason for rejecting *creatio ex nihilo* and
the sense of the envisioned alternative. The *reason* for rejecting a "transcendent
creator" is that this creator refers precisely to that particular ontotheological ruler
who arbitrarily disposes over communication. The attendant notion of "creation
out of nothing" is merely the logical expression lurking behind the mask of the
transcendent creator. In this sense, the omnipotent God is the *origin of coercive
power* insofar as God determines the *conditions* of communication from "his" her-
metic dominion. Yet Whitehead considers this very understanding of God itself
to be an expression of actual coercive power and a projection of the legitimization of human power. The *sense* of the alternative reference to "immanent creativity" or "self-creativity" is obviously to develop—contra the ontotheological
power fantasy—a *relational concept of creation* that renounces power and violence
precisely because such renunciation ultimately derives from the very essence of
God (§28). The analysis of "creativity" has already identified it as the noncoercive, power-free communion of *universal intercreativity* or *divine matrix* (§32).
The fact that in "an air of paradox, or of pantheism" Whitehead chooses no longer
to mention God as the subject of creative power is *not* to be taken as a dissolution of God into creativity—such would constitute pantheism, which Whitehead
rejects in any case (§26), rather than a *paradox*. What he is doing instead is
addressing an important function as a signal of precise theological language.
Commensurate with the *sixth antithesis*, it is the *same* self-creativity—*as* intercreativity—that creates God and world (§31).

Process theology did, however, choose an interesting but problematic expression to refer to this relational and noncoercive alternative to *creatio ex nihilo*,
namely, *creation out of chaos*. Cobb and Griffin's assertion that "process theology
affirms instead a doctrine of creation out of chaos" (Cobb and Griffin 1979, 64)
did not fail to evoke vehement objection, its opponents suspecting it of conceal-
ing what was in fact a turn away from the specifically Christian concept of the
creator and a revitalization of Plato's demiurge, who created not "out of nothing," but out of the unformed (Maassen 1991b). Jürgen Moltmann articulates
the programmatic opposition to this notion in his assertion that "[i]f the idea of
the *creatio ex nihilo* is excluded, or reduced to the formation of a not-yet-actualized primordial matter, 'no-thing,' then the world process must be just as eternal
and without any beginning as God himself. But if it is eternal and without any
beginning like God himself, the process must itself be one of God's natures"

(Moltmann 1993, 78). In that case, however, process theology—so Moltmann—
has no creation doctrine at all, but only a doctrine of maintenance and order
(Moltmann 1993, 78). A more differentiated assessment must first address four
questions involving the metaphor of "creation out of chaos": (a) What exactly
does "creation out of chaos" mean in the context of process theology's discourse
concerning coercive power? (b) How do process theologians in their own turn
ground the metaphor of "chaos"? (c) What does "chaos" itself mean in Whitehead's cosmology? (d) To what extent does this chaos metaphor correspond to
Whitehead's theopoetic alternative of "immanent creativity"?

(1) The *sense* of the metaphor concerning "creation out of chaos" emerges from
process theology's goal of providing an alternative to the ontotheological
metaphor of coercive power understood as inherent in the doctrine of "creation
out of nothing." If the root of creation is characterized by coercive power, then
the world itself is ruled by such power. How would it reveal itself as a world cor-
rupted by coercive power or violence in this sense? The innermost *creative motor*
of the world itself would be *violence*, that is, ruthless coercion, hopeless compulsion, oppression, repression, suppression, and heteronomy (Loomer 1976a). The
fundamental metaphor here would be the one-sided determination of the conditions of communication, omnipotent autocracy, relationless substantiality, creation from *nothing*—isolated (needing only itself) and relationless (absolutely
one-sided) dictate (Keller 2003). The *theology of nonviolence* counters "unilateral
power" with "relational power" (Keller 2000), which persuades rather than
coerces, lures rather than compels, liberates rather than oppresses (Ford 1986b;
1978a). God and world correspond in the countermetaphor of "creative chaos."
God is the *Eros* of the world (primordial nature) who is attractive through God's
ideas, the potentials God opens up to the world (eternal objects), the goals God
bequeaths in caring concern (initial aim), the alternatives with which God lures
toward freedom (AI, 253; Loomer 1976a). The world is accordingly never "nothing," but rather the *coming about of self-value* and for that reason conceivable only
as a *self-creative happening* which God releases and values (Mesle 1993) (§§15–16,
32). Theopoetic difference expresses the notion that God determines *everything*—
and is in this sense the creator of all events—*except* the *self*-creativity of each event
(Griffin 1992) (§27). In this sense, every event is free—at liberty to determine *itself,*
a notion from which process theology then develops an "ontology of freedom." This
"radical self-creative capacity" refers to the dignity of the irreducible freedom and
unconditional self-value of every event and indeed of the world as a whole. The
term "chaos" expresses this freedom and dignity of creation, its spontaneous self-
creativity, which *ex nihilo* would autocratically undermine (Keller 2003). It is no
accident that process theology developed further precisely as a theology of liberation, as political theology, and as feminist theology by adducing this irreducible dignity of freedom, freedom that, inasmuch as it applies to the cosmos as a whole
beginning with creation itself, now doubtless acquires inalienable significance in *all*
spheres of life (Cobb 1983; Keller 1997). "Chaos" expresses the fact that God
cannot transform the world into nothing, since God never destroys freedom,

albeit not because God does not want to do so, but because doing so belongs *neither* to the essence of God *nor* to that of the world. Hence "chaos" always refers to freedom contra *autocratic* order that through its repressive arrangement and with the power of its closed structure would otherwise cripple freedom. Moltmann's charge that "creation out of chaos" ultimately divinizes the world or even understands it as "one of God's natures" proves to be wrong. In fact, quite the *opposite* is the case. As the central theopoetic passage in *Process and Reality* attests, God encompasses the process with God's natures such that in the "intermediate process" of the world, the world can be *wholly world* precisely because it stands in freedom, and because in the face of this "chaos" God's creative power, rather than coercing, instead continually communicates (§32).

(2) Process theology *grounds* the metaphor of "creation out of chaos" in the paradigm of the *thoroughgoing evolution* of the universe. Here Whitehead juxtaposes *two fundamental cosmological models*—that of Plato and that of Newton—ultimately taking the side of Plato (Rust 1987) (§15) because Newton's *Scholium* "made no provision" (PR, 95) for a thoroughgoing evolution of the world and thus for evolution of matter—precisely the path taken by Plato's *Timaeus* in its understanding of the evolutive world of events emerging from ideas (forms), the demiurge (defining act), and the "wherein" (*khora*) (Maassen 1991b) (§2). Whitehead adopts Plato's cosmology at precisely the point at which within the context of contemporary physical cosmology (in light of the theory of relativity, quantum mechanics, and contemporary theories of evolution) it provides a relational theory of the origin of the world, its development, and its grounds (Kann 2001). It offers the archetypical alternative to the notion of an arbitrary creation of this world that breaks through all relationality. Whereas Newton assumed that the world *either* "with its present type of order, is eternal," *or* "came into being, and will pass out of being, according to the fiat of Jehovah" (we know that Newton delivered the latter), Plato by contrast traced "the origin of the present cosmic epoch . . . back to an aboriginal disorder, chaotic according to our ideals" (PR, 95). Whitehead understands this position as the "evolutionary doctrine of the philosophy of organism" (PR, 95). In that sense, so Whitehead, it represents the alternative to the "Semitic theory of a wholly transcendent God creating out of nothing an accidental universe" (PR, 95). These efforts to establish a nonsubstantialist view of the world prompted Moltmann to object theologically that the metaphor of "creation out of chaos," by taking the notion of the eternity of the world as its point of departure, thereby erects the world itself as the anti-God (Moltmann 1993). But this objection too misses the mark. Rather, the "chaos" metaphor provides an *evolutive metaphor* of the creation of the world under the conditions of a *thoroughgoing* evolution of all types of order (including natural laws) and even of matter itself (Kann 2001). It is noteworthy that Whitehead, rather than finding the *true* alternative to the evolutive view in an eternal world, instead formulates this alternative contra *both* "creation out of nothing" *and* the "eternity" of the world (PR, 95). Even though the implication is that Whitehead allows for multiple "cosmic epochs" ("many universes"), the goal is nonetheless *not* the "eternity" of the world (PR, 91ff., 111ff., 197ff.).

Notwithstanding that even process theologians themselves are occasionally less than unequivocal on this point (Cobb and Griffin 1976), "chaos" *actually* neither directly *opposes* the "nothingness" of the world nor *advocates* the notion of the "eternity" of the world, insisting instead on the *thoroughgoing relationality* of the world as summarized in the *ecological reminiscence* (§31).

The *theological support* for this metaphor of "creation out of chaos" is drawn from the *biblical doctrine of creation*. As a matter of fact, the notion of "creation out of nothing" is *not* a biblical doctrine at all, but the result of the later philosophical reflections of Irenaeus of Lyon and other church fathers (May 1994). The biblical understanding of creation includes the metaphor of the *formless sea*, whose unfathomable depths represent the "beginning" of the world. Catherine Keller demonstrates how in Genesis 1:2 the sea as *chaos* is antecedent to all creation acts *through which* God from Genesis 1:3 on is creatively active (Keller 2003). Genesis 1:2 reads: "The earth was a formless void (*tohuwabohu*) and darkness covered the face of the deep (*tehom*), while a wind from God (*ruach*) swept over the face of the waters" (NRSV). Two mythological terms associated with chaos characterize the act of creation, namely, the chaos of the land (*tohuwabohu*) and the chaos of the sea (*tehom*). It is *within* them that God creates. The text *never* says that God creates them. They are instead the consistent, *unspoken presuppositions* of creation. The initial situation is that of darkness, of dark, profound stillness prior to creation itself. *Moreover,* God's creative power—the spirit—is there, hovering above the abyss of chaos. This stillness is the point of departure for creation. Not until verse 3 does the action of creation itself commence, namely, "God said" (Faber 2001c). Here "chaos" is revealed as a *nothingness of formlessness* or, put differently, as the nothingness beyond all form or shape, as an unfathomable depth "in which" everything hovers over the abyss (Keller 2000). Creation happens biblically *in* chaos (Eissfeldt 1966; Kaiser 1962). The metaphor of "creation out of nothing" occurs biblically *only* in 2 Maccabees 2:7, which refers *not* to *creatio ex nihilo*, but to *re*-trieving into being *that which is past*, the eschatological resurrection of that which has *already* existed (Faber 2000h). Moltmann's objection that process theology's adherence to "creation out of chaos" supplies it not with a doctrine of creation, but with a doctrine of maintenance, is faulty, for it is precisely the biblical doctrine of *creation* that understands itself not merely as a doctrine of maintenance; but neither does it oppose "chaos," that is, the assumption of primal chaos does not run counter to a genuine biblical doctrine of creation. What process theology is asserting is merely that the doctrine of *creatio ex nihilo* is not biblically supported and thus at the very least does provide justification for a theological discussion of its motives. The notion of *creatio ex nihilo* in the theology of the church fathers needs to be examined, insofar as it might well imply unbiblical nonrelationality, and the metaphor of "creation out of chaos" needs similarly to be examined to the extent it might biblically reflect the relationality of divine creative power.

(3) In Whitehead's own work, the *meaning of the "chaos" metaphor* emerges from its correlation with the *essential and universal relationality* of the world,

which in fact has several dimensions. "Chaos" refers first of all to the *basic chaotic nexus*, that nonsocial nexus referring to the broadest context of "existence" and alluding to Plato's *khora* (PR, 72, 94f.) (§15). In that sense, it always refers to *relative chaos*; that is, although "chaos" is indeed always formless, it also always expresses *relation,* or that in which communication might be rendered possible (AI, 134). The chaotic "wherein" corresponds to the fundamental relationality of the world, which Whitehead calls *mutual immanence* (§34). And finally "chaos" moves to the center of the evolutive dynamic of creation in the mode of what Whitehead calls the *entirely living nexus,* insofar as it expresses life, which for Whitehead always develops "along the borders of chaos" (PR, 111). As such, it is essential for living beings and for the emergence and unity of persons (§22). The theological ground of this "chaos" is God's own *Trinitarian immanence* in the world, the direct immanence *in which* the chaotic nexus manifests mutual immanence (§§32–34). As such, "chaos" is disclosed as the theological metaphor for the ultimate "wherein" of the world in its *disposition for life and communication.* Hence, Whitehead argues *against* "creation out of nothing," but rather *for* the notion that precisely *because of* God's immanence there can be no "pure chaos" indistinguishable from "nothingness," though also no ultimately static order (PR, 208ff., 339, 348f.). Here Whitehead's use of the "chaos" metaphor emerges as the quintessence of a cosmology formulated nonsubstantialistically, and as such— quite in the sense of Derrida—*nonlogocentrically.* The self-fulfilled presence of a "formal" Logos is countered by "chaos" as the emphatically nonformal, freely moving, living evolution of orders and by a Logos of *living communication* based on God's own nonformal, living Trinitarian immanence. Whitehead's "chaos" metaphor is directed against *all* ontological "givenness" (Wiehl 1990) that depends on the alternative of being or nothingness; that is, it is directed both against the notion of the *eternity* of the world and against that of *ex nihilo* (§13). Just as in Derrida's interpretation of Plato's *khora,* so also is Whitehead's "chaos" *older* than ontological difference, because it neither "posits" self-present being nor, for that reason, "pre-posits" or presupposes nothingness prior to creation (§15). Instead, "chaos"—*beyond the abstraction* of being and nothingness—is not an "absolute beginning," but rather *différance,* that is, beginnings within difference. Although Pannenberg objects that process theology thereby withdraws creation from God's creative power, and Moltmann is suspicious that what is actually presupposed here is "eternal matter," Whitehead in fact refers to God as the *ground* of creation (PR, 225). Because God creates *relationally,* however, creation can *neither* come "from nothing" (pure chaos) *nor* indicate material resistance ("op-position") to God. "Chaos" is instead the *formless activity of communication* that is wholly an *expression of divine perichoresis* (§32).

(4) In assessing process theology's countermetaphor of "creation out of chaos," one must also keep in mind that "chaos" is *not the same* as "immanent creativity" to which Whitehead's new initiative is referring in *Adventures of Ideas* (AI, 236). This becomes evident in the structure of the "ecological reminiscence," where "chaos" refers to that particular "part" of the divine matrix corresponding to

"world," namely, the cosmologically grounding and encompassing chaotic nexus (§32: Figure 4). The "chaos" of the chaotic nexus, however, is *not identical* with the intercreativity between God and world to which the metaphor of "immanent creativity" is referring. Whitehead's reference to "out of chaos," contra "out of nothing," in *Process and Reality* (PR, 95) thus does *not* have the same meaning as the reference to "immanent creativity," contra the "out of nothing" of an "external creator," in *Adventures of Ideas* (AI, 236). The discussion of "chaos" in *Process and Reality* is dealing with an *evolutive cosmology* directed against two modes of cosmological substantialism, namely, the supernaturalism of a creation from will of a transcendent God "out of nothing," and a Spinozism according to which the world emanates out of God "from eternity" by the force of natural necessity (PR, 95). Hence the countermetaphor of "chaos" exhibits a *cosmological meaning* regarding the difference between evolutive and nonevolutive cosmology. By contrast, the countermetaphor of "immanent creativity" in *Adventures of Ideas* is rejecting the notion of an "external creator" of the world and as such thus has a *theological* meaning in speaking about the *theopoetic difference* between God and creativity (AI, 236).

On the basis of this distinction between the *cosmological-evolutive* and *theopoetic* sense of the expression "out of nothing," some process theologians who in fact do cosmologically advocate the notion of "out of chaos" have nonetheless, with respect to theopoetic difference, identified creativity as specifically *divine* creativity, thereby rendering at least conceivable from the perspective of process theology the notion that the world was indeed created "out of nothing." Steven Franklin has concluded that if creativity is never real without its instances (§16), then God as *primordial instance* of universal (self-)creativity must also be understood as its *origin* (Franklin 2000). In his analysis of the primordial activity of God's primordial nature, that is, of the "primordial envisagement" of eternal objects (§33: Trinitarian model II), Lewis Ford finds that it implies a primordial distinction *in* God between form (eternal objects) and act (creativity) without which creation is impossible (Ford 1972). Ford's point of departure is Whitehead's remark that God is "at once a creature of creativity and a condition for creativity" (PR, 31), that is, not only "exemplifies general principles of metaphysics" but also "constitutes" them in a *primordial act of creation* (PR, 40). Ford understands the *cosmologically* uncreated elements "creativity" (activity) and "ideas" (potentiality) *theopoetically* as the result of *creatio ex nihilo* (Ford 1970). For his part, Joseph Bracken maintains that the divine matrix constitutes a field of creativity of the divine persons that God *freely creates* (Bracken 2001) (§32). With such reflections, process theology precisely renders the *sense* of the ancient introduction of the doctrine of *creatio ex nihilo*, namely, that God creates the world freely, without (pre-)conditions deriving "from outside," and without any counterpart of eternal matter.

The key argument in favor of maintaining and acknowledging the reference to *creatio ex nihilo* in the context of process theology is found in the notion of *God's Trinitarian superjectivity* (§34: figure 5). Within the inner conversion or *inversion* of the divine process, God's *superjective nature* is the origin of the *distinction* between act and potency, nature and person, God and world, indeed the *origin of the theopoetic difference* between God and creativity as such. From the *internally divine* perspective, creativity is God's nature, God's self-creativity; *in the world*, however, divine creativity as the "wherein" of communication renders possible the self-creativity of all events. In this sense, both the "radical self-creative capacity" (Pannenberg) and the "not-yet-actualized primordial matter" (Moltmann) are grounded in the primordial act of God's superjective nature. Because of its own lack of ground, it appears simultaneously as the internally divine and world-creative *source ground* (Faber 1997). This enables the notion of God's superjectivity to express the early Christian doctrine of the Father as the *origin* "from which everything" (*ex quo omnia*) arises, for the Father is unbegotten (*agennetos*) "inwardly" (immanently) as the origin of the Trinity (*patrogennetos*) and "outwardly" (economically) as the bearing of the world (*gignomai*) (Schulte 1970). Within the *same* superjective nature, God is "patrogennetically" (*gennaō*/beget) the origin of theopoetic difference *as such* (and with it of the Trinity), and is "theogenetically" (*gignomai*/bear, give birth to) the origin of the world *in* theopoetic difference. In contradistinction to their unilateral view of creation, however, the creation act of God's superjective nature is a *relational* happening *within* the divine matrix (§§28, 32: Figure 4).

    In the light of the divine matrix, the *primordial act of creation* of God's superjective nature can be understood as *relational creatio ex nihilo*. Lewis Ford describes this primordial act of "primordial envisagement," that is, of the primordial differentiation of form and act, as a *creative* happening *directed inwardly*, an act in which God differentiates so that God's "own act of concrescence would [not] exhaust all creativity (Ford 1970, 148), and would instead, as *intercreativity*, render the world possible beyond God. Joseph Bracken speaks about an act *within* the divine matrix of the inner-Trintarian life (in God's nature) that freely allows for "world" (Bracken 2001). Remarkably, from the perspective of God's inverse concrescence, this creative act is, however, *not* an act of impositional or coercive power, nor is it comparable to either productive or destructive physical force, but instead an *act that creates "space"/"khora" inwardly* (§29). "Concrescence" is *per definitionem* an act of "receptivity within," that is, of relationality, rather than "outwardly directed production." Hence, in the *reverse synthesis* (§23) of God's Trinitarian concrescence, through a self-creative act of *self-differentiation*, God first creates that "nothing" *within* the divine matrix *within* which the chaotic nexus can arise (Faber 2000e). Not unlike the "zimzum" (God's "self-limitation") of the Lurian Kabbalah (Scholem 1980), which Moltmann introduces into the creation discourse to show that the divine act of creation *first* refers to the "creation of space" *within* the divine (Moltmann 1993), an understanding of *creatio ex nihilo* now emerges that takes account of process theology's discourse concerning coercive power—that is, of the relationality of the creation act—without abandoning the intentions driving the development of a doctrine of "creation out of nothing." Creation is viewed here as the gracious gift of communication directed outwardly, *not* from sovereign coercive power, but from an *inner-divine* act of tender love that allows for the *Other* (alterity) "within itself."

Given the distinction between the *evolutive* meaning of "chaos" and the *theopoetic* meaning of "creativity," the notions of "out of nothing" and "out of chaos" are not necessarily mutually exclusive. In a new interpretation of the biblical doctrine of God as the beginning and end, as alpha and omega, I understand "chaos" and "nothing" as *two aspects of the same creative happening* (Faber 2000h) corresponding to a *countermovement* arising from the *external conversion* of the processes between God and world (§29) and taking place in the *four creative phases* (§30). God *creates* "*counter*" to the world such that the result is a conversion of *evolutive* "creation out of chaos" and *theopoetic* "creation out of nothing." *Cosmologically* the world can be understood as a process evolving out of chaos. The alpha (α) of the world points back to a past into which its beginnings fade and to an omega (ω) of an open-ended future into which it similarly fades. In this sense, the world can be interpreted as a cosmic epoch alongside of which there can certainly be other, "older" and "future" eons, all representing larger overall rhythms of cosmos and chaos. Here there is neither "absolute beginning" nor "apocalyptic end," but only—critically similar to Derrida's *différance*—"beginnings" and "endings" (Keller 2003). Here creation is "creation out of chaos." From the *theopoetic* perspective, however, God, in a *reversal* of this "*creaturely* process*" (of cosmological evolution) moves toward the world as "*creative* process*." In a fashion moving counter to evolutive time, God's creative process is an *eschatological process* that at once *both* opens up the creaturely process "from the front," *from the future* of the world and of every event in God's primordial nature, *and* rescues it *into the past* of the world in the consequent nature (§§17, 20, 39). Within this creative process, there is an *absolute beginning* of the world (A) that from the perspective of process theology represents the locus of *creatio ex nihilo*, and an *absolute release* (Ω) (in the sense of a *release* of limitations) in God's consequent nature, in which God transforms the "old" into Godself and renews it "back" into the world, in that sense creating it *ex vetere* (from the "old").

Unlike the notion of Whitehead's cosmological difference between "chaos" and "nothing" in *Process and Reality*, the theopoetic difference between "external creator" and "immanent creativity" in *Adventures of Ideas* provides a key reference for the abiding meaning of the notion of "creation out of nothing" in the context of process theology. The characterizing feature of creativity is to be the "origination of novelty," and it is precisely this "absolute novelty" of the creative process that represents the genuine content of "*ex nihilo*" (Faber 2000h). Process theology can thus refer meaningfully both to the notion of "out of chaos" within the creaturely process and to that of "out of nothing" within the creative process—namely, as the *countermovement* of *creaturely* and *creative* processes. Ultimately the two processes coincide within the innermost feature of both "nothing" *and* "chaos," namely, the *absolute novelty* expressed by "*ex nihilo*" (May 1994; Haught 1986). "Chaos" is based on the absolute beginning expressed by "nothing"—the absolute beginning of creation within the Trinitarian matrix, that is, within the creative primordial act of the superjective nature, in the novelty of potentiality (future) of the primordial nature itself, and in the novelty of release of the consequent nature. And precisely this is God's "poetics"; instead of renouncing the idea of a creator God, it represents a nonsubstantial, relational, and noncoercive grounding of universal creative power (§28). It takes nothing from God in the way of God's "absolute novelty" (*ex nihilo*), yet with no detriment to relationality (out of chaos). Within God's "poetic weakness," God's creative power is nonetheless "overwhelming" ("overpowering"); in God's "tender patience" it is nonetheless "rational"; and in its "conceptual harmonization" it is "persuasive" rather than "coercive." As the "origination of novelty," God is that particular "absolute beginning" who within God's *creatio ex nihilo* nonetheless remains a *relational creator*—God's *poiesis* maintains the self-value of the creature, bequeaths to it its self-creativity, and presupposes ("pre-posits") world for itself for creative communication.

§36. PRINCIPLE OF EMPIRICISM (COSMOLOGY, RELIGION, AND REVELATION)

The history of process theology has always had a strong philosophical anchoring. Its pronounced philosophical identity derives not only from Whitehead's ecological cosmology (§2), but also from the empirical theology of Henry Wieman (§3) and the neoclassical theism of Charles Hartshorne (§4). Not surprisingly, many scholars have understood "process theology" as such as a philosophical/metaphysical theology or as a new form of "natural/cosmological theology" (*theologia naturalis*) (Koch 1983), a charge also repeatedly raised from theological quarters. Langdon Gilkey, whose own work owes much to process theology, notes that hardly anywhere in the history of theology have theology and metaphysics been more intimately wedded than in process theology, with metaphysics or speculative theology now assuming a "predominant, if not all-determining, role" (Gilkey 1973, 7). Scheffczyk notes from afar that process theology actually turns into philosophy, that its philosophy is moreover unable to accommodate "Christian theism" and its philosophical implications are unable to acknowledge any divine mystery (Scheffczyk 1984, 104). For its own part, process theology has largely maintained a critical distance from such false conclusions. Although Griffin justifiably points out that theological data and theorems are "in principle universally accessible" (Griffin 1990b) and that every theology tries to articulate itself as an understanding of the world within a context of universal reality and world experience, Daniel D. Williams does nonetheless emphasize that process theology is interested in integrating the "revelatory theology" and "metaphysical theology" rather than replacing the one with the other (Williams 1970). Given the universal quality of the unitexturality of reality, process theology by default finds itself in intercontextual dialogue with philosophy, theology, and the sciences, a position moreover in support of which it can adduce the very origins of Christian theology. From the very first apologetic and systematic attempts at Christian theology in Justin or Origen (Platonism) through Thomas Aquinas (Aristotelianism) and on down to the hermeneutical and existential theologies of the twentieth century (Gadamer, Heidegger), theology has also defined itself through an *integrated understanding of the world* within which it then tries to develop the revelation of God in a more specific sense (Lindsay 1970; Griffin 1990b).

The inclination to distinguish and determine the relationship between philosophy and theology, or between "natural theology" and "revelatory theology," inheres deeply within Whitehead's own metaphysics. (a) Whitehead was first prompted to write his "Essay in Cosmology," namely, *Process and Reality*, at the invitation of the famous Scottish *Gifford Lectures*, which subscribe to "natural theology" (K. Barth, W. Pannenberg, and J. Moltmann presented their creation theology in this context) (Hampe and Maassen 1991b). Here Whitehead presented a *theological* understanding of God, explicitly explicating the "religious function" of God alongside God's "secular function" (Cobb 1952; Lowe 1990; Ford 1984). (b) The dipolarity of God (§25) must be read as a differentiation/juxtaposition of the philosophical and theological aspect of the concept of God, and in this sense dipolar theism makes it evident how a genuinely adequate theology needs both philosophy and theology, reason and revelation (Reeves 1984, 166). The relationship between God's primordial nature (cosmological function) and consequent nature (soteriological function) integrates into a coherent paradigm both the differentiation and the juxtaposed connection between reason and revelation, as required by the First Vatican Council in *Dei filius* contra fideism and rationalism (Pottmeyer 1968). (c) Not least because Whitehead's own theological intuition takes him beyond philosophical speculation concerning God and into the sphere of the central Christian dogmas of the Trinity and the Christ event (§34), process theology understands itself (as John Cobb has shown) as being engaged in disclosing a biblical (processual) access to God beyond the Greek-philosophical (substantialist) overlay of Christian theology (Cobb 1982).

Considering the intimate intertwining of the processes of God and world in intercreative communication (§§29–30), it is not surprising that for many process theologians there is no clear distinction between God's activity in the world in a general-cosmic sense, on the one hand, and the specifically revelatory sense, on the other—and that as a consequence the independent status, import, and meaning of religions over against universal metaphysics becomes questionable. David Pailin paradigmatically describes this situation, maintaining that "God is active in all events. . . . From this it follows that the distinction between natural and revealed theology is alien to a Whiteheadian understanding. . . . A 'process theology' . . . does not provide a case for affirming certain limited affirmations about the reality of God which are then to be augmented by a distinct kind of 'revealed theology'"(Pailin 1984, 285). I consider this particular view—one even shared by many process theologians—to be incorrect (Faber 1999a), for there is a theoretically mediated perspective within process theology from which

I'm a mystic.

one can indeed *distinguish* metaphysics and theology, natural theology and revelatory theology, cosmology and revelation, a perspective from which *specific* revelatory events can be grounded within the paradigm of an ecological cosmology
and interior boundaries of metaphysics adduced in a methodologically reflected
fashion precisely insofar as such metaphysics is itself relative, historical, and of an
ultimately *revelatory disposition.*

Is there a mediated perspective from within process theology from which one
can *distinguish methodologically* between metaphysics and revelation? Yes, in the
principle of concretion (§27), from which follows not only the theoretical irreducibility of the concreteness manifested by events, but also the philosophical
irreducibility of divine revelation. In *Science and the Modern World*, the principle
of concretion appears first of all in its *metaphysical* function as the creative limitation of infinite creativity and infinite form for the concrescence of singular
events. Since *in and of itself,* however, that is, precisely *as* a metaphysical principle, it represents a *principle of ultimate nonrationality* securing the *creativity* and
singularity of every concretion, it also represents a principle of the ultimate
groundlessness of the concrete and of its rationally irreducible *spontaneity* (§§11,
27). Hence Whitehead understands the principle of concretion strictly as the
principle of the distinction between metaphysics and theology, cosmology and religion, nature and revelation, and he explicates the principle of concretion in this
function as a "general principle of empiricism" (SMW, 178). This *principle of
empiricism* "depends upon the doctrine that there is a principle of concretion
which is not discoverable by abstract reason. What further can be known about
God must [therefore] be sought in the region of particular experiences, and therefore rests on an empirical basis" (SMW, 178). The theological consequences of
this assertion are considerable, since what Whitehead does here is provide metaphysical *grounding* for an *empirical* principle of knowledge of God; his metaphysical initiative *requires* a revealed theology (Faber 2000e). This says nothing,
by the way, about which revelation is true—Whitehead mentions several (SMW,
179); what he does instead is ground in principle the *revealed character* of knowledge of God as such, or at least the concrete character—metaphysically irreducible and incapable of abstract reconstruction—of the *historical nature* of
knowledge of God within the ecological paradigm. The principle of empiricism
evokes (in a philosophically rational mode) a historical revelation of God (Faber
1995) and thus requires a revelatory theology. Out of the very center of its own
presuppositions and central theorems, process theology must acknowledge a *nonmetaphysical* root of theology (Faber 2000e). Whitehead (quite contrary to later
fascination with a general theory of the world) confirmed this by adducing the
Christ event, the biblical understanding of God as love, and the Christian doctrine of the Trinity (§§34–35), thereby laying the groundwork for specifically
Christian process theology.

How can *specific revelatory events* be made comprehensible within the paradigm
of ecological cosmology? *Four characteristic features of organic event nexuses* render
this possible (§11). (a) Every (microcosmic) event happening is *singular* and

unique. Commensurate with the principle of concretion, each event is a creative "growing together" (rationally impenetrable and incapable of being rendered in universals) from relations resulting in a unique, singular subject/superject (§§27–28). (b) An event "becomes" *self-creatively* in its singularity and perishes *self-transcendently* in its immediacy (subjectivity) by passing into the becoming of other events (objective immortality). The "real objectivity" with which a singular but past event becomes causally efficacious (transcendent creativity) always involves a loss of its "singularity" (as immediacy) *for itself,* though not necessarily *for others.* That is, as an object in the becoming of other events, the original event, rather than being rendered into universals (pure potentials, eternal objects, possibilities), instead remains efficacious *in its singularity* (§23). Whitehead clarifies this by delineating *two different modes of "presence"* applicable to events *beyond themselves.* In perceiving events, we "conceive in terms of universals" but "feel particular existents" (PR, 230). (c) Singular events acquire *universal* relevance—beyond their own status of having "already happened"—through the *power of repetition,* through which each new event "re-enacts" its past (AI, 192ff.) in order to realize itself more or less creatively on that past (§37). The more the singularity of an event is reactivated in a historical nexus, the more it will remain present in singularity in the tradition (of itself). Following the suggestion of Gilles Deleuze, one should understand this power of repetition or of re-actuation of the singular, that is, the power of its universal agency, not as "repetition," but as the "potentialization" of a genuine event in all its presentations within history. Put differently, this "repetition," rather than adding a second and third time to the first time, as it were, instead carries this (original) first time to the nth degree (Deleuze 1992, 23). Paradoxically, this reactivated, "one-time" singular—in contrast to the generality of universals—is *unrepeatable* and for just that reason also *universally* efficacious (Faber 1999a). (d) The more this "repetition"/"reactivation" of the one-time singular makes the "trace" of its genuine unrepeatability present, the more vibrant will be the tradition of the one-time, singular event in the nexuses. This applies particularly to an *entirely living nexus* (§22), in which the singularity of its event is mediated in the *utmost immediacy,* because the entire nexus is transparent with respect to the singular events that it universalizes (§44). Within this "transparency," singular events become efficacious for the entire nexus in an *immediately universal* fashion (AI, 248). Hence, if an event stands within a living nexus, that event is "repeated" and "reactivated" and thereby becomes "present" in its singularity (§47).

This particular characteristic of events within the ecological paradigm offers a perspective from which now to understand *historical revelation.* Divine revelation always happens by way of *singular* events or event nexuses, that is, in historical events (macrocosmic events), persons (living personal societies), or traditions (living nexuses within the model of "living persons") (§§19, 22). In this sense Whitehead understands the Christ event as a "revelation of the nature of God and of his agency in the world" (AI, 167). Although God is directly and intensively engaged in *all* events, God can nonetheless also be *eminently* engaged in some events and event nexuses (§31), that is, engaged not "more," but "differently," engaged not with respect to the potentials of the world, but *as a self-revelation* of "God's nature" (Ford 1988). It is *within* this historical situatedness of particular revelatory events that God's self-revelation becomes universally efficacious insofar as two "immediacies" meet, namely, *historical* immediacy and *eschatological* immediacy. On the one hand, a historical event of revelation can be conveyed in its singularity over space and time in the *"trace" of a tradition*, that is, in an entirely living nexus (after the mode of a "living person"). In this way, it is able to "potentialize," "re-activate," and thus "representatively evoke (re-present)" itself within other events of the nexus. On the other hand, within the rhythm of the creative phases of the reconciled past of past events within Godself, God bequeaths a uniquely new future in new events (Farmer 1997). Hence, through its release in God's consequent nature, the revelatory event is granted an *eschatological* advent through the agency of the primordial nature (as absolute beginning) in *new* events (§30). In this way, a revelatory event becomes universally efficacious *without*, however, being accessible to abstract reconstruction (Faber 1999a). The *historical understanding of revelation* emerging from these considerations is secured against three dangers: (a) Contra its reduction to *metaphysics*, the ecological paradigm passes beyond general conceptual categories in consistently requiring *singular, unique* events, events that *cannot* be reconstructed in terms of such categories. (b) Contra its reduction to the *divine immediacy* of mystical experience (of the primordial nature), the creative process requires a *historical mediation* of the process of God (four creative phases). (c) Contra reduction to the *eschatological consolation* that God can reveal Godself *entirely* only at the very end, this paradigm counters with God's eschatological agency *within* the event process itself (conversion of the divine process).

A concept of *self-revelation* underlying this specifically historical understanding of revelation now emerges (Waldenfels 1996). Whitehead himself speaks about it in connection with the essential relationality of all reality (§26). An event attains meaning beyond itself only through its perishing, through the "objectification in which it transcends itself" (§23). Whitehead does admittedly refer to this "self-transcendence" as "self-revelation" (PR, 227). (a) Within the conversion of processes, this implies an *inner inversion* in the sense that God's essence within God's primordial superjectivity and reverse concrescence carries out God's own essential relationality (§26) inwardly as *essential self-transcendence* and as such as *inner-divine self-revelation*, which with respect to the threefold character might be designated as *inner-Trinitarian self-revelation* (§34). (b) On the other hand, the conversion of processes also implies an *external reversion*. The communicability of the divine matrix is to be understood as God's free and relational self-revelation (§32), which in its own turn becomes the foundation for God's *particular self-transcendence*, thereby grounding particular revelatory events.

Can *metaphysics and religion* complement each other such that they remain inwardly related without either diminishing the uniqueness of the other? Such is possible within the process paradigm insofar as within it, metaphysics and religion are positioned in a kind of countermovement over against each other, metaphysics always remaining relative and religion always striving for universality (Faber 2000e). Moreover, because ultimately both are based on the *principle of empiricism*, their own correlation within process theology is critically positioned equally against both ontotheological metaphysics/theology and logocentrism.

(1) Although Whitehead does indeed develop his ecological cosmology as metaphysics, that is, as a general theory of the world (or of all worlds), in terms of which, in principle, all experiences can be theoretically interpreted (PR, 3), his recognition of the living, vibrant, open-ended nature of the cosmos as a whole (§24) prompts a clear awareness that even metaphysics itself can never attain any final, conclusive knowledge of the whole. Events cannot be reduced to structures, nor the cosmos to metaphysics; no logocentric termination of thought is possible (Faber 2000e; Poser 1986). Whitehead's cosmology is thus *in principle* open ended, subject to revision, and—despite its rational claims—chaotic in a vibrant, living sense (PR, 8; AI, 144f.; Let., 1f.) (§15). In *Adventures of Ideas*, Whitehead summarizes this final consequence of his principle of empiricism by stating that metaphysics is "a step by step process, achieving no triumphs of finality. We cannot produce that final adjustment of well-defined generalities which constitute a complete metaphysics" (AI, 145). Whitehead understands the opposite view as the "dogmatic fallacy" (AI, 144f.)—his term for logocentrism, that is, belief in the definitive structural self-presence of ultimate principles (Keller 2002). Whitehead does not believe in any antecedently *a-historical structure* of a priori truth, but rather seeks a nonstructural, event-centered, creative "unity" of the whole and of its cognition (§24). It is not some unchangeable, unilateral *logos* of final structure that constitutes the basis of ecological cosmology, but the all-receptive, all-communicative *khora* of living "chaos" (§§2, 15f., 35). This disclosure of the principle of empiricism thus demonstrates how rationality itself is *disposed* toward historical revelation.

(2) The impossibility of general metaphysics in this sense corresponds to Whitehead's understanding of religion (RM, 31; Faber 1999a). Within the development of religions considered by Whitehead in *Religion in the Making*, all contemporary religions (religions within recorded history), though especially the universal religions of Christianity and Buddhism, represent *rational religions*, meaning that in addition to their ritualistic, national, or regional interests, religions also strive to understand the world as a whole (RM, 20ff.). The more any given religion is conscious of this openness for the whole, the more it will also overcome its provinciality and national ties in striving, within the arc of tension between solitariness (RM, 59) and universality (world loyalty) (RM, 16), toward *rational faith*. Such religions derive from *singular, one-time foundational events*, which are then reflected and *universalized* in their rational faith—be it Buddha's enlightenment or the cross of Christ (RM, 31, 55, 130f.). Rational faith consistently seeks to render universally efficacious that one, rationally irreducible element associated with the founding of the religion itself, its source in the *event* (RM, 31, 65). It is within the field of tension between this one-time grounding event, on the one hand, and its universalization, on the other, that rational religion

manifests itself between its genuinely religious intuition (event-centered nature) and universality (metaphysics). It focuses on the "direct intuition of special occasions, and to the elucidatory power of its concepts for all occasions" (RM, 31). Here rational religion is understood as metaphysics deriving from the "supernormal experience of mankind in its moments of finest insight" (RM, 31). Metaphysics understood in this sense, deriving from a religion's experiences, would then represent not a general theory of universal rationality, but a *universalization of genuine events*, inaccessible and irreducible in terms of ahistorical reason (Faber 1999a).

Applied to the countermovement of religion and metaphysics, the principle of empiricism means that process theology is positioned within *essential intercontextuality*. Rather than expressing itself within the earlier substantialist paradigm of the unreconciled juxtaposition of philosophy and theology, reason and revelation, it is characterized by *permeability*. On the one hand, it philosophically develops a *metaphysics-critical cosmology* and opposed to all *logocentricity* of reason; on the other, it is also able to support a *nonmetaphysical revelatory theology* opposed to all ontotheological substantialism in seeking the trace of singular events and acknowledging their universal meaning (Faber 1999a). Whitehead's reference back to God's revelation in Jesus Christ (§35) and his demand that the doctrine of the Trinity emerging from early Christendom should have issued into a system of general metaphysics (§34) acquire *central* significance in this context. Specifically *Christian* process theology is interested, not in dissolving revelatory theology into general metaphysics, but in focusing on the *universal rationality* of the genuine grounding events of Christianity, just as in a reverse fashion its metaphysics is *disposed* to allow for generalizing such genuine events.

Since commensurate within the same principle of empiricism there is not just *one* religion—with its grounding event—that strives for metaphysical universality, nor, on the other hand, any possibility of ahistorical metaphysics capable of developing abstract ideas (such abstractions would have no truth value in any case) (Krämer 1994), then *all* universalizations—philosophical and theological alike—represent universals tied to *particular societies,* that is, valuations of communities (Rohmer 2000). It is at precisely this boundary that process theology—and quite justifiably so—evades the strict separation of contextually independent philosophy, on the one hand, and Christian revelatory theology, on the other, the separation of natural process and revelatory event, of nature and culture, allowing instead for *intercontextual transformation* (Faber 2002e). It can be Christian natural theology, but then also Buddhist natural theology; it can be a specifically Christian revelatory theology, but then also a cultural theology in non-Christian contexts. Like Karl Rahner's "anonymous Christianity," process theology—despite (or even because of) its Christian identity—refuses to abandon its universal (here: multicontextual) claim, while yet understanding itself (in contradistinction to Rahner) not as a transcendental incorporation of that which is Christian on a universal (noncontextual) level, but as a historical matrix, more specifically as an *empirical matrix* capable of learning from other societies (religions, philosophies, sciences, civilizations) and as a *transformational matrix* always formulated in specific societies. As Christian theology however—and in what makes it *genuinely* Christian theology—it remains translatable into other contexts (Cobb 1982a).

§37. SOLIDARITY AND INTERRUPTION (GRACE, SIN, AND REDEMPTION)

In ecological cosmology, the world appears as a *cosmos* positioned within universal relationality, in which everything is coherently related to everything else, everything emerges from everything else, and everything grows together from relationships (§15). God is eminently involved in this process, namely, in all phases (RMn, 94) (§30), embracing the process as a whole (§25) and moving toward it both creatively and in reconciliation (§29). The intimate connection—through mutual immanence—of the processes of God and world (§34) enables one to speak about *universal solidarity* in this context, namely, the solidarity of the processes with each other through being indispensably interwoven, and God's solidarity with the world through God's embrace and interpenetration, solidarity inhering at the very root in God's inner-divine process (PR, 7, 40, 67, 71f., 164ff., 200, 346). Following Bracken's suggestion, one can refer to this "field of solidarity" between God and world as a "divine matrix," which out of God's communicative nature and the medium of communication at the foundation of the world (the "wherein") grounds all solidarity (§32). *Nonetheless* the universe is not a locus of universal harmony, nor a manifestation of shimmering "holistic" relations, nor a paradise of any other sort, since it equally attests perishing and death, change and discordance, indissoluble plurality and mutual obstruction (Suchocki 1995). That is, despite all its solidarity and relationality, the universe clearly does not have the appearance of being *redeemed*. The *chaotic* nexus into which it is embedded makes possible not only living communication, but also turmoil, destruction, and abyss (PR, 244). In this sense, the world by no means represents a simple continuum of solidarity, but, to an equal extent at least, also an *interruption*. Relationality is invariably accompanied by isolation (§24), the organic by the atomistic (§12), and harmony by discordance (§21) (Wiehl 1991). Within theopoetic difference, the category of *creativity* expresses this "contradiction" or "discordance" (§16) as unity and multiplicity within mutual movement and mutual exclusion, as permanence and change, becoming and perishing, coming and going, negation and multiplication—and all of it amid constant upheaval (§16). Creativity allows for these contradictions, as a result of which the world is indeed experienced as unredeemed, and precisely the world's *unredeemed nature* prompts process theology to distinguish between God and creativity within theopoetic difference (§28). Solidarity *and* interruption describe an unredeemed world, the contradiction of indispensable intertwining, on the one hand, and mutual hindrance, on the other (Faber 2000e) (§33).

Because the world appears theologically as a contradiction—as a place of

harmony and sin, freedom and violence, grace and guilt—three theological questions arise with respect to the world process as such (Suchocki 1995). (a) Given
the eminently interwoven nature of God and world as understood by process theology, how can one yet speak about the interruption of God's free *grace*? Does not
God merge into the world precisely in solidarity with it? (b) How is *sin* possible
in a world this intimately "interwoven" with God? What constitutes sin? Within
the horizon of a universe characterized thus by solidarity and interruption, does
sin actually consist in solidarity (in evil) against the gracious interruption of grace
or an interruption of the solidarity of the world? (c) How does God's *redemptive*
activity lead to reconciliation of the world in the face of denied grace and sin?
Does God act redemptively by interrupting "solidarity in evil" or by establishing
"solidarity in grace"?

Because these three question complexes—involving grace, sin, and redemption—stand in a coherent connection with the "contradiction" or "discordance"
of solidarity and interruption, process theology's reflections on them similarly
belong in a *single, coherent context*. Moreover, their answer is based on the *single
principle* underlying Whitehead's understanding of the relationship between solidarity and interruption, namely, that *there is no continuity of becoming, only a
becoming of continuity* (PR, 34). The first consequence is that our attention is
directed toward the elementary correlation between continuity and discontinuity within the creative process, which Whitehead describes as the duality of two
processes, as the swing between transcendent and immanent creativity (§16),
both of which, while indeed standing in an *irreducible connection,* nonetheless
cannot be reduced the one into the other. Hence, continuity emerges only in transition through the interruption of the continuum in new events (concrescence).
The *inner* unity of events in their "becoming" does not derive from the continuum of the past (being) united within it, and yet it is a re-action to that past (AI,
237f.; PR, 27f.: Categoreal Obligation IX). That which interrupts an event in its
becoming establishes it anew as a continuum in its perishing ("coming-to-be")—
as the world expanded by its addition (PR, 21) (§24). A *temporal index* inheres
in the dual process between solidarity and interruption (§14). The future (an
event in its becoming) *interrupts* (as an "epoch") world-time and simultaneously—in perishing—establishes the (macrocosmic) continuum of time (PR,
222, 284f.). This elementary principle describing the creative movement of the
process itself as a *temporal happening* can be applied *theologically* to all three questions above. It defends God's grace as freedom within the process, makes the
emergence of sin and its effects comprehensible, and views the process as such as
disposed toward gracious redemption.

(1) Grace—the Presence of the Future

References to "grace" in the context of process theology are not without problems (AI, 130; Pailin 1981). Whitehead defends his skepticism toward the concept of "grace" in *Adventures of Ideas* with the same reserve that prompted him to
argue against the notion of an "external creator" (§35), namely, its (Augustinian)

inclination to acknowledge a wholly transcendent God who imposes "his partial favours in the world" (AI, 130). Contra an understanding of God according to which the world is merely an "arbitrary imposition of God's will," Whitehead understands God's interwovenness with the world as mutual immanence—immanence that, while not excluding God's transcendence, does not ground God's relationship with the world in God's volition, but in the "nature of an immanent God" (AI, 130) (§26). Ultimately Whitehead does not, however, think the essence of grace is adequately rendered in this concept of impositional power (coercion) attaching to God's relation to the world; instead, he finds that here "the doctrine of Grace has been degraded" (AI, 170). Grace is not an expression of impositional power, but the expression of God's *poiesis*; gracious actions consist in persuading, luring, even *summoning*, out of a world of coercive, physical violence, a kind of *erotic attraction* of the vision of God (§27). The gracious God is the *Eros* leading into a new future (AI, 148). In the conversion of processes, *Eros opens up* or *inaugurates* the world process from an absolute future (§35).

Hence it comes as no surprise that Cobb and Griffin interpret God's grace as "the presence of God in us," a presence whose ultimate gifts are the open-ended adventure of the world as well as eschatological peace (Cobb and Griffin 1976). This twofold "presence," however—over against ontotheological temptation— never refers to God's fulfilled presence in the world, but rather to a "trace" of God, of God's *threefold character* within the process (§33). This presence of the "future" as the agency of God's grace can be described with respect both to the *four creative phases* (§30) of each individual process and to the *creative process* (§35) of the world as a whole.

(a) Within the concrete process, grace manifests itself as God's *universal agency*—perpetually, everywhere, and in everyone (PR, 31f., 93, 111; AI, 148). In the *four creative phases*, God's grace is efficaciously active in its *threefold character*. It is the *beginning* of every process (first phase), insofar as God's primordial nature bequeaths to each event the vision of the whole as possibility. It is *recollection* (third phase), insofar as God's consequent nature takes up or receives the past of an event before. And it is *caring concern* (fourth phase) in the agency of the superjective nature, bequeathing the past to the event as its own future, thereby (and therein) creatively establishing the event. All "three natures" *together*—as vision, recollection, and *caring concern*—effect God's grace. Grace is the *bequeathed future* of every event, the *unincurred beginning* of every process, and thus the *loving opening up* of the enduring adventure of the world process. Grace does *not* take the world's freedom from it, for it is through grace that every event is bequeathed *itself*, that it might then be *self-creative* in concretizing itself out of the *history of its origination* (PR, 244). In the *threefold creative act*, God does indeed embrace both the beginning and the end of every event. In the *intermediary phase* (second phase), however, the world is self-creative, self-responsible, free, *and* every event is positioned within the physical world with its history and its coercive power and violence and its turmoil (PR, 88). Within the threefold creative act of every event, grace and freedom belong inalienably together. Grace establishes concrete

grace as opening

freedom but does not replace it. Nor does it replace the history out of which an event derives. Instead it creates the creative beginning, freely constituting every event *in* its history (Mesle 1993). God's creative grace is the *Eros of the adventure of the world* that is present for every event *as its future* (AI, 148, 295).

(b) Within the world process as a whole, God's grace is manifested as the "creative process" flowing counter to the "creaturely process." The *creaturely time* in which each new event constitutes itself from its history before transcending itself—through its perishing—toward future events, is met by the counterflow of God's *creative time*, which from the future of a world not yet existing creates *new* events and then recollects and delimits them in their perishing (Faber 2000h). Within this counterflowing "time of grace," the world process is suspended in the caring, providing hand of God, whose goal is *intensity, harmony, and reconciliation*. Intensity and harmony (§21) attest the *world orientation* of God's grace, which as the future of the world process wants not its closure, but its existence, that it might, in its adventure, be led to depth and radiance. By contrast, *reconciliation* promises the *final reception* of the world in the kingdom of God, in which it is perceived in its history, valuated, and transformed into divine life (§§30, 33). Within this counterflow of the creative process, "absolute future" (primordial nature) does *not* promise a "new God"— the unconditional "novelty" of the primordial nature does *not* lead out of the history of the origination, nor is it characterized by any "haste" toward that which is "new"—instead it promises a *loyal* God, a God who dispatches Godself anew out of the "re-collection" of the world (consequent nature) by following history in its past in order to remember it (§39). Finally, however, grace is grounded in God's superjective nature, in the *originless primacy or originality of the creative*, in which God not only freely manifests Godself creatively and in reconciliation, but also bequeaths to creatures their own self-creativity (§28).

This notion of the coactivity of God's threefold character can, from the perspective of process theology, give a new interpretation to two classical theological assertions concerning grace. (a) In God's superjective nature, God creates the theopoetic difference in which the existence of the world appears as God's groundless overflowing—as the loving outflow of the purposelessly good, which in its own turn grounds all self-value (*bonum diffusivum sui*) (§21). (b) In the unconditional vision of God's primordial nature, which does not presuppose any specific world, *and* in the re-collection of the concrete world process in God's consequent nature, God *pre*supposes (*pre*-posits) Godself *for the world* "from the front" as absolute beginning, and *pre*supposes (*pre*-posits) the world *for Godself* as relative perception of the world "afterward" (*gratia supponit naturam*) (§17). The fundamental characterizing features of God's grace within the paradigm of process theology are *freedom and relationality*. To the same extent that grace is indeed involved in the world process (since without it, that process is not itself), so also is God's grace free to create, to reconcile, and to act in caring concern. But God's threefold grace is always turned toward the world, toward the process, and is always world sensitive.

(2) Sin—the Presence of the Past

What is the source of sin if God's grace permeates everything? Process theology adduces the internal event structure in explicating this issue. Every event, being dipolar, thus has two "beginnings." The "beginning" of the mental pole is the initial aim, which ultimately comes from God. The "beginning" of the physical pole, however, is the event's own past, the past out of which it "grows together" as the re-collection ("in-ternalization") of its past (Fetz 1981). In its own turn, the initial aim is constantly oriented toward this past, reflecting it with respect to *new event activity* (Rohmer 2000). Hence a new event's first act establishes a *repetition* of its past or a "*re-enactment*" of the past through internal re-collection (AI, 194; Hampe 1990). At the same time, the initial aim makes *difference* over against this past possible by "pre-positioning" before the event an ideal of its self; it is the *perspective* of the highest possible potential of a "becoming" event in view of its past, that it might indeed become that which it is *capable* of becoming (§20). If an event's primordial act emerges out of the *temporal* tensions between poles (albeit not within physical time), that is, out of the difference between physicality (origin) and mentality (future), the arising of events *simultaneously* requires the "presence" of God and world (PR, 88) (§18). But whereas God's "presence" is that of the *future*—the "ad-vent" from the initial aim in which an event is still future for itself—the world's "presence" refers to the *origin* from the past nexus, the past history of an event (Faber 2000h).

This divine-worldly dipolarity of events *predisposes* the ecological world process for sin. Insofar as grace, in bequeathing new events to themselves (in the initial aim), is always positioned in the context of an event's origin, the arising of every event is accompanied by *maximal freedom for the event in relation to its past* (Hauskeller 1994). Depending on the evolutive context, this can range from a simple repetition of its past (as is the case with most physical societies, elementary particles, and fixed macrocosmic things), to minimal spontaneity in events of living societies, on to genuine freedom in entirely living nexuses (§15). Wherever, however, as is the case in a human person (a wholly living nexus with consciousness), God's grace makes *freedom* possible and this freedom is *conscious*, an event will be predisposed for sin whenever it does *not* use this freedom of distance from its past or lags behind the (best) potentials of its initial aim. Whenever a conscious event does *not* make use of its divinely established freedom, it sins against God's grace. The essence of sin consists in an event freely—despite knowing better, and contrary to its conscience—more or less repeating its past *instead* of reflecting it in freedom and in light of its potentials, and instead of developing itself—precisely through this freedom—toward the maximal fulfillment of its subjective aim (Hauskeller 1994). Sin is the *refusal of the creative act*, which empirical theology called "creative transformation" (§3).

Within the paradigm of process theology, sin always has both a *personal* and a *transpersonal* aspect (§23). *Holding fast* to "goods" already attained or *re-activating* the sinful past is the same as refusing the "good" and the grace that enables one to overcome that sinful past (§3). Here, however, an event not only establishes sin "for itself," but also becomes part of the past of *others*, a past that in its own turn is thereby further disposed for sin (Suchocki 1994; 1995). The necessity for an event to re-activate its past, even *before* it is really able to reflect on it and change it, reveals a unique but intimate correlation between free sin and original sin within process theology (Suchocki 1994): *Prior to* the freedom of an event, it is already a re-activation of its past, and this *given condition* constitutes its inherited past, a past for which it can do nothing but which it *must* repeat in order to begin existing (PR, 34, 119, 171, 180f., 224; Suchocki 1995; Hosinski 1993; Kasprzik 1988). Within the presence of the past that *constitutively* grounds an event through its internalizing re-collection, there inheres an "inheritance" predisposing an event to personal sin, which in its own turn acquires causal agency and as such prompts this structural disposition in new events. A refusal of the freedom of the creative act, and the demonic element of the structural prevailing precondition of past decisions, *always* mutually penetrate each other when an event comes about, thereby also shaping the *entire* creative process of events and event nexuses (Williams 1990). Within the specifically *macrocosmic* context, this "diabolical" rhythm of demonic past and sinful freedom develops *sinful structures* whose (causal) power becomes all the stronger the more they are reactivated. Yet the more they are repeated, the more difficult is free resistance to the demonic past in each new event within a sinful nexus (Griffin 1991; Hauskeller 1994). There is thus what may be called *solidarity in sin*. The repetition of the sinful past enlarges or enhances the demonic within the nexus, thereby introducing *structural oppression* and making resistance more difficult.

The essence of sin—situated historically in the origination of an event from its past and ecologically in the structure of the nexus itself—is *sinful continuity* (or the continuity as sin) (Suchocki 1994a). Even though this repetition of the past may well serve to enhance inner intensity, the refusal of the creative act in fact thwarts precisely this, doing so by reducing the critical and creative potential with respect to the past, by reducing constitutive relations out of fear of creative change, and by insulating against any new future out of fear of self-loss (Suchocki 1995). Personal sin and the demonic thus effectively reduce both the intensity and the harmony of self-constitution and of the nexus itself to chaos (noncommunication), coercive force (the destruction of relations), egoism (self-isolation in one's past), and the various forms of "anaesthesia" (through mutual hindrance, discordance, and destruction) (§21). The background to *all* forms of sin is the *will to self-power*. An event, a person, a society believes that by repeating its demonic past it will be able to *maintain* itself, survive, and avoid perishing, to continue through its own power, and thereby to live eternally. And precisely that is the illusion; for sinful continuity merely imprisons one in a demonic past, whose guard it then becomes. Fear of self-loss fails to recognize the "perpetual perishing" that is the presupposition of the creative process *qua* relational process (Suchocki 1995). The world process effects constant change, becoming and perishing, a self-creative process and a process of self-transcendence (§21).

Sin is essentially a *refusal of self-transcendence*, the latter being prepositioned microcosmically in the initial aim as satisfaction (i.e., attainment of the subjective aim) and macrocosmically in the living whole of the nexus of the world (Inada 1975). The nonrecognition or nonacknowledgement of the gracious structure of finitude as the locus of creative self-surpassing generates not only anxiety in the face of loss, but also sin and the demonic as the *interruption of relationality* and thus as the *illusion of "substantiality."* The *sinful continuum of anxiety* generates self-circling (*incurvatio in seipsum*), self-absolutizing (failure to recognize relationality), and coercive power (assertion of one's own continuous substantiality) (Faber 2002d). The sinful continuum generates *relationlessness* in the form of stabilized eternal objects by which, prompted by the fear of self-loss and taken as the foundation of societies, they seek to secure their self-reproduction (§46)—a situation that in its own turn generates ideologies, fundamentalism, xenophobia, and dogmatism, in a word: substantialist dualism (§10).

(3) Redemption—the (New) Future of the Past

Redemption consists in recognizing the substantiality of the sinful continuum, in perceiving one's own relationality and transience, and in acknowledging *creative transformation* into an ever greater future (Beardslee 1972) (§3). This future is itself unhoped-for hope in the power of reconciliation, the power of God as the power of the future. Over against sinful substantiality, God is the "Supremely Related One" (Suchocki 1995, 33), whose creative vivacity disrupts all relationlessness when acknowledged as the *inaugurating future of creative origination* (primordial nature), as the *receptive future of reconciliation* (consequent nature), and as *the power to overcome destructive structures of ideal stability* (eternal objects by which a society sinfully "self-stabilizes" itself). As absolute future (of the primordial nature), God unconditionally transcends the givenness of the world but must nonetheless reflect evil (in the consequent nature) (Suchocki 1995). Within the process itself, God (as superjective nature) sends the reflected (valuated) sinful element of the world as *new* future so that the past does not repeat itself. Within the overall process, however, the perception of receptive, caring concern already provides the foreshadowing for the coming reconciliation, which ultimately consists in a complete release (delimitation) of sinful structures in the kingdom of heaven (Faber 2002f). God's redemptive agency bestows the power of self-transcendence, of creative transformation, which overcomes the anxiety of self-loss and helps resist the demonic repetition of the sinful past. The redemptive God is the *Eros of exodus* leading into a future that bestows *new* future to the *love* unredeemed past.

Like sin itself, so also does redemption have both a *personal* and a *transpersonal* dimension. In contradistinction to sinful freedom, specifically redemptive freedom consists in the self-realization of the person as creative act of self-transcendence. The transpersonal dimension, however, consists in the *delimitation* of the person *beyond itself* in the consequent nature and in the gift of "ethical death" in the world (§23). In this tension between personal freedom and transpersonal delimitation *Christ* is positioned within the doctrine of redemption of process theology. Christ is the divine manifestation of the *interruption* of sinful continuity, the concrete grace through which *solidarity in sin* is overcome (Suchocki 1995). Through his resurrection, he is the concrete figure of the divine vision for a redeemed world and as such is acting in all initial aims of all events precisely as this salutary future that both interrupts and heals (§38). In assignation to Christ ("in Christ"), that is, when we admit Christ as the determinative moment of our initial aim, we are released into God's future and encouraged with respect to entering the world for creative transformation (Cobb and Griffin 1976). Christ is the *transpersonal self-transcendence in person* "in" which we ourselves become "person" *by* transcending ourselves (§38). The embodiment of this redemptive grace "in Christ," as the "body of Christ," as a society shaped by Christ, is *not* simply the "continuum of Christ" (such would typify sinful continuity, which seeks to stabilize its givenness), but rather the continuum established *anew* in every initial aim, a continuum nourished by the *everlasting discontinuity of grace*. Nonetheless, concrete grace does seek *redeemed solidarity* with the world in embodiments of redemption (of the body of Christ) within the adventure of the world (Suchocki 1995; Cobb 1975; Griffin 1990). In contradistinction to sinful continuity, however, which constantly strives for self-preservation, redeemed solidarity is of a *kenotic* nature. Just as God's redemptive process, in kenotic solidarity, moves toward the world process, into its unredeemed past, so also does the kenotic solidarity of events, *through suffering*, strive to perceive discordant reality in order to *transform* that reality—though a creative act by the grace of *interruption*, coming from itself as redemptive future—into a redeemed contrast. This continuity is the *gift* of solidarity through the act of self-transcendence (Inada 1971; 1975).

§38. WISDOM AND SPIRIT
(*SOPHIA*/LOGOS, PERSON OF CHRIST, AND PNEUMA)

Process theology understands itself as a theology that in a genuine way has succeeded in accommodating Christian revelation within its paradigm and has developed Christian doctrine further specifically regarding Christology and pneumatology (§47). Many process theologians have developed "process Christologies" (Sullivan 1987)—across all of process theology's directions: John Cobb (1975; 1986) and David Griffin (1990), Schubert Ogden (1961) and Bernard Loomer (1952), Bernard Lee (1977) and Norman Pittenger (1959) or Marjorie Suchocki (1995). All these theologians can adduce Whitehead's dictum concerning the revelation of God's nature in Jesus and God's direct immanence in Christ (§34). Similarly all have taken, as the basis of a Christology specific to process theology, Whitehead's evocation of Chalcedonian Christology in *Adventures of Ideas* in its assertion that God is in fact *directly incarnated* in the one person of Christ (undivided and unmixed) (AI, 167ff.). The peculiar feature of such process Christology is its attempt *not* merely to consider the classical (and still disputed) contradictions of the "simultaneity" of God and humanity in the person of Christ on an individual basis, but also to make it comprehensible in a *universal* context of ecological cosmology (of the God/world relationship) (Schwarz 1983).

(1) Process Christology is first of all *Sophia-Christology* in its mindfulness of the biblical evocation of wisdom (*Sophia*) as the background of early Christian Logos Christology (Cobb and Griffin 1976). The Johannine evocation of the Logos that is God and has always been in the world (John 1) is based on biblical and Jewish wisdom speculation that attributes to *Sophia* a position as mediator in creation. She is in God prior to all creation, that it might play before God, and embodies the measure of creation according to which creation was formed (Wis. 7; Prov. 8). She responds to the world reason of Mid- and Neoplatonism, describes God's vision of the world in its ideal (reconciled) form, is never entirely absorbed by the world even though she is immanent to the world as its ideal order, but she does know about *this* particular world—with caring concern, ordering, renewing (Pannenberg 1976). From the perspective of process theology, *Sophia* describes God's *primordial nature*, the *ideal vision* of all possible worlds (Schulte 1989), which in its own turn (and in an unequivocally Johannine fashion) characterizes the primordial divine act of concrescence *as well as* the order in and of the world—she *is* God, is *in* God *before* the world, and has always been *in* the world (Cobb 1986).

(a) Insofar as the notion of *Sophia*/primordial nature addresses the *primordial act of divine concrescence* (§§28, 34), she is not merely something secondary in God, but the primordial implementation of precisely that creativity through which God also makes the world possible. Contra the Arian/Neoplatonic tendency not to attribute multiplicity to God, the *Sophia*/Logos is understood not as the "second God" (i.e., merely similar to God), but as the primordial creative act within *Godself*, that is, God's own concrescent "identity" (Cobb and Griffin 1976) (§34: models I, II). Unlike in classical Logos Christology, however, here she is understood not only as representing an order of ideas, but also as designating *living unfathomableness* inaccessible to comprehension through ideas (forms). She refers (initially perhaps shockingly) to the *infinite sea of potentialities* inexpressible by *any* order, appearing instead in her relationality only as an *infinitely living nexus* (Suchocki 1995) (§§35, 34: model II). *Sophia* is (as in Prov. 8) the *reflection* of the primal sea, of the chaotic nexus, *in God*; from the inner-divine perspective, she functions as "primal chaos"—though the latter is pure communication, not "pre-formed" in any sense—pure relationality, the divine origin of the "wherein" (*khora*) (§§15–16, 35).

(b) Although *Sophia*/primordial nature does refer to God's ordering of the world (PR, 88, 108, 244; Cobb and Griffin 1976), she is—unlike in classical Logos Christology—not simply an order of the world, as it were, its immanent "natural law." She is instead the *Eros* that even in her immanence is always transcendent, the *Eros* in which "order" in actually an abstraction to which no real significance or meaning can be attributed beyond concrete, living, processual intensity and harmony (§26). God's wisdom/primordial nature does *not* establish any preformed ideal order (Maassen 1988) according to which the world then mechanically unfolds or to which the world is to accommodate itself morally. Instead she imagines a *living* order of intensity through knowledge of the concrete world itself (§16). *Sophia*/primordial nature refers *not* to accommodation, but to the *exodus into the new* represented by the living process (§19); that is, she grounds the world not in the sense of implementing "pre-posited" antecedents, but as creative transformation, as the adventure of inexhaustible intensification and harmonization.

(c) *Sophia* is immanent to the world as *concrete wisdom* and *caring concern (provisio)* (Cobb and Griffin 1976; Schulte 1989) (§30). Economically *Sophia* is manifested in a *pneumatological* context, insofar as she not only is the act of knowledge and valuation of what is possible within the primordial nature, but she is also—in order to be concretely present within the world as such—receiving knowledge from, and acting as valuation of, the *concrete* world, which God takes up in God's *consequent nature*, the Pneuma, and transforms in the valuation of the primordial nature for the sake of caring concern in turning toward the world itself. Insofar as *Sophia* as God's primordial envisagement is not simply a "pool" of possibilities, but the innerdivine *valuation* of potentials (Suchocki 1995), she is to be understood as God's *Logos* rather than simply as *Chaos* (§40). For the world as such, she is God's overflowing goodness, which in her valuation of the world, rather than imply simply chaotic arbitrariness, instead promises God's *caring concern*, which bequeaths to the world its self-value, its self-creativity, and the strength for self-transcendence (Sayer 1999).

(2) Process theology embraces an *incarnational Sophia/Logos*. *Sophia*/Logos is immanent to the world as Eros, who within the tension between order and novelty "lures" toward intensity and harmony (AI, 148, 253; Cobb and Griffin 1976; Ford 1978; Suchocki 1988). The immanence of *Sophia*/Logos, however, is not that of distant world order, but that of intimate proximity, since it is the beginning of every event (§20). Here the mediatorship of creation becomes concrete insofar as *Sophia*/Logos, by establishing every initial aim of every event in the world, represents the *absolute beginning* of the world in its process (§35). Within the initial aim, *Sophia*/Logos appears to the established event in a *nondifferent* and yet *differentiating* mode. As *différance* within the initial aim, God differentiates Godself from the emergent ("becoming") creature, while in a reverse way the creature itself takes its divine origin there in order to differentiate itself within the world (Faber 2000e and h) (§20). Whitehead refers to this as the *incarnational structure* of the divine engagement in the world, since *Sophia*/Logos is indeed the "incarnation" of the primordial divine envisagement of the world in all that takes place as events (PR, 31f., 67, 189, 344; AI, 198).

The incarnational presence of *Sophia*/Logos is that of *différance*; that is, despite her eminent immanence in all that happens in the world, *Sophia*/Logos is neither *self-fulfilled* as "presence" nor even present *as such* or, certainly, *for her own sake*. (a) Contra all ontotheological interpretation of "presence" of the Logos in every event and in the process as a whole, she is always present as future, as "trace," which is already present at the locus of origination of every event, even before the event becomes (Ford 1988) (§20). By accepting its initial aim, an event becomes self-creative and in a certain sense thenceforth *always* has *Sophia*/Logos "at its back" during its becoming. Like Moses, we can in our own turn only have God "behind" us, "at our back," when God passes by (Exod. 33:18–23). (b) In the initial aim, *Sophia*/Logos never sends herself *as such*, but only by bequeathing the vision of an event to that event as its potential (Cobb and Griffin 1976; Griffin 1990). Hence the "presence" of *Sophia*/Logos never points *toward herself*, being instead consistently *turned toward the world*. In seeking to render possible the becoming of the event, she thus sends it into the world, releasing it thus into its own becoming. That is why *Sophia*/Logos is actually present *only* as a *hidden* beginning of the becoming of world, that is, only for the sake of this very becoming—its intensity and its self-value (Suchocki 1995). (c) In the gift of beginning and in her position as mediator of creation, *Sophia*/Logos is herself pneumatologically mediated. *Sophia*/Logos is present *within the Spirit* when God perceives and releases the event in its past and origin. In this capacity, *Sophia*/Logos mediates an ideal that while allowing for past simultaneously challenges that past and shows to every event a vision of that which in view of its own origination it *could* be if only it would (RMn, 155) (§30). The hiddenness of *Sophia*/Logos within the ideal of events is not something neutral, not a "visionary" presence with only passive status. It is instead an *active* presence that within the Spirit directs the event away from herself to its history, positioning her within its *own* possibility in the tension between historical past and ideal future, summoning it to *decision*, and throwing it back on its *own* future (Cobb and Griffin 1976; Cobb 1986; Griffin 1990a).

Within the general incarnational structure, the Christ event would merely represent a special case, or—as Karl Rahner put it (cosmologically applied)—a singular, one-time ultimate case (Rahner 1976), in the sense of Christology as fulfilled cosmology and cosmology as deficient Christology. The question is, how does a *singular incarnation* of *Sophia*/Logos in Christ arise from the incarnational structure? This question has two aspects. First, what distinguishes the incarnation of *Sophia*/Logos in the flesh (John 1:14) from her immanence in the world (John 1:9f.)? And second, in view of the incarnational structure, must *Sophia*/Logos be incarnated *once for all* (Heb. 9:12: *ephapax*), or could that not in principle happen everywhere and at all times?

(a) The general incarnational structure allows for *Sophia*/Logos to be "present" in a specific way in every event as the origin of self-difference for every event (Ford 1981). *Sophia*/Logos, within the initial aim, carries through that which is the primordial act of (inner-)divine concrescence (§28), that is, the *différance* of form (eternal objects) and act (creativity) is released out of God's nondifference into the self-difference of the event (Ford 1972) (§35). More specifically, *Sophia*/Logos bequeaths herself through the *différance* between self-creativity and the complex eternal object with which she mediates to the event the vision of the developmental space and goal as the potential of its self-development (Faber 2000e).

Hence *Sophia*/Logos is never "objectivized" in the event—in the initial aim—as *Sophia*/Logos, but rather *with respect* to the *différance* bequeathed by *Sophia*/Logos, as the *power* of self-creativity and as the *vision* the event has of itself (Ford 1988). Yet in both, *Sophia*/Logos is hidden (Suchocki 1995) (§48), since in self-creativity the event refers to its innermost individuality, its irreplaceable *actus essendi*, and in its vision always appears only with respect to *its* possibilities (Griffin 1992)—and in both, *Sophia*/Logos is always concealed in nondifference.

In the *incarnation of Sophia*/Logos, however, this *différance* between act and form is sublated into the *nondifference of the conversion* of the divine process (§29). Initially the "direction" of the nondifference of the *Sophia*/Logos event is positioned *converse* to that of all creaturely events (Cobb and Griffin 1976). Whereas in all creaturely events *Sophia*/Logos is present only for the sake of the events themselves, which she creatively releases for their own becoming, in the *Sophia*/Logos event she is present *for her own sake,* as herself, and with regard to herself (Koch 1983). Then the difference between self-creativity and ideal future in the initial aim is *not* differentiated for a creaturely event, abiding instead in *that particular* nondifference of act and form inhering within the *primordial act* of the inner-divine concrescence. Ultimately, precisely *because of* this nondifference, act and form in the event refer not to the event itself, but to *Sophia*/Logos; the act of self-creativity, rather than releasing into creaturely independence, instead makes the primordial act of inner-divine concrescence (carried out by the primordial nature) *transparent* (Cobb 1986). Within the initial aim, the ideal form then represents not an objectification of specific possibilities for this particular event and its history, but rather (commensurate with the view of Pittenger and Cobb) the presence of the *primordial nature* itself (Sullivan 1987). The conversion within the initial aim of the *Sophia*/Logos event means that *Sophia*/Logos is incarnated within it, since in the initial aim of this event she is now present not only as *différance* (toward the world), but *as Sophia*/Logos *herself.*

(b) In what sense is the incarnation *singular, once for all* under these conditions? Obviously it is not the singularity of a *single* event that can ground the one-time, singular incarnation in the world. A *Sophia*/Logos event would make sense only if it arrived as *divine self-revelation* in the world for creaturely event *nexuses,* that is, no *single* event would be incapable of such self-revelation; only an event nexus, a society of events, could function as self-revelation for other (or all) nexuses (Cobb and Griffin 1976) (§37). In the highest degree, however, the living vibrancy of the inner-divine self-revelation can manifest itself in the world *only* in an *entirely living nexus* positioned within personal unity and possessing consciousness, corporeality, and freedom (§§15, 19). The singularity of the incarnation of *Sophia*/Logos can refer only to a *living person* who as a whole would then be the incarnation of *Sophia*/Logos (§22). Historically and theologically, such a claim has been the case with Jesus of Nazareth, as Whitehead remarks in *Adventures of Ideas*: (for Christianity), Jesus is to be viewed as the *self-revelation of God's nature in the world* (AI, 167).

But how is a *single* person to manifest *Sophia*/Logos? Viewed from the perspective of the history of religions, why should the incarnation not also refer to other persons in other societies and religions—for example, the Buddha (RM, 55)? Viewed from the perspective of salvation history, why should the rhythm of the prophets, who proclaim the Word in specific situations, not be included in a higher rhythm within which the Word is *repeatedly* incarnated for the sake of redemption (for example, similar to the rhythm of Buddhas from eon to eon) (Cobb 1975)? What is it that makes the incarnation a *one-time, singular* affair, as Christian theology maintains? Indeed, the real problem in process theology is not to "explain" how Christ can be both divine and human, but to "explain" how Jesus of Nazareth is the "unique manifestation" of God among us (Suchocki 1995, 91f., n. 1). At first glance, this seems to contradict the universal relationality of *Sophia*/Logos as mediator of creation, since *Sophia*/Logos is, after all, "incarnationally" present in every event (PR, 67)—or at least she could be incarnated in *every* living person. Why, then, a *single* person, and why this *particular* person, Jesus of Nazareth?

The perspective changes in light of the self-revelation of God's nature (§30) of the sort *capable* of being articulated within the parameters of process theology. The *historical singularity* of God's self-revelation becomes comprehensible beyond classical Logos theology if God is the *principle of concretion* (§27) underlying a *principle of empiricism* (§36), for in that case God encounters the world only through historical mediation, within contingent contexts irreducible to general metaphysics, and only within concrete revelation theoretically underivable apart from concrete historical origin (SMW, 178; RM, 31). Hence the incarnation of *Sophia*/Logos cannot be theoretically derived beyond the historically given event, being comprehensible instead only in the history of its origin. Biblically it is the mode of God's immanence in the world associated with *Sophia* that makes the designation of Jesus as Logos *comprehensible* within the monotheistic context of Yahwism; it does not, however, make it possible to derive it theoretically from the facticity of Jesus' life (Schulte 1967).

The *Christ event* (the macrocosmic event of the incarnation of *Sophia*/Logos in the person of the human being Jesus) can be understood as a *one-time, singular* "event" because it is both *historically singular* and *universally efficacious* (Faber 2000e). There is no *need* to assume any further incarnation apart from God's historical self-revelation, though such remains theoretically *conceivable* within the concept of the incarnational structure of *Sophia*/Logos and the potentiality of *Sophia*/Logos for singular incarnation. It is commensurate with the principle of concretion, however, that God reveals Godself in a historically singular mode, that is, in an *unrepeatable* mode and precisely through such unrepeatability in a potentially universally efficacious way for *all* events (§36). It is precisely *this* universality (rather than abstract generality) that speaks against everlasting or repeated or multiple incarnation (although tolerating such concepts). It is in this way that the paradigm of process theology can speak about Christ as the singular incarnation of *Sophia*/Logos and can understand the Christ event as the concrete universality (*universale concretum*) of the self-revelation of God's nature.

(3) Process Christology attributes special significance to the *divine-human*

constitution of the *person of Christ*. To a greater degree than have other initiatives drawing on the Chalcedonian Creed concerning the unmixed and unseparated hypostatic union of the human and divine natures, process Christology under-stands itself as a paradigm capable of providing the categories without whose har-mony the contradictions otherwise inhering within this christological confession necessarily remain unresolved (Cobb and Griffin 1976). In responding to the central christological question of how God and humanity are positioned within personal union in Christ, process Christology does not engage the *substantialist* line of thinking responsible for its emergence in the first place, but the *ecologi-cal, processual, and relational categories* unique to process theology itself (Hosin-ski 1993). For, as Marjorie Suchocki puts it, in a process metaphysics of inner relations, contradictions disappear; a process world is an incarnational world (Suchocki 1995, 92, n. 1). This position has two implications. On the one hand, the explication of the contradictory qualities of two incommensurate substances (God and human being) through relational categories corresponds to that which in fact applies to *all* events; there is no need to develop "special metaphysics" for God. On the other hand, these "internal relations" lend to Christology a ratio-nality necessarily denied it by substance-metaphysical conceptions.

The person of Christ is indeed the incarnate *Sophia*/Logos if one can say that in it, all events carry out within the initial aim a *conversion of the nondifference* in which *Sophia*/Logos herself becomes present (Faber 2000e). John Cobb develops this idea further in connection with the divine-human connection within the person of Christ. He points out, *first*, how in Christ the universal immanence of *Sophia*/Logos in all initial aims of the living nexus of the person Jesus, takes on an intensity that "presents" *Sophia*/Logos herself, and, *second*, that the human being Jesus himself also fulfills these initial aims of the events of his person. It is not just that *Sophia*/Logos is present in Jesus (as in all events); Jesus *is Sophia*/Logos (Cobb and Griffin 1976) insofar as all of his initial aims are ulti-mately the *same* "initial aim," namely, God's primordial nature, *and* insofar as the human being Jesus wholly fulfills (satisfies) this *one* "initial aim" in all his events as subjective aim (Cobb 1966).

How is the divine-human constitution of the person of Jesus articulated here? (a) Concerning the *divine* side of the person of Jesus, the essence of a living person is the *self-transcendence of the events of the entirely living nexus* of the person into a *mutual immanence* that constitutes the living unity of a person *beyond* all "charac-ter" (§23). Hence it is conceivable that all events have the *same* initial aim, insofar as in all individual events they wholly permeate one another in mutual immanence (Faber 2000e). If, however, the same, *one* "initial aim" is not to petrify into a "super-character" such that the novelty constituting the self-transcendence of satisfied events into new events is not lost, then this can be the case only if the content of this *one* "initial aim" *is* the *unrestricted novelty of Sophia*/Logos *incarnated* in it (Cobb and Griffin 1976). (b) Concerning the *human* side of the person Jesus, *Sophia*/Logos, rather than "replacing" anything in the events of the living person of Christ, instead fulfills the general creaturely structure of *releasing* creaturely events of the person

Jesus into acts of *self*-creativity with their specific subjective aims. The events of the human being Jesus do not lose their independence (Jesus' personal identity), nor their historical origin from within his surroundings (Jesus' history), nor their freedom (self-creativity), nor their specific situatedness within history (specific initial aims for every situation in the history of the person). That is, the human being Jesus is *free* either to fulfill or not to fulfill his subjective aims, in which *Sophia*/Logos herself is present. Jesus is historically charged with processually fulfilling (not just substantially executing) Sonship in his life (Schulte 1970). The human being Jesus is independent to the extent he is not divested of the self-creative act of *his* personal being, or the self-transcendence of *his* events for mutual immanence (Cobb and Griffin 1976).

This Christology of the divine-human person of Christ, however, should not be misunderstood as a violation of the otherwise *critical* distance process theology maintains from speaking about the "presence" of *Sophia*/Logos in events as ontotheological "fulfilled self-presence" (§§8, 13). On the contrary, it is precisely in the thus characterized presence of *Sophia*/Logos in the mutual immanence of all subjective aims of the person Jesus that the same *différance* is preserved that characterizes God as *eschatological trace* within creaturely happenings. *Sophia*/Logos is incarnated in the person of Jesus as the *eschatological future* in the presence of the *one* "initial aim," which per se is always future. Although *Sophia*/Logos does indeed wholly permeate Jesus, she does so not as fulfilled presence, but as *absolute future* (§35). In that sense, the human being Jesus has his initial aims just as much "at his back" (from that future) as do all other living persons with consciousness, for the initial aim—even if it be *Sophia*/Logos herself—always initiates an event prior to that event "seizing" itself in "becoming" and becoming conscious. The presence of *Sophia*/Logos, rather than overwhelming Jesus' human consciousness or repressing his freedom, instead opens up both; that presence is the unconscious and *hidden anteriority*—in the human being Jesus—that both makes his being human possible *and* in fact demands it.

Here one can draw on the terminology of classical Christology in speaking about a *hypostatic union* of natures. For it is in the *person* that the creative non-difference of *Sophia*/Logos with the events of the person Jesus is united with the free self-creativity of these events (§20). The personal identity of the *hypostasis* of the *Sophia*/primordial nature with the *one* "initial aim" of the events of the human being Jesus, rather than constituting a mixing of humanity and God, instead refers to the identity of the same person amid a simultaneous distinction of divine being and human being, albeit with the human being having been taken up into the *hypostasis* of *Sophia*/Logos. In this point, process theology's concept of hypostatic union corresponds to the concept of *enhypostasis* in the Cappadocian fathers, that is, the concept of the human nature being taken up into the person of the divine Logos (Faber 1995a). The "identity" of a person is a cumulative collection of the satisfactions of that person's life events (§22). In the case of Jesus, however, this cumulation leads into *Sophia*/Logos, who in the *one* "initial aim" of the entirely living nexus is the *unity of person* into which all person-events of the human being Jesus are gathered as to their identity (Faber 2000e). In *enhypostasis*, Jesus' humanity, rather than being sucked up, as it were, is instead positioned in freedom. *Sophia*/Logos makes *true humanity* possible for the human being Jesus, humanity by being *true* even possessing the *power to overcome* violence and sin, demonic past and anxiety in the face of death.

(4) The *soteriological meaning* of the divine-human person of Jesus as the *salutary incarnation* of *Sophia*/Logos (in the flesh of sin) becomes clear in the meaning of God's self-revelation as personal *self-transcendence* (§23). Sinful existence comes about through withdrawal into self, isolation, the refusal of relationality, and ultimately in a *refusal of self-transcendence* (§37). The search for (and obsession with) *self-possession*—a kind of sinful substantialization—perverts the essence of personal existence as an entirely living nexus of personal events characterized by mutual immanence in their living novelty. By contrast, redemption allows for a *radical reversal* of sinful self-identity as absolutistic self-possession, insofar as the person is now able to surpass the self relationally *without* the anxiety of self-loss. Self-transcendence is the very essence of the fundamental relational structure of the world in the divine matrix, whose primary characterizing feature is mutual immanence and perichoretic communicability (§32). Self-transcendence is ultimately based on the *Trinitarian self-transcendence* of the mutual immanence of the divine persons (§34), namely, in the primordial *superjectivity* of the superjective nautre/Father/Mother (§28) as the quintessence of the nondifference (and differentiation) of self-revelation and self-transcendence (§36), in the primordial act of the inverse concrescence of God in the primordial nature/*Sophia*/Logos/Son, and in the unconditional receptivity of the consequent nature/*Pneuma*/Spirit. With respect to the *Christ event* as the locus of *concrete redemption*, self-transcendence emerges as *radical proexistence* (even as far as the cross) for the sake of redeeming both human and cosmic refusal (Faber 1992; 2000e).

In the Christ event divine self-transcendence happens as the *soteriological self-revelation of God's nature,* insofar as God is incarnated into the sinful form of relational refusal precisely that God might disrupt such refusal, for *Sophia*/Logos is incarnated as *Eros*, who *persuades* rather than *imposes* (AI, 166ff.; Ford 1986b). In that sense, it is through faith and conversion that we enter into the kingdom of heaven (Mark 1:14f.). That is why, as Bernard Loomer explicates (1949), the Logos/Eros is incarnated as *agape*, as noncoercive love that disrupts the violent circle of sinful self-possession, moving instead toward the proexistence of "selfless" (self-transcending) love. It is, moreover, in the events of the person Jesus that precisely this *nonviolence of pure relationality* takes place, in opposition to the coercive power of self-absolutizing (§35). In Jesus' own self-transcendence in *Sophia*/Logos, that is, in the *free obedience* (of creative weakness) through which he transforms the initial aims of his nexus into such subjective aims, whereby he also lives out his Sonship as proexistence, he interrupts the continuum of sin with its demonic effects and manifests *Sophia*/Logos as "absolute novelty" over against the sinful repetition of the world's sinful structure (Suchocki 1995). The enduring soteriological significance of the *humanity* of Jesus (his "being human") (Acts 4:12), is that, through embracing his own personal existence, he is to embody what *Sophia/ Logos* as such is from all eternity, namely, proexistence. Without precisely this *human* fulfillment, the incarnation is not really a true incarnation of *Sophia/Logos* (Schulte 1970). In Jesus' own life, as genuinely lived, that particu- lar self-transcendence *fulfills*—as *redemption*—this *one* and *same* "initial aim" that *is Sophia/*Logos herself.

(5) The incarnation of *Sophia/*Logos happens *in the Pneuma*. Process theology identifies God's efficacious power in the world (*dynamis*), the mode of divine imma- nence in the breath/wind (*ruach*), and the Trinitarian person of the Spirit (Pneuma) with God's consequent nature (Suchocki 1995; Keller 2003) (§34). From the per- spective of the economy of salvation, the Pneuma of the world is immanent in a fash- ion different than is *Sophia*—a differentiation deriving from the inner-Trinitarian difference between the creative and receptive dimensions of God's superjectivity. Whereas *Sophia/*the primordial nature refers to God's immanence in the world, the Pneuma/consequent nature refers to the world's immanence in God (§34). In the Spirit, God is in *us* insofar as we are torn away from our self-being and are as a result a "person in the Spirit" (Faber 2000e) (§22–23). The same applies to the person of Jesus and its soteriological significance. In this sense, process Christology essentially implies a certain understanding of pneumatology.

(a) *Sophia/*Logos is *incarnated* in the Spirit. The primordial nature/*Sophia* does not send visions independent of the world, as it were, "divine fantasies," having nothing to do with the history of the world; instead she sends concrete initial aims pertaining to genuine history. This world-sensitive knowledge of history, however, comes about in God's own receptive consequent nature/Pneuma (§30). Hence the incarnational "logicity"/"wisdom" of the world process always happens "in the Spirit" (§30). Such applies to an even greater degree to the incarnation of *Sophia/*Logos herself, which is incarnated in Jesus' personal events "in the Spirit" based on an experience of the real world into which she is incarnated. In this sense it is not just Jesus' own, personal life experiences that are mediated in the person of Jesus (the experiences of his heritage and past), but—within God's universal recep- tivity—the suffering of the world, God's suffering in the world, and God's will to redeem it. On the path that leads to the cross, Jesus suffers "in the Spirit" not only the violent reaction of the world to his own nonviolence, but also the reaction to God's nonviolence in *Sophia/*Logos (Faber 1995). It is "in the Spirit" that Jesus experiences the suffering that the violence in the world has caused in God. In a pro- found sense, *Jesus' suffering* on the cross can be said to be redemptive because it not only bears this violence "in the Spirit" and in so doing manifests God's self- revelation and noncoercive nature all the way through the power of sin, but even more so because through his own suffering Jesus breaks through the suffering of the world under sin (refusal of self-transcendence) and makes possible—indeed, reveals—the creative transformation of the world "in the Spirit."

(b) In the Spirit, the person of Jesus is *resurrected* into God. All the events of Jesus' person are already mediated during his lifetime through the consequent nature. "In the Spirit," the person in the world is already transformed into the "person in God" (§22). In death, however, the person of Jesus becomes wholly a "person in God"; put differently, the human being Jesus is gathered in God wholly into *that particular* person he *is* for God and, in an abiding sense, for the world. Because the person of Jesus is the *hypostasis* of *Sophia*/Logos herself, however, in the Spirit *Sophia*/Logos *becomes* the person she is through her *incarnation*, namely, the person of Jesus Christ. That is, "in the Spirit" incarnate *Sophia*/Logos takes on a new identity, namely, that of the person of Jesus. *Sophia*/Logos now has the name of Jesus Christ and "instills" herself into God's Spirit as Jesus Christ (Suchocki 1995). Here God's historical revelation in the history of Jesus becomes the *history of Godself*, a moment of the *identity* of *Sophia*/Logos in God and as such a determinative moment of the *further* self-revelation of God's nature in the world (AI, 269). The suffering of Jesus and his *sinless disruption* of the connex of sin in the world is taken up into God "in the Spirit" *such that* it also shapes God's own immanence in the world *precisely through* shaping *the world's immanence in God.* The reception or taking up of incarnated *Sophia*/Logos in the inner-divine Pneuma (consequent nature) thus first of all shapes *God* such that the divine transformation of the world into the absolute delimitation of the world in the kingdom of heaven now bears the countenance and form (*morphē*) of the person of Jesus Christ (Suchocki 1995). Put biblically, it is *in the Spirit* that *through* Christ we become "children of God" the Father (Rom. 11:36; 1 Cor. 8:6; Gal. 4:4–7), that we are transformed into his form, the *morphē* of his resurrection (Phil. 3:21) (Faber 1992).

(c) In the Spirit *Sophia*/Logos that has become human is redemptively *active* as the resurrected Christ in the world. Just as God's Spirit is shaped through the person of Jesus, so also does *Sophia*/Logos now appear redemptively "in the Spirit," in which it now forms the countenance of Jesus in us. The *incarnational structure of the world*—the presence of *Sophia*/Logos in all events insofar as she makes their beginning possible—now bears the *form* of Jesus Christ (Suchocki 1995). "In the Spirit," *Sophia*/Logos acts such that every initial aim has always meant "con-forming" (*syn- morphē*) to the image (*eikōn*) of the Son (Rom. 8:29) (Faber 1995a). Like both Ford and Suchocki, I understand the agency of Christ in us (the gift of the initial aim) as the presence of the Pneuma (§34: model II), more precisely, as the *presence of the Son in the Spirit* as power of self-transcendence. As such power, the Pneuma is active in *all* events of the world process. "In the Spirit," God *desires* (Whitehead also speaks of "appetition") that Christ permeates the world process such that he then delimits all nexuses toward self-transcendence, that is, not only making such transformation possible and indeed empowering it in their *initial* aims (potentiality), but genuinely "luring" toward their satisfaction so that *Sophia*/Logos/Christ may acquire form in real event nexuses. It is in this sense that God strives for a creative *transformation of the world* toward the *eikōn* of Sophia (PR, 345ff.). Through interrupting the demonic past and solidarity in sin, through discipleship to Jesus in the establishment of new solidarity in redemption, and through developing a society whose "entirely living nexus" is the Resurrected, the world itself is to be transformed "in the Spirit" into the *cosmic body of Christ* (Cobb and Griffin 1976). In a fashion not unlike that envisioned by Teilhard de Chardin, albeit without his alledged evolutive optimism (§15), the process of the universalization of the body of Christ strives toward *fulfillment*—toward an *Omega point* (Cousins 1972). Unlike in Teilhard, however, this transformation cannot reach that goal in the temporal future of the world, but rather only through the absolute delimitation of the world in God's kingdom of heaven (§§35, 39). At the same time, however, this transformation into the kingdom of heaven "in the Spirit" acquires the countenance of Christ *only* insofar as God's Pneuma is indeed shaped by the figure of Christ *as well as* by a world that through its own self-creative realization becomes the body of Christ.

(6) The Pneuma is the *divine matrix.* The Pneuma is that *mode of immanence* of the transcendent God (the divine superject) in the world through which God *longs for* the world, enters into it *kenotically,* and takes it up in *delimiting* it that it might become the universal body of Christ. The Spirit strives for a fulfilled body of Christ, for the *pleroma* of Christ. The unique feature of the Pneuma (consequent nature) is *universal receptivity.* Notwithstanding that it is immanent in the world in a different mode than is *Sophia*/Logos (primordial nature), it nonetheless stands not only for the immanence of the world in God, but just as much for the immanence of God in the world. In the Pneuma, these two immanences constitute a *single* continuum of communication between God and world (§32). As the continuum of *salvific communication* within the *pleroma* of Christ, the Pneuma is the *divine matrix.*

(a) The Pneuma is the *de-limiting communication in God.* It is the kingdom of heaven to the extent everything is taken up into it, valuated, judged, transformed, and delimited. Within this *delimiting condition of communication,* the Pneuma stands for the "person" in God in which everything is communicated and joined into a *reconciled nexus* (Faber 2000e). The Pneuma is the *transpersonal person* in which everything has become itself *beyond* itself. Like all living persons, the Pneuma too is *not* determined by a given "character" (form), being instead in what amounts to a virtually archetypical mode an "entirely living nexus" of mutual immanence of *all* events (all nexuses, societies, persons of the world), in which everything mutually permeates everything else in a living, released (de-limited) fashion (§40). It is not without reason that Suchocki has compared the consequent nature with Buddhist "emptiness" (*sunyata*), in which *everything transcends itself* (*annata*), nothing is "something" for itself, and everything mutually allows everything else to be "its self" (Suchocki 1978). This is equally the locus of absolute identity and difference, which Whitehead himself evokes in the form of Plato's "wherein," or *khora* (AI, 150, 295). Like it, so also is the Pneuma *wholly receptive,* the *hypodochē* (the consequent nature knows no negative prehensions). Unlike this *receptive aspect,* however, the "person" of the Pneuma is not "characterless," being instead *communication in love,* the fullness of communication as the *pleroma* of Christ. The Pneuma is thus shaped by Christ, as whose body the world forms itself within the Pneuma into the kingdom of heaven (Suchocki 1995).

(b) The Pneuma is *God's kenotic communication in the world.* Even though at first glance the Pneuma seems to be present only through the mediation of *Sophia*/Logos, it nonetheless is active as God's direct immanence in the world by prehending the past, something that happens not only "in God," but also *in* the world, as it were *on* the past of the world. Within the *conversion* of processes, *Sophia*/Logos is incarnated as future (*from* the creaturely future as its creative beginning) in order to *follow* the world *into* its perishing (§35). This "following" happens within the Pneuma itself such that—according to Griffin—the *kenotic* form of God's presence becomes visible, namely, as the enduring and bearing of the world only *in* its perishing (Griffin 1997).

(c) The Pneuma is the *universal locus of communication in God and world.* From the *inner-divine* perspective, it is first of all God's self-creativity that stands for this communication, that is, God's communicative nature. From the *inner-Trinitarian* perspective, each of the three persons (the three characters or "natures") fulfill this communication in a unique way. The superjective primordial act is the difference between creativity and form, nature and person; it is the primordial act of personal self-transcendence and mutual immanence. *Sophia*/Logos is the primordial act of God's ideal concrescence, the primordial vision, the communication of the ideas. As such, it is the *khora* in God. Within *Sophia*/Logos, the infinite abyss of eternal objects—the "primordial chaos" in God (PR, 7?) (§40)—is positioned in relational communication. The Pneuma is the primordial act of receptivity in which everything communicates. As such, it is the *hypodochē* in God. Within the Spirit, the chaos of the world (the chaotic nexus) stands in reconciled communication (§40). God's nature (inner-divine self-creativity) is nothing apart from the *perichoresis* of the three persons, and as such is shaped by *all three persons* in this characteristic feature through which they fulfill communication (§34). To the extent the *receptivity* of God's nature is meant—that is, of the "threefold character"—God's mutual immanence refers (or as in classical theology, is "appropriated") to the Pneuma. From the perspective of the *economy of salvation*, the Pneuma thus refers to receptivity, mutual immanence, and communication as the ground of the world. The *hypodochē* in the world (the chaotic nexus) and the *hypodochē* in God mutually reflect each other (Faber 2000e).

(d) The Pneuma is the *"person" of intercreativity* (§34: Figure 5). In it, communication is fulfilled in God, in the world, and between God and world. In that sense, the Pneuma refers to the "person" in which *all* nexuses communicate and are integrated into the unity of divine receptivity. The Pneuma appears as the *gift of life*, as the *"person" of the divine matrix* (Bracken 1981; 1997; 2001) (§32). Within the Pneuma, the divine matrix appears as a *bond of love*—borne by the *yearning* for the *pleroma* of Christ. In the Pneuma, creation sighs with longing until it is revealed as the body of Christ (Rom. 8:18–30). The divine matrix is the bond in which God and world are mutually immanent, one in the other, in which world time and God's everlasting time mutually permeate each other, in which alpha and omega are positioned within a reconciled continuum, and in which the body of Christ in the world and the kingdom of heaven are united into an

Omega point. As the "person" of the divine matrix, the Pneuma is thus the *fore-shadowing of completion.*

§39. THE HARMONY OF HARMONIES (AD-VENT/FUTURE, PEACE, AND ADVENTURE)

The poet of the world, which becomes visible in theopoetics, is an *eschatological God* (§35). In delimitation over against standard twentieth-century eschatological models, the fundamental conviction underlying process theology's development of eschatology is that God's self-revelation is *not* found primarily (1) in *nature*—as one might suppose given process theology's orientation toward cosmology—that is, as the supporting "ground" of the world; nor (2) in *history*—as one might suppose, given process theology's consistently historical mode of thinking—that is, as the God of a certain people, tradition, or path of faith; nor (3) in the extremes of human *existence* itself, which believes it senses God's presence in "border situations," in the face of death, or as the "inner ground of the soul." Instead, process theology delimits itself over against presentist eschatology (liberal theology, Schweitzer), existentialist eschatology (Althaus, Barth, Bultmann), and historical eschatology (Pannenberg, Moltmann) by understanding God's self-revelation from the perspective of the *temporal form of the process* itself (Moltmann 1995). From the perspective of the unitexturality of reality, process theology understands the world as a nexus of temporal events and God as a *dipolar temporal process* (§25) (Faber 2000h). Hence process eschatology is essentially a *theology of time* (Faber 2002f). In this capacity, it not only engages various natural, historico-theological, and existentialist aspects of other eschatologies—not surprising, given the intensive interconnection between the natural, historical, and existentialist aspects (§§3–6) in process theology's organic cosmology (§36)—it also transforms the key postmodernist critique of the presentist thinking of ontotheology (§8) into the temporal structure of God's *diachronic presence* as *différance* and *process*—God's temporally extended, diachronically temporal, oscillating dipolar, transcendent immanence (§25) (Faber 2002e; 2000e). Within God's dipolar temporal presence, each event discloses itself within the extended tension between future and past (§12) and God, doing so both (with respect to the primordial nature) as the *eschatological future* of the world as well as (with respect to the consequent nature) as the *eschatological delimitation of the past* in God (§35). Within eschatology itself, precisely because of its concern with the "last things" and with the completion of the world in God, there inheres precisely that particular *temporal index* formulated within God's dual temporal process which thus prompts process theology to pose a *dual* eschatological question. First, *what* is this *future,* and *how* does the world relate to it? That is, is this future, as something yet outstanding, something that will come only through becoming present, or is it already exerting some sort of agency within the world process even now? And second, what will happen with the world's *past*, with that which perishes and indeed has already perished? These are the key eschatological questions to which specific answers of process theology have been developed. These questions involve *universal* and *individual* eschatology viewed from a temporal theological perspective (Suchocki 1988). These answers essentially critically follow Whitehead's initial intuition with respect to the dipolar concept of God and God's radical orientation toward the world, the universal relationality of his cosmology, and the relational soteriology of his theology as summarized in the concluding vision of his later work, *Adventures of Ideas*, in an "eschatology" of the "Harmony of Harmonies" (§24).

To understand the process's eschatological "time form," one must first address the theological question concerning the temporal nature of the eschaton itself and its *relation* with the world process. Insofar as beginning and end coincide in theopoetics and indeed are even interchangeable according to certain rules, process theology's eschatology emerges within a *mirroring* of creation theology (§35). And to the extent process theologies develop varying creation theologies with varying focal points, one also encounters a series of basic eschatological models that can be reduced to three types.

(1) Not unlike creation theology within the same framework, "eschatology" oriented toward classical *empirical process theology* envisions only a *cosmology of endless process*, a position attesting the heritage of liberal theology, which in its own turn wholly opposed the traditional (neoscholastic) eschatology that acknowledged the possibility that God might intervene supernaturally in ongoing cosmic time and arbitrarily interrupt the world itself (Moltmann 1995). There thus inheres within this "eschatology" an element of *critical naturalism* to the extent it opposes the inclination to look *beyond* the world and understand God as arbitrary, as well as the inclination to divert the attention of theology itself away from this world, a world theology seeks to understand, change, and reconcile. Such "eschatology" is reflected by the lack of interest in (n.b., not the impossibility of) creation theology insofar as it was inclined to pass beyond the *creatio continua* (in inquiring a *beyond* the world itself). Soteriological considerations prompt its character as a *radically world-oriented* eschatology of the presence of God within that particular process through which the world takes place as such; in this capacity, it also advocates a *soteriology of creative transformation* (§§3, 5).

(2) Eschatology deriving from classical *rational process theology*, and especially theology in the tradition of Hartshorne, developed a *dual eschatology* focused especially on the *dipolarity* (physicality/mentality) of the *duality of process* (subjectivity/superjectivity) (§33) and the four-phase creative process (§30). This position seeks to take eschatological account both of God's immanence in the world and of the world's immanence in God, but to do so without sundering the relationality of the world, one of the fundamental convictions of process theology. With respect to *God's immanence in the world* through *Sophia*/Logos, the point of departure is an *endless world process* of successive cosmic epochs (§32). With respect to the *world's immanence in God* in the Pneuma, the point of departure is the reception and delimitation of the world in God's *kingdom of heaven* (Suchocki 1988; Cobb and Griffin 1976) (§34). Mirroring creation theology, dual eschatology corresponds to the

thesis of "creation out of chaos"——by critically opposing any ontotheology beholden to the notion of coercive power in positing an absolute beginning and a definitive end (§35). Most specifically Christian process theologies of the existentialist, speculative, and postmodern variety concur that the deconstruction of this focus on coercive power in the background of *creatio ex nihilo* inevitably also prompts a deconstruction of the notion of an *apocalyptic eschatology* that envisions a violent cessation of the world. In this regard, Keller considers it in the interest of any postmodern process theology rigorously to carry through the notion of *différance* that envisions only *relative* (relational) beginnings and ends (Keller 1997).

(3) Process theologies deriving more narrowly from *Christian tradition*, that is, those driven less by the internal consequences of Whitehead's ecological cosmology than by the particularity of the Christian revelation itself, articulate the question of eschatology more unequivocally as that regarding the *eschaton*—an individual and universal completion of the world in God (Suchocki 1995). Without denying the inner rationality of dual eschatology as the paradigm of process theology might otherwise well suggest, and often even without denying dual eschatology as such, this position—in a fashion not unlike that of Thomas Aquinas—tends to give precedence to a revelatory theology. It is especially the representatives of *speculative process theology* who take this path, insofar as they tend to go furthest in reconstructing the ecological paradigm with respect to Christian revelatory theology (§7). Commensurate with the mirroring of eschatology with creation theology, this position countenances a *creatio ex nihilo* and thus equally an eschaton in which the world as a whole is renewed. Now the eschatological God can be understood as the *eschatological future* of the world (Suchocki 1988), brought into dialogue with corresponding future-oriented theologies of history (Ford 1977c with Pannenberg; Bracken 2002 with Moltmann), or can be conceived simply as the God of the final consummation and completion (Hosinski 1993). Some of these theologians adduce the *renewal of poles* in support of their eschatology (Suchocki 1988) and also reacknowledge God's *freedom* with respect to both the creation act and the eschaton as a presupposition of the soteriological meaning of references to God (Bracken 2001). Although in the following discussion I draw on the motifs of the first two groups, I will be specifically developing further the third (Faber 2000h). But any process eschatology will be shaped by the following critical and constructive considerations: (a) with respect to the first group, a *world-oriented eschatology* directed against all nonrelational supernaturalism; (b) with respect to the second group, a *dual eschatology* directed against all unilateral focus on coercive power; and (c) with respect to the third group, a *converse eschatology* directed against any abbreviation of eschatology to cosmology.

The key eschatological question concerning the completion of the world in God is a *temporal question* that speaks about the eschaton in the categories of God's *diachronic presence*. Process eschatology is thus a theology of time whose presuppositions of process theology include the principles of concretion (§27) and empiricism (§36), the conversion of processes (§29), and God's superjectivity (§28). Its specific medium for mediating a dual eschatology of the temporal world and completion in God—cosmos and kingdom of heaven—is the divine matrix

3-fold
creation
encompasses
eschaton

(§32). Hence this process eschatology is formulated as a *dual, diachronic, converse eschatology*, whose central thesis is that God is *eschatologically present* in the world in God's "threefold character" insofar as God approaches or moves toward the world *from the future of the world* in order to complete it by taking it up in reconciliation *into God's future* (Faber 2000h).

The *threefold creative act* (as addressed in the *primary passage on theopoetics*) and the *four creative phases* of every event (§30) attest events as *happening in time*: the event's grounding in the *future* of itself; the creative process through which it becomes present beyond physical time (in the wholeness of its mental pole), albeit while taking up its own temporal past into this very process; its perishing in its wholeness by which it grounds a quantum of physical time (becoming a causally efficacious moment of temporal past), and simultaneously its reception as superject in God's consequent nature (PR, 244). That which happens in time in this sense is positioned within a twofold duality of time. The *first duality* is that between immanent and transcendent creativity. Although in its immanence an event is indeed positioned "within becoming," it is not "in (physical) time"; only in its self-transcendence does it become a moment in physical time. The *second duality* is that between world-time and God's time. Within the world, the *past* influences the present of an event, thereby acquiring future in it; in God, however, the *future*   from which God releases Godself in order to bequeath to the event its own self as future—influences the present of an event's self-creativity, which in its own turn perishes "into God's consequent nature." The creative act realizes two "temporal modes," namely, the transition of "outside" (physicality) to "inside" (mentality), of past into future, and the transition of "above" ("God's time") to "below" (world-time), of future into past. The first temporal mode is the *creaturely time* of the world process, the time in which all processes are temporal and move toward a (self-transcending) future. The second temporal mode is the *creative time* of the process of God, in which God eternally circles and simultaneously, everlastingly takes up the world into God's circle. The temporal mode of the process of God *opens up* and *grounds* the temporal mode of the world process (Figure 6).

Figure 6: The Conversion of the Temporal Modes of the Processes of God and World

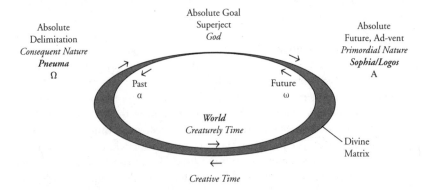

With regard to the *world process*, the two temporal modes appear as variants of the *conversion of processes*. God's "time," with its "threefold character," moves toward the world. (a) God is the *source of the time* of the world (Moltmann 1995; Link 1989). From the perspective of world-time, God opens up its prevailing future through *approaching* it from what is an *absolute future* over against that world. God, however, is also the *guardian of world-time*, since it is God who keeps that time open in God's own *approach* (coming near) or *ad-vent* (becoming present). God's "movement toward" in this sense is an act of *Sophia*/Logos, which instead of *coming, withdraws*—like a horizon—to provide creaturely time-"space" for each new world future. (b) God is the *release of time* insofar as God follows it even in its perishing in order to rescue it into God's "presence." From the perspective of world-time, God is the absolute *delimitation of time* and as such the *future of the past* beyond itself. God is the *preserver of time that has already happened* insofar as God's approach, in its proximity, enables time to reacquire itself *beyond* itself. This is an act of God's Pneuma, through which God not only preserves the world "in Godself," but also vivifies it as past time (that has already happened). (c) As the absolute origin of theopoetic difference and thus of the temporal process of both temporal modes, the superjectivity of God is also the absolute aim of time in which all "departure" is gathered into the goal again. In this sense, God's superjectivity makes it possible to understand God not as that which "underlies" time (*sub*-ject), but as the "approaching goal" (*super*-ject), since it is *in* the superject that all processes are nondifferent. Whereas the temporal modes are *undistinguished* in God (inseparably one), in the world they are distinct and move counter to each other (§§28, 35). Whereas in God there is only the everlasting circling of the Trinitarian movement in which the "three natures" mutually presuppose one another (regardless of the "direction" in which we might conceive them as moving), in the world there is a distinction between the movements of God's *Trinitarian creative act* and the *threefold creative act* of creatures. (d) The *relation* between God and world is the *divine matrix*. In God, it is the nondifferent Trinitarian communication in which the persons mutually interpenetrate one another; in the world, however, it emerges as the field of tension between the processes of God and world positioned in mutual counter-movement (§32). In God's superjectivity, the divine matrix is a "field" of *nondifferent perichoresis*; in the world, however, the divine matrix emerges as the "field" of *différance* in the form of countermoving temporal modes.

Through this conversion of temporal modes, the God of process theology emerges as a *wholly eschatological* God. All "three natures" essentially formulate the creative difference between God and world as *eschatological difference*. (a) *Sophia*/Logos stands for *eschatological ad-vent* or *approach* (becoming present); in it, God appears to the world as the source of time, as the openness of the time-"space" of creation, as the infinitely moving "locus" of that which is possible in the future. Through *Sophia*/Logos, the world is led out beyond itself into the transcendence of the novel from within the divine power of the absolutely novel. Through *Sophia*/Logos, God is present to the world *as* future (§38). Because the primordial nature is the measure of all that is possible, its gift of the future (with no regard for every merely possible relative world) is absolute. As the measure of intensity and harmony, *Sophia*/Logos awakens within the world process a striving for living, vibrant movement, unrestricted novelty, and incessant life. (b) The Pneuma stands for the *eschatological delimitation of the past* (§38). Within the conversion of the temporal modes—and precisely this is the distinctive feature of process eschatology—we anticipate the eschaton not *in* the future of the world, but *as the future of its past* (Faber 2000h; 2002f). In a *reversal of times*, our *eschatological hope* anticipates not that which is "coming," but that which *was*—that which has died, perished, is irretrievable, decomposed (Faber 2000h). We worry about its future and hope in its return to life. The Spirit of God is the "place" that God "grants" to or provides for the world in God, the place in which God grants life to the dead and future to that which is past, and in which God preserves and releases into universal communication that which is past, communication constituting God's own Trinitarian *perichoresis*. And in it, God is subjected in suffering to the world and knows about the world's suffering. In it, the world is promised *eschatological life*. (c) The superjective origin stands for *eschatological completion beyond the difference of creation and creator* (§28). The "origin" of theopoetic difference is its goal, not as "retrieval into the beginning" or as its sublation, but as its inexhaustible fountain. That is, in the goal we are simultaneously at home *and* at the origination of the entire process. The nondifference of processes in God's superjectivity opens up to us access to a *mystical* vision of God of the sort found in the tradition of Dionysius the Areopagite, Nicholas of Cusa, and Meister Eckhart (Faber 2001c), aiming at the Godhead *beyond* the difference of God and world, where beginning and end utterly lose significance, where everything "is" in everything else and God is the "space" of nondifference (§40).

The positioning of process theology's understanding of God *in principle* within an *eschatological horizon* makes it possible to enter into conversation with other Christian eschatologies with respect to critical differences.

reversal of time

(1) Although the fundamental assumption of a *reversal of time* in process eschatology was posited a century ago, it was never really developed further with any abiding effects. Various concepts that were indeed present *in nuce* in process eschatology without exerting any seminal influence—and which thus had to be, as it were, reinvented elsewhere—include the eschatological significance of *time* "at the foundation" of history and nature, the differentiation between *temporal modes* and their *counter-movement*, and certainly the consequences attaching to the notion that God does indeed reveal Godself *through time "from ahead"* (Faber 2000h). Karl Rahner and Paul Tillich make similar demands for an eschatological God of temporal power. Rahner suggests an eschatological understanding of time in opposition to an evolutive one. Whereas in an evolutive understanding of time the "end" (the future) is already contained in the "beginning" (the origin/the past), for him Christianity understands God as the *absolute future* that approaches from the eschaton in a fashion neither predetermined nor derivable.

Rahner, without developing the theological implications of the notion, understands God's *absolute novelty* as the absolute unincurred nature of grace over against the inability of nature to effect redemption or completion itself. The eschatological God of "absolute future" is the absolutely free God. Soteriological hope is grounded in God's freedom in this sense and is then explicated theologically with respect to time (Rahner 1970). In his own turn, Tillich distinguishes between the protological time of "being" and the eschatological time of "becoming." In the paradigm of "being," the *proton* already contains the *eschaton*. In the paradigm of the "becoming," by contrast, that which happens is bequeathed to itself in underivable novelty only from the perspective of the end (Tillich 1963). Both theologians position a gracious God who freely comes in redemption *from* the eschaton—over against the world's own power to redeem itself.

(2) In their theologies of history, Pannenberg and Moltmann develop an understanding of eschatological time not from the substantialist-ontological perspective of the beginning and its subsequent unfolding, but from an event-ontological perspective of the end. The point of departure for Pannenberg's *universal-historical* eschatology is the notion that the world is yet developing toward wholeness that, once having become whole, will correspond to the arrival of the kingdom of God (Pannenberg 1987). Pannenberg—similar to Jüngel—thus understands God's "being" as still "in becoming." God acts *from the perspective* of that whole—the eschatological future of the world—which God "is" as salvation and even now is *proleptically* "becoming," especially in the resurrection of Jesus, in which salvation/wholeness already became present (Pannenberg 1993). In his own turn, Moltmann opposes the continuity of becoming in Pannenberg's schema, that is, its inherent teleology, since it belittles the actual suffering of the world, and because in so doing—here Moltmann follows the lead of Walter Benjamin—it in fact writes a "victor's history" (Klappert 1997). Moltmann, by contrast, roughens up, as it were, Pannenberg's "developmental" eschatology *apocalyptically* by understanding the eschaton as God's temporal inbreaking into the world. Adducing the biblical divine name YHWH and its self-revelation in Exodus 3:14, Moltmann defines God as a God of time who "is what God will be," who, as it were, freely withdraws *into* the future and simultaneously promises God's underivable loyalty *for* the future. Revelation 1:4 interprets this God "who will be" as the one "who is and who was and who is to *come*." Within a breach of symmetry of times, God relates to the past and present in the mode of being (*einai*) and to the (eschatological) future in the mode of coming (*erchestai*). The eschatological God comes from the future of the world (*futurum*) whereby God's "ad-vent" (*adventus*) brings novelty, freedom, and completion (Moltmann 1995). Unlike Pannenberg, process eschatology understands the cosmos not according to the mode of *one* event with its inner teleology, but as a *chaotic nexus* of open order without any obvious goal (§19). As a result, it too does not write a "victor's history" and, in contradistinction to evolutive models, does not refuse "limited time" (Metz 1993). Unlike Moltmann, however, process eschatology no longer projects the eschaton *into* the future and similarly no

longer understands the transcendence of the future as a soteriological "goal," anticipating instead the soteriological eschaton from *God's passage into the past* of the world, from its *rescue* into God's being "behind us" rather than "ahead of us" (Faber 2000h).

In the conversion of times, process eschatology develops a *dual eschatology* in which the eschatological future of the past (in God's kingdom of heaven) must *not* necessarily contradict a cosmic future of the world (out of God's future that "provides space"). Put differently, the world must not come to its "end" in order to be eschatologically reconciled (Faber 2000h; 2002f). Hence, for process eschatology, the determinative categorial questions of eschatology (concerning individual and universal completion) are concentrated in the question of the relationship between the *kingdom of heaven* and the *adventure of the world*, and between *ultimate reconciliation* in God and the *openness of the cosmic world process* (in the succession of cosmic epochs). This, however, is a question concerning the relationship between *Sophia*/Logos and Pneuma (§38) and the *intercreativity* generated by that relationship (§16). Whitehead interprets this inner-divine relationship between *Sophia*/Logos and Pneuma as that between *creative Eros and eschatological Peace*, and interprets the attendant eschatological relationship between God and world as the *harmony of harmonies* (§24).

(1) *It is in the Pneuma that the world attains its eschatological Peace.* The Pneuma is God's kingdom of heaven, into which all events are taken up and delimited (PR, 340, 346; AI, 296). This completion or consummation in the Spirit fulfills existence as self-transcendence (§§23, 38) because it is perceived by God precisely *in its status as that which is already past*, in its superjectivity, in which it "exists" *beyond* itself, which God, after perceiving it, awakens to new life in God *in* its "beyondness" in this sense (§23). The Spirit is the reality of resurrection into which everything is taken up with its historicity as that which it "has become" (Suchocki 1978). Everything acquires life in its *corporeality* (*sōma pneumatikon*) and attains its eschatological *identity* by perichoretically permeating everything else relationally "in God" (Suchocki 1995). As *eschatological Peace*, God is the *intensive harmony* of the world. This *eschatological harmony* has three aspects.

(a) *Eschatological vivacity (prehension).* Within the ongoing world process, the self-transcendent superject is efficaciously active as an object. That is, though it perishes in its subjective immediacy ("for itself"), it is causally efficacious "externally" (§§21, 41). Events that prehend it can perceive it in its singularity but not as a whole (§§11, 36–37). In contrast to the world process, the process of God stands in *intimate proximity* to every event (§30). Whitehead speaks about how God alone stands in a "unison of becoming" (PR, 124, 128, 320, 322, 340, 345f., 350f.) with all event happenings, that is, how God *alone* perceives all event happenings in their perishing exactly as they have become within their inner, subjective immediacy (Suchocki 1977). Hence nothing is lost in God's prehension of the world into the Pneuma, since God has no negative prehensions (Orf 1996; Franklin 1990; Christian 1967). Because God prehends through "ideal completion" (Maassen 1988; Ford 1973), God need exclude *nothing*, being capable instead of experiencing everything from God's comprehensive perspective of "re-enacting" it in its entirety (§36). God is an inclusive actuality that takes up everything in the *subjective wholeness* and *living integrity* of that which it has become (§29). In contrast to the world-agency of superjects, which Whitehead calls "objective immortality" (§23), in their *divine prehension* event happenings are able to attain a redeemed identity that must no longer do without immediacy. Suchocki and Ford refer to this reconciled resurrection of events as "subjective immortality" (Ford and Suchocki 1977).

(b) *Eschatological judgment (transformation).* Just as event-happenings within the world process find their identity only through self-transcendence, thereby becoming positioned relationally within a nexus or society, so also is the context of all events in the world received within the divine nexus their situatedness within the Pneuma (Suchocki 1995). Events attain their "identity" only in the context of the nexuses in which they have stood in the world and with respect to which they have actualized themselves self-creatively (aesthetically) and in self-transcendence (ethically). That identity is *at risk*, however, to the extent events in personal societies (such as human persons with consciousness and freedom) can also *sin*, that is, both lag behind their initial aim in their self-creativity or take a position of refusal with respect to their self-transcendence, thereby fostering the demonic in the world (sinful structures) both for themselves and for other persons and societies. The sinful "person in God" lags behind itself, behind its possibilities, and behind its relationality, and remains but a fragment in its sinful events (§37). Therefore when the *identity* of a "person in God," within the *collection* of all its life events, culminates in its perichoretic presence (§22)—its superjectivity *as* person—it cannot on its own power assemble itself into eschatological "wholeness" without first *reconciling* all the fragmentary, crumbling, and encrusted events (Suchocki 1988). Similar to Pannenberg's reflections on judgment, the eschatological "gathering" or "collection" of a person demands a *reconciling transformation* of its events into a whole of the sort that can be *only* the gift of grace in the Pneuma (Pannenberg 1993). In this *final judgment*, every person is *transcended to* its heavenly identity (PR, 346). Reconciliation in God is something that *happens*—a *suffering* of sinfulness through God's Pneuma and a *disruption* of sinfulness through divine suffering (§38).

Just as *Sophia*/Logos cannot be active in the world in caring concern as wisdom without the Pneuma (§38), however, so also, in a reverse fashion, the Pneuma cannot judge in God without *Sophia*/Logos. *Sophia*/Logos is both the measure of God's universal vision of a world in intensity and harmony (§21) and the measure of the personal vision of the self-value of every event (§23). Her judgment is *just* because it is not influenced by any interest, but rather solely by the intensity, harmony, and value underivable from *any* world and wanting nothing other than the creature itself, for its own sake. Judgment in the Pneuma, however, is not disinterested, but rather *sym-pathetic* insofar as it derives from the knowledge and re-enacted feeling of events "from their perspective" and as such serves the self-acquisition of persons. Judgment in the Pneuma is gracious, merciful, compassionate, not condemning, and is such because—as Whitehead explicitly emphasizes in *Process and Reality* with respect to the consequent nature— it is characterized by an element of "tenderness" that "loses nothing that can be saved" and "with tender care" is intent on seeing "that nothing be lost" (PR, 346). Finally, in a Christian context judgment bears the *countenance of Christ*, for he is the concrete *Sophia*/Logos; Christ is judge in the Spirit (§38), judging the world out of his own self-bequeathing, suffering love for the world (Suchocki 1995).

(c) *Eschatological peace (delimitation)*. The identity of events is fulfilled through their self-transcendence into the nexuses to which they belong. In their own turn, these event nexuses attain their identity through self-transcendence beyond their "own" coherent context within the whole of the reconciled world in the Pneuma. All societies, though especially persons, are delimited within the Pneuma into the divine nexus. Whereas living persons have an entirely living nexus at the center of their self-unfolding, whose *essence* consists in the self-transcendence of their events (§22), the Pneuma is that particular "living person" of God in which everything is delimited into an *entirely living nexus of all-reconciliation* (Suchocki 1978) (§38). The Pneuma is the *person of the universal self-delimitation* into *living whole- ness*. In the Pneuma, personal existence attains its *transpersonal meaning* (§23). The Pneuma is universal communication, and in the delimited nature of this communication it is *the* "transpersonal person," the universal unity of living per- sonal existence at its very "origin"—divine unity as *hypodochē* (universal recep- tion) (§38). In it, however, every event, every event nexus, every entirely living nexus, every living person simultaneously attains its final, ultimate identity (Faber 2002a). God's *kingdom of heaven* consists in the ultimacy and finality of this universally delimited, radically communicative, and everlastingly reconciled identity. Whitehead refers to its delimited relationality as "peace" (AI, 284ff.).

This universal delimitation into *eschatological peace* happens within the *inter- twining or interpenetration of Pneuma and Sophia/Logos*. *Sophia*/Logos, as the measure of intensity and harmony, is the divine "wherein" of God's vision of the world. The *khora* of *Sophia*/Logos corresponds to the *hypodochē* of the Pneuma (§38). It is in the infinite, living, enduringly open-ended vision of *Sophia*/Logos delimitation within the Pneuma acquires its potentiality. In eschatological peace, *Sophia*/Logos is the *Eros* of vibrant life, ideality, potentiality, the *Eros* of the high- est intensity and harmony, of the greatest self-value of creatures. In *Sophia*/Logos, everything is released into that which it is capable of being (PR, 346). And it is *in Christ* that this release acquires its ultimate soteriological significance as *resur- rection*—delimited, corporeal identity (Suchocki 1995). Yet since delimitation in Christ is also *judgment*, the question arises concerning the *form of reconciliation* in Christ. Process eschatology tends to hope for universal reconciliation (*apokatastasis pantōn*). Because every event is positioned within universal rela- tionality, process eschatology has difficulty entertaining the notion of hell as a "place" or "condition" of eternal torment, eternal exclusion in obduracy, or eter- nal punishment for sinful *incurvatio in seipsum*. Given the corporeality (the tem- poral and spatial interwovenness) of *every* event not only within its own nexus, but also with everything in everything, no single event ever belongs *solely* to merely a *single* nexus as its "possession." Through self-delimitation, *each* of my own life events also belongs (through recollection, experience, or agency) to *other* persons. Where, then, would these events of a person actually be if the person were in hell? Would not part of us all (our recollection of others or love for others) be in hell in that case? And would not part of those who were in hell *not* be in hell? Where is the boundary, the breach in the relational resurrection corpo-reality (*sōma pneumatikon*) (Faber 2002f)? Whitehead thus conceives of the pos-sibility of God *limiting* or leaving in *self-limitation* within the Pneuma those events that are "purely self-regarding" and *cannot* be redeemed, simultaneously delimiting, however, the salutary effects in others, thereby redeeming them *in other* events. In Christ, the Pneuma delimits everything capable of such, while limiting (Whitehead speaks of "dismissing") the self-limited as the "triviality of merely individual facts" (PR, 346). Here "hell" means above all relativizing an irremediable event into pure facticity, into a past that is now *left* in its status as past and that as a consequence disappears from living recollection. Although uni-versal reconciliation allows for a final separation between good and evil (and thus for a "hell"), it understands such separation anew against the background of *uni-versal solidarity* within the Pneuma and through Christ (Suchocki 1995).

(2) *In Sophia/Logos, the world is granted space for the eschatological Adventure.* *Sophia*/Logos is the *Eros* of the inalienable element of life in the world. Because *Sophia*/Logos "provides" or frees up time, her eschatological agency from the future is also that of self-limitation. Here the biblical notion of the Son's *kenosis* (Phil. 2:7)—his self-emptying—acquires theological meaning with respect to *time.* The creative emergence of the world happens *out of the nothing of Sophia/Logos* (*ex nihilo Filii*), God's *self-withdrawal*, through which God releases or frees up difference, the *khora*, the "wherein" of the world (§38). "Nothingness" in God appears in *Sophia*/Logos in its character as "locus" of potency—of the power of that which is *possible*. The primordial nature as the quintessence of the possible is per se the *provision of space* for actualizations. This *creative act toward the interior* of God (§35), reminiscent of kabbalistic zimzum (God's self-limita-tion) (Scholem 1980) and Nicholas of Cusa's *contractio* (God's self-contraction) (Haubst 1991), is of an *eschatological* nature. Through this creative provision of space for world-time from the future, God bequeaths Godself in an unending, unlimited, and essential way such that future has no end but is an unending beginning. The *eschatological goal* of this provision of space by *Sophia*/Logos is the world's enduring adventure. The expression "*ad/venture*" contains the future as the *ad-vent* in which creaturely time *is opened up* within *Sophia*/Logos (Figure 6). In the Pneuma, *Sophia*/Logos transfers eschatological *peace* to the world as *essential self-transcendence*. In the *Eros*, self-transcendence is actualized as *Adven-ture*, as displacement into the new that consistently extends beyond itself into God's vision. Peace and Adventure realize this rapturous displacement (White-head speaks of "zest" and "self-forgetful transcendence") (AI, 296). Hence both in and of themselves as well as together, Peace and Adventure represent wholly

valid realizations of the eschaton. Dual eschatology emerges from the relation between *Sophia*/Logos and Pneuma, their Harmony in the *perichoresis* within God's *superject, the* primordial transcendence as alpha and omega.

(3) *The completion and endlessness of the world converge in the Harmony of Harmonies*. Whitehead understands the eschatological concurrence of Peace and Adventure as the Harmony of Harmonies. His great work, *Adventures of Ideas*, concludes with a vision of the world, with all its processes, as a beginning "within a dream of youth" and an end in a "harvest of tragedy." An essential lack of ultimate reconciliation attaches to the world process, which Whitehead calls "tragic Beauty" (AI, 296) (§45). "Beauty" is the harmony of intensities in events (aesthetic process) and in event nexuses (ethical process) of self-surpassment. This myriad of processes and process nexuses is "tragic" because it issues in "perpetual perishing" (PR, 29, 147f., 210, 340). Paradoxically, beauty and tragedy are codeterminative insofar as the finitude and transience of events *alone* secures their *essential* relationality (and vice versa)—otherwise we end in substantialism (§13). Wherever the world process becomes *conscious* of the yearning for the reconciliation of tragedy and beauty, however, and indeed strives for such, the vision of God as Harmony of Harmonies opens up as hope in a *reconciled relationship* between finitude and relationality, process and reality, limitation and delimitation. It is *felt* as a "sense of Peace" (AI, 296). God is ultimately "the secret of the union of Zest with Peace," in which suffering "attains its end in the Harmony of Harmonies" (AI, 296). In the unreconciled world process, by contrast, God is manifested in the "immediate experience of this Final Fact," in which the "union of Youth and Tragedy" is already established as the "sense of Peace" (AI, 296). With respect to this reconciliation, God is the "Supreme Adventure" (AI, 295).

The *dual eschatology of Adventure and Peace* converges in the *Harmony of Harmonies* such that one can equate the eschatological goal of world not with its end, but with a striving for Peace *though* the Adventure and as a striving for Adventure *through* the experience of Peace (Figure 6). Although the question of the "end" of the world is in that sense not crucial to process eschatology, neither must it be eliminated entirely. The *point of departure* is the *essential transience* (impermanence) of the world, which Whitehead calls "perpetual perishing." It is there that the unreconciled nature of the world process comes to expression theologically with respect to time insofar as events realize novelty and in so doing perish. Time is a becoming (subjective process), but also a perishing (superjective process), in effect a *dual* process in the swing between immanent and transcendent creativity (§16). Reconciliation could be found where becoming was possible *without* perishing, that is, where—as Whitehead emphasizes in the soteriological concluding chapter of *Process and Reality*—there was "novelty without loss" (PR, 340). And this is the yearning not for Peace, but for Adventure without tragedy, an end to loss and perishing. Meanwhile, the answer to this "ultimate evil" of the temporal world is the Harmony of Harmonies, the reconciled *convergence of the duality of the process*—of process and reality, flux and permanence, immanence and transcendence, actuality and activity (§31)—but *not* its "end." Whitehead's response—more fertile than his own systematic vision could accommodate and more varied than his reception among process theology— adduces *three possibilities for a reconciled convergence* of Adventure and Peace in the Harmony of Harmonies, three visions of an ultimate eschatology (Faber 2000e).

(1) *The kingdom of heaven (in the Pneuma).* Beyond consideration for the continuing world process, the kingdom of heaven within the consequent nature/in the Pneuma can be understood as the attainment of a Harmony of Harmonies to the extent that novelty and loss are reconciled within it. Whitehead speaks about the consequent nature as a "place" where "there is no loss, no obstruction" and the world is felt in a "unison of immediacy" (PR, 340, 345f., 350). This vision corresponds to the notion of an eschatological Peace of universal delimitation in which the duality of superjectivity (self-transcendence) and subjectivity (immediacy) is reconciled. Whitehead does *not* consider this reconciliation incomplete (in view of the continuing world), since *all* possibilities are given in the vision of *Sophia*/Logos and God is thus not "enriched" through "new" possibilities through the processual reception of the world into the Pneuma (Maassen 1988) (§32). The ongoing Adventure neither diminishes God's own perfection nor endangers reconciliation as the processual element of life within the kingdom of heaven (RMn, 154) (Suchocki 1995). This is the widely accepted solution of dual process eschatology.

(2) *The new eon (in Sophia/Logos).* Whitehead himself also countenances the possibility that the temporality characterizing the world in which we live and providing the backdrop against which ecological cosmology was developed must not necessarily be the only possible one (PR, 340) (§§15, 19). First of all, this particular cosmology in any case already entertains the notion of an infinite world process, or at least a process allowing for different cosmic epochs variously representing a universal nexus in which eternal objects might be realized in a unique way at all levels—nexuses in which *other* natural laws could apply (an assumption largely shared by contemporary physical cosmology). In this context, Whitehead surprisingly conjectures that "there is no reason, of any ultimate metaphysical generality," why there should not be an eon in which the *present* might be experienced as a "unison of becoming among things." "Why," he asks further, "should there not be novelty without loss of this direct unison of immediacy among things" (PR, 340)? The concrescent relationality in which the present is experienced as immediacy might, after all, structure a cosmic epoch such that time might well *not* also mean a loss of the past (PR, 340). This solution reflects rudimentary aspects of biblical-mythological references to several different eons—the eon prior to the flood (2 Pet. 3:5f.), that of the Noachian covenant (Gen. 9), the coming eon of the "new heaven and a new earth" without "waters" (Rev. 21:1; 2 Pet. 3:7). But this solution too is of a dual nature, insofar as the difference between heaven and the new eon would continue to obtain, without converging into nondifference. What, however, becomes of the preceding eons? How are they redeemed?

(3) *The heavenly reconciliation of all cosmic epochs (in the divine superject).* The

complex question concerning what happens to the earthly past after it passes away is one that process eschatology has by no means yet completely resolved. One view is that the past "is" superjectively (qua being real in the past) and as such (in objective immortality) affects coming earthly events (Sayer 1999) while *simultaneously* being prehended in God, thereby becoming "heavenly" (Suchocki 1988; Faber 2000e) (§23). Nonetheless, the problem remains—one few process theologies have even recognized as such—that the prehension of events in the Pneuma *cannot* be identical with the cosmic locus of the past of events (Christian 1967), since, *first*, prehension is in any case always a reception of that which (in its subjective form) remains *external* to the prehension (the "objective datum" of reception), and, *second*, the past itself is efficaciously active precisely in a real mode out of its *past status or being*, not out of its prehension in God (Frankenberry 1983). Where, then, *is* the earthly past (Sherburne 1971)? Though its heavenly prehensions may well be reconciled, the past itself remains unredeemed "in the past." Whitehead must have sensed this discrepancy when he remarks that God acts with respect to the "perishing occasions in the life of each temporal Creature" such that God not only prehends *its* prehensions of past events, but also offers the "transformation of Itself," that *the event itself* might become "everlasting in the Being of God" (PR, 351). This in its own turn presupposes that there will be a *convergence* of the kingdom of heaven and the world process (Faber 2000e).

I consider this convergence to be realized—*without relinquishing* dual eschatology—in the *continuity* of the processes of God and world within the *divine matrix* (§32), in which the processes of God and world, while indeed perpetually diverging, also converge. The universal communication linking God's communicative nature (reconciled *perichoresis*) and the world's own communicative nature (unreconciled Adventure) thus represents a *continuum* between Adventure (*Sophia*/Logos) and Peace (Pneuma). In the divine matrix, they are *processually reconciled*. *The divine matrix* itself is the Harmony of Harmonies: the *nondifference* of God and the world, of the threefold nature of God and of their intercreativity.

§40. MYSTERY
(LIFE, NONDIFFERENCE, AND INSISTENCE)

Process theology is occasionally charged with failing to acknowledge or allow for the "mystery of God" (Scheffczyk 1984, 104). The specifically *rationalistic* version of process theology, along with all those process theologies that view Whitehead in proximity to Hegel's "conceptual process" (Kline 1990) may have given this impression (§4). But a consideration of the other predominant version of process theology, namely, *empirical* theology, fundamentally relativizes this impression. In contradistinction to Hegel's understanding of the goal of the processes of God and world, namely, the sublation of the process itself in God's "absolute (self-)concept," Whitehead nowhere presents this sort of rationalistic resolution of the mystery of the world and God (or of the world *in* God) (Wiehl

1986). Whitehead, empirical theology, naturalism, speculative theology, and deconstructive postmodern process theology consistently give priority to life before thought, event happenings (actualities) before structure (eternal objects), *différance* before presence, creativity before rationality (Wiehl 1986; Rohmer 2000), process before reality (PR, 7), open wholeness before crystalline facticity, a feeling for the singular before (conceptual) thought (universals) (Keller 2002).

The *mysterium* is deeply etched both into Whitehead's own cosmology and into process theology itself, namely, as the mystery of life, the event, creativity, process, as the "mysticism" of the unspoken (MT, 174). The theological expression is the *principle of concretion*, which a priori renders God's own concretion inaccessible to any structural elucidation, rational comprehension, or theoretical articulation (§29), since concretion, being perpetually *creative*, remains inaccessible to formal explication or understanding. This theological expression also includes the *principle of empiricism*, by virtue of which God's temporal, historical, and creative self-revelation is not preformed by any rational disclosure or predetermination (Faber 2000e) (§36). From the *theopoetic* perspective on God, God's mystery emerges in three aspects, namely, God's *life*, *nondifference*, and *insistence*.

(1) The Mystery of God's Life

Within the complex interpenetration of the processes of God and world (part IV of this book), God's life is manifested as *world-oriented relationality*. But can one speak about God's life such that it is *not* exhausted by self-transcendence toward the world process? That is, does God have a life "for Godself"? And if so, what can process theology say about *God's inner life* without in its own turn being "comprehended" as a kind of "theosophy" (*alleged* knowledge of God's being in and of itself)? The following fundamental contours emerge regarding the indissoluble intertwining of divine life within world-orientation or world-anteriority.

(a) The *mystery of originless life*. That God's life "(in and) for itself" is by no means exhausted through God's self-transcendence "for us" is evident from the conversion of processes in its multiple form, namely as a creative (vs. the creaturely) process of creation (§35), as God's eschatological release of time (§39: Figure 6), and as inner conversion (inversion) of the divine process (§30). God's process is perpetually characterized by an inner abundance that is never wholly emptied or resolved into the world process (§31) based on God's primordial superjectivity, which is *without* origin but from which every process nonetheless derives its origin. This primordial superjectivity refers us to the *pre-* of God's life prior to any "grounding" of world (Faber 1997).

(b) The *mystery of revealed life*. God's life "for us" discloses God's life "for itself" (Faber 1995a), since God's self-revelation bequeaths itself not arbitrarily, but rather in an *essentially relational* fashion. Hence God's *inner* life is indeed revealed in God's self-revelation precisely in its *alterity* and as *revealed mystery* (§29), which, rather than being exhausted by that revealed status, instead is revealed precisely in its *mysteriousness*.

(c) The *mystery of intercreative life*. God's life "in itself" is revealed "for us" in its *alterity*, insofar as it appears as the *essential element of life* at the "ground" of the world. The ultimate expression of that element of life and vitality in the world is the *entirely living nexus*, in which the unity of the world (§24) and of personal being (§22) is disclosed in transparency with respect to the mystery of God's life. Within the *divine matrix*, the living element of the chaotic nexus and of personal being is both the *possibility* (in the case of the chaotic nexus) and *reality* (in the case of personal being) of the highest, nonformally graspable intensity of life (§32: Figure 4).

(d) The *mystery of nonformal life*. A *Trinitarian* consideration of God's life (§38) reveals the extent to which this *life*, in its unfathomable nature, bears witness to God's mystery. It is with *Sophia*/Logos that a glimpse is provided into the abyss of potentials in all their primordiality, in all their *primordial chaos*. And with the Pneuma a glimpse is provided into God's eschatological vitality as the wholly delimited living nexus of all actualities within *eschatological chaos*, the delimited Peace *beyond* all order. In this sense, *Sophia*/Logos and Pneuma demonstrate the unfathomable quality of their life as *khora* and *hypodochē* (§39).

(e) The *mystery of the indifference of life*. The *alterity* of God's life "in itself" refers to something that is *not* immediately world-oriented, obtaining instead "for itself" prior to any world (Faber 2000e). This is God's "primordiality" (God's "primordial nature") (§28), the creative beginning of God's concrescence, in which God is a *nonsocial nexus* (PR, 72) that in its *primordiality* ("for itself") seeks "intensity, and not preservation" (PR, 105) (§38). Because this intensity is primordial, there is nothing to preserve, neither anything old nor anything new in God; instead, everything "is" solely with regard to the depth of God's life:

> [God], in [God's] primordial nature, is unmoved by love for this particular, or that particular; for in this foundational process of creativity, there are no preconstituted particulars. In the foundations of [God's] being, God is indifferent alike to preservation and to novelty. [God] cares not whether an immediate occasion be old or new, so far as concerns derivation from its ancestry. [God's] aim for it is depth of satisfaction as an intermediate step towards the fulfilment of [God's] own being. [God's] tenderness is directed towards each actual occasion, as it arises. (PR, 105)

As Gregg Lambert has shown, God's love and tenderness appear in God's primordiality only as an interim stage on the way to the intensity and depth of God's inner life (Lambert 2001). In the process of God's *inner self-creativity*, that is, in God's primordial superjectivity, that is, God's *process of creativity* providing the *foundation* for God's being (§28), God *peers through* every form and every event at Godself, and this creativity *arises prior* to any world and *independent* of it. Notwithstanding that God moves toward the world as novelty and future within this "nonsocial" creativity, God's intensity and depth are not determined by novelty for, or origin of, the world—that is, by or from the perspective of *any* world, whatever the nature of that world might be. Although in the world-oriented conversion of the divine process God does indeed yearn for the physical fulfillment of God's primordial creative vision, and although divine "appetition" does strive for "enjoyment" (PR, 348), nonetheless "for itself" God's life is positioned beyond old and new as *pure intensity* indifferent to the world and yet living the satisfaction of the life of the world "for itself." The *mystery of God's indifference* provides a glimpse into the life of God beyond love "for us."

(2) The Mystery of God's In/difference

God's indifference *simultaneously* manifests itself in love "for us" (Faber 1995b), that is, *as* God's superjective self-transcendence, as self-revelation, as God's essential relationality, as intercreative communication. Hence the mystery of God's "indifference" is ultimately that of the *nondifference* of God's "for Godself" and "for us" (Beierwaltes 1980)—something I call God's "*in/difference*" (Faber 2002b). Three steps lead from the mystery of "indifference" to the mystery of God's "in/difference," steps constituting a genuine expression of the tradition of mystical theology—a tradition reaching far back into the Neoplatonic articulation of "negative theology" among the Cappadocian fathers and Dionysius the Areopagite and reaching its preeminent expression in the theology of Meister Eckhart and Nicholas of Cusa (Haubst 1991; Faber 2001c).

(a) God's *essential relationality* is grounded in the *mystery of nondifference* between God and world, disclosed in what for process theology constitutes the fundamental *theopoetic difference* between "God" and "creativity" (§28) and finding its integrative expression in the *indistinctiveness* (undifferentiated status) of God and world (Beierwaltes 1980) as expressed in the *divine matrix* (§32). Although intercreativity does imply a "pantheistic nimbus" within process theology (§35), it does genuinely express the indistinctiveness of God and world. It is not without good reason that Bracken found the theopoetic difference between "God" and "creativity" prefigured in Meister Eckhart's distinction between "God" and "Godhead" (Bracken 1995). Whereas in Meister Eckhart (as in Whitehead) "God" stands for the *difference* between God and world—for God as creator and the world as creation—he understands the "Godhead" (as does Whitehead with "creativity") as a sphere of *nondifference* between God and world. In Meister Eckhart's German sermon *Beati pauperes spiritu*, it stands "over all being and beyond all difference" (Quint 1969, 308). Hence in the "Godhead" there is no distinction between God and creature—albeit *not* because God and creation are *identical*, but because the "Godhead" *precedes* and *grounds* the difference between God and world (Faber 2001c).

God's nondifference in this sense is part of *theopoetic difference*. Initially one can (with Rahner) understand the "pantheistic sphere" with respect to "intercreativity" or the "divine matrix" (similar to Meister Eckhart's reference to the "Godhead") as an expression of God's *self-differentiation* (§35). In this sense, there is no "difference" *between* God and world in which God might be distinguished *from the perspective of the world*, since every difference between God and world is a *self*-difference of God (from the world) that precedes all *capacity* for distinguishing on the part of the creaturely world itself (Rahner 1976). God differentiates Godself from the world *in precisely such a way that* God is neither positioned "over against" the world (in some ultimate dualism) nor "identical" with it (in some ultimate pantheism). Instead, God does *not distinguish* Godself from it. God's transcendence is God's *self*-difference from the world, which ultimately *comes forth* from God's radical nondifference from the world. *This is why* God's *alterity* (God's "own" life in "indifference" toward the world) consists in *radical relationality, loving proximity* to the world (Faber 2000e). Nicholas of Cusa referred to this radical alterity of God with what for him was one of the highest divine names, namely, God as the "non-other" (*non aliud*). In God's nondifference, God is *so* "different" that no other contrast or opposite to God can be adduced (Faber 2001c). This *non aliud* comes to expression in the *intercreativity* of the divine matrix insofar as God's *self*-creativity bequeaths itself to the world as the world's *own*, innermost self-creativity. Within the *nondifference of the divine matrix*, God comes forth (paradoxically) precisely *as* God, and the world *as* world (§32).

(b) The "indifference" (of God's "inner life") discloses itself within the Trinitarian mystery of the *nondifference of the "threefold character"* (§34) and in God's Trinitarian love "for us" (§38). In light of the *non aliud*, *Sophia*/Logos "in herself" is God's primordial concrescence because she represents the primordial nondifference of form and act and thereby carries through "for us" the primordial difference of form and act that renders the world possible as creation—precisely in the nondifference between God and world and as the *source* of the difference between God and creature in the initial aim (Faber 2000h). In light of the *non aliud*, the Pneuma "in itself" is the primordial delimited condition in which everything in God is "God," and thereby simultaneously—"for us"—the *reconciled nondifference* of creature and God in eschatological Peace (Faber 2000e). In light of the *non aliud*, God's *superject* is the primordiality in which God grounds the nondifference of nature and person, act and actuality "for Godself" and carries through the primordial difference of nature and person "for us" (Faber 2000e).

This "inner" divine life (God's "indifference") is nothing other than the *Trinitarian nondifference of love*. Nicholas of Cusa described this connex in *De venatione sapientiae* with the succinct Trinitarian formulation deriving from the notion of *non aliud*, namely, that the "non-other (*non aliud*) is nothing other (*non aliud*) than the non-other (*non aliud*)" (Gabriel 1989, 65). Reference to this subtle Trinitarian formula of the *non aliud* is simultaneously reference to God's indifferent life "for Godself" *and* the radical, nondifferent intimacy of God's love "for us." This paradoxical distance (God's "inner" life) and intimacy (God's love for creation) attaching to God's nondifference comes to expression in the fact that everything *in God* is Trinitarian nondifference and *in the world* bears the Trinitarian character of God's life (*vestigium Trinitatis*) (§33). Nicholas of Cusa speaks about this movement of nondifference in which everything in God is "God" and in the world is "itself" as a "complication" (*complicatio*) of God through which God has *enfolded* everything in Godself, and as an "explication" (*explicatio*) through which God is *unfolded* in everything in the world (Flasch 1998). This Trinitarian "complication" and "explication" (exchange of life and love) that *is* the divine matrix is the mystery of continuity between God and world that is intercreativity (Faber 2001a).

(c) God's "in/difference" refers to the *mystery of the nondifference between difference and nondifference* in God. "In/difference" is the loving origin of all difference, the real expression and operation of the "foundational process of creativity" in God, that is, of God's superjectivity (§28). The event of God's superjectivity *is* the event of "in/difference," and the latter the "source" of all difference—even that between difference and nondifference. In his final essay, "Immortality" (1941), and largely unnoticed by process theology, Whitehead discloses the theopoetic difference between God and creativity in precisely this fashion, namely, as the in/difference between the *personal difference* of God and world and the *transpersonal nondifference* of creativity in God and world (§28). "God" appears as the ground of the valuation process—of the "World of Value," which provides both aesthetic and ethical relevance, intensity and harmony in difference (Imm., 90). By contrast, "creativity" appears as the ground of the creative process—of the "World of Creativity," of the self- and intercreativity within which both world and God "live" their spontaneity nondifferently (Imm., 79). Whitehead views both "worlds" and their "grounds" "for themselves" as an *abstraction* from the *one* universe, from the *one wholeness of the process itself* (Imm., 80) (§12).

Theopoetic difference is grounded ultimately in *theopoetic in/difference*. That is, God not only is *the* nondifference beyond all differences as such ("Godhead," creativity, *non aliud*); God also has *no* juxtaposed or opposite "counterpart"—not even that of a theopoetic difference between difference ("God") and nondifference ("creativity") (Faber 2002b). Here Whitehead's "one totality of the process" takes its place within the tradition of mystical theology (Beierwaltes 1980). Nicholas of Cusa "defines" God not only as *non aliud* (nondifference), but "prior to all differences . . . even prior to the difference of indifference and difference" (Flasch 1998, 608). This is what I refer to as God's "in/difference," which is *beyond* the difference of "God" and "creativity," "God" and "Godhead," "value" and "creativity", "difference" and "nondifference" (Faber 2001c). It is here, in *theopoetic in/difference,* that the circle is completed between the "indifference" (of God's life "for itself") and the divine intimacy of "nondifference" (as love "for us"), both ultimately *expressing* the same in/difference.

(3) The Mystery of God's Insistence

Theopoetic in/difference *happens* as differentiation *and* nondifferentiation and refers to the *primordial act of God's superjectivity*, that is, the *creative in/difference of self-creativity and self-transcendence* generating (*explicatio*) and simultaneously gathering within itself (*complicatio*) all difference and nondifference (Faber 2001a). I borrow a term from Gilles Deleuze in referring to this *movement of God's superjective in/differentiation* as the mystery of God's *insistence* (as opposed to *ex-sistere,* existence) (Faber 2000b). God, precisely in God's alterity, being all-relational and acting *creatively* within the primordial process of "in/differentiation," can thus be referred to as the primordial act of *différance*, an act no longer comprehensible in the categories of "essence"/"existence"; at this point, even reference to "God" as such thus becomes in/different.

(a) For the "negative theology" of the mystics, God is the "One" beyond all categories (of being). In its emphasis on God's alterity, however, and on the basis of God's in/difference, this negative assertion paradoxically requires that because God is indeed *nothing* beyond all differences, God thus appears only *in* difference. The negative "One" is paradoxically *simultaneously* already the *world-oriented* "All-One" (Faber 2001c). The "All-One" is *all-relational* (Helander 1996). This mystical paradox of the "coincidence of opposites" (*coincidencia oppositorum*) brings the theopoetic in/difference to genuine expression by describing the element of God's self-relatedness simultaneously as *essential relationality*. This is God's "insistence," namely, superjective in/difference as pure *agape*, God's self-creativity as pure self-transcendence.

(b) This superjective in/difference, as the primordial *process* of "in/differentiation" (*complicatio* and *explicatio*), is the primordial creative act that God "is" (Faber 2001a). For the superjective in/difference is already the creative *origin* of the difference between difference ("God," "value," "person") and nondifference ("Godhead," "creativity," "nature") and thus the *source of all* difference. The essential relationality of God's essence, which effusively moves beyond itself in the communication of the divine matrix, is grounded in the paradoxical countermovement of the creative "in/differentiation" of *complicatio* and *explicatio*. Because theopoetic in/difference has no intention of being something "for itself" without at the same time being such "for others" as well (principle of relativity), that is, has no intention of being some dark mystery "behind all differences," it is always already living *as* self-transcendent, creative love; that is, God's creative in/difference *in-sists* (Faber 2002b).

(c) Theopoetic in/difference is the origin of, that is, insistence on, *différance*. Like the latter, it too—as Derrida puts it—is "older" than ontological difference; because it does *not* refer back to any sort of "foundation," it is not comprehensible in categories of "ground," "presence," "being," or "existence." Although Whitehead is well aware of the cosmological, teleological, and ontological proofs for God's existence, he rejects them as being incapable of reaching God (PR, 93; MT, 113) (Connelly 1962; Phillipson 1982; Faber 2000e). Although rationalistic process theology was tempted to adduce Anselm of Canterbury's ontological argument (Hartshorne 1962) (§4), a consideration of the mystery of superjective in/difference shows this to be impossible. Because God's primordiality is what differentiates the categories of form and act, person and nature, being and nothingness in the first place, it cannot be comprehended with their aid. As in the mystical theology of Nicholas of Cusa, the *coincidencia oppositorum* and the *non aliud* are *antecedent* to the difference between being and nothingness (Faber 2001c). That is why one can speak about them in the form neither of "existence" nor of "essence." Contra references to God's "ex-sistence," the mystery of in/difference is better served by understanding God as a *superjective event that insists by loving*, as that which in the primal act of primordial differentiation (primordial envisagement)—which one can understand with Ford as corresponding to originless origin in God (the Father) (§34: model II)—first creates the difference between being and nothingness through which it is itself thus *not* comprehensible (Ford 1986). And yet it is still "present" insofar as it *insistently loves*, freely giving of itself as *agape* (Faber 2002b). Contra references to God's "hyperessence" (Almond 2000), which ultimately understands God (in Derrida's sense) as fulfilled presence (§18), God is now understood as that particular *eschatological event that insists insofar as it remains the "supreme Adventure"* (§39). It delimits everything into God (*complicatio*) by simultaneously opening up *différance* and insisting *within* it (Faber 2001a).

(d) In this theopoetic in/difference, language reaches the boundaries at which negative and positive theology begin to flow into each other (Faber 2001c). Nicholas of Cusa encountered this final consequence of mystical theology in his last great work, *De apice theoriae* (1464), by considering the most extreme alterity (negativity) of the *non aliud* and its radical world-orientation (positivity) by then trying to articulate these beyond the difference between negation and position. Here he "de-fines" (de-limits) God in pure positivity as "can itself" (*posse ipsum*) (Flasch 1998; Faber 2001a). This is the crowning step beyond all difference within in/difference insofar as it manifests itself wholly *in differences*. Here God is interpreted as *can* (*potency*), as the *in/difference of possibility and power*. Such is attained in theopoetic in/difference insofar as God is understood as *creative insistence* in the form of a primordial creation of the difference between idea and creativity. Here insistence comes to express theopoetics itself, since God's *poiesis* is in fact God's threefold *posse*, the superjective in/difference of the *creative power of primordial possibility* (of that which provides space for that which is real) within the primordial nature and the *delimitation of all power into its eschatological possibility* (that which redemptively enfolds everything toward its highest possibility) in the consequent nature.

VI. Frontiers

Programmatic Alternatives

A process theology primarily focused on *essential relationality* also understands itself as an *empirical matrix* and as a *transformational matrix* (§36); as such, it understands positions more as transitions at whose boundaries it tries to create an interface of mutual communication. Process theology is thus characterized by a dynamic of *intercontextual transformation*, integrating complexity, differentiating itself multicontextually, and manifesting itself through interdisciplinarity (Faber 2002e). Three central intuitions shape process theology's interwovenness with a theory of the world as a whole, namely, relationality, concrescence, and creativity (Introduction; Faber 2000e).

Relationality. All realms of reality are ultimately positioned within a coherent interrelationship or context—be it ever so complex, discordant as a result of mutual hindrances, or at first glance seemingly even irreconcilable. Ultimately, a *universal harmonics* regulates all these coherent contexts, at the very least also generating a dynamic prompting a search for these contexts.

Concrescence. These interrelated contexts cannot be comprehended logically or structurally, but rather only through a focus on events. Its "Logos" is itself a life happening (event) that cannot be "grasped" through any structure (i.e., through universals). All harmony comes about through events. A "context" (*contextus*, a joining together, from *contex(ere)*, to join by weaving) is always a "growing together" (concrescence) into a unity of events (Fetz 1981).

Creativity. The moving order of the whole in manifesting itself in events is always a unity toward ever *new* unities. Harmonics is a creative process of unexpected concurrence and of movement that never becomes fixed.

This *universal harmonics* ("doctrine of Harmony," AI, 148), characterized by relationality, concrescence, and creativity, provides a counterpoint for developing process theology's programmatic alternative resisting equally the dualism of matter and spirit and the identification of structural rationality with living nexus. Ultimately it is grounded in the *divine matrix*, in which everything is related through living communication such that it is always itself both within and out of the whole of the matrix. This position involves considerable consequences for the correlation of the various spheres of reality in which and for which theology is now articulated *sub ratione Dei*. Process theology thus posits interdisciplinary accents with theological alternatives: in the theory of perception, process theology's unique understanding of the experience of God (§41); in epistemology, its relational (soteriological and eschatological) understanding of truth (§42); in the theory and philosophy of science, its integrative access to both the natural sciences and the humanities (§43); in the theory or philosophy of mind, its non-dualistic understanding of mind and body, consciousness and person (§44); in the theory of evil, its understanding of the problem of theodicy (§45); in the theory of civilization, its ethical impulse toward self-transcendence (§46); in (meta)theology, its tension between relationality and normativity (§47); and finally with respect to a spirituality, its focus on creative transformation (§48).

§41. CAUSAL PERCEPTION
(SYMBOLISM, SEMIOTICS, AND THE EXPERIENCE OF GOD)

The question concerning the possibility, form, and particular nature of an experience of God within a relational, concrescent, and creative universe is directed to a *theory of perception* positioned within the framework of organic cosmology (Klose 2002). And indeed, Whitehead himself develops a theory of perception in his book *Symbolism: Its Meaning and Effect* (1927) alongside and parallel to *Process and Reality* (Lachmann 2000), though he had already broached the topic of a theory of perception in his theory of events in *Concept of Nature* (1920). What one finds is that Whitehead's later understanding of "event" emerged from his theoretical consideration of perception with respect to the "percipient event" (§9) and then, from the perspective of the fully developed theory of events and the organic cosmology based on it, that understanding reflexively exerted an influence back onto a theory of perception. This explains why the same critical impulse inheres within Whitehead's theory of perception as within his event theory and his cosmology in the larger sense; indeed, to a certain extent it represents the beginning of Whitehead's critique of the omnipresent dualism of substantialism and subjectivism (§10) and thus also the beginning of his own essential relationalism—with all the attendant implications for relational process theology (Hampe 1990) (§26). Hence, with respect to the question of the experience of God, this critical dimension in Whitehead's theory of perception will be especially fruitful from the postmodern perspective in a critique of "self-presence," since here experience of God is a mystery rather than fulfilled presence (§40). It speaks about that particular differentiated "presence" of God as the "Harmony of Harmonies" (§39) in whose *ambivalence*—which can never be entirely resolved (in this world) (§§24, 45)—it nonetheless does possess aesthetic, ethical, soteriological, and eschatological meaning.

In his book *Symbolism*, Whitehead analyzes human perception against the backdrop of his event theory as a complex happening that he calls "symbolic reference" (S, 18ff.; PR, 178ff.). Its particular nature ultimately consists in the realization that we can never adequately—that is, unequivocally and unambiguously—distinguish between the *perception* of reality, that which we ourselves neither are nor generate (*extra nos*), on the one hand, and the *interpretation* of such reality (in the projection of our thought, feelings, and wishes onto reality), on the other (Lachmann 1990). And precisely that is the dilemma confronting any theory of perception: do we really (actually) perceive that which we feel and think, or are we already interpreting it through our own (projective) categories? Kant's "Copernican turn," according to which all metaphysics is already determined by the categories of thought, represented merely an initial step toward becoming conscious of this problem (PR, XIII, 155f.), and the linguistic turn in post-Wittgensteinian analytical philosophy and the postmodern linguistic critique in deconstructionism and poststructuralism merely underscored the impossibility of distinguishing adequately between perception and interpretation (Rorty 1991). The question then becomes whether there is *any* reality beyond language and symbols (Keller 2002). Its negative and critical answer, invoking a markedly antirealistic and nonfundamentalist consequence, is that there is *no* reality beyond interpretation. Any reference to reality is symbolically determined (Faber 2000e). Whitehead thus understands the "symbolic reference" of human perception as a *reciprocity* between reality and symbolization (e.g., in language) and thus as the *irresolution* of the question of what is actually symbol (interpretation) and what is reference (reality) (Hauskeller 1994) (§12). The nexic complex or the complex of eternal objects either can refer symbolically to the other and be a reference for the other. It is here that the *problem* of truth first emerges (Hampe 1998) (§42).

Whitehead considers the ground of this reciprocity and irresolution to be the fact that the "symbolic reference" actually overlays two different modes of perception, of which one—perception in the mode of "causal efficacy" (S, 30ff., 37ff.; PR, 168ff.)—refers to the nexic complex within perception; the other—perception in the mode of "presentational immediacy" (S, 13ff.; PR, 311ff.)—refers to the eternal objects (Hauskeller 1994; Hampe 1998). Whereas in the perception of *causal efficacy* the world is perceived as an event complex of becoming and perishing, concrescence and transition, subjectivity and superjectivity—as causal event reality in its temporal, integrative, and differentiating arc of tension—reality in *presentational immediacy* appears as an integrated complex of ideas, patterns, and objects, that is, in a "present" that, by *fading out* the temporal and causal origin and future of the event complexes, in return acquires *form* whereby they themselves become integrated (PR, 27: Categoreal Obligation VI: Transmutation; Rust 1987). Whereas in the perception of the *nexic complex* its multiple events are felt with their inherent emotional tone in their difference, their causal relationships to one another, and their creative movement within time, perception in *presentist forms* reduces this causal complex to an "image" of reality, an image that—devoid of its emotional tenor—can be understood conceptually (§18). That is, we recognize the form of an object, but we no longer recognize its complexity and movement as event nexus. Instead of the diffuse multiplicity of events, we now perceive a clear form (Hauskeller 1994; Hampe 1990).

And as a matter of fact, the emergence of this second mode of perception—that of "presentation"—did provide an evolutionary advantage for living organisms by enabling them to distinguish between (what for survival or prevailing interests are) important and unimportant data, this awareness of forms in its own turn then contributing not inconsiderably to the emergence of consciousness (PR, 52f., 108f., 188, 241ff.; Busch 1993). At the same time, however, it also results in a displacement of perception's center of gravity to sense data, structures, and an alleged *presence* of that which is actually causally and temporally past and future. It results in a loss of the emotional tone of reality in the causal efficaciousness of the various event nexuses. The *conscious perception* of sense experience through clear, distinct, and objectively grasping consciousness overlays (and represses) the *un- and preconscious perception* of the universal relationality of causal processes at the level of event complexes that, while certainly grounding such forms of sense and concept, are however *not* exhausted by them. Whitehead's critique enters at just this point. The theories of perception put forward by Locke, Hume, and Kant consistently focused only on sense perception and conceptual consciousness, not on the underlying causal relations between events (PR, 130ff., 144ff.; MT, 122; Hampe 1990). As a result, these theories are essentially *substantialist*, acknowledging solely "things in external relation" rather than "relational events." They consequently fall prey to the "simple localization" of matter in space without acknowledging the event-field of mutual immanence that first grounds such "locality" (§14). Moreover, they mistake the concrete for the abstract, events for objects (§12), the singular or unique with the general and universals (Hosinski 1994) (§11).

Here the circle closes with the critical nondualism of the early theory of perception found in *Concept of Nature*, which ultimately led to the event theory underlying the distinction between the modes of perception in *Symbolism* (§9). The mode of *perception* there attests a "percipient event" as a *moment* in the relational structure of the world surrounding it, as a "factor" in the "fact" of nature (§12). It is only in the mode of *thought*, of conscious formative construction, that something is extracted from the complex (i.e., simplified and abstracted) such that it now appears as an isolated "thing" or (underlying) "sub-ject," that is, as a substance with arbitrary attributes (Lotter 1990). But because—recalling the implications of "unitextural reality"—*all* events have a *percipient* structure, Whitehead develops them later after the model of "percipient events" as *prehensive happenings* (§§13–14). All events feel their past and their perishing into a future that passes beyond them; events are panrelational and are interrelated with one another within a causal process (AI, 191ff.). This rediscovery of the perception of these *causal event nexuses* "at the ground" of world structures effectively undoes the restrictions imposed on consciousness by its conceptual focus, the fixation on sense perception, the reduction of the unique and singular to universals, and the substantialism of traditional theories of perception (Hampe 1990; Klose 2002).

In opening the door to a colorful world of "fellow creatures" (PR, 50), to a feeling of the vibrations of the causal event nexuses surrounding and determining us, Whitehead also opens the door to a kind of critical realism (Maassen 1991a; Faber 2000e). For it is only in the mode of "(re-)presentation" that we are trapped in symbols, feeling cut off from "reality" in an infinitely mutual cross-reference of interpretations and in a sphere of what seem to be arbitrary reality and truth references of the sort with which someone like Derrida is often accused or which his disciples follow. Similar, however, to the way Derrida prefers *not* to restrict perception of reality to the interplay of symbols (Kemuf 1991), and similar also to the way Deleuze tried to sound out the "chaosmos" of the event world beyond our symbolizations (Deleuze 1994), so also did Whitehead rediscover in the mode of causal perception the causal character of the event world at the boundary of our consciousness as a primal feeling of the world (Keller 2002a).

> In the dark there are vague presences, doubtfully feared, in the silence, the irresistible causal efficacy of nature presses itself upon us; in the vagueness of the low hum of insects in an August woodland, the inflow into ourselves of feelings from enveloping nature overwhelms us; in the dim consciousness of half-sleep, the presentations of sense fade away, and we are left with the vague feeling of influences from vague things around us. (PR, 176)

We do not create the world through our interpretations *ex nihilo*, being ourselves instead continually *relationally positioned* and *causally produced* by it, albeit within a creative self-surpassment of all that is already extantly given (Hauskeller 1994). Although Whitehead knows, as does Derrida, that the "vague presence" that comes with the causal feeling of reality cannot be had in any pure fashion and beyond symbolizations, he does believe that these symbolizations must be accessible to deconstruction such that in them that "beyond" of those symbolizations does become visible. Catherine Keller has pointed out how Derrida's *différance* exhibits the same sense as Whitehead's *process*, namely, that it is only within the contexts of differentiations in which everything is already positioned so that significance beyond symbols can be perceived, since otherwise something would be significant "for itself" (in isolation) in a fashion that substantializes it without interpretation, without context, and without relation (Keller 2002a). The "reality" that *différance* and *process* open up for us beyond symbolization, however, as Keller explicates further, is that which Julia Kristeva calls the "semiotic." The "semiotic"—in contradistinction to Lacan's "symbolic"—"cries out for interchange with Whitehead's odd doctrine of 'causal feeling'" (16). Like the latter, it is associated with Plato's *khora*—the *formless* locus of vibration, intercreativity, communication, and creative chaos. Here nothing is "preformed" or "presented" through forms, moving instead within a "rhythmic presymbolic process" (Keller 2002a, 16).

Hence Whitehead's demand for causal perception rather than "presentation" is his most powerful weapon not only against the "self-presence" of substance in classical metaphysics, but also against the metaphysics of God's fulfilled omnipresence in classical theology (§16). From the perspective of process theology, God is never experienced at the level of "presentation"; God can never become an object of our experience capable of being grasped conceptually within the clarity of consciousness (Suchocki 1995) (§18). Instead, the perception of God *already* happens within the mode of causal event constitution insofar as God bequeaths *Godself* (reveals Godself) in the *initial aim of every event*, with which God releases every event into its self-creativity (Haught 1986) (§20). Through such experience of God, God is never "present"; or better, God is "present" not as "presence" within our own present, but rather such that God has already *passed by* ("was there") before and precisely so that an event becomes, and such that God "re-presents" every event's future (as ad-vent) and as the recollection of its past (Ford 1981). In this sense, God is perceived soteriologically and eschatologically, historically and temporally, and always in *diachronic transcendence*, never as straightforwardly or simply "presence" (Faber 2000b and e) (§36).

Four characteristic features attaching to the experience of God follow from the particular nature of causal perception. Together they reveal the form of the experience of God to be that of a pneumatological Christology (§38) such that every event appears as *logos spermatikos* and as spiritual delimitation.

(1) God is always perceived as being *present but concealed, insubstantially present* (rather than as an object), and as *withdrawn even in God's presence*. Because God "encounters" an event at the very beginning of the "existence" of every event, God is—as Suchocki has shown (1995)—deeply concealed within it, being "recognizable" or "discernible" neither at its arising (being always antecedent to it) nor in its reflection on itself, since no event can reflect itself "in itself," the event being able to feel "itself" only in a new event upon perishing. Because God is preconsciously and presensually revealed within this experience, God can never appear as an "object" of our experience, but rather can only be felt as the nonobjective Eros of our becoming (§24). As future in the sense of advent, God is thus consistently the space of opening from which Godself, however, always remains withdrawn(§§35, 38). In this creative concealment God is encountered as creative *Sophia*/Logos—as the beginning of the *logoi spermatikoi*.

(2) God is perceived only through *historical* and *social mediation*. Because in

every event God has already acted before and indeed in order that the event becomes in the first place, God can be perceived only as a "trace" in the fulfillment of the initial aim (§§13, 20). By contrast, the *subjective aim*—the fulfillment of the initial aim through satisfaction—can be causally efficacious in its singularity only with respect to future events and thus be perceived historically. God's "presence" reveals itself as "trace" in the past—though now only in the *ambivalence* of historical events. This is why God can be experienced only *in the relation* between events and *amid* concrete event nexuses, that is, through specifically social, contextual, and "empirical" mediation. Such experience of God is always mediated *corporeally* (in the body of Christ) and *pneumatologically* (the body in God's Pneuma) (§38).

(3) God is always perceived within a *creative* and *dynamic* impulse, since the experience of God is always characterized by a certain direction, namely, toward the self-creativity of the events, nexuses, and societies posited free as creatures (Faber 2000e; Cobb 1974). As a result, God is never experienced statically; there is no "enjoyment" of God's presence. It is instead the release into a world through which every event (depending on stage and nexic context) is placed into its own responsibility. Hence we experience God precisely where in creative transformation we structure world and renew it "with ourselves." This releases a dynamic of action that is manifested *not* in some passive vision of God, but precisely—and solely—through the active structuring and forming of world. This is the *incarnational dynamic* of *Sophia*/Logos (§38).

(4) God is always perceived in *soteriological relevance* and *eschatological difference*. The experience of God is never "neutral," "objective," or distant. Instead it consistently confronts us with decision for salvation and is always reconciliatory—the mirror of our (perfect) self as possible only in God (RMn, 155). At the same time, however, we are aware of being positioned within an eschatological difference of nonpresence (§47), but toward the completion of the experience of God, as which God is already moving toward us (ad-vent) within the premonitory light of hope (§39). And again, God's "present absence" in this sense, God's "presence in withdrawal," consistently positions us in the sphere of hope, in the responsibility of freedom, and under the admonition of conversion. The experience of God is consistently the grace of hope that redeems and delimits and that happens as promise. In this respect, the experience of God constitutes a moment of God's own *dynamis*, of the delimitation of the Pneuma (§38).

The experience of God as conceived against the background of causal, concrescent, and creative perception of the process background exhibits a *dual character*. On the one hand, it conceives every event as a *moment within the divine matrix*. The event emerges within and then enters back into it. Hence the experience of God is from one perspective not so much the perception of God "in Godself" as of God within the divine field of intercreativity, creative chaos, and loving communication "at the foundation" of the world (§32). On the other hand, it is not "Godself" that we perceive within the matrix, since its *direction* is that of God's own world-orientation (§38). In the initial aim, God comes toward the world from the future of God's primordial nature (Faber 2000h). Hence a meditative practice might well be conceivable in which one might experience God "at the beginning" of our existence (in each of our personal events)—as it were, in the "solitude" of the beginning, as Suchocki puts it (§48). Within the *incarnational dynamic* of such mystical experience, however, we would have to "turn around" in order to experience God, that is, reverse our own gaze that we might *look in God's direction*. Through such reversal, however, we are then looking precisely *not* at God, but at the world (Faber 2002c). This is why within the divine matrix the experience of God does *not* consist in mystical meditation on a vision of God that turns *away* from the world; it is instead the vision of God's own view toward the world. It frees the mystical gaze *as* an impulse of reversal and conversion (*metanoia*) (§48), as world ethics (§46). From the perspective of the theopoetics of God's creative and salutary embrace—in the field of tension "between" *Sophia*/Logos and Pneuma—the divine matrix represents a delimitation, a setting free for creative, promising, reversing, and active self-creativity and experience of God; as such, it is thus an *act of self-relativizing, incarnational, and kenotic self-transcendence* directly into the world. Within the divine matrix, the gift of the highest Eros becomes an act of *agape*.

§42. AESTHETIC COGNITION
(TRUTH, HYPOTHESIS, AND ESCHATON)

Whitehead's theory of perception addresses the *problem* of truth on the basis of the complexity of our cognition as a process of "symbolic reference" in the overlapping of two "pure" modes of perception—the *clear* consciousness of sense, concepts, and forms in "presentational immediacy," and the *vague* feeling of the relational world surrounding and permeating us in its causal and diachronic field of tension (§41). Our cognitive situatedness is characterized by projection, deception, and falsehood as well as by the often painfully perceived subjectivity, discomfiting relativity, and confusingly profuse contextuality in which we must formulate the problem of truth epistemologically. Whitehead's epistemology offers two opposing points of departure for resolving the problem of truth. On the one hand, he advocates *non-fundamentalism* with respect to the question of cognition, seeking to overcome the Cartesian dualism of subjectivity and objectivity, subject and reality, rationalism and empiricism (§11), from which perspective the ideal of cognition is an irreducible *fundamentum inconcussum*. Here Whitehead opts for the wholly postmodern, deconstructionist, poststructuralist, and relativistic thesis regarding the *universal interpretability of reality* (Faber 2000e). On the other hand, he advocates a *realism* that is keen on overcoming the Kantian "Copernican turn," according to which cognition always bears the form of the subjective cognitive forms of the agent of cognition; this "turn," so Whitehead, inevitably ends—as postmodern constructivism demonstrates—in a skepticism concerning *whether* there is any reality at all (Lotter 1990; Busch 1993). Contra the covert subjectivism and antirealism of this epistemology, for which all knowledge of truth consists either in the projection of subjects (subjectivism) or in the manipulation of signs (deconstructionism), Whitehead suggests returning to the "pre-Kantian modes of thought" (PR, XI) that, as, for example, Leibniz previously, do not sublate reality into an interpretive circle and have not yet lost contact with reality (Keller 2002a).

This context of *nonfundamentalism* (contra premodern dogmatism) amid simultaneous *realism* (contra postmodern constructivism) permeates every fiber of Whitehead's event theory. In his *reformed subjectivistic principle* (§10), he formulates this correlation as an axiom of the "unitexturality of reality" (§11), according to which knowledge and being in fact have the *same texture* (PR, 3f.). Therefore every event, in its becoming, is the concrescence of extant facts, which in their own turn were *prehensive processes of cognition* now received in the mode of the past. The causal event process is an *interpretive process* insofar as, although that which is past is indeed causally efficacious, it is also *creatively* received (process principle) (Lachmann 1990). Within the swing of concrescence and transition, everything that has happened *can* be perceived (relativity principle). At the same time, nothing is grasped *merely* abstractly, that is, *merely* with respect to its incarnate ideas, universal forms, patterns, concepts, or figures; instead it is felt in its singularity (ontological principle) (§13). Whitehead believes that his "hypothetical realism" overcomes both the trap of *subjectivism*, for which ultimately everything is a self-present projection and construction, as well as the trap of *sensualism*, which alleges to have access to uninterpreted facts (PR, 142f.; Wiehl 1971; Hampe 1990). Contra Francis Bacon's program, nothing is merely "given"; everything is *tuned* and yet—contra post-Kantian and postmodern constructivism—never merely "construed" (PR, XIII).

These two *epistemological directions* shape Whitehead's resolution of the problem of truth. Knowledge is *truth-relative* insofar as it expects—nonfundamentalistically—no preinterpreted or (in the sense of Derrida) self-present reality. At the same time, however, knowledge is always *truth-realistic,* insofar as it always refers to a reality that is *not* first generated or produced within cognition itself. Hence, as Catherine Keller has demonstrated, truth ultimately has the character of *khora,* referring not to *symbolic* knowledge, but to *semiotic* knowledge—knowledge not in the mode of forms, ideas, figures, concepts, and propositions, but in the mode of creative causality, concrescence, emptiness, and communication (Keller 2000) (§41). *Between chaos and communication,* the divine matrix is the locus of truth, and yet for just that reason also the perspective from which truth is called into question. The divine matrix addresses truth as a *problem* insofar as it is the "harmony of harmonies" that, on the one hand, makes a *reference to reality* possible and, on the other, demands cognition as a *creative interpretation* of the matrix. Within the divine matrix, truth is always *relational,* that is, communicatively based, *contextual,* that is, never "abstractly" universal, being instead consistently related to events, and *creative,* that is, pointed toward future, *never* fixated on the past (Bracken 1995; 2000) (§32).

Within the divine matrix, cognition has an *aesthetic* character, and truth a *harmonic* sense—both deriving from the *prehensive structure of concrescence*. In the original sense of *aisthēsis* (as perception), every event is, in a radicalized form, a "system of all things" (PR, 28, 36) growing together in the movement of creative harmonization—an aesthetic process of contrast and development of intensity (§21). This *aesthetic harmonics* of event structure has a "threefold character" (§33) such that the harmonic sense of truth emerges within process theology's typical *interwovenness* of truth dimensions—correspondence, coherence, and consensus. Because, on the one hand, every event emerges from others precisely through the *latter's* integration, truth has a *referential* sense (physical pole). Because, on the other hand, every event represents the *creative* integration toward new unity, truth simultaneously has a *coherent* sense (mental pole). And because, finally, the superjective meaning of an event depends on its reception within the organic nexus in which it becomes and perishes, truth has a *pragmatic* sense (superjective character) (Hosinski 1994; Farmer 1997; Keller and Daniell 2002).

Whitehead, however, integrates all three modes of truth—correspondent-theoretical truth (between cognition and object), coherent-theoretical truth (pertaining to the agreement and logicity of the various thematic elements of that which is true), and consensus-theoretical truth (pertaining to the acceptance of a truth community)—in a unique way. To the extent the physical nexus in the event is grasped in a physically *conformational* mode, there is *correspondence*—such grasping then being either *true* or *false*. To the extent it is a matter of integrating physical and mental prehensions, there is *coherence*—a "judgment" then being *correct, incorrect*, or *suspended* (postponed) (PR, 190f.). The symbolism of real knowledge, however—in the overlay of causal (physical, conformational) and ideal (mental, coherent) modes of cognition and truth—is what decides the *success* concerning truth—such then being *pragmatically* either *justified* or *unjustified* (PR, 181). Hence, since in symbolic reference perception and cognition are always in tension and the overlay of the correspondence and coherence of truth thus always *ambivalent*, what is required is for truth to exhibit a pragmatic sense—that is, one must ascertain whether truth *succeeds*.

This is the context in which Whitehead's famous dictum is to be understood concerning how "in the real world it is more important that a proposition be interesting than that it be true. The importance of truth is, that it adds to interest" (PR, 259). There has been considerable speculation whether Whitehead here is not advocating a kind of pragmatism oriented toward the mere evolution of truth (Keller and Daniell 2002; Auburger 2001; Lucas 1989; Busch 1993; Wiehl 1986; Kasprzik 1988). If one bears in mind, however, that Whitehead is arguing against both fundamentalist dogmatism and relativistic constructivism (Keller 2002a; Welker 1985), then this correlation between truth and interest constitutes nothing other than an explication of the *concrete threefold character of truth in the divine matrix*. Correspondence and coherence necessarily remain ambivalent as long as communication *and* chaos determine the event process. Propositional truth is thus always related to the process of intensity and self-relativization through which an event both becomes and perishes within a *nexic context*. Its own "succeeding" is withdrawn from it, as it were; that is, its satisfied intensity acquires significance *beyond* the event's self and as such belongs to the *history of its truth*. The reverse side is that no event can expect to be recognized "the way it was," being able to hope instead to contribute to the creative intensification of the process. It will, however, contribute all the more to the intensity of others the more it is perceived in its own intensity, and to that extent, its truth enhances the intensity of other events and thus ultimately that of its own truth within the view that the whole has of its "having been" (Busch 1993). But does that nonetheless still constitute pragmatic dissipation of the past in favor of creative novelty?

Whitehead's *theological understanding of truth* now comes into play. Truth is not, as one might think, exhausted in pragmatic relevance and evolutive success, demanding instead some *ultimate, final status* in which the truth concerning an event is decided. Here truth is opened up soteriologically, eschatologically, and theologically. Correspondence and coherence remain ambivalent only as long as truth is not *justified*. Justification, however, demands *finality*, "for the pragmatic test can never work, unless on some occasion—in the future, or in the present—there is a definite determination of what is true on that occasion" (PR, 181). The finality of justification, however, reveals that the truth concerning an event is in fact a process of *soteriological delimitation* and an *eschatological determination* of the justified in God's Pneuma/consequent nature (Auburger 2001). Ultimately, then, the sense of truth in the event theory is fulfilled in *theological truth* within the "Harmony of Harmonies"; it is in this sense that it has *harmonic* meaning (§39). The *reconciliatory* meaning of a creative harmonization of the *past* must *not* be forgotten; the victims of history, rather than being relativized, are to be *remembered* in their history and precisely *therein* delimited toward their redeemed *pleroma* (Suchocki 1978; 1988; 1995) (§39). Hence the preeminent eschatological locus of truth is ultimately the final *judgment of justification*, for "truth itself is nothing else than how the composite natures of the organic actualities of the world obtain adequate representation in the divine nature" (PR, 12; Auburger 2001).

The theological consequences of this *relationalistic understanding of truth* are as follows: (a) *Truth coherence as decision*. Although there are indeed eternal ideas, there are no "eternal truths" (Krämer 1994) (§38), meaning that truth is not identical with an eternal idea of God (an eternal object), always being positioned instead *with reference to an event* and within a *concrete* (event) context. Truth is thus also not a matter of logical coherence within a "truth whole," but rather the *event-oriented concrescence* of eternal ideas in *Sophia*/Logos. The coherence of truth is never given in principle, never disclosed systematically, never valid in abstraction; instead, it is *decided* in events (Rorty 1983). (b) *Truth correspondence as contextuality*. Truth, rather than being independent—the substantialist fantasy—is instead always *contextual* and thus *historical*. And this contextuality in its own turn, rather than demonstrating the relative nature of truth, instead attests its nexic anchoring. The historical nature of truth announces that something remains true within such event orientation only if recollected; that is, truth requires a historical tradition of truth. Rather than relativizing truth, this historically one-time or singular element instead secures, as it were, its very universality, since only the singular can have universal significance (§§11, 27, 36). And precisely this is the real meaning process theology attaches to the correspondence of truth, namely, that the singular, as Whitehead puts it in his book *Symbolism*, imposes an *obligation of correspondence* on the universe; that is, the singular yearns for universal significance to which the universe must accommodate itself (S 26). (c) *Truth consensus as redemption.* Ultimately there is truth only in reference to *universal communication.* This is the delimited communication within the Pneuma. Truth consensus is thus always a *soteriological* category, the pragmatism of truth being focused not on evolutionary survival (on "success"), but on *reconciliation.* Hence cognition or recognition of truth is always—quite in the sense of St. Paul in 1 Corinthians 8:2f.—an act of love, of self-transcendence, and of universal community. (d) *Truth harmonics as eschaton.* In its theological anchoring, truth is ultimately an *eschatological* rather than an ontological category (Auburger 2001). All three modes of truth converge in God's eschatological nature (Peukert 1988), with *correspondence* preserving the singularity of all events in God's memory, *consensus* obtaining in God's judgment as the justification of the universal community, and *coherence* referring to the reconciliatory harmonics of divine release into eschatological Peace (§39).

Regarding what in (systematic) theology is the key status of truth propositions and propositional truth, in process theology an interesting picture emerges. Propositional truths can never lead to a *correspondence* with the mystery of God's revelation, because they always remain embedded in the ambivalence of symbolism. Put differently, their correspondence is never available "isolated"—as it were, substantialistically "in and for itself"—but only through the *inner coherence* of the *nexus mysteriorum* (Faber 1992). On closer examination, one finds that coherence and correspondence are positioned in an irresolvable dialectic. *On the one hand,* truth is *appropriated* from tradition (commensurate with the event of origin); *on the other hand,* however, the truth of every event is *decided* only within the coherent context with everything else. That is, there is no such truth without its systematic reconstruction (Pannenberg 1988) (§47).

From the perspective of the theopoetics of the universal *creative and eschatological harmonics of truth,* preference is given to *event-theoretical coherence* (creative presentation in God's reconciling judgment) over correspondence (memory of that which is past) and consensus (release of the community in eschatological peace). The *consensus* of the community within reasonable discourse—whose locus is theology itself—presupposes internally that only that which in principle (or to a greater degree) concurs, is consistent, and is therefore coherent is in fact *capable* of consensus. The disjunctive and disconnected, the contradictory and disruptive, cannot prompt consensus, or can at most coerce it under adverse conditions. Consensus implies coherence (PR, 181). Although coherence can indeed also be the expression of projection, there can be no *correspondence* with any *pre-*

determined or presupposed truth *unless* such be grasped *as* truth through the medium of cognition. Cognition, however, strives to discern coherent relationships, grounds or reasons, and the coherence of such grounds. There is no correspondence without coherence (Wiehl 1971) (PR, 190f.). Everything is thus positioned within *universal relationality*, which acquires *harmonious coherence* in God's embrace. Indeed, nothing situated *beyond* such relationality can be said to *exist* (PR, 3f.). That is, nothing "is" without relation or reference. It is the coherence within the whole that first renders propositions regarding existence *possible* in the first place and, with them, correspondence between rationality and existence. Moreover, the eschatological fulfillment of this whole of all relations "in the divine nature" (PR, 12) is nothing other than the fulfillment of that which we expect in every consensus as salvation, namely, universal salvific consensus. In summary, then, it is the harmonious coherence within the whole that first makes consensus possible as salvific happening, and only thus is consensus meaningful at all.

§43. RESONANCE WITH THE SCIENCES (ENERGY AND INTENSITY)

The interdisciplinarity of process theology is a coherent consequence of its fundamental ecological disposition—the postulate of the "unitexturality of reality" and the "essential relationality" of all reality and of cognition and reality. This position has prompted a plethora of initiatives that have tried to overcome dualism, substantialism, and subjectivism in epistemological and scientific theory (Griffin 2000). Although such applies especially to the hiatus between the natural sciences and the humanities, it also prompts reflections concerning the integration of psychology and physiology, ecology and economy, and philosophy and theology in interreligious dialogue (Cobb and Griffin 1976; cf. *Process Studies* 1970ff.). This *nondualistic impulse* of process thought is so fundamental that it has affected even the development of terminology, the categories of research, the understanding of the cosmological framework, and theological language itself. Eloquent testimony to this influence can be found in event theory, with its integration of physicality and mentality, in nexus theory, with its complex, evolutive, and differentiating understanding of the organism and society, and in reflections on the divine matrix, with its integration of cosmological and theological language.

Whitehead's work was from the outset focused on overcoming the "bifurcation of nature" (Maassen 1991a). In his early works on philosophy of science and nature—*An Enquiry on the Principles of Natural Knowledge* (1919), *Concept of Nature* (1929), and *Principle of Relativity* (1922)—he opposed the mechanistic materialism that in his opinion constituted the background of contemporary natural science. His early event theory (what he calls the "passage of nature") tries to overcome the split between mind and matter, mechanism and vitalism, atomism and organicism, and internal and external relations (Lucas 1989) (§9) by drawing on the internal developments going on at the time (and largely still valid today) in the disciplines of logic, mathematics, and physics, all of which were engaged in a paradigm change, and especially on the philosophical implications of the theory of relativity and quantum physics (Stolz 1995; von Ranke 1997; Griffin 1986; Wassermann 1991). In *Science and the Modern World*, Whitehead presents a comprehensive (and widely read) examination, from the perspective of the history of ideas, of the aforementioned "bifurcation" into two realities— a subjective-psychic reality and an objective-scientific reality (Maassen 1991a; Klose 2002), concluding that Descartes's dualism of *res cogitans* and *res extensa* maneuvered the grand cosmological concepts (symbolized by Plato and New-ton) into an irresolvable aporia (§§9–10). What is needed is thus not only a philosophical revision of the atomism, mechanism, and materialism inherent in the natural sciences, but also a comprehensive examination—from the per-spective of the history of ideas—of the way the phenomenon of bifurcation was both prompted and fostered by substantialism. Only a new meta-physics can overcome the split of reality into two systems (Sayer 1999). Here one also finds the original context in which Whitehead integrated the natural sciences and religion into a new, comprehensive understanding of philosophical cosmology on the basis of aesthetics, as well as the first context in which "God" became a key theme of his subsequent reflections (SMW, 178). In his later work—*Sym-bolism* (1927), *Process and Reality* (1929), *Adventures of Ideas* (1933), and *Modes of Thought* (1937)—Whitehead considers ever anew how to integrate in a com-prehensive, coherent, and relational fashion this bifurcation of subject and object within a new theory of perception ("symbolic reference"), event theory ("concrescence"), theory of civilization ("mutual immanence"), and theory of the significant "modes of thought" ("importance") (Hall 1973; Johnson 1958; 1983; Emmet 1966).

The situation within the history of philosophy to which Whitehead's new organic, relational, and nondualistic cosmology is reacting can be understood as the problem of the *unity of the world* (Welker 1988; Keller 2002b). The "bifur-cation" of subjective and objective reality as fixed in Descartes's "two realities" has two sides: *materialism* as the background of the natural sciences, and *historicism* as the background of intellectual history and the humanities (Sayer 1999). Whitehead's key realization was that the two are intimately intertwined, suffer-ing as both do under the *separation* or *disjunction* of perception and perceived, agent and object of knowledge, internal and external reality, *to the extent* they are no longer recognized or discerned as in fact belonging to the *same texture* (Kasprzik 1988). *Mechanistic materialism* supports subjectivism in dialectical dependence, interpreting, for example, "secondary" qualities (such as colors) as subjective experiential projections—over against the "primary" qualities (such as weight) of physical objects. Here, mathematical quantity and mental quality diverge in an irresolvable fashion (Hampe 1990). But if the subjective is closed off into the sensuous cognitive human subject, that subject then becomes the sole locus, not only of subjective experience and feeling, but also of value, freedom, and responsibility. One consequence is that nature then becomes the lifeless arena of the pulls and pushes of vacuous particles, functionally ordered but lacking internal meaning and direction (teleology) (PR, 167). Another consequence is that *relativistic historicism* dethrones the subjective import of the qualities, values, and responsibilities from transmundane, eternal figures of the world to the status of historical and societal variables. In other words, nothing possesses stability. Value and meaning are but projections emerging from subjective inadequacy, and all that remains is to acknowledge the relative, lost status of human beings in an otherwise (in and of itself) meaningless universe (Sayer 1999; Rohmer 2001). The attempts by Hume, Kant, and Hegel to overcome this disjunction of matter and spirit failed. Hume reduced mechanistic causality to a convention of mental repetition, but then naturalized that convention into a toy of meaningless (nonteleological) sense impressions—the result being skepticism (Welten 1984; Lotter 1990). Kant's transcendental philosophy merely entrenched subjectivism, insofar as the causality of mechanistic reality remained untouched while appearing theoretically mediated only in the categories generated by subjects. By contrast, value characters (especially freedom, immortality, and God) remain only as postulates of practical philosophy. They become withdrawn from the world, which is now in its emptiness dualistically positioned over against isolated human beings with their "ethical needs." Subjective reality has lost "real" meaning, that is, with regard to reality, being instead a human projection that merely *imputes* "objectivity" (transcendentally, as the condition of the possibility of ethics) in securing societal cohesion (Wiehl 1990). In its own turn, Hegel's absolute Spirit elevates Kant's transcendental subject to the status of a divine reality. Although doing so enables him to decipher and thus, for the first time, to *mediate* the "objectivity" of physical reality (from the perspective of the natural sciences) as the self-objectivizing of a cognitive subject, his imputation of a teleology of (natural) history as a whole must be viewed as having failed in view of subsequent scientific and philosophical developments (as whose completion Hegel viewed himself). Neither the world as a whole nor even merely as human history proves to be striving toward a divine goal, and the notion that matter is actually a manifestation of self-negating Spirit does not do justice to the nonteleological structure of a physical reality that acts according to its own laws (Lucas 1989; Sayer 1999).

Contrary to these failures of "unification," Whitehead's philosophical impetus manifests itself in his attempt to focus on the problem of the *collapsed* unity of the world and to *relativize* that collapse (concurrently considering its underlying reasons) in a new initiative by *relating* the attendant contradictions and dualisms in a *unity of process* (Welker 1984; Faber 2003) (§§16, 24). Whitehead developed his final processual position over the course of four phases or periods in his work.

The *first stage* of his search for nondualistic unity focused on the significance of *mathematics* in (not) guaranteeing the relationality among multiple worlds. In his early works *On Mathematical Concepts of the Material World* (1905) and *An Introduction to Mathematics* (1911) he finds on the other hand that the "atoms" grounding the world are not isolated objects (particles as substances), but relational events (intersections of relations). On the other hand, he determines that there is not just a *single* mathematics capable of comprehending the world (Stolz 1995). Mathematical relationality can furnish only an abstract unity of the world, constituting a "hypothetical substructure of the universe" that otherwise necessarily ignores all specific perceptions, thoughts, and emotions (IM, 33), thereby ultimately lagging behind the world's concrete plurality (Welker 1984).

The *second stage* focuses on the relationship between *experience and nature*. In his works on the philosophy of nature from the early 1920s, which were not yet really that interested in metaphysical synthesis (Sayer 1999), Whitehead makes the momentous distinction between event and object (§12). This distinction variously infiltrates the question of unity in which the natural sciences are generally accorded a privileged position. Unity itself is no longer defined reductionistically (by way of the natural sciences) within an empty, materialistic universe, since that universe itself consists in a plethora of events with a percipient structure (prehensive events), whereas their structures (objects) represent abstractions from processes of becoming and perishing (passage of nature). This position not only deciphers "abstraction" as such as a mental phenomenon (objects) that is anchored in nature (rather than solely in human beings), it also understands "subjectivity" (events) as a natural phenomenon (Plamondon 1979; Löw 1990).

The *third stage*—Whitehead's later philosophical works from the mid-1920s on—focuses on integrating metaphysically the cognitive (knowing) subject, on the one hand, and known (discerned) reality, on the other (CN, 28) (Beelitz 1991; Lotter 1991). Whitehead's event theory now recognizes the event as that particular nondualistic unity of the world that discloses itself as an *internal* process through which physical and mental relations "grow together" *subjectively* (concrescence) and as an *external* process (transition) through which subjective immediacy is lost (superject) while simultaneously acquiring universal significance in its "objectivity" (objective immortality) (Fetz 1981; Sayer 1999). Everything that happens is now understood as a dual processual unity of matter and mind, subjectivity and objectivity, cognition (knowledge) and reality. *All* reality has the *same texture*, albeit *processually* as the swing between two—internal and external—processes (Faber 2000e) (§16).

In a *late, fourth stage*, which becomes visible at least in its outline in his final works of 1941, namely, "Immortality" and "Mathematics and the Good" (Faber 2000c), Whitehead articulates in complex fashion the final dualities that remain issues (albeit processually mediated) in his thought (AI, 190) and defines their correlation as being nondual. At work in all concrete happenings are the "world of creativity" and "facticity," which allude to the becoming and perishing of events as both *temporal* and *historical process*, and the "world of value" characterizing the creative process as a *subjective and objective process of decision and valuation* (§23). The creative process is self-creative *as* a process of decision grounded on intrinsic self-value that forms objective values in its (past) facticity, values that endure beyond the perishing event as its meaning. The value process, on the other hand, is valuative in this sense not as an abstract order, but rather *only* as a process of decision of concrete events. These two "worlds" are thus nothing "in and for themselves," being instead merely abstractions of the *same* nondual, concrete universe as *world process* (Imm., 87–90).

The processual, relational, and postconstructivist solution at which Whitehead arrives over the course of his investigations thus effectively undermines the traditional dualistic hiatus of nature and spirit, natural sciences and the world of the mind, subjective *psychē* and objective *physis*—which in Whitehead's view are merely *extreme, abstract, static boundary concepts* of the concrete reality of *process*, a process that yet resonated in the Greek concepts of *psychē* as the principle of *life* and *physis* as the inner emergence of world into its organic form (Kann 2001). For Whitehead, the duality of mind and matter, subject and object, measurement and feeling is manifested in the *concrete* world only as a *processual difference of time* (AI, ch. XII). Within the "present of becoming," *every* event (of whatever sort or as belonging to whatever society) represents a happening of *ontological privacy* through which a certain measure of inwardness, immediacy, self-creativity, and self-value is attributed to every event. In the "past of being," however, it witnesses to the *objective public* that can be observed, measured, analyzed, and valuated quite independent of inwardness. Here reality is accessible to the natural sciences and is causally efficacious. In the "future," however, there are no concrete events, but only "eternal objects," *abstract* ideas, possibilities, forms, structures, and potentials *for concrete becoming* (Hampe 1990). Here Whitehead successfully reintegrates value with fact, the functional mechanics of the material with the teleological aesthetics of the mind, indeed the natural sciences with religion, nature with God (Sayer 1999).

The metatheoretical strength of this *processual nondualism* is its *nondifferent category formation and language*. If *all* happening in the world is "unitextural" and "universally relational," then not only does it all share the *same event texture*; it also represents a *single* coherent context of categorial relationality and interpenetrating linguistic transgression (Faber 2000e; 1999c). Because Whitehead's event categories do not apply only to human beings, because value capacity is a natural phenomenon, because subjectivity does not just apply to conscious being, and because decision is not tied to ethics, a certain decoupling takes place between nondualistic language and sphere of application. "Perception" is now understood as a happening applicable to all event happening (Hampe 1990); "feeling" now applies not just to sensitive beings (animals and plants), but equally to elementary particles; and "decision" now represents a fundamental phenomenon applying to all events, even to the virtuality of empty space (Spaemann 1986) (§15). In *Adventures of Ideas*, Whitehead paradigmatically and philosophically critically summarizes this nondualistic "lower deviation" of process language—which *ties together* the entire span of the natural sciences and philosophy by comprehending them in their isolation as an *abstraction* from a common reality—as the *nondifferent, coherent context of complex reality* at the ground of every "event/occasion of experience":

An occasion [event] of experience which includes a human mentality is an extreme instance, at one end of the scale, of those happenings which constitute nature. . . . But any doctrine which refuses to place human experience outside nature, must find in descriptions of human experience factors which also enter into the descriptions of less specialized natural occurrences. If there be no such factors, then the doctrine of human experience as a fact within nature is mere bluff, founded upon vague phrases whose sole merit is a comforting familiarity. We should either admit dualism, at least as a provisional doctrine, or we should point out the identical elements connecting human experience with physical science. . . . The science of physics conceives a natural occasion as a locus of energy. . . . The notion of physical energy, which is at the base of physics, must then be conceived as an abstraction from the complex energy, emotional and purposeful, inherent in the subjective form of the final synthesis in which each occasion completes itself. It is the total vigor of each activity of experience. The mere phrase that 'physical science is an abstraction', is a confession of philosophic failure. It is the business of rational thought to describe the more concrete fact from which that abstraction is derivable. (AI, 184–86)

Although this delimitation of language is both risky and problematic, insofar as it so easily generates distorted notions, it does appear unavoidable in light of the nondualistic project as such (PR, 4–7; Franklin 1990). Mention of the "common element" (e.g., of "complex energy" at the foundation of physical energy and subjective intensity) must be understood as a *reconstruction of concreteness* from the perspective of a dynamic enhancement of a language of "givenness"; it should *not* be misunderstood as referring to new "givens" (Wiehl 1990). The "complex energy" allowing for both an emotional, value-focused language and a quantitative physical language says nothing about "real reality," referring instead to abstractions as *givens* based on a *process* that is more concrete than all givens that make referential propositions possible, that is, references to reality as such. Reference cannot, however, be made to the *process* itself, which already underlies or provides the foundation for all signification (§41). This misunderstanding in its own turn underlies the charge that with his nondualistic language Whitehead is in fact advocating a kind of "panpsychism" (Wiehl 1990; Hampe 1990; Spaemann 1986). Whitehead himself in fact rejects such (Lowe 1963), maintaining not—though some process theologians prefer to think so (Griffin n.d.; 2000)—that all reality is "mental" (animated, inspired), but merely that the *same* reality appearing in its "givenness" as a physical fact represents, in its otherwise nonreconstructable concreteness, a *self-creative process* of which *both* our physical comprehension and our psychological explication represents an *abstraction* (Faber 2000e) in which we are bound to express the *broken* unity of the world.

One cannot underestimate the specifically theological relevance of the claim to develop such a nondualistic language of universal relationality. A theology of creation incapable of relating God to the physical world as the latter is investigated by the natural sciences ultimately isolates God from God's own creation and itself from any discussion about cognition and reality (Sayer 1999; Sander

1991). Hardly any theology has attempted in so radical a fashion to carry on precisely this dialogue. Process theology's claim to comprehend God and world within mutual immanence has generated theological reflections concerning topics as diverse as the theory of relativity and quantum physics with respect to God's agency in the world, and biological theories of evolution and ecology with respect to the meaning of the development of forms and life as such (Löbl 1994; Griffin 1986; 1992; Birch and Cobb 1990; Overman 1967; Mays 1977). In all these considerations, process theology constantly adheres to the principle of *empirical reference*, albeit not for the sake of defending the reality of God in the face of the findings of the natural sciences—an apologetic position presupposing that science represents a threat to theology—but for the sake of speaking about God in the context of reality as a whole (*sub ratione Dei*) in a rationally responsible fashion (Griffin 2000; Pannenberg 1987; Lüke 1994). In this process, the findings of the natural sciences (despite their hypothetically tentative character) are allowed as "checks" on theological ideas. At the same time, however, those same scientific findings are queried with respect to their cosmological presuppositions; their ideological implications are disclosed, and their abstractions rendered transparent as such. In this fashion, the "reality" of the natural sciences is disclosed as an *implication* of the theological *reconstruction of concrete reality*, that is, of *processual* rather than "given" reality, and theology itself disclosed as a *contingent*, that is, historical and hypothetical anamnesis of the mystery (principle of concretion).

I use the expression *resonance with the sciences* to refer to theology's openness to scientific rationality *if* it is accompanied by a *simultaneous, contingent reconstruction of its abstractions* on the basis of its fundamentally relational event-reality (Faber 2002e). The "unitexturality of reality" is sought *not* in any direct influence or certainly identity between scientific and theological conceptuality—as if God were a scientific "given," or physical energy a theological fact (Esterbauer 1996). What is sought instead is, in the Whiteheadian sense of a *broken* "unity" (of world, categories, and language), to *mediate* the methodically and objectively independent sciences or disciplines by means of an "identical moment"—but a moment *processually* presupposed rather than scientifically "given." From the processual perspective, the *metaphysical implications* of the findings of the natural sciences touch on those of theological propositions such that they generate thereby the possibility of a *transformational matrix of mutual immanence* through which they mutually interpret each other without, however, directly influencing each other. Within the prevailing methodological and objective sphere of each discipline, *vibrations* are thereby set in motion that *without* such resonance would in fact not resound at all (§36). The theological ground of this resonance from the perspective of process theology is ultimately the *divine matrix* (Bracken 2001) (§32), in which "energy fields" of a physical nature emerge along with "emotional fields" of mental intensity as "givens" of a communicative divine process—mediated by the chaotic nexus (*khora*), which thwarts both a divinization of the world and a secularization of God, while nonetheless illuminating both processes in a resonance of mutual immanence.

§44. ECOLOGY OF THE MIND
(BRAIN, CONSCIOUSNESS, AND PERSON)

One theologically volatile concretion of this overcoming of the "bifurcation of nature" into mental and physical systems of reality and of the resonance between the sciences and other disciplines is the brain/mind (spirit) problem—a modern form of the body/soul problem (Busch 1993). Essentially two alternative answers have been proposed for this problem. For the *materialistic* interpretation and its *monistic reductionism*, the brain is a material organ to which freedom, inwardness, subjectivity, experiential wealth, consciousness, and identity merely "appear" (as a misfortunate projection), but which in truth is nothing more than a functional, determined physical organ that is quite reasonable from an evolutionary perspective, is mathematically reducible, and can otherwise be wholly illuminated from the perspective of the natural sciences (Popper and Eccles 1997). This interpretation is theologically relevant insofar as it denies the creativity, value capacity, and inwardness of all reality, thereby also ultimately rendering theology itself obsolete. In a reverse fashion, the *idealistic interpretation* with its *Cartesian dualism* is inclined toward a spiritualistic reconstruction of the material givens of the brain as an organ of a "transcendent" spirit or mind, which "in and of itself" can also be conceived as being (existing) "for itself" (Beckermann 1999). Although this position does frequently try to provide a theological foundation (Descartes's idea of God), the disconnect between physical givens leads to isolation with respect to the (natural) sciences (Brüntrup 1996). Hence, from the perspective of process theology, *both* reductionist monism, which reduces the freedom of the human mind to physical causality, *and* spiritualistic dualism, which assumes a reality of the soul (of the mind, spirit, consciousness, or self) independent of natural causality, prove to be nothing more than *forms of the earlier substantialism* of self-sufficient realities capable of "simple localization" (§14)—be they of a material or a mental sort, conceived as the sole reality that reduces the prevailing other to a mere epiphenomenon (monism), or postulated as being autonomous and independent of the other (dualism) (Loomer 1949).

From the perspective of Whitehead's organic cosmology, the fundamental error of both materialistic monism and idealistic dualism, as well as of the substantialism inherent in both, is that they conceive the "mind" or "spirit" or "consciousness" as "thing," "essence," "substance," "independent being" (Brüntrup 1996; Zoglauer 1998). Here monism and dualism do *not* really differ, since both the reduction of the mental to the physical and the assumption of the (relative) independence of the physical and the mental are based on this substantialist presupposition. Whitehead concurs with William James contra Cartesian substantialism, James having determined in his famous piece "Does Consciousness Exist?" (1904) that consciousness represents a "function" rather than an "entity" (SMW, 177ff.; Kann 2001). For Whitehead, "that function is knowing," which is adduced to explain "that things not only are, but get reported, are known" (SMW, 178). Moreover, for Whitehead consciousness and mind are not *res cogitans*—neither in and for themselves nor through difference over against some *res extensa*—but rather *functions of events and nexuses* (Busch 1993; Rohmer 2000). The same applies conversely to the "material substrate" of mind and consciousness, the brain (or the human body in the larger sense). Even material bodies such as the brain are not "things" that can be "simply localized" independently in time and space. They do not represent "inertly naked matter" (SMW, 22) that is merely distributed over the entirety of space in changing configurations, since—as Whitehead argues in *Function of Reason* (1929)—not even their existence (beginning, change, perishing) would have a ground or foundation independent of all "inwardness" (Sayer 1999), and since in any case even their "firmness" ("materiality") must be reconstructed in modern physics as the oscillating conditions of energy fields (Kann 2001; Busch 1993; Wiehl 1991). In Whitehead's ecological reconstruction, even "matter" represents a *function of events and nexuses*—the macrocosmically organized, structurally stabilized, *constant character* of event nexuses (Hampe 1998; Rust 1987). In Whitehead's cosmology, mind and matter are functions of microcosmic events and macrocosmic nexuses. Within the microcosmic process, they are grounded in the *dipolar structure of events*—in their *physicality*, that is, the prehension of real objects (physical objects), and in their *mentality*, that is, the prehension of pure objects (mental ideas). In the macrocosmic process, they are grounded in the evolutionally *differentiated organizational forms* of organism with their "more or less" formal structure (matter), vitality (life), or creativity (mind) (Hampe 1990) (§9).

But Whitehead's process solution also clearly sets itself off from *non*reductionist positions regarding the brain/mind problem—including prominently the position of "nonreductionist physicalism," the "theory of supervenience," and "neutral monism" (Brüntrup 1996). Although he shares their nondualism, he does not accept their—now as before—substantialist implications, which he is intent on overcoming with his own *processual and organic theory of event and nexus*.

(1) *Nonreductionist physicalism* avoids eliminating the phenomenon of the "mental"—including inner perception, subjectivity, consciousness, and reason— or identifying it with material givens (e.g., as does the materialistic theory of identity), instead allowing for a certain independent reality to attach to the mental, albeit strictly tied to biological brain processes and *as* biological processes (Beckermann 1999; Brüntrup 1996). In one of its more prominent forms, John Searle advocates it contra monistic materialism and Cartesian dualism. His motto is that "mental entities," although *dependent* on their underlying "physical entities," cannot be *reduced* to the latter (Searle 1996). This position—often referred as the *emergence theory*—interprets the phenomenon of irreducibility as the unpredictability of new system characteristics of the brain that cannot be derived from physical givens—a form of Gestalt theory for which the whole (mind, consciousness) is always more than its parts (material structures in the brain with their physiological features).

Although Whitehead does certainly acknowledge and commit to emergence theory (PR, 46, 75, 187, 229), he gives it new meaning. Rather than explaining how new features emerge in an increasingly complex organizational form belonging to the macrocosmic "mental whole" and pointing back to microcosmic "material structures," it instead explains how novelty is possible *on every level*—with equal respect to both microcosmic events and macrocosmic organisms (PR, 187). In Whitehead's thought, the principle of emergence derives from the "threefold character" of events (§33) and is disclosed from the principle of creativity as the *processual swing of self-creativity*, that is, from underivable (new) but relational (historically determined) concrescence, and *self-transcendence*, from perishing wholeness and efficacious causality. Hence for Whitehead, emergence never refers to the mind arising from inanimate matter or to freedom arising from causality, being instead a value process (Sayer 1999) (§23). In this sense, the event theory is a theory of the emergence of the *subjectivity* of new events from preceding events (real objects), which then enter into new ones without completely determining them causally (PR, 88), and the emergence of the *superjectivity* of perishing events, which formulate causal patterns in which new events are self-determined. Hence freedom and causality, mentality and physicality, subjectivity and superjectivity (objectivity) inhere in the dipolar events *prior to* any macrocosmic materiality or mentality (consciousness, reason). "Emergence" is describing not the appearance of the free mind from causal matter, but the arising of both matter *and* mind from the dipolar event structure and its irreducible complexity (PR, 229) (Busch 1993). Both represent macrocosmic organizations of their relations among one another, corpuscular societies with a constant pattern of nonliving structure, and living nexuses in living societies—as well as everything in-between against the backdrop of the chaotic nexus (Hampe 1990) (§15).

In Whitehead's conception of *superjectivity* (§28), this emergence theory assumes a *critical stance* contra both its open materialism (physicalism) and its concealed idealism (top-down causality). Contra physicalism, it implies a *sundered concept of causality* (Ford 1983) that consistently includes creativity (as a feature of the concrescent process) without denying scientific objectivity and regularity (as a feature of the transitional process) (Hampe 1990; Wiehl 1991). The superjectivity of events guarantees both (1) the emergence of the novel (PR, 187), since it is always referring to the incipiently arising and causally underivable "wholeness" of a becoming event (PR, 45)—and to this extent it also remains a Gestalt theory (PR, 27–28) (Fetz 1981)—and (2) physical objectivity, since that which perishes attains physical objectivity in space and time. Contra the idealism of the whole, for which the whole is always *more* than its parts (the result being "mental causality" of mental wholeness), superjectivity secures the status of the *perishing of wholeness* into a physical *element* in the becoming of new events (PR, 21). In Whitehead's "Gestalt theory" (Faber 2003)—something taken up again only recently by Bruno Latour (with reference to Gabriel Tardes) (Latour 2001)—the whole is always *less* than its constituent aspects. In this capacity, Whitehead's emergence theory represents a critical, deconstructive theory of demythologization of ideal (and ideological) wholes.

(2) The *theory of supervenience* overcomes the unclear concept of emergence not by assuming some form of "top-down causality" attaching to the whole (of the mind) or its (material) parts, but by speaking of a "surplus" ("supervene"

means "to take place or occur as something *additional*") of the mental within the material (Jaegwon Kim); although the mental can indeed not be reduced to the material, it is always accompanied by material processes and dependent on them (Brüntrup 1996). This theory acquired considerable influence through Donald Davidson in the form of a "token theory of identity." Contra all forms of concealed substantialism, Davidson maintains that there are no "mental entities," only classes of characteristics—including a class of *mental characteristics* (Beckermann 1999). It is always the *same event*, however, to which are ascribed both material and mental characteristics; moreover, those characteristics apply to it such that the material characteristics are of a public nature, that is, of a causal nature and as such accessible to investigation by the natural sciences, whereas mental characteristics are of an individual nature, that is, causally incomprehensible and thus ultimately irrelevant to the natural sciences (Brüntrup 1996).

From the perspective of Whitehead's event theory, however, this theory of supervenience remains trapped in concealed materialism. On the one hand, it conceives material causality in an undeconstructed fashion as self-enclosed causality, while, on the other hand—and for precisely that purpose—understanding the isolation of the mental as singular characteristics of specific physical events for the sake of preserving their scientific irrelevance. Although Davidson does conceive the mind as a characteristic of (physical) *events* rather than as a substantial entity, its strict privatization effectively renders it meaningless within the world process and, by rejecting the concept of emergence, leaves its origination in irrational darkness (Brüntrup 1996). By contrast, Whitehead's emergence theory of the processual dipolarity of events neither presupposes any self-enclosed causality nor has any need of privatizing the phenomenon of the mental for the sake of preserving the prevalence of the natural sciences. Both physical and mental characteristics instead have *macrocosmic relevance* insofar as they actually represent characteristics of *organisms*, and they arise out of the *microcosmic* concrescence of actuality (real objects) and potentiality (pure objects). This perspective avoids the materialistic trap that equates scientific objectivity with "vacuous actuality," since past actuality is now felt in what is also its mental singularity (AI, 219) (Hampe 1990) (§§10, 36, 41). It circumvents the idealistic trap insofar as the ideal presupposition of emergence, rather than being some "realm of ideas" or "absolute spirit," is instead the *mere possibility* of a valuing process, a process that *without* it can be nothing more than an abstraction *of* it (PR, 64). Contra the supervenience (with its concealed "superficiality") of the mental, Whitehead responds with the notion of the *synchronic organism* and the *diachronic process* as the locus of the mind.

(3) *Neutral monism* is to a certain extent an atomistic variant of the idealistic "philosophy of identity" of German Idealism (Popper and Eccles 1997). Like the latter, it believes that matter and mind are basically merely the forms of appearance of a single absolute reality that, although neither mind (spirit) nor matter, can nonetheless appear as both. Whitehead's colleague Bertrand Russell developed this position (Zoglauer 1998). Wholly anchored in the research concerns

of physics in seeking the ultimate entities—"atoms"—and the laws governing their interaction (natural laws), from which the world itself is constructed, Russell understands all atomic happenings as a reality capable of exhibiting either a physical or mental appearance, depending on methodology. "In and of themselves," however, the atoms constituting the world are neither material nor mental, but rather an *ignotum x*. Hence mental characteristics can indeed appear in the organization of the brain that, although inaccessible to the methods of the natural sciences, must not without further ado simply be denied existence for that reason. Despite the risk of falling back into idealism (or of becoming indistinguishable from it), this theory has acquired considerable currency today in its variants because of its varied connections with philosophical and quantum-physical connotations. Indeed, its philosophical arc extends not only to Kant's "transcendental subject" and Schelling's "God," but also to the great Buddhist classic Dogen, with his understanding of the "formless self" (behind all phenomenal forms, both material and mental) (Stambaugh 1999). With Niels Bohr's "Copenhagen interpretation" of quantum reality, whose characteristics are *undeterminable* prior to their determination (measuring), it establishes a connex with contemporary quantum physics (Faber 1999c; Jung 1980; Brüntrup 1996).

Whitehead's *processual and organic event dipolarity* opposes a monism of the unknown because the latter ends in irrationality and skepticism (Lotter 1990). Although he does adopt its nonsubstantialism, according to which the "essence" of the real "atoms" of the world cannot be determined "entitatively" as this or that "given," he resists the irrationalism of an *ignotum x* by locating the presupposition of every essential given in a *process of constitution* whose genesis can be rationally illuminated (process principle) (§26) (Hampe 1990; Fetz 1981). Here Whitehead also eludes the concealed idealism of neutral monism, since unlike the latter he does not view the process of events as being indistinguishable from manifestations of an unknown (absolute) mind or spirit. Instead, that process is capable of clarifying the *conditions* of the emergence of mind— the differentiation of event stages in evolutive organism structures—by clearly distinguishing "ideal reality" as *possibility* within the becoming of organisms, that is, by understanding mind and consciousness *organically* rather than *ideally* (§§9–11).

With his organic cosmology of the evolutive emergence of organism structures increasingly characterized by the element of life and of the corresponding phases of increasing creativity of the events inhering within those structures (§15), Whitehead does indeed develop with respect to the brain/spirit-mind problem a *transformational matrix* for the resonance between the natural sciences, philosophy, and theology (§44). This cosmology understands mind (spirit) as an *ecological* phenomenon, that is, neither as a physical epiphenomenon nor as a reality independent of the body, but as *form of the nexus* of living events arising within the organization of living organisms. In its internal dipolarity of physical and mental, actual and potential aspects of the process, mind arises as a psychophysical happening—and never in any other way (Loomer 1971; 1976b; 1984). Spirit is that particular ecological "whole" of a living organism that emerges from the entirely living nexus embedded within it, that is, which derives or comes *from* that organism, happens *within* it, and simultaneously *surrounds* it by representing its "wholeness" (Loomer 1949). The "form" attributable to the spirit, however, is the *formlessness* of a living nexus rather than the character of a society. The spirit cannot be "simply localized," being instead the *open whole* of a living nexus by means of which—to follow up on a suggestion by Gregory Bateson (1994)—an *organism* is connected *to its surroundings*. That is, it is in the ecological embedding and its wholeness that the "spiritual" aspect of the spirit resides (§24). This spirit acquires *concreteness*, however, not through reason, consciousness, or the freedom of decision (with all of which it tends too precipitately to be identified) but through its preconscious spontaneity and unconscious feeling, its inclination toward intensity and its ecstatic causality, its mutual interpenetration of mentality and corporeality, potentiality and actuality, subjectivity and objectivity, subjective inwardness and rigorous self-surpassing (§41)—and all of these things within a specific ecological intertwinement. This transformational matrix has considerable implications for the connex of brain research, the philosophy of mind, and theology, particularly with respect to the question of the *ecological understanding of personal identity*.

(1) *Consciousness and freedom*. "Consciousness" is not, as some philosophical positions would have it, a higher function in the brain attributable to the cerebral cortex, having instead—as Antonio Damasio has shown—a phylogenetic function in providing alertness for the organism in situations of decision. Corresponding cerebral regions for such "core consciousness" can thus be found in the brain stem, particularly in the reticular formation (*formatio reticularis*). Higher evolutionally developed forms of extended consciousness are then associated with other regions of the brain, including consciousness of action, visual and audio-consciousness, and consciousness of body unity (Damasio 1999). Whitehead's theory of consciousness understands consciousness as a specific mode (subjective form) through which events perceive, that is, "feel" the tension between possibility and reality, where something is that could also be different, or where something is not, even though it is expected (PR, 188, 242; Rust 1987) (§15). It is always the alertness associated with decisions that, if unaccompanied by consciousness, the organism cannot survive, and the circumvention of lethal concrete experiments, which can instead be considered as possibilities rather than simply implemented as such. Hence consciousness can by no means simply be identified with the unity of an organism or its feeling of self (of "I"); it is instead a function of its unity (PR, 58, 162, 178, 236ff.).

Whitehead's ecological model also makes more comprehensible physiological brain experiments that demonstrate how consciousness, instead of being positioned, as it were, at the root of decisions, instead often merely accompanies them or is added only a posteriori to decisions that have in fact already been made. As B. Libet has shown, volitional decisions are made in the brain *before* actually becoming conscious—even though consciousness itself insinuates its own "simultaneity" or even *authorship* of decisions (Roth 2001). Given these findings, can one still speak about freedom, or are we (pre-)determined and merely "informed" of the decisions of our body? For Whitehead, consciousness is a late form of decision *awareness* in the organism, since *every* event already represents a decision process (Rorty 1983). Conscious decision is thus an evolutive achievement of living organisms with an entirely living nexus through which events feel in the subjective form of consciousness (Busch 1993). In that sense, "late-arrival" consciousness militates neither against freedom (and for determination), nor "preconscious freedom" against the authorship of a given organism in its self-identity (identity as "I"). It shows instead that personal identity represents a complex ecological process inseparable from its differentiated organic event nexuses.

(2) *Self-consciousness and personal identity.* The problem of the *unity of self-consciousness* derives from the fragility of "experiential unity" given the physical diversification within the brain itself. Consciousness and authorship of the feeling of "I" cannot be "simply localized" within the physiology of the brain; that is, there are *many* places in the brain that contribute to the emergence of self-consciousness (Rager 2000). But how can such a differentiated unity—a unity with no central location, being strewn instead across the entire brain—be mediated with the powerful feeling of the unity of self-consciousness? This is the "binding problem" (Roth 2001) that the neurosciences have not yet resolved. Roger Penrose, however, has proposed a notable solution based on quantum physics. Its premise is that the unity of self-consciousness is a noncausal, nonmeasured, global quantum state within the brain in which causal brain processes overlap in "quantum entanglement" in merging into a unified arrangement corresponding to "self"-consciousness. One characteristic of "entangled" quantum states is that they represent a noncausal nexus of quantum events that from the perspective of the theory of relativity have no real connection (that is, cannot affect one another), since such connection would have to be faster than the speed of light. What the theory of relativity forbids, however, quantum mechanics demands (and well-supported experimentally), namely, that there be no perceived *distance* with respect to the connectedness between the quantum events entangled in a common quantum state (even if such be light years). This entanglement, to be sure, obtains only as long as it is not measured; any measurement destroys the entanglement itself and "localizes" the quantum events as causally and locally bound events (Penrose 1991).

Whitehead's organism theory was associated with the emergence of the theory of relativity and quantum mechanics and was cognizant of those theories from the very outset (SMW, 129ff.). Whitehead thus understands the event process as such as, on the one hand, "nonlocal" concrescence (events as quantum events), and, on the other, as causal transition. In the *objectivized* condition of transition, events follow the theory of relativity in having finite *causal* velocity (CN, 99ff.; Klose 2002). In the *subjective* condition of concrescence, however, they possess a "unity" allowing for *noncausal* connections between the prehensions and phases of their own emergence; that is, they are not in physical time (PR, 244). The question is now how the entirely living nexus representing the unity of self-consciousness within the organism can be conceived not only within a causal succession of events, but also as the noncausal, nonlocal unity of the nexus allowing that nexus to feel itself as identity.

Whitehead, first of all, identifies a special form of prehension. With this *hybrid prehension* (PR, 245ff.), a new event feels its objectified precursors *physically* (with the physical pole), but with respect to its *mental* decisions (with the mental pole) (Ford 1988). In this way, the entirely living nexus is able to pass on its mental wealth, the treasure of its spontaneity (§15, 22). In one passage in *Adventures of Ideas*, however—a passage I view not as exhibiting a lack of clarity (Griffin 1992), but as a rigorous continued development (Faber 1999c)—Whitehead even speaks of how mental poles are *not* subject to the physical laws of time and causality, such that "measurable time and measurable space are then irrelevant to their mutual connections" (AI, 248). The significant conclusion Whitehead draws from this insight is that "there may be an element of immediacy in its relations to the mental side of the contemporary world" (AI, 248). With respect to an entirely living nexus and its hybrid prehensions, this would mean that a *direct connection* is conceivable between the *mental poles of events within a nexus* implying a *nonlocal and noncausal network* of these events beyond any locality. This insight does indeed make it possible to conceive—in resonance with quantum-mechanical nonlocality and its interpretation by Penrose with respect to consciousness—an entirely living nexus *as* the unity of self-consciousness *and* in personal identity. Within this "unity," the self-creativity of *all* events in this nexus becomes mutually transparent. Although this applies *diachronically* to all events belonging to the history of this entirely living person-nexus, it also applies—even more significantly—to all *presently becoming* events in this nexus, which thus can be conceived as being positioned within a *mutual "entanglement"* (§§22, 38).

(3) *Personal unity in God.* From the perspective of a *cosmologically sensitive theology*, not only does God's agency with respect to *personal identity* become coherently transparent in connection with the physiological givens of the brain; one also acquires something theologically with respect to a new ecological understanding of person. Personal identity can be understood *cosmologically* as the *diachronic and synchronic entanglement of the events of an entirely living nexus within a living organism.* Understood thus, personal identity fulfills the strict criteria of unity heretofore lacking in criticism of Whitehead's theory of event and organism—and of every nonformally grounded personal "theory of identity" (Runggaldier 2000)—with its diachronic and synchronic differentiation (Bracken 1989; 1991; Ford 1986; Rohmer 2000) (§22). It is indeed an *antecedent* but *not* an a priori unity in the sense of a substantial soul or a transcendental subject insofar as it "exists" *solely* together with its constituent events. In this sense as well, it does not represent a stable character or enduring form, but a more specific determination or definition of personal unity as *khora*, as *hypodochē*, as the unity of the chaotic nexus (Faber 2002d) (§24). *Theologically*—and differently than in the case of Bracken's personal "energy field" (2002)—this understanding

of personal identity emerges as a *"unity field" or "khora field" within the divine matrix* (§32). Although in the world it is differentiated organically into brain, body, and history, it is always *emergent* in the gift of divine creativity (PR, 40) and *one* in the solidarity of the entirely living nexus of *Sophia*/Logos. In God, the "person in God" is the reconciled field of unity within the entirely living nexus of the Pneuma (§39). In this sense, *personal being within the divine matrix* completely fulfills the theopoetic axiom of the mutual immanence (§34) of God and world as unseparated and unmixed nondifference. Personal being within the divine matrix is thus the ultimate instance of *process*—the mutual transgression of *explicatio* as *différance* (ecological differentiation) and *complicatio* as *khora* (formless unity) (§40).

§45. HARMONICS OF CREATION
(EVIL, TRAGIC BEAUTY, AND THEODICY)

The question of theodicy constitutes an integral part of Whitehead's thought, constituting the a priori of the introduction of the concept of God into his organic cosmology in the first place (§§26–28, 35, 37). Nonetheless, a peculiar tension is evident between the later interest of process theology in theodicy and Whitehead's own lack of interest in explicitly thinking through the question of theodicy as such. The reason, which precisely this tension renders visible, is that Whitehead understands the "existence" of evil and suffering in the world *not* as a query to God that cries out for God's justification in the face of suffering, but as the *a priori of every possible question* concerning the fundamental structure and meaning of the universe (RMn, 99) (Kreiner 1998). Whitehead responds to the question of theodicy directly (albeit without commentary) with his notion of the *theopoetic difference* between God and creativity, and indirectly with the notion of the nondetermination of the world (§27), God's superjectivity (§28), and his own theopoetic aversion to speaking about God's creative power in terms even remotely implying or evoking any form of coercive power (§35). In Whitehead's theology, God ultimately appears as the "Harmony of Harmonies" into which the harmonics of creation is taken up such that its tragic beauty is confirmed (AI, 286) and evil eschatologically eliminated (RMn, 155) (§39). Here Whitehead neither dissolves evil into God—as a moment in God's becoming—nor views it as an evolutive necessity (PR, 340ff.). Through the notion of the *difference between divine matrix and chaotic nexus* (§35), a theopoetics based on these fundamental considerations provides a theological way to bear the "existence" of evil without despairing of God in the face of suffering in the world, while yet maintaining hope in universal redemption.

Process theology as such has developed essentially two responses to the question of theodicy. The one deriving from the *rationalistic* variant of process theology has received widespread if critical attention, while the one deriving from the *empirical* variant is largely unknown.

In *God, Power and Evil* (1976) and *Evil Revisited* (1991), David Griffin has articulated for *rationalistic process theology* what the majority of process theologians view as the "solution" to the problem of theodicy. This proposal is based on theopoetic difference and as such thus draws on Whitehead's primal distinction between God and creativity in advocating a revision of the idea of God's (the creator's) power. Griffin maintains that the question of theodicy is in fact based on a misconception of God as a simultaneously good, omniscient, and omnipotent being, a position viewed as a late development of substantialist conceptions of God, in terms of which the question of theodicy *necessarily* appears as follows: Given the experiential suffering in the world, God *cannot* simultaneously be good, omniscient, and omnipotent (Basinger 1994). Either God is not good, in which case, while the fact of suffering may well be comprehensible, God's own existence is hardly consistent. Or God is good but not omniscient, in which case, although suffering may well have entered into the world without God's knowledge, it still remains inexplicable. Or, finally, God may well be good and omniscient but not omnipotent, in which case God may be excused for allowing suffering—but at the price of a loss of confession to the "Almighty." And this is the path Griffin takes in understanding God as a good God who knows everything (that can be known), but *not* as an almighty, all-determinative God and thus also *not* as a God with complete responsibility (Griffin 1976). This God is instead a "weak" God—but in that case also a *sym-pathetic*, relational, cosuffering God of solidarity (§35).

The criticism leveled at this "restriction hypothesis" has often been excessively focused on the more obvious part of the thesis—the renunciation of God's omnipotence. A God who is not almighty can allegedly not really be God, lacking as God does the sovereignty enabling God to be not only the creator (*ex nihilo*), but also—and even more importantly—the redeemer of a world suffering under evil (Kreiner 1998). By leveling such charges, however, such criticism remains indebted to precisely the substantialist presuppositions that process theology is criticizing in the first place, and by their overcoming process theology tries to articulate an alternative understanding of God's creative and redemptive power (§45). If, however, one conceives this power in terms *other* than those expressions of coercive power, arbitrary freedom, and absolute sovereignty, *other* than those of nonrelational, ultimately unilateral arbitrariness and decretal dominion—that is, if one conceives this power in terms accommodating a simultaneity of freedom and relationality along with a relational nondifference between God's will and God's nature (AI, 168), then one can understand God's power as poetic (*poiesis*) rather than as coercive (§28). For the question of theodicy, such understanding means that God's power within theopoetic difference is the *power of love*, a power that—and this is a crucial qualification—can no longer be conceived in the categories of "causation" (§28).

Nor must criticism necessarily begin at the deeper level of argumentation, namely, that though this noncausal God is a suffering God, God's own suffering (to the point of *kenosis* on the cross) must not per se or necessarily be viewed as redemptive (Kreiner 1998). One can, of course—as does Karl Rahner—

counter such kenotic theology (of the cross) of the sort developed by Moltmann and von Balthasar with an inner-Trinitarian foundation of suffering (and under which process theology might also be classified) by maintaining that a God in suffering does not possess any redemptive meaning for my own suffering (Faber 1995a). From the perspective of process theology, however, the category of "co-suffering" (sym-pathy) is not necessarily to be understood as a remythologization of suffering and as its "eternalization," as it were, in God's nature, if not conceived from the perspective of the "myth of the suffering God" (Hans Jonas), which—so J. B. Metz—is in any case inclined to stabilize suffering politically and make it merely bearable with respect to God (Kreiner 1998). It can instead be viewed from the perspective of the *essential receptivity* of God's concrescence (§35) (Ford 1977d), which as superjectivity, rather than expressing a suffering (passive) omnipotence, in quite the reverse fashion virtually demands that God be ascribed a *relational* creative and redemptive power (§§28–29).

Criticism of the "restriction hypothesis" of rationalistic process theology needs to begin elsewhere. The sym-pathetic God—particularly in the form of Hartshorne's and Griffin's "society of divine events," which, as Richard Rorty correctly notes, sooner is ahead of the world in a searching fashion than moves toward it in redemption (Rorty 1994)—can do nothing about the evil and suffering in the world, *not only* because Godself is suffering under it and is unable to effect change, since God did not decide on the existence of evil (or is unable to decide differently in any case), *but also* because God *is not permitted the capacity or power to change that suffering*, only to mitigate it (in the consequent nature) (Griffin 1991). Yet even this mitigation itself issues in a new initiative (by the primordial nature) for the process to continue such that the world with its process again contributes to God's being—including in evil and in suffering (Ely 1983; Maassen 1988). At first glance, this consideration seems to quell the theodicy question, since God is effectively removed from the place at which this question first arises. In this sense, the problem of theodicy is rationalized away, and real suffering is blamed on an infinite world process that in its own turn reduces God to a "good" demiurge who is sym-pathetic in God's own impotence (Maassen 1991b; Kann 2000). At second glance, however, the theodicy question merely returns with a vengeance: A God who cannot *want* this world process to be otherwise, since it contributes to God's own inner being, is still—even if God cannot do otherwise—a God who lives from the evil and suffering of the world.

Empirical process theology's largely unknown treatment of the theodicy question, rather than shying away from this *reversal of the theodicy question* as one regarding the *meaning of evil and suffering for God*, instead embarked on this path that to a certain extent is an aporia (Faber 2000a). In his later work *The Size of God* (1977), Bernard Loomer (1987c) developed a theodicy focused *neither* on justifying God in the face of suffering, *nor* on the question of the origin and admittance of evil in the face of a good God, *nor* on sublating the world's "ambiguity" in an eschatological consummation (all these "solutions" can be viewed as having failed) (Welker 1988; Claus 1993). Instead, he accepts the insolubility of the theodicy question as such but *illuminates* it *anew* by asking how the bifurcation of good and evil might be sublated; his response being: through *ambiguity* and *size* (Faber 2000a). "Ambiguity" now becomes the critical principle of theological skepticism; the theodicy problem is now *asserted* as an expression of ambiguity rather than *resolved*. But what does "ambiguity" mean here? It refers to the concretely experienced world in its ambivalence, its dynamics, complexity, and richness, but equally in its unfathomability. Ambiguity is *simultaneously* the condition for living differentiation *and* suffering under the reality of the world. It describes the process of concrescence that must form contrasting relations out of complex and contradictory givens (§21). What is God's "size" in view of this ambiguity? God's "stature" corresponds to the *open wholeness* of the world, which essentially always expresses precisely this ambiguity, never coming to rest in unequivocalness and perfection. Hence God is that particular *concrete actuality* of the whole of the world that is able to "meet" this ambiguity in the hiatus of good and evil, and whose stature "endures" *ever greater* ambiguity without faltering or collapsing under the tension. Because concreteness (concrescence) means living indecision or irresolution, that is, ambiguity, whereas only the dissolution of ambiguity would mean "perfection"—unequivocalness being abstract and dead, insofar as that which is complete *as* something unequivocal is something that is already past—the concrete size of God's everlasting concrescence *corresponds* to *infinite ambiguity*, never dissolving into the past, into perfection, into unequivocalness, structure, and stasis (Inbody 1991). Ambiguity refers to the *irrevocable living element* of the open wholeness of the world, and God as the "mystery of the whole" is precisely that particular *agape* that creatively accepts this ambiguity "into Godself" infinitely (primordial nature) and receives it as saved (consequent nature) (Loomer 1987).

Loomer's theodicy merits attention because, instead of rationalizing the theodicy problem away, it considers it precisely *under the condition of its insolubility*. And indeed, his theodicy proposes no "solution" to the problem that merely trivializes suffering and freezes the uproar it provokes (Welker 1988; Faber 2000a). This proposal, moreover, preserves several elements of conventional solutions. The *unconditionality of divine and creaturely freedom*, for which God "allows" or "admits" evil, is now understood as "temporal stature," as ecstasis between "perfect" (unequivocalness, past, history, causality) and "imperfect" (ambiguity, presence, spontaneity, freedom) (§23). The *delimitation of suffering* is found in God's concrescent "stature" as the *simultaneity* between abundance and receptivity, whose goal is precisely to overcome unequivocalness, abstraction, perfection, and death by opening up the way to vivacity and an identity within it (albeit not in some determinative form) such that identity appears not as "characterlessness" (of the *khora*), but as *stature* in the face of and within the ambivalence of life (§24). The "restriction hypostasis" is now transformed into God's concrescent omnirelationality, which is not understood as a (natural) boundary or as some (voluntary) renunciation of the capacity or desire to overcome evil on God's part, but as the *size* of the saving reception and transformation of the world in God's "identity," God's "formless delimitation" within the Pneuma (Faber 2000a).

This empirical form of theodicy overcomes the weaknesses of the rationalistic theodicy. (a) Here God is understood not as a "weak" God who can do no other, but as a vigorous God whose power is a power of *stature* in the face of evil (Dean 1990). In its size, however, this power, which not only endures ambivalence but indeed *desires* it as an element of life, is God's power of *agapē* (Loomer 1949). (b) God is understood not as a "suffering" God who is *caught* in that suffering, but as a world-sensitive *opposition to the power of death.* In God's "size," evil and suffering are transformed into their unequivocally creative and soteriological alternative. Overcoming the element of the "perfect" within the process of concrescence always means both abundance *and* ambivalence, life *and* suffering. Evil irritates the element of life precisely by siding with *death,* that is, by seeking not the vibrant element of life, but ultimately its very opposite, namely, the unequivocal, the "perfect" element of that which is already past, since it is itself an opponent of the element of life. Hence in "suffering" God does not merely passively suffer or endure, but actively provides an opening toward (ambivalent) life itself (Faber 2000a). (c) Theodicy is not resolved *theoretically* here—a charge leveled at rationalistic process theology from various quarters of more recent political theology (J. B. Metz) (Kreiner 1998)—being positioned instead within a *praxis of creative life* under the power of *agapē*. Its inclination, however, contrary to political theology, is not merely to draw attention to evil in an "anamnesis of the victims" (of evil), but to draw attention to the creative transformation through which the "anamnesis" (of that which is past, of victims, of the deceased) becomes the creative locus of the *good* itself. The stature of the ever active element of life means that good *can* happen, and that the power of life consists in thwarting evil through creative praxis—even if such involves suffering. Hence the ultimate astonishment is that good as such *does* indeed happen (Cobb 1982; Wucherer-Huldenfeld 1997).

Nonetheless, the same query must be put to empirical theodicy as was put to rationalistic theodicy, namely, whether God's size is not *dependent* on the *bifurcation of good and evil* (Ely 1983; Loomer 1949). Does God not overcome evil precisely by *integrating* it into the intensity of God's own concrescence, indeed by *having* to integrate it *as* evil in *contrast* to good for the sake of God's own size? Unlike the rationalistic initiative, the empirical perspective does not conceal this problem. While rationalistic theology operates under the unreflected presupposition of a mutual immanence of the processes of God and world, that in its non-deconstructed and non-"converse" form (to which Griffin and Hartshorne subscribe) understands God as a process that "needs" the world as a physical prehension for God's own concrescence (§31), by contrast, the empirical solution positions this problem at the very center of its reflections. God's size manifests itself in the face of the *separation* or *disjunction* of good and evil. But does disjunction not sooner demand unification rather than overcoming? How can one avoid misusing evil for the sake of God's concrescence and the enhancement of God's process of aesthetic intensity (Maassen 1988)?

Here we are at the center of Whitehead's (presupposed) theodicy. One can indeed already find initiatives toward such aestheticization of evil—for example, in Kitaro Nishida's work *An Inquiry into the Good* (1992), which understands evil as a "part" of divine universality—and Whitehead himself was familiar with the proposal of F. H. Bradley, the English idealist to whom Whitehead acknowledges his own indebtedness in *Process and Reality* (the very title of which was influenced by Bradley's *Appearance and Reality*) (McHenry 1992). Bradley's "absolute idealism" seduces him to distinguish the "whole" from "God" such that, although a certain moral quality is indeed attributed to God (as the presupposition of religious veneration), the "whole" as "absolute" is in fact morally neutral, since it must, after all, accommodate everything. It accordingly encompasses all "appearances" (of the absolute) in *harmonious unity*. Here the absolute is also understood as the aesthetic unity of all evil, ugliness, and error—even though all discordance and destruction is "overruled" in harmony (1930, 432). As far as such *harmony* is concerned, Bradley maintains that the absolute *is* good, manifesting itself by way of various degrees of goodness and badness (1930, 363). But whereas Bradley now concludes that the "God of religion," in its moral limitation to the good, cannot be the absolute, and that even the assumption of God's existence as such thereby becomes an aporia (McHenry 1992), Whitehead draws a completely different conclusion with his introduction of the *theopoetic difference* between creativity and God (SMW, 179; PR, 31f.). Here he dethrones Bradley's "absolute" from any ontotheological substantialization, since as *creativity* it now is the process of self-creativity, which also enables him to entertain a new event concept with respect to God as the primordial process of *value* (Imm., 87ff.) (§40). While in a *theopoetic nondifference* between creativity and value within God's primordiality both thinkers identify God as the superject of creativity (§40), Whitehead's new initiative provided by the notion of *theopoetic difference* can now depart from Bradley's aestheticization of evil within the "absolute." Not only does this move allow for theodicy now to become the presupposition for systematically introducing God into Whitehead's organic cosmology in *Science and the Modern World*; a consideration of its implications also provides a different "solution" to the urgent question of the aestheticization of evil in both proposals for a process theodicy.

(1) Whitehead does indeed position "evil" less in a primarily ethical than an *aesthetic* context, namely, that of the aesthetic event process as a *process of intensity (concrescence) and self-transcendence (transition)* (Lachmann 1990) (§§21, 23). This becomes particularly clear in two passages in which Whitehead poses the fundamental question concerning evil, its essence, and its origin. (a) In *Process and Reality*, Whitehead identifies "ultimate evil"—the evil in which all other evil phenomena ("any specific evil") are subsumed—as the "perpetual perishing" through which the "past fades" (PR, 340). He does not understand the event process itself—the perpetual swing of subjectivity and superjectivity, of internal

becoming and external perishing—through which the past (as the causal frame-work of new becoming) *arises*, as being "evil" *in and of itself.* It is such *only inso-far as* the past *disappears* within it (Faber 2000e). Whitehead is *not* proposing that some "metaphysical evil" attaches to finitude, as does Leibniz (Kann 2000; Maassen 1988); instead he illuminates the metaphysical fact of a dual temporal process within which not only is "becoming" transformed into something that "has become," but also that which "has been" disappears into nonbeing. Such represents a double loss, that is, a loss of the aesthetic abundance of events in their becoming—events needing a complexly differentiated past for their *own* process of intensity if they are not to become impoverished (Welker 1988)—*and* a loss of the "importance" and "value" of that which has become in self-transcendence (Sayer 1999). In this sense, evil is associated with the loss of recollection to life.

(b) In *Adventures of Ideas*, Whitehead describes the emergence of evil in terms of *aesthetic loss*—anaesthesia—within the process of intensity (§21). Here he views beauty and evil as arising unavoidably from one and the same ground and as being bound together within the same happening, namely, the three metaphysical con-ditions under which the event process of concrescence and transition itself takes place. The assumptions are, first, that all events are *finite*; second, that finitude involves the *exclusion of alternative possibilities*; and third, that mental function-ing is intent on introducing into the process possibilities that are in fact *physi-cally excluded*. The problem of evil emerges here as one involving the *harmonics of creation*, in which a "basic disharmony" inheres or obtains within the world process that in its own turn is always directed toward harmony (AI, 259).

(2) Evil proves to be a moment in the process of harmony and intensity (§12). Such is indeed a *process,* insofar as there is no perfect harmony (AI, 257)—per-fection is always the temporal mode of the "perfect," of that which is past. Life by contrast is thus always found only in the mode of the "imperfect," being nec-essarily "ambivalent," unconcluded or open ended, and only as such a process of *intensity* (§21). In this sense the process of harmony and intensity is always an abiding *adventure* (§19) (Johnson 1958; 1983; Hall 1973), with "discord" con-sistently representing an essential part of the process, the causality of the past always appearing as a "struggle" for agency within each new becoming, and the self-creativity of this very "becoming" itself representing as it were a form of "elbow-room within the universe" (AI, 195). And precisely this situation moti-vates theopoetic difference, for Whitehead understands God as a value process that bequeaths to every event that particular initial aim that in its own turn offers the greatest *beauty* within this discordant situation of harmony and intensity—the ultimate situation of balance between intensity and harmony within its event-oriented and nexic situation. Within its process of self-creativity, however, the event itself must decide in this regard. It is in this way that evil can arise from the same ground as beauty, namely, from self-creative decision and causal constraint, from the freedom for creative novelty and the seduction to repeat an overpower-ing past, from solidarity and interruption (Suchocki 1995) (§37).

(3) The notion of aesthetic harmony as the locus of the emergence of evil can

easily be misunderstood as an integration of evil for the sake of enhancing intensity—a charge Ely leveled at Whitehead as early as the 1940s (Ely 1983). At most, Whitehead was willing to acknowledge (and even insist on) the importance of the "imperfect" for the process as such and the necessity of "discordance" for the creativity of the process (AI, 257ff.). Evil, however, consists not in the "discordance" or the "imperfect" as such, but in the causally (in the past) or spontaneously (within self-creativity) grounded inability to *deal creatively* with discordance. It is not the discordance within the process that generates evil, but the inability to attain harmony in that process, specifically, harmony that transforms discordance into a *contrast*; it is the failure of integration that generates evil as a form of *anaesthesia*, aesthetic breakdown (Hauskeller 1994) (AI, 256ff., 275, 285f.). Evil arises as the *aesthetic failure* of the process, indeed as the death of the process, or as Loomer puts it, as the dissolution of ambivalence into deadly, paralyzing, smothering unequivocalness (Loomer 1987)—something that applies all the more to God.

God does *not* "integrate" evil for the sake of enhancing God's own intensity, since evil *fundamentally* always involves a loss of intensity—indeed, the *collapse* of intensive harmony. Moreover, with respect to God's process, one cannot say that God strives to seek an intensity necessarily deriving "externally" or "from the outside." Quite the contrary, the primordial nature, as the measure and standard of all intensity, needs no such enhancement. As Helmut Maassen has shown, what follows is that God is *in and of Godself* "absolute intensity" antecedent to any "physical prehension" of world in the consequent nature, an absolute intensity that no perception of the world—be it good or evil, beautiful or ugly, complete or fragmentary, discordant or well ordered—can either enhance or diminish (Maassen 1988) (RMn, 154). Not only does God *not* "integrate" evil for the sake of "enhancing" God's own intensity; neither does God position good and evil, perpetrator and victim, heaven and hell within a *single* harmony within the releasing contrast formations in the consequent nature. For God's "integration" of God's "physical prehensions" of world happens—as Lewis Ford puts it—not through negating contradictions or discordances for the sake of harmony (like all events in the world), but through "complementing" physical prehensions by the infinite valuation of God's own infinitely intensive primordial nature (Ford 1973) (§39). The primordial nature is the ideal measure of harmony through which all events—both good and evil, beautiful and ugly, complete and incomplete—are brought into a communicative contrast within the consequent nature, that is their release, their delimitation (Maassen 1988) (§38).

The problems attaching to rationalistic and empirical versions of process theology's theodicy can be resolved by reconstructing the underlying theopoetic difference from the *conversion of processes*—as an *inverse* internal and a *converse* external process (§29)—wherein God comes into view as the *superject of creativity* (§28), albeit not without generating new problems. On the one hand, the problems of power, suffering, and the aesthetics of evil within the concept of God as superject of creativity are understood such that the weaknesses of process theology's theodicies are indeed circumvented. (a) God's (omni)potence and power can be interpreted within the conversion of processes as creative power *ex nihilo without* ever being nonrelational, since "chaos" and "nothingness" constitute the countermovement of "creative" and "creaturely" processes (§35). (b) Within the conversion of processes, God's suffering is initially disclosed from the act of creation *ad intra* as the creation of a space for creation *within* God. This *khora* in God corresponds to God's superjectivity as the highest unity of receptivity and spontaneity. It is only *there* that the divine disposition is created for receiving the world into God and thus also for enduring ("suffering") the world (§35). (c) There is no aestheticization of evil here, since within the conversion of processes God grounds intensive harmony such that it does *not* "admit" or "integrate" evil in order to enhance the process of God, but rather *endures* it, since God's process exhibits a "stature" that also surpasses or eclipses both evil and suffering.

On the other hand, however, the notion of God's superjectivity raises the new question of whether a God who releases theopoetic difference out of Godself—that is, first establishes it precisely in God's superjectivity as difference (§28)—is not also responsible for its consequences after all, namely, that there is such a thing as evil and (innocent) suffering in creation. And one could then indeed refer to God as being "guilty" of suffering in the sense that God is responsible for there being a creation in the first place (Schulte 1991). Yet an understanding of God's creative acts not as "causing" the world (God as *causa efficiens*)—as the Thomistic tradition would have it—but as the noncausal grounding of the world's own self-creativity (Garland 1983) (§§28, 35) *transforms* the essence of the theodicy question from a question of the "existence" of *God* to a question of the "existence" of the *world*. Similar to the way the tradition of Albertus Magnus, Dietrich von Freiburg, and Meister Eckhart views creations under the category of *causa formalis,* with God as *forma formatum* (Flasch 1986), Whitehead too chooses to understand creation *aesthetically* rather than "causally," with God as the poet of the world who as Eros lures (and leads) toward self-creativity. To this end, God "first" *insists* on and creates as a medium of communication, the *khora* (§40), as an *environment for the existence* of relations (§32), relations that are not only inner-divine, but also *always* transcend God (§28). Here evil and suffering are not simply the "price of freedom" according to which God must accept evil (Greshake 1978), but the "price of existence" (as fundamentally *relational*)—so that the world process does *not* remain merely a fanciful idea of God (God's "dream"), but is always a *real* process "outside" God, a process of *self-creativity* (of the *Other*)—and that means a process not merely of God's own inner creativity, but always of relational *inter*creativity whose "inter" can *never* be reduced to an "intra." This, to me, seems to be the more profound source of process theology's opposition to *creatio ex nihilo.* In this sense, and commensurate with Whitehead's concluding doxology in *Adventures of Ideas* (AI, 295f.), theodicy is a reference to the *aesthetic essence* of the world process as "tragic beauty," whose creative "harmony" (*harmonia mundi*) refers to the venture of indispensable *interrelationality as process* rather than to some phantasm of inner-divine self-reflection. Or in the terminology of dual eschatology, the world is an *adventure* in God's Eros that *cannot* merely be resolved into *inner-divine peace*. With respect to precisely this "aesthetic goodness" of creation in its *real* "existence," God, in Whitehead's book *Adventures of Ideas*, is the "Harmony of Harmonies" (§31).

It is ultimately *this* particular "inverse theodicy" to which the divine matrix is referring, in which God *creates* the world *non*differently in its *self*-creativity but without ever becoming identical with it; hence it is in the divine matrix that God *insists* on the *reality* of creation as *khora* so that *différance* might genuinely obtain within it. This is why it is necessary to distinguish between the divine matrix and the chaotic nexus, according to which creation within the matrix necessarily develops *relationally* and can never be resolved into *inner-divine* relations. That is, the chaotic nexus of all cosmic epochs, insofar as it cannot be reduced to the divine matrix, secures that particular ambivalence of life in whose "chaos" communication *and* failure, order *and* creativity, aesthetics *and* anaesthesia, beauty *and* evil, harmony *and* discordance are equally grounded. Although God does indeed always nondifferently differentiate the differentiations of the self-creativity of creation (§40)—whereby creation is *différance*—they are for precisely that reason incapable of being retrieved, as it were, through "integration" into inner-divine unity.

§46. CIVILIZATIONAL ETHICS
(FREEDOM, CHARACTER, AND SELF-TRANSCENDENCE)

In Whitehead's organic cosmology, the development of human civilization designates an *aesthetic fact* and an *ethical demand* (Johnson 1958). As an aesthetic fact, "civilization" refers to the evolutive development of societies (of societies) whose character makes it possible to accommodate an entirely living nexus characterized by the most extreme, animated element of life, whose spirituality/intellectuality, creativity, and value structure permit a shimmer of divine reality to become visible, a sensing of the divine matrix in its chaotic/ordered communication, a sheltering within eschatological hope through the conscious interplay of adventure and peace (civilization is ultimately always religious civilization) (AI, 69ff.; Hall 1973; Rohmer 2000). As ethical demand, "civilization" refers to the conscious commitment to the civilizational dynamics of the world process and the responsible acceptance of civilizational dynamics as the universe's *claim* to adventure and peace, intensity and harmony, self-creativity and self-transcendence, freedom and character (AI, 241ff.; Lachmann 1990). Ultimately civilizational ethics serves this dynamic out of the *Eros of creativity*, with its demand for an *ethics of love* in *hope* directed toward the reconciling "Harmony of Harmonies" (AI, 296). The innermost *movens* of this civilizational ethics is thus the civilizational process-contrast of *intensity* and *harmony*, in which aesthetics, ethics, and soteriology combine into the *dynamic unity* of adventure and peace. What this means *philosophically* is that the inner intensity of events and the harmony linking them into the relational whole *beyond* their individuality within the whole of the universe (and of all nexuses and societies in it) determine one another such that none can be without the other—even though none ever attains a "perfect" balance with the other, moving instead consistently toward "unity" *only within the process itself* (AI, 150; Wiehl 1984; 1986) (§§24, 43). It is in this sense that, *theologically,* the aesthetics of inner intensity and the ethics of universal harmony ultimately codetermine each other within the religious hope in a reconciled "Harmony of Harmonies," in which everything enters into a released harmony of Peace (consequent nature/Pneuma) while simultaneously preserving the creative Adventure of ever new intensity (primordial nature/*Sophia*/Logos) (§39). The dipolar God's immanence within *Sophia*/Logos and Pneuma stands for a dynamic permeation of aesthetics and ethics within a civilizational process (§38) that finds its forward dynamic within this dipolar God and is precisely thereby characterized *as civilizational* (and never as anything else) (Johnson 1958).

Whitehead's concept of "civilization" derives first of all from the evolutive dynamic of organisms within the cosmos. The process duality of concrescence and transition obtains within the constitution of organisms themselves. Every event, in and of itself, is an organism that synthesizes itself through its own *inner* process (concrescence) out of organic relations with the world, thereafter constituting in its *external* process (transition) a moment of an organism consisting of events in which it develops causal efficacy beyond its own becoming (§§19–21). The universe, in its organic organization of intensity and harmony, has led toward an evolution of increasingly more complex and simultaneously richer differentiated organisms, to societies and nexuses of living events and living organisms with events characterized by highly intensive freedom, conscious reflection, and visionary power (Busch 1993). The evolutive appearance of humankind represents the birth and breakthrough of this overall dynamic as a civilizational dynamic and thereby as a conscious acceptance of responsibility for the evolution of civilization (Faber 2000e). It intensifies the process through the appearance of *persons* representing the highest form of living societies within this evolutive dynamic (§22), in which self-creativity as a value process *beyond* purposive (functional) and unconscious repetition of values and structures of the past (a form of self-creativity that has in any case always been active within evolution) now acquires the capacity for conscious, free, self-responsible harmonics (§23). Civilizational dynamics describes precisely that process of consciousness, freedom, reason, and responsibility in which persons can develop *as* persons in community by positing and realizing the highest values through social solidarity and individual creativity (Schramm 1991).

Whitehead develops a theory of civilization in his book *Adventures of Ideas* (AI, 241ff.; Johnson 1958). The characteristic feature of "civilization" there is its ideal opposition to coercive power (imposition), savagery, and all forms of "barbarism" (AI, 51). The barbaric in this sense functions as an ideal type for the sake of description, not as a standard of exclusion—it characterizes the relationship betweens persons and societies, on the one hand, and coercive power or violence, on the other. A person or society of persons is civilized to the extent it succeeds in transforming brute, coercive power into the power of ideas, namely, persuasion. *Philosophically* this invokes Plato's discovery of the "freedom of contemplation, and . . . [the] freedom for the communication of contemplative experiences" (AI, 51), for whose significance Plato himself wrote and Socrates died (MT, 173f.). Civilization can develop only after a recognition of the difference between causality and potentiality, energy and ideas, a strategy of coercion and the purposive freedom of reason. Barbarism, however, consists not just in the exercise of brute coercion in implementing particular ideas and interests, but also in ideological barbarism's inclination to force the realization of universal ideas on others—Whitehead refers to this sort as "intellectual barbarism" (AI, 51). Whitehead, however, does not view the emergence of a *culture of persuasion* as a break with evolutive dynamic, in which the civilized element appears first *only* with human beings, but as a move closer to the "delicate splendor of nature" (AI, 51), that is, the innermost process structures of cosmic evolution. *Theologically* the emergence of civilization corresponds to the recognition of God's creative power as the *poetic power of persuasion* (§35), in which God appears not as despot, but as *Eros*. Hence, the development of civilization corresponds to a "fundamental" religious recognition of creatureliness deriving from God's noncoercive relationality, and self-creativity as the noncoercive power of potential, the future, and the novel. This is the *power of beauty* by which Whitehead himself maintains that the "teleology of the Universe is directed to the production of Beauty" (AI, 265), and that this civilizational dynamics refers to the emergence of "persuasive beauty" (AI, 51).

Because this civilizational dynamic is from the outset already contained as potential within the organic evolution of the cosmos, Whitehead understands civilization as arising and developing neither *dualistically* as a new stage of evolution *over against* the mechanisms of subhuman evolution (sooner as its immanent consequence), nor in the sense of *monistic* reduction as the fulfillment of an evolutive dynamic causally *deriving from* the subhuman development (FR, 6ff.; Rohmer 2000) (§44). Whitehead is thus a representative neither of dualistic substantialism, according to which the specifically human element (the soul) simply falls into the world, as it were (and quite independent of how evolution itself may be developing), nor of monistic materialism that reduces civilizational ethics "biologistically" (Kann 2001) (§44). As a result, Whitehead's understanding of evolution is critical not only of advocates of Darwinist selection and mutation in claiming they have the only valid explanation, but also of the application of these mechanisms to societal questions (sociobiology) (Lachmann 1990). Whitehead, quite to the contrary, instead charges Darwinist reductionism of being wholly unable to explain adequately the emergence of life and of the more complex forms of evolution (Rust 1987). He thus considers the Darwinist notion of the "survival of the fittest" and "natural selection" to be an "evolutionist fallacy" (FR, 7). For as a general type, "survival" applies more to *rocks* than to living organisms, given the latter's considerable fragility and vulnerability over against their surroundings (FR, 7). In this sense, Whitehead views "survival" more as an attribute of that which is dead (FR, 5); it cannot possibly be the goal of the living and thus also not the ground of the appearance of life. Instead, for Whitehead evolution serves the "Art of Life," whose goal is not survival, but to live well and to live better (FR, 8). Hence the survival of the fittest and best adapted cannot possibly provide the standard for societal ethics—especially considering the consequences of the dominion of the coercive power of the "fit" over the "less fit" and of the well adapted (the rabble) over the nonconforming. The dynamic element in evolution is not *adaptation*, but *formative shaping*. The greater the degree of intensity and of the element of life, the more will a society strive *not* just to adapt to its surroundings, preferring instead to *seduce* those surroundings to itself, formatively shaping them as the environment of its own life and spirit (FR, 8) (§15). The adventure of civilizational ethics, therefore, is to attain and develop and cultivate freedom and relational communication in this sense, taking its orientation from life, beauty, harmony, seduction, and love (AI, 148f.). Civilizational ethics is grounded in the aesthetics of a *civilization of harmony and love*, that is, it effects a turn to *civilizational noncoercion*, whose content is the "harmonizing of harmonies" *and* the development of "authentic reality" (AI, 292). These two aspects belong inextricably together in referring to the dipolarity of intensity and harmony within the civilizational dynamic as the development of *harmonic "order"* and *personal "love"* (AI, 292), that is, as the mutual permeation of *personal* intensity and *transpersonal* harmony, of self-creativity and self-transcendence (§§22.–23).

One important element in the development of civilization for Whitehead is therefore the evolutive emergence of *reason* and its civilizing as a *persuasive medium* of ethics over against coercive, impositional power (FR, 37ff.; Rohmer 2000; Lachmann 1990). Within this evolutive dynamic driving the emergence of civilization, reason thus refers to the "gradual development of Persuasive Agencies in the communal life of mankind" (AI, 69) and to a sphere of communication in which "an environment has been provided within which the higher mental activities and the subtler feelings can find their use and their enjoyment" (AI, 69). The evolution of reason is tied to the faith in and as recognition of a "world of civilized order" (AI, 25), that is, a conviction that the "victory of persuasion over force" (AI, 83)—as Plato discovered—is *not* an illusion entertained by certain life forms (of consciousness and freedom), but the reality *out of which* this life form has developed as both conscious and free, for the world shows itself to be a "cosmos" insofar as in it, "lowly, diffused forms of the operations of Reason" (FR, 26) have always been at work. Theologically, faith in a "world of civilized order" corresponds to the conviction of the "creation of the world" (AI, 25) through God's poesy, for which "the divine persuasion is the foundation of the order of the world," even though in an aesthetics of free and persuasive reason it "could only produce such a measure of harmony as amid brute forces it was possible to accomplish" (AI, 160). This insight points out how reason is positioned within a context of historicity and creativity, always developing within and out of specific societies toward which it remains historically oriented, *and*—commensurate with the principle of concretion and empiricism—that no *absolute* grounds for concrete reason in a civilization can be adduced (no metaphorical *creatio ex nihilo*)

(Keller 2000), reason instead always being *relatively* positioned with respect to the creative development of the society accommodating it. Reason, as the counterweight to the causality of the world, is thus not an expression of the repetition of physical and historical "givens," but a *movens* of contrafactual *creativity* at the level of "personal" civilization (Wiehl 1986). There it always obtains within a horizon of potentials that set themselves off in relief from the simple facticity of the given, luring toward novelty and displacing into a new future. There Eros manifests itself in holding up the mirror of the Not Yet and summoning to its realization.

In *The Function of Reason*, Whitehead juxtaposes two evolutive functions of reason with respect to the development of civilization. The *reason of Ulysses* is practical reason; pragmatic and goal-oriented, it seeks to render effective purposes both conscious and accessible to reflection (FR, 33, 37). Its eminent evolutive importance in the development of higher organisms is that it enables organisms, through entering into a "converse relation" to the traditional understanding of Darwinist adaptation (FR, 7), to seduce, adapt, or shape their environment *to themselves* rather than vice versa. By contrast, the *reason of Plato* encompasses theoretical, speculative reason; it is purposeless and characterized by "disinterested curiosity" (FR, 38). Its evolutive importance for the development of civilization is that it enables organisms to resist being coerced by purposes, rendering them free; in and of itself, "abstraction," it protects self-creativity, novelty, the unrealized future, and the vision of fulfillment (FR, 37ff.; Rohmer 2000). It is this ultimate "nonobjectivity" of reason, the *khora*, in which it grounds civilization *aesthetically* as free and communicative and *ethically* as the interwovenness of personal freedom and transpersonal solidarity (Lachmann 1990). These two modes of reason together constitute a civilizational ethics linking creative, formative shaping and solidarity for the sake of attaining the goal of a noncoercive civilization. The *reason of Ulysses* involves the ecological renunciation and technological sublimation of power. In coming to an understanding, through *ecological* awareness, of our relationality and embeddedness in environmental processes—that is, civilization as a society of societies within societies and out of societies—we formatively shape for ourselves, through *technology*, an environment in which a civilization can "live better *with* all creatures in their environment." This renunciation of coercive power based on our situatedness within an ecological network corresponds to the sublimation of coercive power in technologies that learn to engage physical power to *serve* and *enrich* the fragility of civilized life and its ecological surroundings rather than destroy it (AI, 75ff.). In the *reason of Plato*, however, there does dwell the critical thorn of freedom from purpose, through which we defend ourselves against civilizational utilitarianism and the subtle return of coercive power through ecology (mere adaptation) and technology (mere transformation). With this reason, rather than repeating the past (tradition) or yielding to the needs and enjoyments of the present (interests), we are positioned in the future of potentiality, of the negative, the other, the novel, the alien, the unimagined (Lachmann 1990; Rohmer 2000). In its critique of mere ecologizing and mere mechanization, of mere adaptation and the mere formative reshaping of civilization, the "speculative" character of the reason of Plato preserves an element of intellectual freedom that prevents self-creativity and self-transcendence from being functionalized either way—functionalization in this sense being the mechanization of coercive power.

Civilizational ethics unfolds within the *processual duality* of *personal* and *transpersonal* dimensions, both of which are as intimately connected as are con-crescence and transition, event and nexus, organism and environment. They interpenetrate each other without ever being capable of being resolved or reduced one into the other. Persons are themselves living societies positioned in a history of value formation and creative intensity, so much so that Whitehead views them as the highest form of organic intensity (AI, 186ff., 208; PR, 350; Hampe 1990; Busch 1993). The essence of the unity of persons, however, is that of the *khora*, the vitality of the chaotic nexus itself in form of the intensity of an entirely liv-ing nexus (§22). It thus stands in a creative self-transcendence as the ethical death (§23), through which it is transparent within *each* of its personal events in respon-sibility toward the "environment." This universal relationality, in which the per-sonal society renders itself transparent, involves not only its organism, but also the surrounding societies, even to the level of civilization itself and its ecological and technological contexts, from which it constitutes itself in each personal event, that is, from which it acquires its self-creative intensity and for which it tran-scends itself (contributing to its harmony).

Here one finds the grounding not only for the vision of noncoercive civiliza-tion, but also for the failure of the same (§45). Every personal society develops a character, leading to stable structures of harmony protecting its own intensity. At the same time, each person contributes to the transpersonal character of the civ-ilization to which it belongs. Personal style and transpersonal harmony, however, strive not just for the element of life and vitality, but consistently also for stabil-ity (Suchocki 1995). The root of coercive power, however, resides precisely in this structural trap, in which (formal) "harmony" takes over the *function of identity*, pushing the *khora*, a *khora* that fits no form, toward forgetfulness (§35). Here that particular process of separation, substantialization, and egological isolation begins in which relationality is degraded to the status of an attribute of substan-tial power, which in its own turn—given the alleged independence of the sub-stantial—now becomes intent on asserting itself physically (§37). Substantialism constitutes the substrate of that particular coercive power that renders noncoer-cive civilization into a mere vision of universal relationality that for just that rea-son remains conceivable *only* as redemption (Faber 2002a) (§37). Civilizational ethics is thus systematic exercise in ethical death, universal relationality, and cre-ative solidarity in view of the very real chimeras of coercive power, substantial-ism, and self-presence, striving instead for self-transcendence, *différance*, and the creative openness of the *khora*. Ultimately it understands itself as opening up both personal and transpersonal structures toward the divine matrix, in which chaos and communication constitute a creative "unity," that is, nondifference.

In *Adventures of Ideas*, Whitehead develops three theoretical civilizational "schemes" capable of articulating at least in outline form a civilizational ethics involving the problematization of the appropriation and sublimation of coercive power and the freedom from such power. (a) With respect to a civilization committed to noncoercion, he adduces *seven qualities* through whose interplay this freedom from coercive power—through the reason of Plato—can be developed philosophically, namely, the ideas, the physical elements, the psyche, Eros, harmony, mathematical relations, and the receptacle (AI, 275). (b) With respect to the intensive and harmonious "stature" of a civilization, that is, its civilizational "character," he adduces *five qualities* that must determine its process, namely, truth, beauty, adventure, art, and peace (AI, 274). (c) With respect to the living self-transcendence of civilization, he adduces *three concepts* in which such freedom from coercive power creates space for itself, namely, adventure, zest, and peace (AI, 295). In all three theoretical civilizational "schemes," the swing of intensity and harmony, physical and mental moments, self-creativity and self-transcendence, form and formless *khora*, structure and vitality manifests as affected by theopoetic difference and the theological demand for God's *poetic* agency. God and world, creation theology and eschatology, solidarity and interruption, sin and grace all obtain within a coherent context recalling the "ecological reminiscence" at the conclusion of the six antitheses (§31). The *intercreativity* between God and world, that is, the divine matrix, provides the "metaphysical" framework for both the emergence or arising *and* the demise of civilizations. Its ethical *movens* is a creativity whose "power" is freedom from coercive power and that ethically both demands and hopes for such in reconciliation—even when it itself generates coercive power or fails because of it, and even when God is encountered in it only anonymously as creativity.

§47. RELATIONAL THEOLOGY
(ECOLOGY, NORMATIVITY, AND ALTERITY)

The theopoetics of a process theology oriented toward essential relationality and ecological processuality also discloses the outlines for a new theory of theology, a metatheology. The epistemological ideal of *theopoetic theology* is not to search for a Cartesian *fundamentum inconcussum* (Faber 2000e) (§11), but to follow the "trace" of the divine matrix, which manifests itself within cognition *only* non-substantialistically and nonfundamentalistically as relational delimitation (§26) and mutual immanence (§34). The immediate consequences of such *relational theology* (Suchocki 1994a; 1995) are its epistemological orientation toward *creative rationality* (§46) and the *universale concretum*, the singular and concrete in its universal significance (§36).

(1) The substantialist epistemological ideal focuses on the "general," which proves to be a kind of substantialist immunization of the "perpetually same," of the (in this context incorrectly so designated) "eternal," the "stable" (§11); it has this focus because it is accompanied by political interest in power stabilization and by psychological interest in fleeing that which is transient (Faber 1995a) (§46). By contrast, *creative* rationality focuses on the "radically novel" (§17), the "unhoped-for

future" (§39), and the "open whole" (§24). From process theology's perspective, "stability" represents merely *one* form of event happening, namely, the repetition of forms in events; it is the tradition of an enduring "character" (Hampe 1990) (§22). Its "general character" is that of eternal objects and is thus *abstract,* insofar as it acquires concrete meaning only through its ingression in singular events (§12). Its "eternity" is merely the presence of *possibilities* for decisions made in events and as event processes such that significant or meaningful cognition always exhibits *temporal* character (§18). Theological cognition thus always represents reaching for the Not Yet of the whole, whose essence is *adventure* (AI, 172). That "whole"—as Henri Bergson and Gilles Deleuze have shown—*cannot* be reduced to the "totality" of the structural moments of order of that whole; structure has meaning only within the event process. The whole is "open" but *not* undecided, since it "becomes" through the process of concrescent decisions (Rescher 1996; Deleuze 1996; Faber 2000e). This wholeness, like that of the "soul," is a *personal unity,* that is, a unity not of form and its abstract eternity, but of the *khora* and its receptive and creative movement (§22). The "identity" of theological propositions thus ultimately resides not in ontological stability, but in God's *eschatological* ad-vent (coming future)—something applying within the conversion of processes also to propositions concerning creation theology (§35). Theological propositions are eschatological propositions, or, more specifically, *temporal* propositions of an eschatological movement. They possess a temporal or time index (Faber 2000h).

(2) Unlike the fundamentalistic epistemological ideal of the "general," in which structure, order, and the (perpetually and everywhere) applicable is sought, the search for a *universale concretum* focuses on the *universality of the singular* that can never be derived from the general, since—commensurate with the ontological principle—the singular event can never be reduced to the universals inhering within it or even be discerned on their basis (§13). Instead, the singular is positioned within processual relations representing its *true* universality, which is the chaotic nexus. That nexus is the *necessary* relationality of the entirety of all events and their intercreative interrelationality, which bestows on every singular event the *unconditional* universality of its meaning. It is the moving whole of the *khora* —not some structure, of whatever kind, which can be only an abstraction of a single snapshot of the movement of the whole—that discloses truth in the universal meaning of the singular (Faber 1999a). The consequence for theology is that it must always follow the principle of empiricism, that is, of the historicity of cognition and knowledge, of being tied to singular events and their meaning. Such theology, however, is *eo ipso* a revelatory theology (§36), though without abandoning its universal—as it were, cosmological—claim. Unlike various forms of nonfundamentalistic theology—for example, "radical orthodoxy"—*process theopoetics* seeks *relational truth* rather than trying to assert particular (denominational) claims (Crockett 2001) (§42). It is *relational* theology because rather than resolving truth into relativity (of opinions), it preserves within the universal relationality of the cosmos a sensitivity to "unitextural" real-

ity (§41). As such, it is both poststructuralist and postconstructivist (§8). The relational truth of its propositions is of a *temporal* nature, that is, *simultaneously* possessing both a historical and an eschatological dimension (§42). And because it countenances the eschatological relevance of singular historical events, its "unity" in its own turn constitutes a *personal character*. Instead of clinging to abstract structures, it is *creatively loyal to a tradition* of the reception of singular events (Farmer 1997).

This epistemological understanding of theology within *theopoetic process theology* has decisive consequences for a metatheology. If as systematic theology it is always *temporal* theology, then it is positioned within an *event-theological space* as articulated paradigmatically by the divine matrix. As "concretion" (concrescence), it oscillates between *historical reality* (physical pole) and *eschatological rationality* (mental pole), and as "living nexus" (personal intensity with transpersonal harmony), it oscillates between *creative integration* (subjectivity) and *self-transcendent openness* (superjectivity). Within this event-theoretical space, theology is a *normative* discipline, that is, its "general truth" happens both as *concrescence*—as synthesis into an event understood as a *process of decision*—and as *transition*—as the relativization of any systematic unity of its truth in the light of the new "events" (situatedness, systems constructions, temporal contexts) of theology itself. The normative character of theology is thus extremely complex and is by no means exhausted by theoretical universality based on principles of the sort entertained by fundamentalistic theories of truth in their search for a systematic foundation *beyond* interpretation (Krämer 1994; Kasprzik 1988) (§42). Instead, the systematic truth of theology has *event character* (Faber 2000e). There *are* no theoretical systems based on principle that would not simultaneously have a normative aspect—something applying not only to theology, but to *all* disciplines (Göedel's theorem). That is, every discipline, every science has a normative aspect in the form of a moment of *decision* among the possibilities of coherent connections and correlations among principles, which in their neutrality denote mere possibility rather than truth. Truth is always a decision (de-cisioning) among principles with respect to coherence in events (§27) and is, therefore, as such always a *value process* (Faber 2000e).

Theology as a decision in this sense *toward* systematic truth is of a *temporal* nature, that is, it is *historical, creative,* and *relational.* (a) To the extent this "systematic decision" toward event coherence refers to singular events, the normativity of theology is concerned with preserving the original intuition of its founding events. (b) To the extent it focuses on alternative possibilities and is positioned in the light of the eschatological Not Yet, it is *creative* and inclined to *break forth* toward ever new systematizations. (c) To the extent it is in transition, that is, maintains a *relative* posture over against other system constructions and their event connectedness, it is *relational*—albeit not (substantialist-fundamentalistically) contextual, but (nonsubstantialist/relationalistically) *intercontextual* (Faber 2002e). Hence as a relational theology, and commensurate with the "threefold character" (of events and event nexuses), theopoetic process theology develops three metatheological characteristics (§33). With respect to its historicity, it is *dogmatic* theology, with respect to its eschatological breadth, *negative* theology, and with respect to its wholeness, *ecological* theology.

(1) *Dogmatic theology.* Relational theology lives as the disclosure of its own foundational events, in which are manifested the *singular element* of the experience of God and the *eph' hapax* of divine agency (Hauskeller 1994), which in the subsequent history of both influence and reception acquire universal and irreplaceable relevance. Contra the "neutral" (theoretical) universality (based on principles) (Krämer 1994) of truth, theology focuses *historically* on its foundational events such that it is forced to break through (philosophical or ideological) "generalizations" in favor of its own, singular religious intuitions (§3). If, as Whitehead suggests in *Religion in the Making*, such singular intuitions cannot be reduced to general metaphysics, constituting instead—commensurate with the principle of empiricism—a "metaphysics of singular events," deriving "from the supernormal experience of mankind in its moments of finest insight" (RM, 31) (§36) and elucidating the "direct intuition of special occasions" for "its concepts for all occasions" (RM, 31), then its theoretical task consists in disclosing *dogmatically* that singularity over against all systematic intrusion and imposition. This *normative universalization* of singularity, in its *consistently critical posture over against principles*, is "dogmatic" (Faber 2000e), insofar as "dogmas," for Whitehead, rather than seeking to enclose and restrict thinking, instead are intent on remaining true to their foundational events, that they might thereby *disclose* those events in their *singularity* and "formulate in precise terms the truths disclosed in the religious experience" (RM, 57) of those events. When Christian theology discloses the Christ event universally in Christologies—something process theology is also intent on doing (§38)—it can in so doing not be reduced to philosophy, nor can the nongeneral or nonuniversal element of Christology provide grounds for objection, since *no* singular event can be reduced to or reconstructed on the basis of universal principles. On the contrary, *solely* through the open disclosure of the feeling of its singularity it can acquire *universal* significance. "Christ gave his life. It is for Christians to discern the doctrine" (RM, 55). This *event-theological normativity* (dogmatics), however, does *not* constitute "dogmatism," since on the basis of its transgressive "character" it can never attain the status of "dogmatic finality" (AI, 162). The "dogmatic fallacy" arises only through the negation of event-theoretical truth construction and through theoretical fundamentalism focused on principles (RM, 126; Lucas 1989). Hence for John Cobb, the loyalty of Christian dogmatics to that foundational event—the Christ event—consists not in asserting theoretical truths based on principles (general, eternal truths), that is, not in maintaining the *one* true Christology, but in "Christologies," as such maintaining their *event-oriented loyalty* to the Christ event (Cobb 1974/75; Farmer 1997). Historical loyalty, however, thus always develops different forms, whose mutual perception must always be guided by the question of how they disclose the universality of the singular. Within a "living nexus" of theology of this sort, dogmaticity and plurality, rather than mutually excluding

each other, instead remained linked within a *living process of the ongoing histori-cal disclosure of truth*.

2) *Negative theology*. Relational theology understands itself as being focused on an eschatological whole (§39) on whose reconciling "rationality" (§42) it reflects and in whose withdrawn presence (§41)—the loving, withdrawn nature of the "divine Eros" (§35)—it, through its own event-theoretical disposition, sunders all systematization (Faber 2000e). In the light of this eschatological Not Yet, every systematic and dogmatic universalization of singular foundational events not only possesses the character of decision, but also effects that decision as an irreducibly *creative* process. Systematization can remain loyal to its histori-cal founding only by simultaneously representing a creative synthesis within a specific event situation. Although the "novel" element in that synthesis *cannot* derive (solely) from that original event, it nonetheless constitutes the only form of *living, ongoing loyalty* to that event (Cobb 1974/75). Within this creative and thus itself historical synthesis, dogmatic truth—as Pannenberg has noted with considerable acumen—necessarily always remains *hypothetical* (Pannenberg 1988) (§42). The reason for this has nothing to do with some relativity of truth, but with the meaning that history possesses for the eschatological synthesis through that the historically singular first attains event-theoretical universality (Pannenberg 1987; 1996). From the perspective of process theology, the "history of reception" represents a moment in the *effect* exerted by the singular event *itself* (e.g., the Christ event) and is, therefore, as such an inalienable part of its *eschatolog-ical identity* (Farmer 1997) (§39). What this means is that the multiple Christolo-gies represent *fully valid* moments of the eschatological truth of the Christ event, and in their creativity *genuine* manifestations of the effect of that event, whereas their *harmony* represents an eschatological act of *the* "Harmony of Harmonies." This sort of *creative* theology in its own turn, however, subject to the *eschatological reserve or difference* (§41) disclosed through precisely such *events*, is also always specifically *neg-ative* theology, for it knows God to be consistently *beyond* all of its own systemati-zations while simultaneously never shying away from systematizations but obtaining precisely *within* them (§29). Systematizations, rather than serving to "grasp" ("com-prehend") God, instead make it possible to *speak* about God in the first place, though always with an awareness of the hyper-systematic living nature of God (Faber 2000e) (§§27, 36, 42). Just as theology in this sense represents a *living nexus* of theologies engaged in perpetual self-transcendence, so also does such event-centered systematic theo-logy demonstrate *practically* that the *event* of God exceeds *all* systematization (just as an event exceeds its universals). That is, "systems" always remain mere possibilities among which not only a *normative* decision must be made, but which also must repeatedly be *creatively* sundered—in view of the *negativity* of God's living nature. This negative theology, however, to the extent it is con-cretized through events in ever new systematizations, is not only beyond fixating images; it also discloses the *spheres of possibility* with respect to its eschatological identity in being historically linked. It is precisely the potentials of "possible the-ologies" that allow for critical distance from the allegedly "value-free factual,"

thereby making possible a valuating, self-creative synthesis, a creative reception precisely of that which is past, for the sake of an authentic interpretation through universalizing the singular (Faber 2002c).

(3) *Ecological theology.* Relational theology is paradigmatically *"concrescence,"* that is, neither turned *solely* toward the past nor being *solely* future oriented, neither *solely* conservative nor progressive, focused neither *solely* on preserving values nor on being revolutionary. Instead, it represents the harmony of both "poles"—precisely in their tension—insofar as they enhance intensity (AI, 258ff.). But relational theology is also *"transition,"* emerging through events only by being aware of its own self-transcendence, through which its systematic synthesis acquires relational character, thereby avoiding any substantializing with the power interests immanent within it. As such, it is a critical, world-oriented, inverse, and ecological theology. (a) *Critically* it directs itself against the *attained* intensity and harmony through knowing about its own "perishing" and agency in *new* forms of theology, for whose form it seeks to provide material and—in the best-case scenario—for whose form its own intensity will be transmitted as if in a living nexus. (b) As *world oriented*, relational theology manifests itself through an awareness of the *temporal relativity* of the interpretation of the past toward which it is itself oriented and of the sphere of the future in which it creatively recollects that past; it is also characterized by *extensional relativity* with respect to the nexuses in which it is itself positioned—referring not only to the "theologies" in which it is contextualized, but also to the *real* societies with which it deals, which it "feels," and for which it thinks. It flees neither into the past nor into negative theology, viewing itself instead as consistently world *sensitive* and world *relevant*. (c) Given this world relativity, a theology in theopoetic difference can—in the words of Walter Benjamin and Theodor W. Adorno—be referred to as *inverse* theology (Faber 2002c). It still encounters in the godless a form of non-theology and in the oppressed a form of secular *kenosis*—God in the form of world-oriented, kenotic, nondifferent creativity (Faber 2002c) (§40). (d) Finally, relational theology is *ecological* theology, to the extent it views itself not only as "theology," as reflection on God, and thereby also—since Feuerbach and with Rahner—as "anthropology" (Rahner 1976) concerned with human salvation, but also as *cosmology* concerned with human beings within the *whole* of the world, with the organic interwovenness of all societies within the chaotic nexus. The ecological element in relational theology should not be confused with "eco-theology" (Lüke 1997), insofar as it maintains "anthropocentric" by relativizing human beings within the ecological network. Relational theology instead focuses on the wider, *mutual cross-reference* between all character forms of "societies" and "societies of societies" within both micro- and macrocosmic immanence as the genuine locus of divine revelation and encounter (§36). It is cognizant of the interwoven, interpenetrating nature of that which from the substantialist perspective is separated, namely, nature and history, grace and freedom, immanence and transcendence, time and eternity, the personal and the transpersonal, self-creativity and self-transcendence, God and creativity (Faber

2000e). Metatheologically, it is thus inclined to construct bridges of under-standing rather than walls of separation, to create a *transformative matrix* (§42) in which (even mutually alien) traditions can enrich one another through their mutual novelty as new spheres of possibility *without* losing the normative refer-ence to their own foundational events. In this sense relational theology is a gen-uinely *ecumenical* theology (Cobb and Griffin 1976; Faber 2002e) (§32).

§48. TRANSFORMATIVE SPIRITUALITY (SOLIDARITY, CREATIVITY, AND PEACE)

Process theology has never viewed itself solely as theology, that is, as the theoret-ical reflection of a certain praxis or as the vision of a relational world. It has also consistently viewed itself as praxis—not just as ethical praxis, but as specifically *spiritual* praxis (Suchocki 1996; Loomer 1949). From the very outset, empirical theology focused not merely on an ethical praxis of "creative transformation" (§3), but on understanding such praxis as a spiritual encounter with God, indeed even as the preeminent locus of an encounter with God and of a fundamental orientation of existence within a certain understanding of life. The understand-ing of God's dipolarity was consistently developed on the basis of the *feeling* of a creative and reconciling embrace of the world process by God (§25). The under-standing of God's unique intimacy toward the world in the divine matrix clearly demonstrates process theology's basis for a spiritual theology and praxis (§32). Within these conceptions, the *eminent spiritual experiences* with which process theology is concerned radiate clearly, namely, the concrescent and transitory ten-sion between solidarity and creativity, crisis and identity, decision and gift, adven-ture and peace.

In *Religion in the Making*, Whitehead identifies the tension between solitari-ness and solidarity or world loyalty as one of the key elements driving the emer-gence and development of "rational religion"—religion characterized by universalistic features (RM, 95) (§46). For Whitehead, the two are linked, simi-lar to the way singularity and universality will be linked later—with respect to Whitehead's later event theory—by individualizing self-creativity (the internally directed process of subjectivity) and universalizing self-transcendence (the self-divesting process of superjectivity) (§23). Within the innermost recesses of a per-son's solitude, where each of us is alone with our irreplaceable singularity, each of us is *simultaneously* wholly displaced and self-transcendently directed toward a whole *beyond* ourselves (Sayer 1999). Wherever this dialectic is misunderstood (in a sinful process), the dipolar structure collapses into egoism (isolation) and altruism (self-surrender). Where the two poles are connected, however, they gen-erate a spiritual dynamic whose center, from the perspective of process theology, represents the moment of *creative transformation* (between the two poles) (Cobb and Griffin 1976). Such transformational spirituality has developed in two basic directions—depending on which pole comes to represent the focus of spiritual praxis from which, through a kind of countermovement, to conquer the *other* pole. On this basis, one can distinguish the following tendencies with respect to process spirituality.

(1) *The hidden God in the solitariness of the beginning.* In Marjorie Suchocki's view, the analysis of the God who is active in the initial aim not only indicates a theory of God in the narrower sense, but also evokes the living Spirit, insofar as we should seek God through spiritual praxis—on a path back to the beginning of our existence (Suchocki 1995). This beginning, however, rather than lying in our *past*, instead is "present" (as future) in every moment of our self, in each one of our personal events in which we received an initial aim as a gift from God and from which we then develop our self-creativity. But in the initial aim God is present *as beginning*, not in "fulfilled presence" of any sort. God has always already been present in our "beginning," and our self-creativity is the "trace" of God (§20). And it is precisely as *this* beginning that God is *hidden* from us (§27). Even before we become conscious of the "presence" of the "trace" of God in this sense, we have already generated a nexus of further events through reflection on ourselves (Lango 1972). As "beginning," however, God is not only hidden from us, but also unconsciously and antecedently "there," as future of ourselves, such that he remains inaccessible through reflection (§35). God, who is "present" (in the mode of ad vent) and "touches" us in *every* event of our personal being—be it the multiple nonliving events of our material body, the living events of our organism, the events of the entirely living nexus of our "soul," or the few conscious events of this living nexus—is nonetheless experientially submerged amid these myriad events (§30). Only a spiritual journey back *into* this beginning—through mystical experience and meditation—may uncover this submerged experience of God (Suchocki 1995). It is not through introspection, reflection, or bringing such to consciousness, but rather—according to Suchocki—only through *pausing within the solitariness* of this beginning, in the moment of the beginning of the immediate spontaneity of our personal being (as being ineffable, incommunicable) in each of its personal events that God may be encountered in "mystical union" (§40). For Suchocki, such is possible where in the most profound loneliness all contrasts with the world that accrue within the concrescence of events—all physical experiences deriving from our history and environment, though also all mental feelings of possibilities and potentials—are leveled to *nothingness*. Perhaps it will then be the case, Suchocki suggests, that a new contrast will emerge that "touches the edges of our consciousness with a sense of divine presence" (Suchocki 1995, 55). Where all the contrasts of the world fall silent, perhaps there the primal contrast between God and self-creativity may emerge at the origin of the self.

This mystical experience, however, exhibits a peculiar *conversion,* leading into a *creative transformation* in which the "inward" (*ad intra*) of the *unio mystica* *reverses* into an "outward" (*ad extra*) of world solidarity (Faber 2001c) (§41). It is in this sense that mystical experience lays bare the temporal countermovement of creative and creaturely time (§39: Figure 6). On the one hand, this *unio mystica* is the gift of the experience of the beginning as nondifference, which is not yet different and is indeed only nascently differentiating itself (§20). It would be the *mystical experience of theopoetic in/difference* as the process of the self-differentiation of God from the nascent event (§40). In this mystical experience, we are directed back toward God's ad-vent out of the "future" of the event (§35), and are touched by God's primordial act as superject of creativity (§28). On the other hand, however, it is *precisely* in this innermost retreat, seclusion, and "divine birth" (Meister Eckhart) that a conversion toward the world itself occurs (Faber 2001a). Within the initial aim, the mystic does not simply experience "God" or experience a "clear vision" of God; instead, one encounters God in the mode of God's self-emission toward the emergent or arising event (Suchocki 1995; Ford 1988). God is experienced with regard to the origination of a creation and its release into the self-creativity of creatures—whence comes a transformation, a reversal of direction and a conversion toward the direction in which God looks at the world. It is here that spiritual experience becomes *practical*, world oriented, becoming thereby also a path into the world itself (Faber 2002c).

(2) *The creative God as "event" in personal decision.* For empirical theology, the spiritual dimension consists primarily in the "discernment of spirits" (1 Cor. 12:10), that is, in a world solidarity in which God and world become distinguishable (Cobb 1982b). This is a spirituality of *conversion*. Within the ongoing value construction of the world processes, it directs its attention not at the good that has already been attained, but at the overflowing Good within the good event. Its spirituality is always engaged in a search for *the* Creative, which cannot be viewed as having been fully attained in *any* good (Inbody 1995). Invariably, when we focus on something that appears good to us, God is already the difference from that which has *not* been attained, namely the *creating* Good over against all *created* good (Wieman 1946). Spiritual experience and praxis consist in discovering within all events, through focusing attention on them, God as the power of the Good that creatively exceeds or moves beyond everything, contra any "fixing" of God. For Henry Wieman, spiritual experience involves the critical and ethical experience of God as *event*, an experience that through confronting a person with existential decision thereby also alters that person creatively (§3). As such an event, God can never be definitively "discerned" or "ascertained," remaining instead the one who comes, the one who is eschatologically withdrawn, yet the one who precisely as such and as the highest Eros lures *beyond* what is already attained. Here too the direction of the *vision ad extra* turns *ad intra*, for the differentiation between historical "world" and the event "God" can happen only in the *existential* process of *decision* constituting our event structure. In creative transformation spiritual experience happens within our personal events, when through encountering God as event they are placed into the *decision of conversion* (metanoia) (§41).

For Bernard Loomer, this spiritual experience of rapture through an encounter with God as creative "event" leads to a spirituality of love, of self-surrendering, kenotic love, in which we follow God on God's path *into* the turmoil and disjunction of the world (§5). Through experiencing God as the *creative event of agapē*—

God's "stature" and "size"—we ourselves are "ex-centrically taken from ourselves" in an *event* (Loomer 1987). Here "spirituality" means being "placed" *within* the "event" of God, under God's "stature," which refers to the breadth and intensity of an event's *integration* of world with the aid of the highest possible mentality (Loomer 1949) (§§44–45). The "spiritual structure" of experience demands that we intensify relationality by "identifying" with others, by taking them up into ourselves with all of their discontinuity and disharmony attaching to them. It is for us to endure this for the sake of transforming it into a new, more intensive, broader, more "spiritual" form. This correlates with God's self-surrender to the world, God's suffering along with it, God's "sacrifice" (Loomer 1949, 195). The highest form of spirituality is to be understood as the capacity *yet* to integrate into oneself the world with all its discordance, with all its tragedy, with all its disharmony, and with all its failings. And such happens through encountering God as *event*, that is, through experiencing oneself *in the midst* of God's "stature," whereby we ourselves are redefined or determined anew existentially in our own lives and thereby turned, through creative transformation, toward an existence in *agapē*.

(3) *The embracing God in the experience of future (as ad-vent) and delimitation.* One of the primal spiritual experiences of a processual, relational "positioning ourselves within the world"—positioning *not* distorted substantialistically—is the experience of God as "embrace" (§25). God's embrace, through the primordial and consequent natures, reflects not only the entire world process, but also every event in its most profound character, in its complex process structure of dipolarity, dual process, and the threefold character of the process itself (§33). The *theopoetic spirituality* growing out of *this* experience—an experience in which God's processuality and relationality are manifested in their unique, creative, liberating, and reconciling intimacy within the world process—will come to expression especially through *meditation on creatureliness*, the perception of creatures *as* God's creations in their interwovenness with distinction from God's own ad-vent from the future of the Not Yet, and in their reconciliation in God's delimiting eschaton; and it will come to expression through "feeling" the interwoven, interpenetrating nature of the creative and eschatological form of God's own loving inclination toward the world, through becoming *self*-aware, *self*-perceptive in the "*creative* time" with which God happens counter and toward the world's "creaturely time" (§39). Within this meditation, we sense ourselves *within* the divine matrix: "lured" by *Eros* into ecstatic eccentricity toward the adventure with the world with no return, moved within *God's own memory* toward sym-pathetic, coformative solidarity with the world, and set free within *intercreativity* for responsible *self-creativity*. Within the divine matrix, we sense ourselves positioned within *theopoetic in/difference* (§40): in the *personal difference* of the personal God, who addresses us and challenges us, tearing us away for self-transcendence within the highest act of valuation, and in *transpersonal nondifference*, through which we experience ourselves as being bequeathed to ourselves, as being self-creatively delimited for infinite meaning, and as a process of self-value and self-valuation.

This spirituality of self-immersion in the embracing divine matrix takes the form of a theopoetic mystery of creatureliness. Within theopoetic in/difference, its *personal* dimension immerses us into a Trinitarian form of the mystery (§38), and its *transpersonal* dimension into an empty form of the mystery (§39). (a) Through *personal* immersion into God's Trinitarian embrace, we experience ourselves bequeathed as creatures in *Sophia*/Logos, in the Pneuma, and in the mystery of God's superjectivity. In the Wisdom of God, we feel enraptured into "paradise" and into the "utopia" of the divine primordial vision and primordial harmony—with its unfathomability of infinitely moved, living logicity—and yet simultaneously, without fleeing the world, *thrown back* onto the world itself; posited into Eros and set free *for* the world. In the Pneuma we experience being enraptured into the eschaton of the divine final vision and final harmony—with the unfathomability of divine suffering in the delimitation of the world (Faber 2002a)—and yet simultaneously, without fleeing the world, and in each new, event beginning of our selves, being *placed back* into the world. We experience being enraptured into the primordial act of divine superjectivity, of the primordial unity and primordial difference between self-creativity and self-transcendence—with its unfathomability of the "harmony of harmonies," of the unity of creation and redemption—and yet simultaneously, through following God's own view, being *placed* into the *différance* of the world. (b) Through *transpersonal* immersion into the embrace of the divine matrix, that is, of the intercreativity between God and world and everything in the world, we experience ourselves "at the grounding of the world," within the *khora*, at the locus of emptiness, placed into primordial communication in all its formlessness (§40). Here we are aware of being connected with everything, of being woven into the process as a whole. Here we experience the finitude and perishing of all forms, their abiding and their delimitation within the divine memory. Indeed, here we experience ourselves within the "Godhead" about which Meister Eckhart spoke: within the "ocean of God" (Faber 2001c) and yet simultaneously wholly within the world, within its unity of form and emptiness and the oscillation of the process of events (§§16, 24, 35). Here we are aware of being within the infinite adventure of the finite world and yet simultaneously elevated and sheltered within the peace of universal relationality. Here we are aware of being embraced—as a personal and transpersonal moment of the "Harmony of Harmonies."

Postscript: Theopoetics and the Divine Manifold

If in its investigation of the worlds of process philosophies and process theologies there is to be found any single place of inspiration for this book, it obviously is Whitehead's concept of God as "poet of the world." While I have laid out the conditions, implications, and consequences of this concept as it reconstructs process thought for contemporary discussions, its importance is much more far reaching. Such "theopoetics" not only hold this book's themes and discourses together; theopoetics transcends process theology as a viable alternative in the landscape of voices of contemporary theologies. In this postscript, let me explore theopoetics further, using two pairs of concepts and their interrelations: *theopoetics* and *multiplicity* as well as *theoplicity* (or the divine Manifold) and *polyphilia*, respectively.

First, however, I want to draw attention to the *matrix* of this book in its analytic and synthetic intention, its constructive and deconstructive endeavor, its limitations due to its intention and some underlying themes that are the most basic expression of its theopoetics but, *as* its matrix, might in their pervasiveness not be as obvious on first reading. Four underlying discourses are essential for the theopoetic synthesis this book attempts: process theology, constructive theology, Whitehead's philosophy, and the interface of philosophy and theology (not to be confused with a philosophy *of* religion). Following a theopoetic impulse, I intend always to seek to roughen up unified appearances by differentiating the various deep-lying, multiple voices hidden under various powerful contenders of an alleged "orthodoxy" of content, method, and direction of thought; this is the *deconstructive* agenda sharpened by French poststructuralist and deconstructive thought, especially that of Gilles Deleuze and Jacques Derrida. Within this book, this "dramatically" appears through the conceptual "persona" of *différance*. In the interrelation of the diverse discourses, I seek problematization instead of solution; in other words, I always seek to conjure up the questions that supersede the momentary solutions. This is my *analytic* agenda, implying that analysis must always aim at infinite differentiation of an unspoken, undeconstructed, and undisclosed background full of seemingly self-evident presumptions that are truly no more than unconscious limitations.

The *synthetic and constructive* impulses of the book, on the other hand, can best be described as finding new ways to address the different levels of disclosure in their interaction by creating a *matrix of possibilities*. In this manner, I want to do more than integrate a multidimensional field of questions and solutions; I wish to hold open a "moving whole" that never, at any point, closes up against revision and progression of thought. In other words, constructively I try to lay out a *landscape* of interactions, interfaces, and intersections informed by Deleuze's rhizomatic approach to "system" as a "plane of immanence" of always moving concepts (see Deleuze and Guattari, 1994). To do this, I first deploy a *mode of construction* with its emphasis on "concrescence," namely, that of a *formless "place" of synthesis* instead of a formal principle of unification—that is, in invoking Plato's *khora* to which Whitehead, and Deleuze and Derrida after him, has drawn increasing attention. I then work in a mode of *synthesis* that always differentiates the multiple (often suppressed or faint) voices *within* a field and *through* their interaction. Thus, I avoid potential solutions that discard earlier solutions or that ignore their own limitations resulting from the particular questions or interests. This way of synthesizing gives orientation, like directions to travel a landscape with map without losing sight of the diversity of ways to travel the same landscape alternatively. "*Mille viae ducunt hominem per saecula Romam* (a thousand ways lead human beings evermore to Rome)," an old saying goes, but no way *must* pass through Rome or ever end there. While the six parts of the book unfold the matrix of these four fields of interest, they are disposed, differentiated, and transformed by the four modes of accessing their multiplicity—deconstruction and construction, analysis and synthesis.

1. The first field of investigation, *process theology*, is obviously at the heart of the book. This exploration, however, is neither isolated from the other fields of interest—constructive theology, Whitehead's philosophy, and the interface of philosophy and theology—nor a justification of a *past* mode of theology known as "process theology." This theology of about the last hundred years was conceived as a form of liberal theology and hence confined by its limitations, such as not being compatible with Catholic (and more evangelical) theologies or being confined to certain labels like "doctrinally heterodox" or "culturally relativistic" or

"white, American, Protestant, liberal" (see Livingston and Schüssler Fiorenza 2006). On the contrary, I have pointed to process theology as more than a single movement (to be either accepted or denounced), by opening up the cauldron of the astonishing diversity of traditions. Process theology can thereby regain its inherent diversity and at the same time interconnect with a plenitude of contemporary and traditional voices in the theological scene. This readily explains the importance I lay on the recognition of the *many* process theologies and their diversity of philosophical, theological, cultural, and intellectual roots that weave a network of fluent procedures, methods, doctrines, worldviews, and impulses between Protestant denominations and Catholic traditions, liberal theology and orthodox Christianity, pragmatism and existentialism, postrationalism and poststructuralism, Christianity and Buddhism, transreligious confluences and nonreligious intellectualism, science and religion, philosophy and theology, traditional tendencies and radical movements, feminist, ecological, and postcolonial reformations.

2. The second field of *constructive theology* is crucial for the understanding of the book insofar as its whole architecture is leading up to a treatment of major questions, themes, and discussions connected to the traditions of Christian systematic theology in probing into the ability of a reconstructed process theology to become a contemporary voice of innovation. Conversely, I induce these questions, themes, and discussions into the internal structures of "traditional" process theologies in order to open up their closed argumentation where it arises and to bundle interests so as to view constructive theology as indispensable for a viable process theology today. Since this impulse of creative transformation works both ways, the constructive result will always be in peril of being misconceived as either not fitting the presumed needs of systematic theology (and thereby being heterodox) or by seemingly betraying the "identity" of process theology in the particular fights it has picked against certain traditional doctrines or denominational boundaries. However, the intention to *connect* with traditions in a way that transforms *all* sides only follows the basic conviction of all process theologies, namely, to be the prime expression and the always moving (and moved) agent of *process*.

3. The treatment of the third field of exploration, *Whitehead's philosophy*, reveals the hidden method of reconstruction (deconstruction and construction) of process thought. When I wrote my first book on process theology (Faber 2000e), I became convinced that there is a discrepancy between process theology and its utilization of (or viewing itself as being the most consequent expression of) process philosophy, on the one hand, and the most creative source of its constant renewal, namely, Whitehead's philosophy, on the other hand, that has to be addressed aggressively, in order to free its creative impulse for contemporary discussions. This "tension" has at least three dimensions. First, while process theologies always point back to Whitehead, the implementation of his philosophy has led to a very confined set of approaches to this thought as a somehow "completed system" (a term Whitehead reserved for God!). Whitehead's thought in its own development and interconnections shows his own intuition to be well

beyond any confined system of thought (see Faber 2004). Whitehead's tentative imaginings are always complex, beyond any possible simplifications of alleged systems, and thoroughly self-defeating if taken as dogmatic statements. Process theology must always be liberated from dogmatist petrifications. Second, Whitehead's philosophy—not without irony—often was conceived as self-contained truth, as the doctrine that has to be just applied rightly in order to save everything. Instead of being a fragile, philosophical investigation into the "nature of things" that cannot be asserted outside their processes, Whitehead's thought had become a worldview that his followers thought must be promoted because of its salvific qualities. Instead, his philosophy must be liberated from its self-referential overstatements and be viewed as interrelated to streams of thought that influenced Whitehead and that he has influenced—between Plato and Aristotle; Descartes, Hume, and Kant; and James, Bergson, Latour, and Deleuze.

Third, Whitehead's philosophy is neither *a* nor *the* process philosophy. The creation of a unified tradition called process philosophy is flawed because it either forgets (or if recognizing it, has to include) the longstanding tradition of Heraclites, Nietzsche, and Hegel, or it constitutes itself as a narrow creek of Whiteheadian-Hartshornean thought contrary to (or if recognized, in contrast to) the pragmatism, pluralism, and evolutionism of Bergson, James, and Alexander. Even if taken as a genus of which it then becomes a species—as was proposed by Nicolas Rescher—it misses the point that any great philosopher is unique and cannot be repeated in a movement, but has always to be recreated in other philosophies to come. To liberate Whitehead's "philosophy of organism" is also to free it of its alleged perfection and to reveal its limitations as "essential" to any philosophical thought—as Whitehead himself clearly knew (see PR, 7-8).

4. The exploration of the fourth field of interaction, that *between philosophy and theology,* is not only necessary in the context of the tension between Whitehead's philosophy and its implicit theology. It is made particularly necessary by the widely hostile, contemporary division of discourses among (a) *philosophies,* in their self-understanding as *not* related to questions of salvation and religion in general; (b) *hermeneutics of suspicion* that, regarding Christian sensitivities in particular, understand theology as a form of biased ideology constituting (uncritically) the identity of certain social bodies (churches); and (c) *theologies* as consciously socially located discourses of human (and natural) wholeness, which often understand philosophies to be at the same time detached from questions of meaning and intrusive by invasive measures of neutrality. In this context, I view Whitehead's approach (and he is not the only one, to be sure) as drawing on the "tender elements" in these discourses to be opened up to one another without erasing differences, but multiplying them on the level of a manifold of subconnections and floating elements moving freely under the seemingly secured borders. It is this *transgressive* nature of Whitehead's thought that attracts me to blur the borders in many and fruitful ways (see Faber 2006b).

Within this book, these four fields of investigation go hand in hand, and they have been fruitful in developing theopoetic "themes" further and beyond themselves. If forced to name some of these underlying themes, I would choose the concepts of the *divine matrix*, the *chaotic nexus,* and the *mystical dimension of in/difference*. All three of them are employed in order to overcome dichotomies in both classical theology and process theology, but all three of them are directed toward the construction of a reconstructed process theology on the basis of a *relecture* of Whitehead's philosophy (beyond its systematic limitations). While the divine matrix implies a *fundamental field of indispensable, essentially multiple, and ever incompatible differences* of what Whitehead called the *mutual immanence* of everything connected, especially God and the world (and besides that nothing is or becomes), the *chaotic nexus* indicates the radical implication of Whitehead's view of the *constitution of becoming* as being bottomless, groundless, and lawless. Not that there are no grounds and laws—there are in fact many of them, hierarchies likewise of evolution and oppression—but they always have to be reconstructed as modes of becoming (as did Nietzsche before, and Deleuze after, Whitehead). The importance of the *mystical element of in/difference*—meaning that which is *beyond* any difference of identity and difference but actually *only in* differences—connects Whitehead's theopoetics with many streams of secular immanence, religious mysticism, and interreligious sensitivities—all dimensions of his thought that allows me to reconstruct all the remaining dualities of Whitehead's thought, for example, that of actuality and possibility, of mentality and physicality, of the primordial and consequent aspect of God—without implying a new point of essential unity beyond the multiplicity of aspects it opens up.

Multiplicity, then, in avoiding essential dualism and any substantialized One, plays a fundamental role in constructing and deconstructing, analyzing and synthesizing the whole matrix of theopoetics. Multiplicity erects a conceptual framework for this book by working through all the questions, themes, and connections employed. But its application is also limited (within the four interrelated fields of investigation) because of my intention to recreate process theology as a viable constructive alternative in the landscape of contemporary theologies. In other words, since the original publication of *God as Poet of the World* in German in 2003 and its republication in 2004, I have tried to explore this multiplicity as *the* essential element of a contemporary interpretation of Whitehead's philosophy and a *theopoetics of the future*. In superseding my interest in a reconstruction of systematic theology from the perspective of a contemporary process theology, multiplicity now becomes visible as the most basic expression of Whitehead's critique of the whole history of Western philosophy as critique of the One (and its hidden dualism)—one might think specifically of the role of creativity *instead of any symbol* of divine Oneness in Whitehead's revolution of thought (see Faber 2005a).

In light of this theopoetic multiplicity—as mani*fold*ness, not as sheer plurality of un-relation!—the *divine matrix* must be deconstructed again regarding its interest of invoking God-language (cf. Thatamanil 2006); the *chaotic nexus* becomes a root metaphor that "secures" the radical openness of the indispensable "groundlessness" of becoming I now call *in/finite becoming*; and *mystical* *in/difference* must more than ever avoid the implication of a hidden Oneness of the divided—be it that of identity and difference as such—and indicate more than ever the *khora*, the formless "unity" of what is united only in mutual difference (see Faber, in 2006a). The concepts with which I indicate this continuation and supersession are, again, the essential connection of theopoetics *and* multiplicity; the justification of any remaining God-language as indicating a *divine Manifold*, that is, *theoplicity*; and the motive of its employment as being the most pro/found, that is, groundless, expression of the mundane Manifold indicated by *polyphilia*, which in its meaning might be understood as restatement of what could be called "(divine) Love." I understand this Love to be the only, and in this sense, irresistible, reason to retain God-language, and I find it to be the true motive of Whitehead's resistance to the traceless disappearance of the divine in the infinite process of the two abstract worlds of creativity and value he calls "the Universe" (see MG, 105–6).

What lies beyond *God as Poet of the World* would be my own theopoetic project on the basis of Whitehead, Deleuze, and others regarding the *function* of multiplicity: the theme of the fold, virtualities, rhizomes, immanence, nonsystematic theopoetic approaches, building more radically on a Whitehead-inspired than Whiteheadian "theology." I would wish to resist solutions that would be too easy or restricted within a defined process tradition and to be freed of the necessity of being bound to the superiority of Whitehead over against legitimate successors like Deleuze, Latour, Serres, and many emergent creative philosophies in the making right now.

In drawing the lines of continuation and supersession, let me begin by my understanding of the characterization of the constructive proposal of this book, namely to formulate process theology as theopoetics, by making two disclaimers. First, with the concept of theopoetics I do not intend to make the general suggestion that all God-language is *metaphoric*—as proposed, for example, by Sally McFague and Gordon Kaufman. Second, I do not wish to suggest that process theology is *poetic in nature* and that all theology must be a *poetics of the divine*. These two options are, in my constructive matrix, but pitfalls of aesthetic reductions of irreducibly complex matters. What I do mean, however, is that Whitehead's formulation of God as "poet of the world" captures the *intuition* of such a reconstructed process theology as being a *theopoetics*, and that the paradoxical implications of its meaning—as analyzed throughout the book—are necessary expressions of its character. Regarding the two pitfalls mentioned, this is to say that, first, all God-language is indicated by and indicating (not "signifying," however) *poiesis,* that is, a creative event of construction and synthesis (Whitehead would say "concrescence") that cannot be reconstructed out of its elements without losing its novelty; which, however, can be analyzed and deconstructed only *post factum*, but then in infinite ways. Where this event *happens,* it calls for a theopoetic interpretation *insofar* as it is irreducible to any mundane phenomenon. Any event in its *poiesis* is the insistence of *divine* poetics, or conversely, the only justification of God-language (in what form ever) is any event's irreducible novelty as not being reducible to any causation (necessary reason) or reason (sufficient reason). Hence, any invocation of God-language is always *more* than metaphoric in relation to this event's *poiesis*, since the insistence of the divine poet as such is not metaphorical at all; but it is always also *less* than metaphorical, since it is always *beyond* language in being the insistence of the unspeakable *in* language, at the same time. Since no language can capture the *poiesis* of the event, no God-language is more or less metaphoric in relation to a purer mode of conceptualization, and no conceptualizing is more or less metaphorical in relation to the *poiesis* of the event. It is the wrong category! Furthermore, the *poiesis* of an event is not a "poetics" of the divine—in contrast, for example, to its dramatization or conceptualization—but precisely that which *cannot* be grasped in *aisthesis*, that is, in the act of perception (physical prehension) or its aesthetic valuation (mental prehension). It cannot be reduced to aesthetics or even one of its artistic expressions—like "poetry." Rather, it is the *unconditioned condition* of perception and valuation.

The closest we can come to Whitehead's understanding of his unprecedented and singular phrase of God as "poet" of the world in *Process and Reality* is Whitehead's remark in *Science and the Modern World* that it is precisely a "poetic rendering of our concrete experience, [when] we see at once that the element of value, of being valuable, of having value, of being an end in itself, of being something which is for its own sake, must not be omitted in any account of an event as the most concrete actual something. 'Value' is the word I use for the intrinsic reality of an event" (SMW, 93). This remark indicates that *poiesis* is about the irreducibly intrinsic reality of an event, its self-value, that cannot be given to it but also cannot be created by it. Neither is it external, nor is it any mode of self-possession; it indicates its *immanent, creative givenness to itself.* A second remark from *Modes of Thought*, on the other hand, indicates the intrinsic connection between *poiesis* and the mystical in/difference that happens in the creative act. There, Whitehead insists not only that "philosophy is akin to poetry" (in finding this intrinsic creativity of the event) but also that "philosophy is mystical. For mysticism is direct insight into depths as yet unspoken" (MT, 137). The depth of *poiesis* always remains *unspoken*, but it is precisely the ever unspoken novelty that is the gift of the intrinsic creativity of the event.

There is a fine but important complication in Whitehead's phrase of God as "poet of the world" relevant to the theopoetic paradox of the immanent gift of self-creativity. Whitehead is very clear on the distinction between the self-creative act of an event in its becoming and God's *poiesis*, which Whitehead never equates with the immanent creativity of the event. In *Adventures of Ideas*, Whitehead radically proposes that "the word Creativity expresses the notion that each event is a process issuing in novelty. Also if guarded in the phrases Immanent Creativity, or Self-Creativity, it avoids the implication of a transcendent Creator" (AI, 236). This is what I have reserved for the *poiesis* as a divine *insistence* on *self*-creativity. Indeed, it is not the novelty *as such* that leads Whitehead to understand God as poet of the world—because he has reserved this function to the metaphysical principle of creativity—but something else. In *Process and Reality*, Whitehead names this supplementation "God" as being the "poet of the world" who "does not create the world, [God] saves it . . . , with tender patience leading it by [God's] vision of truth, beauty, and goodness" (PR, 346). Without explaining this phrase, which is the matrix of this book, only one moment has to be highlighted: that the *poiesis* is *theopoetics* not because it "creates"—again, Whitehead differentiates the invocation of God-language from this self-creativity—but because this *poiesis* "saves," that is, because it "determines" infinite creativity to indeed become a concrescence, a synthesis, a construction precisely by *evoking* the "for-itself," the intrinsic "for-its-own-sake," the "self-value" of what is not yet self-creative. God is not the *event*, but the *gift* of *self*-creativity. In the three-dimensional field of divine matrix, chaotic nexus, and mystical in/difference—the underlying themes of the book—*poiesis* is the in/difference of the intrinsic gift of self-creativity, enfolding in the irreducible novelty of a chaotic nexus of events that in its irreducible insistence on the difference between events encounters a divine dimension of the process of its in/finite becoming that *saves this difference by releasing it as irreducible to any unification under the Law and Logic of the One.*

Hence, *theopoetics is about multiplicity!* "God" is the *name for the insistence of the event on irreducible multiplicity.* This is the event: the multiplicity, the manifold of diverse trajectories and movements that it is impossible to achieve. This impossibility that, insofar as it *happens,* is always only gift and grace may be called *poiesis,* and this *poiesis* may be understood as the never "singular" but always "unique" *insistence* on a self-creativity that is itself never mundane, that is, part of the world, it saves from the One.

While many consequences follow from such a theopoetics on a theological level—and I have given a wide variety of them in the corpus of the book—I understand this theopoetics as constructive proposal of a contemporary process theology because it creates a counterdiscourse that insists on the priority and primacy of in/finite becoming. Insofar as the Manifold is held beyond the Logic of the One that always tries to close the process down into static Law or eternal order, theopoetics harbors *a divine insisting on multiplicity that saves the Manifold from any controlling power of unification.* In other words: the deepest concept of *salvation* of the multiverse in process theology is the *insistence on multiplicity.* In a Deleuzian context, we could say that this insistence on the ever-becoming variety of irreducible manifoldness, on this process of infinite "folding, unfolding, refolding" (Deleuze 1992, 137), constitutes the "Chaosmos" wherein God "becomes Process" and is precisely that *poiesis* that in any "process . . . at once affirms [all of its] incompossibilities and [at the same time] passes through them" (ibid., 81).

If there is any reason to hold on to a divine dimension of this process of in/finite becoming, it is because of the insistence on *unsuppressed multiplicity,* where unity is not lost but liberated of any Logic of the One with its power of manipulation. Because of this retreat from any concept of power, the *poiesis* is not "creation" but supersedes the notion of creation. It supersedes it completely, because it retains the original meaning of God as Creator—the Council of Nicaea calls God *pantōn poietén*!—by insisting on its exclusive meaning as *salvation* of the Manifold of self-creative becoming. And in undercutting any statement of *poiesis* as one of power, the only alternative to understand this insistence on multiplicity as divine ingression in the process of in/finite becoming is that of divine Love, which, then, must be interpreted as *love for* the mundane Manifold or as divine *polyphilia*.

Since in the corpus of the book I was mainly concerned with the transformation of both the tradition of systematic theology and process theology's approaches to this matter of God as "creator," I was interested in models to address this transformation beyond the simple alternative of God as actor and the divine matrix as anonymous activity of self-creation or of "independent self-creativity" and "divine self-limitation." In fact, these alternatives wanted to be brought into the *theopoetic in/difference of both* so as to allow for a "third space," in which the ambiguity of both statements could become obvious and productive by insisting on a multiplicity of ways to express the inexpressible mystery of creation. Beyond the limitation of this interest, however, I feel convinced to go even more boldly beyond any of these metaphorical statements in addressing the mystery of the divine *poiesis* in no way as process of unification, even viewed as *generation* of differences (be that between God and creativity, God and the divine matrix, between the divine matrix and the chaotic nexus, the chaotic nexus and the many ordered universes, and so on; see Faber 2005b) but *strictly* as *saving insistence* on the diversification of the many folds of the never united but always many-folded multiverse. A consequence may well be that this divine insistence can neither be expressed adequately as divine matrix nor as act of God, neither as the impulse of an entity called God nor as the inexplicable activity of a mysterious field of creativity, but always only as *mystery of the resistance to closure*. This, if at all, is what I mean with *polyphilia*: the insistence on the ever multiplying manifold of in/finite becoming as counter-"agency" to any power of closure—be it ontological, cultural, social, or political.

If it is about "power *or* love," the opposition is between the Logic of the One (in whatever form it might appear) as primordial sin, especially when identified with "God," and the divine *polyphilia* as indication of God's "nature" to be *beyond any concept of power*. Here, I understand my theopoetics to relate to, but also to differ from, both Kaufman's "serendipitous creativity" (Kaufman 2004) and Caputo's "weak force" (Caputo 2006). While I agree with Kaufman's utilization of Henry Nelson Wieman's adoption of Whitehead's creativity, I cannot follow their collapse into God because of the difference of salvation. While I agree with Caputo in God-language as articulation of the event of salvation, I differ insofar as I increasingly tend to radically refute the collapse of power and love— even in the form of a "weak force of love." And by this differentiation, I wish also to supersede Whitehead's ways of reconciliation of love as "power . . . in its absence of force" (RM, 57) or as "persuasive agency" (AI, 169). In order to renounce *any* infection with the possessiveness of the One, whenever invoking

God-language, it must be counterbalanced with "God's reality" *not being defined in any way by the One, but only by pure multiplicity.* Hence, I call *this* theopoetic statement of the *poiesis* that is *polyphilia* not "God" but *theoplicity.*

"God" is *the* Manifold, but the divine Manifold is not "identical" with the mundane manifold—although it is not different from it! The world is the "complication"—the unfolding and enfolding—of theoplicity. But instead of Nicolas of Cusa's two distinct infinites—of the world and God—theoplicity supersedes its dualism not by collapsing both into "one" (which would be another mode to reintroduce the monistic fallacy of the Logic of the One!), but by *insisting on the deconstruction* of the "complicity" of our God-language to be always inflected with dualism and the Logic of the One. The intricate metaphoric of "God's insistence on mundane manifoldness" still lives from the duality of God and the world, while the notion of the divine *polyphilia* undercuts this duality by resisting to any notion of "power" that conjures up the "One" again—the "God-entity," the "divine activity," the intention of "one" direction over another—and by transforming all theological metaphoric into the absolute emptiness of the gift of this love for manifoldness. *Only theoplicity can be polyphilic, and only universal polyphilia is unrestricted theoplicity!* But this hypermetaphoric insistence on *unrestricted manifoldness* that *is* the divine Manifold (and besides that it is nothing!) not only forbids us to reinvent the metaphoric of the "One" but compels us even more critically to deconstruct our always remaining "complicity" in the metaphoric of the "One."

In an odd application of Henry Nelson Wieman's early insight in a Whiteheadian theopoetics that God *is* creativity (see Wieman 1927b), I take that not to mean that he "identifies" God and creativity but that he urges us *never to worship the creatures instead of the creator.* This "creator," however, cannot anymore in any sense be "identified" as unity called "God" in difference from the diversifying creativity as gift of novelty. Instead of an "identification" of God and creativity, however, a theopoetic in/difference of both metaphors wants only to warn us against the complicity of *any language* with the "One." Theoplicity *takes away* from us the ability to "identify" the creative insistence on self-creativity as expressible by any term other than the negativity of our *inability* to express its *poiesis* by any creature and, hence, by any metaphoric that induces the Logic of the One. If theoplicity insists on the divine Manifold, it also becomes the theopoetic "instrument" by which we discover the remaining sedimentations of our complicity to the "One." Theoplicity *subtracts* itself from any language, but it does so by *critically insisting* on the in/finite becoming of its expressions. Hence, a theopoetics of theoplicity is not mere "negative theology"; rather, it is a disturbing complication of our all-too-easy self-reinforcing reverence of all things creaturely instead of theoplicitous.

In a stunning similarity to Tillich's being-itself, theoplicity is not *existing* but *insisting;* but in difference from Tillich's divine "essence," it is *insisting as* the process of in/finite becoming *itself* that *is* the insistence on the manifold that *is* divine polyphilia. And while Tillich indicates that all God-language is symbolic except the expression that God is "the ground of being," theoplicity cannot be symbolized at all and is the ultimate point of reference of any divine metaphoric without being itself metaphoric (cf. Tillich 1973). Theological metaphoric is nothing but the complicity in which we, as creatures of theoplicity, desire power more than love, desire the One more than pure multiplicity, desire static stability of perseverance more than in/finite becoming, desire to articulate the divine in terms of the creatures of divine *poiesis* more than its subtractive positivity in which theoplicity always saves us from the idolatry of the "One" for the pure manifoldness.

If there is a future of theopoetics, it will be its articulation of theoplicity. It will be deconstructive by relentlessly uncovering our complicity with simplifications. It will be constructive, however, in seeking ways to overcome the "metaphoric of creatures" by way of a *pure affirmation of multiplicity*. Whitehead has gone far in doing so; Gilles Deleuze has gone even further by invoking pure immanence, but he might have fallen back behind pure multiplicity again by articulating its "unity" as "univocity of Being." Here, theoplicity never *closes* immanence by excluding transcendence per se but supersedes both of their tendencies to unify. But with Deleuze, and more hidden but persistently with Whitehead, the event of theoplicity must be that of the *pure affirmation of in/finite becoming*. It, therefore, can only be expressed *in multiple, mutually irreducible ways* as *pure subtraction* and *pure affirmation*, as pure immanence and pure transcendence, as purity of complication and impurity of complicity, as insistence and existence, and even more importantly, by the mutual irreducibility of theoplicity, polyphilia, and multiplicity (as never being "the same"). Indeed, nothing is the same; but all is affirmed on its own terms, which means unending mutuality of the process of creative syntheses of the in/difference of multiplicity with theoplicity, of theoplicity with polyphilia, and of polyphilia with multiplicity without ever becoming "One."

The future of this theopoetics will be a *process* theology of in/finite becoming. Even if it fails, it must insist never to become less! In this sense, I still affirm the ending of the section of this book on *Mystery* (§ 40) that the divine *poiesis* is the pure affirmation of the *posse;* but I would add now that this *posse* must be deprived of its complicity with "power," thereby becoming erased into *pure polyphilia without any power* and *pure theoplicity without leering at the wrinkleless "One."* To remind us a last time of Whitehead's line on the "poet of the world," the *posse* of the divine *poiesis* must *completely subtract itself from the complicity of "creation"*— God as being "someone" creating, a "self" being subject of self-creativity, a "force-field" of creativity, a "divine" matrix—and *affirm nothing but the salvation of the manifold, that is, insist only as/on infinite manifoldness.*

Roland Faber, Desert Hot Springs, California, March 2008

Bibliography

Abe, Masao. 1985. "Mahayana Buddhism and Whitehead." In *Zen and Western Thought*, ed. W. R. La Fleur, 152–70. Honolulu: University of Hawaii Press.

———.1990. "Kenotic God and Dynamic Sunyata." In *The Emptying God: A Buddhist-Jewish-Christian Conversation,* ed. J. Cobb and C. Ives, 3–68. New York: Maryknoll.

Alexander, Samuel. 1920. *Space, Time and Deity.* 2 vols. London: MacMillan & Co.

Almond, Ian. 2000. "How Not to Deconstruct a Dominican: Derrida on God and 'Hypertruth.'" *JAAR* 68/2: 329–44.

Altizer, Thomas J. J. 1966. *The Gospel of Christian Atheism.* Philadelphia: Westminster Press.

———. 1975. "The Buddhist Ground of a Whiteheadian God." *PS* 5/4: 227–36.

Auburger, Leopold. 2001. *Wahrheit und Weisheit in der Metaphysik von Alfred North Whitehead und in den beiden Enzykliken 'Fides et ratio' und 'Veritatis splendor' von Papst Johannes Paul II.* Würzburg: Ergon-Verl.

Auxier, R. E. 1998. "God, Process, and Person: Charles Hartshorne and Personalism." *PS* 27/3–4: 175–99.

Balz, Albert. 1964. "Whitehead, Descartes and the Bifurcation of Nature." *Journal of Philosophy* 31: 281–97.

Basinger, David and Randall. 1994. "The Problem with the 'Problem of Evil.'" *Religious Studies* 30: 89–97.

Bateson, G. 1985. *Ökologie des Geistes. Anthropologische, psychologische, biologische und epistemologische Perspektiven.* Frankfurt: Suhrkamp.

Bayer, Oswald. 1999. "Schöpfer/Schöpfung VIII: Systematisch-theologisch." *TRE,* 326–48.

Beardslee, William. 1972. *A House of Hope: A Study in Process and Biblical Thought.* Philadelphia: Westminster Press.

Beckermann, Ansgar. 1999. *Analytische Einführung in die Philosophie des Geistes.* Berlin: Walter de Gruyter.

Beelitz, Thomas. 1991. *Die dynamische Beziehung zwischen Erfahrung und Metaphysik. Eine Unter-suchung der Spekulativen Philosophie von Alfred North Whitehead im Interesse der Theologie.* Frankfurt: Peter Lang.

Beierwaltes, W. 1980. *Identität und Differenz.* Frankfurt: Klostermann.

Birch, Charles, and John B. Cobb. 1990. *The Liberation of Life: From the Cell to the Community.* Denton, TX: Environmental Ethics Books.

Bloch, Ernst. 1978. "Tendez, Latenz, Utopie." In *Gesamtausgabe der Werke.* Frankfurt: Suhrkamp.

Bogaard, Paul, and Gordon Treash, eds. 1993. *Metaphysics as Foundation: Essays in Honor of Ivor Leclerc.* Albany: SUNY.

Böhme, Gernot. 1980. "Whiteheads Abkehr von der Substanzmetaphysik." In *Whitehead. Einführung in seine Kosmologie,* ed. Ernest Wolf-Gazo, 45–53.Freiburg: Alber.

Bonhoeffer, Dietrich. 1997. *Widerstand und Ergebung. Briefe und Aufzeichnungen aus der Haft*, ed. E. Bethge. Munich: Kaiser.

Bracken, Joseph. 1978. "Process Philosophy and Trinitarian Theology I." *PS* 8/4: 217–30.

———. 1981. "Process Philosophy and Trinitarian Theology II." *PS* 11/2: 83–96.

———. 1985. *The Triune Symbol: Person, Process and Community*. Lanham, MD: University Press of America.

———. 1989. "Energy-Events and Fields." *PS* 18/3: 153–65.

———. 1991. *Society and Spirit: A Trinitarian Cosmology*. London: Associated University Press.

———. 1995. *The Divine Matrix: Creativity as a Link between East and West*. New York: Orbis Books.

———. 1997: "Panentheism from a Process Perspective." In *Trinity in Process: A Relational Theology of God*, ed. Joseph Bracken and Marjorie Suchocki, 95–113. New York: Continuum.

———. 2001. *The One in the Many: A Contemporary Reconstruction of the God-World Relationship*. Grand Rapids: Eerdmans.

———. 2002. "Whitehead and the Critique of Logocentrism." In *Process and Difference: Between Cosmological and Poststructuralist Postmodernism*, ed. Catherine Keller and Anne Daniell, 91–110. Albany: SUNY.

———. 2003. "Intersubjectivity and the Coming of God." *JR* 83: 381–400.

Bracken, Joseph, and Marjorie Suchocki, eds. 1997. *Trinity in Process: A Relational Theology of God*. New York: Continuum.

Bradley, Francis. 1897. *Appearance and Reality*. 2nd ed. with appendix, 1893. London: Swan Sonnenschein.

Bradley, James. 1994. "Transcendentalism and Speculative Realism in Whitehead." *PS* 23/3: 155–91.

Brown, Delwin. 1977. "Gott verändert sich. Konzepte und Entwicklungen der Prozeßtheologie in den Vereinigten Staaten." *EvK* 10: 595–97.

Brown, Delwin, and Sheila Greeve Davaney. 1990. "Methodological Alternatives in Process Theology." *PS* 19/2: 75–84.

Brown, Delwin, Ralph James, and Gene Reeves, eds. 1971. *Process Philosophy and Christian Thought*. Indianapolis: Bobbs-Merrill Co.

Browning, Douglas, ed. 1965. *Philosophers of Process*. New York: Fordham University Press.

Bruck, Michael von, and Whalen Lai. 1997. *Buddhismus und Christentum. Geschichte, Konfrontation, Dialog*. Munich: Beck.

Brüntrup, Godehard. 1996. *Das Leib-Seele Problem. Eine Einführung*. Stuttgart: Kohlhammer.

Buckley, James J. 1997. "Revisionists and Liberals." In *The Modern Theologians: An Introduction to Christian Theology in the Twentieth Century*, ed. David Ford, 327–42. Cambridge, MA: Blackwell Publishing.

Buri, Fritz. 1970. *Gott in Amerika. Amerikanische Theologie seit 1960*. Frankfurt: Katzmann.

Busch, Elmar. 1993. *Viele Subjekte, eine Person. Das Gehirn im Blickwinkel der Ereignisphilosophie A. N. Whiteheads*. Würzburg: Könighausen & Neumann.

Caputo, John. 2006. *The Weakness of God: A Theology of the Event*. Bloomington: Indiana University Press.

Carnap, Rudolf. 1961. *Der logische Aufbau der Welt. Scheinprobleme der Philosophie*. Hamburg: Felix I.

Case, Shirley J. 1914. *The Evolution of Early Christianity: A Genetic Study of First-Century Christianity in Relation to Its Religious Environment*. Chicago: University of Chicago Press.

Casti, John. 1989. *Paradigms Lost: Tackling the Unanswered Mysteries of the Modern Science*. New York: Harper.

Chopp, Rebecca S., and Mark Lewis Taylor, eds. 1994. *Reconstructing Christian Theology*. Minneapolis: Augsburg Fortress.

Christian, William. 1964. "The Concept of God as a Derivative Notion." In *Process and Divinity: The Hartshorne Festschrift*, ed. William Reese and Eugene Freeman, 181–204. La Salle, IL: Open Court.

———. 1967. *An Interpretation of Whitehead's Metaphysics*. New Haven, CT: Yale University Press.

Clarke, Bowman. 1984. "God as Process in Whitehead." In *God and Temporality*, ed. Bowman Clarke and Eugene Long, 169–88. New York: Paragon House.

Clarke, Bowman, and Eugene Long, eds. 1984. *God and Temporality*. New York: Paragon House.

Clarke, W. Norris. 1988. "Comments on Professor Ford's Paper." In *The Universe as Journey: Conversations with W. Norris Clarke, S.J.*, ed. Gerald McCool, 159–70. New York: Fordham University Press.

Claus, Ina. 1933. *Intensität und Kontrast. Eine Auseinandersetzung mit der Gottesvorstellung ausgewählter Entwürfe der Prozesstheologie*. Heidelberg: Lit-Verlag.

Clayton, J. 1985. "Charles Hartshorne." *TRE* 14: 464–69.

Cobb, John B. 1957. "Heidegger and Whitehead—A Comparison." CPS files.

———. 1964. "Is the Later Heidegger Relevant for Theology?" In *The Later Heidegger and Theology: New Frontiers in Theology 1*, ed. John B. Cobb, 177–97. New York: HarperCollins.

———. 1966. "The Finality of Christ." In *The Finality of Christ*, ed. Dow Kirkpatrick, 122–54. Nashville: Abingdon.

———. 1971. "The 'Whitehead without God' Debate: The Critique." *PS* 1/2: 91–100.

———. 1971a. "A Whiteheadian Doctrine of God." In *Process Philosophy and Christian Thought*, ed. Delwin Brown, Ralph James, and Gene Reeves, 215–43. Indianapolis: Bobbs-Merrill Co.

———. 1974. *A Christian Natural Theology: Based on the Thought of Alfred North Whitehead*. Philadelphia: Westminster Press.

———. 1974/1975. "The Authority of the Bible." *Drew Gateway*, 188–202.

———. 1975. *Christ in a Pluralistic Age*. Philadelphia: Westminster Press.

———. 1982a. *Beyond Dialog: Toward a Mutual Transformation of Christianity and Buddhism*. Philadelphia: Fortress Press.

———. 1982b. *Process Theology as Political Theology*. Philadelphia: Westminster Press.

———. 1983. "Freedom in Whitehead's Philosophy." In *Explorations in Whitehead's Philosophy*, ed. Lewis S. Ford and George L. Kline, 45–52. New York: Fordham.

———. 1986. "Christology in 'Process-relational' Perspective." In *Process Theology and the Christian Doctrine of God*, ed. Santiago Sia, 79–94. Petersham: St. Bede's.

———. 1989. "A Process Concept of God." In *Concepts of the Ultimate: Philosophical Perspectives in the Nature of the Divine*, ed. Linda Tessier, 39–51. New York: Macmillan.

———. 1990. "On the Deepening of Buddhism." In *The Emptying God: A Buddhist-Jewish-Christian Conversation*, ed. John B. Cobb and Christopher Ives. Maryknoll, NY: Orbis Books.

———. 1993. "Process Theism." In *Process Theology: A Basic Introduction*, ed. C. Robert Mesle, 134–47. St. Louis: Chalice Press.

———. 1996. "The Multifaceted Future of Theology." In *The Future of Theology: Essays in Honor of Jürgen Moltmann*, ed. Miroslav Volf, Carmen Krieg, and Thomas Kucharz, 196–204. Grand Rapids: Eerdmans.

———. 1997. "The Relativation of Trinity." In *Trinity in Process: A Relational Theology of God*, ed. Joseph Bracken and Marjorie Suchocki, 1–22. New York: Continuum.

Cobb, John B., and David Ray Griffin. *Process Theology: An Introductory Exposition*. Philadelphia: Westminster Press, 1976.

———. 1979. *Prozesstheologie*. Göttingen: Vandenhoeck & Ruprecht.

Cobb, John B., and Christopher Ives, eds. 1990. *The Emptying God: A Buddhist-Jewish-Christian Conversation*. Maryknoll, NY: Orbis Books.

Connelly, George E. 1962. "The Existence and Nature of God in the Philosophy of Alfred North Whitehead." Ph.D. diss., St. Louis University.

Cousins, Ewert. 1971. *Process Theology: Basic Writings*. New York: Newman Press.

———. 1972. *Hope and the Future of Man*. New York: Fortress Press.

Crockett, Clayton. 2001a. "Introduction." In *Secular Theology: American Radical Theological Thought*, ed. C. Crockett. London: Routledge.

———. 2001b. *Secular Theology: American Radical Theological Thought*. London: Routledge.

Dalferth, Ingolf. 1986a. "The One Who Is Worshipped. Erwägungen zu Charles Hartshornes Versuch, Gott zu denken," *ZTK* 83: 484–506.

———. 1986b. "Die theoretische Theologie der Prozessphilosophie Whiteheads." In *Religion im Denken unserer Zeit*, ed. Wilfried Härle and Eberhard Wölfel, 127–91. Marburg: Elwert.

———. 1989. "Prozesstheologie." In *Historisches Worterbuch der Philosophie*, vol. 7, ed. Joachim Ritter, 1562–65. Basel: Schwabe.

Damasio, Antonio. 1999. *The Feeling of What Happens: Body and Emotion in the Making*. New York: Harcourt.

Dean, William. 1990. "Empirical Theology: A Revisable Tradition." *PS* 19/2: 85–102.

Dean, William, and Larry Axel, eds. 1987. *The Theology of Bernard Loomer in Context*. Macon, GA: Mercer University Press.

Deleuze, Gilles. 1992. *Differenz und Wiederholung*. Munich: Fink.

———. 1992. *The Fold: Leibniz and the Baroque*. Minneapolis: University of Minnesota Press.

———. 1996. *Die Falte. Leibniz und der Barock*. Frankfurt: Suhrkamp.

———. 1997a. *Das Bewegungs-Bild — Kino 1*. Frankfurt: Suhrkamp.

———. 1997b. *Henri Bergson zur Einführung*. Ed. Martin von Weinmann. Hamburg: Junius.

Deleuze, Gilles, and Felix Guattari. 1994. *What Is Philosophy?* New York: Columbia University Press.

Derrida, Jacques. 2000. "Chora." In *Über den Namen,* 123–70. Vienna: Arcade.

———. 1978. *Writing and Difference*. London: Routledge & Kegan Paul.

Doud, Robert. 1993. "Matter and God in Rahner and Whitehead." *Philosophy and Theology* 8: 63–81.

Eissfeldt, O. 1983. "Gott und das Meer in der Bibel." *Kleine Schriften* 3: 256–64.

Ely, Stephen Lee. 1983. "The Religious Availability of Whitehead's God." In *Explorations in Whitehead's Philosophy*, ed. Lewis S. Ford and George L. Kline, 170–211. New York: Fordham.

Emmet, Dorothy. 1966. *Whitehead's Philosophy of Organism*. New York: Macmillan.

———. 1984. "Whitehead's View of Causal Efficacy." In *Whitehead und der Prozessbegriff. Beiträge zur Philosophie Alfred North Whiteheads auf dem Ersten Internationalen Whitehead-Symposion 1981*, ed. H. Holz and E. Wolf-Gazo, 161–78. Munich: Karl Alber.

———. 1986. "Creativity and the Passage of Nature." In *Whiteheads Metaphysik der Kreativität. Internationales Whitehead-Symposium Bad Homburg 1983*, ed. Friedrich Rapp and Reiner Wiehl. Freiburg: K. Alber.

———. 1991. "Whitehead und Alexander." In *Die Gifford-Lectures. Materialien zu Whiteheads 'Prozess und Realität' 2*, ed. M. Hampe and H. Maassen, 100–120. Frankfurt: Suhrkamp.

Esterbauer, Reinhold. 1996. *Verlorene Zeit—wider eine Einheitswissenschaft von Natur und Gott*. Stuttgart: Kohlhammer.

Faber, Roland. 1992. *Freiheit, Theologie und Lehramt. Trinitätstheologische Grundlegung und wissenschaftstheoretischer Ausblick*. Innsbruck: Tyrolia.

———. 1995a. *Der Selbsteinsatz Gottes. Grundlegung einer Theologie des Leidens und der Veränderlichkeit Gottes*. Würzburg: Echter.

———. 1995b. "'Über Gott und die Welt . . .' Struktur analoger Gottesrede und prozeßtheologische Perspektive." In *Variationen über die Schöpfung der Welt*, ed. E. Schmetterer, R. Faber, and N. Mantler, N., 118–42. Innsbruck: Tyrolia.

———. 1997. "Trinity, Analogy and Coherence." In *Trinity in Process: A Relational Theology of God*, ed. Joseph Bracken and Marjorie Suchocki, 147–71. New York: Continuum.

———. 1999a. "On the Unique Origin of Revelation, Religious Intuition, and Theology." In *PS* 28/3–4: 273–89.

———. 1999b. "Prozesstheologie." *LTK³*, 681–82.

———. 1999c. "The Two Times Theorem—Structures of Quantum Indeterminacy and the Ecological Entanglement of Physics, Philosophy, and Theology." Lecture presented at Griffith University, Brisbane, Australia. In CPS files.

———. 2000a. "Ambiguität und Größe. Überlegungen zu einer skeptischen Theodizee." *Impulse* 56/4: 3–6.

———. 2000b. "Insistenz—Zum, 'Nicht-Sein' Gottes bei Levinas, Deleuze und Whitehead." *Labyrinth: International Journal for Philosophy, Feminist Theory and Cultural Hermeneutics* 2.

———. 2000c. "The Infinite Movement of Evanescence—The Pythagorean Puzzle in Plato, Deleuze, and Whitehead." *AJThPh* 21: 171–99.

———. 2000d. "Nicht-Ich und Nicht-Wiedergeburt. Zur Entmythologisierung des Reinkarnationsgedankens in Buddhadasas Dhamma-Sprache und A. N. Whiteheads Ereignissprache." *Ursache und Wirkung* 10/1: 42–48.

———. 2000e. *Prozesstheologie. Zu ihrer Würdigung und kritischen Erneuerung.* Mainz: Matthias Grünewald-verlag.

———. 2000f. "Theopaschismus." *LTK* 9: 1464–65.

———. 2000g. "Toward a Hermeneutics of the Unique." Paper presented at Chapman University, Orange County, CA.

———. 2000h. "Zeitumkehr. Versuch über einen eschatologischen Schöpfungsbegriff." *TP* 75: 180–205.

———. 2001a. "Creation as Differentiation: Toward a Third Space-Concept of Creation as 'Self-Differentiating In/Difference' in Dialogue with Mystical and Process Theology." Conference paper presented at Drew University, New Jersey.

———. 2001b. "God's Love without God? The Nondifference of God as Mystical Solution of Feuerbach's Antinomy of Love." Presented at American Academy of Religion Annual Meeting. Denver.

———. 2001c. "Gottesmeer—Versuch über die Ununterschiedenheit Gottes." In *"Leben in Fülle": Skizzen zur christlichen Spiritualität*, ed. Thomas Dienberg and M. Plattig, 64–95. Münster: Weismayer.

———. 2001d. "Introduction to Charles Hartshorne's Handwritten Notes on A. N. Whitehead's Harvard Lectures 1925–26." *PS* 30/2: 289–300.

———. 2001e. "Wahrheit und Maschine: Wider das transsylvanische Argument von der Gewalt im Erkenntnisdiskurs." *Labyrinth: International Journal for Philosophy, Feminist Theory and Cultural Hermeneutics* 3.

———. 2002a. "Apocalypse in God: On the Power of God in Process Eschatology." *PS* 31/2.

———. 2002b. "De-Ontologizing God: Levinas, Deleuze, and Whitehead." In *Process and Difference: Between Cosmological and Poststructuralist Postmodernism*, ed. Catherine Keller and Anne Daniell, 209–34. Albany: SUNY.

———. 2002c. "Messianische Zeit. Walter Benjamins 'mystische Geschichtsauffassung' in zeittheologischer Perspektive." *MTZ* 53.

———. 2002d. "Personsein am Ort der Leere." *NZSTh* 44: 189–198.

———. 2002e. "Der transreligiöse Diskurs. Zu einer Theologie transformativer Prozesse." *Polylog* 9.

———. 2002f. "Zeit. Tod. Neuheit. Gedächtnis – Eschatologie als Zeittheologie. Teil I: Zeit und Tod." *FZPhTh* 48/1–2: 190–213.

———. 2003. "Entmythologisierung als radikale Reduktion. Zum Programm einer holistischen Reduktion in Whiteheads Ereignistheorie." ESPT 2.

———. 2004. "Whitehead at Infinite Speed: Deconstructing System as Event." In *Schleiermacher and Whitehead: Open Systems in Dialogue,* ed. Christine Helmer, Marjorie Suchocki, and John Quiring, 39–72. Berlin: DeGruyter.

———. 2005a. "'O bitches of impossibility!'—Programmatic Dysfunction in the Chaosmos of Deleuze and Whitehead." In Andre Cloots and Keith Robinson, eds., *Deleuze, Whitehead and the Transformation of Metaphysics,* 117–28. Brussels: Flemish Academy of Sciences.

———. 2005b. "God's Advent/ure: The End of Evil and the Origin of Time." In Joseph Bracken, ed., *World without End: Christian Eschatology from Process Perspective,* 91–112. Grand Rapids: Eerdmans.

———. 2006a. "Prozesstheologie." In Giancarlo Collet et al., *Theologien der Gegenwart,* 179–97. Darmstadt: Wissenschaftliche Buchgesellschaft.

———. 2006b. "Transkulturation. Dogmatische Überlegungen zum 'Wesen des Christentums' im Fluss." In Rupert Klieber and Martin Stowasser, eds., *Inkulturation: Historische Beispiele und theologische Reflexionen zur Flexibilität und Widerständigkeit des Christlichen,* 160–87. Vienna: LIT.

Fagg, Lawrence. 1995. *The Becoming of Time: Integrating Physical and Religious Time.* Atlanta: Scholars Press.

Farmer, Ronald. 1997. *Beyond the Impasse: The Promise of a Process Hermeneutic.* Studies in American Biblical Hermeneutics 13. Macon, GA: Mercer University Press.

Felt, James. 1974. "The Temporality of Divine Freedom." *PS* 4/4: 252–62.

Fetz, R. L. 1981. *Whitehead. Prozessdenken und Substanzmetaphysik.* Freiburg. Symposion.

———. 1986. "Kreativität: Eine neue transzendentale Seinsbestimmung?" In *Whiteheads Metaphysik der Kreativität. Internationales Whitehead-Symposium Bad Homburg 1983,* ed. Friedrich Rapp and Reiner Wiehl, 207–25. Freiburg: K. Alber.

Fiddes, Paul. 1988. *The Creative Suffering of God.* Oxford: Oxford University Press.

Fitzgerald, Paul. 1972. "Relativity Physics and the God of Process Philosophy." *PS* 2/4: 251–73.

Flasch, Kurt. 1986. "Productio et imago. Das Hervorgehen des Intellekts aus seinem göttlichen Grund bei Meister Eckhart, Dietrich von Freiburg und Bertholt von Moosburg." In *Abendländische Mystik im Mittelalter,* ed. Kurt Ruh, 125–34. Stuttgart: J. B. Metzler.

———. 1998. *Nikolaus von Kues. Geschichte und Entwicklung.* Frankfurt: Klostermann.

Ford, David, ed. 1997. *The Modern Theologians: An Introduction to Christian Theology in the Twentieth Century.* Cambridge, MA: Blackwell.

Ford, Lewis S. 1968. "Boethius and Whitehead on Time and Eternity." *IPhQ* 8: 38–67.

———. 1970. "The Viability of Whitehead's God on Time and Eternity." *Proceedings of the American Catholic Philosophical Association* 44: 141–51.

———. 1972. "Neville on the One and the Many." *Southern Journal of Philosophy* 10: 79–84.

———. 1973a. "Is There a Distinctive Superjective Nature?" *PS* 3: 229f.

———. 1973b. "The Non-Temporality of Whitehead's God." *IPhQ* 13/3: 347–76.

———. 1973c. "Process Philosophy." In *New Catholic Encyclopedia* 16: 363–65. Washington: Catholic University of America.

———. 1974. "Process Theology." In *New Catholic Encyclopedia* 16: 365–67. Washington: Catholic University of America.

———. 1975. "Process Trinitarianism." *JAAR* 43: 199–213.

———. 1977a. "An Appraisal of Whiteheadian Nontheism." *Southern Journal of Philosophy* 15/1: 27–35.

———. 1977b. "Can Freedom Be Created?" *Horizons* 4/2: 183–88.

———. 1977c. "A Whiteheadian Basis for Pannenberg's Theology." *Encounter* 38/4: 307–31.

———. 1977d. "Whitehead's Transformation of Pure Act." *Thomist* 41/3: 381–99.

———. 1978a. *The Lure of God: A Biblical Background for Process Theism.* Philadelphia: Fortress.

———. 1978b. "In What Sense Is God Infinite? A Process Perspective." *Thomist* 42/1: 1–13.

———. 1981. "The Divine Activity of the Future." *PS* 11/3: 169–79.

———. 1983a. "Afterword." In *Explorations in Whitehead's Philosophy,* ed. Lewis S. Ford and George L. Kline, 305–45. New York: Fordham.

———. 1983b. "An Alternative to Creatio ex Nihilo." *Religious Studies* 19/2: 205–13.

———. 1983c. "Neville's Understanding of Creativity." In *Explorations in Whitehead's Philosophy,* ed. Lewis S. Ford and George L. Kline, 272–79. New York: Fordham.

———. 1984a. *The Emergence of Whitehead's Metaphysics 1925–1929.* Albany: SUNY.

———. 1984b. "Notes toward a Partial Reconciliation of Tillich and Whitehead." *Union Seminary Quarterly Review* 39/1-2: 41–46.

———. 1985. "Whitehead and the Ontological Difference." *Philosophy Today* 29: 148–55.

———. 1986a. "Creativity as a Future Key." In *New Essays in Metaphysics,* ed. Robert C. Neville, 179–97. Albany: SUNY.

———. 1986b. "Divine Persuasion and Coercion." *Encounter* 47/3: 268–73.

———. 1986c. "God as Temporally-Ordered Society: Some Objections." In Tulane Studies in Philosophy 34. *Hartshorne's Neoclassical Theology,* ed. Forrest Wood and Michael DeArmey, 41–52. New Orleans: Tulane University.

———. 1988. "Inclusive Occasions." In *Process in Context: Essays in Post-Whiteheadian Perspective,* ed. E. Wolf-Gazo, 107–36. Bern: Peter Lang Publishing.

———. 1990. "Efficient Causation within Concrescence." *PS* 19/3: 167–80.

———. 1993. "Perfecting the Ontological Principle." In *Metaphysics as Foundation: Essays in Honor of Ivor Leclerc,* ed. Paul Bogaard and Gordon Treash, 122–49. Albany: SUNY.

———. 1997. "Contingent Trinitarianism." In *Trinity in Process: A Relational Theology of God,* ed. Joseph Bracken and Marjorie Suchocki, 41–68. New York: Continuum.

———. 2000. *Transforming Process Theism.* Albany: SUNY.

Ford, Lewis S., and George L. Kline, eds. *Explorations in Whitehead's Philosophy.* New York: Fordham.

Ford, Lewis S., and Marjorie Suchocki. 1977. "A Whiteheadian Reflection on Subjective Immortality." *PS* 7/1: 1–13.

Fowler, Dean B. 1975. "Whitehead's Theory of Relativity" *PS* 5/3: 159–74.

Frankenberry, Nancy. 1983. "The Power of the Past." *PS* 13/2: 132–42.

Franklin, S.T. 1984. "Panentheism." In *Evangelical Dictionary of Theology,* ed. W. A. Elwell, 818–20. Grand Rapids: Baker Book House.

———. 1990. *Speaking from the Depth: Alfred North Whitehead's Hermeneutical Metaphysics of Propositions, Experience, Symbolism, Language, and Religion.* Grand Rapids: Eerdmans.

———. 2000. "God and Creativity: A Revisionist Proposal within a Whiteheadian Context." *PS* 29/2: 237–307.

Gabriel, Leo, ed. 1989. *Nikolaus von Kues: Philosophisch Theologische Schriften I.* Vienna: Herder.

Garland, William. 1983. "The Ultimacy of Creativity." In *Explorations in Whitehead's Philosophy,* ed. Lewis S. Ford and George L. Kline, 212–38. New York: Fordham.

Gilkey, Langdon. 1973. "Process Theology." *Vox Theologica* 43: 5–29.

Green, Thomas. 1968. "The Idea of Novelty in Peirce and Whitehead." PhD diss., University of Notre Dame.

Greshake, Gisbert. 1978. *Der Preis der Liebe.* Freiburg: Herder.

———. 1983. "Theologie—eine Wissenschaft? Ein Gespräch mit Thomas v. Aquin über die Theologie als Wissenschaft vom Heil." In *Gottes Heil—Glück des Menschen. Theologische Perspektiven.* Freiburg: Herder.

Griffin, David Ray. "Pantemporalism and Panexperientialism." Unpublished paper, CPS files.

———. 1976. *God, Power, and Evil: A Process Theodicy.* Philadelphia: Westminster Press.

———, ed. 1986. *Physics and the Ultimate Significance of Time.* Albany: SUNY.

———. 1987. "Creation ex nihilo, the Divine Modus Operandi, and the Imitatio Dei." In *Faith and Creativity: Essays in Honor of Eugene H. Peters,* ed. George Nordgulen and George W. Shields, 95–123. St. Louis: CBP Press.

———. 1989a. *God and Religion in the Postmodern World: Essays in Postmodern Theology.* Albany: SUNY.

———. 1989b. "Reply: Must God Be Unlimited? Naturalistic vs. Supernaturalistic Theism." In *Concepts of the Ultimate: Philosophical Perspectives in the Nature of the Divine,* ed. Linda Tessier, 23–31. New York: St. Martin's Press.

———. 1990a. *A Process Christology.* Lanham, MD: University Press of America.

———. 1990b. "Process Theology as Empirical, Rational, and Speculative: Some Reflections on Method." *PS* 19/2: 116–35.

———. 1991. *Evil Revisited: Responses and Reconsiderations.* Albany: SUNY.

———. 1992. "Hartshorne, God, and Relativity Physics." *PS* 21/2: 85–112.

———. 1993. "Charles Hartshorne." In *Founders of Constructive Postmodern Philosophy: Peirce, James, Bergson, Whitehead, and Hartshorne,* ed. David Ray Griffin et al., 197–232. Albany: SUNY.

———. 1997. "A Naturalistic Trinity." In *Trinity in Process: A Relational Theology of God,* ed. Joseph Bracken and Marjorie Suchocki, 23–40. New York: Continuum.

———. 2000. *Religion and Scientific Naturalism. Overcoming the Conflicts.* Albany: SUNY.

Griffin, David Ray, William A. Beardslee, and Joe Holland. 1989. *Varieties of Postmodern Theology.* Albany: SUNY.

Griffin, David Ray, et al. 1993. *Founders of Constructive Postmodern Philosophy: Peirce, James, Bergson, Whitehead, and Hartshorne.* Albany: SUNY.

Hahn, Lewis E., ed. 1991. *The Philosophy of Charles Hartshorne.* La Salle, IL: Open Court.

Hall, David. 1973. *The Civilization of Experience: A Whiteheadian Theory of Culture.* New York: Fordham.

Hampe, Michael. 1990. *Die Wahrnehmungen der Organismen: Über die Voraussetzung einer naturalistischen Theorie der Erfahrung in der Metaphysik Whiteheads.* Göttingen: Vandenhoeck & Ruprecht.

———. 1991. "Einleitung: Alternativen zu einem monolithischen Universum." In *Prozess, Gefühl und Raum-Zeit. Materialien zu Whiteheads 'Prozeß und Realität,'* vol. 1, ed. Michael Hampe and H. Maassen, 92–100. Frankfurt: Suhrkamp.

———. 1998. *Alfred North Whitehead.* Munich: Beck.

Hampe, Michael, and H. Maassen, eds. 1991a. *Prozess, Gefühl und Raum-Zeit. Materialien zu Whiteheads 'Prozeß und Realität,'* vol. 1. Frankfurt: Suhrkamp.

———. 1991b. *Die Gifford-Lectures. Materialien zu Whiteheads 'Prozess und Realität',* vol. 2. Frankfurt: Suhrkamp.

Hanselmann, Johannes, and Uwe Swarat, eds. 1986. *Fachwörterbuch Theologie.* Wuppertal: Brockhaus.

Hardt, Michael. 1995. *Gilles Deleuze: An Apprenticeship in Philosophy.* Minneapolis: University of Minnesota Press.

Hardwick, Charley D. 1996. *Events of Grace: Naturalism, Existentialism, and Theology.* Cambridge: Cambridge University Press.

Harris, James. 1992. *Logic, God and Metaphysics.* Studies in Philosophy of Religion 17. Dortrecht: Kluwer Academic.

Hartshorne, Charles. 1937. *Beyond Humanism: Essays in New Philosophy of Nature.* Lincoln: University of Nebraska Press.

————. 1948. *The Divine Relativity: A Social Conception of God.* New Haven, CT: Yale University Press.

————. 1953. *Philosophers Speak of God.* Chicago: University of Chicago Press.

————. 1962. *The Logic of Perfection.* La Salle, IL: Open Court.

————. 1965a. *Anselm's Discovery: A Re-examination of the Ontological Proof of God.* La Salle, IL: Open Court.

————. 1965b. "The Development of Process Philosophy." In *Philosophers of Process,* ed. Douglas Browning, v–xxii. New York: Random House.

————. 1967. *A Natural Theology for Our Time.* Indianapolis: Open Court.

————. 1977. "Bell's Theorem and Stapp's Revised View of Space-Time." *PS* 7/3: 183–91.

————. 1984a. *Omnipotence and Other Theological Mistakes.* Albany: SUNY.

————. 1984b. "Whitehead's Revolutionary Concept of Prehension." In *Creativity in American Philosophy,* ed. Charles Hartshorne, 103–13. Albany: SUNY.

————. 1991a. "Peirce, Whitehead und die sechzehn Ansichten über Gott." In *Die Gifford-Lectures. Materialien zu Whiteheads 'Prozess und Realität,'* vol. 2, ed. Michael Hampe and H. Maassen, 194–216. Frankfurt: Suhrkamp.

————. 1991b. "Some Causes for My Intellectual Growth." In *The Philosophy of Charles Hartshorne,* ed. Lewis E Hahn, 3–45. La Salle, IL: Open Court.

————. 1991c. "Whitehead's Idea of God." In *The Philosophy of Alfred North Whitehead,* ed. Paul A. Schilpp, 513–60. La Salle, IL: Open Court.

————. 2001. *Notes on A.N. Whitehead's Harvard Lectures 1925–26.* Transcribed by Roland Faber. *PS* 30/2: 301–73.

Hartshorne, Charles, and William L. Reese. 1976. *Philosophers Speak of God.* Chicago: University of Chicago Press.

Haubst, R. 1991. *Streifzüge in die cusanische Theologie.* Münster: Aschendorff.

Haught, John F. 1986. *What Is God? How to Think about the Divine.* New York: Paulist Press.

————. 1995. *Science and Religion: From Conflict to Conversation.* Mahwah, NJ: Paulist Press.

Hauskeller, Michael. 1994. *Whitehead zur Einführung.* Hamburg: Junius.

Henry, Granville, C. 1983. "Whitehead's Philosophical Response to the New Mathematics." In *Explorations in Whitehead's Philosophy,* ed. Lewis S. Ford and George L. Kline, 14–30. New York: Fordham.

————. 1993. *Forms of Concrescence: Alfred North Whitehead's Philosophy and Computer Programming Structures.* Cranbury, NJ: Associated University Presses.

Holz, Harald, and Ernest Wolf-Gazo, eds. 1984. *Whitehead und der Prozessbegriff. Beiträge zur Philosophie Alfred North Whiteheads auf dem Ersten Internationalen Whitehead-Symposion 1981.* Freiburg: Alber.

Holzhey, Helmut, Alois Rust, and Reiner Wiehl, eds. 1990. *Natur, Subjektivität, Gott. Zur Prozessphilosophie Alfred North Whiteheads.* Frankfurt: Suhrkamp.

Hosinski, Thomas. 1993. *Stubborn Fact and Creative Advance: An Introduction to the Metaphysics of Alfred North Whitehead.* Lanham, MD: Rowmann & Littlefield.

Inada, Kenneth. 1971. "Whitehead's 'actual entity' and the Buddha's anatman." *Philosophy East and West* 21/3: 303–16.

————. 1975. "The Metaphysics of Buddhist Experience and the Whiteheadian Encounter." *Philosophy East and West* 25: 465–88.

Inbody, Tyron. 1991. "Religious Empiricism and the Problem of Evil." *AJThPh* 12: 35–45.

————. 1995. "The Constructive Theology of Bernard Meland: Postliberal Empirical Realism." In *The Constructive Theology of Bernard Meland,* 109–42. American Academy of Religion Studies in Religion 69. Atlanta: Oxford University Press.

Johnson, A. H. 1937. "Actual Entities—A Study of A. N. Whitehead's Theory of Reality." PhD diss., University of Toronto.

————. 1958. *Whitehead's Philosophy of Civilization.* Beacon Hill: Dover.

————. 1963. *Whitehead's Theory of Reality.* Kansas City: Beacon Press.

————. 1983. *Whitehead and His Philosophy.* Lanham, MD: University of America Press.

Joranson, Philip, and Ken Butigan, eds. 1984. *Cry of Environment: Rebuilding the Christian Creation Tradition.* Santa Fe: Bear & Co.

Jung, W. 1958. Review of Ivor Leclerc, "Whitehead's Metaphysics: An Introductory Exposition." *PhR* 6: 219–25.

————. 1965. "Zur Entwicklung von Whiteheads Gottesbegriff." *ZPhF* 19: 601–36.

————. 1980. "Über Whiteheads Atomistik der Ereignisse." In *Whitehead. Einführung in seine Kosmologie,* ed. Ernest Wolf-Gazo, 54–104. Freiburg: Alber.

Kaiser, O. 1962. *Die mythische Bedeutung des Meeres in Ägypten, Ugarit und Israel.* BZAW 78. Berlin: Alfred Töpelmann Verlag.

Kaku, Michio. 1994. *Hyperspace: A Scientific Odyssey through Parallel Universes, Time Warps, and the Tenth Dimension.* New York: Oxford University Press.

Kann, Charles. 2001. "Fußnoten zu Platon. Philosophiegeschichte bei A. N. Whitehead." *Paradeigmata* 23.

Kasprzik, B. 1988. "Whiteheads metaphysische Option." *Allgemeine Zeitschrift für Philosophie* 13: 19–36.

Kaufman, Gordon. 2004. *In the beginning . . . Creativity.* Minneapolis: Fortress.

Keller, Catherine. 1986. *From a Broken Web: Separation, Sexism and Self.* Boston: Beacon.

————. 1997. *Apocalypse Now and Then: A Feminist Guide to the End of the World.* Boston: Beacon.

————. 2000. "No More Sea: The Lost Chaos of Creation." In *Christianity and Ecology. Seeking the Well-Being of Earth and Humans,* ed. Dieter T. Hessel. Cambridge: Harvard University Press.

————. 2002a. "Introduction: The Process of Difference, the Difference of Process." In *Process and Difference: Between Cosmological and Poststructuralist Postmodernism,* ed. Catherine Keller and Anne Daniell, 1–30. Albany: SUNY.

————. 2002b. "Process and Chaosmos." In *Process and Difference: Between Cosmological and Poststructuralist Postmodernism,* ed. Catherine Keller and Anne Daniell, 55–72. Albany: SUNY.

————. 2003. *The Face of the Deep: Genesis and Chaosmos.* New York: Routledge.

Keller, Catherine, and Anne Daniell, eds. 2002. *Process and Difference: Between Cosmological and Poststructuralist Postmodernism.* Albany: SUNY.

Kemuf, Peggy, ed. 1991. *A Derrida Reader: Between the Blinds.* New York: Columbia University Press.

Klappert, Bertold. 1997. *Worauf wir hoffen. Das Kommen Gottes und der Weg Jesu Christi.* Gütersloh: Kaiser.

Kline, George. 1983. "Form, Concrescence, and Concretum." In *Explorations in Whitehead's Philosophy,* ed. Lewis S. Ford and George L. Kline, 104–48. New York: Fordham.

————. 1990. "Begriff und Konkreszenz: über einige Gemeinsamkeiten in den Ontologien Hegels und Whiteheads." In *Whitehead und der Deutsche Idealismus,* ed. G. Lucas and A. Braeckman, 145–61. Bern: P. Lang.

Klose, Joachim. 2002. *Die Struktur der Zeit in der Philosophie Alfred North Whiteheads.* Freiburg: Alber.

Koch, K. 1983. "Schöpferischer Lockruf im Prozess der Welt. Perspektiven der Gottesfrage in der amerikanischen Prozesstheologie." *Theologische Berichte* 12: 129–71.

Krämer, Felix. 1994. *Der Zusammenhang der Wirklichkeit. Problem und Verbindlichkeitsgrund philosophischer Theorien: Eine Untersuchung in Auseinandersetzung mit Fichte und Whitehead.* Amsterdam: Rodopi.

Kreiner, Armin. 1998. *Gott im Leid. Zur Stichhaltigkeit der Theodizee-Argumente.* Freiburg: Herder.

Küng, Hans. 1980. *Does God Exist? An Answer for Today.* Garden City, NY: Doubleday.

————. 1994. *Das Christentum. Wesen und Geschichte.* Munich: Piper.

———. 1996. *Ewiges Leben?* Munich: Piper.
Lachmann, R. 1990. *Ethik und Identität. Der ethische Ansatz der Prozessphilosophie A. N. Whiteheads und seine Bedeutung für die gegenwärtige Ethik.* Freiburg: Alber.
———. 2000. "Einleitung." In *Kulturelle Symbolisierung,* by Alfred North Whitehead, 7–55. Frankfurt: Suhrkamp.
Lambert, Gregg. 2001. "On Whitehead's proposition 'Life is robbery.'" In *Secular Theology: American Radical Theological Thought,* ed. Clayton Crockett, 92–103. London: Routledge.
Lango, John. 1972. *Whitehead's Ontology.* Albany: SUNY.
Lansing, J. 1973."The 'Natures' of Whitehead's God." *PS* 3/3: 143–52.
Latour, Bruno. 2001. "Gabriel Tarde und das Ende des Sozialen." *Soziale Welt* 52/3: 361–75.
Leclerc, Ivor. 1978. *Whitehead's Metaphysics: An Introductory Exposition.* 1958. Reprint, Atlantic Highlands, NJ: Humanities Press.
Lee, Bernard. 1977. "Sacramental Model in Process Christology." Unpublished, Chicago.
———. 1997. "An 'Other' Trinity." In *Trinity in Process: A Relational Theology of God,* ed. Joseph Bracken and Marjorie Suchocki, 191–214. New York: Continuum.
Lindsay, James E. 1970. "An Interpretation of Whitehead's Epistemology." ThD diss., Union Theological Seminary in Virginia.
Link, C. 1989. "Die Transparenz der Natur für das Geheimnis der Schöpfung." In *Ökologische Theologie. Perspektiven zur Orientierung,* ed. Günther Altner, 190ff. Stuttgart: Kreuz.
Livingston, James, and Francis Schüssler Fiorenza, eds. 2000. *Modern Christian Thought,* vol. 2: *The Twentieth Century.* Upper Saddle River, NJ: Prentice Hall.
Löbl, Michael. 1994. *Wissenschaftliche Naturerkenntnis und Ontologie der Welterfahrung. Zu A. N. Whiteheads Kosmologiemodell im Horizont von Relativitätstheorie und Quantentheorie.* Frankfurt: Lang.
Loomer, Bernard. 1944. "Ely on Whitehead's God." *JR* 24: 162–79.
———. 1948. "Neo-Naturalism and Neo-Orthodoxy." *JR* 28: 79–91.
———. 1949. "Christian Faith and Process Philosophy." *JR* 29: 181–203.
———. "Christology." (Unpubl.) CPS files.
———. 1968. "Empirical Theology within Process Thought." In *The Future of Empirical Theology,* ed. Bernard Meland, 149–73. Chicago: University of Chicago.
———. 1971. "Christian Faith and Process Philosophy." In Delwin Brown, Ralph James, and Gene Reeves, eds., *Process Philosophy and Christian Thought,* 70–98. Indianapolis: Bobbs-Merrill.
———. 1976a. "The Conceptions of Power." *PS* 6/1: 5–32.
———. 1976b. "Dimensions of Freedom." In *Religious Experience and Process Theology,* ed. Harry Cargas and Bernard Lee, 323–39. New York: Paulist Press.
———. 1978a. "The Future of Process Philosophy." In *Process Philosophy: Basic Writings,* ed. J. Silbey and P. Gunter, 515–45. Washington: University of America Press.
———. 1978b. "The Web of Life." In *The Nature of Life,* ed. William Heidcamp, 93–109. Baltimore: University Park Press.
———. 1984. "A Process-Relational Conception of Creation." In *Cry of Environment: Rebuilding the Christian Creation Tradition,* ed. Philip Joranson and Ken Butigan, 312–28. Santa Fe: Bear.
———. 1987a. "On Committing Yourself to a Relationship." *PS* 16/4: 255–63.
———. 1987b. "Process Theology: Origins, Strength, Weakness." *PS* 16/4: 245–54.
———. 1987c. "The Size of God." In *The Theology of Bernard Loomer in Context,* ed. William Dean and Larry Axel, 42. Macon, GA: Mercer University Press.
Lotter, Maria-Sibylla. 1990. "Subject-Superject: Zum Verhältnis von Privatheit und Öffentlichkeit." In *Natur, Subjektivität, Gott. Zur Prozessphilosophie Alfred North Whiteheads,* ed. Helmut Holzhey, Alois Rust, and Reiner Wiehl, 169–97. Frankfurt: Suhrkamp.

————. 1991. "Erfahrung und Natur. Von der Philosophie der Naturwissenschaft zur pragmatischen Metaphysik der Erfahrung." In *Die Gifford-Lectures. Materialien zu Whiteheads 'Prozess und Realität,'* vol. 2, ed. Michael Hampe and H. Maassen, 234–75. Frankfurt: Suhrkamp.

————. 1996. *Die metaphysische Kritik des Subjekts. Eine Untersuchung von Whiteheads universalisierter Sozialontologie.* Hildesheim: Georg Olms.

Löw, R. 1990. "Zeit und Ereignis. Überlegungen zum Zentralteil von A. N. Whiteheads 'Der Begriff der Natur.'" In Alfred North Whitehead, *Der Begriff der Natur,* 159–73. Weinheim: VCH.

Lowe, Victor. 1963. "The Concept of Experience in Whitehead's Metaphysics." In *Alfred North Whitehead: Essays in His Philosophy,* ed. George Kline, 124–33. Englewood Cliffs, NJ: Prentice-Hall.

————. 1985. *Alfred North Whitehead: The Man and His Work,* vol. 1, *1861–1910.* Baltimore: Johns Hopkins University.

————. 1990. *Alfred North Whitehead: The Man and His Work,* vol. 2, *1910–1947,* ed. J. B. Schneewind. Baltimore: Johns Hopkins University.

————. 1991. "The Development of Whitehead's Philosophy." In *The Philosophy of Alfred North Whitehead,* ed. Paul Arthur Schilpp, 15–124. La Salle, IL: Open Court.

Lucas, George. 1989. *The Rehabilitation of Whitehead: An Analytic and Historical Assessment of Process Philosophy.* Albany: SUNY.

Lucas, George, and Antoon Braeckman, eds. 1990. *Whitehead und der Deutsche Idealismus.* Bern: Herbert Lang.

Lucas, Hans-Christian. 1990. "Substanz-Subjekt-Superjekt. Überlegungen zu Hegels und Whiteheads Abwendung von der Substanzmetaphysik, besonders im Hinblick auf Spinoza und Aristoteles." In *Whitehead und der Deutsche Idealismus,* ed. George Lucas and Antoon Braeckman. Bern: Herbert Lang.

Luhmann, Niklas. 1989. *Gesellschaftsstruktur und Semiotik. Studien zur Wissenssoziologie der modernen Gesellschaft,* vol. 3. Frankfurt: Suhrkamp.

Lüke, Ulrich. 1997. *Als Anfang schuf Gott . . . : Bio-Theologie Zeit Evolution, Hominisation.* Paderborn: Schoningh.

Maassen, H. 1988. *Gott, das Gute und das Böse in der Philosophie A. N. Whiteheads.* Frankfurt: Lang.

————. 1991a. "Einleitung: Natur als Aktivität." In *Prozess, Gefühl und Raum-Zeit. Materialien zu Whiteheads 'Prozeß und Realität,'* vol. 1, ed. Michael Hampe and H. Maassen, 35f. Frankfurt: Suhrkamp.

————. 1991b. "Offenbarung, Mythos und Metaphysik." In *Die Gifford-Lectures. Materialien zu Whiteheads 'Prozess und Realität,'* vol. 2, ed. Michael Hampe and H. Maassen, 217–33. Frankfurt: Suhrkamp.

Mathews, Shailer. 1915. "Theology and Social Minds." *Biblical World* 46/4: 201–48.

————. 1923. "Theology from the Point of View of Social Psychology." *JR* 3/4: 350f.

————. 1931. *The Growth of the Idea of God.* New York: Macmillan.

————. 1940. *Is God Emeritus?* New York: Macmillan.

May, Gerhard. 1994. *Creatio ex Nihilo: The Doctrine of 'Creation out of Nothing' in Early Christian Thought.* Edinburgh: T.&T. Clark.

Mays, W. 1961. "The Relevance of 'on Mathematical Concepts of the Material World' to Whitehead's Philosophy." In *The Relevance of Whitehead: Philosophical Essays in Commemoration of the Centenary of the Birth of Alfred North Whitehead,* ed. Ivor Leclerc, 256–62. London: Allen & Unwin.

————. 1977. *Whitehead's Philosophy of Science and Metaphysics: An Introduction to His Thought.* The Hague: Martinus Nijhoff.

McCool, Gerald, ed. 1988. *The Universe as Journey: Conversations with W. Norris Clarke, S.J.* New York: Fordham.

McHenry, Leemon. 1992. *Whitehead and Bradley: A Comparative Analysis.* Albany: SUNY.

Meland, Bernard. 1963. "A Long Look at the Divinity School and Its Present Crisis." *Criterion* 1/2: 25.

———, ed. 1968. *The Future of Empirical Theology*. Chicago: University of Chicago.

———. 1976. *Fallible Symbols and Other Essays*. Philadelphia: Fortress.

Mellert, Robert. 1975. *What Is Process Theology? An Introduction to the Philosophy of Alfred North Whitehead, and How It Is Being Applied to Christian Thought Today*. New York: Paulist Press.

Mesle, C. Robert. 1993. *Process Theology: A Basic Introduction*. St. Louis: Christian Board of Publication.

Metz, Johann B. 1993. "Zeit ohne Finale." *Conc* 29: 458–62.

Moltmann, Jürgen. 1993. *God in Creation: A New Theology of Creation and the Spirit of God*. Minneapolis: Fortress.

———. 1994. *Trinität und Reich Gottes. Zur Gotteslehre*. Gütersloh: Piper.

———. 1995. *Das Kommen Gottes. Christliche Eschatologie*. Gütersloh: Kaiser.

Moser, L. 1975. *Die Dimensionen des Dynamischen im Seinsbegriff. Versuch, das whiteheadsche Wirklichkeitsverständnis für einen dynamischen Seinsbegriff auszuwerten*. Frankfurt: Lang.

Neville, Robert C., ed. 1986. *New Essays in Metaphysics*. Albany: SUNY.

———. 1995. *Creativity and God: A Challenge to Process Theology*. Albany: SUNY.

Nishida, Kitaro. 1992. *An Inquiry into the Good*. New Haven, CT: Yale University Press.

———. 1999. *Logik des Orts. Der Anfang der modernen Philosophie*. Darmstadt: Wissenschaftliche Buchgesellschaft.

Nobo, Jorge Luis. 1978. "Whitehead's Principle of Relativity." *PS* 8/1: 1–20.

———. 1986. *Whitehead's Metaphysics of Extension and Solidarity*. Albany: SUNY.

———. 1998. "From Creativity to Ontogenetic Matrix: Learning from Whitehead's Account of the Ultimate." *Process Thoughts* 8.

Nordgulen, George, and George Shields. 1987. *Faith and Creativity: Essays in Honor of Eugene H. Peters*. St. Louis: CBP.

Ogden, Schubert. 1961. *Christ without Myth: A Study Based on the Theology of Rudolph Bultmann*. New York: Harper.

———. 1980. "Faith and Freedom." *Christian Century*, Dec. 12, 1980: 1241–42.

———. 1988. *Process Metaphysics and Hua-Yen Buddhism: A Critical Study of Cumulative Penetration vs. Interpenetration*. Albany: SUNY.

———. 1991. *The Reality of God and Other Essays*. 1964. New York: Harper & Row.

Oomen, Palmyre. 1998a. "Consequences of Prehending God's Consequent Nature in a Different Key." *PS* 27/3–4: 329–31.

———. 1998b. "The Prehensibility of God's Consequent Nature." *PS* 27/1–2: 108–33.

Orf, Eberhard. 1996. *Religion, Kreativität und Gottes schöpferische Aktivität in der spekulativen Metaphysik Alfred North Whiteheads*. Egelsbach: Hänsel-Hohenhausen.

Overman, Richard H. 1967. *Evolution and the Christian Doctrine of Creation: A Whiteheadian Interpretation*. Philadelphia: Westminster Press.

Pailin, David. 1984. "God as Creator in a Whiteheadian Understanding." In *Whitehead und der Prozessbegriff. Beitrage zur Philosophie Alfred North Whiteheads auf dem Ersten Internationalen Whitehead-Symposion 1981*, ed. Harald Holz and Ernest Wolf-Gazo, 273–99. Freiburg: Alber.

Pannenberg, Wolfhart. 1976. *Grundzüge der Christologie*. Gütersloh: Haus G. Mohn.

———. 1986. "Atom, Dauer, Gestalt. Schwierigkeiten mit der Prozeßphilosophie." In *Whiteheads Metaphysik der Kreativität. Internationales Whitehead-Symposium Bad Homburg 1983*, ed. Friedrich Rapp and Reiner Wiehl, 194. Freiburg: K. Alber.

———. 1987. *Wissenschaftstheorie und Theologie*. Frankfurt: Suhrkamp.

———. 1988. *Systematische Theologie*, vol. 1. Göttingen: Vandenhoeck & Ruprecht.

———. 1993. "Die Vollendung der Schöpfung im Reich Gottes." In *Systematische Theologie*, vol. 3., 572ff. Göttingen: Vandenhoeck & Ruprecht.

———. 1996. *Theologie und Philosophie. Ihr Verhältnis im Licht ihrer gemeinsamen Geschichte*. Göttingen: Vandenhoeck & Ruprecht.

Penrose, Roger. 1991. *The Emperor's New Mind: Concerning Computers, Minds, and the Law of Physics*. New York: Oxford University.

Peters, Eugene Herbert. 1966. *The Creative Advance: An Introduction to Process Philosophy as a Context for Christian Faith*. St. Louis: Bethany Press.

Peukert, Helmut. 1988. *Wissenschaftstheorie, Handlungstheorie, Fundamentale Theologie*. Düsseldorf: Detmos.

Philipson, Sten. 1982. *A Metaphysics for Theology: A Study of Some Problems in the Later Philosophy of Alfred North Whitehead and Its Application to Issues in Contemporary Theology*. Atlantic Highlands, NJ: Humanities Press.

Pittenger, Norman. 1959. *The Word Incarnate: A Study of the Doctrine of the Person of Christ*. New York: Harper.

———. 1968. *Process Thought and Christian Faith*. New York: Macmillan.

———. 1969. *Alfred North Whitehead*. New York: Lutterworth.

———. 1971. "A Strictly Personal Account." *PS* 1/2: 129–35.

———. 1981. *Catholic Faith in a Process Perspective*. Maryknoll, NY: Orbis.

Plamondon, Ann. 1979. *Whitehead's Organic Philosophy of Science*. Albany: SUNY.

Popper, Karl, and John Eccles. 1997. *Das Ich und sein Gehirn*. Munich: Piper.

Poser, Hans. 1986. "Whiteheads Kosmologie als revidierbare Metaphysik." In *Whiteheads Metaphysik der Kreativität. Internationales Whitehead-Symposium Bad Homburg 1983*, ed. Friedrich Rapp and Reiner Wiehl, 105–26. Freiburg: K. Alber.

Pottmeyer, Hermann. 1968. *Der Glaube vor dem Anspruch der Wissenschaft*. Freiburg: Herder.

Price, Lucien. 1954. *Dialogues of Alfred North Whitehead*. Boston: New American Library.

Quint, Josef. ed. 1969. *Meister Eckhart. Deutsche Predigten und Traktate*. Munich: Goldmann.

Rae, Eleanor. 1984. *The Holy Spirit in Whiteheadian Process Theologians*. New York: Fordham.

Rager, Günter. 2000a. "Hirnforschung und die Frage nach dem Ich." In *Ich und mein Gehirn. Persönliches Erleben, verantwortliches Handeln und objektive Wissenschaft*, ed. Günter Rager, 13–52. Freiburg: Alber.

———, ed. 2000b. *Ich und mein Gehirn. Persönliches Erleben, verantwortliches Handeln und objektive Wissenschaft*. Freiburg: Alber.

Rahner, Karl. 1970. "Die Frage nach der Zukunft." *SzTh* 9: 524–25.

———. 1976. *Grundkurs des Glaubens. Einführung in den Begriff des Christentums*. Freiburg: Herder.

Ranke, Oliver von. 1997. *Whiteheads Relativitätstheorie*. Regensburg: Roderer.

Rapp, Friedrich. 1990. "Das Subjekt in Whiteheads kosmologischer Metaphysik." In *Natur, Subjektivität, Gott. Zur Prozessphilosophie Alfred North Whiteheads*, ed. Helmut Holzhey, Alois Rust, and Reiner Wiehl, 143–68. Frankfurt: Suhrkamp.

Rapp, Friedrich, and Reiner Wiehl, eds. 1986. *Whiteheads Metaphysik der Kreativität. Internationales Whitehead-Symposium Bad Homburg 1983*. Freiburg: K. Alber.

Rauschenbusch, Walter. 1917. *A Theology of the Social Gospel*. New York: Macmillan.

Reese, William. 1991. "The 'Trouble' with Panentheism—and the Divine Event." In *The Philosophy of Charles Hartshorne*, ed. Lewis Edwin Hahn, 187–202. La Salle, IL: Open Court.

Reese, William, and Eugene Freeman. 1964. *Process and Divinity: The Hartshorne Festschrift*. La Salle, IL: Open Court.

Reeves, Gene. 1984. "God as Alpha and Omega: Dipolar Theism." In *God and Temporality*, ed. Bowman Clarke and E. Long, 155–68. New York: Paragon.

Reeves, Gene, and Delwin Brown. 1971. "The Development of Process Theology." In *Process Philosophy and Christian Thought*, ed. Delwin Brown, Ralph James, and Gene Reeves, 21–64. Indianapolis: Bobbs-Merrill.

Reitz, Helga. 1970. "Was ist Prozesstheologie?" *KD* 16: 78–103.

Rescher, Nicholas. 1996. *Process Metaphysics: An Introduction to Process Philosophy*. Albany: SUNY.

Rohmer, Stascha. 2000. *Whiteheads Synthese von Kreativität und Rationalität. Reflexion und Transformation in Alfred North Whiteheads Philosophie der Natur*. Freiburg: Alber.

———. 2001. "Einleitung." In A. N. Whitehead, *Denkweisen*, 7–42. Frankfurt: Suhrkamp.

Rorty, Richard. 1983. "Matter and Event." In *Explorations in Whitehead's Philosophy*, ed. Lewis S. Ford and George L. Kline, 68–103. New York: Fordham.

———. 1990. "Das subjektivistische Prinzip und die Wende zur Sprachanalyse." in *Die Gifford-Lectures. Materialien zu Whiteheads 'Prozess und Realität,'* vol. 2, ed. Michael Hampe and H. Maassen, 276–312. Frankfurt: Suhrkamp.

———. 1994. *Contingency, Irony and Solidarity*. Cambridge: Cambridge University Press.

———. 1995. "Response to Hartshorne." In *Rorty and Pragmatism: The Philosopher Responds to His Critics*, ed. Herman J. Saatkamp, 29–36. Nashville: Vanderbilt University Press.

Roth, Gerhard. 2001. "Die neurobiologischen Grundlagen von Geist und Bewusstsein." In *Neurowissenschaft und Philosophie*, ed. Michael Pauen and Gerhard Roth. Munich: Fink.

Ruether, Rosemary Radford. 1993. *Sexism and God-Talk: Toward a Feminist Theology*. Boston: Beacon Press.

Runggaldier, E. 2000. "Die Fortdauer (Identität) des Ich durch die Zeit." In *Ich und mein Gehirn. Persönliches Erleben, verantwortliches Handeln und objektive Wissenschaft*, ed. Günter Rager, 161–238. Freiburg: Alber.

Rust, Alois. 1987. *Die organismische Kosmologie von Alfred N. Whitehead. Zur Revision des Selbstverständnisses neuzeitlicher Philosophie und Wissenschaft durch eine neue Philosophie der Natur*. Monographien zur philosophischen Forschung. Frankfurt: Athenäum.

Sander, Hans-Joachim. 1991. *Natur und Schöpfung. Die Realität im Prozess. A. N. Whiteheads Philosophie als Paradigma einer Fundamentaltheologie kreativer Existenz*. Frankfurt: Peter Lang.

Sayer, Rowanne. 1999. *Wert und Wirklichkeit. Zum Verständnis des metaphysischen Wertbegriffs im Spätdenken Alfred North Whiteheads und dessen Bedeutung für den Menschen in seiner kulturellen Kreativität*. Würzburg: Ergon.

Scheffczyk, L. 1984. "Prozesstheismus und christlicher Glaube." *MTZ* 35: 81–104.

Schilpp, Paul Arthur, ed. 1991. *The Philosophy of Alfred North Whitehead*. La Salle, IL: Open Court.

Schmetterer, Eva, Roland Faber, and Nicole Mantler, eds. 1995. *Variationen über die Schöpfung der Welt*. Innsbruck: Tyrolia.

Scholem, Gershom. 1996. *Die jüdische Mystik in ihren Hauptströmungen*. Frankfurt: Suhrkamp.

Schramm, Michael. 1991. *Prozeßtheologie und Bioethik. Reproduktionsmedizin und Gentechnik im Lichte der Philosophie A. N. Whiteheads*. Freiburg: Herder.

Schulte, R. 1967. "Die Heilstat des Vaters in Christus." In *Mysterium Salutis. Grundriss heilsgeschichtlicher Dogmatik III/1: Das Christusereignis*, ed. J. Feiner and M. Löhrer, 49–88. Einsiedeln: Benziger.

———. 1970. "Die Vorbereitung der Trinitätsoffenbarung." In *Mysterium Salutis. Grundriss heilsgeschichtlicher Dogmatik III/I*, ed. Johannes Feiner and Magnus Löhrer, 49–84. Einsiedeln: Benziger.

———. 1989. "Eine neue Denkform im Glaubensverständnis?" In *Rationalität. Ihre Entwicklung und ihre Grenzen*, ed. Leo Scheffczyk, 315–66. Freiburg: Alber.

———. 1993. "'Schöpfung' und 'Natur.' Theologische Erwägungen zum Verständnis und zur aktuellen Frag-Würdigkeit des christlich-theologischen Gehalts zweier Schlüsselbegriffe für Wissenschaft, Theologie und ökologisch-ethische Bestimmung." In *In unum congregati*, ed. Augustinus Mayer and Stephan Haering, 361–87. Metten: Abtei.

Schwarz, H. 1983. "Die christologische Forschung in der gegenwärtigen nord-amerikanischen Theologie." *NZSTh* 25: 41–49.

Searle, John. 1996. *Die Wiederentdeckung des Geistes*. Frankfurt: Suhrkamp.

Sherburne, Donald. 1971. "The 'Whitehead without God' Debate: The Rejoinder." *PS* 1/2: 101–13.

Silbey, Jack, and Pete Gunter, eds. 1978. *Process Philosophy: Basic Writings*. Washington: University Press of America.

Spaemann, Robert. 1986. "Welche Erfahrungen lehrt uns die Welt verstehen? Bemerkungen zum Paradigma von Whiteheads Kosmologie." In *Whiteheads Metaphysik der Kreativität. Internationales Whitehead-Symposium Bad Homburg 1983*, ed. Friedrich Rapp and Reiner Wiehl, 169–82. Freiburg: K. Alber.

Stambaugh, Joan. 1999. *The Formless Self*. Albany: SUNY.

Stegmair, W. 1988. "Klassiker Whitehead? Zu neuen Sammelbänden über Whiteheads Philosophie der Innovation." *Allgemeine Zeitschrift für Philosophie* 13: 61–77.

Stokes, Walter. 1960. "The Function of Creativity in the Metaphysics of Whitehead." PhD diss., St. Louis University.

Stolz, Joachim. 1995. *Whitehead und Einstein: Wissenschaftsgeschichtliche Studien in Naturphilosophischer Absicht*. Frankfurt: Lang.

Störig, H. J. 1997. *Kleine Weltgeschichte der Philosophie*. Frankfurt: Fischer.

Suchocki, Marjorie. 1975. "The Metaphysical Ground of the Whiteheadian God." *PS* 5/4: 237–46.

———. 1977. "The Question of Immortality." *JR* 57: 288–306.

———. 1978. "The Anatman and the Consequent Nature." In CPS, Conference on Buddhism and Process Thought.

———. 1988. *The End of Evil: Process Eschatology in Historical Context*. Albany: SUNY.

———. 1994a. *The Fall to Violence: Original Sin in Relational Theology*. New York: Continuum.

———. 1994b. "God, Sexism, and Transformation." In *Reconstructing Christian Theology*, ed. Rebecca S. Chopp and Mark Lewis Taylor. Minneapolis: Fortress Press.

———. 1995. *God—Christ—Church: A Practical Guide to Process Theology*. 1982, rev. 1989. New York: Crossroad.

———. 1996. *In God's Presence: Theological Reflections on Prayer*. St. Louis: Chalice.

———. 1997. "Spirit in and through the World." In *Trinity in Process: A Relational Theology of God*, ed. Joseph Bracken and Marjorie Suchocki, 173–90. New York: Continuum.

Sullivan, John Anthony. 1987. *Explorations in Christology: The Impact of Process/Relational Thought*. New York: Lang.

Takeda, Ryusei, and John B. Cobb. 1974. "'Mosa-Dharma' und Prehension: Nagarjuna and Whitehead Compared." *PS* 4/1: 26–36.

Tanaka, Y. 1987. "Einstein and Whitehead: The Principle of Relativity Reconsidered." *Historica Scienciarum* 32: 43–61.

Tessier, Linda, ed. 1989. *Concepts of the Ultimate: Philosophical Perspectives in the Nature of the Divine*. New York: St. Martin's Press.

Thatamanil, John. 2006. *The Immanent Divine: God, Creation, and the Human Predicament*. Minneapolis: Fortress.

Tillich, Paul. 1951. *Systematic Theology*, vol. I. Chicago: University of Chicago Press.

———. 1963. "Der Widerstreit von Zeit und Raum." In *Gesammelte Werke*, 6:140–48. Stuttgart: de Gruyter.

Tracy, David. 1990. "Kenosis, Sunyata, and Trinity: A Dialogue with Masao Abe." In *The Emptying God: A Buddhist-Jewish-Christian Conversation*, ed. John B. Cobb and Christopher Ives, 135–54. Maryknoll, NY: Orbis.

Van der Veken, Jan. 1986. "Kreativität als allgemeine Aktivität." In *Whiteheads Metaphysik der Kreativität. Internationales Whitehead-Symposium Bad Homburg 1983*, ed. Friedrich Rapp and Reiner Wiehl, 197–206. Freiburg: K. Alber.

Volf, Miroslav, Carmen Krieg, and Thomas Kucharz, eds. 1996. *The Future of Theology: Essays in Honor of Jürgen Moltmann*. Grand Rapids: Eerdmans.

Waldenfels, H. 1996. *Einführung in die Theologie der Offenbarung*. Darmstadt: Wissenschaftliche Buchgesellschaft.

Wallack, F. Bradford. 1980. *The Epochal Nature of Process in Whitehead's Metaphysics*. Albany: SUNY.

Wassermann, Christoph. 1991. *Struktur und Ereignis. Interdisziplinäre Studien in Physik, Theologie und Philosophie*. Geneva: unpublished; CPS files.

Welker, Michael. 1984. "Whiteheads Vergottung der Welt." In *Whitehead und der Prozessbegriff. Beiträge zur Philosophie Alfred North Whiteheads auf dem Ersten Internationalen Whitehead-Symposion 1981*, ed. Harald Holz and Ernest Wolf-Gazo, 249–72. Freiburg: Alber.

———. 1985. "Die relativistische Kosmologie Whiteheads." *PhR* 32: 134–55.

———. 1988. *Universalität Gottes und Relativität der Welt. Theologische Kosmologie im Dialog mit dem amerikanischen Prozessdenken nach Whitehead*. Neukirchen: Neukirchen Verlag.

———. 1992. "Prozesstheologie." in *EKL*³: 1363–66.

Welsch, Wolfgang. 1995. *Vernunft. Die zeitgenössische Vernunftkritik und das Konzept der transversalen Vernunft*. Frankfurt: Suhrkamp.

Welten, Willibrord. 1984. "Whitehead on Hume's Analysis of Experience." In *Whitehead und der Prozessbegriff. Beiträge zur Philosophie Alfred North Whiteheads auf dem Ersten Internationalen Whitehead-Symposion 1981*, ed. Harald Holz and Ernest Wolf-Gazo, 386–403. Freiburg: Alber.

Wessell, Leonard. 1990. *Zur Funktion des Ästhetischen in der Kosmologie Alfred North Whiteheads*. Frankfurt: Lang.

Wiehl, Reiner. 1971. "Einleitung in die Philosophie A. N. Whiteheads." In A. N. Whitehead, *Abenteuer der Ideen. Einleitung von Reiner Wiehl*, 7–71. Frankfurt: Suhrkamp.

———. 1984. "Prozesse und Kontraste. Ihre kategoriale Funktion in der philosophischen Ästhetik und Kunsttheorie auf der Grundlage der Whiteheadschen Metaphysik." In *Whitehead und der Prozessbegriff. Beiträge zur Philosophie Alfred North Whiteheads auf dem Ersten Internationalen Whitehead-Symposion 1981*, ed. H. Holz and E. Wolf-Gazo, 315–41. Munich: Karl Alber.

———. 1986. "Whiteheads Kosmologie der Gefühle zwischen Ontologie und Anthropologie." In *Whiteheads Metaphysik der Kreativität. Internationales Whitehead-Symposium Bad Homburg 1983*, ed. Friedrich Rapp and Reiner Wiehl, 141–68. Freiburg: K. Alber.

———. 1990a. "Aktualität und Extensivität in Whiteheads Kosmo-Psychologie." In *Die Gifford-Lectures. Materialien zu Whiteheads 'Prozess und Realität*,' vol. 2, ed. Michael Hampe and H. Maassen, 313–68. Frankfurt: Suhrkamp.

———. 1990b. "Whiteheads Kant-Kritik und Kants Kritik am Panpsychismus." In *Natur, Subjektivität, Gott. Zur Prozessphilosophie Alfred North Whiteheads*, ed. Helmut Holzhey, Alois Rust, and Reiner Wiehl, 198–239. Frankfurt: Suhrkamp.

Wieman, Henry Nelson. 1926. *Religious Experience and Scientific Method*. New York: Macmillan.

———. 1927a. "Professor Whitehead's Concept of God." *Hibbert Journal*: 623–30.

———. 1927b. *The Wrestle of Religion with Truth*. New York: Macmillan.

———. 1946. *The Source of Human Good*. Chicago: University of Chicago Press.

Wilber, Ken. 1996. *A Brief History of Everything*. Boston: Shambhala.

Williams, Daniel-Day. 1970. "Prozess-Theologie: Eine neue Möglichkeit für die Kirche." *EvTh* 30: 571–83.

Williams, Daniel-Day, and Stacy Evans, eds. 1990. *The Demonic and the Divine*. Minneapolis: Fortress.

Wilmot, Laurence. 1979. *Whitehead and God: Prolegomena to a Theological Reconstruction*. Waterloo, ON: Wilfrid Laurier University Press.

Wolf-Gazo, Ernest. 1980. *Whitehead. Einführung in seine Kosmologie*. Freiburg: Alber.

———. 1988a. "Introduction: Whitehead and the Process Perspective." In *Process in Context: Essays in Post-Whiteheadian Perspective*, ed. Ernest Wolf-Gazo, 15f. Bern: Lang.

———, ed. 1988b. *Process in Context: Essays in Post-Whiteheadian Perspective*. Bern: Lang.

Wood, Forrest. 1986. *Whiteheadian Thought as a Basis for a Philosophy of Religion*. Lanham, MD: University Press of America.

Wucherer-Huldenfeld, Augustinus. 1997. "Das Weltübel als Einwand gegen Gottes Dasein." In *Ursprüngliche Erfahrung und personales Sein. Ausgewählte philosophische Studien II*, ed. Augustinus Wucherer-Huldenfeld, 75–104. Vienna: Böhlau.

Zoglauer, Thomas. 1998. *Geist und Gehirn*. Göttingen: Vandenhoeck & Ruprecht.

Index

receptivity
  creativity and, 77–80
  divine matrix and God-world contin-
    uum, 170–79
  personal being and, 107–8
reciprocity of God and the world, six
  antitheses and, 157–70
reconciled nondifference, 132
reconciling process, ecology of love and,
  152–57
reconstructive theology, 42
  Whitehead and, 319–27
redemption
  creativity and, 143
  future of past in, 227–28
Reeves,Gene, 5–6
reformed history of philosophy, 49–53
reformed subjectivistic principle, 52–53
  space-time and, 66–70
reformed-subjectivstic epistemology,
  54–58
relationality
  chaos and, 209–10
  context of, 263
  of creative process, 161–62
  creativity and, 141–46, 158–59
  divine matrix and, 172–73
  essential relationality, 126–32
  God's alterity and, 149
  God's creativity and, 122–26, 144
  God's threefold character and,
    182–91
  mystery of God's life and, 255–56
  process theology and, 12–14
  solidarity and interruption and,
    221–28
  transcendentalism and, 131–32
  Whitehead's concept of, 23, 62–66
relational theology, 305–11
relationships, organic nature of, 47–49
relativistic historicism, 277–81
relativity, theory of
  philosophy and, 276–81
  process theology and, 40–41, 288–90
relativization, intensity and, 98–102
religion, empiricism and, 214–21
religion, philosophy of, 21

Religion in the Making, 20, 24
  coercive power of God in, 203
  concretion discussed in, 134
  creativity in, 141–42
  dogmatic theology and, 308
  immanence in, 128–32
  metaphysics in, 219–21
  nontemporality of God in, 107–8
  transformative spirituality and, 311
  Trinitarianism in, 196
religiophilosophical principles, divine
  matrix and, 175
repetition, revelatory theology and power
  of, 217–21
res cogitans, 50, 276
res extensa, 50, 276
restriction hypothesis, 291–99
restrictive unity, reconstruction of personal being and, 104–5
revealed life, mystery of, 255
revelatory theology, 306–7
  empiricism and, 214–21
reverse process of, 149–51
Roman Empire, 203
Rorty, R., 40, 147
Ruether, Rosemary Radford, 176
Russell, Bertrand, 48, 93, 285–86

salvation, Trinitarianism and economy of,
  193–94
Santayana, George, 8
Sartre, Jean-Paul, 108
satisfaction
  creative process and, 152–53
  primordial, 150
Scheffczyk, Leo, 127, 214
Schelling, 286
science
  process theology and, 21–25
  reconstructed philosophy of, 46–49
  resonance with, 275–81
  Whitehead's philosophy of, 60–62
Science and the Modern World, 21, 59–60,
  67, 71, 93
  bifurcation discussed in, 276–81
  coercive power of God in, 203
  concretion discussed in, 134, 216